Wilderness and Natural Areas in the Eastern United States:

A Management Challenge

To

Pam, Aron, Anders and Arika,

and

Jeanne, Melanie, Erik and Jeffrey

Wilderness and Natural Areas in the Eastern United States:

A Management Challenge

David L. Kulhavy

Center for Applied Studies
School of Forestry
Stephen F. Austin State University
Nacogdoches, Texas

Richard N. Conner

Wildlife Habitat and Silviculture Laboratory
Southern Forest Experiment Station
USDA Forest Service
Nacogdoches, Texas

PUBLISHED BY:

Center for Applied Studies
School of Forestry
Stephen F. Austin State University
Nacogdoches, Texas

First Edition
1 2 3 4 5 6 7 8 9

Printed in the United States of America

ISBN 0-938361-00-7

Publication supported by:

    Center for Applied Studies
    School of Forestry

    USDA Forest Service
       Southern Forest Experiment Station
       Southeastern Forest Experiment Station
       National Forest System, Region 8

    T.L.L. Temple Foundation, Inc.

FOREWORD

by
Kent T. Adair

The purpose of this symposium is not to debate either the concept of wilderness or the amount of wilderness appropriate for the United States. These are not debatable issues for present purposes. The Congress has spoken twice. The Wilderness Act of 1964 (PL 88-577) and the amendments of 1975, known as the "Eastern Wilderness Act" (PL 93-622), both set-aside existing areas as wilderness and established procedures for consideration of additions to the wilderness system. The purpose of this symposium is to consider the management of wilderness areas over time. In a very real sense, if those areas established as wilderness today deteriorate significantly over the next century, the people in the year 2085 A.D., and after, will probably blame the managers, not the good intentions of those who worked to have these areas set-aside in the year 1985.

It is for that reason that this symposium was designed as a communications vehicle for those individuals charged by law with the management of wilderness. Basically, the question is "now that we have wilderness, what do we do with it?"

It is not enough to do nothing and allow nature to run its course. That is not fair to those whose purpose in setting these areas aside was to maintain unique environments. It is also not fair to adjoining property owners who can be damaged by natural forces that may be detrimental to their desires. So, doing nothing is not the answer.

The answer, it seems to me, is to use designated wilderness areas to fill the greatest number of social needs possible while maintaining and enhancing the purposes for which each area has been set aside. Thus, each wilderness area should play its maximum possible role in the development and enhancement of society.

For all wants are ultimately human wants. And the mosaic of these wants defines societal demand. The desire for preserving rare and endangered species is a human want. The desire to protect unique habitats is a human want. So is the desire for recreation, solitude, wood products, minerals and every other thing produced or enjoyed by people.

It is these trade-offs among competing human wants that makes wilderness management a special challenge because the lure of wilderness to many people is emotional rather than rational. Perceptions outweigh facts. What is believed is more important that the legal and biological realities of wilderness management.

For example, what management activities are required to produce a feeling of solitude among users of the wilderness? Or, how does management create the perception of primitive recreation in an intensively utilized primitive recreation area? These and similar questions illustrate the difficulty of managing wilderness in such a way as to produce a specific effect on the minds of users.

No other form of land use management has to meet this challenge as intensively as does wilderness management. It is a much different and more difficult problem than defining the legal and biological limits to management because it deals with the esteem people attach to the activities of management rather than the specific outcomes in terms of habitat enhancement or legal percepts.

The population of the United States is becoming increasingly urban and uninformed about the physical world in which it lives. The beauty of a wilderness scene is easily grasped and supported by those having some idea of what one is talking about. It is more difficult, if not impossible, to gain even emotional support from someone who knows little or nothing of nature and natural resources management.

Therefore, I formally issue a challenge to this symposium to find ways in which the Wilderness System of the United States can fill its role as an educational resource.

Nothing less than the long-term survival of the wilderness system is at stake in this effort. A caring and knowledgeable population will make the difference between a successful wilderness management effort for America and one that falls short of its potential.

This means educating people about the technology of wilderness management as well as the need for wilderness. A population that assumes we know how to accomplish specific goals in wilderness management can only attribute failure as a lack of political and emotional resolve. Such a society is capable of demanding performance which cannot be delivered. The result is alienation.

Therefore, as you discuss the various problems in wilderness management that are with us today, I challenge you to add education to all levels.

The Wilderness System is an educational resource. I challenge you to use it as such.

PREFACE

Management issues in wilderness and natural areas encompass many facets of resource management. Topics presented include wildlife, ecology, forest protection, visitor needs and user impacts, vegetation ecology and management, and resource management issues, including fire, minerals, and public perceptions. Keynote presentations encompassed overviews of legal, social, and management perspectives, Forest Service administration and historical perspectives, and critical needs for wilderness.

The mandate of the 98th Congress and the continued need to plan for wilderness and ecologically sensitive areas dictates that increasing acreages will come under scrutiny for wilderness consideration. As these acreages increase, additional personnel will be needed to maintain these areas and to provide for judicial management of these resources in the future. This conference drew together professional managers and researchers to discuss and plan for the future. Ideas brought forth in this volume are the culmination of planning sessions with session moderators and planning boards. The overall objective was to provide a document useful to both the manager of these areas and potential user groups.

We wish to acknowledge the School of Forestry, Center for Applied Studies, Stephen F. Austin State University, Southern Forest Experiment Station, Southeastern Forest Experiment Station, the National Forest System, Region 8, USDA Forest Service, and The Wilderness Society for cosponsoring the symposium. The School of Forestry, the Southern and Southeastern Forest Experiment Stations, and the National Forest Service System, Region 8 and the T.L.L. Temple Foundation deserve special recognition for supporting the publication.

We thank the authors for their prompt attention to editorial reviews and the session moderators for their assistance in the program. Dr. Kent T. Adair, Dean, School of Forestry, Mr. John E. Alcock, Regional Forester, Region 8, and Dr. Thomas H. Ellis, Director, Southern Forest Experiment Station, provided tacit and provocative welcoming addresses. Special thanks to our conference host, Tim Weller, Manager of the Ramada Inn in Nacogdoches. Ms. Betty Morrow kindly spent many hours typing the manuscripts and Ms. Jinnie Fleming handled fiscal affairs. Jan Warren and Frances Main deserve special acknowledgement in editing. Lisa Knauf, Juan Torres and Ashley Snipp provided additional assistance. Robert Biesterfeldt, Southeastern Forest Experiment Station provided critical manuscript editing. Glenn Millard and Morris Lang, Computer Center, Stephen F. Austin State University, provided key technical assistance. Ben Carter provided production assistance. Rene Alcaniz, J. Howard Williamson, Myrna Johnson, Steve Tracy, Karen Cathey, Jim Mitchell, Jim Meeker, Jim Bing and Karen Middlebrooks assisted at the symposium. Bob Murphy gave insights at the banquet. Larry Phillips, National Forest System, Region 8, provided guidance and coordination throughout the conference. Dr. Kent T. Adair, Dean, School of Forestry, Stephen F. Austin State University, provided insight, advice and encouragement throughout the entire process.

David L. Kulhavy
Richard N. Conner
Nacogdoches, TX

**Ramada Inn
Nacogdoches, Texas
May 13-15, 1985**

Sponsored by:

**School of Forestry,
Center For Applied Studies,
Stephen F. Austin State University**

Southern Forest Experiment Station

Southeastern Forest Experiment Station

National Forest System, Region 8

The Wilderness Society

CONTENTS

SECTION 3: FOREST PROTECTION

SECTION 4: MANAGEMENT ISSUES

SECTION 5: VISITOR NEEDS AND IMPACT

SECTION 6: VEGETATION

SECTION 7: GRASSLANDS AND SAVANNAHS

SECTION 8: SUMMARY

An Introduction To Wilderness And Natural Area Management

by
David L. Kulhavy, Richard N. Conner, Fred E. Smeins, and Michael H. Legg

Management issues in wilderness and natural areas are many faceted. Managers must interact with and be aware of information from scientific disciplines, user groups and agency policies. In addition to actual land management problems concerning vegetation, wildlife, and pest species, management must address the needs of and problems created by wilderness users. Water and air quality are important issues in wilderness management and will probably increase in importance as populations near wilderness areas and wilderness use increases. Complex problems related to oil and mineral rights that exist in some wilderness areas will inevitably conflict with other wilderness values.

How to manage the complex of resources and recreation values in wilderness areas is a basic question. Thus a philosophy of "no management" can lead to many user and environmental problems. Change is the rule in natural communities. How we manage vegetation will affect the type of wilderness we have, what wildlife is present, and what potential pest problems may arise. The wilderness areas we have today are not the pristine "natural" communities our forefathers encountered. They are a product of the alterations we have made on them combined with the effects of surrounding land use patterns. Land use patterns around wilderness areas may limit our ability to use certain management techniques such as fire to manage for "fire-climax" plant communities.

We must also deal with complex issues such as southern pine beetle control and endangered species. These two problems also create incredible challenges to the wilderness manager. All of our management solutions to problems must, however, be tempered by the initial intent of wilderness legislation and the concept of "minimal tool use." We must learn to use the least management necessary to achieve our goals while still preserving the true wilderness character of each area.

WILDLIFE

Wildlife is an important part of wilderness and natural areas. Indeed it is often the wild beasts that give

wilderness its true character. The bugling of an elk or call of a loon disturbing the silence of the evening more than anything else represents one of the greatest values of wilderness. The wildlife that lends its character to wilderness is dependent on the wilderness habitat. Eventually, without management, habitat in wilderness areas will be composed mainly of old-growth or climax vegetation. Such vegetational conditions are important to many species of wildlife, particularly those that need mature forests to meet their life requirements. In a time when human population centers, agriculture, and timber and mineral needs have dominated or claimed most of the eastern wild lands, it is of particular importance that large areas of roadless, old-growth habitat for species such as the gray wolf, mountain lion, black bear, and wolverine be preserved.

Also, choice of wilderness management strategies affects habitat. A strategy of no management may produce a plant community that is different from a strategy that favors active management to return a wilderness area to its primeval condition. A "no management" strategy will permit plant succession to occur if an area is not currently at climax vegetationally. Species diversity and composition of the wildlife community is tied directly to the type of plant community. Thus, what we permit to happen or actively manage for on wilderness and natural areas will determine wildlife species composition.

Vegetation management may also present legal conflicts if an endangered species inhabits a wilderness area. A "no management" policy or even a "minimum management" strategy may cause plant community changes that adversely affect an endangered species. Which law takes precedent, laws protecting wilderness, or laws protecting endangered species? A timely resolution to such conflicts is needed that protects both wilderness quality and endangered species.

FOREST PROTECTION

Biological organisms coexist in a dynamic ecological system. This system is subject to both subtle, slow changes and tumultuous wrenching perturbations. As a forest matures, trees within the system compete for resources, such as light, moisture, rooting space and nutrients. Competition leads to stress within each plant and within the system.

Stress may also arise due to physical changes in the system. One such example is a mature pine forest located on sites subject to alternating periods of flooding and drought. If these oscillations are coupled with disturbances (that is, lightning, tornadoes or hurricanes), the system generally responds in proportion to the disturbance. Small disturbances (a single lightning strike) usually lead to small changes; large disturbances (multiple lightning strikes) may lead to rapid changes. One organism central to the forest protection issue, and responding to these disturbances, is the southern pine beetle. Questions include its relationship to endangered species (for example the Red-cockaded Woodpecker), limits of the Wilderness Act and interpretation of the National Environmental Policy Act. Additional issues include the mosaic of ownership patterns in the forest community and the interaction of special interest and management groups.

In the context of the IPM (Integrated Pest Management) model (see Hertel, Mason and Thatcher, this volume), four items should be considered when deciding to take (or not take) management action against forest pests: 1) the resource manager must determine the potential effect on the resource; 2) the consequence of control (or no control) actions must be ascertained; 3) affects on the forest ecosystem must be included; and, if warranted, 4) further needs for research and development, impacts and benefits of management decisions, must be included. There are no easy answers to these management issues--the purpose of this volume is to consider potential solutions for these long term wilderness management issues.

VEGETATION

The forest, prairie and forest inclusions such as savannahs, glades, barrens, bogs, marshes and others are dynamic entities that constantly vary in response to natural physical and biotic factors as well as man-made impacts. Disturbances due to periodic fires, climatic flucuations, animal activities and other variables have interacted to produce, and are often necessary to maintain, the diverse communities of the region. Of course, many of these communities have been greatly altered or destroyed by man's activities. Conversion to urban and agricultural use, clearcutting, introduction of exotic species, and cessation of naturally occurring fires, have permanently changed the structure, composition and integrity of many communities. Certainly those communities that occur in restricted, unique habitats suffer most from these impacts.

Braun in her classical 1950 treatment, Deciduous Forest of North America, divided the forest into 9 regions:
1. Mixed Mesophytic Forest: Southern Appalachian plateau and mountains, diverse composition, includes botanical elements found in nearly all other forest regions.
2. Western Mesophytic Forest: West of Mixed Mesophytic (Tennessee, Ohio) drier, less diverse version of Mixed Mesophytic.
3. Oak - Chestnut Forest: Eastern margin of Mixed Mesophytic chestnut largely eliminated by chestnut blight.
4. Oak - Pine Forest: Piedmont from Virginia to Texas, pines dominate secondary forests.
5. Southeastern Evergreen Forest: Coastal plain from New Jersey to Texas historical fires and current fires and logging perpetuate pine forests.
6. Beech - Maple: Southern margin of Great Lakes (Michigan, Ohio).
7. Hemlock - White Pine - Northern Hardwoods: Northern part of Great Lakes region into southern Canada.
8. Maple - Basswood: Narrow belt between forest and grassland in Minnesota and Wisconsin.
9. Oak - Hickory: Western margin of deciduous forest, forming westward the transition to the central grasslands - western limits expressed as the Cross-Timbers from Kansas to Texas.

Grasslands to the west of the forest are characterized by wide-ranging species such as big and little bluestem, Indiangrass, switchgrass and other tall and midgrasses. Management is essential to maintain and, in many cases, to restore the natural communities of this region. Enlightened, multiple - resource management based upon sound ecological information is needed to allow for not only use of the resources of these communities, but also to conserve and preserve their natural diversity and productivity.

VISITOR USE AND IMPACT

Wilderness is made up of three parts: a natural land base, a potential recreational experience, and a national heirloom to be protected forever. Wilderness management is faced with the multiple challenges of protecting and preserving the physical resource while not reducing, or allowing the users to reduce, the quality of the recreation experience. In many cases the greatest threat to the environmental quality of a wilderness is not the natural pests or disturbances that occur periodically, but the users themselves. They trample, pollute and erode the very resource they came to enjoy. The quality of the wilderness experience more than any other form of recreation is tied directly to the undisturbed environmental quality of the area.

The role of visitor management is to accomplish the maximum of resource protection with a minimum of intrusion upon the user. Maximum acceptable intrusion varies with the initial expectations of the visitor. Long lists of rules and regulations can infringe upon the wilderness experience that emphasizes the absence of restrictions and solitude from the limits of modern society. Attitudes, previous experiences, and level of knowledge about natural resources are all characteristics that determine the goals and benefits that recreationists expect to achieve with a wilderness recreation experience.

The challenge of management is to provide the information necessary to insure that visitors have realistic expectations of a wilderness experience. Information can be used to insure that the users are knowledgeable enough to either voluntarily protect the resource or to help them understand the need for regulations.

Wilderness: Important Legal, Social, Philosophical And Management Perspectives

by
John C. Hendee

ABSTRACT--Growth of the Wilderness System nationwide and in the Eastern United States has resulted from public demand, and expresses values rooted in American culture. Current trends in our society support an extended application of the wilderness concept. Wilderness management offers resource professionals a chance for leadership in something the public thinks is important. The public's involvement in wilderness has grown beyond decision-making to also include work in wilderness management. Wilderness managers need to increase their skills in working with the public, recognize wilderness values beyond just recreation, and apply established management principles to insure that eastern areas are fully integrated into the National Wilderness Preservation System.

KEYWORDS: wilderness, management, minimal tool rule, philosophy, public involvement.

This is a timely book. Wilderness in the East has grown rapidly--in size, in public appreciation of its values, and in public involvement in its protection. Managing wilderness areas in the East reflects the broader challenges of managing the entire National Wilderness Preservation System. The public and resource professionals need to work together for one national Wilderness System and to manage our system skillfully, wisely, and with foresight about the ultimate values of wilderness to our nation and humankind.

As our Wilderness System has grown in size and variety, we have begun to value the diversity it includes. Particularly in the East, wilderness areas are smaller, and may have more historic human impacts than have western areas. Our challenge is to fully integrate all designated areas into the National Wilderness Preservation System, all as full members of our national family of wilderness areas, each special for its own unique qualities.

Surely we have the skills to do this. The presence of scientists, highly trained resource managers, eager students of resource technology, and our management traditions all testify to the many management alternatives we can generate and the analytical power we can focus on them. Yet, our breadth of vision may be challenged. Will we apply our wilderness management technology with wisdom and foresight toward the highest, long-term values of the Wilderness System? Will we listen to and learn from the growing public awareness that wilderness values are deep-rooted in our nation's psyche and central to our traditions?

These questions must be the heart of our discussions. We could easily divert our attention to short-term prob-

lems, conflicts, and immediate policy issues. Obviously, we must deal with immediate problems. But the essence of wilderness management is its long-term focus, embracing the protection of both ecosystems and related human values.

I want to offer some important legal, social, and philosophical perspectives on wilderness, and relate those perspectives to management. My purpose is not to instruct you on management methods. Many of the nation's leading wilderness management experts and most experienced managers are available to do that. I want to provide background and perspective for your more technical discussions with them. More than anything, my purpose is to urge you to listen to what the public says is valuable in wilderness, and to inspire you to **let those wilderness values guide our management** under the Wilderness Act.

OVERVIEW

First, I want to review the dramatic growth of the National Wilderness Preservation System, nationwide and in the East. Recent Wilderness Classification Acts may imply a dilution of wilderness allocation criteria. In some cases they provide unique management direction. How do we cope with these evolving requirements while maintaining the integrity of the National System?

Second, I will review some social dynamics I think are related to the growth of wilderness appreciation. When we relate growth of the Wilderness System to other social trends, it is clear that wilderness is no passing fad and that trends are toward more of it.

Third, I want to review some values people place on wilderness, which I believe drive the growth of wilderness and must be the outputs of its management. Our success in managing the National Wilderness Preservation System to produce the highest aggregate values for our nation and all humankind depends on wilderness management that embraces these values. The public is watching resource professionals closely as we face this challenge.

Fourth are some management implications that derive from these legal, social, and philosophical perspectives. The future looks exciting. We are experiencing a transformation in how we manage wilderness. There is greater public involvement and partnership in wilderness decisions and management. This trend is also making wilderness values more accessible and meaningful to the American people.

Finally, I will press for simplicity and biocentric direction in wilderness management--and adherence to its fundamental principles. That is: do only what is necessary to meet wilderness objectives; apply a nondegradation concept; involve the public in setting objectives in area plans; and when management actions are necessary, use only the minimum tools, force, or regulations to meet those objectives.

LEGAL IMPLICATIONS: EVOLVING DEFINITIONS OF WILDERNESS

The definition of wilderness in terms of area size, naturalness, and solitude has been weakening since the days of the American frontier when mountain men roamed millions of acres. Aldo Leopold said in 1921 that to be wilderness, an area must be able to absorb a 2-week pack trip (Hendee *et al.* 1978, p. 9). In 1939, Forest Service U-regulations required 100,000 acres (40,470 ha) for an area to be called wilderness. The Wilderness Act of 1964 (PL 88-577) reduced the qualifying size to 5,000 acres (2,025 ha). The so-called "Eastern Wilderness Act" of 1975 (PL 93-622) reduced the qualifying size still further, and also allowed inclusion of areas with more human impacts. Of course, as the size criteria for wilderness decreased, the amount of land eligible for classification increased. Still, Senator Frank Church of Idaho, a leader in the passage of the Wilderness Bills, said in 1977 that he had anticipated an ultimate Wilderness System of about 40 to 50 million acres (16 to 20 million ha)--far short of what was by then developing (Church 1977, p. 6). The Wilderness Act had proved to be more a beginning than an end of the thrust for wilderness--especially as the wilderness concept was applied to National Forest roadless areas.

In 1971, the Forest Service began a Roadless Review and Evaluation (RARE I) to determine which of the remaining National Forest System roadless areas should be committed to wilderness study. RARE I resulted in 274 wilderness study areas containing 12.3 million acres (5.0 million ha).

But many felt that RARE I criteria were too stringent, particularly in the East. Ultimately these views prevailed.

Early in 1975, the so-called "Eastern Wilderness Act" (PL 93-622) expanded wilderness classification in the East, where only four areas had yet been designated. This legislation classified 16 National Forest areas--some 207,000 acres (83,800 ha)--as wilderness, and directed wilderness study for 17 other areas--an additional 125,000 acres (50,600 ha). Because of some areas included, it implied a change in minimum wilderness eligibility standards for size, naturalness, and solitude. Two of the new Act's wildernesses, and seven of its study areas, were smaller than 5,000 acres (2,025 ha). Some had been previously impacted by low-standard roads, logging, or homesteading. The Endangered American Wilderness Act of 1978 (PL 95-237) added still more roadless areas that were not selected for wilderness study in RARE I, and some that had not even qualified as roadless areas in the RARE I inventory. The need for another look at the roadless areas was apparent.

In early 1977, the Forest Service initiated a second roadless area review and evaluation, RARE II, which was intended to be more decisive and to include more areas in the Eastern United States. Based on a review of areas which Congress had classified as wilderness since passage of the 1964 Wilderness Act, RARE II guidelines permitted one-half mile (0.8 km) of improved Forest Service road per 1,000 acres (405 ha), and timber harvesting within the past 10 years on 20 percent of the area.

Under these more liberal criteria, RARE II found 1,921 remaining roadless areas on the national forests totaling 65.7 million acres (26.6 million ha). The majority were in the West; 2.3 million acres (0.9 million ha) were in 23 eastern states. President Carter proposed wilderness designation for 15.4 million acres (6.2 million ha) of National Forest lands--proposals that would have doubled the amount of wilderness in the East.

Action on the RARE II proposals developed steadily in the 96th Congress (1979-80), but dwarfing all other wilderness legislation was the Alaskan Lands Bill (PL 96-487), which nearly tripled the Wilderness System's size by adding 56 million acres (22.7 million ha), 5 million of them on RARE II lands.

Many thought action on the remaining RARE II proposals would lag with the new and conservative Republican administration. However, several wilderness bills took shape along state lines during the 97th Congress, often with strong bipartisan support. Five of them passed, designating wilderness in Indiana, Georgia, Missouri, Alabama, and West Virginia, but totaling less than 84,000 acres (34,000 ha). But the 98th Congress went on to pass 21 wilderness bills establishing or adding to new areas a total of about 8.3 million acres (3.4 million ha) in 22 states, including 52 areas totaling 513,000 acres (207,600 ha) in the East. In 1984, Congress increased classified wilderness in 12 southern states from 18 areas to 59 (Warren 1985).

All these Wilderness Classification Acts have liberalized the legal definition of wilderness because, in a pragmatic sense, as former Assistant Secretary of Agriculture Dr. Rupert Cutler stated, "Wilderness is whatever the U.S. Congress designates as wilderness" (Roth 1984, p. 1).

Some of these wilderness area classification acts also imposed special management direction to deal with controversial issues in particular areas. Two things are important here. First, Congress' willingness to defer to local differences and preferences, case by case, when the groups involved and their state delegations reach a consensus on how to handle controversial management issues; second, Congress' unwillingness to change the Wilderness Act just to resolve local problems.

For example, the Endangered American Wilderness Act (PL 95-237) provided for vault toilets serviced by helicopter in the Lone Peak Wilderness, which is an important municipal watershed. The Colorado Wilderness Act (PL 96-560) mandated guidelines for grazing of livestock in new wilderness areas in that state, and those guidelines have been adopted in several subsequent state bills. The Boundary Waters Canoe Area Wilderness Act (PL 95-495) allowed motorboat use to continue on some lakes, ended it immediately on others, and phased it out gradually on the rest.

A few of the state acts even attempt to clarify policy for the entire System. For example, the New Mexico (PL 96-550) and Colorado Wilderness Acts (PL 96-560) state that Congress does not intend the creation of buffer zones around wilderness, and this wording has been included in most subsequent wilderness classification acts.

This evolution of wilderness criteria illustrates the still expanding vision of the public, expressed through Congress, of the breadth and importance of the Wilderness System it desires. The public, it seems, wants to conserve many wilderness areas in the East that still approximate natural conditions while there is time to protect that natural heritage. This desire poses special management challenges, since many of these are smaller and more impacted than those in the West. But in other respects they are special as wilderness. Most western wilderness areas represent a residual--land remaining after allocations to all other uses. Many areas in the East have historically experienced logging, homesteading and ORV use, and have evolved to wilderness status because the public believes that is their highest and best use. Further, wilderness areas in the East are close to people; they are diverse ecologically and aesthetically, and many have potential through careful management to increase their wilderness qualities, thus becoming even more special relative to surrounding lands. Clearly, the public seems to trust that nature can restore natural conditions to areas in the East--given wilderness protection.

SOCIAL DYNAMICS RELATED TO WILDERNESS APPRECIATION

Several trends in U.S. society are related to and feed the growing wilderness appreciation. These include growing education levels of the public, wilderness-related education in colleges and universities, public involvement in resource decisions, political decentralization and conservatism, and wilderness as a rallying point and symbol for conservation.

A More Highly Educated Public

Research has shown a strong association between increased education, environmental values, and wilderness appreciation and use. In 1970, we attributed the surging increase in wilderness appreciation and use to educational gains during the 50's and 60's. But the Bureau of Census reports that during the 70's larger proportions of Americans than ever before graduated from high school, attended college for at least 1 year, and graduated from college.

These educational gains helped fuel appreciation of environmental values. Yet environmental values have become more than a luxury for those educated to appreciate them. Surveys reveal that a majority of Americans across all categories of education, race and ethnic background, political party, ideology, age, and income support the environmental movement--a movement for which wilderness provides symbolic meaning (Hendee 1984). The validity of these survey data is more pragmatically expressed in the widespread wilderness allocations by Congress.

Wilderness-Related Education in Colleges and Universities

A recent study found 417 colleges and universities with wilderness-related courses, addressing such things as wilderness values, benefits, use skills, and management (Hendee and Roggenbuck 1984). Where these courses are taught may be as important as their numbers--45 percent are in education schools, with much smaller percentages in resource management or biological sciences. Further, the education-based courses that most often focused on wilderness appreciation, use, and enjoyment had rising enrollment more often than wilderness protection and management courses. Broad support is apparent for wilderness appreciation as something we want to teach our youth, and as something they want to learn.

Public Involvement

One of the most important social trends influencing the wilderness concept, and which should therefore influence our wilderness management, is growing public involvement in resource policy. RARE II generated more than seven times as many public comments as RARE I (Hendee et al. 1980). Each new plan for managing a National Forest, or altering a natural area, seems to bring more public involvement than the one before.

Public involvement is also extending beyond decision-making to the work itself. Volunteerism in National Park and National Forest management is mushrooming. Wilderness is a favorite focus of volunteers--so much so that managing volunteers was one of the important "Issues in Wilderness Management" addressed at the recent national conference (Frome 1985). Volunteer rangers, wilderness information specialists, HOST programs, wilderness "cleanups" and "adopt a trail" projects--even the trend toward private contracting of trail construction and maintenance--all increase the involvement of citizens in wilderness work. The greatest value of these volunteer efforts goes beyond supplementing diminishing budgets; it is the involvement of the public in the day-to-day management of their public lands (Greer 1985). This involvement is making public facilitators out of wilderness managers.

Political Decentralization and Conservatism

We hear a lot these days about "Megatrends", one of which is decentralization, as people assert their right to more local self-determination. This trend is seen in the many State Wilderness Classification Acts passed in recent Congressional sessions. Three statewide acts, including the Alaskan Lands Bill (PL 96-487) designating 56 million acres (22.7 million ha) of wilderness, were passed by the 96th Congress (1979-80). Three more were passed by the 97th; and 21 acts, including 18 statewide Wilderness Acts, were passed by the 98th Congress ending in 1984. In each case, when state Congressional delegations agreed on areas in their states worthy of wilderness designation, they were supported by the rest of the Congress. Clearly this trend has facilitated local resolution of disputes,and, as mentioned earlier, some of these Acts include special management direction to deal with individual area conflicts.

The continued public support for wilderness during America's recent conservative renaissance has confounded those who consider environmental and wilderness values the luxuries of liberal thinking. Recent public opinion polls have shown majority support for the environmental movement, for the wilderness idea, and for the addition of millions of acres to the National Wilderness Preservation System.

No one would expect free market conservatives who seek short-run commercialization of resources to embrace wilderness, but the wilderness idea is not in conflict with broader conservatism. Listen carefully to the values the public espouses for wilderness. What is more conservative than leaving parts of our country "untrammeled by man . . . retaining their primeval character and influence"--at least until the resources they protect are more urgently needed? What better way to resist change for change's sake--a bedrock conservative attitude--than to guarantee that some of our heritage will remain intact for future generations? What more truly reflects conservative concerns for traditional values than retaining some wilderness as a "a natural reference point from which civilized people can take stock of their beginnings and regain touch with the natural balances that govern them"? (From a sign at Lake Butte Overlook, Yellowstone National Park.)

Wilderness as a Rallying Point for Conservation

America's natural resources, and more particularly our wilderness, strike a deep chord in our nation's psyche. Debate over altering a natural area symbolizes the development versus protection dilemma. Wilderness symbolizes

what has been lost; what has been saved; what is still natural, balanced, and whole; and thus what might be ideally pursued in man's relationship with the natural world. It is thus not surprising that wilderness has been one of the most important rallying points for the environmental movement, and a focal point for shaping our nation's conservation ethic. Wilderness has contributed to our culture, first by shaping our national character through its conquest, and more recently by inspiring in us an ecological awareness and conscience. The rallying force of wilderness helps mobilize action on a broad range of conservation concerns such as toxic wastes, soil loss, and pollution, to name a few.

The love of Americans for wilderness is so strong that it has become identified internationally as a hallmark of this country. This was a key factor in attracting the 4th World Wilderness Congress to Colorado in 1987, with the theme, "Wilderness as a rallying point for world conservation." Dr. Ian Player (1984), widely decorated international conservationist, claims: "The U.S. Wilderness idea and conservation know-how are America's most valuable gifts to the rest of the world."

We should appreciate the importance of wilderness in the social fabric of our country, and its growing international significance. And we should be proud of our affiliation with wilderness as resource professionals; it's an opportunity for leadership in something a large and growing public believes is important, a chance to be " . . . identified with resources that are highly valued by society, and that are perceived to be in some danger (Heinrichs 1985, p. 279)."

PHILOSOPHICAL PERSPECTIVES

The values of wilderness are subtle but real in the support they generate. Some derive from direct use; others are vicarious and symbolic. While some of these values have been converted through econometric gyrations into dollar values, their real worth defies such conversion.

Much has been written about wilderness values, and your list may be different from mine. But everyone's list includes more than just recreation. We need to understand the values--both real and symbolic--that attract millions of people to wilderness: to recreate in it, to work for it as volunteers, to study and read about it, to join organizations that promote it. We need to understand the appeal of the wilderness idea--the notion that we should retain some areas of our country in their natural state. This concept inspires broad endorsement by a majority of Americans, and intense commitment by a fervent minority. All these values, however we might describe or measure them, are the products desired from the National Wilderness Preservation System. The success of our wilderness management efforts depends on how clearly we understand these wilderness values and how effective we are in protecting and producing them.

I think we often assign too much weight to recreation, and too little to the indirect, vicarious, symbolic, and spiritual meanings that wilderness has to millions of people. Consequently, we have been surprised at Congressional wilderness allocations that exceeded our analyses of what is needed. It is fair to ask whether our wilderness management programs are similarly biased toward providing recreation use.

Wilderness Values

We know a lot about wilderness **recreation** use and how to manage it, because recreation is the most easily measured and studied wilderness use or value. Wilderness hiking, camping, climbing, and river running are increasingly popular, but only a small percentage of the population takes part in wilderness recreation. Nevertheless, more than half of all Americans endorse the wilderness idea. Obviously, recreation use is not the most widespread source of wilderness values.

Educational values of wilderness are extremely important. In addition to the numerous college level courses mentioned earlier, there are thousands of youth **environmental education** programs and summer camps run by institutions such as the Boy Scouts, YMCA, and churches of every denomination. Their information sources and study locations may not be wilderness dependent, but many of their most inspiring examples and case studies come from the intact natural processes whose strongest protection is in classified wilderness.

Many **experiential education** programs--Outward Bound, National Outdoor Leadership School (NOLS), Wilderness Vision Quest, and a host of others use wilderness as locations for education, **leadership development** and **personal growth**. These programs serve people who share the deep-seated American belief that wilderness experiences provide the most important lessons of life and thus shape the most important attributes of American character. Many are aimed at special and disadvantaged populations. They help people in crisis or transition find personal renewal and cope with change. They help those dealing with the trauma of domestic instability and chaos or abuse, those adjusting to emotional losses such as death and broken relationships, those recovering from alcoholism, drug abuse, and delinquent behavior. The importance of such programs is illustrated by a National Conference on Wilderness Therapy, September 13-17, 1985, Colorado Outward Bound Leadville Mountain Center, Leadville, Colorado.

All these programs derive from a belief that, in the natural environment (ideally in wilderness), away from the social pressures, excessive stimuli, and diversions that choke our lives, we can confront ourselves in depth, identify our values and priorities, and recover a sense of wholeness. This belief is part of our heritage from native, tribal people before us who drew spiritual and psychological strength from wilderness. Those people employed sophisticated rituals and exercises similar to those used in current programs. These programs reflect a modern-day search for essential human values. They reflect a

quest for one of the central beliefs of the founding fathers of our Wilderness System that the character building values of wilderness are vital to our society (Scott 1984). Do these personal growth and therapy programs depend on wilderness? Perhaps not. But their effectiveness is related to the presence of naturalness and solitude in which to pursue self-discovery with the fewest possible artificial distractions. Where but in wilderness are such conditions guaranteed?

These recreational, vicarious, educational, therapeutic, and personal growth uses do not exhaust the list of wilderness values. In an interdependent world economy where industrial impacts extend to every corner of the globe, areas like wilderness with intact natural processes are increasingly scarce. Wilderness areas are valuable assets: as **natural baselines** that reveal the extent of impacts elsewhere; for **scientific research** to discover and describe natural processes; as **gene pools** reflecting the incredible diversity of nature, and maintaining a gene reservoir we are only now developing the technology to use; and as **protected reserves for endangered or wilderness-dependent and associated flora and fauna**. They are valuable in their own right, but even more valuable to humankind as part of the natural baselines and gene pools that wilderness protects.

Finally, there are **symbolic and spiritual values** of wilderness. In a world characterized by rapid change and complexity that are both exciting and frightening, wilderness represents comforting stability and simplicity. The existence of wilderness reflects self-imposed limits on the technological imperative that we must subdue all the earth just because we can.

All these values--direct, indirect, vicarious, and symbolic--are the products of wilderness management. We need to embrace them all in our management strategies, not just focus on recreation.

MANAGEMENT IMPLICATIONS

Wilderness areas in the East exist because the public desires not only to preserve the few natural areas left in that region, but also to insure the recovery as wilderness of some areas already impacted by early settlement and use. What should the management principles be for wilderness in the East, given that many of these areas are smaller and many contain less initial naturalness and solitude than larger areas in the West? How do we embrace them as part of the National Wilderness Preservation System as Congress has mandated?

In my opinion, five fundamental management principles apply--bearing in mind that they are guides and that a "rule of reason" must govern their application. (These principles appear in a different order in Chapter of the textbook "Wilderness Management", Hendee, Stankey, and Lucas 1978.)

1. **Be biocentric in orientation.** The distinctiveness of wilderness is in the integrity of its natural processes, and

therein lies its values for people as well as its own protection. Wilderness managers must be guardians, not gardeners. The distinctiveness of wilderness recreation depends on naturalness and solitude; in short, on wilderness conditions. We must keep the wild in wilderness.

2. **Do only what is necessary.** Wilderness management means doing only what is necessary to maintain those thresholds of naturalness and solitude that distinguish an area as wilderness and that led to its classification. Do not let management presence or practices dilute the wilderness.

3. **Apply a nondegradation concept.** Each wilderness area stands as its own benchmark of naturalness and solitude. Wilderness management's purpose is thus to prevent further area degradation, or in some cases to upgrade wildness if it is determined to be below an acceptable wilderness threshold. Wilderness areas vary in their wildness, and management of the Wilderness System can protect that diversity, and need not aim at its lowest denominator of wildness.

4. **Involve the public in settling objectives for area plans.** Proposed management actions should be necessary to meet clearly defined objectives that describe desired wilderness conditions. These objectives and actions should be set forth in individual area management plans prepared with full public involvement. Public involvement and support are essential for management's success.

5. **Use minimum tools.** When management actions are necessary to meet planned objectives, use approaches, methods, and techniques that minimize impacts and regulation. This is the "minimum tool rule."

CONCLUSION

Where do we stand now, as resource management professionals, in recognizing and protecting what the public values in wilderness? Resource management has traditionally been concerned with directly harnessing natural resources for human consumption and use. When we implemented the Wilderness System, we never anticipated how much it would grow. With almost 88 million acres (35.6 million ha) of wilderness, we may be approaching a midlife crisis in resource management. Psychologist Carl Jung taught that midlife crisis resulted when the single-mindedness leading to success in early life repressed the normal development of the whole self that is essential to coping with later life. The solution, he believed, was not a swing to the other extreme, but a search for balance that fosters wholeness.

Similarly, resource management in America has spent its early years establishing efficient organizations and developing technology for natural resource consumption. Our success has helped make this one of the most prosperous societies in the world, and we are rightfully proud of that contribution. During those years we also gave birth to the wilderness idea and implemented a Wilderness System, and we are proud of that too. But in the early days wilderness was pure and vast, and solitude was truly solitude--wilderness had absolute qualities. The world has changed and so has the public appeal of wilderness. It now includes relative qualities of naturalness and solitude sometimes diluted compared to our pure, earlier standards. With growth, we have experienced growing pains. That is why we are here. Resource management has matured and our wilderness child has grown and changed; we must learn to adjust to a new relationship with it.

Jung's advice for midlife crisis was increased openness to the intangibles and spiritual values of life in a search for balance and wholeness. Similarly, as resource managers, we must allow the intangible values of natural resources, such as wilderness, to reach full bloom in balance with our other programs.

As a forester I believe--as most of you do--that wilderness must coexist and be managed in reasonable balance with programs for wildlife, forest products, water, recreation, and range. We need sound professional management of all those resources, not in competition with public concerns, but in alignment and harmony with them. That harmony can come through greater public involvement, and it is in wilderness that the public is most involved, helping us decide what to do and helping us do it.

We are experiencing a transformation in which resource professionals are becoming facilitators of the public--where the public will share not just management decisions, but the work as well. It is already happening in wilderness. It will be exciting to work and learn with the public to ensure that the wilderness values that inspired our forebearers will be there to guide our descendants. Through your efforts we will succeed in both the eastern and western United States.

ACKNOWLEDGMENTS

I want to thank the following colleagues for their review comments on earlier drafts: Paul Barker, Michael Brown, Millie Buchanan, Bill Coleman, Ken Cordell, Ed Krumpe, Vance Martin, Joe Roggenbuck and Paul Winegart.

LITERATURE CITED

Church, F. 1977. Wilderness in a balanced land use framework. First Annual Wilderness Resource Distinguished Lecture, Univ. Idaho Wilderness Res. Center, March 21. Reprinted as "Whither Wilderness," Am. For. 83:11-12, 38-41.

Frome, M. 1985. Issues in wilderness management. Westview Press, Boulder, Colo.

Greer, J.D. 1985. How to run a volunteer program. J. For. 82:660-662.

Heinrichs, J. 1985. Pinchot's heirs. J. For. 83:277-279.

Hendee, J.C. 1984. Public opinion about forestry and what to do about it. J. For. 82:340-344.

Hendee, J.C. and J.W. Roggenbuck. 1984. Wilderness-related education as a factor increasing demand for wilderness. *In* Proc. International For. Cong., Soc. Am. For., Quebec City, Canada.

Hendee, J.C., Z.G. Smith, and R.M. Lake. 1980. Public involvement in resource decisions: RARE I and RARE II and their implications for the future. pp. 217-232. *In* D.D. Hook and B.A. Dunn, (eds.). Proc. Multiple Use Symp., Clemson, South Carolina.

Hendee, J.C., G.H. Stankey and R.C. Lucas. 1978. Wilderness management. USDA Misc. Publ. 1365.

Player, I. 1984. A plan for the 4th World Wilderness Congress in Colorado, September 12-19, 1987 (draft). Available from Mr. Vance Martin, Congress Exec., Colorado State Univ., Coll. of For. Nat. Res., Ft. Collins, Colo.

Roth, D. 1984. The wilderness movement and the National Forests: 1964-1980. USDA For. Serv., FS-391.

Scott, D.W. 1984. The visionary role of Howard Zahniser. Sierra 69:40.

Warren, B.J. 1985. Why we need to control pine beetles in wilderness areas. For. Farmer 44:6-8.

What's In A Name: Perspectives On Wilderness Management

by
Paul F. Barker

ABSTRACT--Wilderness areas must be managed in accordance with the Wilderness Act. Each area is unique, but part of a national system.

KEYWORDS: 1964 Wilderness Act, management challenge.

What's in a name? In Shakespeare's play Othello, (Act III, Scene III) Iago says:
"Good name in man and woman, dear my Lord,
  Is the immediate jewel of their souls:
  Who steals my purse steals trash; 'tis something, nothing;
  'Twas mine, 'tis his, and has been slave to thousands;
  But he that filches from me my good name
  Robs me of that which not enriches him,
  And makes me poor indeed."
To Iago his good name and reputation were all important and all controlling, as I suspect they are to most of us. So What's in a Name? What's in the name "wilderness?" Is the integrity of the name "wilderness" as cherished as the integrity of our own name? I submit to you that it is. Not only is it as cherished, but it can be damaged in the same fashion.

We have heard and will continue to hear that wilderness in the East is different than wilderness in the West. Hogwash! Wilderness is wilderness! John Hendee (1985) in his keynote address referred to the "so called Eastern Wilderness Act." Scientists pride themselves on being exact and Dr. Hendee is exactly correct. It is the "so called" Eastern Wilderness Act because the Act does not have a name. That, in itself, is somewhat unique among legislative acts, but in this case, it is not only unique; it is very significant. I believe that Congress by design left the Act without a name to ensure that we would not in the future attempt to differentiate between eastern and western wilderness. The clear intent was to create one wilderness system throughout the United States, not an Eastern Wilderness System and a Western Wilderness System. A system that would give this country some "Islands in Time" to remind us of our great heritage, history, and opportunity in this fantastic country--to set aside for future generations areas of the United States where the land would not be modified. And so we have today a wilderness system spread across the country. Not a Eastern Wilderness System and a Western System.

Yes, the Paddy Creek Wilderness in Missouri differs from the Bob Marshall in Montana, just as the Bob Marshall differs from the Santa Lucia Wilderness in California. The portions of the country where they are located only partially explain the differences. What makes each area different is its individual characteristics. Wilderness is wilderness and must be managed as such, or we will besmirch the name wilderness and rob it of its good name.

From an administration standpoint how do we handle, or administer wilderness? We administer each area differently, but we manage all areas under the same philosophy and law. Each unit of the wilderness system is slightly different from any other unit, and we have to consider those unique wilderness values. Yet the sideboards within which we operate are exactly the same, regardless of which wilderness area we may be talking about. The difference in wilderness management from one area to another should only be the exceptions clearly allowed for in specific legislation such as mining, airstrips, fire control, etc.

What is that legislation? Each wilderness area falls under the umbrella of the 1964 Wilderness Act and the specific act that created the particular area. If you are going to discuss wilderness management you need constantly to carry one or possibly two instruments with you. One is the 1964 Act and the other is the Act that created the particular wilderness. If an area came into the wilderness system after 1964, then you need both instruments.

Forest Service Chief Max Peterson used the following example in his address at the University of Idaho Wilderness Conference. He mentioned that Justice Frankfurter, who was a great constitutional Supreme Court Justice, always carried a copy of the Constitution in his pocket because the Justice said, "I have observed that over time people get the idea that the Constitution says what they would like for it to say." The Chief went on to say, "There is also a great tendency for us to convert the Wilderness Act to what we would like for it to say or to remember only the part that we would like to remember." We constantly need to remind ourselves, whether we like to or not, that the Wilderness Act gives some pretty specific guidelines on what wilderness is and how it is to be managed. It is also equally specific in granting certain exceptions, and they are as important to remember as the rest of the Act. If it were not for the exceptions, it is debatable whether we would have a Wilderness Act today.

When the Wilderness Act finally passed it was after eight full years of Congressional debate and carefully worked out conditions. As professional land managers we have to be true to both aspects of the Act. Biblical scholars constantly stress the point that the Bible must interpret itself. In other words, one section of the Bible must be understood in connection with all the other sections. The same is true of the Wilderness Act. We do not have the luxury to manage wilderness according to what we may wish the Act said. We have the professional and legal responsibility to manage wilderness according to what the particular Acts actually say. As reasoning human beings we should, most of the time, be able to agree on what has been written in the law. We may not personally agree with what was written, but we must be guided by it in our management.

Our direction in the Secretary of Agriculture's Regulations and the Forest Service Manual are based on the philosophy and the wording of the Wilderness Act. Every time I reread the Act, the regulations, or the manual it seems I discover something new or that I had passed by on previous readings. In the Secretary's Regulations it states that "National Forest Wilderness resources shall be managed to promote, perpetuate, and where necessary, restore the wilderness character of the land and its specific values of solitude, physical and mental challenge, scientific study, inspiration and primitive recreation. To that end: (a) Natural ecological succession will be allowed to operate freely to the extent feasible.--" In previous reading the word **"restore"** had not jumped out at me, but there it is: "and where necessary restore the Wilderness character of the land and its specific values of solitude...." It is interesting that those words were written soon after the 1964 Act was passed and are not a recent addition. They speak well of the individuals who spent weeks working together to draft the Secretary's Regulations after passage of the 1964 Act. It would have been nice, convenient, and a lot easier if the criteria for managing wilderness as spelled out in the Act had also been the criteria for establishing wilderness areas. But they were not, so we have added **challenges to manage** some areas so that we restore the wilderness character of the land and its specific values of solitude, physical and mental challenge, scientific study, inspiration, and primitive recreation.

How do we do this? By constantly keeping in mind what the Act says: "In order to assure that an increasing population, accompanied by expanding settlement and growing mechanization, does not occupy and modify all areas within the United States . . . and these shall be administered for the use and enjoyment of the American people in such manner as will leave them unimpaired for future use and enjoyment as wilderness, . . . "wilderness is further defined in the Act as that" . . . which is protected and managed so as to preserve its natural conditions and which (1) generally appears to have been affected primarily by the forces of nature, with the imprint of man's work substantially unnoticeable; . . . " Yes, we have areas in the system where the imprint of man's work is noticeable. Where that exists, our challenge as professional land managers is to allow the natural processes to operate as freely as possible to restore those natural conditions of ecological freedom, solitude, and primitive recreation. One of the values of wilderness is scientific study and wilderness is occasionally used as a benchmark of natural conditions as well it should be. In areas where man's work is noticeable, what better place for scientists to study the natural recuperative power and process of the land unaltered by man's influences.

Wilderness management is challenging, it is difficult, and sometimes it is controversial. Some people believe wilderness requires no management--just leave it alone. That is not possible, nor was that the intent of Congress, which went into a fair amount of detail on uses of wilderness, prohibitions, and special provisions. Wilderness areas are to be used and enjoyed by the American public. Use implies that some changes will occur. We must be sure those changes caused by use do not detract from the enduring wilderness resource.

MANAGEMENT CHALLENGES

I mentioned earlier we have a challenge in some areas to restore. We must also permit use, recognizing that use will cause changes. Are there conflicts here? There could be if we ignored our management responsibility and took a hands-off approach. Change will occur simply through natural ecological process, which is one reason wilderness areas were established. At times, nature is not too gentle in its actions and the Act permits intervention by man in some cases. But the long-term changes, intrusions and uses of wilderness by man have the greatest potential to adversely alter wilderness areas over time.

Thirty years from now we will still have areas called wilderness: but will they be any different than any other tract of land that is void of roads? They can be and will be if we critically look at each decision we make in relation to what the law states, as well as its long-term cumulative effect. As an example, we constantly get requests for various types of electronic, radio transmission sites in wilderness. Each proposed addition would have little impact. The small structure would be painted to blend with the landscape and the majority of people would not even know it was there. For each individual request that is true. However, when you add all those individual requests together it becomes clear that soon there would be few mountain tops unoccupied. Sometimes it is difficult to see the long-term cumulative effect in relation to the request for use of a single peak.

How does the Wilderness Act address this issue? First: Congress' purpose in establing wilderness areas was: "In order to assure that an increasing population, accompanied by expanding settlements and growing mechanization, does not occupy and modify all areas in the United States.--" The purpose is to assure that we do not occupy all areas.

Second, the Act states "there shall be no temporary roads, no motor vehicles, motorized equipment, or motorboats, no landing of aircraft, no other form of mechanical transport, and no structures or installations in any such area." That is pretty clear, but the same section of the Act makes exceptions for existing private rights and exceptions as necessary to meet minimum requirements to administer the area for the purpose of the Act. We need to be sure that as administrators of wilderness areas we read all the words of the Act. The exceptions are not for administration of areas as wilderness, but for only **the minimum** needed for administration.

As we look at the next 20 years we need to be sure that we educate ourselves and those who use wilderness areas in the wilderness law and philosophy. If we are to have an enduring resource of wilderness I believe this is critically necessary, and a job that can never stop. If we stop, we will have constant problems managing according to what we think or would like wilderness to be rather than what the law says it should be. And we will have stolen the integrity of the name wilderness.

This book and others like it are a valuable part of that process. Our job is to understand what wilderness is and to administer it accordingly, not to redefine wilderness.

LITERATURE CITED

Hendee, J.C. 1986. Wilderness: Important legal, social, philosophical, and management perspectives. pp. 5-11 *In* D.L. Kulhavy and R.N. Conner (eds.). Wilderness and natural areas in the eastern United States: A management challenge. School of Forestry, Stephen F. Austin State Univ., Nacogdoches, Tex.

Wilderness Management Issues And Recommended Solutions

by

Larry N. Phillips

ABSTRACT--When the United States was being settled, wilderness was a barrier to progress and development. It was a place hostile to anyone except Indians. Today, wilderness represents an island in time, a source of inspiration, and primitive recreation for present and future Americans. There are several principles that must be followed if wilderness is to remain an enduring, untrammeled resource.

KEYWORDS: principles of wilderness management, limits of acceptable change.

The Chief of the Forest Service R. Max Peterson, recently stated "he had observed over time that many interpretations of the Wilderness Act are made in the context of what we personally would like for it to say; sometimes reading only the parts of the act that support our opinions."

We all have our preconceived image of what wilderness really is before we read the act, and most of us read the act, rather than studying it. The traditional or provincial idea of wilderness is a far cry from what is actually described in the Wilderness Act. The word "wilderness" itself derives from Old English "wildor," wild beast. In ancient times, it was a place hostile to man. The Bible equates it with "desert," the last refuge for outcasts, into which one drove the scapegoat laden with the sins of mankind. The Puritan settlers brought this concept with them across the Atlantic. To them, everything beyond the cleared area of the settlements was:

A waste and howling wilderness

Where none inhabited

but hellish fiends, and brutish men

that devils worshipped. (Brooks 1980)

In Europe, this attitude took a sudden turn in the late 18th century, beginning with philosophers like Jean Jacques Rousseau and culminating in the romantic movement, with Wadsworth as its English prophet. The American pioneer, however, had no time for enjoying the daffodils dancing in the breeze. He toiled with the land, which appeared to be limitless. He believed that taming the wilderness, and making it work for him was doing God's work. As Jehovah said unto Noah after the flood: "The fear of you and the dread of you shall be upon every beast of the earth and upon every bird of the air and upon everything that creeps on the ground and all the fish in the sea. Unto you they are delivered" (Brooks 1980).

It is not difficult to understand how the Christian ethic had come to weigh so heavily upon the land. Jumping to a more contemporary view of wilderness, an English wag once described wilderness as **"A cool, damp place where birds fly about uncooked."**

MANAGEMENT ISSUES

There are several areas where there seems to be more conflict and misinterpretation than understanding and agreement when management decisions are made, or when wilderness management philosophy is discussed. At one time or another, many of us have stated that specific Wilderness Areas were either too small or had the imprint of man's activities. This is the pure view or the nonrenewable resource philosophy. In the Forest Service, this concept was emphasized back in 1924, when the Gila Primitive Area was placed in a wilderness category to protect its pristine qualities. The areas that were later designated wilderness and primitive by the Forest Service up until the 1964 Wilderness Act, conformed to this philosophy that wilderness was a nonrenewable resource. This philosophy was discussed when Chief John McGuire testified on March 26, 1974, about eastern wilderness legislation. He stated, "In interpreting the Wilderness Act, the Forest Service has placed emphasis on areas which have retained their primeval character and influence. Prior to the Wilderness Act, and now under its definition, we have considered wilderness as unique, nonrenewable, predominantly undisturbed natural resource."

Since passage of the Wilderness Act and the 1975 (Eastern) amendment to the Act, the nonrenewable resource concept has faded somewhat. Popular and congressional support of vastly modified lands, particularly in the East, has redefined wilderness as a resource that can be created by man.

This renewable resource concept is supported by the fact that the National Forests of the East have been put together from the "lands nobody wanted." They were purchased piecemeal from small private owners. The result is a patchwork ownership of public and private lands. Much of this land had been abused, poorly protected, or ignored before being acquired. Today, the same land is healing and has a natural appearance.

The 1964 Wilderness Act did not absolutely confirm the nonrenewable concept. Section 2C states, "A wilderness is so designated . . . to preserve its natural conditions and which (1) generally appears to have been affected primarily by the forces of nature with the imprint of man's work substantially unnoticeable . . . " It goes on to say, "A wilderness area has at least 5,000 acres (2,025 ha)--or is of sufficient size as to make practicable its preservation and use in an unimproved condition."

If wilderness managers are to protect, enhance, promote, and perpetuate this wilderness resource, they need a set of principles or guidelines. The practice of wilderness management is not a precise science. Seldom are there clear and precise answers for managers faced with problems. They must interpret information and choose among alternative solutions to problems. (Hendee *et al.* 1978)

SOLUTIONS

On a daily basis, wilderness managers are confronted with difficult decisions. I want to discuss a set of principles of wilderness management that offer a logical and consistent framework on which to base decisions. These should be used as basic concepts and fundamental assumptions to guide the development of more specific management direction for individual Wilderness Areas. They can be referenced in our management documents. More detail on these principles is found in Chapter 7, Wilderness Management by John C. Hendee. George H. Stankey and Robert C. Lucas *et al.* 1978.

Wilderness Is On One End Of The Environmental Scale

Wilderness is less modified than nonwilderness, but may provide many of the same uses. When an area is classified as wilderness, many forces can still erode the primeval qualities of naturalness and solitude. Some activities that will erode the environmental spectrum are trail biking, overnight shelters, comfort stations, and retreats for teaching religion, mountaineering, survival and environmental education. Management must maintain the thresholds between wilderness and other lands. Any pressure to increase environmental modification of wilderness must be resisted. Wilderness cannot meet all the demands made upon it without either directly violating provisions of

the act or compromising the qualities that distinguish wilderness from other lands.

Wilderness Management Is Related To Adjacent Lands

Management outside and inside of wilderness cannot be done in a vacuum. Many examples illustrate the interrelationships between inside and outside lands. Timber harvesting next to a wilderness boundary may open up new access routes to the wilderness, dramatically affecting the amount and character of recreation use. The development of high-density recreational facilities next to a boundary may generate serious management problems.

Impacts can also move from wilderness to nearby nonwilderness areas. Natural fire in wilderness may cause a smoke problem on the outside. Insect and disease attacks may spread outside the boundary. Relating the management of wilderness to that on adjacent land is a complex and controversial issue. Buffer zones have been suggested, but we do not recommend these. We recommend explicitly defined use zones to help protect against overdevelopment near wilderness boundaries. These use zones are described in the "Recreation Opportunity Spectrum User Guide Handbook" as primitive, semiprimitive, nonmotorized, semiprimitive motorized, roaded natural, and rural. This zoning will prevent managers from responding to every increase in use with a development to accommodate it, such as a large parking lot at the edge of a wilderness. Also, it will help prevent the construction of trails in areas visited only by cross-country travelers seeking the greatest possible isolation, and may even prevent the construction of trails in very small wildernesses. The above Forest Service Handbook guides the recreation resource input to land and management planning. Land management plan incorporates the recreation opportunity spectrum as the basic framework for inventorying, planning, and managing the recreation resource in accordance with the Forest and Rangeland Renewable Resource Planning Act of 1974 (RPA), as amended by the National Forest Management Act of 1976 (NFMA).

Wilderness Should Be Managed As A Distinct, Composite Resource With Inseparable Parts

Although to the early settler the abundant wilderness was something to be eliminated, it has now achieved a measure of utility and value. The 1960 Multiple Use Sustained Yield Act recognized wilderness as a resource in Section 2, when it stated, "The establishment and maintenance of areas of wilderness are consistent with the purpose and provisions of this act". From a management standpoint, one important attribute of the wilderness resource is the natural relationship among all its ecological parts; vegetation, water, forage, wildlife, and geology. It is a composite resource with inseparable parts, and the central focus of its management must be on the interrelationships of the whole, not on those component parts. This is why the wilderness management document must not develop isolated management direction for vegetation, water, recreation, and wildlife, but must respond to the interrelationships among these and all other component parts of the resource.

How does wilderness fit into the renewability perspective? As Senator Frank Church noted in 1972: "This is one of the great promises of the Wilderness Act, that we can dedicate formerly abused areas where the primeval scene can be restored by natural forces." To do this, the focus has to be on protecting the naturalness of relationships between its ecological parts.

Wilderness Management Is To Produce Human Values

The Wilderness Act stated, "It is . . . the policy of the Congress to secure for the American people of present and future generations the benefits of an enduring resource of wilderness." How these benefits are derived from wilderness is an important and controversial question.

Direct benefits may result to wilderness visitors from the pleasure of therapy coincident to their wilderness recreation. Others may vicariously appreciate or indirectly benefit from wilderness, simply by knowing it is there or by reading about it. It is from the primeval attributes of wilderness that its human values and benefits are derived; attempts to facilitate their enjoyment by making them easier, more convenient, or simultaneously accessible to too many people at one time can ultimately diminish them. Management philosophy also must be applied wisely to avoid extreme purity. The wise manager will not allow public use to the point that the natural forces of the wilderness and its solitude are affected.

Wilderness Preservation Requires Management Of Human Use And Its Impact

The principal goal of wilderness preservation is the maintenance of long-term ecological processes. Thus,

wilderness management is basically concerned with management of human use and influence to preserve natural processes. Recreational impacts are currently among the most critical unnatural influences in wilderness. However, ecological problems are also growing, and wilderness managers are being challenged to monitor the naturalness of wilderness. We also need to restore fire closer to its historical role.

Establish Goals And Objectives For Wilderness Management In Individual Management Documents

Because wilderness management covers so many inter-related resources, objectives must be developed for each resource. It is a very difficult job to write clear objectives for all the various aspects of wilderness management. Clear objectives will guide judgements about what management actions are necessary, will provide continuity when managers are replaced, and will prevent independently conceived decisions. Poorly conceived management actions can be as damaging to wilderness values as the absence of necessary management.

Carrying Capacity Constraint Or Limits Of Acceptable Change

The concept of carrying capacity, which is the use an area can tolerate without unacceptable impacts occurring, offers a framework for limiting use in order to preserve wilderness qualities. Carrying capacity has two important parameters when applied to wilderness. They pertain to the physical impacts that an ecosystem can sustain without showing evidence of unnatural impacts, such as soil compaction and vegetative destruction around campsites. The second parameter pertains to the social or psychological impacts that an area can accommodate before the solitude is diminished.

Limiting the number of users to a carrying capacity is only one solution available to wilderness managers. They may also set limits of acceptable change in wilderness planning (Stankey et al. 1985). Such limits provide many other alternative courses of action to the manager. Use can be regulated by this process if the limits of acceptable change and the methods for monitoring them have been defined. In effect, this process defines desired wilderness conditions, and management actions to maintain or achieve these conditions.

Selectively Reducing Physical And Social-Psychological Impacts Of Use

This principle calls for selective restriction. Use reductions should focus on specific use impacts in the wilderness environment and the wilderness experience of other visitors. Across-the-board restrictions should not be applied everywhere in a wilderness to solve problems that might be only local or temporary in nature.

Apply Only The Minimum Regulation Necessary To Achieve Wilderness Management Objectives

This principle of minimum regulation calls for the use of only that level of control necessary to achieve a specific objective. If, for example, managers wish to bring about a more even use distribution, they might seek the coopera-

tion of informed users. To achieve this, they might provide users with information about current use distributions, alternative trailheads or other areas they might use, times when concentrations are lowest, and so forth. However, if current impacts are so severe that this light handed, indirect approach seems inadequate or if it fails to bring about the desired redistribution of use, then a more restrictive direct action approach might be needed. A manager might need to limit camping at damaged sites, assign entry quotas for each trailhead, or even assign campsites.

The Nondegradation Concept

Basically, the nondegradation concept calls for the maintenance of present environmental conditions if they equal or exceed minimum standards, and the restoration of below-minimum levels. Where existing conditions are judged to be below minimum acceptable levels, an appropriate priority of management is to promote restoration of the wilderness to a minimum quality level. This does not imply the active manipulation of the resource, such as scarifying campsites. It normally will involve the control of use numbers or the timing of use.

Wilderness-Dependent Activities Should Be Favored

Wilderness serves as a setting for many activities, ranging from scientific study to recreational pursuits, such as fishing, backpacking, and hunting. Conflicts among competing wilderness uses should be solved by favoring those that are highly dependent on a wilderness setting. It may be a tough job separating the dependent wilderness activities. However, the key to favoring wilderness dependent activities in classified wilderness is the availability of alternative non-wilderness lands where the inappropriate activities may be diverted

SUMMARY

In conclusion, wilderness is a special place, a special resource, and a renewable resource that requires special sensitive treatment by the manager and user. These principles are not comprehensive nor do they insure quality wilderness management. They do provide a broad conceptual foundation that can guide management decisions. They provide a means for consistent management goals and objectives that will promote, perpetuate and renew our wilderness resource.

LITERATURE CITED

Brooks, P. 1980. The wilderness ideal. Living Wilderness, September 1980.

Hendee, J.C., G.H. Stankey and R.C. Lucas. 1978. Wilderness management. Chapter 7, Some principles of wilderness management.

Stankey, G.H., D.N. Cole, R.C. Lucas, M.E.Petersen, and S.S. Frissell. 1985. The limits of acceptable change (LAC) system for wilderness planning. USDA For. Serv. Gen. Tech. Rep. INT-176.

Why Have Wilderness?

by

Peter C. Kirby

ABSTRACT--The goal of wilderness management is to maintain and enhance the special wild values for which areas are designated as wilderness. From the starting principles of "why wilderness," agencies and the public can assess the adequacy of present and proposed management direction. Basic reasons for wilderness include: (1) preservation of a representative range of the nation's biological diversity, (2) opportunities for recreation in an unmodified natural setting, (3) protection of relatively large blocs of undisturbed wildlife habitat, (4) assured protection of important watersheds for the benefit of users and sensitive fish species, (5) expression of the "land ethic," and (6) model for the world on the above issues. In light of these reasons, conservationists consider two current Forest Service programs as unsound and ill-advised: timber cutting in wilderness to seek to control the southern pine beetle and the proposed doubling and tripling of roading and timbering in draft forest plans in the eastern and southern United States.

KEYWORDS: wilderness, southern pine beetle, RARE II, ecological diversity, wildlife habitat, land ethic, need for wilderness, value of wilderness.

As one of the cosponsors of this symposium, the Wilderness Society appreciates this opportunity to become more involved with federal agency land managers, academicians and researchers in seeking common solutions to the increasingly important challenges of wilderness management in the East. With a membership of over 135,000 at last count, the Society is the only national conservation group dedicated exclusively to wildlands protection and management of the federal lands. Headquartered in Washington, D.C., we presently have nine field offices, including two permanent offices in the East. (Ronald Tipton, Southeast Regional Director is located at 1819 Peachtree Rd., N.E., Atlanta, Ga. 30309, (404) 355-1783. Sarah Muyskens, Northeast Regional Director, is located at 20 Park Plaza, Boston, Mass. 02116, (617) 350-8866. In 1985 Mike Anderson is working on wilderness and forest planning issues in Michigan. He is located at 115 West Allegan, Lansing, Michigan 48933, (517) 484-2372).

The Wilderness Society has always had a special place in its heart--and its agenda--for eastern wilderness. We were founded 50 years ago, in 1935, following an animated discussion by four men in the forests outside Knoxville, Tennessee. United in opposition to a then-proposed highway through the Smokies, they agreed to form an organization to save wildlands in the West and East and established The Wilderness Society. In addition to much work on the 1964 Wilderness Act itself, the Society played a major leadership role in the passage of the 1975 Eastern Wilderness Act and the host of additional bills passed in 1980, 1982 and 1984 that established the wilderness areas under discussion at this symposium.

In the last year, the Society has further committed major resources to influencing proper management of the national forests, including wilderness areas, by the creation of a new Resource Planning and Economics Department. Combining the expertise of foresters, economists, lawyers (like myself) and other analysts, the Department seeks to reorient the Forest Service towards more balanced multiple-use management by reviewing the annual Forest Service budget, the long-range RPA Program, individual NFMA forest plans and other agency actions. Most recently, we have prepared detailed critiques of the draft plans for the White Mountain and Cherokee National Forests in the East. Along with the Sierra Club and the Texas Committee on Natural Resources, we have also sued the Forest Service in Texas to try to stop the cutting of timber in designated wilderness areas in connection with the southern pine beetle infestation.

With many new national forest areas established as wilderness in 1984, this is a very timely occasion to examine the expanded management challenge for the Forest Service. The 98th Congress (1983-84) added about 6.8 million acres of new forest wilderness, bringing the total acreage in the National Forest System to about 32.1 million acres. This represented about a doubling of the number of areas: 163 areas were added in 1984 to the pre-existing l64. About 17 percent of the total National

Forest System of 191 million acres is now managed as wilderness.

In 1984, Congress passed a number of statewide RARE II bills in the East: Wisconsin (24,000 acres, 9,713 ha); Vermont (41,000 acres, 16,593 ha); New Hampshire (77,000 acres, 31,162 ha); Pennsylvania (10,000 acres, 4,047 ha); Virginia (56,000 acres, 22,163 ha); North Carolina (69,000 acres, 27,924 ha); Texas (34,000 acres, 13,760 ha); Arkansas (91,000 acres, 36,828 ha); Mississippi (5,500 acres, 2,226 ha); Florida (50,000 acres, 20,235 ha) and Georgia (14,000 acres, 5,666 ha). Less than statewide bills included: southern Tennessee (25,000 acres, 10,118 ha) and Missouri (16,500 acres, 6,678 ha). While releasing other roadless areas to multiple-uses other than wilderness, these bills also made some lands wilderness study areas and left other areas to the RARE II restudy process. A map and table for all the new areas are displayed as Attachment One.

All told, wilderness in the East (Regions 8 and 9) now totals about 1.7 million acres (0.69 million ha). The national forest ownership for these regions is about 24 million acres (9.7 million ha). Thus, in the East, only 7 percent of the national forest land is now managed as wilderness, compared to 17 percent for the System as a whole. In the Eastern Region (No 9), there are presently 31 wilderness areas, totalling 1.2 million acres (0.49 million ha) of federal ownership out of the Region's 11.4 million acres (4.6 million ha) for a share of 10.2 percent. The biggest single area is, of course, Minnesota's Boundary Waters Canoe Area at 800,000 acres (323,760 ha). In the Southern Region (No 8), there are presently 56 wilderness areas, totalling 522,736 acres (211,551 ha) of federal ownership out of the Region's 12.6 million acres (5.1 million ha) for a share of about 4 percent.

As these numbers suggest, there are some important geographical gaps that remain to be filled in the East. In the Eastern Region, statewide wilderness legislation is much needed for Michigan, where there is currently **no** designated forest wilderness. Individual area designations are also needed for the Daniel Boone and White Mountain National Forests. In the Southern Region, major wilderness legislation will be sought for Tennessee, where no wilderness has been designated yet in the northern portion of the Cherokee National Forest, and for the Chattahoochee National Forest. Forest plans will also be studying many individual areas for possible wilderness in Alabama, North Carolina, Virginia, South Carolina and Puerto Rico.

Even if all the areas sought by conservationists are designated, still only a very small percent of national forest land in the East will be managed as wilderness. Thus, it becomes crucially important that these lands and other federal lands are managed to protect and enhance their natural values. To determine the correct policies for Forest Service management of wilderness and other natural areas, we need to ask: "Why Have Wilderness?" at all. From these starting principles, we can review the adequacy of present and proposed management direction.

REASONS FOR WILDERNESS PRESERVATION

Ecological Diversity

One of the foremost reasons for preserving wild land in its natural condition is to save intact a representative range of the nation's biological diversity. The benefits of protecting the integrity of a wide range of ecosystems are many and varied. Among the scientific benefits is the preservation of a natural laboratory for medical and scientific study that can lead to better health and an improved quality of life. For example, plant and animal species existing in their natural habitats have been vital in the development of drugs to fight heart disease, antibiotics, anticancer agents, hormones and anticoagulants. More than 40 percent of modern pharmaceuticals are derived from natural substances, and only 1 percent of known plant species have been studied thoroughly for possible human benefits.

Also of benefit is the maintenance of gene pools for diversity of animal and plant life. Each species is an important link in the intricate web of life. Wilderness provides an irreplaceable habitat for wildlife and plants in their natural state; it serves as a perpetual yardstick for measuring and assessing the impact of human activities on the environment in other areas. Writing in *Wilderness* magazine (Summer 1984), Professor Edward O. Wilson of Harvard warns of the steep decline in biological diversity:

"In our own brief lifetime humanity will suffer an incomparable loss in aesthetic value, practical benefits from biological research, and worldwide biological stability. Deep mines of biological diversity will have been dug out and carelessly discarded in the course of environmental exploitation, without our even knowing fully what they contained."

Wilderness serves a crucial role by allowing us to save some of the ecological pieces of America as we tinker wholesale with our natural endowment, to paraphrase Aldo Leopold. To date, wilderness has helped protect samples of somewhat less than half of the nation's basic ecosystems for scientific and educational use. In 1982, George Davis estimated that of the 233 distinct ecosystems in the United States, as defined by the Bailey-Kuchler method, 81 were represented in the wilderness system. By a very rough use of Davis' tables, I would estimate that in 1984 Congress added areas that represent another 25 ecosystems, bringing the total to 106. Of the 127 ecosystems not yet represented, Davis' article would indicate that another 77 can be found on federal land.

Thus, an urgent remaining need is to add important and missing ecological pieces to the wilderness system. For, as Davis counsels: "If we are not willing to set aside representative samples of the earth's complex systems that we know and are a part of, our future understanding of natural processes and our flexibility will be unnecessarily limited." If its potential is fully realized, the wilderness system could eventually represent samples of almost three-quarters of all the distinct and diverse ecosystems found in our country.

Wilderness

Record of the 98th Congress

ARKANSAS

Black Forest Mountain: 7,568
Dry Creek: 6,310
Poteau Mountain: 10,884
Flatside: 10,105
Upper Buffalo: 1,504 (addition)
Hurricane Creek: 15,177
Richland Creek: 11,822
East Fork: 10,777
Leatherwood: 16,956

FLORIDA

Bradwell Bay: 1,170 (addition)
Mud Swamp/New River: 7,800
Big Gum Swamp: 13,600
Alexander Springs: 7,700
Juniper Prairie: 13,260
Little Lake George: 2,500
Billies Bay: 3,120

GEORGIA

Ellicott Rock: 2,000 (addition)
Southern Nantahala: 12,439
    (addition)

MISSISSIPPI

Black Creek: 4,560
Leaf: 940

MISSOURI

Irish: 16,500

NEW HAMPSHIRE

Pemigewasset Area: 45,000
Sandwich Range: 25,000
Presidential Range-Dry River:
    7,000 (addition)

NORTH CAROLINA

Birkhead Mountains: 4,790
Catfish Lake South: 7,600
Ellicott Rock: 3,680 (addition)
Joyce Kilmer: 2,980 (addition)
Linville Gorge: 3,400 (addition)
Middle Prong: 7,900
Pocosin: 11,000
Pond Pine: 1,860
Sheep Ridge: 9,540
Shinning Rock: 5,100 (addition)
Southern Nantahala: 10,900

PENNSYLVANIA

Allegheny Island: 368
Hickory Creek: 9,337

TENNESSEE

Big Frog: 5,055
Citico Creek: 16,000
Bald River Gorge: 3,887

TEXAS

Turkey Hill: 5,400
Upland Island: 12,000

Big Slough: 3,000
Indian Mounds: 9,946
Little Lake Creek: 4,000

VERMONT

Breadloaf: 21,480
Big Branch: 6,720
Peru Peak: 6,920
Lye Brook: 1,080 (addition)
George D. Aiken: 5,060

VIRGINIA

Beartown: 6,375
Kimberling Creek: 5,580
Lewis Fork: 5,730
Little Dry Run: 3,400
Little Wilson Creek: 3,855
Mountain Lake: 8,253
Peters Mountain: 3,326
Thunder Ridge: 2,450
James River Face: 200(addition)
Ramseys Draft: 6,725
Saint Mary's: 10,090

WISCONSIN

Porcupine Lake: 4,235
Headwaters: 20,104

To derive the fullest benefits from ecosystem representation, land managers need to be guided by the goal of preserving natural integrity unimpaired. In the Society's 1982 policy statement (Appendix I) on wilderness management, our Governing Council's first principle was that:

"The purpose of wilderness management should be the maintenance and, if need be, the restoration of a dynamic equilibrium of natural forces. Nondegradation of and noninterference with natural processes are fundamental. The goal is **free play** of natural forces, **not** any particular static condition."** A related point is that wilderness areas, especially in the East where they have been relatively small to date, need to be larger in size so that natural processes, like fire and insect infestation, can be allowed to function freely without human interference.

In short, management is needed to ensure first and foremost that the natural integrity of wilderness is protected in perpetuity and that other uses are kept consistent with this primary objective.

Primitive Recreation Opportunities

Probably the reason most commonly given for wilderness is the recreation experience offered by an unmodified natural setting. Much fabled by legend and song, the "wilderness experience" typically features "outstanding opportunities for solitude or a primitive and unconfined type of recreation," to quote the Wilderness Act itself. To directly experience wilderness on-site, a visitor can day-hike, backpack, ride a horse, or float in boats, canoes and rafts. Within a national forest wilderness, a visitor can hunt, fish, study nature, swim, ski, camp or simply do nothing.

Forbidden is the use of mechanical transport or motorized equipment. Film and print narratives also extend indirect wilderness experiences to millions. A fine example is Mike Edward's (1985) article in the *National Geographic* about his trek through Montana's spectacular Bob Marshall Wilderness.

The benefits of wilderness recreation are as varied and unique as the individuals at this conference. From "outstanding opportunities for solitude" can flow a physical and spiritual tranquility and an eventual humility and insight from contemplation of the natural. And from "outstanding opportunities for . . . a primitive and unconfined type of recreation" can come a testing of backcountry skills and self-reliance, physical training and restoration, a closeness to the elements and the earth, and a sense of freedom from society and its artificialities. No doubt each of us could attest to these benefits in our own lives, and I wish we had the time to sit around a campfire tonight and do just that.

For my own part, I would probably be a municipal bond lawyer in downtown Manhattan were it not for many golden experiences on the Appalachian Trail and in wilderness West and East during a year off from law school. One further illustration: I was fortunate enough to attend the signing of the Central Idaho Wilderness Act at

the White House in the summer of 1980. It was during the Iranian hostage crisis and Jimmy Carter emerged stern and haggard to say a few words. After acknowledging the hard work of Cecil Andrus and others, he began to reminisce about the 1978 float trip down the Middle Fork of the Salmon River he took with Andrus through the newly created River of No Return Wilderness. Within moments, his eyes misted over and he whispered that the trip had been the happiest week of his Presidency.

Also significant about on-site wilderness recreation (hiking, camping, hunting, fishing) is that it is the **only** use of wilderness that the Forest Service assigns an economic value to be considered in evaluating alternative forest plans. Many of the other benefits are not quantified but are theoretically taken into account. As for recreation, a visitor day (12 hours) of use is calculated to be worth $16 in the Southern Region and $18 in the Eastern Region, according to the 1985 RPA Program (Draft at F-6). Yet, despite large cumulative increases in use expected in the years ahead (which implies an increasing scarcity of wilderness recreation opportunities), the Forest Service makes no increase in the real dollar value of wilderness recreation for purposes of forest planning.

As with ecosystem representation, important additions must still be made to the wilderness system in the East to meet the rising demand for wilderness recreation. The Regional Guide for the South (1984) makes a number of very significant findings:

"Wilderness recreation visits in the Southern Region increased an average of 5 percent per year from 1975 to 1979. This compares to a 2.5 percent increase nationally during the same period. Since 1979, recreation use of wilderness in South has increased approximately five times faster than during the 1975-79 period. The 1980 RPA Program projects national wilderness use to increase 2 percent per year for the next several decades. Wilderness use in the South is expected to continue to exceed national trends, with an average annual growth rate of 4 percent over the next two decades.

It is estimated that all of the proposed RARE II wilderness areas and 55 percent of the further planning areas would require wilderness designation to meet 1980 RPA Program targets. Even with proposed additions, however, wilderness use restrictions may be necessary at popular areas. The supply of wilderness experiences also may be extended through the use of lands outside of classified wilderness areas that are suitable for primitive recreation."

The Regional Guide for the South also notes that many existing wilderness areas have already reached their carrying capacity for recreation. The Guide points to potential wilderness areas in the Southern Appalachian Mountain forests as helpful in meeting increased demand. The Regional Guide for the Eastern Region also states that the rate of growth for wilderness recreation may be higher than the national rate in future years and that a number of existing areas already have higher than the desirable level of visitor use.

To achieve the greatest benefits from wilderness recreation, *"visitor freedom should be a management goal,"* according to The Wilderness Society's policy statement. Concepts such as the traditional "carrying capacity" and the more recent "limits of acceptable change" should be carefully used to provide the highest quality wilderness experience possible consistent with keeping visitor impacts at acceptable levels. Direct regulation, permits and quotas should be used as the last resort. A top priority continues to be needed expansion of the wilderness system to provide for primitive recreation opportunities.

Undisturbed Wildlife Habitat

A third reason for wilderness is to assure the preservation of relatively large blocks of undisturbed wildlife habitat. Particularly in the East, there is a pressing need to set aside federal lands for the re-emergence of old-growth forests so lacking in the region. Such old-growth habitat is crucial to the maintenance and possible expansion of species like bear, moose, marten and others that rely on wilderness-type settings. As was pointed out by Shands and Healy in their 1977 book on the eastern national forests, *The Lands Nobody Wanted*, "As private forest lands are cleared for agriculture or modified for urban or recreational use, federal lands will become more important as wildlife habitat particularly for species that can survive only when isolated from man and his noisy artifacts." They recommend that the national forests should provide large blocks of climax forest habitats and thereby "raise the diversity of wildlife throughout the region as a whole."

The black bear is a good example of the type of wildlife that benefits from the protection of wilderness on the national forests in the East. According to Dr. Michael Pelton, an internationally recognized expert at the University of Tennessee, in the East the bear now largely exists only on public lands that provide necessary food, cover and protection. In the Southeast the Forest Service controls most of the remaining occupied bear habitat. In reviewing the draft Cherokee National Forest plan, Dr. Pelton concluded that the alternative that would best suit the needs of the black bear was alternative 5. It contained the maximum wilderness recommendation and provided the greatest amount of hard-mast food and the least amount of new roaded access, both crucial factors for the bear. In describing the areas under wilderness study on the forest, e.g, Jennings Creek, the Forest Service repeatedly states that "the bear population would benefit most under wilderness management."

The distinguished wildlife biologist A. Starker Leopold (1978) also documents the important role for nongame wildlife from the old-growth forest. In reviewing studies from Europe and the United States, Leopold found that the number of bird species and the total bird population peaked in mature forests. He counsels that: "The point is evident that to maintain the full spectrum of native vertebrates, it is necessary to preserve or create areas representing all stages of forest succession, particularly the mature forest." Thus, wilderness, which preserves old-growth, serves to protect an indispensable niche in the overall biological diversity of the nation.

Finally, wilderness contributes to the understanding of wildlife in an unmanaged setting so that wildlife in a managed environment can be compared and more intelligently regulated. Dr. Maurice Hornocker of the Idaho Cooperative Wildlife Research Unit explained this wilderness value in a recent address to the Forty-Third North American Wildlife Conference: "Relatively unexploited wildlife populations," he said, "can provide an insight into intrinsic behavioral mechanisms that can and should form the basis for any management program outside wilderness ... In short, wilderness populations can provide the baseline data, an understanding of which is essential if we are to prevent the list of endangered species from becoming even longer." Wilderness is increasingly recognized as a wildlife management tool. It conserves old-growth habitat for the species that rely on it and is a benchmark for understanding wildlife that exists in a managed setting. As noted earlier, larger wilderness areas are needed in the East so that wildlife populations can be studied and preserved in large unmodified ecosystems that largely replicate original conditions.

Fisheries and Watershed Protection

Another purpose of wilderness is to provide assured protection of important watersheds for the benefit of downstream and on-site users and for sensitive fish species. In the West, over 50 percent of the volume of all flowing water used by ranchers, farmers, industry and others originates in the national forests. Many major river systems, such as the Colorado, the Snake, the Columbia and the Missouri, begin in national forests, often on wilderness lands. Over 1,000 municipal watersheds are contained on national forest land. In the East, one of the central purposes for the acquisition of the national forests under the 1911 Weeks Act was to protect watershed.

Undisturbed forests, such as the old-growth wilderness stands in the Northwest, produce pure water both for human use and for fish and wildlife, thus saving communities the costs and health impacts of chemical treatment. As scientist Glenn Juday explains, "old growth watersheds produce the highest quality water for human consumption. In addition, beds of gravel in sediment pools, where the stream is free to circulate oxygen-rich water unclogged by fine sediment, are prime anadromous fish spawning areas." During the formulation of RARE II legislation for Washington State, Representative Mike Lowry (D-WA) identified key fish habitat that needed protection and introduced a "fish" wilderness bill for 1.9 million acres. Such an approach helped educate the delegation and the public about the watershed values of wilderness and, in fact, contributed to the designation of some areas.

Wilderness watersheds also establish a benchmark against which to judge the impacts of development activities elsewhere. Several years ago I toured Weyerhaeuser lands in Southeast Oklahoma in response to concerns of the Oklahoma Wildlife Federation about water quality, species conversion and other issues. The mountain streams on their lands ran muddy with the siltation from road-building and timbering. I understood the exact extent of the degradation only by visiting a wilderness candidate area on the nearby Ouachita National Forest where the mountain stream ran crystal-clear through the roadless area. So too, wilderness waters are being used to conduct important studies on acid rain in the Rockies, the East and elsewhere. Because these waters are largely free of the background disturbance of human activity, they can provide vitally needed baseline data about the effects of atmospheric pollution.

Land Ethic

In summing up the many practical benefits of wise land stewardship, Aldo Leopold went one step further and proposed a land ethic for "saving the wilderness remnants in America." "A land ethic," he urged, "reflects the existence of an ecological conscience, and this in turn reflects a connection of individual responsibility for the health of the land." And what is this ecological conscience? "A thing is right when it tends to preserve the integrity, stability and beauty of the biotic community. It is wrong when it tends otherwise."

Leopold saw in wilderness a keen expression of the land ethic--for cultural, recreational, wildlife, scientific and aesthetic reasons. But more than that, it captured the essence of the humility that underpins the land ethic. In *Sand County Almanac*, Leopold concludes his chapter on wilderness as follows:

"Ability to see the . . . value of wilderness boils down, in the last analysis, to a question of intellectual humility. The shallow-minded modern who has lost his rootage in the land assumes that he has already discovered what is important; it is such who prate of empires, political or economic, that will last a thousand years. It is only the scholar who appreciates that all history consists of successive excursions from a single starting-point, to which man returns again and again to organize yet another search for a durable scale of values. It is only the scholar who understands why the raw wilderness gives definition and meaning to the human enterprise."

Cost-efficiency

Those who are not reached by a fundamental land ethic appeal may be interested in the cost-efficiency of preserving wilderness. Managing roadless lands in the national forests for wilderness use may often be more economically sound than managing the land for commodity use. In its analysis of the management situation on the Cherokee National Forest, for example, the Forest Service found that "wilderness management has an extremely high benefit/cost ratio when compared with full resource development." The reasons given for the "dramatically higher" benefit/cost ratio for wilderness compared to development were: "(1) the benefit/cost ratio for resource development was lowered because of low timber values combined with extremely high roading costs; (2) the benefit/cost ratio for wilderness is raised

because of low administration costs coupled with a very high assigned value for wilderness recreation." As a result, the Forest Service concluded that the maximum present net value of the roadless land would be achieved by allocating all of this land to wilderness management. In the mountainous forests where many unprotected roadless areas remain, the Cherokee lesson is quite typical. Moreover, because many of the other benefits of wilderness cannot be quantified, the value of wilderness compared to resource development becomes even higher.

Model for the World

As Rod Nash and others have fully documented, the United States has taken the international lead in both inventing and popularizing the concepts of national parks and wilderness preservation. The need for our country to continue as a pace-setting model is more urgent than ever. Many recent reports, such as the Global 2000 Report (1980), have ominously warned that hundreds of thousands of species - perhaps as many as 20 percent of all species on earth - may be lost by the year 2000 as their habitats vanish. Most of these losses will be in developing countries, as tropical forests are cleared. The United States should seek to serve as a model to such countries by continuing to set aside portions of our wildlands for reasons of ecological diversity, wildlife, watershed, recreation and other purposes. Our wilderness areas can be teaching tools to government leaders from other countries as to why they should likewise preserve these dwindling lands.

ANTI-WILDERNESS PROGRAMS

Before concluding, let me discuss two Forest Service programs in the East, both quite controversial, which undercut the basic reasons for preserving wilderness. The first is the current Forest Service program of timber cutting **within** designated wilderness in an attempt to control the southern pine beetle and prevent its spread outside the areas. Such a program interferes with the dynamic equilibrium of natural forces within these areas and degrades their ecological diversity. The second is the proposed program of the Forest Service to dramatically increase timbering and roadbuilding on nonwilderness areas in the Eastern national forests. Taking the Southern Appalachians as an example, these proposed forest plans will destroy the wild character of tens of thousands of acres and further concentrate primitive recreation use into the few designated wilderness areas. This result will make it even more difficult to achieve visitor freedom as a management goal within wilderness.

Southern Pine Beetle Timber Cutting

The Wilderness Society is strongly opposed to recent Forest Service logging in wilderness areas to control southern pine beetle infestation. This unprecedented timber cutting has and is taking place in the newly established wilderness areas in Texas--Upland Island, Turkey Hill, Indian Mounds, Big Slough and Little Lake Creek--and in the Kisatchie Hills Wilderness in Louisiana and may soon take place in the recently established Black Creek Wilderness in Mississippi. Along with the Sierra Club and Texas Committee on Natural Resources, we filed a lawsuit on April 16th, 1985 in East Texas against this program. (*Sierra Club, et al.* v. *Block.*)

Our suit contends that the cutting program violates the Wilderness Act, which charges the Forest Service with the "responsibility for preserving wilderness character." The suit also contends that the cutting program violates the Endangered Species Act, by adversely modifying habitat of the endangered Red-cockaded Woodpecker (*Picoides borealis*)and thereby jeopardizing the continued existence of the species. Finally, our suit contends that the implementation of the cutting program without a full environmental impact statement violates the National Environmental Policy Act. Among other failings, the environmental analysis to date has failed to study appropriate alternatives to the cutting program, including use of integrated pest management or artificial pheromones, reduction of pine density in areas immediately outside wilderness and other potential preventive measures.

In addition to the unnecessary damage occurring in Texas, Louisiana and Mississippi, another concern we have about this method of insect control is that it sets a very dangerous precedent for the wilderness system. Other wilderness areas in the South and West are susceptible to bark beetle infestations. In addition, infestations of other forest pests that are now occurring, including the balsam woolly aphid, spruce budworm, and the gypsy moth, mean that under current direction other national forest wilderness areas are potentially at risk of being cut.

By interfering with the free play of natural forces within the areas, we are losing important values of biological diversity that justified the establishment of these areas as wilderness in the first place.

Proposed Forest Plans

As noted earlier, the Forest Service projects that the demand for wilderness recreation will continue to rise steadily in the decades ahead in the Southern and Eastern Regions at levels exceeding the national rate of increase. In addition to establishing new wilderness areas, the Southern Regional Guide suggests that, "The supply of wilderness experiences also may be extended through the use of lands outside of classified wilderness areas that are suitable for primitive recreation." Despite these findings, however, the recent wave of draft forest plans under the National Forest Management Act proposes dramatic increases in roading and logging on forests that are heavily used for primitive recreation.

On the White Mountain National Forest, for example, the Forest Service is proposing to double the annual timbering rate and double the miles of new permanent road. Among the other impacts, this will destroy the wild character of over 150,000 acres of currently roadless land and further shrink the base for primitive recreation opportunities. On six southern mountain forests as well, the draft plans are proposing to more than double the level of annual timber harvests and almost triple the size of the permanent road system.

Our Attachment Three sets out the current and proposed timber and road levels for the six forests that comprise the Southern Appalachian Highlands. On the Cherokee National Forest, for example, almost 80 percent of the forest is zoned for roading and clearcutting in order to achieve the high timber goals. In these draft southern mountain plans, very little land is put in any intermediate category between wilderness and timber cutting. If these plans are implemented as proposed, those seeking an unmodified and roadless natural setting for their recreation will more and more have to use designated wilderness areas and the already heavily travelled Appalachian Trail. This will compound the management problems of visitor overuse and make the goal of visitor freedom in these areas probably impossible to realize. We urge the Forest Service to scale back these high timber and road goals and leave more nonwilderness lands as roadless. This approach is needed to make possible opportunities for solitude and unconfined recreation within the outstanding wilderness areas already set aside.

Let me close by emphasizing, as did our Vice Chair Arnold Bolle at the First National Wilderness Management Workshop (1983), that The Wilderness Society strongly supports increased professionalism and funding for the field of wilderness management. Conservation groups often play a key role in getting areas established as wilderness and more and more have an obligation to see that they are managed to preserve their special qualities. We look forward to working closely and cooperatively with the Forest Service and other federal land agencies in the years ahead to produce the highest quality wilderness management.

LITERATURE CITED

Bolle, A. 1985. Public groups turn to management issues. *In* M. Frome (ed.). Issues in Wilderness Management. Westview, Boulder, Colo.

Davis, G. 1984. Natural diversity for future generations. *In* J. Cooley (ed.). Natural Diversity in Forest Ecosystems. Institute of Ecology, Athens, Ga.

Edwards, M. 1985. A short hike with Bob Marshall. Natl. Geogr. Mag. 167:664-689.

Juday, G. 1978. Old growth forests: A necessary element of multiple use and sustained yield National Forest management. *In* Environmental Law 523-38.

Leopold, A. 1949. A Sand County Almanac and Sketches Here and There. Oxford University Press.

Leopold, A.S. 1978. Wildlife and forest practice. *In* H.P. Brokaw (ed.). Wild. and Am. Counc. Environ. Qual. Washington, D.C.

Nash, R. 1978. International concepts of wilderness preservation. *In* J.C. Hendee, G. Stankey and R. Lucas, (eds.). Wilderness Management, USDA For. Serv. Misc. Pub. No. 1365.

Pelton, M. 1985. Black bears in the Southern Appalachians: Some General Perspectives, In The Wilderness Society. March, 1985, A Critique of the Cherokee National Forest Plan. Washington, D.C.

Shands and Healey, 1977. The lands nobody wanted. The Conserv. Found. Washington, D.C.

Wilson, E. 1984. Million-year histories: Species diversity as an ethical goal, Wilderness (Summer), Washington, D.C.

USDA. 1983. Regional Guide for the Eastern Region, Sept., 1983. Milwaukee, Wis.

USDA. 1984. Regional Guide for the Southern Region, June, 1984. Atlanta, Ga.

Wilderness Society. 1985. A critique of the Cherokee National Forest Plan. March, 1985. Washington, D.C. and Atlanta, Ga.

Wilderness Society. 1985. A critique of the White Mountain National Forest Plan, February, 1985. Washington, D.C. and Boston, Mass.

APPENDIX I
THE WILDERNESS SOCIETY MANAGEMENT OF WILDERNESS USE

Statement Of Problem

Wilderness designation alone does not suffice to ensure the preservation of wild places. Proper management of use is imperative to prevent the degradation of the values for which wilderness areas were designated; otherwise, they may become empty shells -- wilderness in name only. Recreation overuse or misuse may result in areas being "loved to death." Overdevelopment to accommodate excessive use or inappropriate types of use can also erode wilderness. "Nonconforming" uses legally allowed under special conditions -- such as livestock grazing and administrative activities -- can also impair wild character. Management is needed to ensure first and foremost that the natural integrity of wilderness is protected in perpetuity and that other uses are kept consistent with its primary objective.

Discussion

As defined in the 1964 Wilderness Act, "A wilderness, in contrast with those areas where man and his own works dominate the landscape, is ... recognized as an area where the earth and its community of life are untrammeled by man, where man himself is a visitor who does not remain." Wilderness areas, according to the Act, ... shall be administered for the use and enjoyment of the American people in such a manner as will leave them unimpaired for future use and enjoyment as wilderness, so as to provide for the protection of these areas (and) the preservation of their wilderness character.

In other words the Act directs the managing agencies to maintain the processes of nature essentially uninterrupted, with man as an observer who does not interfere with, and certainly does not degrade, the wilderness resources. Furthermore, the Congress has made no distinction regarding wilderness characteristics of areas in different regions of the country or managed by different agencies (although the special exceptions in section 4 of the Act do not apply to the National Parks or Wildlife Refuges). Because of a variety of growing pressures, however, effective management of use is increasingly needed to meet the "non-degradation" mandate of The Wilderness Act.

The single greatest threat to wilderness is its potential invasion by exploration and development of fossil fuels and minerals. Permission for such use by the government would destroy quintessential wilderness qualities or, at best, require decades or centuries to restore. The Wilderness Society is unalterably opposed to government action which might open wilderness areas to such destructive use.

Except for this new threat, recreation use is the foremost pressure on wilderness with a steady increase of about 7 percent in visitation each year (1980 assessment). In many cases soils at campsites are becoming compacted and eroded, and vegetation is being damaged or destroyed. Wildlife may suffer from harassment, most of it unintentional; quiet and solitude may be difficult to find in some places, almost impossible in others. Concentration of

U.S. Forest Service Road Construction and Annual Timber Harvests on Six Southern Appalachian National Forests

National Forest	Timber Harvests		Level of Increase	Existing Roads	New Road Construction	Level of Increase
	Current	Proposed				
	(millions of board feet)			(miles)		
Chattahoochee/Oconee*	95	206	117%	1,271	769	61%
Cherokee	41	130	217%	1,540	1,412	92%
Jefferson	21	64	205%	1,043	1,980	190%
Nantahala/Pisgah*	64	117	83%	2,037	7,246	356%
Sumter	65	135	108%	1,100	301	27%
TOTALS	286	652		6,991	11,708	

*The Forest Service manages the Chattahoochee and Oconee forests in Georgia as one unit and the Nantahala and Pisgah forests in North Carolina as one unit.

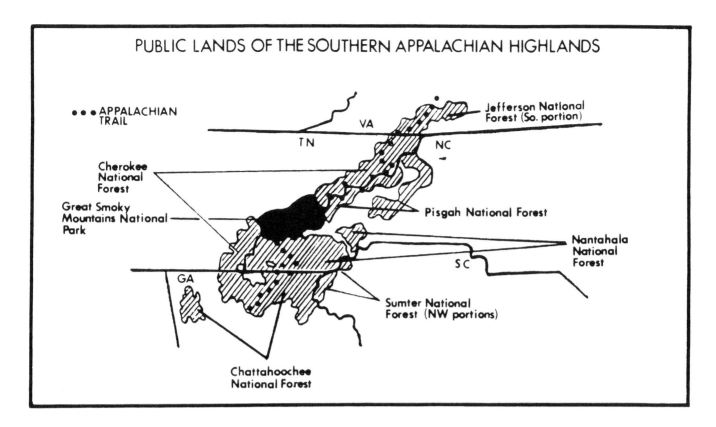

PUBLIC LANDS OF THE SOUTHERN APPALACHIAN HIGHLANDS

• • • APPALACHIAN TRAIL

Jefferson National Forest (So. portion)

VA

TN

NC

Cherokee National Forest

Great Smoky Mountains National Park

Pisgah National Forest

Nantahala National Forest

SC

GA

Sumter National Forest (NW portions)

Chattahoochee National Forest

recreation pressure is compounded in some cases by inadequate measures to disperse visitor use patterns. Also, many existing trails were built years ago for fire control and are poorly located for resource protection or a quality visitor experience. In still other cases, there has been a tendency to design and install trails and other visitor facilities that are excessive in scope and, as such are inconsistent with the preservation of wilderness character.

The Wilderness Act also grants the managing agencies considerable latitude for the protection of wilderness and its visitors when and where necessary by maintaining, for example, minimum sanitation facilities, fire protection necessities, and structures for administrative use. The agencies in the past have vacillated between overly strict and overly permissive views of what activities are appropriate given the general mandate to ensure an enduring wilderness resource.

Congress provided for continued livestock grazing in wilderness where such grazing was established prior to designation of the area as wilderness. In 1980, House Report 96-1126 set forth some policy guidelines for the agencies to follow in administering such grazing. The thrust of these guidelines is to provide for reasonable continuation of such grazing -- so long as the range resource is not deteriorated -- while minimizing impacts on wilderness values.

Policy Statement

The many valid benefits we derive from wilderness depend on the preservation of its undisturbed natural integrity. Management of wilderness ecosystems and their related uses should be judged against the goal of preserving natural integrity unimpaired and should be

guided by the following principles. (The Wilderness Society has already addressed the question on mineral activities in its policy statement adopted on June 5, 1981.)

1. **The purpose of wilderness management should be the maintenance and, if need be, the restoration of a dynamic equilibrium of natural forces**. Nondegradation of and noninterference with natural processes are fundamental. The goal is **free play** of natural forces, **not** any particular static condition. For example, The Wilderness Society generally supports a policy of allowing natural fires to play their ecological role in wilderness, with due regard for public health, safety and welfare in surrounding nonwilderness areas. (In addition, careful experimental burning may be considered to restore the natural equilibrium in fire-dependent ecosystems where decades of fire exclusion by man has led to unnatural conditions.)

2. **Administrative activities should be guided by the concept of the "minimum tool."** Managers should use only those tools, structures, equipment or practices that are the **minimum necessary** to protect the wilderness resource. Equipment used in such circumstances should be those that cause the least impact on wilderness values. Motorized access or other motorized equipment should be used only in emergency situations where necessary to protect visitor health or safety or the wilderness resource. Minimum necessary structures, such as trails or bridges, should be designed to blend into the wilderness environment to the maximum extent possible.

3. **Necessary management actions should be based on clearly defined objectives that describe desired wilderness conditions and are set forth in individual area management plans prepared with full**

public involvement. Formal plans are needed to establish clear objectives for each Wilderness Area and to define policies and actions by which these objectives will be pursued. The Wilderness management plan must be for a wilderness as a whole and indivisible unit and not subdivided by agency administrative units. Regulations and overall management objectives must be consistent over an entire Wilderness Area. The plans are useful in facilitating continuity in management policies and practices, despite changes in administrative personnel or agency. Each plan should address specific issues, such as fire, insect, and disease, recreation trails, permits, access, fish and wildlife, and give special attention to commodity uses such as grazing, mining or oil and gas leasing for the period during which they may be legally permitted.

4. **Visitor freedom should be a management goal.** Wildernesses are to provide "outstanding opportunities for solitude or a primitive and unconfined type of recreation." Wilderness management must recognize "unconfined" recreation as one of the major appeals of wilderness. Wilderness use capacities of wilderness areas should be carefully determined to provide the highest quality wilderness experience possible consistent with keeping visitor impacts at acceptable levels. Regulation and control of visitors should follow the "**minimum tool**" concept (policy 2, above).

5. **Management should include a rigorous system of monitoring of use as well as the provisions for managing use.** Such monitoring should provide the basis for preventing resource damage or deterioration as well as the basis for improving management. The purpose of management is to restore past damage and to prevent future damage from occurring. Monitoring can provide the information to test how well the management actions are working and also serve as an early warning system to detect damage in its initial stages. Such knowledge is fundamental to making the adjustments needed to sound management.

Does Public Involvement Help Wilderness Management Decisions?

by
Howard Orr

ABSTRACT--The public must be involved in making management decisions. The involvement may take different forms ranging from personal contact to formal documents.

KEYWORDS: media, public involvement, wilderness management.

The title of this segment poses the $64,000 question-- not just for wilderness management, but for public administration in general. Public participation, public involvement, or citizen participation (whichever term you choose) is not new. Few decisions are ever been made in a democratic society without some form of citizen input. It has only been in the last couple of decades, however, that public involvement has been defined by law and practice and institutionalized.

Debates over its usefulness in decision making have continued to this day. Survey 10 decision makers and you will find their opinions spread across the board. Some view it as a moral responsibility--essential to a free society. Others see it as an obstacle--a hindrance to decision making that more often than not generates unnecessary controversy. Most, however, fall between these extremes. Somewhere in that range also lies the truth.

Does public involvement help wilderness management decisions? The answer appears to be a definite "maybe." Hans and Anne Marie Bleiker, two leading authorities on citizen involvement, sum up the problem this way: "Citizen participation is neither inherently 'good' nor is it inherently 'bad'; it is a complex and ill-understood phenomenon, and has the potential of playing either a constructive or a destructive role in public and private decision-making."

Despite the fact that public involvement increases the element of uncertainty in the decision making process, it is legally required for most land managing agencies today. Decisions on minor or purely administrative matters are often exempt, but decisions about land use or allocation usually are not. Even though it is often legally required, there are other, practical reasons why public involvement is useful for managers in making decisions about wilderness.

Without public consent, it has become almost impossible to implement public policy. The nature of pub- lic administration has changed over the last 20 years. People have become very sophisticated in their dealings with government, and the effect has been gradual restriction in the discretion that public agencies can exercise. Public involvement is the best tool we have to gain public consent for our actions. We use public involvement in making decisions, then, not just because it seems like the right thing to do, or because it is required by law, but also because we need it to get the job done. This is especially true when we are deciding how to manage America's wilderness, a subject dear to the hearts of many--perhaps most--Americans. Without public consent, wilderness management will exist only on paper.

Public involvement might help you make better wilderness management decisions. We have certainly seen examples of that in the Forest Service. Unfortunately, public input will not always give you that new piece of missing technical information needed to solve a knotty management question. It does make such decisions possible, however. It gives them legal legitimacy and the necessary atmosphere of consent.

Public involvement in wilderness management decision making offers no guarantees. Just because you have involved the public does not mean your policies will be accepted. Sometimes the issues are just too sharply polarized to be resolved within an agency's technical planning process. Public participation will not solve these problems (although it may help).

At other times, public involvement may be part of the problem, rather than the solution. The Bleikers have noted that public involvement may be destructive. Sometimes this may happen for no clear reason, but often it results from problems in the way public input was gathered, analyzed, used, or documented. If these problems can be overcome, the chances for successful public involvement can be increased.

The key to this success is proper planning. This is a

cliche as old as government itself, but it is still true. How many times have public agencies set out on the public involvement journey with no clear idea of where it was they wanted to go, how they intended to get there, or what they wanted to do once they arrived? I have seen it happen, and it is a formula for failure.

The first step should be to set well-defined objectives for the public involvement process. Just what do you want to accomplish: "The law says we've got to have public comment on this, so let's go out and get some." Or how about "Let's ask the public if they have information we haven't been able to find." Or "Let's find out what the public thinks."

I am afraid that if you looked at most of the public involvement, these three objectives would be as far as the planners ever got. I am not belittling these objectives because all three are legitimate. But a public involvement program based on these nonspecific goals can not succeed. It may, in fact, destroy the technical planning process it was designed to support.

Participation can help you achieve many of your objectives with the public--objectives that are necessary for your project to succeed. One objective especially relevant to wilderness management involves what planners refer to as the null or no action alternative--the alternative where no changes are made from current direction. If you want to but cannot convince the public that doing nothing will lead to unacceptable results, then your wilderness management proposal is in trouble. People like the status quo. This preference for no action is particularly strong where wilderness is concerned. Overcoming this resistance is a **key** step in building consent for any wilderness management decision. Yet, it is rarely identified as an objective for public involvement. There are many other objectives that may have a bearing on wilderness management. Identifying them must be the first step in designing a public involvement process that will be useful for wilderness managers.

Two other public involvement technicalities that seem to give us a lot of trouble are the scope of the public involvement process and the selection of techniques.

How much public involvement is enough? There is no clear answer. Each case needs to be approached individually. Some wilderness management decisions need just a little, while others need an extensive amount. Learning how to strike the delicate balance between too little and too much is important. Erring in either direction can cause serious problems for your project.

So can choosing the wrong public involvement techniques. Frankly, this is often where public involvement processes run into trouble. After you have carefully identified what you want your public involvement to achieve and decided what level is appropriate, equal care should be exercised in choosing the public involvement techniques. These techniques should be viewed as tools, each best suited for a specific job. No tool performs all tasks, and neither are there any public involvement techniques that match all situations. Trying to use a pipe

wrench to drive a nail can cost you a mashed thumb. Overreliance on one or two public involvement techniques can lead to failure, increased controversy, and a torpedoed project.

In wilderness management and other natural resource decision making, there is a tendency to rely solely on just a few techniques such as public hearings, meetings or media campaigns. These usually occur at the expense of other less formal techniques such as one-on-one contacts, small group meetings, telephone calls, field trips, and other forms of personal contact. The formal meetings are usually more expensive. If the atmosphere is highly emotional or politically charged, such meetings tend to fan the flames. The result: public involvement may be destructive.

Personal, less formal contacts, when properly documented, may be better suited. However, care must be used to prevent charges of excluding the general public from the involvement process. The point is this: reliance on only one kind of activity is dangerous and should be avoided. Different tools allow you to reach different kinds of audiences. You get a broader picture of public opinion, and it is far more likely that the objectives you set for your public involvement will be achieved.

Another factor that has a bearing on how you design your public involvement process is the nature of the decision itself. Is it an emergency decision, or is it routine? If it is an emergency, then public involvement will have to be done quickly. This does not mean it should be approached with less care. Public involvement must be just as carefully planned--perhaps even more carefully planned--when the management decision must be made in a hurry. The greatest threat to your management decision is a veto by the public. This threat is magnified during an emergency because (1) the stakes are higher and (2) delays cannot be tolerated. Using public involvement in an emergency will affect the techniques you use. There will not be time to plan public meetings. Frequently all you will have time for will be telephone calls or quickly arranged visits to the field for a few key leaders. If you are thorough, the public will have a good understanding of the need for emergency action. It is possible with the right approach to build public consent to a wilderness management decision within a matter of days (sometimes in hours). There is simply no excuse for doing slipshod public involvement or no public involvement at all just because you are faced with an urgent situation. What about fire or threat to human life types of emergencies? These should have been prepared for by public involvement in a so-called proclamation decision analysis well in advance. This leads me to two key problems--problems that frequently deprive decision makers of full benefit of the public involvement process.

The first involves public understanding of the public participation process. Simply stated, public ignorance and misconceptions about your public involvement processes are your worst enemies. Chief among these problems is misunderstanding about the role involvement will play in your decision process. Many people, including many pub-

lic officials, confuse the advisory role of public involvement with decision making itself. It must always be made clear that input from the public is advice. The authority for the decision still rests with the agency. This sounds simple, but in too many cases the public mistakenly believes that if one side or the other sends in the most mail, or gets the largest delegation to the public meetings, then the decision will be automatically influenced in that direction. The public must always understand the constraints you are operating under. They must realize that despite public opinion, some management principles must come first. People must realize that legal requirements must also be met. The responsibility for preventing these kinds of problems rests with you, and it should be one objective of your public involvement process.

The best way to prevent misunderstanding about the public involvement process is to be able to clearly tell the public how its input will be used. This brings me to the most critical problem wilderness managers and other decision makers have with public involvement.

Frankly, we are all pretty good at getting public comment. Where we have a real problem is integrating it

into the decision making process. "Now that I've got this stuff, what do I do with it?" Well, I have a simple answer, but I do not have an easy one. The answer is meticulous documentation.

Each issue raised by the public must be displayed. It must be traceable back to its sources, and traceable forward through the decision process, so that the public can see how each issue affected the final decision. Each issue should be considered by the planning team, and accepted or rejected, and the rational should be displayed. If this sounds like a lot of work, it is, particularly if your project has received a lot of public attention, and therefore a mountain of public comment. But it still must be done. It is on this point that the public most often loses faith in a public agency. If the public begins to believe that its input will not be seriously considered, it will find other, less pleasant ways to drive its message home.

I can not begin, in a short presentation, to adequately cover all the ins and outs of a subject as complex as public involvement. Books have been written about it; college level courses are taught in it. But I wanted to cover a few of the key points that are relevant to the field of wilderness management--points where we often come to grief.

I started this talk with the question, "Does public involvement help wilderness management decisions?" The answer was maybe. But we must remember that usually it is required when wilderness management decisions are made--either from a legal standpoint, or from a practical, political standpoint. However, it is necessary, so we should be working hard to make it useful. Public involvement can help us make better wilderness management decisions. We must make sure that it does.

2

Wildlife In Eastern Wilderness And Natural Areas: An Introduction

by
Richard N. Conner

Wildlife has always been an integral part of wilderness. Historically, the word "wilderness" takes its meaning from the term "habitat of wild creatures" (Schoenfeld and Hendee 1978). Idealistically wilderness and natural areas are places where natural processes and wildlife can exist without man caused restraints and alterations. A basic question is to manage or not to manage these areas. An absence of management will allow gradual plant succession in many areas. In southern pine forests, for example, succession may produce a hardwood forest, conditions quite foreign to what probably existed in pre-historic times. With this vegetation will be a community of wildlife that is different from the wildlife that would be present if the prehistoric fire climax pine forest was present. Re-creation of the primeval conditions of southern pine forest necessitates management with prescribed fire. Thus, depending on the philosophical approach to wilderness, we manage to produce the primeval vegetational condition of a geographical or regional area, or do not manage, and let wilderness character be determined by modern day "natural" conditions and processes as affected by surrounding land use patterns.

Endangered species are of particular concern in wilderness areas. Laws that suggest that minimum or no management be implemented in wilderness may conflict with laws assuring the survival of threatened and endangered species. Solutions compatible with both wilderness and these species are needed. Wilderness management of Red-cockaded Woodpeckers (*Picoides borealis*) is an example of this particular problem.

Wilderness should provide excellent habitat for most mature forest bird species as well as most cavity nesting birds. Because of the eventual abundance of snags and decayed trees, the best way to manage for most forest dwelling cavity nesters is to provide oldgrowth forests.

Windthrow and insects will cause portions of wilderness areas to revert to early stages of forest succession. Such areas will be used by early succession nongame bird species. However, most forested lands outside of wilderness designated areas will regularly provide habitat for these species because of the frequency of clearcutting. Such species do not need wilderness to provide refuges for them.

Where large tracts of wilderness exist in the western United States (and a few in the East), the possibility of realizing naturally functioning ecosystems is more closely achieved than in the East where most wilderness and natural areas are typically smaller in size. Natural processes and wildlife in the smaller eastern wilderness areas have a greater chance to be influenced by surrounding land use patterns and in turn influence surrounding private and public lands because they have a higher average edge length to area ratio. The relatively small size of many eastern wilderness areas presents a special problem for large carnivores such as the black bear (*Ursus americanus*) and the cougar (*Felis concolor*). These species have very large home ranges and would be most benefited by wilderness because of their shy secretive nature and their vulnerability to excessive hunting pressure. The area requirements of such species suggest a need for larger wilderness areas in the eastern United States than those already designated. This is especially true if we desire populations of sufficient size to prevent genetic problems (Franklin 1980).

Wilderness and natural areas have the potential to provide much for wildlife and human use of wildlife. Wilderness areas can be used as laboratories to study natural processes with minimal disturbance from man. The areas can serve as genetic preserves for a variety of fauna and flora, and as refuges for all oldgrowth wildlife and plant species that are sensitive to habitat alteration. Wilderness should also provide a refuge for many raptorial birds that often suffer greatly from illegal shooting in areas where human population densities are high.

The absence of vehicular travel in wilderness areas will reduce hunting pressure particularly in the more central portions. This will create unique opportunities for nonconsumptive uses of wilderness wildlife such as photography or plain "animal-viewing" because of a reduction in wildlife's fright response. Alternatively, the few, hardy hunters and trappers who penetrate the depths of wilderness after game and furbearers will be rewarded with the unique experience of a truly natural setting and minimal contact with other humans.

The articles on wildlife in this book address species or species groups of wildlife that may be of special concern because of their status as an endangered species, importance as a game species, or uniqueness as a wildlife group. Special topics of concern relevant to wildlife species in wilderness such as disease and a dynamic landscape approach to habitat management are also presented. The main objective of the wildlife section is to identify potential wildlife-wilderness problem areas and suggest management recommendations to solve these problems. No management is always a viable option in wilderness and natural areas. However, if active management to solve wilderness-wildlife problems is chosen as the course of action, it is hoped that the papers presented herein provide solutions, and other *minimal* management techniques to prevent major problems from occurring.

LITERATURE CITED

Franklin, I.R. 1980. Evolutionary changes in small populations. pp. 135-149 *In* M.E. Soule' and B.A. Wilcox (eds.), Conservation biology, an evolutionary-ecological perspective. Sinauer Assoc. Inc., Sunderland, Mass.

Schoenfeld, C.A. and J.C. Hendee. 1978. Wildlife Management in Wilderness. Boxwood Press, Pacific Grove, Calif.

Wilderness Management: A Perspective On Furbearers

by
Edward P. Hill

ABSTRACT--Aspects of wilderness policy and management and their effects on some of the furbearers of the Eastern United States are discussed from one individual's perspective. Suggestions are made for additional policy to address the needs for compensatory management actions to fulfill the roles of top predators whose removal has altered the natural balance of animal systems on most wilderness areas. Aesthetic value, potential for recreational use, suggestions for compensatory management, and precautions are offered for several of the important furbearers.

KEYWORDS: policy, mammals, preserves, parks, restrictions, hunting, trapping, compensatory management.

The more than 100 areas designated as wilderness in the eastern United States vary in latitude, altitude, size, public use, and vegetative cover. They average about 40,000 acres (16,200 ha) in size, the largest four being the Everglades in Florida, the Okefenokee Swamp in Georgia, Isle Royale in Michigan, and the Boundary Waters Canoe Area in Minnesota. A wilderness is a different thing to different people, but has been defined by Congress in the Wilderness Act of 1964 as "an area where the earth and community of life are untrammeled by man, where man himself is a visitor who does not remain." Most Wilderness Areas in the eastern United States are administered by the U.S. Forest Service (FS), U.S. Fish and Wildlife Service (F&WS), or the National Park Service (NPS). The Bureau of Land Management also has some wilderness responsibilities, but they have been intermittent (IAF&WA 1976) and are minor compared to the magnitude of responsibilities among the three other Federal agencies.

With the possible exception of policies on grazing and fires, those affecting the flora of eastern wilderness areas are relatively free of controversy. In contrast, policies that affect animals and birds are a continuing source of public debate, media coverage, and concern among agencies that administer wilderness. Although policy among all these agencies is derived primarily from the Wilderness Act of 1964, differences that are related primarily to agency goals exist with respect to furbearers. This paper reviews wilderness policies among agencies, presents a perspective on management of animal systems in eastern wilderness, and offers some suggestions for management strategies for individual furbearers in eastern wilderness areas. Among the perspectives addressed are aesthetic value, potential for recreational use, suggestions for compensatory management, and management precautions.

Stated perspectives are those of the author, and are not intended to address wilderness areas in Alaska and other western states.

WILDERNESS POLICY

National Park Service

The National Park Service does not, as a general policy, "allow consumptive utilization of renewable or nonrenewable resources" except under situations where prior rights and privileges exist (USDI 1978). In a separate paragraph of the policy, hunting and trapping were specifically prohibited. Moreover, "where consumptive uses are permitted by law, and where it can be demonstrated that they are detrimental to the purposes of a park, the Service will recommend their elimination, limitation, curtailment, or modification through the legislative process."

Under Management Policies that govern animal populations, the Park Service policy is responsible to "perpetuate the native animal life of the parks for their essential role in the natural ecosystems." Such management, "will strive to maintain the natural abundance, behavior, diversity, and ecological integrity of native animals in natural portions of parks as part of the park ecosystems."

The policy also states: "Natural processes shall be relied upon to regulate populations of native species to the greatest extent possible. Unnatural concentrations of native species, caused by human activities, may be regulated if those activities causing the concentrations cannot be controlled. Non-native species shall not be allowed to displace native species if this displacement can be prevented by management. The need for, and results of, regulating animal populations, either native or non-native, shall be documented and evaluated by research studies." The policy further defines "native species as those that occur, or occurred due to natural processes" and not those that have moved into park areas "directly or indirectly as the result of human activities."

The policy further specifies that "Native animal life in the National Park System shall be given protection against harvest, removal, destruction, harassment, or harm through human action." Three pertinent exceptions occur when: (1) hunting and trapping are permitted by law (2) control of specific populations of wildlife is required for the maintenance of a healthy park ecosystem, and (3) removal or control of animals is necessary for human safety and health.

U.S. Forest Service

Paragraph 2323.3 of the U.S. Forest Service Manual (USDA 1976) is pertinent to this discussion because it contains philosophy related to animal populations. It states "The native wildlife and fish in National Forest wilderness should exist and compete in an environment where the forces of natural selection and survival operate with optimum feasible freedom." "Wildlife may be harvested under state regulations in an orderly manner, fisheries management will be consistent with wilderness values, and direct fish and wildlife control measures will be applied only upon a showing of need." Paragraph 2323.31 states "The proper balance of game animals with their habitat may be achieved by managing public hunting." Paragraph 2323.31c states that "In some instances, wildlife species once native to the wilderness have been forced from their original habitat by the encroachment of man and his activities. To the extent that these factors can be altered or managed within the intent of the Wilderness Act, species no longer part of the wilderness scene may be reintroduced and managed as a part of the wilderness resource."

With respect to control of predators, paragraph 2323.32 provides the following guidelines: "Where control of predators is necessary to protect threatened or endangered wildlife species or on a case-by-case basis to prevent special and serious losses of domestic livestock, it will be accomplished by methods which are directed at eliminating the offending individual(s) while at the same time presenting the least possible hazard to other animals or to wilderness visitors. Poison baits or cyanide guns are not compatible. Control programs will be carried out by or under the direction of the Fish and Wildlife Service, the Forest Service, or State game agencies in those States which have traditionally conducted control programs on National Forest lands."

Paragraph 2323.34 of the U.S. Forest Service Manual (USDA 1976) states that "Under state laws, trapping of furbearers, such as mink, marten, beaver, and muskrats is a compatible wilderness use when population levels justify a harvest program. Commercial trapping will not be permitted." Another paragraph on rodents contains provisions for "control of overpopulations that pose a serious threat to other wilderness values."

Fish and Wildlife Service

Update No. 12 - Policy concerning management of wilderness areas (USDI 1977) and the guidelines in the Refuge Manual (USDI 1982) contain some identical language in their respective sections on Public Use. "A wide variety of activities, such as hiking, bird watching, hunting, fishing, wildlife observation, and photography, may be permitted on a wilderness area so long as they are compatible with refuge objectives."

The format guides in the Service Refuge Manual and Policy Update No. 12 for development of wilderness management plans provide separate numbered paragraphs where hunting and trapping use and restrictions are to be covered. Generally, policy and guideline language governing furbearers at most upper administrative levels give only cursory attention to the subject, and to the best of my knowledge, management considerations of individual furbearers on individual areas have not been addressed.

Differences among Agencies

The major policy difference among agencies are: (1) that almost no consumptive use of furbearers is allowed in National Park wilderness except where permitted by earlier laws; (2) the U.S. Forest Service provide for consumptive and recreational use (hunting, trapping with stated prohibition of commercial trapping) in accordance with laws and regulations of the respective states and their conservation agencies; and (3) the U.S. Fish and Wildlife Service policy provides for consumptive use programs (hunting and trapping) on an area-by-area basis. The relative paucity of furbearer policy in documents emanating from upper administrative levels of the U.S. Fish and Wildlife Service could have been designed to ensure flexibility needed in development of wilderness plans for individual areas. The disadvantage however, of less than a well defined policy is that strategy on a separate area may begin to reflect the philosophies of its manager.

Generally, the management of fur resources has been ranked secondary to other fish and wildlife considerations in most state and federal planning and budgets. Similarly, it seems that wilderness policies pertaining to fur resources have been given only cursory treatment.

WILDERNESS PERSPECTIVES

Policy for Altered Wilderness Systems

Occupying a multitude of niches, furbearers constitute major components within wilderness animal systems. Policy for wilderness animal systems is therefore policy for the resident furbearers. Policy documents across agencies generally seem to express an intent to insure that wilderness areas are protected and managed to preserve their natural conditions. Within the National Park system, policy directs that "natural processes should be relied upon to regulate populations of native species to the greatest extent possible" (USDI 1978). "To the extent possible, wildlife species in National Forest wilderness should be allowed to maintain a natural balance with their habitat and with each other" (USDA 1976). "Predators should be able to survive and compete with other species, free from the unregulated interference of man and his traditional pursuits of sport and bounty" (USDA 1976). "It is the policy of the U.S. Fish and Wildlife Service to manage wilderness areas so as to preserve the wilderness resource for the use and enjoyment of Americans now and in the future" (USDI 1977).

These policy statements appear to fall well within the context intended in the Wilderness Act. However, in my judgement, they do not go far enough to cover problems associated with differences in interpretation. Policy is often interpreted as an obligation to intercede when man or his interests are threatened, yet to avoid any tampering with the same natural system to compensate for human induced alterations. Restoration to completely natural conditions and processes, though noble, is impossible or impractical on most wilderness areas. With possible exception of the four large wilderness areas mentioned earlier, few, particularly in the eastern United States are large enough to function as pristine natural systems; the home range of most of the top native predators (cougars and wolves) exceeds the size of most wilderness areas; maintaining a population of these large predators usually requires an area many times the 5,000 acres (2,025 ha) minimum required for wilderness area establishment. Whether even the large areas containing top predators can function without man's control has been questioned (Mech 1985).

The problem encountered as natural system philosophies are implemented, stems from prior removal or human infringement upon the role of top predators such as wolves and cougars that have system-dependent functions in animal ecosystems. The direct, secondary, tertiary, and deeper effects that ripple through natural systems when major predators are removed are complex and not well understood, yet are often dramatic. The removal or reduction of large predators can directly influence abundance in several prey species, some furbearers, most ungulates, and indirectly alter or influence abundance of multiple species of fauna as well as flora.

Some professional biologists and teachers, who espouse using natural processes for regulating wilderness animal populations, do not recognize that animal systems divested of their top predators, have been so altered as to no longer function naturally. A few would go as far as to propose poaching and highway mortality as substitute means of controlling ungulate populations, a classic example of nonmanagement or mismanagement.

It seems inconsistent to control a species that may threaten livestock and at the same time fail to control the density of another species that damages habitat or constitutes a driving hazard. Managers who tolerate illegal

poaching for ungulate reduction rather than support public hunting may subject agencies to charges of conflict of interest and loss of public support. If top native predators have been controlled or removed suddenly, or over an extended period because of their threat to man's interests, then compensatory management strategies should be implemented to fulfill the roles left vacant in the altered system. In my judgement, there is need for policy that mandates compensatory management strategies, if the native top predators can not be restored and maintained. Such a policy may help prevent the frequently occurring "unnatural concentrations of native species caused by human activities" (USDI 1978). It also seems prudent that compensatory management actions within animal systems should be accomplished economically through some form of consumptive use, that has the least impact on floral systems.

Policies of the U.S. Forest Service and Fish and Wildlife Service contain provisions for activities such as hunting and trapping. However, I could find no policy mandating compensatory management of animal systems that have been altered through removal or disappearance of the top native predators. Assessment of how effective compensatory management actions are in restoring balance to wilderness animal systems is beyond the scope of this paper, but should be done as part of wilderness management plans. Support for compensatory management strategies directed at altered natural systems may help individual wilderness managers maintain the desired balance within their respective areas.

Furbearer-Wilderness Relationships

Plant Succession - Maintenance of wilderness areas for plants is much easier than for animals. Compared to animals, plant communities are relatively easy to characterize and locate. Soils, climate, and animal populations exert their influence on plant species composition, rates of growth, and stem density, yet change in plant communities is generally a gradual, predictable progression toward the climax stages, except when periodic catastrophic events set back succession. In contrast, animal populations may fluctuate dramatically over short periods of time. Plant communities generally determine the furbearers that will be present and the densities that will prevail. Since wilderness areas managed to preserve natural conditions will usually provide a pristine floral appearance that goes with their respective climax succession, those furbearers that fit the niches within respective climax forest, marsh, prairie, or other types associated with a particular wilderness will flourish. A wilderness area can not provide the ideal or even good habitats for all the species of fauna that are present (Poole 1976). The goals of a particular wilderness may religate some species to very low densities and in some cases local absence. Species that require early successional stages may occur only in small pockets where wildfire or some other event sets plant succession back. Wilderness policy that provides for some wildfire will enhance diversity of plants and those furbearers that require early plant successional stages to produce their cover and food supply.

Wilderness custodians or managers should consider both the vegetative and animal components of wilderness to avoid neglecting a portion of their responsibility and public trust. Wilderness policy could mandate that areas be staffed with trained individuals competent to deal with both the floral and faunal components of wilderness.

Wilderness managers should employ appropriate techniques for estimating relative densities of wildlife, and seek indices of population imbalances and other potential problems. Maintenance of harvest records, trend information, and catch or harvest per unit of effort should be part of management of a designated wilderness, particularly those where the top predators have been extirpated. Wilderness managers are often the first to identify research needs and should be encouraged though policy mandate to point out problem areas.

Research and Education

Wilderness areas are some of the last places where plant and wildlife relationships can be studied under natural conditions. Documentation and understanding of animal and plant relationships are the basis for planning and implementing management strategies. Policies and decisions that affect the conduct of research should have local input, but also should be elevated to such levels as to expedite and facilitate research endeavors.

It is important to inform the public and in particular the users of wilderness areas about the complexities of wilderness and animal system relationships, the need for compensatory management actions, and their associated rationale for both plant and animal systems. Innovative and interpretive approaches could employ illustrations of food chain pyramids depicting animal systems without their extirpated predators and the compensatory management actions taken to maintain balance.

FURBEARERS

Furbearing mammals that have historically, or presently occur on areas now designated as wilderness in the eastern United States include: a marsupial, the opossum (*Didelphis virginia*); three rodents, beaver (*Castor canadensis*), muskrat (*Ondatra zibethicus*), and nutria (*Myocastor coypus*); and 21 carnivores, coyote (*Canis latrans*), gray wolf (*Canis lupus*), red wolf (*Canis rufus*), red fox (*Vulpes vulpes*), gray fox (*Urocyon cinereoargenteus*), black bear (*Ursus americanus*), racoon (*Procyon lotor*), marten (*Martes americana*), fisher (*Martes pennanti*), weasels (*Mustela erminea, M. nivalis,* and *M. frenata*), mink (*Mustela vision*), wolverine (*Gulo gulo*), badger (*Taxidea taxus*), striped skunk (*Mephitis mephitis*), spotted skunk (*Spilogale putorius*), river otter (*Lutra canadensis*), cougar (*Felis concolor*), lynx (*Felis canadensis*), and bobcat (*Lynx rufus*). The black bears, wolves, and the cougar (puma, mountain lion, Florida panther) will not be included except for mention of roles of the latter two as upper level predators in natural systems.

Furbearers are often grouped by biological or practical considerations. Wolves, cougars, wolverines, fisher, pine marten, and lynx are often considered or perceived by the public as wilderness wildlife because they occur chiefly in areas of sparse human populations, (Allen 1966, Hendee *et al.* 1978). Most of the other furbearers are widely distributed in wilderness and nonwilderness areas, a relationship that does not diminish their aesthetic value. Furbearers are also grouped according to their habitats or where they are trapped. For example, beaver, mink, muskrats, otter, and nutria are grouped as aquatic or water-trapped furbearers; bobcats, lynx, wolves, coyotes, the foxes, the skunks, the weasels, badgers, and opossums are grouped as terrestrial or land-trapped furbearers. Raccoons are often included in both groups. The equipment for aquatic and terrestrial trapping is quite different. Most trappers, who devote substantial time to the endeavor, concentrate on one of the other during a given period, whereas a weekend trapper may trap both land and water furbearers at the same time (Bailey 1980, Hardisky 1985).

SPECIAL CONSIDERATIONS BY SPECIES

A detailed discussion of each furbearer with respect to varied policies, the multitude of vegetative successional stages, area differences associated with size, visitor use, latitude, political and special interest pressures, and climate is beyond the scope of this paper. It seemed appropriate, however, to address some of the peculiarities and special considerations for several species.

Opossum--The opossum is a shy, secretive, mostly nocturnal species that is an omnivore, a carrion feeder, and an opportunistic predator of nestlings and eggs of ground nesting birds. Although a component of most eastern wilderness animal systems, its occurrence as a common furbearer throughout most of the eastern United States diminishes its image as wilderness wildlife. It is preyed upon by mid-level predators (Gardner 1982), and is not known to have caused animal system imbalances because of overabundance. It is a species that is taken incidentally during terrestrial recreational trapping and is not apt to be overharvested by this activity as currently regulated in most states. I consider the opossum comparatively unimportant aesthetically, and to have limited values for food and sport. It seems inappropriate that it be given more than casual consideration in the scheme of wilderness management.

Beaver--Historically, the beaver is one of the furbearers that has been overharvested. It is easily located and trapped because of its dependence on water and the abundant sign it leaves. Because of its relative scarcity except in areas of sparse human habitation, the beaver, until recently, exemplified wilderness wildlife. Management and restoration programs have restored the beaver to most of its former range, and although considered a pest in many places, it still has high aesthetic values. Beaver signs such as cuttings and remains of habitat modification such as dams, pools, and lodges can be aesthetically pleasing and contribute aesthetic value to wilderness. The beaver is a species that must have compensatory harvest in wilderness areas, where timber wolves have been extirpated. If wilderness policy dictates maintenance of beaver in a pristine wilderness setting, one or perhaps two beaver per colony, depending on the availability of winter food, should be removed each year. Otherwise, beaver will over utilize the winter food supply and be forced to move to new areas, subjecting steep watersheds and riparian areas to erosion when non-maintained beaver dams are breached by high water (Yeager and Rutherford 1957). In some eastern wilderness areas, climax southern bottomland hardwoods are unique and should be preserved. This climax type is not considered good beaver habitat because of the relatively low-quality food supply. However, extensive hardwood stands in flat terrain are often stressed or killed by inundation resulting from beaver activity. Wilderness managers should be prepared to prevent the establishment of beaver colonies in such situations through consumptive use or damage control trapping. Similarly, control measures may be necessary to retain northern deciduous forests consisting primarily of aspen (Populus tremuloides) that, in contrast to deciduous climax forests of oak-hickory, are excellent winter food.

Beavers, depending on rates of natural predation, should be subjected to compensatory harvest through some recreational outlet. However, such harvests should be closely regulated through an appropriate quota or trapline management system to insure an evenly distributed harvest and to prevent overharvest.

Muskrat--This aquatic rodent inhabits fresh and saltwater wetlands and waterways in every North American state and province except Florida (Deems and Pursley 1983). The muskrat is dependent on aquatic habitats containing non-woody vegetation, and is therefore relatively scarce on small streams flowing through pristine wilderness forest, except streams closely associated with beaver ponds or similar openings. Like other rodents, this prey species serves as food for many mammalian and avian predators. It often becomes overpopulated and may damage marsh wilderness for several years through "eat-outs" (Perry 1983).

Custodians of coastal or inland marsh wilderness should be prepared to recognize potential muskrat eat-outs and take actions to prevent their associated disruptions to marsh ecosystems. Recreational trapping can be helpful in addressing this problem without likelihood of overharvest. I consider the aesthetic value of the muskrat to be less than its recreational value as a trappable renewable furbearer.

Nutria--This large round-tailed South American rodent, has spread from releases to at least 15 states. It now occurs in coastal marshes and major rivers of the Gulf and Atlantic coasts from Texas to Maryland as well as Ohio and Wisconsin (Wilner 1983). I perceived the nutria as having low aesthetic value, because of its "huge rat" appearance. If possible, it probably should be controlled in wilderness under policy dictating, "Non-native species shall not be allowed to displace native species." Intensive recreational and commercial trapping have been helpful in controlling nutria.

Coyote--This canine is mid-size between a wolf and fox. Although its diet consists primarily of rabbits, small rodents, and vegetable matter, it has been known to limit deer densities through fawn predation (Gardner et al. 1976, Cook et al. 1971), and is suspected of having similar influences on some pronghorn antelope (Antelocapara americana) and big-horn sheep (Ovis canadensis) herds (Frank Grogen 1984 pers. commun.). The spread of the coyote through the southeastern states has been substantially enhanced by releases for the purpose of chase with hounds. In my judgement, it should be controlled under existing policies affecting non-native species. Because of its adaptability, shrewdness, and role as an upper level predator, I consider the coyote's aesthetic value to be medium to high, diminished somewhat by its secretive behavior and pest attributes. Coyotes are displaced or killed by wolves (Mech 1970, Carbyn 1982) and do not compete well with the cougar (Bekoff 1983).

They are not known to occur with the wolf in true wilderness systems. In a grassland prairie wilderness divested of wolves, the coyote displaces red foxes (Johnson and Sargent 1977, Sargent et al. 1980, Wooding 1984). These relationships, in my judgement, dictate the need for compensatory control on most wilderness areas where the top predators have been extirpated. Although coyotes are comparatively difficult to trap, experienced trappers and predator hunters can help keep population levels from becoming excessive. There is little apparent danger of overharvest even during years of intense control pressure.

Red and Gray Foxes--These two furbearers have similar roles in animal food chains preying on rabbits, small rodents, invertebrates, and fruit. I would judge their aesthetic value as high because of their beauty and their predation on mice and rats. Two major differences are in their ranges and preferred habitats, with the red fox prospering in areas with a greater component of open land and occurring throughout most of Canada and Alaska, whereas the gray fox is limited primarily to the United States and seems to thrive in interspersed and forested habitats (Samuel and Nelson 1983). Another important difference is that gray foxes can cohabit agricultural and interspersed habitats with coyotes (Hill and Wooding 1984, Wooding 1984), where they remain closely associated with woodlots, whereas the red fox is displaced as coyotes increase. Finally, both species are subject to periodic population crashes. Red foxes are vulnerable to sarcoptic mange, where gray foxes are vulnerable to canine distemper (Nicholson and Hill 1984). Distemper epizootic in gray foxes is believed often to be tied to their population density and related to fluctuations in raccoon populations that are suspected as vectors of the disease (Nicholson and Hill 1984). Fox predation can influence populations of ground nesting birds (Johnson and Sargent 1977) and fox densities should be monitored in altered wilderness areas to insure that their numbers do not become excessive. Both the red and gray foxes have excellent recreational value for trapping and predator hunting; neither seems subject to overharvest by regulated consumptive use.

Raccoon--This highly adaptable species consumes a variety of invertebrates, fruits, crops, and eggs. It has extended its range northward across southern Canada and exists at high density levels in some urban areas. It has been a subject for many artists and has high aesthetic value. Protected racoon populations often increase rapidly and prey heavily on the eggs of ground and marsh nesting birds and other aesthetically important and endangered species such as sea turtles. Raccoon populations in many upland habitats of predominantly deciduous forests can be excessively harvested by legal and illegal hunting (Johnson 1970, Minser and Pelton 1982). They are also subject to respiratory and canine distemper diseases that are associated with high population densities (Johnson 1970). These relationships should be considered in compensatory management planning for wilderness. In addition, populations should be monitored for indications of conditions that may vector canine distemper into gray foxes (Nicholson and Hill 1984). To be effective, compensatory actions to reduce raccoon populations must be timed to avoid periods of severely cold weather when the raccoon is usually sedentary. Its potential for regulated consumptive use by both hunters and trappers is excellent. Hunting is more effective and a greater threat to overharvest than trapping (Minser and Pelton 1982, Atkeson and Hulse 1953).

Pine Marten--In contrast to most other furbearers, this little-known carnivore prefers in climax boreal coniferous forests or mixed forest stands (Strickland *et al.* 1983b) feeding on voles, mice, and other small rodents, birds and their eggs, and other vertebrates. It has high aesthetic value, is generally considered a wilderness species, and its well being should rank high when wilderness management strategies are considered. Marten populations should benefit from wilderness where associated with northern climax coniferous forests. It is a species that should be restored to areas where it has been extirpated. Its recreational potential, in my judgement is high, predominantly for regulated trapping, and nonconsumptive uses. Although excessive logging and the effects of fire are blamed for its disappearance in many areas, the pine marten is subject to overharvest by trapping. This consumptive use activity is compatible in wilderness areas, but should be carefully planned and supervised.

Fisher--This large member of the weasel family is associated with mature and climax coniferous forests, mixed hardwood-softwood forests, and occasionally burned and cutover areas. The fisher is primarily carnivorous, taking prey as large as porcupines, foxes and raccoons, but will utilize carrion and a wide variety of small vertebrates, fruits, and nuts. Its rareness on areas other than wilderness increases its high aesthetic value as a wilderness species and a mid-level carnivore. The fisher has high aesthetic value and is a good candidate for restoration to wilderness areas where it has disappeared. Like the pine marten, its well being should rank high when wilderness management strategies are considered. It has recreational potential in regulated trapping and nonconsumptive uses. Like the pine marten, it is easily baited and trapped (Strickland *et al.* 1983a), subjecting it to overharvest unless this activity is carefully supervised.

Weasels--These three small carnivores occupy a variety of habitats and feed mostly on mice and other small rodents. I consider them aesthetically valuable in wilderness, but believe they should be given only minor consideration in the scheme of wilderness management.

Mink--This small aquatic carnivore preys on a variety of small rodents, rabbits, fish, birds, and small invertebrates. The mink may reach high populations along some coastal wildernesses, but is usually not abundant in climax forests. It is mostly nocturnal, and I would estimate its aesthetic value to be moderate. Like the weasels, it is not a species that should be given undue consideration in policy formulation. Where it is abundant in prairie or coastal wilderness, its recreational potential is primarily for trapping and nonconsumptive uses.

Wolverine--This small bear-like member of the weasel family exemplifies wilderness wildlife of boreal forests of Canada and Alaska and some of the higher elevations in western states. It does not occur in high densities, but has high aesthetic value bolstered by its legendary aggressiveness and strength. It is a species that is extremely rare, and if restored in eastern wilderness areas where it has been extirpated (Wilson 1983), should be protected until well established.

Badger, Striped Skunk, and Spotted Skunk--These three terrestrial furbearers are more openland carnivores that attain optimum densities in habitats other than climax deciduous and coniferous forests. Collectively, they are important predators on eggs of ground nesting birds, and consume a variety of small vertebrates and invertebrates. The skunks are colorful and their fur has moderate value some years, but because of their offensive odors, the skunks have relatively low aesthetic value. Their recreational potential is believed relatively low because of their nocturnal activity and relatively low densities in most wilderness habitats. The badger has moderate aesthetic value, but its fur has low value. It seems appropriate that the badger and the skunks should be given only minor consideration in the management strategies for wilderness areas.

River Otter--This aquatic furbearer is abundant in most coastal wilderness, and in other wilderness areas where fish are available for food. Upland wilderness streams and lakes may also hold population densities proportional to their respective fish populations. The maintenance of beaver populations at levels consistent with their food supply will insure that beaver ponds are maintained as foraging areas for river otters. The river otter has a very high aesthetic value because of its close association with water and playful behavior. Its fur is highly valued and is the standard against which other fur is judged. It is often caught during trap-out programs directed at nuisance beaver, but compensatory management trapping for beaver can be accomplished with relatively little threat of taking river otter. The river otter is an excellent candidate for reintroduction into wilderness areas where it has disappeared. I believe its recreational potential is excellent, as much for nonconsumptive uses as for regulated harvest. In some areas the river otter is subject to over harvest; trapping activities are compatible in wilderness areas, but should be clearly regulated to prevent over harvest.

Lynx and Bobcat--Both of these upper level predators prey on birds and small mammals such as rabbits and hares, mice, squirrels, fawn, raccoon, opossum, and other vertebrates. The lynx is particularly dependent on the snowshoe hare (*Lepus americanus*). The climax forest wilderness does not provide ideal habitat for these felines: they require an interspersion of forest age classes and associated edges. Therefore, they do not reach their optimum population densities in wilderness. They tend to be solitary and to many people, the lynx and bobcat are some of the last symbols of "true wilderness" (Miller 1980). Although they are generally nocturnal or crepuscular, they have high aesthetic value. Unlike many other furbearers the relative abundance of the lynx and bobcat is dependent upon prey availability, a condition that produces cycles in lynx populations in Canada. The recreational potential for both species is high for hunting with dogs, trapping, and nonconsumptive uses. Consumptive use of these midsize cats in wilderness should be closely regulated.

SUMMARY

Eastern wilderness areas should be beneficial to several furbearers, and offer some unique opportunities to restore and maintain such species as the wolverine, pine marten, river otter, and fishers. Some of the more common furbearers will decrease as the plant succession on newly established areas moves toward climax stages.

Eastern wilderness areas can provide opportunities for consumptive and nonconsumptive use of furbearers. The regulation of consumptive use of the furbearers discussed above can be accomplished by limiting the number of participants, their equipment, the duration of harvest, and through establishment of seasonal and participant harvest quotas.

ACKNOWLEDGMENTS

R.J Esher, G.A. Hurst, H.A. Jacobson, R.J. Muncy, C.H. Halverson, and R.E. Reagan offered editorial comments on early drafts of the manuscript. Manuscript reviews from the U.S. Forest Service, National Park Service, and U.S. Fish and Wildlife Service were provided by E. Bloedel, J. Dennis, and R. Goforth respectively, C. Mills typed the numerous revisions of the manuscript.

LITERATURE CITED

Allen, D. 1966. The preservation of endangered habitats and vertebrates of North America. pp. 22-37 In F.F. Darling and J. Milton (eds.), Future Environments of North America, Biology, Management and Economics the Natural History Press, Garden City, N.Y.

Atkeson, T.Z. and M.C. Hulse. 1953. Trapping versus night hunting for controlling raccoons and opossums within sanctuaries. J. Wildl. Manage. 17:159-162.

Bailey, T.N. 1980. Characteristics, trapping techniques, and views of trappers on wildlife refuges in Alaska. pp. 1905-1918 In J.A. Chap and D. Pursley (eds.), Proc. Worldwide furbearers Conf., Vol. III. Univ. of Maryland, Frostburg, Md.

Bekoff, M. 1983. The coyote (*Canis latrans*). pp. 447-459 In J.A. Chapman and G.A. Feldhamer (eds.), the Wild Mammals of North America, Biology, Management, and Economics, Johns Hopkins University Press. Baltimore, Md.

Cook, R.A., M. White, D.O. Trainer, and W.C. Glazner. 1971. Mortality of young white-tailed deer fawns in South Texas. J. Wildl. Manage. 35:45-56.

Carbyn, L.N. 1982. Coyote population fluctuation and spatial distribution in relation to wolf territories in Riding Mountain National Park, Manitoba, Can. Field-Nat. 96:176-183.

Deems, E.F. and D. Pursley. 1983. North American furbearers, a contemporary reference. International Association of Fish and Wildlife Agencies and Maryland Department of Natural Resources - Wildlife Administration.

Gardner, A.L. 1982. Virginia Opossum (*Didelphis virginiana*). pp. 3-36 *In* J.A. Chapman and G.A. Feldhamer (eds.), Wild Mammals of North America, Biology, Management, and Economics. Johns Hopkins University Press, Baltimore, Md.

Gardner, G.W., J.A. Morrison, and J.C. Lewis. 1976. Mortality of white-tailed deer fawns in the Wichita Mountains, Oklahoma. Proc. Ann. Conf. Ssoutheast Assoc. Fish Wildl. Agencies 30:493-506.

Hardisky, T.S. 1986. Trapper characteristics, fur harvest, sex and age structure of trapped bobcats in Mississippi. M.S. Thesis. Mississippi State Univ., Mississippi State: (138 pp.).

Hendee, J.C., G.H. Stanley, and R.C. Lucas. 1978. Wilderness management, USDA Forest Service Misc. Publ. No. 1365. U.S. Govt. Printing Office, Washington, D.C.

Hill, E.P. and J.B. Wooding. 1984. An ecological study of the coyote (*Canis latrans*) in some bottomland hardwood and coastal plain ecosystems of west Alabama and east Mississippi. Final Report Pittman-Robertson Project W-46, Jobs A, B, and C. Alabama Dept. of Conservation and Natural Resources, Game and Fish Div., Montgomery, Ala.

IAF&WA. 1976. Policies and guidelines for fish and wildlife management in wilderness and primative areas. Ann. Rept. Int. Assoc. Fish Wildl. Agencies. Washington, D.C.188-195.

Johnson, A.S. 1970. Biology of the raccoon (*Procyon lotor*) in Alabama. Bull. 402 Agr. Exp. Stn., Auburn University, Auburn, Ala.

Johnson, D.H. and A.B. Sargent. 1977. Impact of red fox predation on the sex ratios of prairie mallards. U.S. Fish and Wildl. Serv. Wildl. Res. Rept. 6.

Mech, L.D. 1970. The wolf: The ecology and behavior of an endangered species. Univ. of Minnesota Press, Minneapolis, Minn.

Mech, L.D. 1985. How delicate is the balance of nature. Nat. Wildl. 23:54-58.

Miller, S.D. 1980. Ecology of the bobcat in South Alabama. Ph.D. Diss., Auburn University, Auburn, Ala.

Minser, W.G. and M.R. Pelton. 1982. Impact of hunting on raccoon populations and management implications. Bull. 612, Dept. Forestry, Fisheries, and Wildlife. Univ. Tennessee, Knoxville, Tenn.

Nicholson, W.S. and E.P. Hill. 1984. Mortality in gray foxes from eastcentral Alabama. J. Wildl. Manage. 48:1429-1432.

Perry, H.R. 1983. Muskrats (*Ondatra zibethicus* and *Neofiler alleni*). pp. 282-325 *In* J.A. Chapman and G.A. Feldhamer (eds.), Wild mammals of North America, Biology, Management, and Economics, Johns Hopkins Univ. Press, Baltimore, Md.

Poole, D.A. 1976. Wilderness values and wildlife. An address to Allegheny Section Winter Meeting, Soc. Amer. Foresters,Dover, Delaware, Feb. 6, 1976. Wildlife Management Institute, Washington, D.C.

Samuel, D.E. and B.B. Nelson. 1983. The foxes (*Vuples vulpes*) and Allies. Chapter 22. pp. 475-490 *In* J.A. Chapman and G.A. Feldhamer (eds.), Wild Mammals of North America, Biology, Management, and Economics, Johns Hopkins University Press, Baltimore, Md.

Sargent, A.B., J.D. Hastings, and S.H. Allen. 1980. Coyotes and red fox spatial relationships on the northern Great Plains. 41st Midwest Fish and Wildl. Conf., St. Paul, Minn. 42:108.

Strickland, M.A., C.W. Douglas, M. Novak, and N.P. Hunziger. 1983a. Fisher (*Martes pennanti*) pp. 586-598 *In* J.A. Chapman and G.A. Feldhamer (eds.), Wild mammals of North America, Biology, Management, and Economics, Johns Hopkins University Press, Baltimore, Md.

Strickland, M.A. C.W. Doublas, M. Novak, and N.P. Hunziger. 1983b. Marten (*Martes americana*) pp. 599-612. *In* J.A. Chapman and G.A. Feldhamer (eds.), Wild mammals of North America, Biology, Management, and Economics, Johns Hopkins University Press, Baltimore, Md.

USDA 1976. Title 2300 Recreation Management., Chapter 2320-Wilderness, Primitive Areas, and Wilderness Study Areas. USDA For. Serv. Manual (as amended March 1983).

USDI 1977. Policy update No. 12 - Policy concerning management of wilderness areas. U.S. Fish Wildl. Serv., Washington, D.C.

USDI 1978. Management Policies, National Park Service Sect. IV and VI.

USDI 1982. Wilderness Area Management, Refuge Manual. National Wildlife Refuge System.

Wilner, G.R. 1983. Nutria (*Myocaster coypus*) pp. 1059-1076 *In* J.A. Chapman and G.A. Feldhamer (eds.), Wild mammals of North America, Biology, Management, and Economics, Johns Hopkins University Press, Baltimore, Md.

Wilson, D.E. 1983. Wolverine (*Gulo gulo*). pp. 644-652 *In* J.A. Chapman and G.A. Feldhamer (eds.), Wild Mammals of North America, Biology, Management, and Economics, Johns Hopkins University Press, Baltimore, Md.

Wooding, J.B. 1984. Coyote food habits and the spatial relationship of coyotes and foxes in Mississippi and Alabama. M.S. Thesis, Mississippi State Univ., Mississippi State, Miss.

Yeager, L.E. and W.H. Rutherford. 1957.An ecological bases for beaver management in the Rocky Mountain region. Trans. North Am. Wildl. Conf. 22:269-299.

1 - This paper is a contribution of the Mississippi Coorperative Fish and Wildlife Research Unit, Mississippi State University Department of Wildlife and Fisheries, Mississippi Department of Wildlife Conservation, the Wildlife Management Institute, and the U.S. Fish and Wildlife Service, coorperating. MAFES publication 6102.

Wilderness Preserves And Small Mammals In The Eastern United States

ABSTRACT--About 80% of the wilderness preserve units in the eastern United States are distributed in four major geographic regions south of the Mason-Dixon line. The small mammal fauna (insectivores, bats, rodents) of these four regions is documented and found to be representative of the fauna in the entire United States. Wilderness preserves provide a natural laboratory for the scientific study of small mammals. Unfortunately, our knowledge of most wilderness areas is insufficient to accurately assess their significance for small mammal conservation and management.

KEYWORDS: endemic species, endangered species, faunal similarity.

There are approximately 122 Wilderness Preserve Units in the eastern United States, about 80% of which are located south of the Mason-Dixon Line. The majority (about 75%) of these southerly distributed units are situated in four major geographic regions: (I) northern Arkansas and southern Missouri; (II) southeastern Texas and Louisiana; (III) the southern Appalachian Mountains; and (IV) Florida and southern Georgia (Fig. 1). The number of wilderness preserve units in these four areas, respectively, is 18, 7, 30, and 24.

The purpose of this paper is to document the small mammal fauna (insectivores, bats, and rodents) in each of these four regions with respect to species diversity and composition, number of endemic elements, and any endangered or threatened taxa that might be present. While perusing the literature to prepare this article, I did not locate a single published paper concerning the mammalian fauna of specific wilderness units. Thus, our present information base is too meager to permit detailed comparisons of the small mammal fauna among the various wilderness units themselves.

Information for this paper concerning the distribution of small mammals was taken from the following sources: eastern United States (Hamilton and Whitaker 1979, Hall 1981), Region I (Sealander 1979, Schwartz and Schwartz 1981), Region II (Lowery 1974, Schmidly 1983), Region III (Barbour and Davis 1974, Hamilton and Whitaker 1979), and Region IV (Layne 1979, Hamilton and Whitaker 1979).

SMALL MAMMAL FAUNA OF THE FOUR WILDERNESS PRESERVE REGIONS

A total of 74 species of small mammals have been recorded from the four geographic regions in Figure 1. These include 14 insectivores, 18 bats, and 42 rodents (Table 1). All but four of the 67 species of small mammals recorded from the eastern United States (east of the Mississippi River) have been recorded in one or more of these regions. Regions I and II, which are west of the Mississippi River, contain seven species (*Blarina hylophaga*, *Notiosorex crawfordi*, *Peromyscus attwateri*, *Baiomys taylori*, *Reithrodontomys megalotis*, *Reithrodontomys fulvescens*, and *Reithrodontomys montanus*) characteristic of the arid southwest, Great Plains or southern tropics.

There are substantial differences in the taxonomic composition of the small mammal fauna in these four geographic regions. Region III, with 45 species, has the greatest diversity, followed closely by Region I (44 species). Regions IV (33 species) and II (32 species) have a substantially lower species richness. Interestingly, the small mammal fauna of Region IV (Florida-Georgia) includes six endemic species (*Geomys pinetis*, *G. cumberlandius*, *G. colonus*, *Oryzomys argentatus*, *Peromyscus floridanus*, and *Neofiber alleni*) whose entire geographic range is encompassed within the region. There are no species of small mammals endemic to any of the other three regions.

The Appalachian Region (III) is rich in species of insectivores as well as sciurid, microtine, and zapodid rodents but there are relatively few cricetine rodents and no species of geomyid or heteromyid rodents in this area. The East Texas - Louisiana Region (II), in contrast, has fewer insectivores and sciurid rodents, a greater proportion of geomyid-heteromyid and cricetine types, fewer microtine rodents, and no zapodids. The Arkansas -

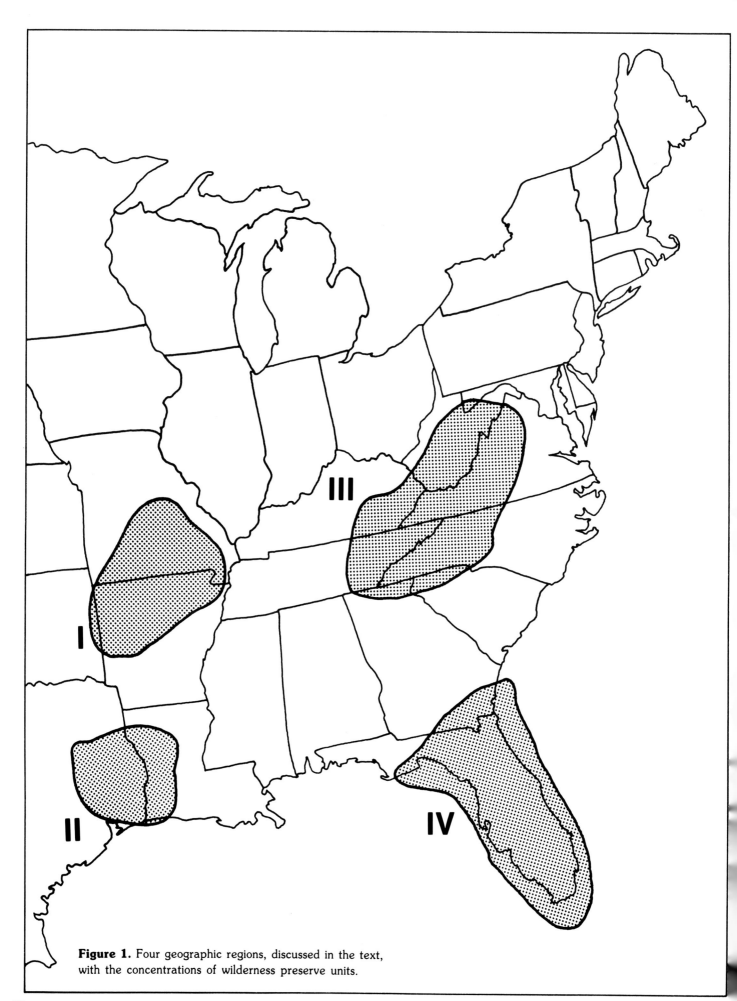

Figure 1. Four geographic regions, discussed in the text, with the concentrations of wilderness preserve units.

Table 1. Checklist of Small Mammals (Insectivores,
Bats, and Rodents) Occurring in the Four Geographic
Regions Depicted in Figure 1.

Order Insectivora—Moles and Shrews	
Family Soricidae—Shrews	
Sorex cinereus, Masked Shrew	*III*
Sorex longirostris, Southeastern Shrew	I, IV
Sorex palustris, Water Shrew	III
Sorex fumeus, Smoky Shrew	III
Sorex dispar, Long-tailed Shrew	III
Microsorex hoyi, Pygmy Shrew	III
Blarina brevicauda, Short-Tailed Shrew	III
Blarina carolinensis, Southeastern Short-Tailed Shrew	I, II, IV
Blarina hylophaga, Southwestern Short-Tailed Shrew	I
Notiosorex crawfordi, Desert Shrew	I
Cryptotis parva, Least Shrew	I, II, III, IV
Family Talpidae—Moles	
Parascalops breweri, Hairy-Tailed Mole	III
Scalopus aquaticus, Eastern Mole	I, II, IV
Condylura cristata, Star-Nosed Mole	III
Order Chiroptera—Bats	
Family Vespertilionidae—Vespertilionid Bats	
Myotis lucifugus, Little Brown Bat	I, III
Myotis austroriparius, Southeastern Myotis	II, IV
Myotis grisescens, Gray Bat	I, III
Myotis leibii (= *M. subulatus leibii*), Small-Footed Bat	I, III
Myotis sodalis, Indiana Bat	I, III
Myotis keeni, Keen's Myotis	I, III
Lasionycteris noctivagans, Silver-Haired Bat	I, II, III
Pipistrellus subflavus, Eastern Pipistrelle	I, II, III, IV
Eptesicus fuscus, Big Brown Bat	I, II, III, IV
Lasiurus intermedius (= *Nycteris intermedia*), Northern Yellow Bat	II, IV
Lasiurus borealis (= *Nycteris borealis*) Red Bat	I, II, III, IV
Lasiurus seminolus (= *Nycteris seminola*), Seminole Bat	II, IV
Lasiurus cinereus (= *Nycteris cinerea*) Hoary Bat	I, II, III, IV
Nycticeius humeralis, Evening Bat	I, II, IV
Plecotus townsendii, Townsend's Big-Eared Bat	I, III
Plecotus rafinesquii, Rafinesque's Big-Eared Bat	I, II, III, IV
Family Molossidae—Free-Tailed Bats	
Tadarida brasiliensis, Brazilian Free-Tailed Bat	II, IV
Eumops glaucinus, Wagner's Mastiff Bat	IV
Order Rodentia—Rodents	
Family Sciuridae—Woodchucks, Chipmunks, and Squirrels	
Tamias striatus, Eastern Chipmunk	I, III
Marmota monax, Woodchuck	I, III
Spermophilus tridecemlineatus, Thirteen-lined Ground Squirrel	I

Sciurus carolinensis, Gray Squirrel	I, II, III, IV
Sciurus niger, Fox Squirrel	I, II, III, IV
Tamiasciurus hudsonicus, Red Squirrel	III
Glaucomys volans, Southern Flying Squirrel	I, II, III, IV
Glaucomys sabrinus, Northern Flying Squirrel	III
Family Geomyidae—Pocket Gophers	
Geomys breviceps, Louisiana Gopher	I, II
Geomys lutescens, Yellow Pocket Gopher	I
Geomys pinetus, Southeastern Pocket Gopher	IV
Geomys colonus, Colonial Pocket Gopher	IV
Geomys cumberlandius, Cumberland Island Pocket Gopher	IV
Family Heteromyidae—Pocket Mice	
Perognathus hispidus, Hispid Pocket Mouse	II
Family Castoridae—Beaver	
Castor canadensis, American Beaver	I, II, III, IV
Family Cricetidae—Native Rats and Mice	
Oryzomys palustris, Marsh Rice Rat	I, II, III, IV
Oryzomys argentatus, Cudjoe Key Rice Rat	IV
Reithrodontomys humulis, Eastern Harvest Mouse	I, II, III, IV
Reithrodontomys montanus, Plains Harvest Mouse	I
Reithrodontomys megalotis, Western Harvest Mouse	I
Reithrodontomys fulvescens, Fulvous Harvest Mouse	I, II
Peromyscus maniculatus, Deer Mouse	I, III
Peromyscus leucopus, White-Footed Mouse	I, II, III
Peromyscus polionotus, Oldfield Mouse	IV
Peromyscus gossypinus, Cotton Mouse	I, II, IV
Peromyscus floridanus, Florida Mouse	IV
Peromyscus attwateri, Attwater's Mouse	I
Ochrotomys nuttalli, Golden Mouse	I, II, III, IV
Baiomys taylori, Northern Pygmy Mouse	II
Sigmodon hispidus, Hispid Cotton Rat	I, II, III, IV
Neotoma floridana, Eastern Wood Rat	I, II, III, IV
Cleithrionomys gapperi, Gapper's Red-Backed Mouse	III
Microtus pennsylvanicus, Meadow Vole	III
Microtus chrotorrhinus, Rock Vole	III
Microtus ochrogaster, Prairie Vole	I, II
Microtus pinetorum, Pine Vole	I, II, III, IV
Neofiber alleni, Round-Tailed Muskrat	IV
Ondatra zibethicus, Muskrat	I, II, III
Synaptomys cooperi, Southern Bog Lemming	III
Family Zapodidae—Jumping Mice	
Zapus hudsonicus, Meadow Jumping Mouse	I, III
Napeozapus insignis, Woodland Jumping Mouse	III
Family Erethizontidae	
Erethizon dorsatum, Porcupine	III

Missouri Region (I) has the greatest number of bats and cricetine rodents and a relatively rich sciurid fauna, but there are not many microtines and no zapodids in this region. The Florida Region (IV) is relatively low in species for the insectivore, chiropteran, sciurid, microtine, and zapodid categories, but the number of geomyids - heteromyids and cricetines is relatively high.

Table 2. List of Endangered and Threatened Taxa of Small Mammals Occurring in the Four Regions Depicted in Figure 1.

Taxa	Status Category	Region of Occurrence
Sorex longirostris eionis	2[a]	IV
Sorex palustris punctulatus	2	III
Microsorex hoyi winnemana	2	III
Blarina carolinensis shermani	2	IV
Sciurus niger avicennia	2	IV
Sciurus niger shermani	2	IV
Glaucomys sabrinus coloratus	2	III
Glaucomys sabrinus fuscus	2	III
Geomys pinetis goffi	2	IV
Geomys colonus	2	IV
Geomys cumberlandius	2	IV
Oryzomys argentatus	2	IV
Oryzomys palustris sanibeli	2	IV
Peromyscus polionotus allophrys	1[b]	IV
Peromyscus polionotus decoloratus	3A[c]	IV
Peromyscus gossypinus allapaticola	1	IV
Peromyscus floridanus	2	IV
Neotoma floridana smalli	1	IV
Microtus ochrogaster ludovicianus	2	II
Myotis grisescens	E[d]	I, III
Myotis sodalis	E	I, III
Plecotus townsendii ingens	E	I
Plecotis townsendii virginianus	E	III

[a] Taxa for which USFWS does not have substantial data to support a proposed rule.

[b] Taxa for which USFWS has substantial information to support listing as endangered or threatened.

[c] Taxa for which USFWS has pervasive evidence of extinction.

[d] Taxa listed as endangered by USFWS.

Sixteen species of small mammals have been recorded in all four wilderness preserve regions. Thirty-three species are restricted in distribution to one of the four regions. These include 16 species in region III, eight in region IV, seven in region I, and only two in region II. I used Burt's coefficient of faunal similarity to assess the faunal relationships of the four regions; the 16 ubiquitous species were eliminated from consideration since they offered no information relative to this question. The highest faunal similarity (37.5%) was between regions II vs IV. Similarity values were high and virtually identical between region I vs II (29.4%) and I vs III (29.54%). The lowest faunal similarities were between region I vs IV (12.5%), II vs III (6.66%), and III vs IV (0.00%). The biogeographic affinities of regions II and IV are expected since both are a part of the Coastal Plain regions of the southeastern United States. The lower faunal similarity of region II to the other areas may be attributed to the large number of northern boreal elements which inhabit the southern Appalachian Mountains but do not occur on the Coastal Plains.

Twenty-three small mammal taxa (species and/or subspecies) from the four geographic regions discussed (Table 2) are listed as endangered or are being considered for addition to the list of Endangered and Threatened Wildlife by the Fish and Wildlife Service. Almost two-thirds of these taxa are listed as category 2 species. This refers to taxa for which information now in hand indicates that proposing to list the species as endangered or threatened is possibly appropriate, but for which substantial data are not currently available to biologically support a proposed rule. The list includes 14 taxa from Region IV, six in Region III, three in Region II, and only one in Region I.

In summary, the four geographic wilderness regions support a small mammal fauna that is representative of that found in the entire eastern United States. The Appalachian Region (III) supports the greatest diversity of species and is faunistically the most distinct region, but Region IV (Florida - southern Georgia) has the greatest number of endemic elements. A substantial number of the small mammals in these regions can be viewed as having some sort of biological problem that potentially threatens their existence.

IMPORTANCE OF WILDERNESS PRESERVES FOR SMALL MAMMAL CONSERVATION

Wilderness preserves serve to protect natural diversity, although their capacity for preservation is limited by a number of internal and external factors. These areas can be envisioned as ecological islands, or areas of resource protection surrounded by a "sea" of environmental alteration. The ability of preserves to protect natural diversity depends upon a number of interacting factors. Some of these include (1) the size of the protected area; (2) their geographical distribution; (3) system and area configuration; (4) the amount and kind of site development; (5) management objectives and practices; and (6) environmental influences (Carls 1984).

Wilderness is especially valuable for the protection of threatened and endangered wildlife. Habitat loss coupled with some direct detrimental human influences is generally responsible for the critical status of most species. Therefore, for the most part, the problem of rare and endangered species boils down to the problem of rare and endangered habitats. The survival of these species is synonymous with protection and proper management of their habitats.

We simply do not know enough about most small mammals. There are numerous gaps in our knowledge of the distribution, populations, and other aspects of their life history and ecology. Efforts to preserve and enhance the populations of species that are now threatened or endangered, and prevent still other species from declining to these critical levels, must be based on a thorough understanding of the biology of each species. Thus, there is an urgent need for greatly expanded research on many small mammals. In this regard wilderness lands are extremely important because they provide a natural laboratory for scientific study. Such inquiry can lead to an improved understanding of mammalian biology, and is potentially of vital importance to mammalian conservation and management.

Unfortunately, our knowledge of most wilderness areas is insufficient to accurately assess their significance for small mammals. For most preserves we do not know the composition of the mammalian fauna let alone anything about the dynamics of the small mammal community. There is an immediate need to inventory the fauna of as many preserve units as possible. Managers of wilderness preserves should encourage biologists to make use of these lands for long-term ecological studies. Special attention should be devoted to the identification of those units with unusually rich species diversity and/or which support populations of rare, endangered, or threatened species.

LITERATURE CITED

Barbour, R.W., and W.H. Davis. 1974. Mammals of Kentucky. Univ. of Kentucky Press, Lexington, Kentucky.

Carls, E.G. 1984. Texas natural diversity: the role of parks and preserves. pp. 51-60. *In* E.G. Carls and J. Neal (eds.). Protection of Texas Natural Diversity: An Introduction for Natural Resource Planners and Managers, Tex. Agric. Exp. Stn. Bull. MP-1557

Hall, E.R. 1981. The mammals of North America. N.Y. Wiley-Interscience, New York, N.Y.

Hamilton, W.J., Jr., and J.O. Whitaker, Jr. 1979. Mammals of the eastern United States. Cornell Univ. Press, Ithaca, N.Y.

Layne, J.N. (ed.). 1979. Rare and endangered biota of Florida. Volume One: Mammals. Univ. Press, Gainesville, Fla.

Lowery, G.H., Jr. 1974. The mammals of Louisiana and its adjacent waters. Louisiana State Univ. Press, Baton Rouge, La.

Schmidly, D.J. 1983. Texas mammals east of the Balcones Fault Zone. Texas A&M Univ. Press, College Station, Tex.

Schwartz, C.W., and E.R. Schwartz. 1981. The wild mammals of Missouri. rev. ed. Univ. Missouri Press, Columbia, Missouri.

Sealander, J.A. 1979. A guide to Arkansas mammals. River Road Press, Conway, Arkansas.

Habitat Needs Of Black Bears In The East

by
Michael R. Pelton

ABSTRACT--The historic range of black bears (*Ursus americanus*) in the Eastern United States has declined significantly in the wake of deforestation and heavy exploitation. The species now exists on only 5 to 10 percent of its former range in the Southeast; increasing human densities and continuing agricultural developments create more and more patchy and fragmented populations. The highly adaptable black bear has survived and continues to survive in the Southeast primarily due to federally owned lands containing designated or de facto wilderness; undoubtedly the species would have been extirpated from the region were it not for these federal "refuges." Loss of the American chestnut (*Castanea dentata*), elimination of protective travel corridors and fall feeding areas, increased permanent road development, increased hunting efficiency, and increased numbers of hunters and incentives to kill bears in and around occupied bear habitat, emphasizes the importance of resource agencies to recognize the pressure and potential plight of this sensitive species on its remaining habitat. The species future existence depends on the availability of a diversity and abundance of late successional (greater than 100yrs) oaks and alternate fall seed•erry species, old growth forests (minimum 5 to 10%) distributed throughout its range, limited future permanent road development, greatly increased educational and enforcement activities by all responsible resource agencies, and regular and systematic population monitoring. Because of the inherent nature of the species and its inevitable interactions with people, management actions (control) will have to be conducted on an occasional basis, even on the smallest of populations with closely monitored harvests on larger populations, and establishment of bear sanctuaries where necessary. A stable core of wilderness, de facto or not, remains at the heart of this species' needs and will become even more important in the future.

KEYWORDS:road impacts, old growth, mast, late succession, hunting, black bear, *Ursus americanus*.

The historic range of black bears (*Ursus americanus*) covered the entire forested areas of North America (Hall 1981:950). As it is true for many forest-dependent species, when the forests receded in the wake of expanding human populations, so did the range of black bears (Maehr 1984). A combination of dramatic habitat loss and exploitation now results in the species being relegated to primarily forested public lands in the eastern United States. In terms of strong population viability, only a few areas in the northeastern United States now enjoy sustained, healthy and substantially harvestable populations (Maehr and Brady 1984). A combination of factors including low and static or even decreasing human population densities, and limited agricultural development has provided the necessary food, cover, and protection requirements needed by black bears in the Northeast; changes do continue to occur in this region, but not at a rate comparable to those in the Southeast.

In contrast, black bears now occupy only 5 to 10% of their former range in the Southeast (Maehr 1984). Occupied black bear habitat in this region is predominantly under federal ownership of the U.S. Forest Service, National Park Service, and U.S. Fish and Wildlife Service. The change in the status of this large mammal in the Southeast over the past 100 years is alarming but understandable considering the human population pressures and loss of forest habitat. It is particularly disconcerting to realize that this species, unlike many other forest species, would now likely be totally extirpated in this region were it not for federal lands, containing designated wilderness or de facto wilderness.

PROBLEMS AND BIOLOGY OF BLACK BEARS

Black bears in the Southeast are relegated to two basic habitats--mountain, and bottomland or coastal areas. A predominant feature of the species' range in the mountain habitat type is a federally-owned "peninsula" covering parts of six states in the southern appalachian mountains and consisting of two national parks and six national forests (Maehr 1984). This habitat "unit" in the Southeast provides the largest, strongest, most viable bear population, and therefore, has the potential for being the most secure stronghold for this species in the region; however, this primarily depends on future U.S. Forest Service management strategies on the six national forests in the area. Also, it should be noted that even this unit has been fragmented into two "islands", north and south. The only other occupied mountainous habitat in the Southeast consists of two national forests in Arkansas; even though this area is large, the relative strength of this population has yet to be completely documented.

In contrast to the Northeast, the so-called sunbelt continues to attract people and undergo extensive agricultural development. The results are a well-documented, rapid loss of the bottomland or coastal habitat type. The consequences of these losses are well illustrated by the patchy and fragmented remains of what used to be an extensive range.

There are few areas of occupied habitat on private lands in the Southeast, and unless such areas are adjacent to public lands or connected to them by a relatively secure or permanent dispersal corridor, resident populations will likely become extirpated from them in the next 25 to 50 years.

The inherent biological characteristics of black bears must be understood and appreciated in order to put into proper perspective the species' basic habitat needs in the East. From an optimistic and positive standpoint, black bears are remarkably adaptable large carnivores exhibiting mental capabilities second only to primates and physical capabilities that characterize them as omnivores and generalists rather than true carnivores. These attributes have allowed the species to survive in the wake of incredible human impacts where their less adaptable cousin, the grizzly bear, has succumbed. Special adaptations such as induced ovulation, delayed implantation, physiological and metabolic alterations associated with winter carnivorean lethargy, tree-climbing ability, color vision, long memory, dexterous use of their moveable lips, tongue, and toes, an omnivorous diet dominated by vegetable material, their relative shy, secretive nature and wide adaptability in selection of winter den sites are some major characteristics that have contributed to the survival of this species. When these adaptations are combined with their formidable size, speed, strength, agility, mobility, and keen sense of smell, the species presents a challenge to managers when it comes in conflict with man's interests, whether these interests be livestock, beehives, picnic tables, garbage cans, or backpacks. Consequently, from a more pessimistic and negative standpoint, the species has some attributes working against it. Their great mobility and large home range sizes frequently bring them in contact with people. Therefore, no matter how fragile and small a particular population may be, management actions will always be necessary on an occasional basis.

In addition black bears are classic "K" selected species. That is, they exhibit inherently slow reproductive rates and turnover rates. Typically, females are not sexually mature until four years of age and usually produce only two cubs every other year. Exploitation rates of black bear populations cannot normally exceed 15 to 25% without causing a population decline; recovery from population declines can be very slow.

Outside the confines of publicly-owned lands, greater numbers of people result in more and more roads, houses, and agricultural development. Increasingly fragmented and patchy, occupied bear habitat gets squeezed tighter and tighter as potential dispersal corridors between occupied sites or to alternate fall feeding areas on the periphery and surrounding the public lands are reduced or eliminated. Mixing of gene pools is substantially lessened or totally stopped between cohorts of populations. These increasingly isolated populations should focus attention even more intensively on the needs of the animal on occupied federal lands. The adaptability and resiliency of black bears have been, are presently, and will be tested to their limits as an increasing array of pressures is placed upon them.

In recent years, new roads, both within and surrounding publicly-owned lands, particularly national forests, have increased access into bear habitat or along its perimeter. Accompanying this access also is an increased use of modern technology by bear hunters; the availability of CB radios, 4-wheel drive vehicles, ATV's, and radio-collared hunting dogs has led to increasing efficiency in harvesting bears. Growing numbers of other kinds of hunters also put pressure on the resource. In addition, there are added economic incentives to kill bears for their hides, claws, teeth, cubs, and more recently, gall bladders; the latter are being used by some Asiatic groups for reputed medicinal purposes.

Another kind of impact was loss of the American chestnut (*Castanea dentata*), a valuable fall food source in many parts of the species' range in the East and a consistent and heavy producer of high energy food for wildlife. High energy demands of bears and other forest wildlife species during the fall place important emphasis on the regular availability of a variety of species of high energy foods such as oak acorns. Periodic years of poor acorn production result in increased movements and home range sizes as bears forage for food; their movements out of designated or de facto wilderness areas leads to an increasing incidence of contact with people, particularly when traditional foraging areas and dispersal corridors disappear, and this, in turn, leads to increased mortality due to illegal hunting, legal hunting, depredation kills, and road kills. These fall feeding forays often are coincidental with hunting seasons (squirrel, deer, bear, etc.). During years of scarcity of fall foods mortality due to malnutrition among the cub/yearling age classes may be as high as 90% and adult females may not produce cubs at all. On the other hand, survival may be greater than 90% following a fall season of good food production and the incidence of birth of triplets or even quadruplets among some adult females is common.

Thus, considering the species' low biotic potential, the loss of traditional dispersal corridors and/or feeding sites outside the confines of federally-owned land, increased access into presently-occupied habitats, the increased efficiency of harvest, and enhanced incentives to kill bears, it is very important for the federal agencies that manage the occupied range of black bears to be particularly aware of and sensitive to the needs of this animal. In recognition of the above, all the national forests in the Southern Appalachians have chosen the black bear as a Management Indicator Species (MIS).

NEEDS OF BLACK BEAR

What are the basic needs of black bears for this region and what can resource agencies do to protect and enhance these needs? A questionnaire survey conducted in 1972 to determine the status and distribution of black bears in the Southeast yielded the first comprehensive information about this species for the region (Pelton and Nichols 1972). Among the facts and figures submitted by state game and fish personnel in characterizing black bear habitats and habitat needs, four common ingredients

emerged: (1) a relatively thick, impenetrable understory, (2) limited permanent road access, (3) abundant berry and nut crops, and (4) relatively large areas over which to roam with limited disturbance. These basic needs translate into food, cover, and protection.

Food

Although black bears are omnivores, their diet is predominantly berries and nuts. Berries are the predominant food source in summer throughout the black bear's range in the Northeast and Southeast. Although this food source is small and often scattered and thus, requires considerable energy to forage for and consume, it is normally diverse and abundant enough under a variety of cover types and management strategies (wilderness or not) to provide necessary energy and nutrition for body maintenance and growth during the active period after spring. Blackberries, raspberries (*Rubus* spp.), blueberries (*Vaccinium* spp.), huckleberries (*Gaylussacia* spp.), serviceberries (*Amelanchier* spp), and many other species may be available and ripened at different times under different conditions through the summer and early fall.

However, fall (late August into November) is a different matter. Bears begin to make physiological and behavioral adjustments that allow them to accumulate body fat. In order for this to occur, they often must abandon their typical crepuscular summer feeding patterns and home ranges and begin foraging almost continuously over extensive areas. It is not uncommon for individual bears to gain one to two pounds of fat per day during the peak of this so-called "feeding frenzy." Throughout most of their range in the East (particularly the Southeast), nut crops are their predominant source of food; oak acorns must provide most of their energy needs. As pointed out earlier, without abundant high energy food sources, bears are impacted significantly and sometimes quite dramatically. They must accumulate enough fat to carry them through three to four months of winter and denning, plus another month of scarce spring foods, often referred to as the "negative foraging period."

Obviously in foraging for fall foods such as acorns, bears must compete among themselves and with other wildlife species depending to greater or lesser degrees on the same food source, i.e., white-tailed deer (*Odocoileus virginianus*), raccoons (*Procyon lotor*), turkeys (*Meleagris gallopavo*), hogs, gray squirrels (*Sciurus carolinensis*), and a wide variety of other small nongame birds and mammals. In order to accommodate the needs of bears and other wildlife species, hardwood forests within federal lands must be allowed to reach late successional stages to produce maximum yields of mast before harvest. Rotation lengths will need to be increased from 60 to 80 years to over 100 years. To lessen the impacts of periodic mast shortages, a variety of species of oaks must be maintained at different elevations, slopes, and aspects, and light-seeded species also must be maintained in or near the stands to provide vital alternative food sources, i.e., ash, gum, dogwood, grape, etc. The "bottom line" is that increased acorn yields result in decreased fall movements, therefore decreased mortality, increased natality, and consequently an increase in the number of bears that can be legally harvested without detrimentally affecting the population.

Cover

As the area of occupied habitat shrinks and/or access into such habitat increases, the necessity of thick cover becomes more important to bears. The cover needs of black bears in the East vary between spring/summer/fall (active periods), and winter (inactive period). During the active periods, the needs for adequate cover change with the changing sources of food. Movements of bears are much more restricted in spring and summer as compared to fall, consequently bears are generally less vulnerable; during this period they may safely locate and feed in berry patches. Maintaining traditional travel corridors to and from feeding areas becomes particularly critical in fall when bears move more.

Winter cover needs are for prime denning sites. Black bears are adaptable enough to den in a number of different kinds of sites. However, the needs of adult females for highly protected sites is greater than that of males. Most of the more protected sites are associated with old growth forests-under the root mass or in cavities of large living or dead trees, either standing or fallen. As pressures on a population intensify, the need for more secure den sites increases. Males take advantage of thickets created by the effects of large old trees falling or timber cutting activities. It is now evident from years of telemetry data in both mountain and swamp or lowland areas that bears prefer old growth as a vital part of their habitat needs. Ages of large trees containing cavities big enough to hold a female and her young range from 150 to 400 years. It is generally felt that a minimum of 5 to 10% of the occupied habitat should contain an old growth component, assuming adequate distribution over the area.

Protection

Protection essentially equates with access, and access with roads, and roads with open, unrestricted roads into occupied bear habitat. Present telemetry data on bears from a variety of locations in the East present differing results regarding the relationship between roads and bears; these reports range from roads actually attracting some bears (i.e., the paved transmountain road through Great Smoky Mountains National Park, and bears feeding on berry crops along restricted forest logging roads), to total avoidance of roads. It is felt that most of the variation in response by bears to roads is associated with the type of road in question and/or the relative use or abuse of a road by people. Our preliminary telemetry data indicate that bears may begin to avoid local National Forest roads in the southern Appalachians at a road density of 0.5 km per square km of forest, under present cultural conditions (Brody 1984). Many national forests already equal or surpass this road density. If open road densities equal or exceed the above, responsible resource agencies should adopt a very conservative approach in construction of new, permanent roads. Some resource agencies have created bear sanctuaries that have helped compensate for

the increased pressures that have occurred primarily as a result of road construction and increased access (i.e. Tennessee and North Carolina). This concept provides pockets of protected habitat in which breeding age females, who are relatively sedentary, can produce young without undue disturbance. Most of these sanctuaries are associated with areas of low road densities to no roads at all.

The future welfare of black bears in the East is related to cultural factors as well as biological or habitat factors. Sometimes it is the cultural factors that need to be addressed more than the biological ones. In order to do so, the responsible resource agency needs to recognize and institute effective educational and enforcement programs. Most state wildlife agencies have long recognized the tripartite value of management, education, and enforcement. Until all three of these areas are adequately addressed, the cultural problems regarding black bears will continue to be a potentially serious limiting factor on populations.

SUMMARY

The needs of black bears in the East include (1) Management for a much greater quantity and quality of late successional oaks on a variety of sites with rotations greater than 100 years, (2) Provision for alternate fall foods in the form of light-seeded hardwoods and other seed or berry producers (3) Provision for well-distributed pockets of old growth covering a minimum of 5 to 10% of the occupied range, (4) Because of their immediate scarcity on most sites, preservation of large (3+ ft, or 1+ m DBH) trees as potential den trees, (5) Restriction of road development where open road densities begin to exceed 0.5 km of road per square km of forest, (6) Establishment of bear sanctuaries within hunted areas inside or outside designated wilderness to protect a nucleus of breeding age females, (7) Development of much stronger educational and enforcement components to alleviate the cultural pressures (illegal hunting and depredation kills) on the resource, (8) Population controls will always be necessary on this species; this should be accomplished with systematic harvests on larger more secure populations and occasional control activities on an individual basis on less secure smaller populations. In conjunction with the above, responsible resource agencies should (9) Establish a regularly conducted system of population monitoring such as the Bait Station Index conducted annually in the Southern Appalachians (Johnson 1984).

It has been said that without designated wilderness there would be no grizzly bears in the lower 48 states. Similarly, without federally-owned lands there would be no black bears in the Southeast. Additionally it is no coincidence that designated wilderness or de facto wilderness has contributed significantly to the survival of black bears in the East. Wilderness in the East has insured some degree of stability in a system where instability may have extirpated the species. Considering all the factors affecting black bears, limited access in the form of wilderness, de facto or not, remains at the core of the species' needs. If such a stable core does not exist within the habitat of the remaining patchy populations, the future viability of those populations will be jeopardized.

LITERATURE CITED

Brody A.J. 1984. Habitat use by black bears in relation to forest management in Pisgah National Forest, North Carolina. M.S. Thesis, Univ. Tennessee, Knoxville, Tenn.

Hall, E.R. 1981. The mammals of North America. John Wiley and Sons. N.Y.

Johnson, K.G. 1984. Bait station surveys to determine relative density, distribution, and activities of black bears in the southern Appalachian region. Annu. Prog. Rep., Dep. Forestry, Wildlife & Fisheries, Univ. Tennessee, Knoxville, Tenn.

Maehr, D.S. 1984. Distribution of black bears in eastern North America. p.74. In D.S. Maehr and J.R. Brady (eds.). Proc. 7th eastern workshop on black bear management and research. Florida Game and Fresh Water Fish Comm., Gainesville, Flor.

Maehr, D.S. and J.R. Brady. 1984. Status reports. pp.2-3 In D.S. Maehr and J.R. Brady (eds.). Proc. 7th eastern workshop on black bear management and research. Florida Game and Fresh Water Fish Comm., Gainesville, Flor.

Pelton, M.R. and R.G. Nichols. 1972. Status of the black bear in the Southeast. pp. 18-23. In R.L. Miller (ed.). Proc. 1st eastern workshop on black bear management and research. New York State Dep. Environ. Conserv., Delmar, N.Y.

Wilderness Areas: Impact On Gray And Fox Squirrels

by
Jimmy C. Huntley

ABSTRACT--Although their food and cover requirements are similar and their ranges are sympatric, fox and gray are most abundant in different habitats. Fox squirrels are more numerous in xeric upland forests or fragmented forests such as woodlots and prairie riparian zones. These forests are usually open, with sparse woody understories that are often fire-adapted. In contrast, gray squirrels are most abundant in unfragmented bottomland and mesic upland hardwood forests with closed canopies and denser woody understories. In wilderness and natural areas, plant succession will change forest conditions and may improve or adversely impact squirrel habitat. Successional changes that increase the oak-hickory component of forest are generally beneficial to squirrels. Ultimately plant succession will favor gray squirrels over fox squirrels. Prescribed fire can be used to maintain fire-adapted ecosystems that contain habitat more suitable to fox squirrels.

KEYWORDS: Natural areas, *Sciurus carolinensis*, *S. niger*, wilderness management.

Tree squirrels are a major recreational, ecological, and aesthetical resource of the eastern United States. Hall (1981) describes five subspecies of the gray squirrel (*Sciurus carolinensis*) and 10 subspecies of the fox (*S. niger*). This paper discusses what impact wilderness or natural area designation may have on gray and fox squirrel populations. Squirrel life history and successional changes plant communities undergo must be understood to form assumptions about the impact of natural area preservation on squirrel populations. I discuss ranges and life histories of both species with emphasis on factors that limit population growth, long-term vegetational changes that affect limiting factors, and management practices that may reduce negative impacts of wilderness areas. The information and assumptions that I present are based primarily on review of literature and secondarily on personal research and field experience.

There are over 1.6 million ha of natural areas in the eastern United States. Designated wilderness areas within The National Wilderness Preservation System contain a large percentage of this acreage. As of April 1985, in the 32 states east of a line from Minnesota to eastern Texas, about 1.5 million ha were in wilderness areas. The five largest areas; the Everglades, Boundary Waters Canoe Area, Okefenokee, Isle Royale, and Shenandoah; contain 1.1 million ha. Of the remaining areas, 89 percent are smaller than 6,000 ha and 34 percent are smaller than 2,000 ha.

RANGE

Gray and fox squirrels are sympatric from Florida to eastern Texas and north to North Dakota and southern New York. Gray squirrels range into Southern Canada and farther north throughout New England except northern Maine. Fox squirrels range from 320 to 640 km farther west than gray squirrels along riparian forest to eastern Montana, Wyoming, Colorado, western Oklahoma, and west-central Texas (Hall 1981). In Texas, Spencer (1981) found that the western limits of gray and fox squirrel range were, respectively, near the 914 mm and 508 mm mean precipitation line. In the eastern states, the fox squirrel's range is declining and one subspecies is federally listed as endangered (Flyger and Gates 1982).

LIFE HISTORY

Madson (1964) and Barkalow and Shorten (1973) presented general reviews of squirrel life history. Regional life histories are also available (Allen 1943, Brown and Yeager 1945, Uhlig 1956, Goodrum 1961). More recently, Flyger and Gates (1982) summarized the biology of fox and gray squirrels. Because the life histories of gray and fox squirrel are similar, they will be discussed together and, unless otherwise noted, comments pertain to both species.

Reproduction

Squirrels have a high reproduction potential and can quadruple their population in one year. Squirrel survival is high because most young are born in secure nest dens in tree cavities high above the ground and are vigorously defended by protective mothers. Squirrels have a winter and summer breeding period. Females over 1-year-old have 1 or 2 litters per year, but younger squirrels usually have 1 litter at about 10-months-old. Factors that control or limit squirrel reproduction and survival are disease, predation, squirrel behavior, and the habitat's ability to provide food, cover, and water.

Infectious and Parasitic Diseases

If well nourished, squirrels suffer little from infectious or parasitic diseases. Although coccidioidomycosis, adiaspiromycosis, fibromatosis, listeriosis, and eastern encephalitis have been reported in squirrels (Davis et al. 1970), infectious diseases probably do not limit squirrel populations and do not become epizootic. Of the many parasites that infest squirrels, mange causing mites are probably the most life threatening (Sweatman 1971). Infestations by larvae of the botfly Cuterebra emasculator are common in the Southeast, but apparently do little damage to the squirrels. The internal and external parasites known to infest squirrels are listed by Flyger and Gates (1982).

Predation and Hunting

Predation is not considered a serious limiting factor on squirrel populations. Although many predators occasionally prey on gray or fox squirrels, they are not a staple food item in any common carnivore's diet. The squirrel's well developed senses, arboreal habit, agility, and aggressiveness make them very difficult prey. Predation is probably highest when squirrel movement is increased by food shortages and dispersion. Lack of den trees with suitable nest cavities may also increase predation.

The greatest predator of squirrels is man. Hunters harvest over one million squirrels annually in many states and some 40 million nationally (Flyger and Gates 1982). Most state wildlife agencies consider the squirrel an under-harvested resource because less than 20 percent of the fall population is normally harvested in extensive forested areas. The harvest percentage can be much higher in smaller woodlots, but squirrel populations recover quickly to preharvest levels (Fouch 1961, Mosby 1969, Jordan 1971). Although hunting accounted for 55.2 percent of the annual mortality on an intensively hunted public area in southeast Ohio, populations fluctuated mainly in response to the mast crop the preceding fall (Nixon et al. 1975). Hunters kill few squirrels when populations are low because hunting success and effort decrease.

Life Requirements

The dominant limiting factor on squirrel populations is habitat quality or the availability of food, cover, and water. Food and cover are the primary determinants of habitat quality for both gray and fox squirrels. Suitable cover provides protection from weather and predators and sufficient food enables good physical condition that improves reproduction, disease resistance, and ability to escape predators. Intraspecific social activity as influenced by population density and food supply also affects squirrel population levels.

Cover--Squirrels are restricted to habitats that contain trees, which supply food and cover. External leaf nests and dens located in tree cavities are used for escape from predators, shelter from weather, and reproduction of young. A scarcity of dens limits squirrel populations most often in young forests and forests intensively managed for wood production. Most squirrel dens are partially excavated by woodpeckers. Tree conditions most suitable for nest cavity excavation by woodpeckers were described by Conner et al. (1976) and Evans and Conner (1979) and are most prevalent in older trees that have developed in forest stands. The number of dens needed to maintain maximum squirrel populations is dependent on food supply and weather severity, both of which vary areally and temporally.

Because squirrels can survive and raise young in external leaf nests, the value of dens for maintaining populations is a subject of some controversy. In general, gray squirrels use leaf nests for rearing young more in the summer than in the winter, but dens are preferred year round and insufficient dens can reduce squirrel numbers (Uhlig 1955, Goodrum 1961). Fox squirrels raise young more often in leaf or twig nests than gray squirrels. Nixon et al. (1984) believed this successful use of nests was an adaptation to shelter-poor landscapes made possible by the fox squirrel's larger body size, which enables it to maintain body heat more efficiently during cold weather. Although the larger fox squirrel is less dependent on dens than the gray squirrel, the survival and reproduction of both species are maximized when sufficient dens are available because they provide better protection than leaf nests. This need for better shelter is most critical during the winter.

Food--If sufficient dens are available, lack of food usually limits squirrel populations. Although squirrels eat many foods that vary seasonally, they are most dependent on tree seeds, primarily large nuts such as hickory nuts, acorns, beechnuts, and walnuts (Martin et al. 1951:232-233, Nixon et al. 1968). Because of their wide distribution and abundance, oaks (Quercus spp.) and hickories (Carya spp.) are most important in the squirrel's diet. Acorns and nuts are scatter-hoarded and utilized throughout the year. Mast producing species have large fluctuations in annual fruit yield that cause large annual fluctuations in squirrel density (Allen 1943, Uhlig 1956, Goodrum 1961, Longley 1963). Winter survival of adult squirrels and their reproduction depend mainly on the abundance of mast produced the prior fall and also on the severity of the winter (Havera and Nixon 1980, Smith and Barkalow 1967).

Although food habits of fox and gray squirrels are

similar (Bakken 1969, Smith and Follmer 1972), some differences in food habits occur because fox squirrels occupy more open habitats and forage farther from trees than gray squirrels. Corn, wheat, and seeds of open growing trees are often major food items in fox squirrel diets (Fouch 1961, Longley 1963, Korschgen 1981). Gray squirrels, which occupy closed canopy forests, rely more heavily on hickory, oak, and beech (*agus grandifolia*) mast (Korschgen 1981, Nixon *et al.* 1968). Many wildlife species in addition to squirrels compete for acorns.

Water--Open water is not normally a limiting factor, especially for fox squirrels (USDA 1971). Although squirrels readily drink open water, they can survive with no apparent detrimental effects for 1 to 2 months without free water (Uhlig 1955). Nevertheless, gray squirrels utilize habitats with open water sources more than those without water.

Behavior

Squirrel behavior and social organization assist in the regulation of squirrel populations (Armitage and Harris 1982, Nixon *et al.* 1984). Squirrels interact with conspecifics to form a social hierarchy in which adults are dominant over immatures and males over females, except near den trees. Pregnant and nursing females aggressively defend nesting areas. During fall, when density is maximum, young squirrels often disperse because of intraspecific intolerance. Thompson (1978a, 1978b)

speculated that the density at which dispersion takes place may be controlled by proximate factors, such as food availability. Dispersal helps to regulate population size because survival of dispersed animals is low, especially during years of low mast production. Fox squirrels seem to be more asocial than gray squirrels and have developed a dispersed social system that limits annual recruitment (Armitage and Harris 1982, Nixon *et al.* 1984).

Fox squirrels forage in more open areas than gray squirrels. Smith and Follmer (1972) speculated that this difference in foraging behavior was a mechanism for niche diversification that adapts fox squirrel for open forest and forest edges and gray squirrel for dense forest. Fox squirrels also forage more during the middle of the day.

Gray Squirrel Population Dynamics

Nixon *et al.* (1975) reported some of the results from a 10-year study on a 505 ha public hunting area in southeastern Ohio. Their paper explained squirrel population dynamics by determining the effects of hunting, mast production, prior density of squirrels, and behavior on gray squirrel density.

The major conclusion was that heavy hunting affected subsequent squirrel densities, but density fluctuated mainly in response to mast crops the preceding fall. Response to good mast crops were: (1) improved survival of summer-born young, (2) a lower rate of emigration of both juveniles and subadults, (3) an increase in fecundity of breeding females, and (4) a higher rate of survival of adult gray squirrels in response to increases in the hickory nut crop. The importance of hickory mast to adult squirrels was demonstrated by a 10 to 15 percent survival increase when hickory nut production increased 11.2 kg/ha.

Intraspecific social behavior was important in survival of adult females and subadults of both sexes, the population segments most sensitive to high density levels. As density prior to breeding increased, survival of subadult squirrels decreased. The survival of adult females appeared affected more by density level than by hunting mortality. Their survival was highest when preseason squirrel densities were less than 70/40 ha and low when densities exceeded 100/40 ha.

HABITAT PARTITIONING

Although gray and fox squirrels can inhabit the same woods, each species is best adapted for slightly different habitats. Because they have similar food and cover requirements, adaptation to different habitats probably occurred to reduce competition between the two species (Brown and Batzli 1984 and references therein). The size and pattern (patchiness) of forest distribution and density of woody understory appear to be major determinants in habitat selection between the two species (Taylor 1974). Brown and Batzli (1984) concluded that in Illinois forest patch size influenced distribution more than understory and that understory cover was simply correlated with forest size because of differential grazing. Flyger and Gates (1982) stated that as the percentage of woodland increases the ratio of gray to fox squirrels increases, and if 70 percent or more of an area is wooded, fox squirrels are absent. Nixon et al. (1984) believed the fox squirrel has adapted to more resource-limited environments, such as fire-adapted savanna forests, than the gray squirrel. This assumption appears valid because fox squirrels appear to be more abundant in resource-limited environments throughout the ranges of the two species.

The range of fox squirrels extends farther west into areas where forest resources are restricted to narrow riparian zones and savanna woodlands separating prairie from forest land. In the Midwest, the cutting and agricultural conversion of the original forest into small woodlots greatly favored the fox squirrel over the gray (Allen 1943). Gray squirrels greatly outnumber fox squirrels in areas with extensive hardwood forest, where fox squirrels are found mostly along the forest edge or on upland xeric sites with pine (Pinus spp.) or open hardwood overstories and sparse woody understories. On The Coastal Plain and Piedmont, fox squirrels are more abundant on pine uplands where preferred food and cover occur in scattered patches and linear strips of hardwoods along small drainages. Gray squirrels predominate in extensive bottomland hardwoods, except in the Mississippi Delta Re-

gion of Arkansas, Mississippi, and Louisiana, where a small fox squirrel subspecies (S. n. subauratus) is also abundant. Because of differences in habitat preference, the preservation of wilderness and natural areas will have different impacts on each species.

IMPACTS OF WILDERNESS DESIGNATION

Wilderness or natural area designation can have positive or negative impacts on squirrel populations. The type of impact will depend on what future land use or forest management was planned for the area and on plant successional changes that will occur. Squirrels benefit if wilderness designation prevents conversion to nonforest land uses or forest management practices that reduce or destroy suitable squirrel habitat. Many forests are now managed under an even-aged management system with short rotation ages. These young forests support few or no squirrels because of insufficient dens and food. The superiority of wilderness and natural areas as squirrel habitat if compared to nonforest land uses and forests managed to maximize wood production is obvious and require no further discussion. But forests can be actively managed to produce better squirrel habitat than that found on many wilderness areas where most management activities are not allowed.

Designation as a wilderness or natural area will not preserve forest conditions in their present state. Plant succession will proceed and produce changes that will alter the fox and gray squirrels' habitats and may favor one species over the other. Although the effects of disease, predation, and hunting on squirrel populations may change within wilderness areas, these changes are not expected to be of major consequences. Habitat changes that affect the availability of suitable food and cover determine squirrel population levels regardless of whether forests are managed for wilderness or nonwilderness uses.

Successional Change

Tree Size and Age--Most wilderness areas in the East contain second growth forest stands in some seral stage of development. These forests will not remain in their present state forever. Trees will grow older, larger, and fewer in number. Aging and growth of existing trees strongly affect production of squirrel food and cover. As trees age, tree decay becomes more prevalent and the number of sites suitable for cavity excavation increases. Therefore as wilderness stands grow to maturity and beyond into old-growth conditions, den availability should increase. However, an increase in dens may favor gray squirrels over fox squirrels because fox squirrels appear to be better adapted to living and reproducing in environments scarce of dens (Nixon et al. 1984).

Mast production is usually higher in middle-aged to mature stands than in old-growth stands. The relationship between tree size and acorn production has been intensively studied. Acorn production in most tree-size oaks begins at 20 to 25 cm d.b.h. and increases with size until trees become large (greater than 66 cm d.b.h.) and senescent. Although larger trees produce more acorns, acorn yields per unit of land area are usually greatest when stands contain trees 41 to 56 cm in diameter (USDA 1971, Table 1). As wilderness stands approach old growth, squirrel density may decrease because of lower food production, but population levels will remain higher than those in younger stands (less than 39 cm d.b.h.) or in stands with insufficient dens.

In upland hardwood stands on the Cumberland Plateau in Tennessee, Huntley (1983) found that squirrel populations were higher in second growth forest than in old-growth (Table 2). Dens were plentiful in old-growth forests, but mast production by oaks and hickories was poor to fair. Baumgartner (1943) also found that climax forests in Ohio supported fewer squirrels than subclimax forests or secondary forest types. The two causes he suggested were that old trees appear to supply fewer food resources than younger trees and that most climax forests are the beech-maple type, which supplies a good mast crop only once every 3 to 5 years.

Forest Composition, Structure, and Pattern--As trees in the existing stands become senescent, lose vigor and die from natural causes and disturbances, canopy gaps are created. Often the gaps are filled by species dif-

ferent from these that died, therefore forest composition changes. These changes affect the food and cover available for squirrels. Compositional changes should not greatly affect den availability, but food production could be increased or decreased depending generally on whether oaks and hickories become more or less abundant in the succeeding stands.

The vegetational development within eastern wilderness areas will vary greatly because of wide scale past disturbances by man and local differences in topography, soil, and moisture regimes. The interrelationships among these and other factors often produce a polyclimax community of different forest types with numerous species in close proximity. Therefore, ecologists familiar with the local area are best qualified to predict successional changes that may occur on each wilderness or natural area.

The most comprehensive interpretation of the eastern forest was presented by Braun (1950), and potential natural vegetation was mapped by Kuchler (1966). Although eastern vegetation is complex and varies with many factors, some general trends are apparent. Without disturbances, southern yellow pine forests will advance through a mixed pine-hardwood sere ultimately to a predominately oak-hickory forest. The continued existence of pine forest on southern wilderness areas will depend on disturbances, such as fire, that prevent hardwood

Table 1. Acorn Yields (Air Dried Weight in kg) per 1 m^2 of Basal Area of Trees in Various Size Classes. Adapted from USDA (1971).

d.b.h. (cm)	Species of Oak						
	Chestnut	White	N. Red	S. Red	Scarlet	Black	Water
25	8.8	6.3	3.4	2.9	22.0	9.8	3.9
30	18.1	9.3	13.7	4.9	23.9	10.7	12.7
36	22.0	12.2	24.4	6.8	24.9	10.3	16.6
41	22.0	15.1	34.7	9.8	27.8	9.8	24.9
46	22.0	23.4	39.1	13.2	32.7	9.3	19.5
51	19.5	23.4	35.2	17.6	33.2	8.8	19.5
56	18.1	21.0	31.7	22.5	32.2	8.3	19.0
61	15.6	19.5	23.9	28.3	27.8	8.3	18.6
66	13.7	17.6	18.1	31.7	24.4	7.8	
71	12.2	14.6	14.2		21.0	7.3	
76	10.7	12.2	9.8		18.1	6.8	

Table 2. Density of Gray Squirrels Determined by Time-Area Counts in Upland Hardwood Stands on the Cumberland Plateau in Tennessee. (Number/40 ha)

Forest Age & Location	Den Trees	1979		1980		1981	
		May	Oct.	May	Oct.	May	Oct.
Second-growth							
Undulating upland	320	11	9	44	54	0	29
Upland drainage	230	14	21	79	67	12	17
South Cove	160	10	49	7	32	6	0
North Cove	120	10	74	26	54	0	4
Old-growth North Cove	270	1	34	4	89	1	0

encroachment. Oak-hickory forests may remain so or succeed to forests characterized by a greater number of species or by species other than oaks and hickories. On mesic sites, a major successional tendency in central and southern hardwood stands is an increase in species richness (Braun 1950, Quarterman and Keever 1962). Because these species often are not oaks or hickories, the food supply available to squirrels can be reduced. Oaks and hickories will be more abundant on xeric sites. In northern forests, sugar maple (*Acer saccharum*), American beech, American basswood (*Tilia americana*) and eastern hemlock (*suga canadensis*) are major dominants in older forests. These forests usually support smaller squirrel densities than oak-hickory forests.

The successional trends in bottomland hardwoods are complex and difficult to predict. Although species composition is site specific and associated with soil and water characteristics, a great variety of species can become dominant on moist, well-drained sites. Generally the oaks, most of which are only moderately tolerant of shade, follow a pioneer forest of intolerant species, and are gradually replaced by more shade tolerant species as the forest reaches climax stage.

The climax forest is more stable and less likely to change species composition than the preceding seral stages. Although no forest is completely stable, climax forests are resilient and revert to earlier stages only after major man-made or natural disturbances. Without man-made disturbances, the major portion of wilderness areas will ultimately reach the climax stage, which may be better, similar, or worse squirrel habitat that the current stage of the forest. Successional trends from pine to hardwood forest and from open forest to denser forest will be more favorable to the gray squirrel than to the fox squirrel.

Succession to the climax condition also impacts forest pattern. All man-produced openings will revert to forest land. Natural disturbances will produce forest openings, but most of the openings will remain in or quickly revert to woody growth. Most savannas, shrublands, and grasslands in the East are dependent on fire or grazing and will probably succeed to forest without active management. Naturally occurring fires will probably not be of sufficient extent or frequency to maintain fire dependent ecosystems. The widespread use of fire by aboriginal Americans and lightning-caused fires played a major part in the development of fire-dependent ecosystems. The succession to forest will decrease landscape diversity and this decrease in forest patchiness and edge will favor gray squirrels over fox squirrels.

Detrimental Impacts on Fox Squirrel

Because successional changes will ultimately produce habitat more favorable to gray squirrels, fox squirrel populations in wilderness areas will decrease and may be extirpated by competition from the gray squirrel. The loss of fox squirrel habitat will be most critical in the southeast where fox squirrel populations have greatly decreased (Flyger and Gates 1982). Typical is the status of the fox squirrel (*S.n. niger*) in South Carolina (Wood and Davis 1981), where forestry and wildlife professionals generally thought the fox squirrel was scarce and most perceived declines in fox squirrel numbers.

Another eastern subspecies, the Delmarva fox squirrel (*S.n. cinereus*) is restricted to four counties on the Eastern Shore of Maryland and was placed on the first official "Federal Endangered Species List" (Lustig and Flyger 1976). The Delmarva fox squirrel, similar to other eastern subspecies, prefers open forests with mature pine and sparse understory (Taylor 1974). Increased competition from gray squirrels because of changing habitat conditions seems to be a major factor causing the decline of the Delmarva squirrel. The Delmarva squirrel has attained its highest density on an island void of gray squirrels by utilizing all available habitat including that normally occupied by gray squirrels (Taylor 1974, Lustig and Flyger 1976). Although Maryland has forbidden hunting and established a refuge for the Delmarva fox squirrel, Taylor (1974) believed that this subspecies faces total extinction unless more positive actions are developed. Management planners for wilderness areas, especially those in the southeast, should consider reducing competition from gray squirrels by retaining some portion of the area in forest conditions more favorable to fox squirrels.

MANAGEMENT

Although successional changes may decrease gray squirrel populations below their present levels, direct management practices are not needed to maintain viable and thriving gray squirrel populations on most wilderness areas. On many areas, gray squirrels will increase and may replace fox squirrels if the management strategy of simply allowing plant succession to proceed to climax conditions is adopted. To maintain fox squirrel populations, a management policy to maintain some earlier successional seres should be implemented. In the southeast, one such management policy could be to maintain pine forests on some upper slopes and ridges. Doing so would prevent the development of a continuous hardwood forest that would greatly favor the gray squirrel. Within the constraints imposed by the Wilderness Act, planned ignition of fires, letting unplanned fires burn, and grazing are management practices that may maintain habitat more favorable to fox squirrels. Repeated light burning and cattle grazing during spring and early summer to reduce underbrush were suggested as the most promising way to manipulate habitat to favor the endangered Delmarva fox squirrel (Lustig and Flyger 1976). If agencies adopt management policies to maintain and restore the fire dependent ecosystems now present on wilderness and natural areas, a greater diversity of vegetation types will be preserved and fox squirrels and other animals adapted to these systems will benefit.

Whether or not squirrel hunting is allowed should have little impact on squirrel populations or on the environment. Squirrel hunting is enjoyed by many people and wilderness areas offer excellent opportunities for high quality, secluded hunting not available on other public land. Squirrel hunting should not be allowed on areas that contain endangered or threatened fox squirrel populations.

LITERATURE CITED

Allen, D.L. 1943. Michigan fox squirrel management. GameDiv. Publ. 100. Michigan Dept. of Conserv. Lansing,Mich.

Armitage, K.B. and K.S. Harris. 1982. Spatial patterning in sympatric populations of fox and gray squirrels. Am. Midl. Nat. 108:389-397.

Bakken, A. 1959. Behavior of gray squirrels. Proc. Southeast. Assoc. Game and Fish Comm. 13:393-406.

Barkalow, F.S. Jr. and M. Shorten. 1973. The world of the gray squirrel. J.B. Lippincott Co., New York, N.Y.

Baumgartner, L.L. 1943. Fox squirrels in Ohio. J. Wildl. Manage. 7:193-200.

Braun, E.L. 1950. Deciduous forest of eastern North America. The Blakeston Co., Philadelphia, Penn.

Brown, B.W. and G.O. Batzli. 1984. Habitat selection by fox and gray squirrels: a multivariate analysis. J. Wildl. Manage. 48:616-621.

Brown, L.G. and L.E. Yeager. 1945. Fox squirrels and gray squirrels in Illinois. Ill. Nat. Hist. Surv. Bull. 23:449-536.

Conner, R.N., O.K. Miller, Jr., and C.S. Adkisson. 1976. Woodpecker dependence on trees infected by fungal heart rots. Wilson Bull. 88:575-581.

Davis, J.W., L.H. Karstad, D.O. Trainer. ed. 1970. Infectious diseases of wild mammals. Iowa State Univ. Press, Ames, Iowa.

Evans, K.E. and R.N. Conner. 1975. Snag management. pp. 214-225 *In* R.M. DeGraaf and K.E. Evans (Compilers), Proceedings of the workshop, management of north central and northeastern forest for nongame birds. USDA For. Serv. Gen. Tech. Rep. NC-51.

Flyger, V. and J.E. Gates. 1982. Fox and gray squirrels. pp. 209-229 *In* J.A. Chapman and G.A. Feldhamer (eds.), Wild mammals of North America. The John Hopkins Press, Baltimore, Maryland.

Fouch, W.R. 1961. Mast crops and fox squirrel populations at the Rose Lake Wildlife Experiment Station. Game Div. Rep. No. 2332. Mich. Dept. Conserv., Lansing, Mich.

Goodrum, P.D. 1961. The gray squirrel in Texas. Texas Parks and Wildl. Dept. Bull. No. 42, Austin, Tex.

Hall, E.R. 1981. The mammals of North America, Volume I. John Wiley & Sons, New York, N.Y.

Havera, S.P. and C.M. Nixon. 1980. Winter feeding of fox squirrel populations. J. Wildl. Manage. 44:41-55.

Huntley, J.C. 1983. Squirrel den tree management: reducing incompatibility with timber production in upland hardwoods. pp. 488-495 *In* E.P. Jones (ed.), Proc. second biennial southern silvicultural research conference, USDA For. Serv. Gen. Tech. Rep. SE-24.

Jordan, J.S. 1971. Yield from an intensively hunted population of eastern fox squirrels. USDA For. Serv. Res. Pap. NE-186.

Korschgen, L.J. 1981. Foods of fox and gray squirrels in Missouri. J. Wildl. Manage. 45:260-266.

Kuchler, A.W. 1966. Potential natural vegetation. National Atlas Map. USDI Geol. Surv., Washington, D.C.

Longley, W.H. 1963. Minnesota gray and fox squirrels. Am. Midl. Nat. 69:82-98.

Lustig, L.W. and V. Flyger. 1976. Observations and suggested management practices for the endangered Delmarva fox squirrel. Proc. Southeast. Assoc. Game Fish Comm. 29:433-440.

Madson, J. 1964. Gray and fox squirrels. Conserv. Dept., Olin Mathieson Chemical Corp. East Alton, Ill.

Martin, A.C., H.S. Zim, and A.L. Nelson. 1951. American wildlife & plants a guide to wildlife food habits. Dover Publication, Inc. New York, NY.

Mosby, H.S. 1969. The influence of hunting on the population dynamics of a woodlot gray squirrel population. J. Wildl. Manage. 33:59-73.

Nixon, C.M., S.P. Havera, and L.P. Hansen. 1984. Effects of nest boxes on fox squirrel demography, condition, and shelter use. Am. Midl. Nat. 112:157-171.

Nixon, C.M., M.W. McClain, and R.W. Donohoe. 1975. Effects of hunting and mast crops on a squirrel population. J. Wildl. Manage. 39:1-25.

Nixon, C.M., D.M. Worley, and M.W. McClain. 1968. Food habits of squirrel in southeast Ohio. J. Wildl. Manage. 32:294-305.

Quarterman, E. and C. Keever. 1962. Southern mixed hardwood forest: climax in the southeastern Coastal Plain, U.S.A. Ecol. Monogr. 32:167-185.

Smith, C.C. and D. Follmer. 1972. Food preferences of squirrels. Ecology 53:82-91.

Smith, N.B. and F.A. Barkalow, Jr. 1967. Precocious breeding in the gray squirrel. J. Mammal. 48:328-330.

Spencer, G.E. 1981. Final report of job number 27: squirrel distribution investigations. Federal Aid Project No. W-108-R-4, Texas Parks and Wildlife Dept., Austin, Tex.

Sweatman, G.K. 1971. Mites and pentastomes. pp 3-64 *In* J.W. Davis and R.C. Anderson (eds.), Parasitic diseases of wild mammals, Iowa State Univ. Press, Ames, Iowa.

Taylor, G.J. 1974. Present status and habitat survey of the Delmarva fox squirrel (*Sciurus niger cinereus*) with a discussion of reasons for its decline. Proc. Southeast. Assoc. Game Fish Comm. 27:278-289.

Thompson, D.C. 1978a. The social system of grey squirrel. Behaviour 64:305-328.

Thompson, D.C. 1978b. Regulation of a northern grey squirrel (*Sciurus carolinensis*) population. Ecology 59:708-715.

Uhlig, H.G. 1955. The gray squirrel; its life history, ecology, and population characteristics in West Virginia. Pittman-Robertson Project 31-R. Conservation Commission of West Virginia.

Uhlig, H.G. 1956. The gray squirrel in West Virginia. Div. of Game Manage. Bull. No. 3. 83 p. Conservation Comm. of West Virginia.

USDA. 1971. Wildlife habitat management handbook. Southern Region, USDA For. Serv. FSH 2609.23R.

Wood, G.W. and J.R. Davis. 1981. A survey of perceptions of fox squirrel populations in South Carolina. For. Bull. No. 29, Dept. of For., Clemson Univ.

White-Tailed Deer In Eastern Wilderness Areas

by
Lowell K. Halls

ABSTRACT--Historically, the white-tailed deer (*Odocoileus virginianus*) is a biological component of eastern mature forests. After a near demise in the late 1800's, the whitetail now thrives throughout its former range and beyond. Whether hunted or not, whitetails are now present in most wilderness areas, however, they are not wilderness-dependent. The wilderness areas can provide a quality hunting experience, but because of limited access the hunter take is apt to be light. Predators other than man may be the main consumer in lightly hunted areas. Livestock and big game animals are not likely to compete strongly with whitetails in wilderness areas except that the moose may be adversely affected by meningeal worms and liver flukes carried by deer. Because of a wide variety in habitat conditions and public desires and sentiments, the wilderness-deer management plan should be area-specific.

KEYWORDS: climax forests, quality hunting, predators, meningeal worms, liver fluke, competition with cattle and moose.

Since, by definition, "wilderness is an area of undeveloped land retaining its primeval character and influence without permanent improvements of habitation . . . and which generally appears to have been affected primarily by the forces of nature with the imprint of man's work substantially unnoticed," I will briefly review historical information about the white-tailed deer in the so-called primeval forests, ie., forests unmolested by white man in his colonization and agricultural development.

Whitetails were prevalent throughout most of North America prior to settlement by the white man. The literature is filled with accounts by adventurers who penetrated the wilderness and appraised the variety and number of wildlife; white-tailed deer were mentioned prominently in many of the earliest records. Whitetails abounded in climax forests, such as those of central New England (McCabe and McCabe 1984). Evidence of deer abundance in the virgin forests of east Texas is described by Truett and Lay (1984), "Deer rivaled wild turkey in their plenty. Stephen F. Austin in his first trip from Nacogdoches to San Antonio in 1821 killed deer daily for food, despite his hurry. Traveler Amos Parker reported that east Texas Indians traded mainly in deer skins in the 1880's. North of Houston in 1841, William Bollaert saw parties of three or four hunters shoot thirty to forty deer in a day. Near Silsbee in Hardin county in the mid 1800's, parties of sport hunters sometimes killed as many as 70 deer a day." Additional evidence of the abundance of whitetails in pristine North America comes from early trade records (McCabe and McCabe 1984).

The number of deer in early settlement days is speculative. Seton estimated 40 million, probably an optimistic assessment. Elder (1965) wrote, "There is little doubt that deer are much more numerous today than under primeval conditions. Logging, clearing, alternating periods of fire control have greatly increased the carrying capacity of modern deer range in the United States." However, McCabe and McCabe (1984) disagree with the assertion that whitetail abundance is greater today than it was under "primeval conditions" or during the "Indian era." They estimate that the number of whitetails prior to the sixteenth century could have been more than double the current population of approximately 14.2 million. Some writers have concluded that whitetails did not occur extensively in the vast tracts of mature virgin forests.

Regardless of the disparity in estimated deer numbers, they were numerous and contributed a substantial part to the Indians' welfare and culture. On this enormous wildlife resource the Indians had little if any negative effect - their needs were dwarfed by the magnitude of the supply (Trefethen 1975). A major effect that the Indians had on the deer's well being was in the burning of the woodlands and prairies. The grassland and parklike forests which explorers found in many parts of the eastern forests could only have resulted from repeated burning. When the Indian set torch to the forest he let the fire burn itself out. Repeated burning provided a wide variety of game that otherwise could not have existed in the virgin forest. In essence, the effect of Indian-set fires was quite likely what one would expect to find from lightning caused fires that spread unchecked in wilderness areas of today.

Although deer were common around most every white settlement, the bountiful days soon passed with colonization, destruction of forests, and unrestricted hunting. Within a relatively few years deer numbers were severely reduced throughout their range and decimated in many areas. The low point in deer numbers probably occurred between 1870 and 1890. East of the Mississippi there were only scattered patches of deer range in the Appalachians, the northern counties of the lake states, and scattered swamps and mountains throughout the southern states. Total numbers east of the Great Plains probably did not exceed 500,000 and may have been as low as 350,000 in 1890 (Trefethen 1975).

Substantial positive efforts towards deer restoration began with the passage of the Pittman-Robertson Act in 1937, but the situation remained bleak for the whitetail until after World War II. Since then, deer recovery and expansion has been remarkable. It is truly one of the most outstanding wildlife restoration accomplishment efforts in North America.

So, here we are today. Whitetail numbers now probably exceed 14 million and are found in huntable populations throughout their original range, and in some cases beyond. With a few exceptions, there are plenty of whitetails. In many cases too many. Often the critical problem is not how to increase the deer population but how to keep it down, in balance with the habitat.

How do these so-called "wilderness areas" fit into the immediate and future needs of deer?

We are quite certain that whitetail herds can exist in the mature natural forest. History attests to that fact. In terms of deer numbers the climax forests may not be the most productive of the habitats, but they do contain the food and cover necessary for deer reproduction and survival.

The extent to which the forest will produce food for deer is largely dependent on the timber stand structure, the size and spacing of trees, the density of low cover, and on the overhead composition and density. Relatively speaking the disturbed forest is likely to produce a

greater number of deer than pristine forests. Lay (1964) indicated that a mixture of tree species, age classes, and clearings could yield more food for deer than uniform treatment of a large block of even-aged pines. In an east Texas pine-hardwood forest the forage yields decreased with the exclusion of fire and timber cutting (Halls and Boyd 1984). In Mississippi, forage from woody plants generally increased as the hardwood component of the stands increased and was inversely related with pine tree density (Hurst et al. 1979).

It is quite obvious that the white-tailed deer is not a wilderness-dependent species. Being highly adaptable and versatile it can and does exist in many habitats other than the primeval forest. In terms of the overall perspective, the wilderness areas will have little impact on the population of whitetails in the eastern United States. For example, the current 60 wilderness areas in the southern forests comprise only 5 percent of the 10.4 million acres (4.2 million ha) of national forests and 0.3 percent of the 193.3 million acres (78.2 million ha) of commercial forests in the southern United States. There may be instances, however, where refuges, which closely resemble wilderness situations, are needed to perpetuate a particular subspecies of whitetail such as the key deer of southern Florida.

Let's examine some of the situations that might exist in the wilderness forest and how they might affect the deer herd. What happens when hunting is excluded, such as is usually the case in national parks? It is not necessary that deer populations be harvested. Most wildlife biologists and managers can point to situations where deer have not been hunted yet do not fluctuate greatly or cause damage to vegetation (McCullough 1984). If deer are already present they are probably reasonably in balance with their habitat.

Although deer reach over population status in some park situations, the surprising thing is how many parks have no critical deer problem. In the Great Smokey Mountain National Park white-tailed deer were generally considered to be in balance with the ecosystem throughout the park, except where agricultural management was used to maintain open vistas and a cultural landscape (Bratton 1979). In "Lessons from the George Reserve" McCullough (1984) suggested that stable environments can sustain equilibrium relationships between residual deer populations and densities at which the number of recruits declines to zero. In extremely fluctuating environments hunting is not necessary because environmental variation regularly results in the population being below the carrying capacity.

Where hunting by man is restricted, natural predators are especially important in population regulation. Hunting in moderately fluctuating environments may not be necessary if a good complement of natural predators is present. Natural predators are better at reducing chronic mortality than are human hunters. The deer reproductive rate will likely be low, but a large proportion of those surviving the first year will reach maturity. Thus, the age structure will

strongly reflect the older age group, with a sex ratio only slightly in favor of does. In south Texas, predator control resulted in a two-fold increase in white-tailed deer population densities and the studies pointed out that if deer are not controlled by hunting or predators the result will be poor physical condition and the likelihood of a population crash (Kie et al. 1983).

Most wilderness areas will be hunted and the hunting pressure will undoubtedly affect the deer. As a general rule where hunting pressure is high the deer population is apt to be near or below the habitat carrying capacity, the reproductive rate per doe is likely to be high, the age-class at relatively low levels, and the buck/doe ratio rather high. If too many deer are killed, the reduced residual population will have increased recruitment. This tends to force the population back towards the original balance point. If too few deer are killed, the increased residual population has a low recruitment, and the population tends to decline back to the original balance point (McCullough 1984).

It is unlikely that deer hunting pressure will be high except along the edges of the wilderness. High hunter densities along the perimeter will probably be acceptable in heavy cover that conceals both deer and hunter, and among relatively unskilled hunters who depend on chance to see a deer. Hunters who place great emphasis on harvesting a deer are more likely to consider high hunter density acceptable than those who emphasize quality of the hunt (McCullough1984).

Deer hunting in the interior portions of large wilderness areas is not likely to be undertaken by a large number of hunters. Only a few will leave the roads and trails to go any great distance in the woods. Deer hunters just aren't going to venture very far into a forest devoid of roads and camping and parking areas. Even less appealing are areas devoid of foot trails (Thomas et al. 1976).

The reason some hunters prefer the wilderness is a quest for solitude. They want to get away from people, to avoid congestion that frequently is found on easily accessible public lands. Hunters who employ skill by stalking and selecting carefully considered stands are not likely to want encounters with other hunters. It is the stalk that lingers in the mind, the killing is a secondary thing, the anticlimax wherein the prize is plucked as proof of where they have been and what they have done (Schoenfeld and Hendee 1978).

Even though the wilderness area hunter is more apt to be interested in "quality" rather than "quantity" deer hunting, the realization that he may have to drag the slain animal through rough terrain and dense vegetation for a mile or so may temper his enthusiasm. Undoubtedly there is a dedicated core who enjoy these vicissitudes and challenges. Such situations may be especially appealing to primitive weapons hunters. However, the take will be light, and the central portions of wilderness areas, especially the larger areas, will essentially be the same as non-hunted areas. Predators other than man may be the main consumers in these lightly hunted areas, and under harvesting may contribute to large seasonal die-offs among some sex-age classes, and a late-age harvesting of bucks (Short 1972).

It is ironic that areas possessing many of the attributes desired by "quality" hunters may not have quality deer. Many of the poor quality deer are found in "big woods" country where deer populations are usually high. In such situations bucks are apt to be of smaller-than-normal body size with poor antler development (Matscke et al. 1984).

Whether to have either-sex or buck-only hunting also concerns the wilderness hunter. Under heavy buck-only hunting, bucks of more than 3.5 years of age may be eliminated and an abnormally high number of does will lead inevitably to a high percentage of small antlered young bucks than would otherwise exist (Matscke 1984). Some trophy bucks are obtained under buck-only hunting but they are relatively few. Management for maximum sustained yield will produce the greatest number of bucks, and because of rapid growth rate they will reach maximum size in a short time (McCullough 1984). If one wants to maintain a high residual population of deer for tourists, nature study groups, etc., but also wants some hunting, buck-only hunting is probably a good strategy. Nevertheless, most biologists recommend either-sex hunting as a practical means of keeping the herd healthy and productive and in balance with the habitat.

In all probability there will be movement of deer in and out of the wilderness area. The extent and direction will depend largely on hunting pressure. At the Crab Orchard National Wildlife Refuge social pressure within the refuge manifested itself in the dispersal of yearling bucks, many of which were cropped in the surrounding area, thus helping to prevent an overpopulation within the refuge. The percentage of deer moving off the study area was directly related to population levels. Even though there was only one controlled harvest since the herd began in 1942-43, the program resulted in a healthy deer herd with little detriment to the habitat by 1971 (Hawkins, et al. 1971). At a refuge in Georgia (Kammermeyer and Marchinton 1975) three major patterns of deer movement were apparent: (1) relatively sedentary movement of resident refuge deer, (2) dispersal of 1.5 and 2.5 year-old bucks from the refuge, coincident with the onset of rut, and (3) migrations of a large contingent of deer (mainly does) onto the refuge coincident with the opening of deer hunting season.

Livestock presence, mainly cattle, adds another dimension to deer management in wilderness areas. Cattle left on range yearlong may be quite competitive with deer, especially in winter and early spring when green forage is scarce. Little competition exists if cattle are restricted to late spring and summer grazing and the numbers properly regulated according to forage availability. Serious problems exist when the cattle or deer, or both, exceed the carrying capacity of the range. Fortunately, unregulated livestock grazing is essentially a thing of the past on most National Forests and serious conflicts are unlikely to occur in the future.

Moose is the most likely big game competitor of whitetails in the northern wilderness areas. They often consume similar foods and range over a common habitat. Although direct competition between them is generally minimal it may be serious where forage has been seriously depleted and where weather conditions are severe. Probably the most damaging aspect of deer-moose coexistence is in their response to the meningeal worm (*Parelaphosptrongylus tenuis*) and the liver fluke (*Fascioloides magna*). The deer are normal hosts to the meningeal worm and suffer no apparent harm from its presence, but the worm invades the brain area of the moose often leading to its death. Likewise, the liver fluke produces no clinical disease in whitetails, but moose in close association with deer may become affected, with adverse results (Franzmann 1978).

Regardless of how the deer herd is managed or what restrictions are placed on hunter activity in wilderness areas, it will be impossible to completely satisfy all segments of society. There is too wide a variety in habitat conditions and public desires and sentiments to make a blanket recommendation for all areas. Wilderness-wildlife management plans will need to be area-specific, and the real down-to-earth decisions reconciled pretty much on a local basis. McCullough (1984) has suggested that "One can manage for deer hunter satisfaction or for protectionist group satisfaction, but any one program cannot achieve all biological and social goals simultaneously."

LITERATURE CITED

Bratton, S.P. 1979. Impacts of white-tailed deer on the vegetation of Cades Cove, Great Smokey Mountain National Park. Proc. Ann Conf. S.E. Assoc. Fish and Wildl. Agencies 33:305-312.

Elder, W.H. 1965. Primeval deer hunting pressures revealed by remains from American Indian Middens. J. Wildl. Manage. 29:366-370.

Franzmann, A.W. 1978. Moose. Pp. 61-81, In J.L. Schmidt and D.L.Gilbert (eds). Big Game of North America. Stackpole Book, Harrisburg, Penn.

Halls, L.K. and C.E. Boyd. 1982. Influence of managed pure pine stands and mixed pine/hardwood stands on well being of deer. USDA For. Serv. Res. Pap. SO-183. South. For. Exp. Stn., New Orleans, Louis.

Hawkins, R.E., W.D. Klimstra and D.C. Autry. 1971. Dispersal of deer from Crab Orchard National Wildlife Refuge. J. Wildl. Manage.35:216-220.

Hurst, G.H., D.C. Guynn, and B.D. Leopold. 1979. Correlation of forest characteristics with white-tailed deer forage. Proc. Ann. Conf. S.E. Assoc. Fish and Wildl. Agencies 33:48-55.

Kammermeyer, K.E., and R.L. Marchinton. 1975. The dynamic aspects of deer populations utilizing a refuge. Proc. Ann. Conf. S.E. Assoc, Game and Fish Comm. 29: 466-474.

Kie, J.G., M.White, and D.L. Drawe. 1983. Condition parameters of white-tailed deer in Texas. J. Wildl. Manage. 47:583-594.

Lay, D.W. 1964. The importance of variety to southern deer. Proc. Ann. Conf. S.E. Assoc. Game and Fish Comm. 18:57-62.

Matscke, G.H., K.A. Fagerstone, F.A. Hayes, W. Parker, R.F. Harlow, V. F. Nettles, and D.O. Trainer. 1984. Population influences. Pp. 169-188, In L.K. Halls (ed.). White-tailed deer: ecology and management. Stackpole Books, Harrisburg, Penna.

McCabe, R.E. and T.R. McCabe. 1984. Of slings and arrows: a historical retrospection. Pp. 19-72, In L.K. Halls (ed.). White-tailed deer: ecology and management. Stackpole Books, Harrisburg,Penn.

McCullough, D.R. 1984. Lessons from the Georgia Reserve, Michigan. Pp. 211-242, In L.K. Halls (ed.) White-tailed deer: ecology and management. Stackpole Books, Harrisburg, Penna.

Schoenfeld, C.A. and J.C. Hendee. 1978. Wildlife management in wilderness. The Boxwood Press, Pacific Grove, Calif.

Short, H. L. 1972. Ecological framework for deer management. J.For. 70:200-203.

Thomas, J.W., J.D. Gill, J.C. Pack, W.H. Healy, and H.R. Sanderson. 1976. Influence of forest land characteristics on spatial distribution of hunters. J. Wildl. Manage. 40:500-506.

Trefethen, J.P. 1975. An American crusade for wildlife. Winchester Press, New York, NY.

Truett, J.C., and D.W. Lay. 1984. Land of bears and honey. University of Texas Press, Austin, Tex.

Moose In Eastern Wilderness--A Role For Prescribed Fire

by
Hewlette S. Crawford

ABSTRACT--Moose are bulk feeders and require the large volume of forage that in boreal and sub-boreal forests is found only in early seral stages. Prescribed burning is a feasible way to create or maintain early seres in eastern wilderness areas. Prescribed burning can be conducted effectively and safely in the heavy fuels of spruce-fir forests. Burning techniques are discussed.

KEYWORDS: *Alces alces*, white-tailed deer, spruce budworm, burning technique.

The moose (*Alces alces*) is the largest of cervids (Franzmann 1981). It is circumpolar in distribution and occupies the boreal and sub-boreal forests. Peterson (1974) accepts one species with seven geographic races. One race, *A. a. americana*, is found in the northeastern United States and eastern Canada and merges with *A. a. andersoni* in western Ontario.

Moose are common in Maine, Minnesota, and Isle Royal in Michigan, and are increasing in northern New Hampshire and northern Vermont. Occasional sightings have been reported in northeastern New York, Massachusetts, and Connecticut. Maine and Minnesota have a moose season and New Hampshire is considering one. The most recent population estimate for Maine is in excess of 20,000 animals (K.I. Morris, pers. comm. 1984).

Depending on your perspective, the moose is a noble-appearing animal or ugly as a mud fence. With its massive body perched on long, thin legs, the moose is seemingly ungainly, yet this animal amazes you with the effortless and graceful way it moves quickly through heavy logging slash and dense regrowth. Exhibiting unimaginable coordination, moose have charged me twice during my course of work. At these times, the mud fence perspective prevailed--1000 pounds of blood-shot eyes, laid-back ears, and axe-like hooves. The other perspective is obtained when canoeing a wilderness river and gliding up to a 1200 pound, heavily antlered bull wading the shallows and feeding on aquatic plants. The second perspective is probably held by most. How accurate is this perspective of moose in a wilderness setting?

DESIRABLE HABITATS OF EASTERN MOOSE

Balsam fir (*Abies balsamea*) is the food most often eaten by moose during winter (Peek 1974). Brassard *et al.* (1974) found that mountain maple (*Acer spicatum*) was important in winter in Quebec. During other seasons, several early successional species are eaten. These include white birch (*Betula papyrifera*), fire cherry (*Prunus pensylvanica*), quaking aspen (*Populus tremuloides*), willow (*Salix* spp.), raspberry (*Rubus* spp.), beaked hazel (*Corylus cornuta*), and other deciduous species. Some herbaceous species, including aquatics, also are eaten. Aquatics rich in sodium are important dietary supplements on some ranges (Fraser *et al.* 1984).

Moose are bulk feeders. Estimates of the weight of food ingested per day have ranged from 1.3 to 27.0 kg wet weight (Gasaway and Coady 1974). Penned moose ate 23 to 27 and 18 to 23 kg wet weight per day of cut browse during summer and winter, respectively (Verme 1970). Moose are not highly selective in their diet. In our studies (Lautenschlager and Crawford 1983), tamed moose found an area with abundant vegetation and fed there. By contrast, tamed deer on the same area wandered and searched for food. Forage quantity is more important than quality to moose, and early successional stages provided quantity. Dodds (1974) reported that before European settlers arrived, fires, blowdowns, and perhaps forest insects and disease created early seral stages beneficial to moose. After settlement, human-caused fires and forest cutting created desirable vegetation.

Snow depths influence the value of forest cuttings for moose. As snow accumulation exceeds 70 cm, moose require a protective forest canopy to intercept snowfall. Snow depths greater than 100 cm substantially limit their movement and decrease their ability to forage.

MOOSE IN WILDERNESS

Eastern wilderness areas in late successional stages will provide only limited habitat for moose unless natural disasters create early seres. However, the limited size of eastern wilderness areas will create pressures to limit natural factors such as wildfire, insect irruptions and pathological organisms. Adjoining landowners or state agencies will demand early controls to limit the spread of any natural disaster that could affect their land. Options for uncontrolled fire or insect outbreaks may not exist. Advanced seral stages will continue to provide suitable habitat for deer, favoring the transmission of *Parelaphostrongylus tenuis*, the brainworm, to moose. *P. tenuis* has decreased moose populations, while deer populations increased (Anderson and Lancaster 1974), however, in recent years moose populations have increased in the presence of deer.

To favor moose over deer, large areas in early seral stages subject to snow depths between 50 and 100 cm must be abundant. Depths above 50 cm limit deer movement. In areas of deep snow, advanced successional seres favor deer over moose. Snow depths are lessened under dense canopies and deer are able to move and search for food--much of which falls from the tree canopy through the action of wind or clipping by squirrels, porcupines, and birds.

PRESCRIBED FIRE TO FAVOR MOOSE

Prescribed fire is a feasible way to create or maintain moose habitat in eastern wilderness. A prescribed burning program will favor several species of wildlife in addition to or at the expense of moose. Beaver create desirable aquatic habitat for moose. Conversely, deer may transmit parasites. In northerly latitudes, numerous small fires of 10 ha or less over a period of years will benefit beaver, deer, grouse, and woodcock, and create diversity in woodland passerines. However, to favor moose, managers should create a burned area of 100 ha or larger. If it is impractical to burn a large area in one year, clustering successive yearly burns should provide good habitat. Up to 50 percent of the total area should be in early seral stages. Adequate burns can be conducted with conservative burning technology and control measures that will not mar the area's wilderness aspect. Following are some suggestions.

Objectives
The objective of prescribed burning to favor moose in the East is to maintain early seres that provide substantial quantities of food for moose. I do not recommend prescribed burning to remove conifer overstory. Crown fires are unpredictable with our present state of knowledge. However, it is possible to take advantage of other natural disasters that remove the overstory, such as spruce budworm (*Choristoneura fumiferana*), by using fire to halt subsequent plant succession before it advances too far to be useful to moose. Spruce budworms generally reach epidemic levels at approximately 40 year intervals. Natural succession to a new fir stand occurs rapidly following defoliation by spruce budworm since fir regeneration usually is abundant before defoliation is complete. Once the overstory opens, advanced fir regeneration is released. On average sites, the vegetation probably is available to moose for about 20 years.

Prescribed burning on a 15-year cycle after the initiation of understory response would result in continuing availability of food. Fire in sapling-small pole stands is manageable. A burning frequency of approximately 15 years would keep the zone of growing points and photosynthetic activity within reach of moose and enhance the cycling of nutrients and energy between habitat and animal. There should be little loss of nutrients with proper burning. Repeated burning will likely remove fir. However, pioneer hardwoods should remain in the stand and continue to provide desirable forage.

Burning Technique
Time of year-- I used spring burns in a prescribed fire program on the Moosehorn National Wildlife Refuge in eastern Maine. My objectives were (1) to reduce the depth of the organic mat covering the mineral soil by about half, (2) to consume as much logging debris as possible, and (3) to initiate hardwood succession. The area had been logged during a spruce budworm outbreak; tops and fallen unmerchantable trees were scattered over the site. There are two options for spring burning: wait for the organic material to dry following snowmelt and burn at that time, or allow greater drying of above-surface litter and logging debris and rely on rainfall to remoisten the organic layer to prevent excessive depth of burn. Spring burning also offers the advantage of having a source of water nearby for fire pumps.

Barriers-- During spring, numerous wet areas in northern latitudes provide useful firebreaks. Swamps with little understory growth are common and prevent the spread of fire when the edges adjacent to the burn are sprayed with fire hoses just before ignition. Streams wider than four to five meters and rivers provide natural breaks. Continuous stony outcrops also can serve as a fire line. Marshes with dried emergent growth can be burned early in the spring while snow remains in the shaded woods nearby, and can be used as firebreaks when woodland areas are burned later. Road boundaries of the smaller wilderness areas also make a satisfactory firebreak for controlled burns. Areas with light fuels can be sprayed with hoses or sprinklers and form a satisfactory firebreak with proper burning technique.

Weather-- Weather conditions must be evaluated with fuel load in mind. If fuels are heavy, be conservative. One might attempt burning on successive days beginning one day after a heavy rain. Light fuels dry faster and can be ignited before heavy fuels. Light fuels adjacent to a firebreak will dry sooner than light fuels located toward the interior of the area to be burned. By attempting ignition periodically as the fuel dries, one can find the point at which fine fuels will burn for several meters into the fuel bed and extinguish because the remaining fuel is too wet to burn. In this manner, a wider firebreak is created because the dangerous fine fuels have been eliminated. One can burn the remaining fuel later when it has dried enough to provide the desired intensity of combustion. It is important not to burn all of the fine fuel before the larger fuel can be ignited because it may then be impossible to ignite the large fuels.

We used this technique to burn logging slash of about 168 tons (M)/ha, with only a four-meter-wide fire line separating the burned area from standing dead fir trees on three sides. Flame heights reached 15 m, but we had minimal spotting only on the downwind side when using strip head fires.

We burned with relative humidities from 30 to 50 percent. Relative humidities under 30 percent are dangerous. Relative humidity at 50 percent at our latitude will still carry a fire and is safer with fine fuels. You need not consume all of the fuel--burning enough to stimulate growth near the ground will provide a favorable habitat response.

Light steady winds are most favorable. Winds over 24 km/hour are dangerous. Calm conditions with high relative humidity may not support continuous ignition and will result in a spotty burn, though a spotty burn can produce good habitat. An escaped fire caused by heavy winds may also produce favorable habitat, but it will be detrimental to a continuous burning program. You can burn heavy fuels if you are cautious, but watch the wind!

Ignition Patterns-- Ring burns, whereby the entire perimeter is ignited progressively around a circle are satisfactory for small areas--perhaps a hectare or two--but are difficult to control on larger areas. An area might look small before ignition but it seems to grow as flame heights become higher and the smoke becomes more dense. Strip head fires offer a greater degree of control and usually produce more uniform burns because most of the fuel is consumed by head fires. With ring ignition, some fuel is exposed to head fire and some to backing fire. Backing fires may remove most of the organic mat and expose mineral soil. Head fires with a uniform wind and proper fuel moisture generally burn only a portion of the mat.

The design of strip head fires allows fire ignited along a strip to burn with the wind into a previously burned strip. A series of strips are ignited progressively. The width and length of the strip should depend on fuel load. Again, be conservative; if fuels are heavy, the strip width may be only 50 m or less. Backfire initially from a good firebreak. Start the headfire from the upwind side of the first strip to create enough updraft to draw the backfire toward the headfire. This lessens the heat and smoke along the base firebreak where firefighters are stationed with hoses and backpack pumps to extinguish spot fires. Start igniting the second strip after the first strip is about half ignited and continue the process until the area is burned.

Clean up-- After the fire has burned over the area, begin extinguishing any fuel left around the perimeter that could flare up and transport sparks to unburned areas. This is also a good time to reburn areas missed by the flames, if desired. Two persons with drip torches can cover a considerable area in a short time. The area should be watched until it is safe to leave unattended. We usually check our burned areas for three days after the fire if there was insufficient rainfall to thoroughly extinguish any smouldering fire. Avoid burning in deep organic fuels that can smoulder indefinitely.

Other considerations

In some years, excessive or limited rainfall may make it impossible to burn. Burning programs must be ready when all conditions are correct. The burning window for a season may be only a few days at most. Fire plans, equipment, and crews must be ready. When all is in readiness with eager crews and observers poised, the responsible fire boss should not hesitate to say "no" if all conditions are not correct. I have heard it said that one is not a "real" burner if he has not had a fire escape. I am not a "real" burner and do not recommend that anyone become one. I do recommend safe burning for improving the habitat of moose in eastern wilderness areas.

Technical reviews by R.A. Lautenschlaer, K.I. Morris and R.W. Wein improved the content of this paper.

LITERATURE CITED

Anderson, R.C. and M.W. Lancaster. 1974. Infections and parasitic diseases and arthropod pests of moose in North America. Nat. Can. 101:23-50.

Brassard, J.M., E. Audy, M. Crete, and P. Grenier. 1974. Distribution and winter habitat of moose in Quebec. Nat. Can. 101:67-80.

Dodds, D.G. 1974. Distribution, habitat and status of moose in the Atlantic provinces of Canada and northeastern United States. Nat. Can. 101:51-65.

Franzmann, A.W. 1981. *Alces alces*. Mamm. Species 154:1-7.

Fraser, D., E.R. Chavez, and J.E. Palokeimo. 1984. Aquatic feeding by moose: selection of plant species and feeding areas in relation to plant chemical composition and characteristics of lakes. Can. J. Zool. 62:80-87.

Gasaway, W.C. and J.W. Coady. 1974. Review of energy requirements and rumen fermentation in moose and other ruminants. Nat. Can. 101:227-262.

Lautenschlager, R.A. and H.S. Crawford. 1983. Halter-training moose. Wildl. Soc. Bull. 11:187-189.

Peek, J.M. 1974. A review of moose food habits studies in North America. Nat. Can. 101:195-215.

Peterson, R.L. 1974. Moose: yesterday, today and tomorrow. Nat. Can. 101:1-8.

Verme, L.J. 1970. Some characteristics of captive Michigan moose. J. Mammal. 51:403-405.

The Effects Of Wilderness On The Endangered Red-Cockaded Woodpecker

by

Jerome A. Jackson, Richard N. Conner, and Bette J. Schardien Jackson

ABSTRACT-The endangered Red-cockaded Woodpecker (*Picoides borealis*) is endemic to mature, open pine forests of the southeastern United States. Approximately 100 colonies exist on presently designated wilderness areas, but potential for increased numbers and the significance of these populations is high. Problems associated with the species on wilderness areas relate to its specific habitat requirement of large acreages of mature open forest. Aboriginally, these forests were kept open by lightning caused fires. Human influences limit such fires today and wilderness managers should strive to re-create aboriginal conditions. Data on frequency of electrical storms in the southeast suggest that such fires occurred during the summer months, as opposed to the cooler winter fires that are now generally used during prescribed burns. The lack of fire has resulted in development of dense hardwood understories and dense stands of pines, both unfavorable to the Red-cockaded Woodpecker. In addition, the dense stands of pines provide conditions favorable to the southern pine beetle (*Dendroctonus frontalis* Zimm.), a species capable of destroying large tracts of pine forests. A fire regime favorable to the Red-cockaded Woodpecker would not only open up the habitat, but would also help control some insects harmful to pines.

KEYWORDS: Red-cockaded Woodpecker, wilderness, southern pine beetle, fire climax, pine forest, prescribed fire, population viability, pheromones.

The Red-cockaded Woodpecker (*Picoides borealis*) is an endangered species that is endemic to the mature, open pine forests of the southeastern United States. Its populations are thought to include between 3,000 and 10,000 individuals, with perhaps as many as 80% of those occurring on public lands (Jackson 1971, 1978; Lennartz *et al.* 1983a). Habitat needs and the unusual ecology of this species have been summarized by Hooper *et al.* (1980). Briefly, these include a unique social system, home ranges averaging about 80 ha (200 acres), low fecundity, use of living pines 75+ years old for cavity excavation, use of living pines for 90+% of foraging activities, strong site tenacity, and a proclivity to abandon sites when the understory grows to reach the lower branches of cavity trees. The species seems as dependent on fire in its natural environment as the pines in which it lives (Garren 1943).

In this paper, we examine the known distribution of the species on wilderness areas in the southeastern United States and the potential effects of wilderness and wilderness management on the species. Particular emphasis will be placed on wilderness size, the role of fire in southeastern wildernesses, and problems with southern pine beetles (*Dendroctonus frontalis* Zimm.).

WILDERNESS AREAS AND RED-COCKADED WOODPECKERS IN THE SOUTHEASTERN UNITED STATES

Distribution

For the purpose of this paper we identify a wilderness as an area designated as such by the congressional mandate of the Wilderness Act or by similar actions of a state. Some other areas, such as the Big Cypress Preserve in Florida and some back country National Park lands, will be discussed because of their similarities (relative to Red-cockaded Woodpeckers) to designated wilderness.

A cursory review of federal lands in the Southeast that have been designated as wilderness reveals that most are bottomland, swamp, or island environments that do not include suitable habitats for Red-cockaded Woodpeckers. The few wilderness areas that do include populations of Red-cockaded Woodpeckers are identified in Table 1.

Of federally designated wilderness areas with Red-cockaded Woodpeckers, the U.S. Fish and Wildlife Service administers one, and the U.S. Forest Service administers nine (Table 1). In addition, one state-designated wilderness (McCurtain in Oklahoma) includes the woodpeckers.

Major wilderness populations of Red-cockaded Woodpeckers are those on Texas National Forests; the Kisatchie Hills Wilderness, Kisatchie National Forest, Louisiana; Okefenokee National Wildlife Refuge, Georgia; and the McCurtain County Wilderness Area, Oklahoma.

The McCurtain County Wilderness Area in southeastern Oklahoma includes one of the largest "wilderness" populations of Red-cockaded Woodpeckers. Wood and Lewis (1977) found 29 active colonies there and suggested that the population had been relatively stable throughout recent history.

There are historical records of Red-cockaded Woodpeckers from the vicinity of some other wilderness areas and in some areas that have been proposed for wilderness status. A small population of Red-cockaded Woodpeckers occurs in the Great Smoky Mountains National Park (Tanner 1965), part of which has been proposed for wilderness listing (Anon. 1971). Whether or not official wilderness status is gained, the remoteness, terrain, and National Park status probably assure "wilderness-like" habitat associated with these colonies.

Table 1. Distribution and Status of Red-Cockaded Woodpecker Colonies on Wilderness Areas in the Southeastern United States.

| Wilderness Area | No. of Colonies | | | Area of Wilderness (ha) |
	Active	Inactive	Unknown	
U.S. Forest Service				
Alabama				
Sipsey		4		7,766
Cheaha		4		2,752
Kentucky				
Daniel Boone NF	1	1		7,248
Louisiana				
Kistatchie Hills			19	3,521
South Carolina				
Francis Marion-				
Sumter	1	3		6,873
Texas				
Upland Island	2	4		4,856
Indian Mound			1	4,025
Little Lake Creek			12	1,619
Big Slough			1	1,214
Turkey Hill	1			2,185
U.S. Fish and Wildlife Service				
Georgia				
Okefenokee National				
Wildlife Refuge			26 +	143,254
State				
Oklahoma				
McCurtain				
(Wood and				
Lewis 1977)	29			5,701

Although there are no known Red-cockaded Woodpecker colonies in the Everglades National Park, there are approximately 40 colonies just north of the park in the Big Cypress Preserve, which has a wilderness-like character (Patterson and Robertson 1981; JJ and BJ, pers. observ.). Maturation of pine forests in proposed wilderness areas of the Everglades National Park (Anon. 1971) could produce habitat into which the birds could expand. Prior to logging early in this century, Red-cockaded Woodpeckers were known from the Everglades (Howell 1921, Holt and Sutton 1926).

Although Red-cockaded Woodpeckers have been reported (Wilson 1961, Mengel 1965) from the vicinity of proposed wilderness (Anon. 1971) in Mammoth Cave National Park, there have been no recent sightings of the species there. Prior to wilderness designation, there was one sight record of a Red-cockaded Woodpecker from Horn Island, off the coast of Mississippi (USDI 1968).

Wilderness size and population viability

Perhaps the most dense population of Red-cockaded Woodpeckers known is that on the Francis Marion National Forest, South Carolina, where Lennartz and Henry (1985) reported 406 colonies on 66,755 ha of suitable habitat. A colony never includes more than one breeding pair, although male offspring from previous nesting efforts may remain with the pair as helpers. Three birds per colony have been used as an average in estimating population sizes (e.g., Jackson 1971). Assuming such a density approaches the maximum possible for the species, most wilderness areas on which Red-cockaded Woodpeckers have been reported could support fewer than 300 birds, even if their entire acreage was suitable habitat. Most of these areas include a variety--and some a majority--of habitats unsuitable for the species. Such a population size falls far short of the minimum of 500 breeding individuals thought needed for population viability by population geneticists (Franklin 1980).

When compared to the species' estimated total of 3,000 to 10,000 birds, the numbers known on wilderness areas seem insignificant. But are they? When dealing with an endangered species whose populations are becoming increasingly fragmented, the genetic variability of all populations of the species may be important for its survival. We know that the species has declined at the hands of man and it is quite possible that current management efforts on behalf of the species will be unable to change population trends. If crucial elements of the Red-cockaded Woodpecker's aboriginal environment are not being provided by modern forestry, the species' salvation might rest in restoring the primeval conditions through protection and management of wilderness. It is our opinion that in the interests of seeking to assure a future for this endangered bird, and more importantly, for the ecosystem into which it was born, at least one major population of the species should be managed in a manner as much like the prehuman environment as possible. To assure ecosystem viability, based on the minimum viable population of Red-cockaded Woodpeckers as suggested by Lennartz and Henry (1985), such a wilderness may need to include at least 20,235 ha (50,000 acres) of fire-climax pine forest.

The wilderness that was here before man's arrival in the Southeast cannot be re-created solely by legislative protection of set aside areas. Man has changed Southeastern environments such that to reproduce the Red-cockaded Woodpecker's natal environment will require an understanding of the natural forces that sustained it and the human disturbances that brought about changes in it.

THE ROLE OF NATURAL FIRE AND NEED FOR PRESCRIBED FIRE FOR RED-COCKADED WOODPECKERS IN WILDERNESS AREAS

One of the environmental factors which most influences the Red-cockaded Woodpecker and its environment is fire. Fire plays several significant roles in the maintenance of the pine forest ecosystems of the Southeast: it (1) prevents hardwood encroachment, (2) prevents overcrowding of pines, and (3) kills some pathogenic fungi (Parmeter and Uhrenholdt 1974). These effects all result in a healthier, less stressed forest. As a secondary result, the pines are less susceptible to attack by the southern pine beetle and other insect pests (Wahlenberg 1946a, Belanger and Malac 1980) because of their increased vigor and the increased dispersal distance between trees for the insects. The southern pine forests to which Red-cockaded Woodpeckers are endemic are fire-climax ecosystems. Without fire, succession would result in replacement of pines by fire intolerant hardwood ecosystems.

Since the arrival of early Indian cultures in the Southeast, man has burned the forests deliberately and accidentally (Wright and Bailey 1982). Deliberate burning has included fires used to facilitate hunting, to maintain grassy understories for grazing, to move back the wilderness for safety reasons, and more recently, to manage for production of pulp and lumber.

Prior to such human intervention, lightning-caused fires likely swept through the forests as frequently as annually in Florida (Bancroft 1976) and at less frequent intervals to the north (Heinselman 1981). It is difficult to collect data on the frequency of prehistoric fires, but much can be inferred from our knowledge of species' habitat requirements and modern climatological data. These inferences are important to an understanding of the dynamics of wilderness ecosystems today. The comments below are predicated on the assumptions that (1) the habitat needs of Red-cockaded Woodpeckers and southern pines and (2) climatic patterns, particularly the frequency of electrical storms, have not changed dramatically since the arrival of the first human cultures in the Southeast.

Modern fire records in the Southeast suggest that today only about 4% of forest fires are caused by lightning, with most of the rest being caused by man (Anon. 1979, 1980). These statistics cannot be taken as indicative of prehistoric lightning-caused fire rates, however, for two main reasons: (1) man-caused fires reduce natural fuels, and thereby reduce the potential for lightning ignition of those fuels; and (2) modern forests are much younger than the old-growth that would have been characteristic of primeval forests, and as trees mature, they produce proportionately more litter which falls to the forest floor (Kittredge 1948). For example, Kittredge (p. 171) demonstrated a linear increase in litter depth in stands of loblolly pine (*Pinus taeda* L.) varying from 10 to 70 years old. Finally, the average acreage burned by individual wild fires in the Southeast today can be anticipated to be much less than what would have been burned before the arrival of European man. Each road that is built acts as a firebreak to restrict the potential extent of wildfires.

Stone (1965), Ghiselin (1974), and Parsons (1977) document the need for fire to play its natural environmental role if wildernesses are to be naturally functioning ecosystems. Unfortunately, the traditional approach to "preservation" of wildernesses and natural areas has usually involved suppression of fires (Heinselman 1970, Stone 1965).

Since the primeval frequency of fires in southeastern forests would have been dependent on the frequency of ignition of forest fuels by lightning, a primary clue to the dynamics of prehistoric fire is the frequency of electrical storms in the areas. Figures 1-3 (from Anon. 1952) illustrate variation in annual, winter, and summer frequency of electrical storms in the United States. The extreme southeast has one of the highest electrical storm frequencies in the world, with that frequency decreasing clinally to the north and west. Examination of electrical storm frequency by month further reveals that few storms occur during the winter months (Fig. 2) and most occur during summer (Fig. 3). Although there are other factors involved (Fuquay *et al.* 1972, 1979), the magnitude of the difference in seasonal frequencies suggests that fires might have been more frequent in summer than at other times of year.

Winter and early spring fires tend to be cooler and have been used most frequently by forest managers, with

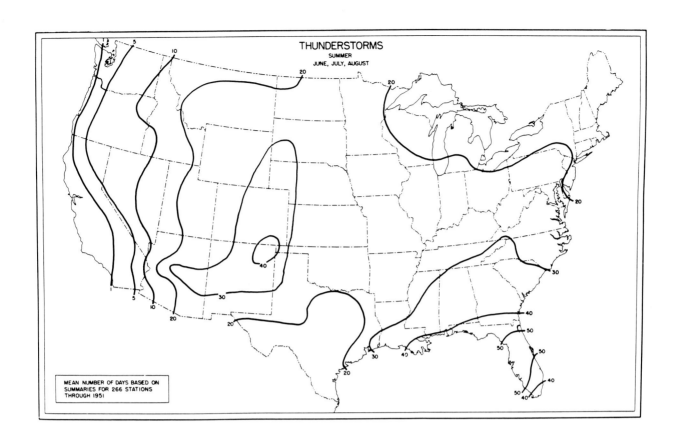

THUNDERSTORMS
SUMMER
JUNE, JULY, AUGUST

MEAN NUMBER OF DAYS BASED ON
SUMMARIES FOR 266 STATIONS
THROUGH 1951

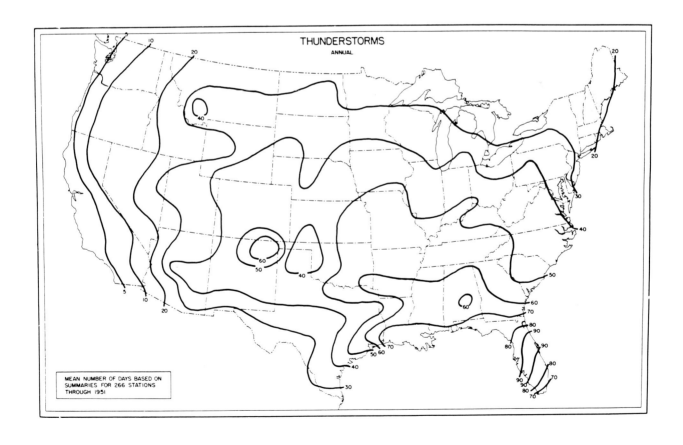

THUNDERSTORMS
ANNUAL

MEAN NUMBER OF DAYS BASED ON
SUMMARIES FOR 266 STATIONS
THROUGH 1951

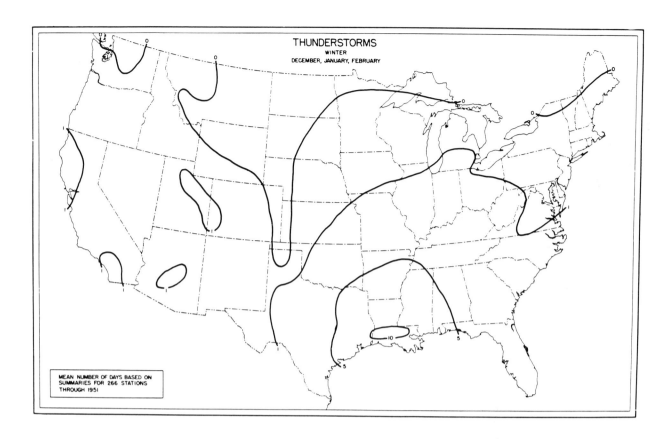

THUNDERSTORMS
WINTER
DECEMBER, JANUARY, FEBRUARY

MEAN NUMBER OF DAYS BASED ON
SUMMARIES FOR 266 STATIONS
THROUGH 1951

the resulting decrease in litter precluding natural fires in summer. When hardwoods become an exceptional problem in areas managed for pine, prescribed burns in summer are used (Riebold 1955, Lotti 1956, Bruce and Nelson 1957). It seems likely that the unique and extreme adaptations of longleaf pine (*Pinus palustris* Mill.) to fire (e.g., Wahlenberg 1946b, Hare 1965) may be the end product of a long association with periodic hot summer fires. The apparent preferences of the Red-cockaded Woodpecker for longleaf pines and open forest habitats also seem linked to such fires (Jackson 1971, Hooper *et al.* 1980, Lennartz *et al.* 1983a).

Another factor facilitating frequent fire, is the well-drained sandy soil of the southern coastal plain. To the north, increased clay content results in poorer drainage and more moist, less flammable litter on the forest floor. This, accompanied by a rapidly decreasing incidence of electrical storms (Figures 1-3), would have resulted in less-extensive and less-frequent natural fires. Chapman (1952) discusses the differing tolerances and needs of pines for fire, and the ranges of the various southern pine species reflect the general pattern of intensity of electrical storm activity.

Away from the coastal plain, pine forests and Red-cockaded Woodpeckers in wilderness areas may be perpetuated even with limited fire suppression (e.g., McCurtain County Wilderness Area, Oklahoma; Wood and Lewis 1977). In such areas, the steepness of some slopes assures that hardwoods will not reach the lower

branches of some pines and that some pine regeneration can occur. Fire is likely a necessary component of these pine ecosystems, although needed with lesser frequency. Elimination or extensive suppression of fire from such areas could result in the loss of Red-cockaded Woodpecker populations as pine reproductive success decreases following closure of forest canopies. Jackson *et al.* (1976) noted such problems on the Daniel Boone National Forest, Kentucky, and Wood and Lewis (1977) suggested that subtle vegetative changes may be resulting from the limited fire suppression efforts in the McCurtain Area.

SOUTHERN PINE BEETLES AND RED-COCKADED WOODPECKERS

Just as the pines and fire are characteristic of the Red-cockaded Woodpecker's environment, so too is the southern pine beetle. Southern pine beetles and their larvae are regularly eaten by Red-cockaded Woodpeckers (JJ, pers. observ.), although they are apparently not an especially significant food resource. However, the southern pine beetle has been of increasing concern to forest managers of the Southeast (e.g., Hedden 1978) and has been a problem in Red-cockaded Woodpecker colonies (e.g., Nicholson 1980, pers. observ. JJ, RC, BJ). These beetles have wrought extensive destruction in some southern wilderness areas and areas under consideration for wilderness status. Their control in these areas has been the subject of considerable controversy (e.g., Warren 1985). We will here limit our discussion to the habitats favored by the southern pine beetle, historical factors that have facilitated massive destruction by the beetles in wilderness areas, and the relationships between the beetles and the Red-cockaded Woodpecker.

Hedden and Billings (1979), Ku et al. (1980), Lorio (1980), and others have documented site and stand conditions associated with southern pine beetle infestations to include slower growing trees stressed by overcrowding, lightning strike, and logging activities. Pine beetle sites also had a higher pine/hardwood ratio and less understory. Thatcher et al. (1982) noted that the southern pine beetle "prefers pure pine stands" and that "a mixture of pine and hardwood species reduces the potential" for infestations. Hicks et al. (1981) also found that pines in low, wet sites were more associated with southern pine beetle attack than were pines on better drained sites.

Gara and Coster (1968) found that 5.5 m (18 feet) was the maximum distance over which infestations were able to spread from tree to tree and concluded that expansion of a local infestation was unlikely when average tree spacing was 6.1-7.6 m (20-25 feet). These results were reaffirmed by those of Johnson and Coster (1978), but they also noted that tree spacing was less critical when the beetles are colonizing trees rapidly. These and numerous other studies have demonstrated that high densities of pines--in excess of 34 square meters/ha (150 square feet/acre)--are conducive to the development of southern pine beetle infestations. In contrast, the Red-cockaded Woodpecker shows a strong preference for low pine basal areas--averaging between 9.2 and 13.8 square meters/ha (40 and 60 square feet/acre) (JJ, pers. observ.; RC, unpublished data; Thompson and Baker 1971). Lennartz et al. (1983b) include a wider range of basal areas, and DeLotelle et al. (1983) much lower basal areas for active Red-cockaded Woodpecker colonies, but in our experience their extremes represent suboptimal habitat for the birds. Because of a lack of fire, high basal area pine stands exist on many of the southern wilderness areas today, providing marginal or poor habitat for Red-cockaded Woodpeckers and prime habitat for southern pine beetles.

Prehistoric pine forests in the South most preferred by Red-cockaded Woodpeckers were probably low basal area (in the range of 9.2-13.8 square meters/ha) pine stands on drier sites. At least, longleaf pine habitats were likely maintained by intense summer fires. Such open stands, if present in abundance, were probably less vulnerable than modern forests to southern pine beetles. Southern pine beetle attacks undoubtedly still occurred, but were more restricted to small pockets of loblolly or other pines that were densely packed in moist transition zones between longleaf on dry uplands and the hardwood bottoms (Wahlenberg 1960, Schowalter et al. 1981, Coulson et al. 1983). These small southern pine beetle spots probably served as a food source for Red-cockaded

and other woodpeckers (Kroll and Fleet 1979, Kroll et al. 1980).

There are probably about 100 active Red-cockaded Woodpecker colonies on all wilderness areas (Table 1), and many of these colonies exist in areas of low basal area longleaf pine. Management in wilderness areas relative to Red-cockaded Woodpeckers and southern pine beetles should involve crisis prevention strategies rather than crisis treatment strategies (Stark 1979). This should include prescribed fire and, where necessary, an initial thinning to reduce high basal areas. Since tree damage resulting from use of heavy equipment can increase stand susceptibility to southern pine beetle infestation, we recommend the use of helicopters during thinning operations near active colonies. Any thinning activities should be accomplished outside of the woodpeckers' breeding season (approx. March-July),. Following such initial treatment, low basal areas should be maintained by natural or prescribed summer fire as needed.

We suggest that cavity tree protection from beetles in vulnerable areas should only be considered a viable option as a last resort, and then only for active woodpecker colonies with a high basal area (greater than 25 square m/ha '110 square ft/acre'). The sole purpose of this minimal control should be to prevent extirpation of Red-cockaded Woodpeckers in wilderness areas so that a population is available to recolonize the fire-climax pine ecosystem when it is restored. Use of any beetle control technique should be based on its statistically proven effectiveness and a proven lack of negative impact on the woodpecker. The probability of successful beetle control must be weighed against a high probability of colony abandonment by Red-cockaded Woodpeckers if the beetle management involves cutting of mature pines which might serve for cavity excavation and as prime foraging habitat. Such cutting might also isolate cavity trees, making them more vulnerable to windthrow or lightning strike. Any beetle control efforts during the Red-cockaded Woodpecker's breeding season would have the greatest risk of causing colony abandonment or loss of a year's reproductive effort.

Alternative control measures for southern pine beetle infestation may soon be available. These control techniques use pheromones to alter beetle invasion behavior (Payne and Richerson 1985). If used when beetle spots on wilderness are still small (less than 30 trees), pheromone control may be very effective. The pheromone verbenone is the chemical signal released by southern pine beetles when a tree is "full" of infesting adults and as such inhibits attack by other adult beetles. Application of verbenone to a buffer of healthy trees where southern pine beetles are advancing may inhibit the progression of the infestation. At the same time, a small application of "frontalure," a pheromone attractant for the southern pine beetle (Billings et al. 1981, Payne et al. 1985)., to dead pines behind that advancing infestation may further depress the progression of an infestation by luring the beetles away from the verbenone treated live trees to already dead pines (Richerson *et al.* 1980, Billings *et al.* 1981, Payne *et al.* 1985). The use of pheromones to control beetle spots around Red-cockaded Woodpecker colonies as well as other places in wilderness and natural areas follows the concept of *minimal control* more than any cutting technique and would leave little or no evidence of human intervention. When and if pheromone control techniques become available, they would be the best beetle control measure to use in wilderness areas because they create the least habitat disturbance, could be used during the Red-cockaded Woodpecker's breeding season, and do not require that pines be cut.

The entomological data have told us that the beetles are a problem in even-aged, high density, stressed stands. Fire has been excluded for intervals that are too long on many southern wilderness areas. Fire under a natural regime would have thinned both pines and hardwoods, opening up the forest to create better habitat for Red-cockaded Woodpeckers and exerting some preventative control on beetle populations. Problems with beetles on wilderness areas can be greatly reduced if we restore fire, with the frequency and time of its occurrence under primeval conditions, to those portions of wilderness areas that would have naturally supported fire climax ecosystems.

LITERATURE CITED

Anonymous. 1952. Mean number of thunderstorm days in the United States. U.S. Dept. of Commerce, Weather Bureau Technical Paper No. 19.

Anonymous. 1971. Preserving wilderness in our National Parks. National Parks and Conservation Association, Washington, D.C.

Anonymous. 1979. 1977 Wildfire statistics. USDA, Forest Service.

Anonymous. 1980. 1978 Wildfire statistics. USDA, Forest Service, FS-343.

Bancroft, L. 1976. Natural fire in the Everglades. pp.47-60, *In* Proceedings, Fire by Prescription Symposium. U.S. For. Serv., R-8.

Belanger, R.P. and B.F. Malac. 1980. Southern pine beetle handbook. Silviculture can reduce losses from the southern pine beetle. USDA Combined Forest Pest Res. and Dev. Prog., Agri. Handb. No. 576.

Billings, P.D., E.A. Roberts, and T.L. Payne. 1981. Controlled-release device for southern pine beetle behavior chemicals. J. Ga. Entomol. Soc. 16:181-185.

Bruce, D. and R.M. Nelson. 1957. Use and effects of fire on southern forests: Abstracts of publications by the Southern and Southeastern Forest Experiment Stations, 1925-1955. Fire Control Notes 18:67-96.

Chapman, H.H. 1952. The place of fire in the ecology of pines. Bartonia 26:39-44.

Coulson, R.N., P.B. Hennier, R.O. Flamm, E.J. Rykiel, L.C. Hu, and T.L. Payne. 1983. The role of lightning in the epidemiology of the southern pine beetle. Zeit. angew. Entomol. 96:182-193.

DeLotelle, R.S., J.R. Newman, and A.E. Jerauld. 1983. Habitat use by Red-cockaded Woodpeckers in central Florida. pp. 59-67, *In* D. Wood, (ed.). Red-cockaded Woodpecker Symposium II Proc. State of Florida Game and Fresh Water Fish Commission, Tallahassee, Florida.

Franklin, I.R., 1980. Evolutionary changes in small populations. pp. 135-149. *In* M.E. Soule' and B.A. Wilcox, (eds.). Conservation Biology, An Evolutionary-Ecological Perspective, Sinauer Assoc., Inc., Sunderland, Mass.

Fuquay, D.M., R.G. Baughman, and D.J. Latham. 1979. A model for predicting lightning-fire ignition in wildland fuels. U.S. For. Serv., Res. Pap. INT-217.

Fuquay, D.M., A.R. Taylor, R.G. Hawe, and C.W. Schmid, Jr. 1972. Lightning discharges that caused forest fires. J. Geophysical Res. 77:2156-2158.

Gara, R.I. and J.E. Coster. 1968. Studies on the attack behavior of the southern pine beetle. III. Sequence of tree infestation within stands. Contrib. Boyce Thompson Inst. 24:77-85.

Garren, K.H. 1943. Effects of fire on vegetation of the southeastern United States. Botanical Rev. 9:617-654.

Ghiselin, J. 1974. Wilderness and the survival of species. Living Wilderness 37(124):22-27.

Hare, R.C. 1965. Contribution of bark to fire resistance of southern trees. J. For. 63:248-251.

Hedden, R.L. 1978. The need for intensive forest management to reduce southern pine beetle activity in east Texas. S. J. Appl. For. 2:19-22.

Hedden, R.L. and R.F. Billings. 1979. Southern pine beetle: factors influencing the growth and decline of summer infestations in east Texas. For. Sci. 25:547-566.

Heinselman, M.L. 1970. Preserving nature in forested wilderness areas and National Parks. Natl. Parks and Conserv. 44:8-14.

Heinselman, M.L. 1981. Fire intensity and frequency as factors in the distribution and structure of northern ecosystems. Pp. 7-57, *In* Proc. Conf. Fire Regimes and Ecosyst. Properties, U.S. For. Serv. Gen. Tech. Rep. WO-26.

Hicks, R.R., Jr., J.E. Howard, K.G. Watterston, and J.E. Coster. 1981. Rating east Texas stands for southern pine beetle susceptibility. S. J. Appl. For. 5:7-10.

Holt, E.G. and G.M. Sutton. 1926. Notes on birds observed in southern Florida. Ann. Carnegie Mus. 16:409-429.

Hooper, R.G., A.F. Robinson, Jr., and J.A. Jackson. 1980. The Red-cockaded Woodpecker: notes on life history and management. U.S. For. Serv. Gen. Tech. Rep. SA-GR 9.

Howell, A.H. 1921. A list of the birds of Royal Palm Hammock, Florida. Auk 38:250-263.

Jackson, J.A. 1971. The evolution, taxonomy, distribution, past populations and current status of the Red-cockaded Woodpecker. Pp. 4-29, *In* R.L. Thompson, (ed.). The Ecology and Management of the Red-cockaded Woodpecker. Bureau of Sport Fisheries and Wildlife, USDI, and Tall Timbers Res. Stat., Tallahassee, Fla.

Jackson, J.A. 1978. Analysis of the distribution and population status of the Red-cockaded Woodpecker. Pp. 101-110, *In* R.R. Odum and L.L.

Landers, (eds.). Proc.of the Rare and Endangered Wildlife Symposium. Georgia Department of Natural Resources, Technical Bull. WL 4.

Jackson, J.A., R. Weeks, and P. Shindala. 1976. The present status and future of Red-cockaded Woodpeckers in Kentucky. Kentucky Warbler 52:75-80.

Johnson, P.C. and J.E. Coster. 1978. Probability of attack by southern pine beetle in relation to distance from an attractive host tree. For. Sci. 24:574-580.

Kittredge, J. 1948. Forest influences. McGraw-Hill Book Co., New York, NY.

Kroll, J.C., R.N. Conner, and R.R. Fleet. 1980. Woodpeckers and the southern pine beetle. USDA Agric. Handbook /No564.

Kroll, J.C. and R.R. Fleet. 1979. Impact of woodpecker predation on over-wintering within-tree populations of the southern pine beetle (Dendroctonus frontalis). Pp. 269-281, In J.G. Dickson, R.N. Conner, R.R. Fleet, J.C. Kroll, and J.A. Jackson, (eds.). The Role of Insectivorous Birds in Forest Ecosystems. Academic Press, New York, NY.

Ku, T.T., J.M Sweeney, and V.B. Shelburne. 1980. Site and stand conditions associated with southern pine beetle outbreaks in Arkansas - a hazard-rating system. S. J. Appl. For. 4:103-106.

Lennartz, M.R., P.H. Geissler, R.F. Harlow, R.C. Long, K.M. Chitwood, and J.A. Jackson. 1983a. Status of the Red-cockaded Woodpecker on federal lands in the South. Pp. 7-12, In D. Wood, (ed.). Red-cockaded Woodpecker Symposium II Proceedings. State of Florida Game and Fresh Water Fish Commission, Tallahassee, Fla.

Lennartz, M.R., H.A. Knight, J.P. McClure, and V.A. Rudis. 1983b. Status of Red-cockaded Woodpecker nesting habitat in the South. Pp. 13-19, In D. Wood (ed.), Red-cockaded Woodpecker Symposium II Proceedings. State of Florida Game and Fresh Water Fish Commission, Tallahassee, Fla.

Lennartz, M.R. and G. Henry. 1985. Recovery plan for the Red-cockaded Woodpecker. USDI, Bureau of Sport Fisheries and Wildlife, Atlanta, Ga.

Lorio, P.L., Jr. 1980. Loblolly pine stocking levels affect potential for southern pine beetle infestation. S. J. Appl. For. 4:162-165.

Lotti, T. 1956. Eliminating understory hardwoods with summer prescribed fires in coastal plain loblolly stands. J. For. 54:191-192.

Mengel, R.M. 1965. The birds of Kentucky. Ornithol. Monogr. 3.

Nicholson, C.P. 1980. Red-cockaded Woodpecker colony in Campbell County, Tennessee. Migrant 51:89.

Parmeter, J.R., Jr. and B. Uhrenholdt. 1974. Effects of smoke on pathogens and other fungi. Tall Timbers Fire Ecol. Conf., Tall Timbers Res. Stn., Tallahassee, Fla. 14:299-304.

Parsons, D.J. 1977. Preservation in fire-type ecosystems. Pp. 172-182, In H.A. Mooney and C.E. Conrad, (tech. coords.), Proceedings of the Symposium on the Environmental Consequences of Fire and Fuel Managment in Mediterranean Ecosystems. USDA For. Serv., Gen. Tech. Rep. WO-3.

Patterson, G.A. and W.B. Robertson, Jr. 1981. Distribution and habitat of the Red-cockaded Woodpecker in Big Cypress National Preserve. National Park Service, South Florida Research Center, Everglades National Park, Homestead, Fla., Report T-613.

Payne, T.L., L.H. Kudon, K.D. Walsh, and C.W. Berisford. 1985. Influence of infestation density on suppression of D. Frontalis infestations with attractant. Zeit. ang. Entomol. 99:39-43.

Payne, T.L. and J.V. Richerson. 1985. Pheromone-mediated competitive replacement between two bark beetle populations: Influence on infestation suppression. Zeit. ang. Entomol. 99:131-138.

Richerson, J.V., F.A. McCarty, and T.L. Payne. 1980. Disruption of southern pine beetle infestations with frontalure. Environ. Entomol. 9:90-93.

Riebold, R.J. 1955. Summer burns for hardwood control in loblolly pine. U.S. For. Serv., Fire Control Notes 16:34-36.

Schowalter, T.D., R.N. Coulson, and D.A. Crossley, Jr. 1981. Role of southern pine beetle and fire in maintenance of structure and function of the southeastern coniferous forest. Environ. Entomol. 10:821-825.

Stark, R.W. 1979. A second reviewer's impression. Pp. 117-118, In J.E. Coster and J.L. Searcy, (eds.). Evaluating Control Techniques for the Southern Pine Beetle. Symp. Proc. USDA For. Serv. Tech. Bull. No. 1613.

Stone, E.C. 1965. Preserving vegetation in parks and wilderness. Science 150:1261-1267.

Tanner, J.T. 1965. Red-cockaded Woodpecker nesting in the Great Smokey Mountains National Park. Migrant 36:59.

Taylor, A.R. 1969. Lightning effects on the forest complex. Tall Timbers Fire Ecol. Conf. Proc. 9:127-150.

Thatcher, R.C., G.N. Mason, G.D. Hertel, and J.L. Searcy. 1982. Detecting and controlling the southern pine beetle. S. J. Appl. For. 6:153-159.

Thompson, R.L. and W.W. Baker. 1971. A survey of Red-cockaded Woodpecker habitat requirements. Pp. 170-186, In R.L. Thompson, (ed.). The Ecology and Management of the Red-cockaded Woodpecker. Bureau of Sport Fisheries andWildlife, USDI, and Tall Timbers Research Station, Tallahassee, Fla.

USDI. 1968. Gulf Islands National Wildlife Refuges annual narrative report. U.S. Bureau of Sport Fisheries and Wildlife, Atlanta, Ga.

Wahlenberg, W.G. 1946a. Longleaf pine. Charles Lathrop Pack Forestry Foundation, Washington, D.C.

Wahlenberg, W.G. 1946b. Longleaf pine. II. Natural distribution of longleaf pine and the role of fire in its regeneration. S. Lumberman 172:64-66.

Wahlenberg, W.G. 1960. Loblolly pine. School of Forestry. Duke University. Durham, N. Car.

Warren, B.J. 1985. Why we need to control pine beetles in wilderness areas. Forest Farmer 44(4):6-8.

Wilson, G. 1961. Additions to "Birds of the Mammoth Cave National Park." Kentucky Warbler 37:7-9.

Wood, D.A. and J.C. Lewis. 1977. Status of the Red-cockaded Woodpecker in Oklahoma. Proc. Annu. Conf. Southeastern Assoc. Fish Wildl. Agenc. 31:276-282.

Wright, H.A. and A.W. Bailey. 1982. Fire ecology. United States and southern Canada. Wiley-Interscience, New York, NY.

Raptors And Eastern Wilderness

by
James D. Fraser

ABSTRACT--Thirty-six species of raptorial birds (Falconiformes, Strigiformes), including wilderness associated species, occur in the eastern United States. Wilderness can protect raptors from human persecution, disturbance, and contamination, and can provide natural habitats and prey densities. Large, diurnal, endangered raptors, such as the bald eagle, are probably in greatest need of these benefits. Most eastern wilderness areas, however, are too small to protect entire populations of such species. In addition, few eastern wilderness areas have large tracts of the open habitats and shoreline habitats needed by many species.

KEYWORDS: Accipitridae, Cathartidae, disturbance, eagle, falcon, Falconidae, habitat, hawk, owl, Pandionidae, shooting, Strigidae, Strigiformes, Tytonidae.

Some 36 species of raptorial birds (Falconiformes, Strigiformes) occur in the eastern United States (Table 1). The predatory nature, sparse distribution, and general shyness of these species cause people to associate them with wilderness. Indeed 6 of 29 (21%) of the wilderness associated wildlife species listed in the RARE II draft environmental statement were raptorial birds (USDA 1978). For many people, populations of such species are the ultimate measure of a wilderness or a wilderness experience (Shoenfeld and Hendee 1978).

Because they are at the top of the wilderness food web, raptors are good environmental indicators; healthy raptor populations suggest a generally healthy wild environment (Curry-Lindahl 1977, Voous 1977). By monitoring wilderness raptor populations, we can ensure that wilderness communities are remaining free of man's unwanted influences. The fact that many eastern raptors are species of special concern, blue listed, or endangered (Table 1) suggests the sensitivity of this group of birds and a need for improved management.

The purpose of this paper is to examine the relationships between raptorial birds and wilderness areas in the eastern United States. I will discuss the importance of wilderness to raptor populations, and approaches to managing raptors in eastern wilderness. I will also mention two characteristics of the eastern wilderness preservation system that limit its usefulness as raptor habitat.

EFFECTS OF WILDERNESS ON RAPTOR POPULATIONS

Wilderness areas may affect raptor populations by limiting direct contacts between raptors and people, by protecting undisturbed habitat and natural prey densities, and by providing a refuge from the contaminating by-products of human society.

Impacts of human contact

Shooting-- Since the beginning of European immigration to North America, people have viewed raptors as competitors, and have attacked them with gun, trap, and poison. In some areas, the fall raptor migration was viewed as an opportunity to practice shooting prior to the game season (Brett 1973). Shooting of some species may have declined in recent years (cf. Fraser 1985), but raptors are still being shot (Redig 1978).

Accurate estimates of the kill of each species are unavailable, but large raptors probably are killed more frequently than smaller birds (Brown 1974), and diurnal species probably suffer greater persecution than nocturnal ones (Glue 1971). Additionally, species that frequent populated areas such as farms and coastal beaches may experience higher shooting pressure than other species.

In assessing the impacts of shooting, it is important to consider not only the induced mortality rate, but also the ultimate effects of shooting on the dynamics of raptor populations. It is well known that populations of large, slowly reproducing species with small clutches and delayed reproduction are more likely to be affected by increased mortality than populations of more fecund species (Young 1968, Anderson and Burnham 1976, Grier 1980). Additionally, very small, local populations are more likely to be affected than large, dispersed populations (Newton 1979).

Bald and golden eagles, because of their long prereproductive period (3-5 years), small clutch size (usually 2 eggs), and affinity for open habitats, are probably more likely to be affected by shooting than any other eastern raptors. The snail kite, the peregrine falcon, and the eastern golden eagle are also jeopardized by shooting due to their very small populations.

Disturbance-- Raptor behavior, reproduction, and survival may be altered by the mere presence of people. Nonbreeding birds may be forced from favorable feeding areas or may expend excessive energy avoiding approaching humans (Stalmaster and Newman 1978,

Table 1.   Raptors of the Eastern United States, and Their Status. Endangered Status Refers to the U.S. Endangered Species List. Special Concern and Blue-List Designations Are from Tate and Tate 1982. Wilderness Associated Designations Are from USDA (1978).

Species	Status[1]
Falconiformes	
Turkey vulture (*Cathartes aura*)	Special concern
Black vulture (*Coragyps atratus*)	Special concern
Mississippi kite (*Ictinia mississippiensis*)	
Swallow-tailed kite (*Elanoides forficatus*)	
Snail kite (*Rostrhamus sociabilis*)	Endangered
Northern goshawk (*Accipiter gentilis*)	Wilderness associated
Cooper's hawk (*Accipiter cooperii*)	Special concern
Sharp-shinned hawk (*Accipiter striatus*)	Blue list
Northern harrier (*Circus cyaneus*)	Blue list
Rough-legged hawk (*Buteo lagopus*)	
Ferruginous hawk (*Buteo regalis*)	Special concern
Red-tailed hawk (*Buteo jamaicencis*)	
Swainson's hawk (*Buteo swainsoni*)	Blue list
Broad-winged hawk (*Buteo platypterus*)	
Red-shouldered hawk (*Buteo lineatus*)	Blue list
Short-tailed hawk (*Buteo brachyurus*)	
Golden eagle (*Aquila chrysaetos*)	Wilderness associated
Bald eagle (*Haliaeetus leucocephalus*)	Cites I, endangered,[2] Wilderness associated
Osprey (*Pandion haliaeetus*)	Special concern
Crested caracara (*Polyborus plancus*)	Special concern
Peregrine falcon (*Falco peregrinus*)	Cites I, Endangered, Wilderness associated
Gyrfalcon (*Falco rusticolus*)	Cites I, Wilderness associated
Merlin (*Falco columbarius*)	Special concern
American kestrel (*Falco sparverius*)	Special concern

Strigiformes	
Eastern screech owl (*Otus asio*)	Special concern
Great horned owl (*Bubo virgininaus*)	
Long-eared owl (*Asio otus*)	
Short eared owl (*Asio flammeus*)	Blue list
Barn owl (*Tyto alba*)	Special concern
Snowy owl (*Nyctea scandiaca*)	
Barred owl (*Strix varia*)	
Great gray owl (*Strix nebulosa*)	
Burrowing owl (*Athene cunicularia*)	Special concern
Boreal owl (*Aegolius funereus*)	
Northern hawk owl (*Surnia ulula*)	
Northern saw-whet owl (*Aegolius acadicus*)	

[1] All falconiformes except the new world vultures, and all strigiforms, except those listed in CITES Appendix I (species threatened with extinction) are included in CITES Appendix II, species that may become threatened with extinction if trade is not strictly regulated.

[2] The bald eagle is considered threatened in Michigan, Minnesota, Oregon, Washington, and Wisconsin and endangered in the rest of the lower 48 states.

Stalmaster 1983, Knight and Knight 1984, Stalmaster and Gessaman 1984). Human intrusions near raptor nests may cause breeding birds to desert nests, to injure eggs or nestlings when flushing from the nests, or to fail to feed or brood their young (Fyfe and Olendorff 1976, Fraser *et al.* 1985, White and Thurow 1985). Additionally, eggs or young exposed while the attending parent is distracted by human intruders are subject to predation. A wide variety of factors apparently affect the response of individual birds to human intrusions, including prey abundance, stage of the nesting cycle, location of the bird during the disturbance, previous experience of the bird, time of day, and specific nature of the disturbance (Fyfe and Olendorff 1976, Stalmaster and Newman 1976, Fraser 1985, Fraser *et al.* 1985, White and Thurow 1985).

The effect of human disturbance on populations of most eastern raptor species is poorly documented. Some species, such as ferruginous hawks, seem particularly susceptible to human disturbance, while others, such as ospreys and great horned owls are extremely tolerant (Fyfe and Olendorff 1976, White and Thurow 1985).

The impact of human activities on the bald eagle has been somewhat controversial with some observers reporting lowered productivity due to disturbance (Murphy 1965, Weekes 1974), while others have failed to find evidence of such impacts (Mathisen 1968, Grier 1969, McEwan and Hirth 1979, Fraser *et al.* 1985). It is reasonably well established, however, that human developments affect the distribution of bald eagle nests, new nests being placed so as to avoid proximity to human activity centers (Andrew and Mosher 1982, Fraser *et al.* 1985). Prevention of disturbance is one of the primary goals of bald eagle management efforts (Mathisen *et al.* 1977). In the absence of evidence to the contrary, the conservative approach for rare or endangered species or species of special concern, is to assume that disturbance by people could have a negative impact on populations and to devise management programs aimed at limiting disturbances.

Effects of Undisturbed Habitats and Natural Prey Populations

Some eastern hawks appear to do best in undisturbed habitats. Goshawks, red-shouldered hawks, and barred owls, for example, favor mature forests (Titus and Mosher 1981, Renolds et. al. 1982, Moore and Henny 1983, McGarigal and Fraser 1984). Snail kites require undisturbed marshes (Sykes 1979), and the burrowing owl requires the presence of burrowing mammals (Coulombe 1971).

Many other raptors, however, are tolerant of habitat alteration. Black vultures and turkey vultures commonly forage over pasture, and consume livestock (Coleman and Fraser, in prep.), and frequently nest in old buildings (Jackson 1983). Red-tailed hawks, great horned owls, and barn owls often nest in agricultural habitats (Orians and Kuhlman 1956, Marti and Wagner 1985), American kestrels and screech owls frequent cities and suburbs (Brown and Amadon 1968, Brauning 1983, Lynch and Smith 1984), and sharp-shinned hawks, Cooper's hawks, and broad-winged hawks nest in second growth forests (Titus and Mosher 1981, Renolds et.al. 1982).

Although these species survive in altered habitats, some observers feel that their populations are sparser in disturbed areas than in pristine habitats (Cade 1969, Newton 1979). Unfortunately, these conclusions are generally based on correlations between raptor densities and prey densities or land fertility, rather than on controlled comparisons of disturbed with pristine habitats. Nevertheless, it seems likely that for many habitat types, prey will be more abundant in wilderness settings than in severely altered habitats, such as row crop areas, and that this will be reflected in denser raptor populations.

Effects of Refuge from Human Contamination

It is well known that raptor populations have been adversely affected by a variety of environmental contaminants. A comprehensive discussion of this area is beyond the scope of this paper and the reader is referred to the review by Newton (1979).

Wilderness areas, which are generally protected from man's intentional or incidental distribution of contaminants can, in theory, provide a contamination-free location in which raptors can survive and reproduce. The eastern species receiving the greatest potential benefit from protection from direct mortality due to toxic substances would be the species that can least tolerate increases in mortality rates, namely the bald eagle and the golden eagle. The species most likely to benefit from lack of biomagnifying contaminants are those at the end of the longest or most contaminated food chains, particularly the bird hawks such as the peregrine falcon, and the piscivorous bald eagle and osprey.

RAPTOR MANAGEMENT IN EASTERN WILDERNESS

The primary objectives of raptor management in wilderness should be to provide natural distributions, numbers, behavior, and population dynamics of raptorial birds, and to obtain other objectives set forth by Schoenfeld and Hendee (1978). A number of standard techniques are available for managing raptors (Call 1979, Olendorff et al. 1980) but some are generally inappropriate for wilderness because they involve altering the natural environment (e.g. installation of nest boxes or nesting platforms) or because they rely on modifications of land management practices generally not conducted in wilderness (e.g. snag retention in timber harvest operations). Nevertheless, many commonly used raptor management techniques can be used effectively in wilderness.

Inventory

A prerequisite to managing raptors in wilderness is information about the species present and location of crucial habitat elements. The detail required will differ among species. For relatively common species which require little or no active management, presence-absence information (or even no information) may be adequate. For particularly rare or endangered species, however, the goal should be to obtain detailed information about nest sites, roosts, hunting areas, annual site occupancy, and reproductive rates. Inventory techniques have been reviewed by Call (1978) and Fuller and Mosher (1981). Estimation of site occupancy and reproduction rates has been discussed by Postupalsky (1974), Grier (1977), Steenhof and Kochert (1982), and Fraser et al. (1983, 1984).

Protection from Disturbance and Persecution

A goal of management of rare and endangered raptors in wilderness, as elsewhere, should be to prevent human disturbance and persecution. This is best accomplished by keeping people away from crucial areas such as nest sites and roost areas. Such protection is particularly important during periods of the year when disturbance is most likely to have deleterious effects, as during the early nesting cycle (Fyfe and Olendorff 1976) or during severe weather (Stalmaster and Gessamen 1984).

This is perhaps most appropriately achieved in wilderness by passive means. Trails can be routed to avoid crucial areas and management personnel can be instructed to avoid revealing nest and roost locations. Some areas, such as popular climbing cliffs that contain peregrine falcon eyries, may have to be closed during the nesting season. Where closure violations are a problem, nest watchers may be posted to aid enforcement. This technique has been used effectively to prevent nestling thefts in some areas. Watchers are often volunteers trained to summon law enforcement officials when necessary.

Information and education programs may also prevent needless disturbance. Programs or documents that inform users about the impacts of disturbing birds at critical times of the year, and teach visitors to recognize disturbance displays, will allow wilderness users to modify their behavior in appropriate ways, and will enhance visitor benefits.

Reintroductions

In some areas, seeking "natural distributions, numbers, and interactions of indigenous species of wildlife" (Shoenfeld and Hendee 1978) may entail reintroducing extirpated species or augmenting populations of depleted species. This can be accomplished by hacking, fostering, or cross-fostering (Olendorff *et al.* 1980). Hacking generally requires construction of towers or boxes that are inconsistent with the wilderness goal of maintaining an environment free from "the imprint of man's work." A reintroduction program, however, is a temporary measure and hacking towers or boxes can be removed after a population has been established. Thus, the long term objective of maintaining natural distributions and numbers of indigenous species can be enhanced at the expense of a short term setback in the objective of maintaining natural physical conditions.

EASTERN WILDERNESS AS RAPTOR HABITAT

Most people perceive wilderness as a haven for wildlife, particularly for wilderness-associated species like raptorial birds. Eastern wilderness areas, however, fall short as raptor refuges because of their small size and limited habitat representation.

The Size Problem

Raptors are wide ranging, sparsely distributed animals. Densities tend to be correlated with body size such that the largest species require 5 to 50 km per nesting pair (Newton 1979). Thus, small eastern wilderness areas which are generally under 50 km (Wilderness Society 1984), can support only small raptor populations. Such populations, when isolated from other populations, are in constant danger of extinction. Thus, although wilderness areas ideally are self-sustaining ecosystems, the raptor populations of many eastern areas may be dependent upon immigration from adjacent habitats.

The Habitat Problem

Many raptorial birds require open grasslands, marshes, or savannas, and others require terrestrial habitats located next to large bodies of water. Included in this number are four of the five raptor species designated as "wilderness associated" by the USDA Forest Service (excluded is the goshawk, a bird of mature forests) and three endangered eastern raptors (USDA 1978, Table 1). In fact, 15 of the 20 eastern raptors that are blue listed, endangered, or species of special concern (Table 1), are associated with open habitats or shoreline. (I exclude from this list the Accipiters, the red-shouldered hawk, and the screech owl.) Yet the open habitats required by these species are substantially under-represented in number and size in eastern wilderness (USDA 1978).

The desirability of including a wide variety of habitats in the wilderness preservation system was recognized during RARE II deliberations (USDA 1978). However, the RARE II environmental assessment failed to identify the importance of terrestrial habitats adjacent to wetlands. The failure to locate potential wilderness areas in grassland and parkland habitats shows up clearly in the draft RARE II environmental assessment (USDA 1978).

CONCLUSIONS

Raptors are important components of eastern wilderness. They enhance human benefits derived from wilderness by accentuating the image of wildness. Although wilderness can protect raptors from human influences, most eastern wilderness areas are too small to protect more than a fraction of a viable population of the largest species. Additionally there are few wilderness areas with important open and shoreline habitats.

LITERATURE CITED

Andrew, J.M. and J.A. Mosher. 1982. Bald eagle nest site selection and nesting habitat in Maryland. J. Wildl. Manage. 46:382-390.

Anderson, D.R. and K.P. Burnham. 1976. Population ecology of the mallard. VI. The effect of exploitation on survival. USDI Fish Wildl. Serv. Resour. Publ. 125, Washington, D.C.

Brauning, D. 1983. Nest site selection of the American kestrel. Raptor Res. 17:122.

Brett, J.J. 1973. Feathers in the wind. Hawk mountain Sanctuary, Kempton, PA.

Brown, L. 1974. Data required for effective study of raptor populations. pp. 9-20. In F.N. Hammerstrom, Jr. et al. (eds.). Management of raptors. Raptor Res. Rep. No. 2, Raptor Research Foundation. Vermillion, SD.

Brown, L. and D. Amadon. 1968. Eagles, hawks, and falcons of the world. p. 945. McGraw Hill, N.Y.

Cade, T.J. 1969. The status of the peregrine falcon and other falconiformes in Africa. pp. 289-322. In J.J. Hickey (ed.). Peregrine falcon populations; their biology and decline. Univ. Wisconsin Press, Madison, Wis.

Call, M. 1979. Habitat management guides for bird of prey. USDI Bur. Land Manage. Tech. Note 338. Denver, Colo.

Call, M.W. 1978. Nesting habitats and surveying techniques for common western raptors. USDI Bur. Land Manage. Tech. Note 316. Denver, Colo.

Coulombe, H.N. 1971. Behavior and population ecology of the burrowing owl, Spetyo cunicularia in the Imperial Valley of California. Condor 73:162-176.

Curry-Lindahl, K. 1977. Introductory address by the chairman. pp. 2-3. In R.D. Chancellor (ed.). World conference on birds of prey, report of proceedings. International Council for bird preservation, Basingstoke, England.

Fraser, J.D., L.D. Frenzel, J.E. Mathisen and M.E. Shough. 1983. Scheduling bald eagle reproduction surveys. Wildl. Soc. Bull. 11:13-16.

Fraser, J.D., F. Martin, L.D. Frenzel, and J.E. Mathisen. 1984. Accounting for measurement errors in bald eagle reproduction surveys. J. Wildl. Manage. 48:595-598.

Fraser, J.D. 1985. The impact of human activities on bald eagle populations--a review. pp. 68-84. In J.M. Gerrard, and T.N. Ingram (eds.). The bald eagle in Canada. White Horse publishers, Headingley, Manitoba.

Fraser, J.D., L.D. Frenzel, and J.E. Mathisen. 1985. The impact of human activities on breeding bald eagles in North-central Minnesota. J. Wildl. Manage. 49:585-592.

Fuller, M.R. and J.A. Mosher. 1981. Methods of detecting and counting raptors: A review. pp. 235-246. In C.J. Ralph and J.M. Scott (eds.). Estimating the number of terrestrial birds. Stud. Avian Biol. 6.

Fyfe, R.W. and R.R. Olendorff. 1976. Minimizing the danger of studies to raptors and other sensitive species. Occas. Pap. 23, Can. Wildl. Serv., Ottawa.

Glue, D.E. 1971. Ringing recovery circumstances of small birds of prey. Bird Study 18:137-146.

Grier, J.R. 1969. Bald eagle behavior and productivity responses to climbing to nests. J. Wildl. Manage. 41:438-443.

Grier, J.W. 1977. Quadrat sampling of a nesting population of bald eagles. J. Wildl. Manage. 43:438-443.

Grier, J.W. 1980. Modeling approaches to bald eagle population dynamics. Wildl. Soc. Bull. 8:316-322.

Jackson, J.A. 1983. Nesting phenology, nest site selection and reproductive success of black and turkey vultures. pp. 245-270. In S.R. Wilbur and J.A. Jackson (eds.). Vulture biology and management. Univ. Calif. Press., Berkeley, Calif.

Knight, R.L. and S.K. Knight. 1984. Responses of wintering eagles to boating activity. J. Wildl. Manage. 43:999-1004.

Lynch, P.J. and D.G. Smith. 1984. Census of eastern screech owls (Otus asio) in urban open space areas using tape recorded song. Am. Birds 38:388-391.

Marti, C.D. and P.W. Wagner. 1985. Winter mortality of common barn owls and its effect on population density and reproduction. Condor 87:111-115.

Mathisen, J.E. 1968. Effects of human disturbance on nesting bald eagles. J. Wildl. Manage. 32:1-6.

Mathisen, J.M., D.J. Sorenson, L.D. Frenzel, and T.C. Dunstan. 1977. Management strategy for bald eagles. Trans. N. Am. Wildl. Conf. 42:86-92.

McEwan, L.C. and D.M. Hirth. 1979. Southern bald eagle productivity and nest site selection. J. Wildl. Manage. 43:585-594.

McGarigal, K. and J.D. Fraser. 1984. The effect of forest stand age on owl distribution in southwestern Virginia. J. Wildl. Manage. 48:1393-1398.

Moore, K.R. and C.J. Henny. 1983. Nest site characteristics of three coexisting Accipter hawks in northeastern Oregon. Raptor Res. 17:65-76.

Murphy, T.R. 1956. Nest site selection of the bald eagle in Yellowstone National Park. Proc. Utah Acad. Sci., Arts and Letters 42:261-264.

Newton, I. 1979. Population ecology of raptors. Buteo Books, Vermillion, S.D.

Olendorff, R.R., R.S. Motroni, and M.W. Call. 1980. Raptor Management--the State of the Art in 1980. USDI Bur. Land Manage. Tech. Note 345. Denver, Colo.

Orians, G. and F. Kuhlman. 1956. The red-tailed hawk and great horned owl populations in Wisconsin. Condor 58:371-385.

Postupalsky, S. 1974. Raptor reproductive success: some problems with methods, criteria, and terminology. Raptor Res. Rep. 2:21-31.

Redig, P.T. 1978. Effects of a program for raptor research and rehabilitation on raptor management. pp. 42-48. In Proc. 42nd John S. Wright Forestry Conf., Purdue Univ., West Lafayette, Ind.

Renolds, R.T., E.C. Meslow, and H.M. Wright. 1982. Nesting habitat of coexisting Accipiter in Oregon. J. Wildl. Manage. 46:124-138.

Shoenfeld, C.A. and J.D. Hendee. 1978. Wildlife Management in wilderness. Boxwood Press, Pacific Grove, CA.

Stalmaster, M.V. 1983. An energetics simulation model for managing wintering bald eagles. J. Wildl. Manage. 47:349-359.

Stalmaster, M.V. and J.A. Gessaman. 1984. Ecological energetics and foraging behavior of overwintering bald eagles. Ecol. Monogr. 54:407-428.

Stalmaster, M.V. and J.R. Newman. 1978. Behavioral Responses of wintering bald eagles to human activity. J. Wildl. Manage. 42:506-513.

Steenhof, K. and M.N. Kochert. 1982. An evaluation of methods used to estimate raptor nesting success. J. Wildl. Manage. 46:885-893.

Sykes, P.W. 1979. Status of the everglade kite in Florida 1968-1978. Wilson Bull. 91:494-511.

Tate, J., Jr. and D.J. Tate. 1982. The blue list for 1982. Am. Birds. 36:126-135.

Titus, K. and J.A. Mosher. 1981. Nest-site habitat selected by woodland hawks in the central Appalachians. Auk 98:270-281.

USDA. 1978. Draft environmental statement: roadless area review and evaluation. USDA For. Serv., Washington, D.C.

Voous, K.H. 1977. Three lines of thought for consideration and eventual action. pp. 343-347. In R.D. Chancellor (ed.). World Conference on birds of prey, report of proceedings. International Council for bird preservation, Basingstoke, England.

Weekes, F.M. 1974. A survey of bald eagle nesting attempts in southern Ontario, 1969-1973. Can. Field Nat. 88:415-419.

White, C.M. and T.L. Thurow. 1985. Reproduction of ferruginous hawks exposed to controlled disturbance. Condor 87:14-22.

Wilderness Society. 1984. Wilderness lands in the United States. Map. The Wilderness Society, Washington, D.C.

Young, H. 1968. A consideration of insecticide effects on hypothetical avian populations. Ecology 49:991-994.

Wilderness As Wild Turkey Habitat In The Eastern United States

by
James G. Dickson

ABSTRACT--Wild Turkeys in the United States were very abundant in colonial times, declined drastically in the late 19th and early 20th centuries and have recently made a remarkable comeback. Suitability of eastern wilderness areas as Wild Turkey habitat depends on conditions in and around wilderness areas, and how these conditions change over time. Unless they are artifically maintained, openings in the grass-forb stage, which are needed for turkey brood habitat, will be rare and short-lived in wilderness areas. Mature stands suitable as fall and winter range would be common in wilderness areas. Wilderness designation should reduce illegal killing of turkeys and enhance the quality of sport hunting by eliminating vehicular traffic. Options for managing forest stands for Wild Turkeys will be limited by wilderness designation.

KEYWORDS: Wild Turkey, habitat, wilderness.

Wild Turkeys (*Meleagris gallopavo*) are an integral part of North American wildlife and provide some of the greatest hunting sport in the world. Turkey hunting is mind altering and addictive.

STATUS

Early accounts by explorers in America documented Wild Turkeys in vast numbers (Mosby and Handley 1943). Apparently forest conditions were ideal for Wild Turkeys during the years of the first white men in North America. Wild Turkey ancestral range included all or portions of 39 states. Wild Turkeys declined throughout their range in the late 1800's and early 1900's and probably reached their low ebb around the 1930's (Mosby 1975). This drastic decline has been attributed to severe overhunting and habitat destruction. Since the 1940's reforestation, better protection, and trapping and transplanting of wild-trapped turkeys have restored the Wild Turkey in the United States and elsewhere. In 1983 there were an estimated 2.5 million Wild Turkeys in 48 states, 80 times as many as in 1940 (Miller and Holbrook 1983).

There are five subspecies of Wild Turkey in the United States. The eastern Wild Turkey (*M. g. silvestris*) is by far the most populous, found throughout the forested eastern United States and elsewhere. The Florida Wild Turkey (*M. g. oceola*) is limited to the central and southern portion of Florida. The Rio Grande Wild Turkey (*M. g. intermedia*) is abundant in Texas, Oklahoma, Kansas, and

other western states where it has been introduced. It thrives only in areas where annual rainfall is 50-80 cm (Bailey 1980). The Merriam's Wild Turkey (*M. g. merriami*) is found in the arid western United States and Canada. The Gould's Wild Turkey (*M. g. mexicana*) inhabits a few canyons along the border between Mexico and New Mexico and Arizona. Since this symposium deals with eastern wilderness my paper will focus on the eastern Wild Turkey and will generally also be appropriate for the Florida Wild Turkey.

INTERACTING FACTORS

Suitability of wilderness as Wild Turkey habitat depends on conditions in and around wilderness areas that are within the range of turkey flocks. The impact of official designation of Wild Turkey range as wilderness depends on several interacting factors. Vegetation presently on an area determines its current suitability as turkey habitat, and changes over time will determine future habitat. Natural succession will ultimately favor tree species that are tolerant of shade and competition, and stands will advance toward climax vegetation. Natural phenomena such as fire, tornadoes, hurricanes, insects, and diseases will alter vegetation (turkey habitat). The size of such openings and the frequency at which they develop will influence how well turkeys fare within wilderness areas.

Size of wilderness areas, adjoining land use patterns, and local landowner and hunter attitudes also will affect

Wild Turkeys. Eastern wilderness areas are generally relatively small, most between 1,200 and 6,000 ha. The annual range of turkeys includes several thousand hectares. In a newly released flock in East Texas, 90 percent of the population ranged within 8,328 ha (Hopkins 1981). Turkeys will likely range outside wildernesses in some seasons if adjoining habitat is suitable. Small wildernesses with adjacent land in openings such as pasture, agriculture crops, or food plots could make excellent Wild Turkey habitat if protection is good. Hens and broods would especially benefit from fields around wilderness for nesting and brood range, but could be very vulnerable to poaching.

NESTING AND BROOD RANGE

Hens nest in a variety of stand types. Their nests are often located in ecotones between vegetation types (Williams *et al.* 1971), and usually are surrounded by abundant shrubs (Healy 1981, Campo 1983). It has not been demonstrated that nesting sites are limited and sites should be adequate around openings within, and along edges of wilderness.

Young poults feed extensively on arthropods. Hurst and Stringer (1975) found that poults less than 2 weeks old ate more animal than plant matter, and animal matter remained a substantial poult diet item for the duration of the study (38 days post hatching). Healy (1978) found that invertebrates accounted for 71 to 98 percent of items eaten by human imprinted poults less than 4 weeks old. The diet of older turkeys (45 to 105 days old) was 15 percent grasshoppers in Alabama (Hamrick and Davis 1971).

Insects and other arthropods in the diet of young turkeys are associated with abundant herbaceous ground cover. Martin and McGinnes (1975) sampled 25 times more insects in clearings than beneath forest canopy in Virginia. Healy (1978) defined brood habitat by dry weight of ground vegetation in West Virginia. Areas with ground vegetation weighing from 600 to 3,000 kg/ha provided adequate brood range. Vegetation with a dry weight less than 460 kg/ha did not provide enough insects or seeds to feed poults, and vegetation denser than 3,000 kg/ha was too dense for poults to traverse (Healy 1981). The dense ground vegetation needed for brood range is normally found in openings, and openings have often been recommended for brood range (e.g. Speake *et al.* 1975, Baily *et al.* 1981). Adequate brood range can also occur on forest sites that are relatively productive or where the overstory is open-grown and the habitat is savannah-like. In northeastern Alabama, brood habitat was characterized by moderate to abundant herbaceous coverage and an open midstory (Metzler and Speake 1985). In eastern Texas, broods frequented pine stands with low-density tree midstories and abundant herbaceous ground cover (Campo 1983). In hardwood

stands in West Virginia, Healy (1978) concluded that areas with a red oak site index of 80 were adequate brood habitat in clearings, 2 and 15-year-old clearcuts, and in mature stands. But on areas with a red oak site index of 65, only permanent openings produced adequate brood range. In another study in West Virginia, broods avoided stands with basal areas over 23 m/ha (Pack *et al.* 1980).

Soon after wilderness designation, early brood range can be expected to decline as canopies close and understory grasses and forbs are shaded out. Thereafter, brood range in wilderness areas will depend on openings created by natural phenomena such as tornadoes, hurricanes, disease and insects which kill trees. Insect epidemics such as outbreaks of southern pine beetles (*Dendroctonus frontalis*) will influence the extent of brood habitat. The rate of tree death and resulting openings should increase over time as trees in wilderness stands age and die. But openings in wilderness may rapidly advance from the grass forb stage to a dense shrub stage, providing suitable brood habitat for only a short time. Bormann and Likens (1979:174) concluded it would take several hundred years after clearcutting before northern hardwood forests would reach a steady state containing the shifting-mosaic of interspersed openings. Most eastern forests are even aged and less than 100 years old.

FALL AND WINTER RANGE

Wild Turkeys shift ranges somewhat in fall, and increase use of older pine-hardwood and hardwood stands (e.g. Speake *et al.* 1975). Stands of large mixed hardwoods with open understories are usually thought of as ideal fall and winter range (Bailey and Rinell 1968:40). Hard mast, especially oaks, shows up prominently in fall and winter food habits studies (Williams 1981:89).

In the short and long term, suitability of each eastern wilderness as Wild Turkey habitat will depend on stand distribution and composition, and how they change with succession and disturbance. For example, in the southern Appalachian Mountains, yellow poplar (*Liriodendron tulipifera*) predominates after disturbances such as tree harvesting. Oaks (*Quercus* spp.) will gradually replace yellow-poplar, improving habitat for turkeys. Conversely, in the Hemlock-White Pine-Northern Hardwoods region of Vermont, New Hampshire, and northwestern Pennsylvania, black cherry (*Prunus serotina*) will be replaced by eastern hemlock (*Tsuga canadensis*), American beech (*Fagus grandifolia*), and sugar maple (*Acer saccharum*), and habitat value for turkeys will decrease.

In the short term, wilderness conditions should generally provide good fall and winter range for Wild Turkeys and excellent range if appropriate openings are present within or around the wilderness areas. Tree age for optimum mast production for most mast producers is generally from 50 to over 100 years (USDA Forest Service

1981). But shading from overstory canopy will reduce fruit yield of understory plants such as flowering dogwood (*Cornus florida*) (Halls and Alcaniz 1968) and reduce vegetation growth near the ground (Blair and Feduccia 1977). These fruits and this vegetation are important components of the Wild Turkey's diet (Kennamer *et al.* 1980, Williams 1981).

In the long term, habitat suitability in each wilderness will depend on succession and natural disturbances. Wind, insects, and diseases may kill trees and create openings that favor fruiting of understory shrubs and trees around openings. Grass and forb production will increase in openings and benefit Wild Turkeys. The great age of trees in wilderness areas may have a negative impact. Mast producing trees may grow beyond optimum productive condition in the long run. Also, many primary mast producers important to turkeys are intermediate in tolerance to tree competition, and could be replaced by more tolerant species less valuable to Wild Turkeys. For example in Virginia, white oak (*Quercus alba*), black oak (*Q. velutina*), post oak (*Q. stellata*), red oaks (*Q.* spp.), American beech, blackgum (*Nyssa sylvatica*), flowering dogwood, and sassafras (*Sassafras albidum*) are listed as prime Wild Turkey mast producers by Mosby and Handley (1943). Of these, only American beech and dogwood are sufficiently tolerant of shade competition to reproduce and develop under dense overstories.

ILLEGAL KILL

Turkey flocks are particularly vulnerable to poachers during summer when hens with broods frequent grassy roadsides in search of arthropods, seeds, grass, and forbs. During fall and winter, flocks prefer native hardwood and pine-hardwood stands in the coastal plains, where they can be vulnerable to some unscrupulous squirrel and deer hunters if a protectionist attitude is not dominant.

Where wilderness designation decreases human access, turkeys should benefit. When Wild Turkey numbers were drastically low in the first part of the twentieth century they were found in remote areas that had limited human access, such as large mature forests of Virginia (Mosby and Handley 1943) and Louisiana (Hollis 1947). In West Virginia, turkeys did not thrive where roads exceeded 6 km per 1,000 ha of turkey habitat (Bailey and Rinell 1968:42). Although turkeys have proven themselves more adaptable to man recently, illegal killing of turkeys has been thought to limit population increases in areas of appropriate habitat (Mosby and Handley 1943:131, Stoddard 1963, Dickson *et al.* 1978). In some areas, such as Louisiana, east Texas, and elsewhere, it appears that a locked gate excluding the general public is the key to viable turkey populations.

HUNTING QUALITY

Wilderness designation of forested areas should improve the sport hunting of turkeys. Road closure and absence of motorized vehicular transportation will limit travel to foot or animal. Hunting pressure on turkeys should be less than on nonwilderness areas with limitless access. Although some hunters will not travel far into wilderness for hunting opportunities, the hunting experience should be more pleasurable for the hunters that hike or pack deep into wilderness areas. They will hunt with less hunter competition and less noise from vehicles. Numerous hunters and vehicles in a hunted areas can seriously degrade a turkey hunting experience. Packing out the harvest is not a problem as it is with large game mammals.

MANAGEMENT

Procedures for managing turkeys in wilderness areas will be curtailed by official wilderness designation. Some practices that are used to maintain and enhance Wild Turkey habitat include prescribed burning, maintaining openings, providing supplemental food or water sources, and controlling forest stand composition through cuttings. Fire was probably important in maintaining Wild Turkey brood habitat before settlement by Europeans. Prescribed burning is often conducted in the southern coastal plain for bobwhites (*Colinus virginianus*), white-tailed deer (*Odocoileus virginianus*), and Wild Turkey. Burning can reduce thick understory and promote the grass/forb vegetation stage with accompanying insects. Winter burns are frequented by turkeys in early spring. Hurst (1975) found more insects in burned than in unburned stands. Openings are important to Wild Turkeys, but they probably cannot be maintained mechanically in wilderness areas. Biological opinions on value of supplemental food vary, but it has been shown to be beneficial in some situations. It appears that corn plots can increase winter survival of turkeys in the northern extremity of their range (Porter *et al.* 1980). Water can limit turkey habitat in the arid west and suitable turkey habitat in the east is well watered. Artificial impoundments, which might improve habitat, would be precluded in wilderness stands.

Timber harvest could be beneficial or detrimental for Wild Turkey populations. Small cuts in contiguous forests and partial cuts in mature stands would open up canopies, increase diversity, and provide more light for understory fruiting and low forage. Under wilderness conditions these manipulations would be left to natural phenomena.

I thank Lowell K. Halls and William M. Healy for reviewing a draft of this manuscript.

LITERATURE CITED

Bailey, R.W. and K.T. Rinell. 1968. History and Management of the Wild Turkey in West Virginia. West Virginia Dep. of Nat. Resour. Bull. No. 6.

Bailey, R.W., J.R. Davis, J.E. Frampton, J.V. Gwynn, and J. Shugars. 1981. Habitat requirements of the Wild Turkey in the southeast Piedmont. pp. 14-23. *In* P.T. Bromley and R.L. Carlton (ed.), Proc. Symp. habitat requirements and habitat management for the Wild Turkey in the Southeast. Virginia Wild Turkey Foundation, Richmond, Va.

Blair, R.M. and D.P. Feduccia. 1977. Midstory hardwoods inhibit deer forage in loblolly pine plantations. J. Wildl. Manage. 41:677-684.

Bormann, F.H. and G.E. Likens. 1979. Patterns and process in a forested ecosystem. Springer-Verlag. New York.

Campo, J.J. 1983. Brood habitat use, reproduction, and movement of recently restocked eastern Wild Turkeys in East Texas. Ph.D. Diss. Tex. A&M Univ., College Station, Tex.

Dickson, J.G., C.D. Adams, and S.H. Hanley. 1978. Response of turkey populations to habitat variables in Louisiana. Wildl. Soc. Bull. 6:163-166.

Halls, L.K. and R. Alcaniz. 1968. Browse plants yield best in forest openings. J. Wildl. Manage. 32:185-186.

Hamrick, W.J. and J.R. Davis. 1971. Summer food items of juvenile Wild Turkeys. Proc. Annu. Conf. Southeast. Assoc. Game Fish Comm. 25:85-89.

Healy, W.M. 1978. Feeding activity of Wild Turkey poults in relation to ground vegetation and insect abundance. Ph.D. Diss. West Virginia Univ., Morgantown, West Va.

Healy, W.M. 1981. Habitat requirements of Wild Turkeys in the southeastern mountains. pp. 24-34. *In* P.T. Bromley and R.L. Carlton (eds.). Proc. Symp. habitat requirements and habitat management for the Wild Turkey in the Southeast. Virginia Wild Turkey Foundation, Richmond, Va.

Hollis, F.D. 1947. The present status of the Wild Turkey in Louisiana. Louisiana Dep. Wildl. and Fish, New Orleans, La.

Hopkins, C.R. 1981. Dispersal, reproduction, mortality, and habitat utilization of restocked eastern turkeys in East Texas. Ph.D. Diss. Tex. A&M Univ., College Station, Tex.

Hurst, G.A. and B.D. Stringer, Jr. 1975. Food habits of Wild Turkey poults in Mississippi. pp. 76-85. *In* L.K. Halls (ed.). Proc. Third Natl. Wild Turkey Symp., Texas Chapter, The Wildl. Soc.

Kennamer, J.E., J.R. Gwaltney, and K.R. Sims. 1980. Food habits of the eastern Wild Turkey on an area intensively managed for pine in Alabama. pp. 246-250. *In* J.M. Sweeney (ed.). Proc. Fourth Natl. Wild Turkey Symp., Natl. Wild Turkey Fed.

Martin, D.D. and B.S. McGinnes. 1975. Insect availability and use by turkeys in forest clearings. pp. 70-75. *In* L.K. Halls (ed.). Proc. Third Natl. Wild Turkey Symp., Texas Chap. of the Wildl. Soc.

Metzler, R. and D.W. Speake. 1985. Wild Turkey poult mortality rates and their relationship to brood habitat structure in northeast Alabama. pp. 103-111. *In* J.E. Kennamer and M.C. Kennamer (eds.). Proc. Fifth Nat. Wild Turkey Symp., Natl. Wild Turkey Fed.

Miller, J.E. and H.L. Holbrook. 1983. Return of a native: the Wild Turkey flourishes again. pp. 166-173. *In* Using our Natural Resources 1983 Yearbook of Agriculture.

Mosby, H.S. and C.O. Handley. 1943. The Wild Turkey in Virginia: Its status, life history and management. Comm. of Game and Inland Fish., Richmond, Va.

Mosby, H.S. 1975. The status of the Wild Turkey in 1974. pp. 22-26. *In* L.K. Halls (ed.). Proc. Third Natl. Wild Turkey Symp., Texas Chapter, The Wildl. Soc.

Pack, J.C., R.P. Burkert, W.K. Igo, and D.J. Pybus. 1980. Habitat utilized by Wild Turkey broods within oak-hickory forests of West Virginia. pp. 213-224. *In* J.M. Sweeney (ed.). Proc. Fourth Natl. Wild Turkey Symp., Nat. Wild Turkey Fed.

Porter, W.F., R.D. Tanger, G.C. Nelson, and D.A. Hamilton. 1980. Effects of corn food plots on Wild Turkeys in the upper Mississippi Valley. J. Wildl. Manage. 44:456-467.

Speak, D.W., T.E. Lynch, W.J. Fleming, G.A. Wright, and W.J. Hamrick. 1975. Habitat use and seasonal movements of Wild Turkeys in the Southeast. pp. 122-129. *In* L.K. (ed.). Proc. Third Natl. Wild Turkey Symp., Texas Chapter, The Wildl. Soc.

Stoddard, H.L., Jr. 1963. Maintenance and increase of the Eastern Wild Turkey on private lands of the coastal plain of the deep Southeast. Tall Timbers Res. Stn. Bull. 3.

USDA Forest Service. 1981. Wildlife habitat management handbook - Southern Region, For. Serv. Handb. 2609.23R.

Williams, L.E., Jr., D.H. Austin, T.E. Peoples, and R.W. Phillips. 1971. Laying data and nesting behavior of Wild Turkeys. Proc. Annu. Conf. Southeast. Assoc. Game Fish Comm. 25:90-106.

Williams, L.E., Jr. 1981. The book of the Wild Turkey. Winchester Press, Tulsa, Ok.

Preferences Of Visitors For Wildlife Species

by

Bruce C. Hastings and William E. Hammitt

ABSTRACT--Recreation visitors to Great Smoky Mountains National Park were asked how much they would like to see each of 33 animals. The most popular species were deer, bears, turkeys, eagles, and raccoons. The least popular animals included snakes, bats, and lizards. Different analyses revealed that preferred groups of animals were often aesthetically pleasing or important culturally and historically. Commonly feared and domestic groups were least preferred.

KEYWORDS: visitor perception, nonconsumptive wildlife use, wildlife observation, Great Smoky Mountains National Park.

Natural areas often possess large numbers of wildlife species, many of which provide opportunities for nonconsumptive enjoyment. Animals have been shown to have an aesthetic value that is greater than other values they possess (Woodin 1966). Nonconsumptive wildlife activities are not only significant in the western United States (e.g. Yellowstone), but have been shown to be very important to people in both the Northeast (More 1979a) and the Southeast (Horvath 1974). The most popular nonconsumptive activity is probably viewing animals (Lime 1976). Managers need to know how different animals are perceived by visitors to facilitate management for public viewing and public education.

An opportunity to evaluate preferences for species in the Great Smoky Mountains National Park was available in the Cades Cove portion of the Park. Although largely managed for its historic significance, the Cove also provides opportunities for visitors to see free-ranging animals and for the National Park Service to inform visitors about wildlife and ecological relationships. The purpose of this study is to determine the degree to which animals and groups of animals living in Cades Cove are preferred for viewing. The results could guide alternatives for the management and interpretation of wildlife for nonconsumptive purposes in natural areas.

METHODS

Study Area Great Smoky Mountains National Park is located in eastern Tennessee and western North Carolina. It is distinguished by its status as an International Biosphere Reserve and its high visitation rate (gt 8 million annually). Cades Cove is a popular area located in the northwestern section of the Park. An 18 km paved loop road through the Cove offers contact with numerous wildlife species and habitats.

Questionnaire A 10-page questionnaire and a self-addressed, stamped envelope were distributed to one occupant in each of 400 vehicles visiting Cades Cove from 30 July to 21 August, 1983. On each of 16 days (i.e. 8 weekdays and 8 weekend days), 25 vehicles were pulled over near the end of the loop road, and the occupants were asked to participate in the survey. Eight parties were contacted each morning between 0800 - 1000 hrs EDT and each evening between 1800 - 2000 hrs; 9 were contacted between 1300 - 1500 hrs. The response rate was 85%, following the mailing of 2 postcard reminders.

Participants were asked how much they would like to see each of 33 animals in Cades Cove regardless of whether they believed that the species lived within the Park. All animals either presently exist or probably existed previously in Cades Cove. Pretesting demonstrated that the majority of people wanted to see most animals; therefore, the following 5-point Likert Scale was used: Strongly Like to See, Like to See, Somewhat Like to See, Neutral, Not Like to See. Additional items in the questionnaire included variables considered most related to species preference: sex, hunting status, and previous visitor experience in Cades Cove.

For statistical analyses, the significance level was set at p lt 0.05 unless otherwise stated; all differences reported below are statistically significant. Student's t-test and one-way Analysis of Variance (with Duncan's Multiple Range Test) were used to test differences in response means. Factor Analysis was employed as a data reduction technique for grouping animals; a species was placed in a category when it had a factor loading of 0.4 or above in a specific factor and at least 0.1 above its next highest value in any other factor. Principle components with orthogonal varimax rotation was the factoring routine used (Nie *et al.* 1975).

RESULTS

Cades Cove visitors wanted to see most animals listed (Table 1). The most popular species were deer, bears, turkeys, eagles, and raccoons; all of these animals received preference ratings that were consistently high (i.e. low standard deviations). The least popular animals were copperheads, rattlesnakes, bats, lizards, and non-poisonous snakes. Although wild hogs and coyotes also possessed relatively low preference means, they demonstrated unusually high variance in how people rated them.

experience at the Cove. Bats, rattlesnakes, and copperheads were rated lowest (31, 32, and 33 respectively), regardless of visitor sex, hunting status, or visitation status.

To reduce the large list of 33 species to a more manageable package for analytical purposes, categories of animals were intuitively developed (Table 2). Aesthetically and culturally important animals were the most preferred, while commonly feared and domestic animals were least preferred. All t-test comparisons of visitor responses to opposing categories (i.e. commonly-feared versus not-commonly-feared, domestic versus non-domestic animals, etc.) were significant at P lt 0.01. In addition, women liked animals which were culturally important, domestic, or commonly seen in Cades Cove more than men liked them. Non-hunters preferred domestic animals more than hunters. People who had never been to Cades Coves before liked predators, commonly-feared-animals, and those considered "pests" more than repeat

Males and females tended to rate animals similarly; however, women rated horses, cattle, rabbits, box turtles, and "other birds" significantly higher and copperheads, rattlesnakes, and wild hogs significantly lower. Hunters rated wild hogs higher then former hunters and non-hunters (those who had never considered themselves hunters); hunters also preferred bobcats, bears, and wild turkeys more than non-hunters. Hunters rated domestic horses, rabbits, box turtles, frogs/toads, domestic cattle, and "other birds" lower than non-hunters. Hunters also rated rabbits, opossums, chipmunks, and "other birds" lower than former hunters. Those who had never visited Cades Cove prior to the day of the interview rated coyotes and wild hogs higher than those who had previous

visitors.

Factor analysis was employed to statistically group animals according to visitor preference. Of the 6 categories that factored, popular game species and small, aesthetic animals were the most preferred, while poisonous snakes and other unappealing species were least preferred (Table 3). Fur species and domestic animals were the third and fourth most preferred groups. Two categories (poisonous snakes and domestic animals) were not considered strong factors since each had only two species, but their correlational values were high enough to warrant inclusion.

Women rated domestic animals higher and poisonous snakes lower than men rated them. Hunters rated

Table 1. Means and Standard Deviations for Preference of Visitors toward Wildlife in Cades Cove, GSMNP, 1983.

	Most Preferred								Least Preferred		
Rank	Animal	Mean[1]	SD	Rank	Animal	Mean	SD	Rank	Animal	Mean	SD
1	Deer	1.25	0.24	12	Groundhog	2.00	0.94	23	Wild hog	2.84	2.11
2	Bear	1.32	0.36	13	Beaver	2.05	1.01	24	Coyote	2.85	2.09
3	Turkey	1.43	0.49	14	Otter	2.06	0.99	25	Vulture	2.87	1.57
4	Eagle	1.43	0.53	15	Bobcat	2.08	1.64	26	Domestic horse	2.95	1.62
5	Raccoon	1.60	0.69	16	Other birds	2.13	1.12	27	Frog or toad	2.98	1.52
6	Owl	1.68	0.66	17	Mink	2.16	1.08	28	Domestic cattle	3.10	1.54
7	Trout	1.77	0.80	18	Rabbit	2.17	0.99	29	Nonpoisonous snake	3.34	1.72
8	Fox	1.84	0.87	19	Box turtle	2.36	1.12	30	Lizard	3.37	1.40
9	Chipmunk	1.89	0.89	20	Opossum	2.58	1.43	31	Bat	3.78	1.41
10	Hawk	1.92	0.95	21	Weasel	2.79	1.79	32	Rattlesnake	4.07	1.61
11	Gray squirrel	2.00	1.01	22	Skunk	2.83	1.74	33	Copperhead	4.14	1.48

[1]For calculation of means, *Strongly Like to See* = 1 and *Not Like to See* = 5.

Table 2. Preference Means for Selected Groups of Wildlife in Cades Cove, GSMNP, 1983.

Animal Group[1]	Mean[2]
Esthetic animals (11)	1.75
Animals important to local culture/history (7)	1.87
Wild animals commonly taken for sport and food or fun (15)	2.00
Most commonly seen animals in Cades Cove (11)	2.15
Predators (17)	2.58
"Pest" species (11)	2.89
Domestic animals (2)	3.04
Commonly feared animals (7)	3.19

[1]Number of animals comprising groups listed in parentheses.

[2]For calculation of means, *Strongly Like to See* = 1 and *Not Like to See* = 5.

Table 3. Preference Means and Reliability Values (Cronbach's Alpha) for Factor Analyzed Groups of Animals in Cades Cove, GSMNP, 1983.

Group (Component Animals)	Index Mean	Alpha Value
Popular game species commonly observed in Cades Cove	1.42	0.70
Deer		
Turkey		
Raccoon		
Small, esthetic animals	2.01	0.86
Groundhog		
Rabbit		
Trout		
Box turtle		
Owl		
Chipmunk		
Other birds		
Fur species	2.20	0.79
Fox		
Otter		
Mink		
Beaver		
Coyote		
Domestic animals	3.04	0.89
Horse		
Cattle		
Unappealing but nonpoisonous animals	3.16	0.83
Lizard		
Bat		
Weasel		
Vulture		
Skunk		
Nonpoisonous snake		
Poisonous snakes	4.11	0.98
Rattlesnake		
Copperhead		

small/aesthetic and domestic animals lower than non-hunters. Hunters also rated small, aesthetic animals lower than did former hunters. Repeat visitors preferred game species commonly seen in the Cove more than new visitors.

DISCUSSION

Deer and bear have been shown to be popular in visitor populations other than in Cades Cove. Idaho residents reported these two animals as their favorites (Fazio and Belli 1977). Kellert and Westervelt (1982) demonstrated that deer were the most common wild animal reported in newspaper articles over a 75 year period. Both deer and especially bear have been very popular in children's books (More 1979b). Lyons (1982) reported deer as being the most popular game mammal among the general population in America. Species preference is probably improved by aesthetics and large size (Kellert 1980, Collins 1976), both of which deer and bear possess.

Eagles were also highly rated in this and other studies (Fazio and Belli 1977, Kellert 1980). Again, size and aesthetics may be relevant to the popularity of both eagles and wild turkeys, but the added dimension of cultural and historic significance (Kellert and Berry 1980) probably provides a better explanation for eagle and turkey popularity. The intuitively developed categories of aesthetically and culturally important species were the most preferred. The majority of the animals in the most preferred groups categorized by factor analysis also appeared to be aesthetically pleasing.

There should be little surprise that snakes, lizards, and bats were least preferred. These animals possess, in general, several characteristics which would reduce their popularity: predatory tendencies (Collins 1976), threat of biting humans (Kellert 1980, Bowd 1983), unfamiliar skin texture (Kellert 1980), heterothermy (Collins 1976), or competition with more preferred species (Dawson et al. 1978).

Cades Cove visitors rated domestic horses and cattle 26th and 28th in preference, respectively. The reaction to horses is considered unusual since horses are often shown to be very popular animals (Collins 1976, Kellert 1980, Kellert and Westervelt 1982). However, Dagg (1974) demonstrated that exotic animals may be less preferred than native animals in specific environments. Thus, Cades Cove visitors probably treated domestic animals as species not belonging in a national park. The fact that wild hogs and coyotes are not native to the Smokies and may compete with more preferred animal and plant species probably reduced their popularity; the high variance in visitor response to these two species may have been due in part to their relatively large size and to their higher rating by people visiting Cades Cove for the first time.

Women preferred domestic and culturally important species more than men. Kellert (1976) found that sex is one of the most important social differentiators of human attitudes toward animals. He showed that women tend to express strong feelings toward pets, which may be related to their attitudes toward domestic and cultural animals such as the horse. The fact that women rated some "hazardous" animals lower than men rated them is not unexpected since women tend to withdraw from dangerous situations more than men (Maccoby and Jacklin 1974).

Hunters tended to be more interested in several prized game species and less interested in domestic and aesthetic animals than others. These preferences may be related to Kellert's (1980) "dominionistic" attitude displayed for animals used in sporting situations.

Explaining differences in preferences between repeat and new visitors is difficult. Perhaps repeat visitors live closer to Cades Cove resulting in stronger biases toward

certain game species and against predators, commonly feared animals, and pests. Their stronger dislike for coyotes and wild hogs may reflect knowledge that (1) these species are not native to the Park and therefore may be competing with native and more desired species; and (2) the Park provides considerable information to the public on damage produced by wild hogs.

CONCLUSIONS

The most appropriate management action necessary for promoting wildlife viewing will depend on the species available, agency policy, and visitor preferences at a specific location. Managers and interpreters may want to concentrate on several highly preferred species for providing better opportunities to view and interpret these animals. However, less preferred wildlife also require more attention. Although managers may not want to increase viewing opportunities for all unappealing animals (e.g. poisonous snakes), tours for some species (e.g. bats) may provide more occasions to improve attitudes toward ecologically important, but unpopular species.

Once managers realize what animals and groups of animals are appreciated or considered negatively, agencies can move toward a broader understanding of visitor perceptions toward wildlife. Management and wildlife education should use a holistic, ecological approach to explain wildlife management and principles (Gilbert 1982, Kellert 1982), and comprehension of visitor preferences can guide this process.

ACKNOWLEDGEMENT

Research was sponsored by the Graduate Program of Ecology, University of Tennessee.

LITERATURE CITED

Bowd, A.D. 1983. Children's fears of animals. J. Gen. Psychol. 142:313-314.

Collins, M.A.J. 1976. Student attitudes towards animals. Am. Biol. Teacher. 38:491-493.

Dagg, A.I. 1974. Reactions of people to urban wildlife. pp. 163-165 In Wildlife in an urbanizing environment, Symp. Proc. Univ. Mass., Amherst.

Dawson, C.P., R.L. Miller, and T.L. Brown. 1978. Trans. Northeast Fish Wildl. Conf. 35:143-153.

Fazio, J.R., and L.A. Belli. 1977. Characteristics of nonconsumptive wildlife users in Idaho. Trans. N. Am. Wildl. Conf. 42:117-128.

Gilbert, F.F. 1982. Public attitudes toward urban wildlife: a pilot study in Guelph, Ontario. Wildl. Soc. Bull. 10:245-253.

Horvath, J.C. 1974. Economic survey of southeastern wildlife and wildlife-oriented recreation. Trans. N. Amer. Wildl. Conf. 39:187-194.

Kellert, S.R. 1976. Perceptions of animals in American society. Trans. N. Am. Wildl. Conf. 41:533-546.

Kellert, S.R. 1980. American attitudes toward and knowledge of animals: an update. Int. J. Stud. Anim. Probl. 1:87-119.

Kellert, S.R. 1982. The relation of human dimensions information to wildlife management, policy and planning. Proc. Fourth Annu. Meet. Organ. Wildl. Planners. 66-74.

Kellert, S.R., and J.K. Berry. 1980. Phase III: Knowledge, affection and basic attitudes toward animals in American society. U.S. Fish & Wildl. Serv. Rep.

Kellert, S.R., and M.O. Westervelt. 1982. Historical trends in American animal use and perception. Trans. N. Am. Wildl. Conf. 47:649-664.

Lime, D.W. 1976. Wildlife is for nonhunters, too. J. For. 74:600-604.

Lyons, J.R. 1982. Nonconsumptive wildlife - associated recreation in the U.S.: identifying the other constituency. Trans. N. Amer. Wildl. Conf. 47:677-685.

Maccoby, E.E., and C.N. Jacklin. 1974. The psychology of sex differences. Stanford University Press, Stanford, Connecticut.

More, T.A. 1979a. The demand for nonconsumptive wildlife uses: a review of the literature. USDA For. Serv., Amherst, Massachusetts.

More, T.A. 1979b. Wildlife preferences and children's books. Wildl. Soc. Bull. 7:274-278.

Nie, N.H., C.H. Hull, J.G. Jenkins, K. Steinbrenner, and D.H. Bent. 1975. SPSS: Statistical package for the social sciences, second edition. McGraw-Hill Book Co., New York. 675 pp.

Woodin, W.H. 1966. Aesthetic values of native animals. pp. 73-76 In J.L. Gardner (ed.). Native plants and animals as resources in arid lands of the Southwestern United States. Symp. Am. Assoc. Adv. Sci., Flagstaff, Arizona.

Wilderness And Animal Disease Relationships

by

Harry A. Jacobson

ABSTRACT--Human and domestic animal diseases have been factors in wilderness preservation because they have made some wilderness areas inhospitable for man. Certain wilderness areas offer disease threats not normally encountered elsewhere because diseases are a function of both habitat and fauna and these may be unique to some wilderness areas. Eradication of most human or domestic animal diseases from wilderness is neither desirable nor practical. Information and education of the public to potential disease threats and preventative measures that can be taken is the most practical solution to most wilderness disease problems.

KEYWORDS: habitat, wildlife, disease-values.

There are few animal diseases that are unique only to wilderness areas. However, disease is a component of any ecosystem and as such can be a force that is constantly operating on the ecological balance of that system. In formulating policy for wilderness management, consideration of the role of diseases in wilderness ecosystems is of concern. In this paper, I will attempt to cover some of the relationships between wilderness areas and human and domestic animal diseases. Interactions between diseases and habitat, wildlife host species, domestic animals, and man are all relevant to wilderness management policy.

DISEASE AND WILDERNESS PRESERVATION

When we conjure up visions of wilderness, we are likely to think of early explorers' accounts of their struggles with the elements, hostile natives, and diseases. Although some may view wilderness as serene, peaceful places, many wilderness areas exist only because meteorologic, geologic, or disease conditions prevented man from inhabiting these areas. The role of disease in the preservation of wilderness has been relatively great. For example, the tsetse fly, a vector of sleeping sickness in man and nagana in livestock, denied man use of an area that may be as great as one fourth of the African continent (James and Harwood 1969: 272). However, recent tsetse fly control efforts have resulted in major ingress of man and his livestock into wilderness areas and subsequent habitat changes in large areas of Africa (MacLennan 1973, Molyneux 1982). Other diseases, such as malaria, yellow fever, leishmaniasis, Chagas disease, plague, dengue, and encephalitis have played similar roles in the preservation of wilderness in many areas of the world. Albeit disease has not had as great an impact on wilderness preservation in North America as some other regions of the world, it can still be thought of as one factor impeding man's encroachment into some areas. For example, human malaria was present in the United States until 1950 (Chandler and Read 1961: 168). The associations between swampland, mosquitoes and other biting insects, malaria, yellow fever, dengue, and encephalitis undoubtedly had some influence on human habitation of swamplands in the southeastern United States.

HABITAT AND DISEASE

Some disease agents may be more specifically regulated by habitat type than by host distribution or density. This fact is particularly true for arthropod vectored diseases, because arthropods may be specifically tied to habitat types. One study germane to the potential impact of wilderness designation on animal diseases in the southeastern United States was conducted by Handrick (1981). In that study, three forest types (pine, hardwood, mixed pine-hardwood) in east-central Mississippi were evaluated for the presence of biting arthropods. Deer flies and horse flies (Tabinids) were found to be most numerous in pine habitats, whereas mosquitoes were found to be most numerous in mature hardwood forests, and ticks were most numerous in mixed pine-hardwood forests (Table 1). This demonstrates that forest types have a major influence on

Table 1. Effect of Forest Type on Species and Number of Biting Arthropods Sampled in East-Central Mississippi.[1]

Forest Type	Tabanids		Mosquitoes		Ticks	
	Total Species	x̄ Number Captured per Sample Period	Total Species	x̄ Number Captured per Sample Period	Total Species	x̄ Number Captured per Sample
Mature hardwoods	8	4.9	16	136.2	0	0
Immature hardwoods	6	1.8	3	0.5	1	0.1
Mature pines	11	7.6	16	6.6	1	0.3
Immature pines	16	19.8	11	3.0	2	0.5
Mature pine-hardwoods	4	3.9	6	3.2	2	1.3

[1] Data compiled from Handrick (1981); Tabanids were sampled by CO_2 baited malaise traps for 24-hour periods. Mosquitoes were sampled by CO_2 baited CDC light traps for 24-hour periods and ticks were samples by cloth drags over 50m transects.

species of arthropod vectors. Thus, replacing a hardwood forest with a managed pine forest could change the entire complex of diseases present. Similarly, allowing natural succession of plant communities can be expected to change the complex of diseases present. Habitat destruction has been a major factor in control of tsetse flies (Molyneaux 1982). Other studies have shown many parasites are more likely regulated by habitat factors than by host densities (Jacobson et al. 1978a; Jacobson et al. 1981). Obvious disease-habitat relationships are the presence of human malaria, dengue, yellow fever, and encephalitis. Because these diseases are transmitted by mosquitoes, their occurrence is largely associated with swampland and the mosquitoes which dwell there. Preservation of wilderness areas also results in preservation of specific habitat types and will be conducive to maintenance of specific diseases associated with those habitats.

WILDLIFE HOSTS AND DISEASE

Although habitat is an important factor in disease prevalence, a second factor in the relationship between wilderness and disease is that the wild animals which dwell there are hosts for agents that cause disease in man and domestic animals. The timber wolf (Canis lupus) and the coyote (Canis latrans) are normal hosts for a small tapeworm (Echinococcus granulosus), the eggs of which can cause a fatal cancer-like disease of man known as hydatid disease (Schiller 1960). The raccoon (Procyon lotor) is a normal host of a large roundworm (Baylisascaris procyonis), the larvae of which can cause a fatal central nervous system disease in other animals and man (Kazacos 1983). The beaver (Caster canadensis) is the normal host of an intestinal protozoan parasite (Giardia lamblia), and this parasite has been implicated in diarrheal outbreaks of humans drinking untreated water in both residential and wilderness areas (Wallis et al. 1984; Taylor et al. 1983). Zimmerman (1971) implicates 104 species of wildlife as hosts for Trichinella spiralis, the causative agent of trichinosis in man and other animals.

Wild animals inhabiting wilderness areas are also reservoirs of important diseases of domestic animals and man. Fifty-seven wild rodent species or their ectoparasites are known to be carriers of plague (Yersinia pestis) in the United States (Olsen 1970) and surveillance data from 1970-1980 has shown evidence of plague infection in 76 species of five mammalian orders (Barnes 1982). This disease, which killed millions in medieval Europe and Asia, has been reported in the western United States since 1908; it has spread eastward and the number of cases has risen from an average of two per year during 1925-1964 to 16 cases per year since 1975 (Barnes op. cit.). The bison (Bison bison) and its maintenance and transmission of tuberculosis, brucellosis, and anthrax has been a source of controversy for the Wood Buffalo National Park in Canada (Broughton 1983, Gainer 1982). Skunks, raccoons, bats, and foxes are all principal wildlife species involved in rabies transmission and maintenance (Sikes 1970). The cottontail rabbit (Sylvilagus floridanus) is the primary reservoir host of Rocky Mountain fever (Davis 1953, Burgdorfer et al. 1974) and also the primary transfer host of tularemia (Francisella tularensis) (Jellison 1974). A large number of other wildlife hosts are also involved in the epidemiology of these frequently fatal diseases of man.

THREAT OF FOREIGN DISEASE

Introduction of foreign diseases and the threat of establishment of these diseases in wildlife inhabiting wilderness is another concern. Foot and Mouth disease, rinderpest, and contagious bovine pleuropneumonia are responsible for losses to millions of cattle outside the United States (McVicar et al. 1981). Introduction of Foot and Mouth disease in California in 1924 resulted in the slaughter of 22,000 black-tailed deer (Odocoileus hemionus) as part of the control effort to prevent this disease from establishing itself in North America (Keane 1926). An additional 20,000 white-tailed deer (O. virginianus) were killed in Florida during a cattle fever tick (Boophilus microplus) eradication campaign (Kistner and Hayes 1970). In the event of foreign disease introduction, dramatic measures may be necessary to prevent their establishment in the United States and certainly wilderness policy should allow for this contingency.

MANAGEMENT OF DISEASE IN WILDERNESS AREAS

Examples of habitat and wildlife importance in maintenance and transmission of human and domestic animal diseases could fill an extensive reference text. However, the few examples mentioned should serve to demonstrate the complexity and concerns for wilderness and disease relationships. The question to be asked is how should these relationships affect our acquisition and management of wilderness areas? First we must recognize that disease is a normal part of the ecology of any wild species. The cottontail rabbit, for example, is the known host for over 175 separate disease agents (Jacobson 1976). Except in the case of foreign diseases, it is almost without exception too costly or impractical to attempt to eradicate diseases that are reservoired in wildlife. However, it is practical to manage some wildlife populations. Large ungulates and some furbearers can be kept at healthy population levels through sport hunting and trapping, and this usually offers the best alternative to limiting disease problems associated with these species. Control of rodent populations in campground areas and other high recreational use areas is also practical in some situations. Most diseases are not as likely to spread in healthy host populations. Additionally, reduction or control of some diseases would require habitat destruction or removal of wildlife host species. These are generally unacceptable alternatives to wilderness preservation. Some measures of disease prevention and control are practical and should be emphasized. These measures include the prophylactic measures of never drinking untreated water or eating uncooked meat. Insecticides and clothing offer personal protection against biting arthropods. Twice-daily personal inspection and removal of ticks before attachment can be an effective deterent to tick-born diseases. Sound trash disposal habits reduce unwanted contacts with wildlife and their external and internal parasites around campsites. Campground construction and campsite locations are also important considerations. Habitat modification, trapping, toxins, shooting, and screening are techniques which can be used in local control efforts (Hawthorne 1980). Perhaps the most important measure is information and education to the public using a particular wilderness area. Information should be provided on diseases endemic to an area which pose a threat to human health or welfare. Almost all diseases that might be encountered in wilderness areas can be prevented or their dangers greatly lessened by precautionary measures and a knowledgeable public.

POSITIVE DISEASE VALUES

Although this paper has concentrated on some of the more negative aspects of disease, we must also think of the positive. There is scientific and biological value to diseases of wildlife. Disease certainly has played and will play a selection role in the evolution of animals and plants, and species fitness is likely to be enhanced by continued exposure to many disease agents. Disease is a prime factor in keeping many wildlife populations in balance with their habitat. There are some diseases that may be important to man in other ways. Botflies (*Cuterebra* spp.) cause maggot infestation (myiasis) of rodents and lagomorphs and incidental infestations of dogs, cats, cattle, hogs, and man (Jacobson *et al.* 1978b). However, the maggots secrete a bacteriostatic agent that prevents secondary infection in its normal host. (Landi 1960). It is conceivable to think that this bacteriostatic agent may some day be of value to medicine. Examples do exist of the use of maggot infestation to clean wounds of soldiers in wartime (James and Harwood 1969: 298).

There is also a psychologic value of disease in wilderness. Disease was part of the wilderness challenge faced by early explorers. Somehow a wilderness that is without disease threats or other such dangers is like Aldo Leopold's mountain without a grizzly bear (Leopold 1949: 145). A mountain without a grizzly bear is considerably different than one that has one; a wilderness that is free of disease threats is somehow also not the same. Finally, we must realize that although wilderness areas have specific disease problems because of the habitat and the animals that dwell there, removal of the wilderness does not remove disease. The habitat may change from woodlawn to asphalt, and diseases like Giardiasis and malaria may change to diseases like emphysema and cancer.

LITERATURE CITED

Barnes, A.M. 1982. Surveillance and control of bubonic plague in the United States. pp. 237-268. *In* M.A. Edwards and U. McDonnel, (eds.). Animal disease in relation to animal conservation. Symp. Zool. Soc. Lond. No. 50. Academic Press Inc., London.

Broughton, E. 1983. Wood Buffalo National Park: A Different Perspective (Wildlife Disease Newsletter, Supplement) J. Wildl. Dis. 19:No. 3.

Burgdorfer, W., J.C. Cooney and L.A. Thomas. 1974. Zoonotic potential (Rocky Mountain spotted fever and tularemia) in Tennessee Valley region II. Prevalence of *Rickettsia ricketesi* and *Francisella tularensis* in mammals and ticks from Land Between the Lakes. Am. J. Trop. Med. Hyg. 23:109-117.

Chandler, A.C. and C.P. Read. 1961. Introduction to parasitology, 10th ed. John Wiley & Sons, Inc. New York, N.Y.

Davis, E. 1953. Studies on rabbits and spotted fever. Trans. N. Amer. Wildl. Conf. 18:188-190.

Gainer, R. 1982. Wood Buffalo Park has problems (Wildlife Disease Newsletter, Supplement). J. Wildl. Dis. 18:No. 4

Handrick, P.J. 1981. Associations between forest management practices and zoonotic disease vectors in east central Miss. M.S. Thesis. Miss. State Univ., Miss. State, Miss.

Hawthorne, D.W. 1980. Wildlife damage and control techniques. pp. 411-440. *In* S.D. Schemnitz, (ed.). Wildlife management techniques manual. The Wildlife Society. Washington, D.C.

Jacobson, H.A. 1976. Investigation of a major reduction in hunter harvest of the cottontail rabbit in southeastern Virginia. Ph.D. Diss. Va. Polytech. Inst. and State Univ., Blacksburg, Va.

Jacobson, H.A., R.L. Kirkpatrick and B.S. McGinnes. 1978a. Disease and physiologic characteristics of two cottontail populations in Virginia. Wildl. Monogr. 60.

Jacobson, H.A., B.S. McGinnes and E.P. Catts. 1978b. Botfly myiasis of the cottontail rabbit, *Sylvilagus floridanus mallurus* in Virginia with some biology of the parasite *Cuterebra buccata*. J. Wildl. Dis. 14:56-66.

Jacobson, H.S. M.S. Hetrick and D.C. Guynn. 1981. Prevalence of *Cuterebra emasculator* in squirrels in Mississippi. J. Wildl. Dis. 17:78-87.

James, M.T. and R.F. Harwood. 1969. Herm's medical entomology, 6th ed. MacMillin Co., Collier-MacMillin Limited, London.

Jellison, W.L. 1974. Tularemia in North America. Univ. of Montana Foundation, Missoula, Montana.

Kazacos, K.R. 1983. Raccoon roundworms (*Baylisascaris procyonis*) a cause of animal and human disease. Purdue Research Foundation, West Lafayette, Ind.

Keane, C. 1926. The epizootic of foot-and-mouth disease in California. Calif. Dep. Agric. Spec. Publ. No. 65.

Kistner, T.P. and F.A. Hayes. 1970. White-tailed deer as hosts of cattle fever-ticks. J. Wildl. Dis. 6:437-440.

Landi, S. 1960. Bacteriostatic effect of haemolymph of larvae of various botflies. Can. J. Microbiol. 6:115-119.

Leopold, A. 1949. A sand county almanac. Oxford Univ. Press Inc., Oxford.

MacLennan, K.J. 1973. A consideration of environmental consequences following anti-tsetse operations in Nigeria. Trop. Ani. Health and Prod. 4:40-45.

McVicar, J.W., F.M. Handy and R.J. Yedloutschnig. 1981. Foreign infectious diseases. pp. 396-412. *In* W.R. Davidson, F.H. Hayes, V.F. Nettles, F.E. Kellogg (eds.). Diseases and parasites of white-tailed deer. Tall Timber Research Station, Tallahassee, Flor.

Molyneux, D.H. 1982. Tryapanosomes, trypanosomiasis and tsetse control: Impact on wildlife and its conservation. pp. 29-56. *In* M.A. Edwards and U. McDonnell (eds.). Animal disease in relation to animal conservation. Symp. Zool. Soc. Lond., No. 50. Academic Press, Inc., London.

Olsen, P.F. 1970. Sylvatic (wild rodent) plague. pp. 200-213. *In* J.W. Davis, L.H. Karstad and D.O. Trainer (eds.). Infectious diseases of wild mammals. Iowa State Univ. Press, Ames, Iowa.

Schiller, E.L. 1960. Echinococcosis in North America. Ann. Inter. Med. 52:464.

Sikes, R.K. 1970. Rabies. pp. 3-19. *In* J.W. Davis, L.H. Karstad, and D.O. Trainer (eds.). Infectious diseases of wild mammals. Iowa State Univ. Press, Ames, Iowa.

Taylor, D.N., K.T. McDermott, J.R. Little, J.G. Wells and M.J. Balser. 1983. Campylobacter enteritis from untreated water in the Rocky Mountains. Ann. Inter. Med. 99:38-39.

Wallis, P.M., J.M. Buchanan-Mappin, G.M. Faubert and M. Belosevic. 1984. Reservoirs of Giardia spp. in southwestern Alberta. J. Wildl. Res. 20:279-283.

Zimmerman, W.J. 1971. Trichinosis. pp. 127-139. *In* J.W. Davis and R.G. Anderson (eds.). Parasitic diseases of wild mammals. Iowa State Univ. Press, Ames, Iowa

The Role Of Eastern Wilderness And Natural Areas As Genetic Preserves

by
W. Alex Wall and Carol K. Evans

ABSTRACT--Genetic variation within populations should be conserved for both human interests and preservation of adaptive potential within species. Eastern wilderness and natural areas can play a significant role as genetic preserves by: 1) preserving locally adapted gene complexes across species distributions, 2) providing necessary mature, stable communities to preserve a broad selection continuum and to allow previously co-adapted species refuge from chronic environmental change, 3) acting as reintroduction sites for captively bred species and refuges for multiple populations of endangered species, and 4) furnishing natural laboratories for studying the genetic processes of populations. Minimum population size, natural selection pressures and gene flow between local populations are generally deemed necessary for retention of adaptive potential within populations. Since many eastern wilderness areas are small, management practices on surrounding lands should be structured to help provide habitat to maintain critical size of core populations contained within wilderness areas and allow gene flow between local populations on surrounding lands. Populations contained within National Forest Wilderness Areas should be excluded from calculations of minimum viable populations.

KEYWORDS: genetic conservation, minimum viable population, wilderness management.

As intensity of land use increases on public, private and corporate lands, continued reduction and fragmentation of naturally diverse communities is inevitable. Intensive forestry and agricultural practices continually disturb successional patterns and reduce community diversity resulting in altered and marginal habitats for some wildlife species. We can assume that in the future, most undisturbed communities in the eastern United States will be confined to Wilderness and Natural Areas (WANA). These areas can play a significant role in preservation of locally adapted gene complexes and the natural processes which maintain them.

In a discussion of genetic conservation and the evolutionary ethic, Frankel (1974) demonstrated the need for conservation of adaptive potential within natural communities. The preservation of gene pools for agriculture, new domesticates, forestry, research and education was named as an anthropocentric need. Frankel concluded that apart from human endeavors "evolution itself has an intrinsic value" and suggested a human responsibility "to keep evolutionary options open." This goal can only be accomplished by giving consideration to genetics during natural resource management practices.

This paper addresses the need for genetic conservation in dynamic communities of all successional stages and the roles WANA can play. Inherent problems related to area size and isolation of WANA such as small population size, minimum viable populations (MVP) and loss of genetic variability are discussed. Possible management solutions and research opportunities are proposed. Complete reviews of genetic conservation may be found in three recent texts: Soule' and Wilcox (1980), Frankel and Soule' (1981), and Schonewald-Cox, et al. (1983)

GENETIC CONSERVATION

The recognition that genetic variation within populations is necessary for maintenance of adaptive potential in wild species and is crucial for genetic improvement of cultivated species came early to plant geneticists. In the 1920's a Russian genticist, Vavilar, described 'centers of diversity' throughout the world as geographical locations of great genetic variation in ancient forms of locally adapted agricultural crops (Harlan 1975). These ancient forms, although low in productivity, were known to contain potential resistant adaptations to disease, insects, and environmental heterogeneity. Since the 1940's, plant breeders have expressed concern about the loss of genetic diversity in agricultural crops due to the use of 'improved', genetically narrow-based, high-yield varieties. In the 1960's world-wide programs were initiated to collect seeds from these primitive land varieties and store them in 'gene banks' for future use (Harlan 1975).

In the 1940's the forestry industry became concerned over the poor quality of naturally regenerated stands resulting from high grading logging practices. Forest tree improvement programs began in earnest in 1950 (Zobel and Talbert 1984). The result has been artificial genetic selection of superior quality trees which can only maximize their gain in volume through intensive forest management practices such as clearcutting (E. Long, pers. comm.). This strategy reduces the genetic base of commercial trees by replacing wild, genetically variable stands with pure stands of highly related trees. These practices create a paradox. Forest tree geneticists have recognized the need to preserve reservoirs of genetic variation in natural stands throughout a species' range while maintaining high productivity (van Buijtenen et al. 1981). Zobel and Talbert (1984) also pointed out that a major objective of tree improvement is to maintain genetic variability within target species. Multiple WANA across biotic regions may provide a source of locally adapted gene complexes throughout a tree species' distribution for future use in tree improvement programs.

Unfortunately, gene banking and breeding programs cannot be applied to most wild faunal species. The application of conservation biology principles are necessary if natural community diversity and adaptive potential are to be retained. This new multiple discipline is considered by Soule' and Wilcox (1980) to be a "new rallying point for biologists" concerned with nature conservation. Population genetics coupled with island ecology theory, two major disciplines of conservation biology, has initiated theoretical discussions regarding design and management of nature reserves (Diamond and May 1976, Frankel and Soule' 1981, Simberloff and Abele 1982, Harris 1984). Of primary concern are the size and number of reserves within biomes and the effective population size of species maintained within these areas. Habitat loss and fragmentation resulting in isolated remnant populations will be a major cause of loss of adaptive potential through inbreeding and genetic drift (Lovejoy 1977, Franklin 1980). Genetic constraints and evolutionary consequences of small population size including inbreeding depression are reviewed by Lovejoy (1977), Franklin (1980), and Harris et al. (1984). Some of the major goals of conservation biology are to determine effective population size necessary to maintain adaptive potential, to establish area size required to maintain viable populations, and to design management strategies to enhance both (Frankel 1974, Diamond and May 1976, Lovejoy 1977, Soule' 1980, Frankel and Soule' 1981, Shaffer 1981, Simberloff and Abele 1982, Frankel 1983).

An excellent example of the problems developed in wild species through loss of genetic variability may be found in cheetahs, (Acinonyx jubatus) (O'Brien et al. 1985) and Brown-eared Pheasants (Crossoptilan mantchuricum) (Anon. 1977). Cheetahs are extremely homozygous at surveyed gene loci and are believed to have passed through a severe bottleneck in recent evolutionary history. Their genetic vulnerability has been demonstrated by the difficulty of breeding in captivity, a high incidence of infant mortality in both captive and wild pop-

ulations, a high percentage of morphologically abnormal spermatozoa and decimation of a previously healthy captive population by a feline viral infection (O'Brien et al. 1985). Most of the Brown-eared Pheasants in the West descended from one male and two females captured in 1864, an extremely small founder population. In recent times most eggs layed have been infertile, however, artificially inseminated eggs produced 53% fertility. This points to a breakdown in breeding behavior believed to be genetically related.

Although many genetics surveys have been conducted on all taxonomic levels of faunal species (Powell 1975, Nevo 1978), little empirical data is available on the genetic effects of management strategies on either game or nongame species. However, the need for and application of genetic considerations to various management strategies has been addressed. Smith et al. (1976) discussed the application of population genetics to management of faunal populations. Computer simulation was used by Ryman et al. (1981) to model the long-term effects of different harvest strategies on allelic heterozygosity in moose (Alces alces) and white-tailed deer (Odocoileus virginianus). Wall and Kroll (unpubl. data, Table 1) have determined that past harvest strategies of buck exploitation in white-tailed deer have maintained a low effective population size in local demes which theoretically decreases the amount of genetic variability through increased inbreeding. Preliminary electrophoretic data suggest a possible loss of genetic variability (Table 2). Deer herds which have been subjected to the most intense buck exploitation for the longest period of time (NB, Mal, and CC-CS, Table 2) have a lower heterozygosity level for transferrin than do the other herds which have had mitigating management. NB and Mal are contiguous populations recently separated by deer proof fence. Although managed essentially the same historically, NB has recently been subjected to intense doe harvest. This has decreased the buck:doe ratio and increased the effective population size. Although no baseline data are available for comparison, it appears that the NB population is becoming more heterozygous, probably due to greater buck dispersal. Thus, management strategies do effect the genetic variability in populations. Long term studies are needed to determine how management policies effect both game and nongame species.

HABITAT CONTINUUM

Natural selection is a synergistic process occurring at the interface of individuals and their multidimensional niches. Lewontin (1974) described a species as "always slightly behind, slightly ill-adapted, eventually becoming extinct as it fails to keep up with the changing environment because it runs out of genetic variation on which natural selection can operate." Maintenance of genetic

Table 1. Calculation of Effective Population Size for Seven Differentially Managed Deer Populations in Eastern Texas.

Population	NB[1]	MAL[1]	DH[2]	FC[2]	CC-CS	TM[3]	WMA[3]
Area size (ha)	3854	2428	1295	5059	2752	2833	4047
Census size (N)	633	600	267	1041	850	467	1000
Buck:doe ratio	1:2	1:6	1:8	1:8	1:11	1:0.85	1:2
Effective population size (Ne)*	563	295	103	409	287	464	888
$\%\dfrac{Ne}{N}$	88.8	49.1	38.7	39.3	33.8	99.4	88.8

*$Ne = \dfrac{1}{(^{1}/_{4}N_m + ^{1}/_{4}N_f)}$ where N_m = # of breeding males and N_f = # of breeding females.

1–2–3 each pair is a contiguous population, NB and MAL, and TM and WMA are divided by deer proof fence.

Table 2. Fixation Index and Heterozygosity of the Transferrin Locus for Seven Differentially Managed Deer Populations in Eastern Texas.

Population	NB	MAL	DH	FC	CC-CS	TM	WMA
Sample size	207	99	127	169	165	89	86
Heterozygosity	.179	.111	.362	.308	.164	.236	.372
Fixation index	.040	.094	.001	.100	.178	.222	.051

variation through selection and its relevance to adaptive potential is still debated (Powell 1975, Nevo 1978). In stable communities two of the driving forces behind natural selection are believed to be competition and predation (Schoener 1982). However, species do not exist only in stable environments, but are differentially adapted along a multidimensional habitat continuum creating specialists and generalists, old-growth, intermediate, and pioneer successional species.

The natural selection process is so complex that it would be extremely difficult to measure the synergistic effect of community diversity on genomes. However, Nevo and Bar (1976) demonstrated differential selection patterns for protein polymorphism along a moisture cline in the white garden snail (*Theba pisana*), a habitat generalist. Nevo (1976) examined the amount of genetic variation in 4 anurans: 1 specialist, 2 intermediates, and 1 generalist. He found a positive correlation between the amount of environmental heterogeneity experienced by each species and the amount of genetic heterozygosity. These results indicate that selection plays a role in the amount of genetic variation within a species. However, Franklin (1980) concluded that population size and balance between mutation and genetic drift probably have a much greater effect on variation than does selection, especially in smaller populations. Thus, it appears from current knowledge, that both large population size and selection pressures are necessary to maintain adaptive potential within populations.

Hendee et al. (1978) categorizes wildlife species into three useful but relative groups: 1) wilderness dependent species, 2) wilderness associated species, and 3) common wildlife found in wilderness. WANA will provide habitat and selection pressures differentially for each group. For example, the Florida panther, (*Felis concolor coryi*), a wilderness dependent species, may depend entirely on the Big Cypress Preserve to provide habitat for maintenance of a population sufficient in size to retain adaptive potential. The black bear (*Ursus americana*), a wilderness associated species, prefers both old and new growth habitat. These bears may depend on wilderness to provide winter denning sites in over mature trees and disperse into surrounding lands the rest of the year. Species of habitat generalists with demes found throughout successional stages may retain greater genetic variation (Chesser 1983). Thus, both wilderness associated and common species may benefit genetically from WANA through retention of larger population sizes and old growth habitat.

Hendee et al. (1978) asserts "classified wilderness in particular protects habitats which have been modified but little from the conditions under which their biotic communities evolved." WANA will provide some mature, stable communities necessary to maintain a broad selection continuum, provide needed habitat for wilderness dependent species, and allow previously co-adapted species a refuge from chronic environmental changes.

ENDANGERED SPECIES

With the world-wide extinction rate of higher vertebrates expected to reach 40 to 400 times that of the history of life (Ehrlich et al. 1977), the need to manage small remnant populations becomes very important. Captive breeding programs for endangered species suffice for immediate survival and reintroductions. However, this strategy is fraught with problems of expense, animal be-

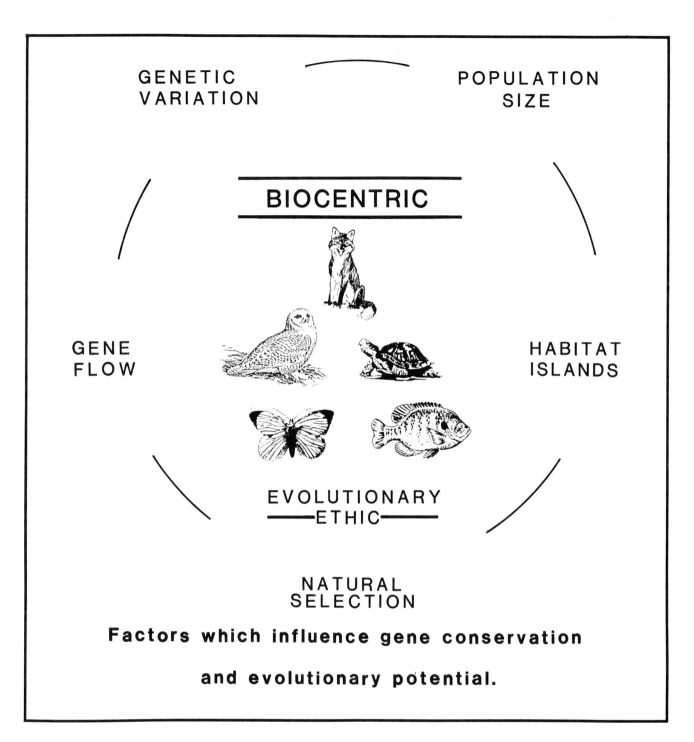

GENETIC
VARIATION

POPULATION
SIZE

BIOCENTRIC

GENE
FLOW

HABITAT
ISLANDS

EVOLUTIONARY
—ETHIC—

NATURAL
SELECTION

Factors which influence gene conservation

and evolutionary potential.

havior, loss of fitness through inbreeding, and genetic drift of chronically small populations (Conway 1980, Kleinman 1980, and Campbell 1980). Wild faunal species must be maintained in dynamic, diverse communities where natural selection and genetic variation work in synchrony to maintain co-adapted gene complexes (Frankel 1974), and behavioral abilities (Campbell 1980).

Most researchers believe that multiple populations of rare species are more desirable than are large, single populations (Soule' 1980, Frankel and Soule' 1981, Chesser 1983). Chesser (1983) noted that exchange of breeding individuals between managed populations will slow the loss of genetic variation. Small populations lose genetic variation quicker than large ones and thus require a

greater proportion of immigration to prevent loss of fitness (Allendorf and Phelps 1981, Allendorf 1983). In cases of endangered species, Frankel and Soule' (1981) have recommended artificial migration of 1-5 reproductively successful individuals per generation among isolated populations to maintain scarce alleles within all populations. Some researchers argue against wholesale artificial migration (Greig 1979, Harris 1984). Most species are composed of multiple locally adapted demes or ecotypes. Exchange between distant demes may upset the balance of locally adapted gene complexes, doing more harm than good. Thus, the importance of maintaining several local populations and allowing natural exchange is accentuated. WANA can provide undisturbed habitat for rare species,

MINIMUM VIABLE POPULATIONS

Due to the small size of most eastern WANA (Table 3), management practices on surrounding lands will have a major impact on species contained within these areas. The National Forest Management Act (NFMA) of 1976 declared that viable populations of all native vertebrate species must be maintained in their natural distribution on all National Forest Service (NFS) lands (Lehmkuhl 1984). Since many WANA are contained within the boundaries of NFS lands, the interpretation and implementation of this policy may have a dramatic effect on vertebrate populations and gene pools in wilderness areas. Franklin (1980) and Soule' (1980) introduced the idea that minimum viable population (MVP) should maintain an effective population size of 50 for short term maintenance of genetic fitness and 500 for long term. Hence, the interpretation of the NFMA changed from viable populations to MVP. These concepts were general and intended only to serve as a starting point for determining population size sufficient for retention of adaptive potential.

Basic to determining the MVP size is calculation of the effective population size (Ne). As stated by Ryman et al. (1981) "effective population size is defined as the size of an 'ideal' population having the same amount of drift and inbreeding as that occurring in the population actually considered." The ideal population is assumed to have a constant census size, nonoverlapping generations, equal sex ratios and random mating (Wright 1978). Census number (N) is usually larger than the effective number (Table 1) depending on population structure and breeding strategy. The idea of MVP is actually based on an effective population of sufficient size to keep the inbreeding coefficient below 1% per generation (Soule' 1980). Generally, the inbreeding coefficient is calculated from effective population size, however other factors are involved. The fixation index is an actual inbreeding coefficient calculated from allelic frequencies (Table 2). Population TM with an effective population size of 464 has the highest fixation index at 22.2%, while DH with an effective size of 103 has the lowest fixation index. This preliminary data demonstrates the problems of calculating MVP strictly from effective population size. Breeding behavior, population structure, density, dispersal rates, and population history can play major roles in the rate of allelic fixation actually occurring. Species may be divided into groups which are adapted to inbreeding and those that are obligate outbreeders with different gradations in between them (Greig 1979). Thus, each species will react to small population size and inbreeding differently. As an alternative to use of MVP, R. N. Conner (pers. comm.), has suggested the use of an ecologically functional population size which is a fraction of maximum population size and includes factors such as reproductive capability, demographic stochasticity, and social reproductive behavior instead of a strictly genetic approach.

At this time, all definitions of MVP are tenuous and lack empirical data, therefore, a conservative approach to the implementation of MVP should be taken. Populations of indicator species contained within WANA should be excluded from calculations of MVP on other NFS lands. If this approach is taken, gene flow between WANA populations and those either scattered or clumped within the National Forest may be possible. However, if MVP are maintained only within and on the periphery of WANA, gene pool isolation may put small populations at greater risk to loss of genetic variation. For current definitions and proposals for determining MVP see Shaffer (1981), Lehmkuhl (1984), and Lacava and Hughes (1984).

INHERENT PROBLEMS AND MANAGEMENT

Loss of community diversity and genetic variation within species contained on WANA will stem from two ecological phenomena: area size and isolation (Wilcox 1980, Soule'1980). Inferences from island ecology (species-area-distance relationships) (Diamond and Mayr 1976, Gilpin and Diamond 1976, Diamond et al. 1976) have been used to predict the rate of extinction of species in refuges (Soule' et al. 1979). Willis (cited in Terborgh and Winter 1980) demonstrated a loss of diversity with data on breeding bird species from three remnant forests in Sao Paulo, Brazil. Deforestation in these areas began about 150 years ago, but isolation probably began 20 to 40 years ago. Of 203 original nesting species, 76, 119, and 175 remain in three respective areas of 21, 250 and 1400 hectares. Many small WANA may follow similar patterns of decreasing species richness depending on area size, degree of isolation and particular species requirements. In addition, Wilcox (1980) described the 'sample effect' for refugia. Extrapolating from observed samples, Wilcox estimated that each 10-fold decrease in area of nature reserves excludes 30% of species within that biotic region.

Gorman et al. (1975) demonstrated effects of chronically small, isolated populations on genetic variation by comparing allelic heterozygosity of two lizard species found on islands of different size. Heterozygosity remained essentially unchanged above 5 ha. Below 5 ha. heterozygosity dropped to almost zero in both species. From these data Soule' (1980) suggested that island area has little effect on genetic variability of a population until a critical size is reached. If this relationship is applicable to other species, then for a particular species, critical size of a refuge will be partially a function of trophic level, body size, and size class within guilds (Terborgh 1974).

A summary of WANA sizes in the eastern U.S. (Table 3) shows approximately 65% of eastern WANA are under 4,000 ha, and 5 of 129 areas contain 71.7% of the total eastern wilderness. This area-size distribution does not allow for maximum genetic conservation. Small

Table 3. Size Classification of Eastern U.S. Wilderness and Natural Areas.

| | Wilderness and Natural Areas | | | |
	All	Under 4,000 (ha)	4,000–20,000 (ha)	Over 20,000 (ha)
Total number	129	84	40	5
Total area (ha)	1,497,903	150,697	273,028	1,074,178
Average area (ha)	11,612	1,794	6,826	214,836
% Total number	—	65.1	31.0	3.9
% Total area	—	10.1	18.2	71.7

WANA surrounded by private or corporate land are at greatest risk for the effects of isolation. In general, large WANA and those surrounded by National Forests will retain greater diversity and more variable gene pools.

Maintenance of genetic diversity can be maximized by three basic management strategies within NFS land surrounding WANA:

1) Exclude populations within WANA from estimates for MVP on surrounding NFS lands (see MVP section)
2) Create buffer zones around small WANA which maximize diversity by containing all stages of succession.
3) Leave travel corridors, especially along riparian zones, for gene flow enhancement between local populations. We offer a general definition of a buffer zone as an area surrounding and approximately one-half the size of a small WANA (under 4000 ha). Hoover and Willis (1984) and Harris (1984) have reviewed the use of silvicultural practices for creating wildlife habitat. A conceptual model for surrounding core conservation areas (such as WANA) by buffers to increasingly intensive management is given by Harris (1984).

The use of travel corridors for gene flow between refuges has been discussed by Soule' (1980) and Frankel and Soule' (1981). Harris (1984: 148-149) has suggested riparian travel corridors eminating from WANA and interconnecting 'old-growth islands' within surrounding National Forest. Implementation of this concept would create multiple travel routes to facilitate dispersal between WANA and populations in surrounding areas.

RESEARCH OPPORTUNITIES

Many theoretical observations and extrapolation of limited empirical data have been applied to major topics involved in conservation biology including refuge design, strategies to maintain adaptive potential, MVP size, and species-area relations (Soule' and Wilcox 1980, Frankel and Soule' 1981, Schonewald-Cox *et al.* 1983). Action for genetic conservation must begin now while genetic diversity still exists. Frankel and Soule' (1981) have stated that reserve management will be a 'seat-of-the-pants' application of general principles until more exacting empirical data can be obtained.

WANA offer natural laboratories for comparisons between undisturbed and chronically disturbed communities. These areas can also provide opportunities for

various research projects, whose results may be applied world-wide in refugia for remnant populations:
1) Long term floral and faunal surveys of replicated community types and species populations within WANA of varying size classes and degrees of isolation will allow estimates of extinction rates within refuge communities.
2) Changing community structure will alter selection pressures (Liu and Godt 1983) for species which remain extant under multiple benefit management. Studies designed to follow the local genetic divergence of populations within WANA and those in surrounding areas may give insight into the disputed way species adapt to changing environments.
3) Multiple small populations of species isolated within different WANA can reveal information on rates of genetic change and evidence of how populations diverge through drift.
4) Comparisons of the genetic variation of isolated populations versus partially isolated ones may yield data on the importance of dispersal to the maintenance of genetic variation.
5) Multiple WANA containing similar species offer an opportunity to test various management strategies including buffer zones, migration corridors, and artificial migration.

CONCLUSIONS

We have briefly reviewed the history of growing concern for gene conservation. Some conservationists fear not only for the extinction of species but for the loss of diverse natural processes which give rise to the biotic diversity on earth. Our species has become a major aspect of the evolutionary process. We can either accept responsibility and leave maximum evolutionary options open or refuse involvement and unconsciously allow the loss of evolutionary potential within many species. Whichever path we chose, man will have a dramatic effect on the evolutionary direction of life.

Hendee *et al.* (1978) in a discussion of wildlife management in wilderness states: "Even more significant, though less obvious, is the role of wilderness as a hidden trove of those recessive genes necessary for genetic adaptability in the face of environmental change." WANA offer an opportunity for preserving small segments of undisturbed habitat for the maintenance of naturally adapted gene complexes and rare alleles within populations. Management policies on lands surrounding these areas will have an effect on the variability of gene pools contained within WANA. Many of the concepts discussed lack empirical data and much research is needed to establish the best methods for retaining adaptive potentials within species and determining MVP. Until more is known about these processes, maximum area and diversity should be preserved, especially for rare species.

ACKNOWLEDGEMENTS

This paper was supported by the Institute for White-Tailed Deer Management and Research and the Center for Applied Studies, Stephen F. Austin State University School of Forestry. The authors wish to thank Dr. David L. Kulhavy for help with the initial idea for the paper and Dr. Richard N. Conner for his consultation and encouragement. Dr. Paul R. Ramsey provided helpful criticism of the manuscript.

LITERATURE CITED

Allendorf, F.W. 1983. Isolation, gene flow, and genetic differentiation among populations. pp. 51-65. *In* Genetics and Conservation. C.M. Schonewald-Cox, S.M. Chambers, B. Macbryde, and L. Thomas (eds.). Benjamin/Cummings Publishing Co., Inc., Menlo Park, Calif.

Allendorf, F.W. and S.R. Phelps. 1981. Use of allelic frequencies to describe population structure. Can. J. Fish Aquat. Sci. 38:1507-1514.

Anon. 1977. Inbreeding and behavior. Oryx 14:309.

Campbell, S. 1980. Is reintroduction a realistic goal. pp. 263-270. *In* M.E. Soule' and B.A. Wilcox (eds.). Conservation Biology: An Evolutionary-Ecological Perspective. Sinauer Associates, Sunderland, Mass.

Chesser, R.K. 1983. Isolation by distance: Relationship to the management of genetic resources. pp. 66-77. *In* C.M. Schonewald-Cox, S.M. Chambers, B. Macbryde, and L. Thomas (eds.). Benjamin/Cummings Publishing Co., Inc. Menlo Park, Calif.

Conway, W.G. 1980. An overview of captive propagation. pp. 199-207. *In* M.E. Soule' and B.A. Wilcox (eds.). Conservation Biology: An Evolutionary-Ecological Perspective. Sinauer Associates, Sunderland, Mass.

Diamond, J.M. and R.M. May. 1976. Island biogeography and the design of nature reserves. pp. 163-186. *In* R.M. May (ed.). Theoretical Ecology. Saunders, Philadelphia, Penn.

Diamond, J.M. and E. Mayr. 1976. Species-area relation for birds of the Solomon Archepelago. Proc. Natl. Acad. Sci. 73:262-266.

Diamond, J.M., M.E. Gilpin and E. Mayr. 1976. Species-distance relation for birds of the Solomon Archipelago, and the paradox of the great speciators. Proc. Natl. Acad. Sci. 73:2160-2164.

Ehrlich, P.R., A.H. Ehrlich and J.P. Holdren. 1977. Ecoscience: Population, Resources, Environment, W.H. Freeman, San Francisco, Calif.

Frankel, O.H. 1974. Genetic conservation: our evolutionary responsibility. Genetics 78:53-65.

Frankel, O.H. 1983. The place of management in conservation. pp. 1-14. *In* C.M. Schonewald-Cox, S.M. Chambers, B. Macbryde, and L. Thomas (eds.). Genetics and Conservation. Benjamin/Cummings Publishing Co., Inc. Menlo Park, Calif.

Frankel, O.H. and M.E. Soule'. 1981. Conservation and Evolution. Cambridge University Press, Cambridge, England.

Franklin, I.R. 1980. Evolutionary change in small populations. pp. 135-149. *In* M.E. Soule' and B.A. Wilcox (eds.). Conservation Biology: An Evolutionary-Ecological Perspective. Sinauer Associates, Sunderland, Mass.

Gilpin, M.E. and J.M. Diamond. 1976. Calculation of immigration and extinction curves from the species-area-distance relation. Proc. Natl. Acad. Sci. 73:4130-4134.

Gorman, G.L., M.E. Soule', S.Y. Yang and E. Nevo. 1975. Evolutionary genetics of insular Adriatic lizards. Evolution 29:52-71.

Greig, J.C. 1979. Principles of genetic conservation in relation to wildlife management in Southern Africa. S. Afr. J. Wildl. Res. 9:57-78.

Harlan, J.R. 1975. Our vanishing genetic resources. Science 188:618-621.

Harris, L.D., M.E. McGlothlen, and M.N. Manlove. 1984. Genetic resources and biotic diversity. pp. 93-107. *In* L.D. Harris (ed.). The Fragmented Forest. Island Biogeography Theory and the Preservation of Biotic Diversity. University of Chicago Press, Chicago, Ill.

Harris, L.D. 1984. The Fragmented Forest. Univ. of Chicago Press, Chicago, Ill.

Hendee, J.C., G.H. Stankey and R.C. Lucas. 1978. Wilderness Management. USDA For. Serv., Misc. Publ., No. 1365.

Hoover, R.L. and D.L. Willis, (eds.). 1984. Managing Forested Lands for Wildlife. Colorado Division of Wildlife in cooperation with USDA For. Serv., Rocky Mt. Region, Denver, Colorado.

Kleinman, D.G. 1980. The sociobiology of captive propagation. pp. 243-261, *In* M.E. Soule' and B.A. Wilcox (eds.). Conservation Biology: An Evolutionary-Ecological Perspective. Sinauer Associates, Sunderland, Mass.

Lacava, J. and J. Hughes. 1984. Determining minimum viable population levels. Wildl. Soc. Bull. 12:370-376.

Lehmkuhl, J.F. 1984. Determining size and dispersion of minimum viable populations for land management planning and species conservation. Environ. Manage. 8:167-176.

Lewontin, R.C. 1974. The Genetic Basis of Evolutionary Change. Columbia University Press, New York, New York.

Liu, E.H. and M.J.W. Godt. 1983. The differentiation of population over short distances. pp. 78-95. *In* C. M. Schonewald-Cox, S.M. Chambers, B. Macbryde and L. Thomas, (eds.). Genetics and Conservation. Benjamin/Cummings Publishing Co., Inc., Menlo Park, Calif.

Lovejoy, T.E. 1977. Genetic aspects of dwindling populations: a review. pp. 275-279. *In* S.A. Temple (ed.). Endangered Birds: Management Techniques for Preserving Threatened Species. Univ. of Wis. Press, Madison, Wis.

Nevo, E. 1976. Adaptive strategies of genetic systems in constant and varying environments. pp. 141-158 *In* S. Karlin and E. Nevo (eds.). Population Genetics and Ecology. Academic Press, Inc., New York, New York.

Nevo, E. 1978. Genetic variation in natural populations: patterns and theory. Theo. Popul. Bio. 13:121-178.

Nevo, E. and Z. Bar. 1976. Natural selection of genetic polymorphism along climatic gradients. pp. 159-184 In S. Karlin and E. Nevo (eds.). Population Genetics and Ecology. Academic Press, Inc., New York, New York.

O'Brien, J.J., M.E. Roelke, L. Marker, A. Newman, C.A. Wrukler, D. Meltzer, L. Colly, J.F. Evermann, M. Bush, D.E. Wildt. 1985. Genetic basis for species vulnerability in the cheetah. Science 227:1428-1434.

Powell, J.R. 1975. Protein variation in natural populations of animals. pp. 79-119 In T.H. Dobzhansky, M.K. Hecht, and W.C. Steere (eds.). Evolutionary Biology Vol. 8. Plenum, New York, New York.

Ryman, N., R. Baccus, C. Reuterwall, M.H. Smith. 1981. Effective population size, generation interval, and potential loss of genetic variability in game species under different hunting regimes. Oikos 36:257-266.

Schoener, T.W. 1982. The controversy over interspecific competition. Am. Sci. 70:586-595.

Schonewald-Cox, C.M., S.M. Chambers, B. Macbryde and W.L. Thomas (eds.). 1983. Genetics and Conservation. Benjamin/Cummings Publ. Co., Menlo Park, Calif.

Shaffer, M.L. 1981. Minimum population sizes for species conservation. Bioscience 31:131-134.

Simberloff, D. and L.G. Abele. 1982. Refuge design and island biogeographic theory: effects of fragmentation. Am. Nat. 120:41-50.

Smith, M.H., H.O. Hillstead, M.N. Manlove, and R.L. Marchington. 1976. Use of population genetics data for the management of fish and wildlife populations. Trans. N. Am. Wildl. Nat. Resour. Conf. 41:119-131.

Soule', M.E. 1980. Thresholds for survival: Maintaining fitness and evolutionary potential. pp. 151-169. In M.E. Soule' and B.A. Wilcox (eds.). Conservation Biology: An Evolutionary-Ecological Perspective. Sinauer Associates, Sunderland, Mass.

Soule', M.E. and B.A. Wilcox, 1980. Conservation biology: Its scope and its challenge. pp. 1-8. M.E. Soule' and B.A. Wilcox (eds.). Conservation Biology: An Evolutionary-Ecological Perspective. Sinauer Associates, Sunderland, Mass.

Soule', M.E., B.A. Wilcox, and C. Holtby. 1979. Benign neglect: A model of faunal collapse in the game reserves of East Africa. Biol. Conserv. 15:259-272.

Soule', M.E. and B.A. Wilcox (ed.). 1980. Conservation Biology: An Evolutionary-Ecological Perspective. Sinauer Associates, Sunderland, Mass.

Terborgh, J. 1974. Preservation of natural diversity: the problem of extinction prone species. Bioscience. 24:715-722.

Terborgh, J.W. and B. Winter. 1980. Some causes of extinction. pp. 119-133. In M.E. Soule' and B.A. Wilcox (eds.). Conservation Biology: An Evolutionary-Ecological Perspective, ed. Sinauer Associates, Sunderland, Mass.

van Buijtenen, J.P., G.A. Donovan, E.M. Long, W.J. Lowe, C.R. McKinley, J.F. Robinson, and R.A. Woessner. 1981. Introduction to practical forest tree improvement. Texas For. Serv. Circ. 207.

Wilcox, B.A. 1980. Insular ecology and conservation. pp. 95-117. In M.E. Soule' and B.A. Wilcox (eds.). Conservation Biology: An Evolutionary-Ecological Perspective. Sinauer Associates, Sunderland, Mass.

Wright, S. 1978. Evolution and the Genetics of Populations, Vol. 4, Variability Within and Among Natural Populations. University of Chicago Press, Chicago, Ill.

Zobel, B. and J. Taltert. 1984. Applied Forest Tree Improvement. John Wiley and Sons, Inc., New York, New York.

The Dynamic Landscape Approach To Habitat Management

by
Raymond D. Dueser, Herman H. Shugart, Jr. and Edward F. Connor

ABSTRACT--We propose a "dynamic landscape approach" to managing wilderness and natural areas. Multivariate habitat descriptions for "target" wildlife species provide a management objective. Vegetation simulation models forecast the changes in habitat structure resulting from the application of a management strategy designed to achieve this objective. Classification functions couple habitat descriptions with habitat simulations to provide predictions about habitat suitability and the probable future occurrence of the target species. Rapid field sampling procedures facilitate the efficient collection of data for model parameterization and for monitoring the consequences of actual on-site application. We outline four tests required for critical evaluation of the utility of the dynamic landscape approach.

KEYWORDS: Animal-vegetation relationships, forest modeling, habitat description, habitat management, landscape ecology, multivariate analysis, wildlife habitat.

Dynamic habitat management represents a major challenge to managers of wilderness areas, natural areas and parklands throughout the United States. Recent interest in management for plant and nongame animal species has served to increase the practical difficulty of this challenge. The statutory and administrative circumstances regulating habitat management vary from one type of natural area to another, with national forest lands subject to extensive periodic manipulation at one extreme and national wilderness areas subject to little or no manipulation at the other. Despite these differences, however, the managers of all such areas face a common challenge: how can we anticipate the probable effects associated with alternative, perhaps even competitive, strategies for habitat management? Having identified the management objective for an area, how do we then implement a practical strategy for achieving that objective? That is, how do we realize a desirable objective in habitat management?

Traditionally, the overseers of wildlands have, by necessity, relied heavily on experience and intuition in seeking answers to these questions. And, again by necessity, the answers often have been prescriptive in nature and narrow in scope relative to the scale and complexity of the problem. Our purpose is to propose a more synthetic approach to answering these questions. This approach, which we shall refer to as the "dynamic landscape approach," builds on three relatively recent developments in forest and animal ecology:
1) multivariate habitat descriptions for game and nongame wildlife species,
2) computer simulation models of forest structure and habitat conditions, and

3) rapid field-sampling procedures, for characterizing forest structure and for efficient monitoring of habitat changes.

These three developments, along with the advent of inexpensive high-speed computers, potentially can equip the wildlands manager with predictive capacity unimaginable only a few years ago.

The "dynamic landscape approach" takes advantage of the strong dependence of animals on the structural characteristics of their habitats. Using the techniques of multivariate habitat description, this dependency is translated into predictive equations that relate the occurrence and/or abundance of a "target" species to the structural characteristics of the habitat. In turn, computer simulation models can be used to predict changes in vegetation structure and habitat characteristics either under conditions of natural succession or under a particular management regime. Coupling multivariate habitat descriptors with a dynamical model of vegetation change permits predictions about the probable presence and abundance of animal species at various times in the future, given specific management regimes. Rapid field-sampling procedures facilitate both the implementation and the monitoring of the management regime under field conditions.

There have been several tentative efforts to couple multivariate habitat description with vegetation simulation models in the single-species case, to predict future probable habitat conditions for a particular species under a particular management regime (e.g., Smith *et al.* 1981a). So far as we know, however, all of these elements have never been brought together in the way and for the purpose which we propose. Our plan is to review each of these developments briefly, to illustrate the application of 1 and 2 in a particular single-species case, and to propose a methodology for implementing the dynamic landscape approach in the more general multi-species case.

HABITAT DESCRIPTION

Multivariate habitat description is a familiar development (Capen 1981). The objective of multivariate habitat description is to determine the habitat conditions favorable for a particular wildlife species or a community of species. Multivariate habitat description is motivated by the realization that animals respond differentially to habitat structure and appearance and that, within the geographic range of the species, habitat structure is perhaps the most reliable indicator of habitat suitability for that species. This procedure routinely includes three steps: 1) population sampling, 2) multivariable habitat sampling, and 3) parsimonious habitat description.

Reliable techniques have been developed for sampling populations of most wildlife species (Taber and Cowan 1971). These techniques tend to be highly specific to particular taxonomic groups, and their review is beyond the scope of the present paper. Two general considerations, however, require mention in connection with multivariate habitat description. First, although specification of the sampling unit (e.g., 0.05-ha forest plot for birds or a trapping station on a grid for small mammals) is dependent to some extent on the species of interest, the spatial scale of both the sampling and the habitat description should be compatible with the structure of the computer simulation model of vegetation dynamics. Recent work by our group at the University of Virginia and others suggests that a great deal of standardization, perhaps even across taxonomic lines, may be possible. Second, sampling programs should be designed with an eye to statistical considerations such as the assumptions of random sampling and independence of observations. Biased or non-independent data may severely restrict the utility of the resulting multivariate habitat description (Johnson 1981).

Habitat sampling is multi-variable in nature because we are interested in describing what James (1971) refers to as the "niche gestalt" of the species, a relatively complete 3-dimensional representation of the "typical" habitat occupied by the species of interest. As with population sampling, the variables selected for measurement may vary with the taxonomic group of interest and the specific research objectives. For example, analyses of forest bird habitats often emphasize vertical habitat complexity more than do studies of mammal habitats (James and Shugart 1970), while the latter may emphasize horizontal complexity at ground level (Dueser and Shugart 1978). Nevertheless, it is encouraging that meaningful, interpretable multivariate habitat descriptions

have resulted from analyses based on both micro-scale variables (e.g., Shugart and Patten 1972) and relatively coarse macro-scale variables (e.g., Anderson and Shugart 1974).

Given a set of habitat measurements, the objective of multivariate habitat description is to describe the habitat (or microhabitat) occupied by the species in an abstract manner but with minimal loss of information. A variety of multivariate statistical procedures are available for this purpose. Perhaps the most commonly employed techniques are principal components analysis (PCA) and discriminant function analysis (DFA) (Shugart 1981). PCA is a procedure for determining the major or most important axes of variation in a multivariate data set. An extension of analysis of variance, DFA is a procedure for determining the major axes of difference(s) among sample groups in a multivariate data set.

As an example of multivariate habitat description, consider the analysis of a breeding bird community in the southern Appalachians by Anderson and Shugart (1974). They described the habitat associations of 28 breeding bird species in the mixed forest on Walker Branch Watershed at Oak Ridge National Laboratory in eastern Tennessee. This watershed had been the subject of intensive vegetation analysis during the past, including both ordination/classification and dimension analysis (Grigal and Goldstein 1971). Using this information, Anderson and Shugart (1974) computed a number of gross habitat variables (e.g., bole, branch and foliage biomass for different size classes of trees) on each of 24 0.08-ha forest inventory plots. They then surveyed the breeding bird species on each plot. The results of their examination of the relationship between these variables and avian species distributions were very revealing. Even with these "coarse" habitat variables, principal components analysis revealed widely dispersed species centroids and "typical" habitat associations for most of the species.

VEGETATION SIMULATION MODELS

The use of computer models to simulate the dynamics of vegetation began in the mid-1960's and emerged as a major research focus in the early 1970's (Shugart and West 1980). This development was motivated both by an applied interest in commercial timber stand projections (Munro 1975) and by a basic interest in ecological succession (Shugart 1984). A variety of model types and over 100 different models have been developed in the past 10 years, but our interest focuses on what are called "canopy gap" models. These models simulate the birth, death, and annual growth of each tree on a small forest plot. The model simulates annual changes in the forest stand by calculating the growth increment of each of the trees growing in the stand, by tabulating the addition of new saplings to the stand through germination and sprouting, and by tabulating the death of trees present in the stand. The simulated plot is scaled to the size of a large overstory tree or to the size of a canopy gap produced by the death of that tree. The gap model thus forecasts successional events on a 0.05-0.08 ha circular plot. An example is the FORET model developed by Shugart and West (1977) to simulate the dynamics of Appalachian deciduous forests.

In the FORET model, the growth of each tree is obtained by solving sets of non-linear differential equations for changes in tree diameter as a function of time, tree size, and several exogenous factors. The model projects the structure and composition of the vegetation on a forest plot through time, based on the establishment, performance, and longevity of individual trees (Fig. 1). Additional factors which may impinge on an individual tree can be incorporated into the model. Subroutines can be incorporated to forecast the consequences of natural events (e.g., pest outbreaks or wildfire) and of specific management activities (e.g., selective thinning or controlled burning).

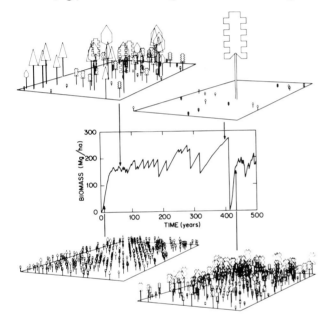

Figure 1. Results of forest simulation using the FORET model. Central figure describes the simulated temporal dynamics of biomass abundance on a forest plot for 500 years. a) Structure of forest at year 5 during regeneration following a clear-cut timber removal. Different symbols represent individuals of different tree species. b) Stand development at year 50, exhibiting increased biomass but reduced tree density. c) Stand structure at year 400, exhibiting dominanace by a single large tree. d) Structure of forest at year 420, approximately 10 years after the death of the dominant overstory tree. Horizontal scales are 2X the vertical scales. (From Shugart 1984.)

The parameters of these equations incorporate information about both the biology of the species of interest and the physical characteristics of the site. Importantly, however, the values of these parameters are relatively easy to measure or estimate. In fact, much of the required

information can be obtained from silvicultural summaries for the species (e.g., maximum height, tolerance, geographic range, etc.). The data required to implement a model such as FORET are thus easily acquired and relatively inexpensive.

Opportunities for independent testing of model predictions are not yet numerous (see Shugart 1984), but several models particularly those based on the FORET concept, have performed well on those tests which have been possible. If one has confidence in the basic forecast ability of the model, and if one can reasonably represent a natural disturbance or management activity in a subroutine, then the models can be used to derive objective answers to the challenging questions which we posed at the outset. In particular, the models can be used to predict the probable consequences of habitat disturbance, for example, or to estimate the probable effects associated with alternative forest managment activities on the structural characteristics of forests that are important to wildlife.

RAPID SAMPLING

Rapid sampling is perhaps the least familiar of the recent developments. It is, nevertheless, a development which promises to become very important in habitat management. The Scandinavians have a long-standing interest in intensive forest mensuration and management. In keeping with this interest, they now seem to be leading the way in applying digital technology to forest sampling. Jonsson (1981) describes an innovative electronic caliper which has tremendous potential for both routine forest inventory and the implementation of a particular habitat management strategy. The caliper has a built-in electronic system for "self-reading" tree diameters. These measurements are stored automatically in a portable computer which is the size of a pocket calculator and weighs less than 0.5 kg. It has 48k of semi-permanent memory and 16k of programmable memory. It also features a 16 character LCD and a 20-key keyboard. With this caliper/computer system, it is possible to record data rapidly and accurately in the field and to transfer it to a central computer by means of an accoustic coupler.

The caliper system is capable of automatic data storage by single keystroke (DBH and species), keystroke data storage (e.g., tree tag number for remeasurement), and programmed interaction with the operator. The computer can be programmed to emit both audible and visual prompts, for example, to "mark every fifth tree with DBH greater than 20 cm DBH." In the hands of a trained operator, this device should increase tremendously both the speed and accuracy of forest inventories, and make it easier to implement habitat manipulations such as tree-thinning and selective cutting. The development of rapid sampling and data transcription techniques is particularly important to the dynamic landscape approach to habitat management because it makes it possible to collect large amounts of detailed habitat information relatively cheaply. This permits both more accurate parameter estimation for the vegetation simulation model and frequent, detailed monitoring of the effectiveness of the chosen management regime.

THE DYNAMIC LANDSCAPE APPROACH

Dynamic Habitat Management

The objectives of dynamic habitat management are to predict structural, compositional, or floristic changes in the habitat resulting from succession following disturbance or from selective management activity, and to assess the probable response of one or more wildlife populations to these changes. The first step in the application of a vegetation simulation model to this task is to adapt or develop a simulation model for the natural area of interest. Models already exist for flatwoods of central Arkansas (Phipps 1979), Mississippi flood plain forest (Shugart 1984), southeastern loblolly pine forest (Shugart 1984), Appalachian hardwoods (Shugart and West 1977), northern hardwoods (Botkin et al. 1972), Puerto Rican rainforests (Doyle 1981), and others. Adaptation of a model to a specific region, forest type, and management situation requires modest investment of time and expertise. Given the model, it is then necessary to incorporate subroutines which simulate the imposition of disturbance or selective management and the dynamics of pertinent habitat variables. Incorporation of the habitat simulator to produce output (i.e., habitat variables) which is directly pertinent to management objectives is relatively straightforward. Experience indicates that even relatively coarse habitat simulators may have considerable predictive capacity. Finally, it is necessary to incorporate subroutines to evaluate the "suitability" of simulated habitat for the species of interest. The development of a practical "classification function" by which the suitability of simulated habitat relative to a particular species or group of species may be judged is a routine application of 2-group discriminant function analysis (Morrison 1967). The development of such a function may, however, require a substantial data base (Rice et al. 1981).

As an example, consider the case of the ovenbird (*Seiurus aurocapillus*) on Walker Branch Watershed in eastern Tennessee. This regionally common species is actually quite rare in this mixed forest. Anderson and Shugart (1974) recorded only 5 observations of this species on their study plots, as opposed to as many as 225 for other species during the same time span. Analysis of ovenbird habitat associations on Walker Branch indicates that its preferred habitat (i.e., well-developed canopy, sparse understory, and little ground cover) is relatively uncommon on the watershed. This raises the question of whether this forest could be managed to increase the availability of prime ovenbird habitat. More

specifically, what would be the probable consequences for the ovenbird of different forest management regimes?

To answer this question, Smith *et al.* (1981a) used the FORHAB model to simulate the dynamics of this forest for 120 years under two conditions: with and without timber harvest. Adapted from the FORET model, FORHAB included subroutines designed to simulate various forest management practices, to compute values of simulated habitat variables, and to classify each simulated forest plot as suitable or unsuitable habitat for the ovenbird. The without-harvest case simply projected the current structure of the forest through time, based on what is known about the biology of the tree species. The with-harvest case was analogous except that in years 1 and 60 of the simulation, a diameter-limit cut was imposed, removing all commercially valuable timber above 22.8 cm DBH. A linear classification function was used to judge the suitability of each simulated plot as ovenbird habitat (Smith *et al.* 1981b).

Simulation without harvest predicted an initial increase of available habitat for the ovenbird for the first 10 years or so, followed by a continual decline through approximately year 60 as the forest matures (Fig. 2).

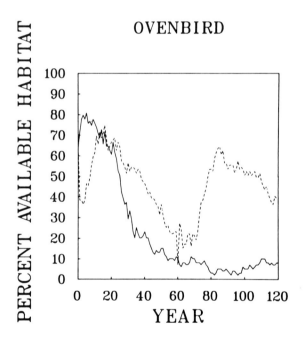

Figure 2. Percentage of available habitat suitable for the ovenbird *Seiurus aurocapillus* on Walker Branch watershed in eastern Tennessee, as predicted by the FORHAB simulation model of forest habitat. Percentage of available habitat is expressed as the percentage of the land area of the watershed. Solid line summarizes the simulation result without timber harvest. Dashed line summarizes the simulation with timber harvests imposed in years 1 and 60. (From Smith *et al.* 1981a.)

Thereafter, the simulation predicted variation in the availability of ovenbird habitat, varying between 3% and 12% of the watershed, through year 120. The simulation with harvest predicted a decrease in available habitat during the first five years following the first cut. Habitat availability subsequently increased to 75% before declining to less than 10% by year 60. The second cut (year 60) produced an increase in available habitat but not to the extent of the first. This initial increase was followed by a slight decline and a secondary increase in available habitat to over 60% by year 80. This increase was then followed by a decline for the remainder of the simulation. Following each cut, then, there was a large increase in ovenbird habitat followed by a gradual decline. At the end of the simulation the managed forest was quite different from the unmanaged, with 45% of the habitat potentially suitable for ovenbirds as opposed to 10%. This exercise both illustrates the probable effects of a particular timber-harvesting procedure on a given forest, and demonstrates the possibility of simulating the dynamics of potential habitats for the ovenbird.

There are, of course, limitations inherent in the procedure. The simulation does not consider the demographic or behavioral ability of the ovenbird population to track these habitat changes, the model does not simulate changes in the habitat preference of ovenbirds, and the model, as run here, does not simulate the interaction of timber management with events such as wildfire. Nevertheless, this habitat simulation clearly represents our best-possible estimate of the influence of this particular forest management strategy on this particular species. Presumably, the same procedure could be used for other, more compelling wildlife species.

A habitat simulation model provides the ability to "test" alternative management strategies relative to a given objective before on-site application. One could then use the results of the simulation study and the rapid sampling methods to implement the prescribed management activity on the ground. These habitat simulation models are still in the developmental stage and important questions remain: Are the predictions produced by habitat simulation models sufficiently detailed to be of practical use to the habitat manager? What are the limitations of the dynamic landscape approach? The simple answer to each of these questions is that we do not yet know. The more compelling answer is that we need to know.

Utility and Reliability

So far we have presented the concept of the dynamic landscape approach, outlined its components, and illustrated its potential application in a single-species case study. When will this approach be useful? And how reliable are its predictions?

The dynamic landscape approach can be useful in developing a management regime for almost any single species or multispecies management program. The key elements for its success are precise multivariable descriptions of animal-vegetation relationships and a well-corroborated model of vegetation dynamics. This approach can be tailored to any management goal for single species or multi-species groups, as long as there is substantial covariation between the animals and the vegetation and, in the multi-species case, also between the different animal species. Because the consequences of different management strategies for various wildlife species can be evaluated rapidly using the computer model and multivariate analysis, the dynamic landscape approach allows the manager to choose the management regime that requires the least effort and yet yields the best results in the shortest time. Even after a management regime has been instituted, successive surveys of the vegetation can be used to update the predicted responses of wildlife and to iteratively improve the management plan.

At present, the dynamic landscape approach could be readily applied to manage birds and mammals in forested habitats. Successful forest dynamic models and considerable information on animal-habitat relationships in forested environments already exist (Shugart 1984, James and Warner 1982). In the future, this approach also may be applicable to grasslands and to landscapes consisting of a mosaic of forested and open habitats.

The reliability of predictions generated by the dynamic landscape approach remain totally untested. The exercise by Smith et al. (1981a) only illustrates how this approach can be used to forecast changes in wildlife habitat in response to habitat management. No management plan was actually instituted to assess the accuracy of the predictions. How then do we determine the reliability of dynamic landscape predictions? What evidence would increase our confidence that this approach will be useful and reliable, or alternatively would impugn this approach?

There are several lines of inquiry that might provide answers to these questions: 1) an assessment of the ability of the dynamic model of vegetation to mimic temporal habitat dynamics on scales of space and time relevant to real-world wildlife populations, 2) a static assessment of the ability of the multivariate analysis to correctly predict the species composition or species abundances of independently investigated units of vegetation, 3) a comparison of dynamic landscape predictions to existing data on the temporal dynamics of wildlife, and 4) full-scale field experiments.

Evidence of the sort mentioned in 1 and 2 above already exists for breeding birds in the deciduous forests of eastern North America. Well-corroborated models of the dynamics of the vegetation are currently in use (Shugart 1984), and multivariate descriptions of bird-vegetation relationships have been shown to account for approximately 70% of the variation in the presence or absence of these bird species (Fig. 2; James and Warner 1982).

The kinds of tests described in 3 and 4 above call for a comparison between observed and "expected" (i.e., modeled) vegetation and wildlife changes on a study area through time. In the interest of efficiency, such a comparison ideally would be based on presently available data on temporal trends in habitat conditions and population status. Unfortunately, because of the data requirements, the opportunities for such comparisons appear to be limited. Information on temporal changes in

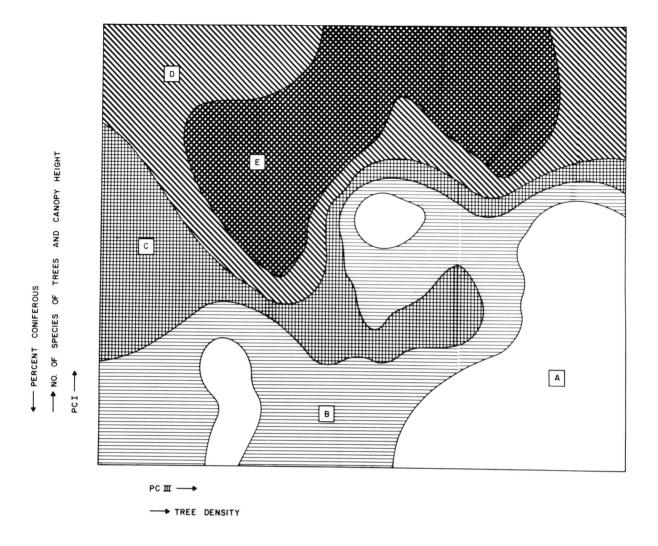

Figure 3. Contour diagrams of the number of territorial pairs of birds (A) and the number of bird species (B) plotted in the bivariate space determined by two principal components. Higher abundances and species richness are indicated by successively darker shading. The interpretations of the principal components in terms of their correlations with habitat characteristics are given on the margins of each plot. Note the substantial overlap between the region of high density and high bird species richness. The data consist of 56 breeding bird censuses from all over the United States and Canada for the years 1973-1977. (From James and Wamer 1982.)

vegetation structure is plentiful, as is information on changes in wildlife populations. However, the two types of information are seldom available for the same site. Remeasurement data from breeding bird survey plots are a likely source of pertinent information (Noon *et al.* 1980). Simulated habitat dynamics would provide the "expected" base for comparison with actual wildlife response. Close agreement between observations and expectations would bolster one's confidence in the practical utility of the dynamic landscape approach. Disparity between ob-

servation and expectations might motivate one to retool the simulator. Even on a small scale (e.g., a single-species case), this comparison would be very enlightening. This validation trial is recommended any time it is feasible, before the implementation of a field trial.

This final approach, a fullscale field experiment, would be the strongest test of all. It would require that dynamic landscape predictions about future changes in wildlife populations be made for specific study plots, that a management goal and management regime be selected and instituted on replicate plots, and that subsequent changes in vegetation and wildlife be monitored on both treatment plots receiving the management regime and control plots receiving no management. If the dynamic landscape predictions are reliable and useful, then the managed plots should approach the management objective more rapidly than the control plots. This will obviously be a large and expensive experiment, but the potential utility of the dynamic landscape approach warrants such an effort.

CONCLUSIONS

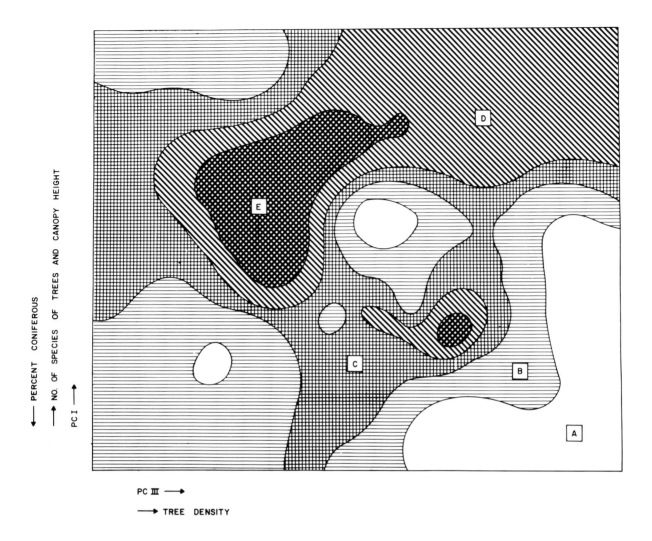

PERCENT CONIFEROUS

NO. OF SPECIES OF TREES AND CANOPY HEIGHT

PC I →

PC III →

→ TREE DENSITY

Although the dynamic landscape approach is untested, we see it as the logical extension of current techniques that have been successfully employed to manage wildlife and vegetation. It is based on the well-established observation that the occurrence of plants and, particularly, animals depends on discernible characteristics of the structure of their habitats, and on the growing repertoire of successful dynamical models of vegetation and habitat change. Futhermore, the kinds of data necessary to parameterize both components of this approach are often already available or easily collected, or at least the techniques for collecting these data are well-established.

If this approach can be shown to make useful and accurate predictions of how plant and animal populations change in response to various regimes of vegetation management, then it will be a valuable tool in managing national forests, national parks, wildlife refuges, and nature reserves, as well as predicting future long term changes of wildlife populations in wilderness areas. Potentially, it can be applied to conservation problems in tropical forests and extended to regional conservation problems encompassing a mosaic of vegetation types. Research to test the reliability of this approach is critically needed.

LITERATURE CITED

Anderson, S.H. and H.H. Shugart, Jr. 1974. Habitat selection of breeding birds in an east Tennessee deciduous forest. Ecology 55:828-837.

Botkin, D.B., J.F. Janek and J.R. Wallis. 1972. Some ecological consequences of a computer model of forest growth. J. Ecol. 60:849-873.

Capen, D.E. (ed.) 1981. The use of multivariate statistics in studies of wildlife habitat. USDA For. Serv. Gen. Tech. Rept. RM-87.

Doyle, T.W. 1981. The role of disturbance in the gap dynamics of a montane rain forest: An application of a tropical forest succession model. pp. 56-73. In D.C. West, H.H. Shugart and D.B. Botkin (eds.), Forest succession. Concepts and application. Springer-Verlag, New York, N.Y.

Dueser, R.D. and H.H. Shugart, Jr. 1978. Microhabitats in a forest-floor small mammal fauna. Ecology 59:89-98.

Grigal, D.F. and R.A. Goldstein. 1971. An integrated ordination-classification analysis of an intensively sampled oak-hickory forest. J. Ecol. 59:481-492.

James, F.C. 1971. Ordinations of habitat relationships among breeding birds. Wilson Bull. 83:215-236.

James, F.C. and H.H. Shugart, Jr. 1970. A quantitative method of habitat description. Audubon Field Notes 24:727-736.

James, F.C. and N.O. Warner. 1982. Relationships between temperate forest bird communities and vegetation structure. Ecology 63:159-171.

Johnson, D.H. 1981. The use and misuse of statistics in wildlife habitat studies. pp. 11-19. *In* D.E. Capen (ed.), The use of multivariate statistics in studies of wildlife habitat. USDA For. Serv. Gen. Tech. Rept. RM-87.

Jonsson, B. 1981. An electronic caliper with automatic data storage. For. Sci. 27:756-770.

Morrison, D.F. 1967. Multivariate statistical methods. McGraw-Hill. New York, N.Y.

Munro, D.D. 1975. Forest growth models. A prognosis. pp. 7-21 *In* J. Fries (ed.), Growth models for tree and stand simulation. Res. Notes 30. Rept. For. Yield Res., Royal Coll. For., Stockholm, Swed.

Noon, B.R., D.K. Dawson, D.B. Inkley, C.S. Robbins and S.H. Anderson. 1980. Consistency in habitat preference of forest bird species. pp. 226-244. Transactions, 45th North American Wildlife and Natural Resources Conference.

Phipps, R.L. 1979. Simulation of wetland forest vegetation dynamics. Ecol. Model. 7:257-288.

Rice, J., R.D. Ohmart and B. Anderson. 1981. Bird community use of riparian habitats: The importance of temporal scale in interpreting discriminant analysis. pp. 186-196. *In* D.E. Capen (ed.), The use of multivariate statistics in studies of wildlife habitat. USDA For. Serv. Gen. Tech. Rept. RM-87.

Shugart, H.H., Jr. 1981. An overview of multivariate methods and their application to studies of wildlife habitat. pp. 4-10. *In* D.E. Capen (ed.), The use of multivariate statistics in studies of wildlife habitat. USDA For. Serv. Gen. Tech. Rept. RM-87.

Shugart, H.H., Jr. 1984. A theory of forest dynamics. Springer-Verlag. New York, N.Y.

Shugart, H.H., Jr. and B.C. Patten. 1972. Niche quantification and the concept of niche pattern. pp. 283-327. *In* B.C. Patten (ed.), Systems analysis and simulation in ecology, Volume 2. Academic Press, New York, N.Y.

Shugart, H.H. Jr. and D.C. West. 1977. Development of an Appalachian forest succession model and its application to assessment of the impact of the chestnut blight. J. Environ. Manage. 5:161-179.

Shugart, H.H., Jr. and D.C. West. 1980. Forest succession models. BioScience 30:308-313.

Smith, T.M., H.H. Shugart, Jr. and D.C. West. 1981a. Use of forest simulation models to integrate timber harvest and nongame bird management. pp. 501-510, Transactions, 46th North American Wildlife and Natural Resources Conference.

Smith, T.M., H.H. Shugart, Jr. and D.C. West. 1981b. FORHAB: A forest simulation model to predict habitat structure for nongame bird species. pp. 114-123. *In* D.E. Capen (ed.), The use of multivariate statistics in studies of wildlife habitat. USDA For. Serv. Gen. Tech. Rept. RM-87.

Taber, R.D. and I. McT. Cowan. 1971. Capturing and marking wild animals. pp. 277-317. *In* R.H. Giles, Jr. (ed.), Wildlife management techniques, The Wildlife Society, Washington, D.C.

3

Forest Protection

by
David L. Kulhavy and David B. Drummond

Insects and diseases are natural, integral components of the forest ecosystem. The forest ecosystem itself undergoes constant change and is subject to perturbations within long-term ecological cycles. As the dynamics of the forest change, so does the response of the organisms feeding (or living) within this system. One such organism in the South, responding rapidly to environmental changes, is the southern pine beetle, *Dendroctonus frontalis* Zimmermann. In the northeast, the gypsy moth (*Lymantria dispar L.*) responds in a similar fashion.

In Texas, populations of the southern pine beetle began to peak at the time wilderness areas were designated by the 98th Congress (October 1, 1984). In 1985, over 15,000 separate southern pine beetle spots (10 or more trees) were detected, many within the boundaries of the wilderness areas. Current management regimes include removing the infested trees from the site plus a strip of uninfested trees (cut and remove); cutting infested trees and a strip of uninfested trees and leaving them in place (cut and leave); or to do nothing (no action). Evidence of extensive activity (feeding) by southern pine beetles if no action is taken occurred both in the Four Notch area of the Raven District of the Sam Houston National Forest (USDA Forest Service) in Texas, and in The Big Sandy unit of the Big Thicket National Preserve administered by the National Park Service.

That something must be done to disrupt southern pine beetle spots is apparent; the question is how to best do this. The "minimum tool" ethic espoused in the Wilderness Act dictates minimal disturbance of wilderness qualities and attributes. However, "measures may be taken as may be necessary in the control of fire, insects, and diseases..." This issue is being addressed by two concurrent lawsuits, currently in district court in Texas and Washington, D.C. An Environmental Impact Statement (EIS), pertaining to control of the southern pine beetle in wilderness areas, is due for public comment in early 1986. The outcome of the lawsuits and the content of the EIS will have far-reaching implications for management of wilderness and natural areas.

The draft EIS, released July 9, 1986, addresses six major issues: impact of proposed alternatives on Red-cockaded woodpecker, *Picoides borealis*; impact on wilderness areas; effectiveness of control techniques; application of control techniques; possible impacts of the southern pine beetle on lands next to wilderness boundaries; and nontraditional control tactics. These major issues will be reviewed with alternatives for control and a preferred alternative recommended.

Management, however, must be prudent, and administered and overseen by professional managers. Wilderness and natural areas must be viewed as a resource to be managed.

Activities Of Insects In Forests: Implications For Wilderness Area Management

by
Robert N. Coulson, Edward J. Rykiel, and D.A. Crossley, Jr.

ABSTRACT--Wilderness areas are unique forested ecosystems only in the sense that they were purposefully designated because of outstanding characteristics associated with the landscape. The persistence of these characteristics through space and time is influenced by the activities of insects and other arthropods. We examine the roles of insects in forest ecosystems and interpret these roles in the context of basic principles of ecological succession, disturbances, and landscape properties. In selecting sites for wilderness preservation, the size of the area, the type of forest ecosystem, and the disturbance regime must be considered because the interaction of these variables may indicate the need for management if the characteristics for which the area was set aside are to be preserved.

KEYWORDS: insects, forest ecosystems, wilderness.

A wilderness area is a unique forested ecosystem only in the sense that it was purposefully selected at a point in time because of an array of outstanding qualities associated with the landscape. The criteria used in selecting a particular area generally include characteristics of physiography as well as attributes associated with plant community composition, diversity, and age structure. As with other forested ecosystems, wilderness areas will change in space and time as a result of the interaction of the biota with the abiotic environment. Therefore, the qualities associated with the wilderness area will also change. To some degree it may be desirable, and even possible, to influence the course of development and rate of change of the ecosystem in a prescribed way, through forest management practices. This issue is the focus of this symposium.

Insects are a common and ubiquitous element of forested ecosystems. Historically, their activities have been considered in the context of forest protection (Coulson and Witter 1984). Viewed in this manner, interest has focused on influence of insect herbivory on plant populations and resulting consequences to community composition, diversity, and age structure of the plant community (Coulson and Witter 1984). However, in recent years the activities of insects have been examined in the context of their influence on basic processes associated with ecosystem function (Mattson and Addy 1975, Mattson 1977, Seastedt 1984, Seastedt and Crossley 1984, Brown 1984, Schowalter 1981 and 1985, Shugart 1984, Schowalter et al. 1986).

In this paper we examine activities of insects, disturbances to forests, and landscape characteristics relative to wilderness area management. Our specific objectives are (1) to review the principal effects of insects on plant populations, communities, and forested ecosystems; (2) to examine the issue of disturbance to forested ecosystems, with particular reference to the special case of excessive herbivory by insects; and (3) to discuss the implication of natural disturbances to wilderness area management practices.

EFFECTS OF INSECTS IN FORESTS

The effects of insects on plant populations, communities, and forested ecosystems are obviously complex. Our intent here is simply to illustrate how insects are involved at each level of ecological organization. Comprehensive reviews on the subject are listed in the introduction of this paper.

At the population level of organization, we are interested in how insects can influence the distribution, abundance, and growth of plant species. A population of a plant species can be viewed from two levels of organization: (1) the individual or genet, and (2) structural modules which comprise the genet. At the first level, the genet, values of population state variables (e.g., the number of individuals) are determined by the operation of the population processes of birth rate, death rate, and dispersal (immigration and emigration). Insect activities influence the distribution and abundance of genets simply by decreasing birth rate and immigration into a site or increasing death rate and emigration from a site. This fundamental statement of population ecology is generally represented as the "demographic equation" and pertains to animal populations as well as plants. At the second level, plant modules, the values of state variables (e.g., number of seeds, biomass of leaves, etc.) are determined by the birth and death rates of the modules. Insect activity that changes the birth and death of structural modules influences both the growth rate and form of a tree.

Coulson and Witter (1984) identified seven principal ways that insect activities influence plants and plant modules:

1. Some feeding groups kill their hosts through excessive levels of herbivory.

2. Herbivory can result in mortality to plant modules such as cones, seeds, leaves, and branches.

3. Insects are responsible for the introduction of various plant pathogenic diseases. Introduction can occur through direct inoculation of the tree by the insect, or the disease inoculum can be transported by the wind and enter through wounds caused by insect feeding.

4. Excessive herbivory can physiologically weaken the tree. Under this circumstance the tree may become susceptible to attack by other insects that would normally be resisted. Physiologically weakened trees are also more susceptible to infection by plant pathogens.

5. Herbivory by insects can structurally weaken host trees. This effect can accentuate damage resulting from wind, snow, or ice storms.

6. Insects play a dominant role in pollination of flowering plants.

7. While feeding and boring, phytophagous insects in dead and dying trees spread inoculum of wood-rotting fungi. These combined activities (boring, feeding, and inoculation) provide the initial conditions that result in decomposition of dead trees.

The plant life cycle model (Fig. 1) is a convenient basis for organizing insect influences on populations of forest trees (Harper 1977, Coulson and Witter 1984). There are four basic components to the model: (1) survival of the seed bank in the soil and litter, (2) recruitment and establishment of individuals of the population from the seed bank, (3) growth of individuals, and (4) reproduction and dispersal of individuals. The various insect feeding groups and different types of herbivory can be assigned to each of these components and the direct effects of the insects on the distribution and abundance of plants (both genets and structural modules) evaluated (Coulson and Witter 1984).

At the community level, the principal effects of herbivorous insects are on the patterns of establishment and growth of plant populations. Direct effects of insects occur during all stages in the life cycles of plant species resident in an area. Insect activities outlined above are involved in regulating the size and composition of the seed bank, the composition and rate of recruitment from the seed bank, the rate of growth and development of trees, and the reproduction and dispersal of propagules (Fig. 1).

At the ecosystem level of organization the roles of insects (and other arthropods) are manifested in the ways they can work to alter or control the functioning of the system (Shugart 1984). Their direct effects center on regulation of ecosystems through influence on energy flow

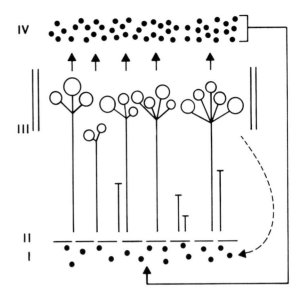

Figure 1. Diagrammatic representation of the plant life cycle, illustrating a tree as a series of modular units (the shoots). There are four basic components of the life cycle: (I) the seed bank, (II) recruitment and establishment of individuals of the population from the seed bank, (III) growth of individuals, and (IV) reproduction and dispersal (From Coulson and Witter 1984).

processes, materials cycling processes, assembly processes, and information control processes (Rykiel 1985a). Figure 2 illustrates a conceptual model of the role of arthropod consumers in elemental cycling, proposed by Seastedt and Crossley (1984), for a terrestrial ecosystem. This model illustrates the relationships between herbivores and detritivores in the mineral cycling process.

In the context of this discussion, with its focus on the role of insects in wilderness areas, we are particularly interested in the assembly process, ecological succession. Although the concept of ecological succession is a subject of continuing development in the ecological literature (see West *et al.* 1981, and Shugart 1984), for our purposes here we define the term simply as the process of ecosystem organization through which a relatively stable community ultimately develops on a newly exposed or disturbed site. Schowalter (1981) and Brown (1984) provide detail on the involvement of insects in the processes.

DISTURBANCES TO FORESTED ECOSYSTEMS

In this section we illustrate basic relationships between insect herbivory, natural disturbances, and the process of ecological succession. These relationships are then inter-

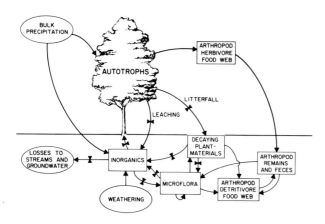

Figure 2. A simplified conceptual model of elemental cycling in a terrestrial ecosystem emphasizing the presence and activities of arthropod consumers. Indirect regulation of elemental movements by arthropods is indicated by the hourglass-shaped valves on these flows. Virtually all fluxes within ecosystems are known or believed to respond to varying levels of arthropod activity (From Seastedt and Crossley 1984).

preted in the context of wilderness area management.

The process of ecological succession is particularly relevant to the issue of wilderness area management because, by definition, a forested landscape is expected to change through time and space. Insects, through the activities discussed above, are involved in regulating certain aspects of the rate and perhaps course of succession. At normal or average levels, the regulating effects of insect herbivory, although extremely important, are only rarely of concern to forest managers. However, excessive levels of herbivory create disturbances that affect the economics of production forestry and may influence the values associated with wilderness areas.

Natural disturbances commonly occur in forested ecosystems and have a profound effect on the process of succession and hence the appearance of the landscape. For our purposes a **disturbance** is defined as a physical force or process that can cause a sudden change in the system. Obviously, the word **sudden** is an important qualifier that is related to the timing and rate of disturbance. There are several important characteristics used to describe a disturbance: (1) initial predominant effect, (2) frequency, (3) spatial distribution, and (4) temporal distribution. These characteristics define the magnitude of the disturbance on the system (White 1979, Rykiel 1985b).

Disturbances create gaps in forested ecosystems that become localized sites (patches) for regeneration and subsequent growth of vegetation. The size of the patch is directly related to the characteristics of the disturbance regime that created it. The original concept of gap phase is attributed to Watt (1947), who used the term to refer to a patch in a forest created by the death of a canopy tree (Shugart 1984). However, the concept applies to larger scales as well--the area created by a bark beetle infestation or that influenced by a hurricane. A mature forested

ecosystem, therefore, can be viewed as a mosaic of patches in various stages of succession. Similarly, the vegetation dynamics of a wilderness area, which has discrete boundaries, can be viewed as a composite of the mosaic elements (gaps) that are associated with the particular landscape and disturbance regime.

NATURAL DISTURBANCES AND WILDERNESS AREA MANAGEMENT

In the preceding sections we have identified three fundamental issues relative to management planning for wilderness areas. First, forested landscapes change in space and time through operation of the ecosystem assembly process, succession. Second, excessive herbivory (and other natural disturbances) can influence the rate and course of ecological succession and hence the appearance of the landscape. Third, the vegetation dynamics of a wilderness are represented as a mosaic composed of gaps which are in various stages of regeneration and growth. We suggest that the suitability of an area as a wilderness can be defined in part by examination of the interaction of landscape characteristics with disturbance characteristics for a particular forested ecosystem.

The ecological issues associated with this suggestion have been treated in detail by Shugart (1984) in his discussion of categories of dynamic landscapes (Chapter 7). In this discussion Shugart identifies two extreme types of landscapes, which are labeled as nonequilibrium and quasi-equilibrium and described by specific properties (Table 1).

Table 1. Some Properties of Effectively Nonequilibrium and Quasi-Equilibrium Landscapes in the Extreme Cases. (from Shugart 1984).

Property	Effectively Nonequilibrium Landscape	Quasi-Equilibrium Landscape
Disturbance size	Large	Small
Landscape size	Small	Large
Forest age structure	Even-aged for frequent disturbances	All-aged
Total landscape biomass	Unpredictable	Regular
Age distributions of populations	Unstable for long-lived organisms	Stable

The impact of disturbances is of greater consequence to the vegetation dynamics of the nonequilibrium landscape relative to the quasi-equilibrium landscape. That is, the attributes of the nonequilibrium landscape will be altered by disturbance to a greater degree than those of the quasi-equilibrium landscape. Of particular importance in this discussion is the relationship of the scale of disturbance to the scale of the landscape (Fig. 3). A large-scale distur-

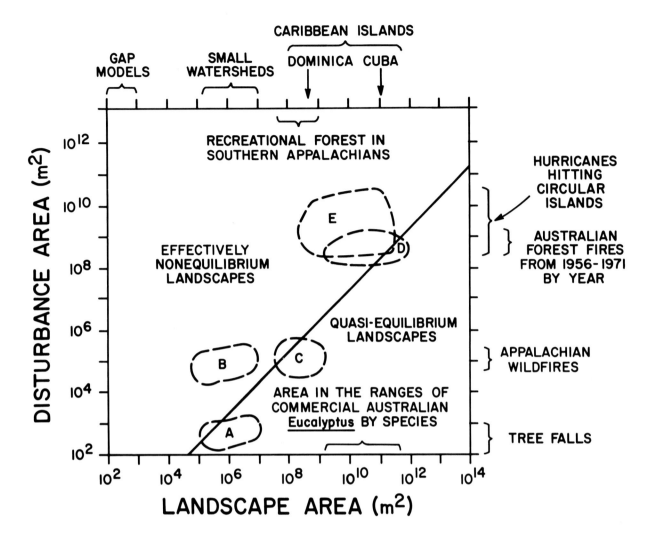

Figure 3. Scale of disturbance and scale of landscape for example ecosystems. The line between the effectively nonequilibrium and the quasi-equilibrium landscapes is based on a 50:1 ratio of landscape area to disturbance area. Combinations of disturbance and landscape scales illustrated include: (a) treefalls on small watersheds, (b) wildfires on small watersheds, (c) wildfires on recreational forests, (d) Australian forest fires on the range of Australian *Eucalyptus* species, (e) hurricanes on Caribbean Islands (From Shugart and West 1981 and Shugart 1984).

bance occurring in a small landscape area will result in a dramatic change in the vegetation dynamics of the forested ecosystem. There will also be corresponding changes in the physical attributes of the landscape, and the subsequent forest may bear little resemblance to its predecessor.

The importance of the relationships between disturbance characteristics and landscape characteristics can be illustrated by examining a case history of southern pine beetle activity in a proposed wilderness site in East Texas, the Four Notch area. This area of about 2500 ha is located in the Raven District of the Sam Houston National Forest in southeast Texas. When the area was proposed as a potential wilderness site, the Four Notch was vegetated primarily with mixed loblolly and shortleaf pines, which had been planted and managed for various purposes throughout the previous half century. The landscape certainly had outstanding physical qualities. However, using the properties in Table 1, the Four Notch would be an ideal example of a nonequilibrium landscape. Eventually the area would be the focus of massive disturbance resulting from excessive herbivory by the southern pine beetle, i.e., massive in the sense that the scale of the disturbance and the scale of the landscape area set aside were the same. Indeed, the southern pine beetle infestation on the Four Notch was the largest ever observed. The specific attributes associated with the landscape, which were used in selecting the site as a potential wilderness, were completely lost as a result of the disturbance.

The consequences of the disturbance event on the Four Notch can be viewed in a number of different ways. First, the recreationist might view the loss of the attributes associated with the old-growth pine forest as a catastrophe. However, because of the attributes of the forest (species composition, diversity, age structure, etc.), the disturbance was highly predictable. The question was not whether the disturbance would occur but when and at what rate. Second, an ecologist interested in ecological succession of forests might view the disturbance as a rare opportunity to observe the operation of ecosystem level processes in the subsequent regeneration of the forest. It is clear that the new forest will not resemble its predecessor in many respects. However, the new forest might also contain outstanding attributes pleasing to a recreationist. Third, the forest manager (and individuals affected by forest economics of the region) might be aghast at the loss of the valuable resource and revenue associated with it. Furthermore, the disturbance created by the bark beetle herbivory creates conditions suitable for a potentially more serious type of disturbance, a forest fire. Indeed, all of these viewpoints were expressed as a result of the events that occurred on the Four Notch.

In conclusion, the ecological concepts presented in this paper are rather fundamental and were all drawn from the published literature. We have identified several relationships between the activities of insects in forest ecosystems; the assembly process, succession; disturbances; and landscape characteristics. In selecting sites for wilderness designation we suggest that the following variables should be considered: the size of the area, the type of forest ecosystem (ranging from nonequilibrium to quasi-equilibrium), and the disturbance regime of the area. In certain cases it will not be possible to retain desirable landscape characteristics because of the interaction of these variables. However, the application of carefully selected forest management practices may provide a way of dampening the effects of the disturbance regime of an area and thereby allow certain desirable wilderness attributes of the landscape to persist.

ACKNOWLEDGMENTS

We acknowledge and thank A.M. Bunting, D. Watkins, and L. Gattis for technical assistance in the preparation of the manuscript. This work was supported by Texas Agricultural Experiment Station Project MS 6009. The opinions expressed herein are those of the authors. This paper is Texas Agric. Exp. Stn. No. 20710.

LITERATURE CITED

Brown, V.K. 1984. Secondary succession: insect-plant relationships. BioScience 34(11):710-716.

Coulson, R.N. and J.A. Witter. 1984. Forest entomology: ecology and management. John Wiley and Sons, N.Y.

Harper, J.L. 1977. The population biology of plants. Academic Press, London.

Mattson, W.J. 1977. The role of arthropods in forest ecosystems. Springer-Verlag, N.Y.

Mattson, W.J. and N.D. Addy. 1975. Phytophagous insects as regulators of forest primary production. Science 190:515-522.

Rykiel, E.J., Jr. 1985a (In press). Ecological disturbances. In Encyclopedia of Systems and Control, Environment Volume, Pergamon Press.

Rykiel, E.J., Jr. 1985b (In press). Ecosystems, disturbed. In Encyclopedia of Systems and Control, Environment Volume, Pergamon Press.

Schowalter, T.D. 1981. Insect herbivore relationship to the state of the host plant: biotic regulation of ecosystem nutrient cycling through ecosystem succession. Oikos 37:126-130.

Schowalter, T.D. 1985. Adaptations of insects to disturbance. pp. 235-252. In S.T.A. Pickett and P.S. White (eds.). The Ecology of Natural Disturbance and Patch Dynamics. Academic Press, N.Y.

Schowalter, T.D., W.W. Hargrove, and D.A. Crossley, Jr. 1986. Herbivory in forested ecosystems. Ann. Rev. Entomol. (In press).

Seastedt, T.R. 1984. The role of microarthropods in decomposition and mineralization processes. Ann. Rev. Entomol. 29:25-46.

Seastedt, T.R. and D.A. Crossley, Jr. 1984. The influence of arthropods on ecosystems. BioScience 34:157-161.

Shugart, H.H. 1984. A theory of forest dynamics: the ecological implications of forest succession models. Springer-Verlag, N.Y.

Shugart, H.H. and D.C. West. 1981. Long-term dynamics of forest ecosystems. Amer. Scientist 69: 647-52.

Watt, A.S. 1947. Pattern and process in the plant community. J. Ecol. 35:1-22.

West, D.C., H.H. Shugart, and D.B. Botkin (eds.). 1981. Forest succession: concepts and application. Springer-Verlag, N.Y.

White, P.S. 1979. Pattern, process, and natural disturbance in vegetation. Bot. Rev. 45:229-299.

Coping With Forest Insect Pests In Southern Wilderness Areas, With Emphasis On The Southern Pine Beetle

by
Ronald F. Billings

ABSTRACT-The protection of wilderness areas in the southern United States from major pest outbreaks is a challenge to wilderness managers. The dense, overmature pine forests that predominate in many of these areas render them extremely vulnerable to destructive insects, particularly the southern pine beetle, *Dendroctonus frontalis*. Several management options for the southern pine beetle have been proposed for use in wilderness areas. These range from letting outbreaks run their course to an aggressive control program aimed at treating expanding infestations soon after detection. The habits of the southern pine beetle as well as advantages and disadvantages of various pest management options for wilderness areas are discussed.

KEYWORDS: direct control, pheromones, pest management, bark beetles, Red-cockaded Woodpecker.

A wide variety of phytophagous insects feeds on forest trees in the southern United States. Many insects are considered economic pests in different stages of commercial forest production. However, once a forested area is set aside as wilderness, all but a few insect species lose their pest status and are no longer of concern. Insect-caused tree mortality, defect, or growth loss are unimportant in wilderness areas because the host trees have no commercial value; the death of individual trees is considered an integral part of natural succession.

A notable exception is damage from the southern pine beetle (SPB), *Dendroctonus frontalis* Zimmermann. This bark beetle attacks and kills all species of southern pine, but loblolly pine (*Pinus taeda* L.) and shortleaf pine (*P. echinata* Mill.) are considered most susceptible. The SPB is notorious for its ability to build large populations in short periods. Because the dense, even-aged pine forests that predominate in many southern wilderness areas had been managed primarily for pure pine sawtimber prior to recent wilderness designation, these areas are more susceptible to SPB outbreaks than natural forests of mixed tree species and age classes. Large infestations that develop under such conditions may threaten the very "wilderness attributes" for which these areas were selected. More importantly, under favorable environmental conditions, beetle infestations may develop to an unmanageable size on wilderness or preserve areas, rapidly spreading to adjacent commercial forests. Experience in Texas (Texas Forest Service 1978, Billings and Varner 1986) has shown that infestations that attain 100-3,000 acres (40-1,200 ha) in size are not uncommon in preserve areas. And once they reach this size, they are

Figure 1. Southern pine bark beetle galleries.

very difficult to bring under control with available technology (Billings 1980, Swain and Remion 1981). Whether or not to manipulate SPB infestations or forest stands within wilderness areas to avoid beetle population explosions has become a controversial issue, particularly in Texas, Louisiana and Mississippi.

This article reviews the biology and infestation characteristics of SPB and discusses options available to wilderness managers for coping with existing or potential beetle infestations. Advantages and disadvantages of different alternatives will be discussed, based on available literature, past experience with the SPB, and forest situations in Texas.

SOUTHERN PINE BEETLE

Southern Pine Beetle Habits

Although five species of bark beetles are native to southern pine forests, the southern pine beetle is considered by far the most destructive (Thatcher *et al.* 1980). Its high reproductive potential and unique attack habits render this species the only bark beetle of concern in southern wilderness areas. Under ideal conditions, SPB development from egg deposition to new adult emergence can take place in as few as 28 days. The number of beetles may increase tenfold in a single generation and up to seven overlapping generations may develop per year in the southern United States.

Outbreak populations of SPB typically occur in multiple-tree infestations, termed "spots." The frequency of spot occurrence and the extent and rate at which active spots enlarge will depend upon the season, the number of infested trees in the spot, and the density and size of pine trees in the stand (Hedden and Billings 1979, Billings and Hynum 1980, Coulson 1980). Spot infestations develop in at least three distinct phases: initiation, expansion, and decline to inactivity.

Spot Initiation Phase--Most large multiple-tree SPB infestations are initiated in the spring, when beetles often attack trees at considerable distances from the spots in which they developed (Billings and Pase 1979, Payne 1980). Pine trees in a weakened condition due to overcrowding, water stress, disease, or injury, serve as centers of initial attack. Attacking female beetles produce a potent pheromone which combines with resin odors from the host tree to draw other flying beetles into the area (Payne 1980). Different pheromones produced by male beetles serve a dual function. At low levels they increase the attractiveness of the female- and host-produced chemicals (Vite' *et al.* 1985) to assure rapid colonization of the tree. At higher concentrations, these chemicals cause arriving beetles to terminate attacks on the initial tree and shift the attack process to adjacent pines within 20-30 feet (6-9 m) (Gara and Coster 1968, Payne 1980).

During the late spring, particularly when aerial beetle populations are high, new infestations may enlarge ex-

tremely rapidly as beetles from outside the immediate area converge on the spot periphery in response to beetle attractants. Since it usually requires 4-6 weeks for the foliage of beetle-killed pines to discolor during the spring (Billings and Kibbe 1978), new SPB spots may range in size from one to several hundred trees by the time they become detectable in aerial surveys. In many cases, due to inherent delays in foliage fading and detection, some spots are rapidly expanding while others may have already been vacated by beetles when they are first detected.

Spot Expansion Phase--The spot expansion phase differs from the spot initiation phase in that most beetles attacking on the periphery of the spot originate from brood trees located within the same infestation. Typically, in spots with 20 or more brood trees, all stages of brood development can be found at any given time. A synchrony becomes established between daily brood emergence near the spot origin and continuous pheromone production at the spot periphery (Gara and Coster 1968). This behavior promotes a self-perpetuating cycle of beetle development and new brood establishment within the same spot. Also, dispersal out of the spot and the resulting beetle mortality is minimized during adverse seasonal periods (hot summer months). The continuous production of pheromones and ample beetle numbers assure that even vigorous, healthy pines are rapidly overcome as the spot expands.

From April through November, large infestations, especially those in dense natural stands, may double in size every 4 to 6 weeks, killing virtually every pine tree in their path if no control is applied. In spots with more than about 100 active trees, beetle density and pheromone production are sufficiently high for infestations to spread in sparse pine stands, in mixed pine/hardwood stands (Johnson and Coster 1978), and through pine stands as young as 5 years of age. The spot expansion phase may continue unabated until cool winter temperatures return, no more pines are available in proximity, or direct control methods (Billings 1980, Swain and Remion 1981) are applied to disrupt pheromone synchrony.

Spot Decline Phase--Admittedly, if left untreated for sufficient time, all SPB spots will eventually become inactive (vacated by beetles), but often not before excessive spot expansion and timber losses have occurred. Uncontrolled spots decline in level of beetle activity for the following general reasons: 1) insufficient number of initially infested trees to establish continual pheromone synchrony; 2) eventual disruption of pheromone synchrony due to insufficient host material in proximity; 3) adverse weather conditions; or 4) other natural causes (Hedden and Billings 1979, Coulson 1980). During the spot decline phase, less than one pine is attacked for each brood tree abandoned in the spot and emerging beetles disperse out of the area or to other spots nearby. The spot eventually becomes inactive, a phenomenon which may occur at any season.

During the fall, many beetles leave uncontrolled infestations to start new spots nearby, while large, well-established infestations may continue to expand as long as temperatures exceed 58 degrees F, the threshold for beetle flight. Thus, the beetle population passes the winter within older active spots and newly infested trees scattered throughout the forest. With the arrival of spring, beetles again will converge into sizeable spots, often in new areas, and the seasonal cycle is repeated.

Not all SPB infestations expand to a large size nor do all spots warrant control. In a study conducted between July 1974 and June 1975, Leuschner et al. (1976) documented that, of 477 SPB infestations detected on the Trinity Ranger District, Davy Crockett National Forest in Texas, 85% contained less than 10 trees in size and only 5% contained 30 or more infested trees. But the few large infestations included 57% of all the beetle-infested trees on the District. Similar relationships have been documented on non-federal lands in Texas (Billings 1980). Hedden and Billings (1979) found that spot growth was sustained primarily in spots that contained more than 20 infested trees in stands having basal areas in excess of 100 sq. ft. per acre (23 sq. m per ha). In turn, the probability that a particular spot would be inactive within 30 days after ground check was inversely correlated with stand density and initial number of active trees. Such relationships have provided the basis for several spot growth models (Billings and Hynum 1980, Turnbow et al. 1982, Stephen and Taha 1981). The ability to reliably

predict which infestations are liable to cause excessive losses in the absence of control has proven valuable for making more intelligent control decisions.

Proposed SPB Control Strategies and Tactics in Wilderness Areas

Five alternatives have been suggested for managing SPB populations in southern wilderness areas: 1) do nothing and let nature take its course; 2) cut a buffer strip immediately outside wilderness areas to prevent the spread of infestations to adjacent land; 3) apply direct control to all expanding infestations that exceed a specified size; 4) use synthetic pheromones to disrupt expanding infestations; and 5) reduce the density of existing pine stands to levels that would no longer support beetle outbreaks. Each approach has certain advantages and disadvantages.

Do Nothing--The approach preferred by many environmentalists is to do nothing to control beetle populations in wilderness areas, allowing natural control mechanisms to operate. This "hands off" approach is favored because it excludes man's activities and, accordingly, does not violate the spirit of the wilderness concept. But, in my opinion, the disadvantages of no control far outweigh the advantages, particularly for those wilderness areas characterized by a preponderance of dense, overmature pine forests (see Billings and Varner 1986 - this proceedings).

Research (Thatcher 1980, Coster and Searcy 1981) and years of practical experience have documented that slow growing, decadent pine forests are extremely susceptible to the occurrence and spread of SPB infestations. To allow nature to run its course in forests that, until very recently, have been managed primarily for pine timber production is to risk losing the very forest for which these areas were set aside. A severe SPB outbreak on these areas is capable of virtually eliminating all pines in the overstory, leaving few hardwoods to occupy the site. Loss of the overstory shade, in turn, will result in rapid invasion of the areas by sun-loving secondary vegetation--brush and weed species. Indeed, many of the areas once occupied by pure pine forests in the Beech Creek Unit of the Big Thicket National Preserve in Texas prior to the 1975-1977 SPB outbreak are still occupied by brush today.

Direct control of expanding infestations and preservation of existing pine forests also are warranted in certain wilderness areas to protect nest trees of the Red-cockaded Woodpecker (*Picoides borealis*), an endangered species that nests only in mature, live pine trees. Finally, and perhaps most importantly, a policy of no control would jeopardize the commercial pine holdings on adjacent land--both federal and private. In Texas, for example, 58% of the land encircling the five recently designated wilderness areas is privately owned (USDA Forest Service, unpublished data). The spread of massive beetle infestations from wilderness land to adjacent private forest is bound to result in personal hardships for adjacent tree farmers and woodlot owners and is likely to precipitate numerous law suits against the USDA Forest

Service. On the positive side, elimination of the dense pine stands on the wilderness areas would alleviate future beetle problems, since beetle-killed stands are likely to be eventually replaced with predominately hardwood forests or mixed pine-hardwood stands less susceptible to SPB.

Cut A Buffer Around Periphery--It has been suggested that a wide buffer should be cut around each wilderness unit, immediately outside the wilderness boundaries. This approach is expected, somehow, to protect neighboring forest lands from the potential spread of SPB infestations off of wilderness areas while preserving the "wilderness attributes" within these areas. The disadvantages of this approach are numerous. As mentioned previously, a majority of the land adjoining wilderness areas, at least in Texas, is privately owned. Most private landowners may be reluctant or unwilling to sacrifice their pine timber for this purpose. Furthermore, there is no assurance that eliminating a strip of pines from the wilderness periphery would have a desirable or lasting effect. Cutting a buffer far in advance of a beetle infestation is not equivalent to a cut-and-leave treatment (Billings 1980), and may have little effect on new spot proliferation on private land. Also, the negative impact of a beetle outbreak within the wilderness area would be the same as that for the no control option -- potential loss of 1) the entire pine component, 2) Red-cockaded Woodpecker habitat, and 3) much of the wilderness attributes that now exist in these areas.

Control Expanding Infestations Within Wilderness--The current USDA Forest Service policy toward control of SPB in Texas wilderness areas is specifically designed to protect nesting colonies of the endangered Red-cockaded Woodpecker and to prevent the development of large expanding infestations capable of spreading to adjoining federal or private land (USDA Forest Service 1983). Infestations with less than 30 currently infested trees are monitored but left untreated unless they 1) are in or immediately adjacent to an active colony of Red-cockaded Woodpeckers, 2) are located on the boundary with private or National Forest land having susceptible pine timber, or 3) have a growth potential to exceed 30 trees within 30 days, based on spot growth projections (Billings and Hynum 1980). Control tactics consist of cut-and-leave, cut-and-remove, or chemical insecticides (Swain and Remion 1981).

Prompt control of certain expanding infestations within southern wilderness areas appears to be a more realistic approach than no control, considering the relatively small size of most areas (less than 10,000 acres, or 4,047 ha), the proximity to managed forest lands, and the inadequacies of current direct control technology to cope with massive beetle infestations. Control strategies during the period May through September are designed to disrupt spot expansion prior to natural beetle dispersal in the fall. Infestations are treated to halt their spread while they are still relatively small and to minimize proliferation of new spots (Billings and Pase 1979).

Cut-and-leave is an effective means of spot disruption during summer months for spots with less than 100 trees.

Spots controlled by cut-and-leave and cut-and-remove are associated with higher levels of new spot proliferation if applied after September (Billings and Pase 1979). Control after September may be necessary, however, to stop the expansion of spots detected during the fall, winter, and following spring. Cut-and-remove (salvage) remains the preferred control tactic for spots with more than 100 active trees, particularly from October through April. The felling and removal of infested trees plus an adequate buffer disrupts the spot and reduces the beetle concentration in the area. Chemical control offers possibilities for reducing beetle densities during the winter in areas where salvage is not possible.

Disadvantages of direct control in wilderness areas are related to violation of the wilderness concept. Although the 1964 Wilderness Act permits control of insect outbreaks, direct control with current technology necessarily requires entry by man, the felling of infested and uninfested, buffer strip trees, and a certain amount of disruption to the area. Salvage, in particular, may cause unsightly destruction to wilderness attributes due to the need for access roads and use of heavy equipment, often when the ground is wet. Paradoxically, the longer control is delayed on expanding spots, the greater the probability that a spot will become inactive without treatment. Yet, certain spots are not likely to be controlled by procrastination, and delayed control of these few large spots will undoubtedly have a much larger negative impact on the total wilderness area than prompt control of numerous small spots. The Four Notch experience is a prime example of the consequences of delayed action (Billings and Varner 1986).

Pheromone Disruption--The primary component of the aggregating pheromone produced by attacking SPB females has been identified and is commonly known as frontalin (Payne 1980). Frontalure, a synthetic attractant composed of frontalin and the host terpene *alpha*-pinene has shown promise as a method for disrupting small SPB infestations. The tactic involves placing synthetic pheromones on nonhost hardwood trees and beetle-killed pine trees near the origin of a spot infestation in order to draw emerging beetles away from natural sources of attraction at the spot periphery. On certain treated spots, the treatment successfully disrupted spot growth processes while untreated spots continued to expand during the course of the experiment (Richerson et al. 1980). More recent experiments have confirmed the efficacy of this approach in Georgia (Dr. C. Wayne Berisford, Univ. of Georgia, personal communication), but similar tests in Texas have been largely unsuccessful to date. More extensive pilot tests in Texas, Louisiana, and Mississippi are now in progress, using improved methods of application.

Although spot disruption using synthetic frontalure remains experimental, the tactic offers considerable promise for future use in southern wilderness areas. Conceivably, small infestations could be treated to disrupt spot expansion without felling beetle-infested or buffer strip trees. Unlike current control tactics, pheromone disruption would cause no adverse effects on site or stand conditions in treated areas. Concurrent development of control strategies using inhibitory compounds produced by male beetles (Payne et al. 1979) may eventually permit treatment of a large number of infestations by aerial application (Vite' and Francke 1976, Billings 1980). Such a strategy would offer definite advantages over conventional mechanical controls for the protection of pine-laden wilderness areas.

Keep in mind, however, that the operational use of pheromones for SPB control must await more conclusive field experiments of efficacy and registration by the Environmental Protection Agency. Costs may prohibit use over extensive forest areas. Perhaps most importantly, one must consider that success under experimental conditions does not assure that a new tactic will become operational. Until pheromone control strategies can be refined and made operational, current cut-and-leave and cut-and-remove tactics are preferred for spot disruption.

Pine Density Regulation--A final approach to the SPB problem in southern wilderness areas that warrants consideration is to reduce the density of pines to levels that would no longer support expanding infestations. Research has shown that both the incidence of SPB infestations and the subsequent rate of spot growth increase dramatically in pine stands when the basal area (a measure of stand density) exceeds 100 sq. ft. per acre (23 sq. m per ha) (Hedden and Billings 1979, Coster and Searcy 1981). By reducing the pine basal areas in newly-designated wilderness areas to levels more characteristic of unmanaged natural stands (e.g., 60-80 sq. ft. per acre, or 14-18 sq. m per ha), future SPB problems would be minimized.

In selecting pines to save, all currently occupied nesting trees and a sufficient number of potential ones would be left to assure protection and perpetuation of local Red-cockaded Woodpecker populations. Openings in the stands created by the elimination of excess pines would seed back to pines or, more likely, to hardwood species. Eventually, mixed pine-hardwood stands of diverse age classes would be created. Such forests are less prone to large scale beetle outbreaks. Bark beetles would continue to infest the remaining pines as they weaken with age or disease, but infestations would be limited to a few trees and provide little threat to adjacent timberland.

Assuming that permission was granted to reduce the pine density in these wilderness areas, the question would become how best to achieve this hazard reduction under these environmentally-sensitive circumstances. I suggest that selected pines be killed by treating them with herbicides injected into basal frills in the stem just as foresters routinely eliminate unwanted hardwoods. This approach would avoid the need to build roads into the wilderness areas or to bring in heavy machinery. The deadened trees would be left standing, becoming host material for secondary bark beetles (Ips engraver beetles), pine sawyers, and cavity-nesting birds. The dead pines would eventually fall to the ground of their own accord,

causing little damage to adjacent trees.

To reduce the possibility of colonization by SPB, unwanted pines could be treated at a time when secondary insects are most abundant and long-range immigration of southern pine beetle into these areas is least likely to occur (e.g. in midsummer). If necessary, invasion of herbicide-treated trees by Ips beetles and sawyers, rather than SPB, could be assured by baiting each tree with appropriate synthetic pheromones--a combination of Ips attractants and southern pine beetle inhibitors (Payne et al. 1979, Texas Forest Service 1980). Unlike the SPB, these secondary insects are seldom capable of invading healthy trees, even at high beetle population levels. Thus, only preselected and treated pines would be eliminated.

If successful, the ultimate result would be a balanced, uneven-aged forest of pine and hardwood that would evolve towards a more stable and natural climax forest ecosystem. In the interim, a sufficient number of large mature pines would remain in these areas for current generations to enjoy. Also, surrounding timberlands would no longer be threatened by the potential for excessive beetle population buildups in these areas.

To my knowledge, such an approach for pine density reduction has never been attempted on a large scale. To pursue this approach short-term studies could be conducted to more conclusively establish the optimal season for herbicide treatment to assure rapid colonization by secondary insects and minimal invasion by SPB. And selected areas with similar stand conditions outside wilderness areas could first be treated as demonstrations. On the negative side, implementation would require short-term vegetative manipulation by man, a decision that could be interpreted as a violation of the wilderness concept.

CONCLUSION

Since long-term preservation of the present forest conditions in these pine-dominated wilderness areas is not possible, wilderness administrators need to decide what the ultimate forest structure should be for these areas. Several scenarios are possible: 1) a wasteland of brush and dead pine snags that may eventually develop into a natural forest ecosystem, 2) an uneven-aged perpetual pine forest or 3) a climax forest of shade tolerant hardwoods, primarily oaks and hickories. Choice No. 1 is perhaps the easiest to obtain. Just exclude beetle control and let a massive SPB outbreak eliminate the existing pine overstory. The increased sunlight on the forest floor would lead to rapid invasion of sun-loving pioneer plants such as sweet gum and other scrub hardwood species, brush or more pine. Should a fire pass over the area within a few years, pine seedlings would sprout near seed sources but more brush would return to most of the area. Succession to a climax hardwood forest might require 50 to 100 years by this route.

Choice No. 2 would likely result if openings in the pine overstory were made over several successive decades.

Such openings are the end result of a direct control of beetle infestations as they occur in these wilderness areas.

A climax forest of oaks, hickories, and other shade tolerant hardwood species (choice No. 3) should perpetuate itself and is likely to offer the fewest management and pest problems. A climax forest will appear in the shortest period of time within wilderness areas now occupied by mature pine forests if the existing overstory of pine is maintained. Indeed, the shade that pines provide is essential for seed germination and early development of desired hardwood species. Protection of the' pine overstory from SPB outbreaks and exclusion of fire will be necessary for at least 10 to 20 years. In summary, then, initial manipulation of wilderness areas by man to reduce pine density and susceptibility to SPB outbreaks (e.g. vegetation management) would seem to offer the least disruptive means to prolong a wilderness appearance in these areas while fostering an understory of climax hardwoods. If vegetative management is to be prohibited, prompt control of both SPB infestations and wildfire offers the next best alternative.

LITERATURE CITED

Billings, R.F. 1980. Direct control. pp. 179-192. In R.C. Thatcher, J.L. Searcy, J.E. Coster, and G.D. Hertel (eds.). The Southern Pine Beetle. USDA For. Serv. Tech. Bull. 1631.

Billings, R.F. and B.G. Hynum. 1980. Southern pine beetle: guide for predicting timber losses from expanding spots in east Texas. Tex. For. Serv. Circ. 249.

Billings, R.F. and H.A. Pase, III. 1979. Spot proliferation patterns as a measure of the area-wide effectiveness of southern pine beetle control tactics. pp. 86-97. In J.E. Coster and J.L. Searcy (eds.). Evaluating Control Tactics for the Southern Pine Beetle-Symp. Proc. Jan. 30-Feb.1, 1979. Many, La. USDA For. Serv. Tech. Bull. No. 1613.

Billings, R.F. and F.E. Varner. 1986. Why control southern pine beetle infestations in wilderness areas? - the Four Notch and Huntsville State Park experiences. pp.129-134. In D.L. Kulhavy and R.N. Conner (eds.). Wilderness and Natural Areas in the Eastern United States: A Management Challenge, Nacogdoches, Tex. May 13-15, 1985.

Coster, J.E. and J.L. Searcy (eds.). 1981. Site, stand, and host characteristics of southern pine beetle infestations. USDA Comb. For. Pest Res. and Dev. Prog. Tech. Bull. No. 1612.

Coulson, R.N. 1980. Population dynamics. pp. 75-105. In R.C. Thatcher, J.L. Searcy, J.E. Coster, and G.D. Hertel (eds.). The Southern Pine Beetle. USDA For. Serv. Tech. Bull. 1631.

Gara, R.I. and J.E. Coster. 1968. Studies on the attack behavior of the southen pine beetle. III. Sequence of tree infestation within stands. Contrib. Boyce Thompson Inst. 24:77-85.

Hedden, R.L. and R.F. Billings. 1979. Southern pine beetle: factors influencing the growth and decline of summer infestations in east Texas. For. Sci. 25:547-556.

Johnson, P.C. and J.E. Coster. 1978. Probability of attack by southern pine beetle in relation to distance from an attractive host tree. For. Sci. 24:574-580.

Leuschner, W.A., H.E. Burkhart, G.D. Spittle, I.R. Ragenovich, and R.N. Coulson. 1976. A descriptive study of host and site variables associated with the occurrence of Dendroctonus frontalis Zimm. in east Texas. Southwest. Entomol. 1:141-149.

Payne, T.L. 1980. Life history and habits. pp. 7-8. In. R.C. Thatcher, J.L. Searcy, J.E. Coster, and G.D. Hertel (eds.). The Southern Pine Beetle. USDA For. Serv. Tech. Bull. 1631.

Payne, T.L., J.E. Coster, and P.C. Johnson. 1979. Development and evaluation of synthetic inhibitors for use in southern pine beetle pest management. pp. 139-143. In. Current Topics in Forest Entomology. USDA For. Serv. Gen. Tech. Rep. WO-8.

Richerson, J.V., F.A. McCarty, and T.L. Payne. 1980. Disruption of southern pine beetle infestations with frontalure. Environ. Entomol. 9:90-93.

Stephen, F.M. and H.A. Taha. 1981. Validation, testing and implementation of a southern pine beetle damage and population prediction model. Pineville, Louisiana. USDA For. Serv., Southern For. Exp. Stn. (unpublished progress report to IPM RD&A Program).

Swain, K.M. and M.C. Remion. 1981. Direct control methods for the southern pine beetle. USDA Agric. Handb. No. 575.

Texas Forest Service. 1978. Texas forest pest activity 1976-1977 and Forest Pest Control Section biennial report. Tex. For. Serv. Publ. 117.

Texas Forest Service. 1980. Texas forest pest activity 1978-1979 and Forest Pest Control Section biennial report. Tex. For. Serv. Publ. No. 121.

Thatcher, R.C., J.L. Searcy, J.E. Coster, G.D. Hertel, (eds.). 1980. The southern pine beetle. USDA For. Serv. Tech. Bull. No. 1631.

Turnbow, R.H., R.N. Coulson, L. Hu, and R.F. Billings. 1982. Procedural guide for using the interactive version of the TAMBEETLE model of southern pine beetle population and spot dynamics. Tex. A&M Agric. Exp. Stn. MP-1518, College Station, Tex.

USDA Forest Service. 1983. Southern pine beetle control in RARE II recommended wilderness and further planning areas, National Forests in Texas: Environmental Assessment Report. Southern Region, July 1983.

Vite' J.P. and W. Francke. 1976. The aggregation pheromones of bark beetles: Progress and problems. Naturwissen. 63:550-555.

Vite' J.P., R.F. Billings, C.W. Ware, and K. Mori. 1985. Southern pine beetle: enhancement or inhibition of aggregation response mediated by enantiomers of endo-brevicomin. Naturwissen. 72:99-100.

Hazard Rating For Southern Pine Beetles On Wilderness Areas On The National Forests In Texas

by
James D. Smith and Wesley A. Nettleton

ABSTRACT--In 1984, Congress designated five areas on the National Forests in Texas as wilderness areas. Hazard rating analysis of these wilderness areas indicates that their timber stands are more susceptible to southern pine beetle attack than managed timber stands. In the absence of preventive management, major damaging outbreaks of southern pine beetles can be expected to continue in these wilderness areas. The results of such outbreaks are severe losses in wilderness and disruption of management on surrounding public and private land.

KEYWORDS: loblolly pine, *Dendroctonus frontalis*.

Forest managers frequently attempt to minimize losses from the southern pine beetle (SPB), *Dendroctonus frontalis* Zimmermann, in two ways: (1) by felling infested trees after an outbreak has been developed (Swain and Remion 1981), and (2) by thinning or removing high-risk stands before outbreaks occur. Stand hazard rating, the key to the second approach, may also be useful for managing other forest pests (Mason *et al.* 1985).

Managing stands and forests to make them less attractive to SPB is an alternative if it is compatible with other long-term management goals. Old, overly dense pure pine stands are especially susceptible to beetle outbreaks. SPB hazard ratings help to identify such stands and justify thinnings or final harvests (Belanger and Malac 1980). Such options are severely limited in wilderness areas, however. Bark beetle control helped create the large, aesthetically pleasing stands of mature pines we now have in most Texas wilderness areas. Where these activities are limited or excluded from Wilderness Areas, the SPB ultimately has the potential to decimate the stands.

Five tracts of land on the National Forests in Texas were designated as Wilderness Areas by Congress in the 1984 Texas Wilderness Act--Bill HR 3788: Turkey Hill and Upland Island on the Angelina Ranger District, Angelina National Forest; Little Lake Creek on the Raven Ranger District, Sam Houston National Forest; Big Slough on the Neches Ranger District, Davy Crockett National Forest; and Indian Mounds on the Yellowpine Ranger District, Sabine National Forest.

For planning purposes, we rated the new Wilderness Areas for SPB hazard. We used the National Forest Risk System (NF RISK) developed for the National Forests in the Southern Region. A rating of high, medium or low risk

is assigned to each stand (Lorio and Sommers 1981). When the wilderness hazard (percentage of acres with high risk) is compared to the hazard of the associated districts, it is easy to see a pattern (Table 1). The Wilderness Areas generally have higher SPB hazard ratings than managed timberlands.

Table 1. Acres (by Percent) of Southern Pine Beetle Hazard Classes[a] within Wilderness Areas and Associated Ranger Districts in Texas.

Wilderness Area/Ranger District	Hazard Class		
	High	Medium	Low
Little Lake Creek	25	53	22
Raven Ranger District	18	21	59
Upland Island	16	41	43
Turkey Hill	42	34	24
Angelina Ranger District	4	15	81
Big Slough	10	17	73
Neches Ranger District	12	20	68
Indian Mounds	13	54	34
Yellowpine Ranger District	6	8	86

[a] This includes all forest types.

Little Lake Creek Wilderness Area had the highest percentage of high and medium acres while the Big Slough had the least. The Upland Island, Turkey Hill, Little Lake Creek, and Indian Mounds Wilderness Areas had more than 50 percent of their acreage in high and medium hazard classes, but none of the Ranger Districts associated with these wilderness areas had more than 50 percent of their acreage in high and medium hazard classes. The Raven Ranger District had the highest percent acreage (30 percent) in the high and medium hazard classes.

The probability of SPB infestation (risk) and the potential for resource loss (hazard) can be used together to estimate future SPB problems for forest stands. We did so by combining Texas Forest Service Grid Hazard (Billings and Bryant 1983), which rates hazard on 18,000 acre (7,285 ha) units based on photo-interpreted stand and landform variables, with an SPB population factor (based on number of spots detected in the past 2 years). The results are "risk rating" values for each grid block (Table 2). SPB

highly susceptible host type for the SPB during endemic periods.

What can we or should we do? Clearly, the pest problems of potential wilderness areas or areas where management is to be limited should be considered before the area is designated. But what of the areas we already have? We believe that the SPB will eventually remove the old-growth pine from these areas and lessen the hazard. In the meantime, managers will have to continue to weigh

Table 2.   SPB Hazard and Risk Rating of Texas Wilderness Areas Using the TSF Grid Block System.

Wilderness Area	Grid Block	Approximate % of WA	SPB Hazard[a]	SPB Risk 1984[b]	1985[c]
Little Lake Creek	316	75%	High	High	Extreme
	266	21%	High	High	Extreme
	265	4%	High	Moderate	Extreme
Upland Island	882	47%	Low	Low	Low
	832	39%	High	Moderate	High
	833	9%	High	High	High
	883	5%	Moderate	Moderate	Moderate
Big Slough	623	75%	Moderate	High	Moderate
	573	25%	Low	Moderate	Moderate
Turkey Hill	684	89%	High	Extreme	High
	685	11%	Low	Moderate	Low
Indian Mounds	690	38%	Low	Moderate	Low
	689	27%	Moderate	High	Moderate
	740	18%	Low	Moderate	Low
	739	17%	Moderate	High	Moderate
	738	Adjacent	High	Extreme	High
	789	Adjacent	High	Extreme	High

[a] Based from an analysis of pine host abundance and suitability for SPB infestations, derived from recent aerial photographs.

[b] Based on a combination of hazard class and 1982–1983 southern pine beetle activity.

[c] Based on a combination of hazard class and 1983–1984 southern pine beetle activity.

activity is expected to be concentrated in grid blocks rated as moderate, high, or extreme risk. Little Lake Creek is the only Wilderness Area where all grid blocks are currently categorized as extreme risk. Ten other grid blocks contain high and moderate risk ratings. Only four grid blocks are categorized as low risk.

The number of SPB infestations/1000 acres during 1984-85 demonstrates the accuracy of these classifications (Figure 1). There were more SPB infestations (spots)/1000 acres in the Little Lake Creek, Indian Mounds, and Turkey Hill Wilderness Areas than on the remainders of the Ranger Districts. During 1984, 96 percent of the acres in Little Lake Creek were classified as high risk. In 1985, 100 percent of the acreage increased to extreme risk. There were 16.7 infestations/1,000 acres in Little Lake Creek compared to 12.5 infestations/1,000 acres on the Raven District in 1984-85. Thus, in this example, when the infestations/1000 acres were analyzed, the results were equal to the hazard and risk classifications .

It is clear that the areas chosen for wilderness attributes are also areas where the SPB can be expected to cause extensive losses. This danger is highly evident during outbreak years which we are now experiencing. More importantly, these areas will continue to provide

the importance of undisturbed wilderness against the economic losses that will be suffered by adjoining landowners during SPB outbreaks.

LITERATURE CITED

Belanger, R.P. and B.F. Malac. 1980. Southern pine beetle handbook: silviculture can reduce losses from the southern pine beetle. USDA Agric. Handb. 576. 17 p.

Billings, R.F. and C.M. Bryant, V. 1983. Developing a system for mapping the abundance and distribution of SPB habitats in east Texas. In: Proc. Symp. on Insect and Host Tree Interactions. 1983 March 29-31; Freiberg, West Germany. Zeit. agnew. Entomol. 96:208-216.

Lorio, P.L., Jr. and R.A. Sommers. 1981. Use of available resource data to rate stands for southern pine beetle risk. In: Hazard rating systems in forest insect pest management: Symposium proceedings. USDA For. Serv. Gen. Tech. Rep. WO-27. pp. 75-78.

Mason, G.N., P.L. Lorio, Jr., R.P. Belanger, and W.A. Nettleton. 1985. Integrated pest management handbook: rating the susceptibility of stands to southern pine beetle attack. USDA For. Serv. Agric. Handb. No. 645. 31p.

Swain, K.M. and M.C. Remion. 1981. Southern pine beetle handbook: direct control methods for the southern pine beetle. USDA Agric. Handb. 575. 15p.

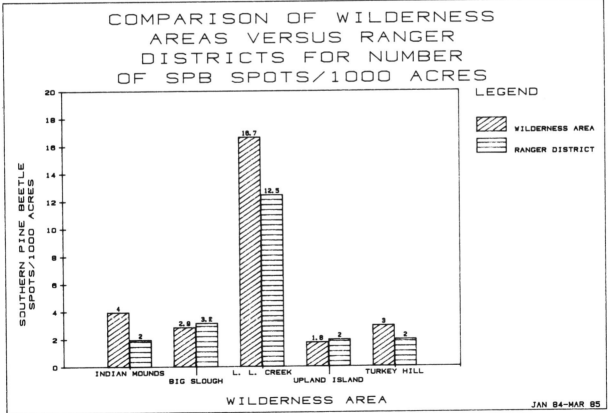

Figure 1. Comparison of Southern pine beetle infestations/1,000 acres during 1984-1985 in wilderness areas and associated ranger districts on the National Forests in Texas.

Why Control Southern Pine Beetle Infestations In Wilderness Areas?
The Four Notch And Huntsville State Park Experiences

by
Ronald F. Billings and Forrest E. Varner

ABSTRACT-The outcomes of two different pest management options available to wilderness managers (no control versus prompt control) for dealing with outbreak populations of southern pine beetle, (*Dendroctonus frontalis*), can be forecast, based on recent experiences in Texas. An initial decision of no control on the Four Notch Further Planning (proposed wilderness) Area within the Sam Houston National Forest ultimately resulted in the devastation of over 3,700 acres (1,500 ha) of prized pine forests, loss of several nesting sites of red-cockaded woodpeckers (*Picoides borealis*), and spread of infestations to adjacent federal and private forest land. In contrast, detection and treatment of infestations of similar potential on the nearby Huntsville State Park in the early stages of outbreak development successfully protected the park's forest and recreational values. In southern wilderness areas comprised of previously managed pine forests, prompt control of expanding beetle infestations is deemed essential and beneficial until a more diverse and stable forest ecosystem is achieved.

KEYWORDS: salvage control, cut-and-leave, pest management, endangered species, loblolly pine, shortleaf pine.

One of the most controversial issues facing management of newly designated wilderness areas in the South is whether or not to control infestations of the southern pine beetle (SPB), (*Dendroctonus frontalis* Zimmermann). Certain environmentalists claim that direct control measures are neither effective nor appropriate in wilderness areas; they prefer to let nature take its course with no interference by man. The USDA Forest Service considers direct control of certain, expanding infestations within wilderness areas as essential 1) to prevent the buildup of massive beetle populations and their subsequent spread to adjacent private and federal forest lands, and 2) to protect nesting sites of the endangered Red-cockaded Woodpecker, *Picoides borealis*. In my opinion, control of SPB infestations also is warranted in wilderness areas to prevent rapid and total loss of the predominate pine overstory that comprises the primary "wilderness attribute" in many of these areas (Billings 1986).

The consequences of two management alternatives for SPB infestations (delayed versus prompt control) were documented in two case studies in Walker County, Texas, during 1983 and 1984: the Four Notch Further Planning Area on the Sam Houston National Forest and the nearby Huntsville State Park. A description of each area and a chronology of events follow.

FOUR NOTCH FURTHER PLANNING AREA

During 1983, a severe SPB outbreak developed in the Four Notch Further Planning Area on the Raven Ranger District, Sam Houston National Forest, about 11 miles (18 km) southeast of Huntsville, Texas. The 6,832-acre (2767 ha) Four Notch tract, a candidate for wilderness designation at the time, was stocked with dense stands of 80-to-100-year-old trees, predominately loblolly (*Pinus taeda* L.) and shortleaf (*P. echinata* Mill.) pines. Infestations expanded from 10 acres (4 ha) in April 1983 to over 2000 acres (810 ha) by the end of the same year. Similar SPB outbreaks occurred on certain units of the Big Thicket National Preserve in southeast Texas in the mid-1970's (Texas Forest Service 1978). These and the Four Notch case demonstrate the destructive potential of epidemic SPB populations when favored with optimal conditions of abundant host type, mild weather, and delayed or inadequate control efforts.

1976--The Texas Committee on Natural Resources (TCONR) filed a law suit to keep the USDA Forest Service from making a timber sale in the Four Notch Area. This legal action resulted in a court injunction, temporarily halting all cutting designated to regenerate even-aged stands on the National Forests in Texas. Although the U.S. Circuit Court in New Orleans eventually reversed the lower court's decision and dissolved the injunction, in the interim the Four Notch Area had been set aside as a further planning area for potential wilderness designation in the RARE II (Roadless Area Review and Evaluation) process. Because of the lawsuit/injunction and RARE II classification, no forest management activity occurred between 1976 and 1983, allowing the pine stands to become even more susceptible to SPB. Beetle infestations detected within the Four Notch unit during the 1970's (Overgaard 1976) were effectively controlled while still small by prompt cutting and removal (Swain and Remion 1981).

1980--The number of SPB infestations on the Four Notch unit increased (Smith 1980), but hot, dry weather that summer kept the spots small, and they eventually went inactive without control.

August 1982--Several multiple-tree SPB spots were detected in the Four Notch unit (Nettleton and Overgaard 1982).

September 1982--USDA Forest Service pest management entomologists from Pineville, Louisiana, made a biological evaluation of the SPB activity in the Four Notch. Based on the abundance of very susceptible host type and active beetle infestations, direct control was recommended (Nettleton and Overgaard 1982). The spots were monitored throughout the winter, but control was delayed due to the area's sensitivity and RARE II designation. Also, since SPB activity had been insignificant in Texas since 1977, there was doubt whether the infestations would develop to an unmanageable size.

April 1983--A mild winter in 1982-83 did little to reduce overwintering beetle populations and, by April, 20-25 infestations were found in the area. Individual spots ranged from less than 1 acre to 10 acres (0.4 to 4 ha) in size. Ironically, prompt control of these relatively small infestations at this time would have caused only minor disruption to the area, but control action was postponed during preparation of the Environmental Assessment required by the area's RARE II status.

April 1983--A USDA Forest Service report (Nettleton and Smith 1983) revealed that 85% of the pine host type in the Four Notch area was rated as high hazard to SPB, based on prevailing site/stand conditions.

In a letter dated April 21, 1983 to the Supervisor of the National Forests in Texas, Texas Forest Service (TFS) Principal Entomologist Ronald F. Billings noted that most proposed wilderness areas, including Four Notch, were located in grid blocks (18,000 acre, or 7,285 ha units) rated as high hazard to SPB. This conclusion was based on a recent TFS evaluation of susceptible pine type, interpreted from aerial photographs (Billings and Bryant 1983). A recommendation was made to control all SPB infestations with more than 100 trees at all seasons and those with more than 30 active trees between September and May, regardless of their location in proposed wilderness areas.

The first set of periodic aerial (35mm) color photographs of the Four Notch infestation was taken by the TFS Pest Control Section on April 11, 1983. Subsequent oblique aerial photos were taken on June 9, July 8, August 2, September 21, October 13, November 11, 1983, February 10, and April 5, 1984 to document progression of the outbreak.

June 1983--Color infrared aerial photographs (scale 1:12,-

000) were taken by the USDA Forest Service on June 8 and October 12, 1983. Similar photo missions were flown by the TFS in July and September, 1983, to document SPB infestation spread and timber mortality. USDA Forest Service pest management entomologists from Pineville, La. completed a second biological evaluation of the Four Notch; 32 multiple tree SPB spots with up to 23,276 currently infested trees were revealed by aerial photography. Prompt control action was recommended (Oliveria et al. 1983).

July 5, 1983--The USDA Forest Service document entitled "Environmental Assessment - Southern Pine Beetle Control in Proposed Wilderness Areas and Further Planning Areas-National Forests in Texas" was completed (USDA Forest Service 1983). The Regional Forester in Atlanta, Georgia approved a decision notice providing for control of SPB infestations in Four Notch and two other Further Planning Areas in Texas. With this approval, preparations for salvage control began in the Four Notch unit. Cutting boundaries were marked around infestations to be salvaged. The first sale was advertised on July 15 and awarded on July 22. By this time, there were 26 active infestations; the largest covered 300 acres (121 ha) and two additional spots were in excess of 50 acres (20 ha) and rapidly growing.

July 9, 1983--The TCONR and the Lone Star Chapter of the Sierra Club made a request to the Chief, USDA Forest Service, to appeal the Regional Forester's decision to initiate SPB control, requesting preparation of an Environmental Impact Statement (EIS). Preparing such a document would have further delayed control efforts for 6-8 more months. These environmental groups claimed that bark beetle control was just a ploy by the USDA Forest Service to destroy the wilderness attributes and disqualify the Four Notch from further wilderness consideration.

July 14, 1983--National Forest personnel held a field tour for local environmental groups and news media to demonstrate the severity of the beetle problem and the need for control action. Despite the growing magnitude of the problem, environmental activists remained unconvinced of the urgent need for control.

July 15, 1983--USDA Forest Service crews marked small infestations bordering private land to be controlled with cut-and-leave (Texas Forest Service 1975). On small spots mechanical shearing of infested trees was effective, but breakouts occurred on several larger spots, where retreatment was required.

July 21, 1983--Request by environmental groups for stay-of-control action was denied by Chief, USDA Forest Service.

August 10, 1983--The Regional Forester issued an amended decision notice which incorporated conservation recommendations of the U.S. Fish and Wildlife Service for protection of Red-cockaded Woodpecker colonies. SPB control could now be initiated in RARE II Further Planning areas for purposes of protecting existing nesting sites of this endangered species.

August 1983--A buffer strip was effectively used to prevent infestation spread through a 13-year-old plantation on the west side of the Four Notch. By mid-August, the largest infestation had merged with two smaller spots, was approaching 1,300 acres (526 ha) in size, and was spreading at 50 feet (15.2 m) per day along a 3 1/2 mile (5.6 km) front. Salvage efforts, begun in late July, were hampered by high rainfall and wet ground conditions. On August 18, Hurricane Alicia further cur-

tailed control operations; high winds blew trees down across roads and high rainfall further inundating the area with rain. Of 18 salvage sales awarded only one was carried to completion. Accordingly, beetles continued to spread, advancing onto federal and private forest land adjacent to the Four Notch unit.

September 1983--Following recommendations of federal and state pest control specialists, chain saw crews brought in from Kentucky, Tennessee, New Mexico, and other states started felling a wide buffer strip along the active

front of the large infestation. The buffer, in this case, consisted of 125 feet (38 m) of freshly-attacked pines and an equal width of green uninfested pines. After 4 weeks (by October 10), the buffer was completed. The buffer stopped the forward progress of the infestation at about 1500 acres (607 ha), although several breakouts required subsequent treatment. In addition, 25 to 30 smaller infestations containing about 500 acres (202 ha), were subse-

quently treated with cut-and-leave (Swain and Remion 1981).

September 3, 1983--Biologists reported that, of 12 known Red-cockaded Woodpecker colonies in the Four Notch unit, five had been infested and eliminated by the beetle, two were threatened, and five remained unaffected.

Meeting at the Raven Ranger District on September 29, state, federal, and Texas A&M University entomologists unanimously recommended continued control efforts during fall and winter with the goal of removing as much of the infested timber as possible prior to beetle dispersal in the spring.

October 6, 1983--The Environmental Assessment was amended to accommodate removal of all infested material, regardless of spot size, to increase the effectiveness of winter suppression efforts. (The original Environmental Assessment specified a 30 infested tree threshold before control would be conducted.) An amendment permitted temporary road construction and improvement within the Four Notch unit and also allowed use of cut-and-leave throughout the year on all sizes of SPB infestations. From the available alternatives, helicopter logging was selected as the preferred means to remove infested trees while minimizing further site disruption and road building. The sale was awarded to Columbia Helicopters of Portland, Oregon.

October 20, 1983--A second appeal by the TCONR and Sierra Club to halt fall and winter control was made to the Chief, USDA Forest Service. This appeal was denied on November 4, 1983.

November 7, 1983--A hearing of the Subcommittee on Public Lands and National Parks, Committee on Interior and Insular Affairs, United States House of Representatives, was held in Washington, D.C., on the Texas wilderness issue. Among those testifying on behalf of continued winter control of SPB in the Four Notch were Congressman Charles Wilson, Raymond Housley (Deputy Chief, National Forest System, USDA Forest Service), David Dailey (Supervisor's Office, National Forests in Texas), Dr. David Drummond (Forest Pest Management, USDA Forest Service), Dr. Ronald Billings (Texas Forest Service), and Dr. Thomas Payne (Texas A&M University). Environmental group representatives, led by George Russell (Lone Star Chapter, Sierra Club), argued for discontinuation of further control.

December 1983--Helicopter salvage operations began in early December and continued until August of 1984. Emphasis was placed on prompt removal of beetle-infested logs within the buffer strip, as well as more recently infested trees in breakout areas and adjacent infestations. Two weeks of subfreezing temperatures in East Texas in late December raised hope that beetle populations would be controlled by natural causes. A survey of overwintering beetle populations by federal and state entomologists following the freeze revealed some beetle mortality, but not enough to solve the beetle problem (Texas Forest Service 1984).

July, 1984--Mild temperatures in January and February 1984 permitted beetle populations to increase, but further expansion of the large infestation had been halted by the buffer strip. Numerous new spots, however, were initiated in neighboring stands damaged by Hurricane Alicia the summer before. By late June, nearly 1000 infestations had been detected throughout the Sam Houston National Forest and on adjacent industrial, state, and private land. By late July 1984, when the helicopter operation concluded, some 27 million board feet of infested and buffer strip trees had been removed from the Four Notch area.

Outcome

According to final USDA Forest Service figures (Dr. F. Oliveria, USDA Forest Service personal communication), 3,736 acres (1,512 ha) were ultimately affected by the SPB outbreak and the efforts to control it. This represents about 55% of the Four Notch Further Planning Area. Of this total, 2,927 acres (1,185 ha) of timber had been salvaged by helicopter or by conventional methods, 77 acres (31 ha) of trees had been felled and left in the woods, and the remaining 732 acres (296 ha) contained dead pine trees that had been killed by the beetle but left standing. For these reasons, the Four Notch unit was eventually excluded from wilderness consideration. On October 30, 1984, five less disturbed areas in East Texas, covering 34,400 acres (13,920 ha), were designated as wilderness. Unfortunately, most of these latter areas

support similar stands of beetle-prone forests, setting the stage for outbreaks like that at Four Notch unless prompt direct control is adopted as a wilderness management option.

HUNTSVILLE STATE PARK

In striking contrast to the Four Notch catastrophe is the SPB control program achieved in 1984 on the Huntsville State Park, located less than 10 miles (16 km) to the west of Four Notch. The Huntsville State Park is a 2083 acre (843 ha) high-use recreation area, including a 300-acre (121 ha) lake, located within an hour's drive of the city of Houston. The forest stands within the park boundaries

consist of mature 60-to-70-year-old loblolly and shortleaf pine stands, mixed in certain areas with hardwoods. On August 18, 1983, Hurricane Alicia passed over the park, blowing down and damaging pines scattered throughout the area. Many of these storm-damaged pines became focal points for SPB infestations in 1984. Six detection flights conducted by the Texas Forest Service (TFS) revealed 49 multiple-tree SPB infestations (spots) within the park boundaries in 1984. The area contained more than 20 multiple-tree spots per 1000 acres (405 ha) of host type, a level far exceeding that which defines an SPB outbreak (one spot per 1000 acres, or 405 ha) or even that present on June 8, 1983, on the Four Notch area (about 6.9 spots per 1000 acres) (Oliveria *et al.* 1983).

The Texas Parks and Wildlife Department, the agency responsible for administering State parks in Texas, was concerned about the spread of beetle infestations and the potential impact of an uncontrolled beetle outbreak on the natural and recreational values of the park. The decision was made to contract with the TFS for evaluation and control needs. TFS employees visited each infestation to establish the level of beetle activity and the need for control, using available evaluation criteria (Billings and Pase 1979). Spot sizes ranged from 20 to 200 active trees in pine stands which averaged 100 to 130 sq. ft./acre (23 to 30 sq. m/ha) of basal area; spot growth potential was high. The larger, expanding infestations were marked for salvage, and timber sales were advertised in local newspapers. In short order, private salvage operators were contracted to fell and remove the marked trees (infested trees plus a buffer). Smaller inaccessible spots were treated by the cut-and-leave method or monitored where spot growth was expected to be negligible (Billings and Hynum 1980). Control activities were closely monitored by TFS technicians to assure correct application and minimal site disturbance.

In all, 29 spots were salvaged, 7 were treated by cutting-and-leaving infested trees, and the remaining 13 were declared inactive. Some 421,900 board feet of sawtimber and 137 cords of pulpwood were salvaged. Averages of 8610 board feet and 2.8 cords were taken per spot. Occasional breakouts were treated by felling a few additional trees. In all, 36 infestations were promptly and effectively controlled and total affected acreage was held to about 80 acres (32.4 ha). Clearly, a potential disaster was avoided by prompt action in the early stages of outbreak development. Similar programs of prompt control have become routine on federal (Smith and Conner 1985), industrial, and small privately-owned forests (Texas Forest Service 1978, 1984) managed for multiple uses and/or timber production.

FOUR NOTCH-HUNTSVILLE STATE PARK COMPARISONS

Examination of the treated areas within Huntsville State Park 1 year after control revealed small openings in otherwise unaffected forest stands. These openings were beginning to revegetate naturally and will eventually increase the age and species diversity of trees within the park. Most visitors are unaware that an intensive beetle control program was conducted to save the park's forest and recreational attributes.

By contrast, a large portion of the Four Notch area was changed drastically by the 1983-4 beetle outbreak. Within 18 months, logged and unlogged areas affected by the outbreak had reverted to brush following the widespread loss of overstory pines and the shade they once provided.

Even in the area where no control had been applied, a one beautiful forest of mature pines had become a wasteland of rotting and falling snags by April 1985. In addition to loss of a potential wilderness area, the delay of SPB control in the Four Notch Area also caused other irretrievable losses, including some **$4 million** in timber revenues, a scenic portion of the Lone Star hiking trail, several colony trees of Red-cockaded Woodpeckers, and untold recreational values for the people of Texas. The uninvited spread of beetle infestations to adjacent federal and private lands also caused severe economic losses and disruption of forest management plans for these "innocent bystanders."

The Four Notch and the Huntsville State Park experiences clearly demonstrate the value of an aggressive protection program based on early detection, proper evaluation, and prompt control of expanding infestations before they attain an unmanageable size.

CONCLUSIONS

Preservation of southern pine forests as wilderness, particularly those forests that are a product of intensive forest management, will necessarily require protection by man to preserve or prolong their valued attributes. Once a more stable condition of mixed tree species and age classes develops, there should be less need for man's involvement (Billings 1986). The experiences detailed here and in many other cases (Morris and Copony 1974, Texas Forest Service 1978, Smith and Conner 1985) show the outcomes of two SPB management options available to wilderness managers (control or no control). Thus, when it comes to the issue of SPB control in wilderness areas, the question is: Have we learned a valuable lesson from past experiences or must history repeat itself in our newly designated wilderness areas?

LITERATURE CITED

Billings, R.F. 1986. Coping with forest insects in southern wilderness areas, with emphasis on the southern pine beetle. pp.120-125. *In* D.L. Kulhavy and R.N. Conner (eds.). Wilderness and Natural Areas in the Eastern United States: A Management Challenge. Nacogdoches, Tex. May 13-15, 1985.

Billings, R.F. and C.M. Bryant, V. 1983. Developing a system for mapping the abundance and distribution of southern pine beetle habitats in east Texas. Z. Angew. Entomol. 96:208-216.

Billings, R.F. and B.G. Hynum. Southern pine beetle: guide for predicting timber losses from expanding spots in east Texas. Tex. For. Serv. Circ. 249.

Billings, R.F. and H.A. Pase III. 1979. A field guide for ground checking southern pine beetle spots. USDA Agric. Handb. No. 558.

Morris, C.L. and J.A. Copony. 1974. Effectiveness of intensive salvage in reducing southern pine beetles in Virginia. J. For.72:572.

Nettleton, W.A. and N.A. Overgaard. 1982. Biological evaluation of southern pine beetle on the Little Lake Creek and RARE II porposed wilderness area and the Four notch further study area on the Sam Houston National Forest. USDA For. Serv., Rep. No. SA 82-2-17 Forest Pest Management, Pineville, La., 16 p.

Nettleton, W.A. and J.D. Smith. 1983. Hazard rating, predicted losses, and control alternatives for southern pine beetle damage on RARE II proposed wilderness and further study areas on the National Forests in Texas. USDA For. Serv. Rep. No. 83-2-15, South. Region. State and Private Forestry, Pineville, La.

Oliveria, F., W. Nettleton, and D.B. Drummond. 1983. Biological evaluation of southern pine beetle on the Four Notch and Chambers Ferry further study areas on the National Forests in Texas. USDA For. Serv. Rep. No. 83-2-19. South. Region. State and Private Forestry, Pineville, La.

Overgaard, N.A. 1976. Evaluation of southern pine beetle infestations on the National Forests in Texas. USDA For. Serv. Rep. No. SA 76-2-18. Forest Pest Management., Pineville, La.

Smith, J.D. 1980. Evaluation of southern pine beetle in the Four Notch

Proposed Wilderness Study area on the National Forests in Texas. USDA For. Serv. Rep. No. SA 80-2-13, Forest Pest Management., Pineville, La.

Smith, J.D. and M.C. Conner. 1985. Post suppression evaluation of the southern pine beetle suppression project on the National Forests in Texas. USDA For. Serv., Rep. No. 85-2-7, Southern Region State and Private Forestry., Pineville, La.

Swain, K.M. and M.C. Remion. 1981. Direct control methods for the southern pine beetle. USDA Agric. Handb. No. 575

Texas Forest Service. 1975. Cut and leave - a method to reduce losses from the southern pine beetle. Circ. 223.

Texas Forest Service. 1978. Texas forest pest activity 1976-1977 and Forest Pest Control Section biennial report. Publ. 117.

Texas Forest Service. 1984. Texas forest pest report: 1982-1983. Forest Pest Control Section biennial report, Publ. 136.

USDA Forest Service. 1983. Southern pine beetle control in RARE II recommended wilderness and further planning areas, National Forests in Texas: Environmental Assessment Report. South. Region, July 1983.

Forest Pathology Considerations In Eastern Wilderness And Natural Areas

by
Paul A. Mistretta

ABSTRACT--Forest pathology is seldom considered when managing wilderness and natural areas because effects of diseases are usually relatively slow and are considered natural processes. Hazard trees should be considered. Saprophytes are necessary as decomposers, yet can cause hazardous situations. Public awareness through education is encouraged.

KEYWORDS: pathology, pathological rotation, hazard trees.

The groups of organisms that cause tree diseases (primarily the fungi and bacteria) are absolutely essential in maintaining a viable forest ecosystem. Saprophytic organisms degrade forest litter, releasing nutrients back into the forest ecosystem to be utilized by the living, growing organisms. Without this decomposition, litter accumulates and vital nutrients are locked up in the debris on the forest floor; nutrient cycling ceases and the forest starves.

Disease in the forest environment must be considered as an extremely volatile ongoing process with very different natural interactions. Climate and local weather conditions often play key roles in disease expression (Hepting 1963). Environmental accidents can also play an important role in disease expression (e.g. location relative to a point source of a pollutant, or proximity of the host to a stressing factor such as shallow soil). Age and vigor of the host are primary considerations in disease processes. Increased age of host generally leads to decreased vigor and hence to increased susceptibility of the host to disease.

Stands that are densely stocked or old are generally more susceptible to infection than are thrifty, well managed stands. Disease can become a driving force in ecological succession.

DISEASE MANAGEMENT

The options available to a manager interested in preventing or controlling disease problems are limited (Berisford and Clark 1982, Hadden 1981, Pirone 1978). They include: (1) sanitizing to remove individual trees or stands (Filip and Goheen 1982, Johnson 1981, Mills and Russel 1981); (2) pruning diseased limbs (Marx 1976, May and Schierber 1976, Scharpf and Hawksworth 1974,

Shigo 1984); (3) burning to reduce the amount of duff and fruiting of pathogenic fungi in an area (Robbins 1984) and to destroy diseased material pruned from infected individuals (May and Schierber 1976); (4) excluding fire from an area to prevent the formation of wounds which can be colonized by a variety of pathogens (Toole 1959a, Toole and Furnival 1957); and, in a limited number of cases, (5) using chemicals to either prevent or control a disease outbreak (Shigo 1984, Robbins 1984).

Pathological rotation is a concept that has special importance in disease management. The concept of pathological rotation is that there is an optimal age for a tree after which it becomes, through completely natural processes, significantly more susceptible to damage and disease problems. Southwide, pathological rotations are about 60 years for southern yellow pines and 80 to 90 years for hardwoods. Beyond these ages rot and decay problems become significant and mechanical tree failures are more common.

WILDERNESS AND NATURAL AREAS

The yardstick by which the impact of a disease is measured in a wilderness is, of necessity, different from that used in managed timber. Damage that is of economic concern to the manager of timberland is often considered aesthetically pleasing (desirable) in a wilderness setting (Small 1979).

Many disease situations in the Southeast and East have primarily aesthetic impact; including most of the needlecasts, needle rusts, and galls (Boyce 1958, Berry and Lantz 1974, Phelps et al. 1978). However, some diseases cause potentially dangerous conditions. Root rot (Filip and Goheen 1982), butt rot (Johnson 1981), bole rot and decay (Wagener 1963, Wallis, *et al.* 1982), and cankers (Brandt 1964, Houston 1966, Barry and Hepting 1969, Phelps and Czabator 1978) create weak points in the structure of trees. These weakened areas can fail under stress. Falling trees or tree parts are often the direct result of disease-caused mechanical failure. Standing snags decay and break up in place resulting in falling bark, limbs and larger pieces of the main stem. Stump decay leaves stump holes as the decay progresses.

Removal of hazards from forest stands is normally proportional to the management use classification of the forest unit. It is most intensive in areas with developed recreation facilities, less intensive in areas managed for dispersed recreation, and extensive in timber areas; it is normally not performed in wilderness areas.

WILDERNESS/NATURAL AREA PATHOLOGY CONSIDERATIONS

Unlike insects, diseases seldom cause catastrophic problems in wilderness or natural areas. The possibility of a pathogen causing the type of devastation that southern pine beetles can cause in a Wilderness Area (Billings 1985) is remote. A pathogen devastated the American chestnut (Diller 1965), but that occurrence was unusual.

Forest disease outbreaks are seldom controlled even in regulated forests. Economical management options are limited in number, and are often used only in situations where trees have an unusually high value. However, the manager of a wilderness area does have a few options that will minimize potential problems without affecting wilderness values directly.

Place parking and other service facilities outside of wilderness or natural areas. This placement will allow maintenance to be performed on these facilities, and will limit preventable mechanical damage to trees in the wilderness/natural area.

Prepare pamphlets and other informative literature to help wilderness users to identify and avoid hazardous situations. Wilderness and natural areas are not designed or managed with the same intensity as city parks. Identifiable hazards within these areas can be avoided with even a little care and knowledge. Take time to help visitors.

Also, educate users about damaging or disfiguring trees. Hacking trees, signing initials on bark, hanging lanterns on trees and lighting campfires at the bases of trees are among the avoidable user-caused conditions that contribute to diseases in woodlands (USDA For. Serv. 1976)

LITERATURE CITED

Berisford, Y.C. and A.L. Clark. 1982. Insect and disease problems of southern urban trees: a guide to descriptive and control literature. CPL Bibl. 72., CPL Bibliographies, Chicago, Ill.

Berry, C.R. and G.H. Hepting. 1969. Pitch canker of southern pines. USDA For. Serv., For. Pest Leafl. 35.

Berry, F.H. and W. Lantz. 1974. Anthracnose of eastern hardwoods. USDA For. Serv., For. Pest Leafl. 133.

Boyce, J.S., Jr. 1958. Needle cast of southern pines. USDA For. Serv., For. Pest Leafl. 28.

Brandt, R.W. 1964. Nectria canker of hardwoods. USDA For. Serv., For. Insect and Dis. Leafl. 84.

Diller, J.D. 1965. Chestnut blight. USDA For. Serv., For. Insect and Dis. Leafl. 94.

Filip, G.M. and D.J. Goheen. 1982. Hazards of root disease in Pacific Northwest recreation sites. J. For. 80:163-164.

Hadden, C.H. 1981. Diseases of trees and their control. Univ. Tenn. Agric. Extens. Serv. Publ. 836.

Hepting, G.H. 1963. Climate and forest diseases. Annu. Rev. Phytopathol. 1:31-50.

Houston, D.R. 1966. Strumella canker of oaks. USDA For. Serv., For. Pest Leafl. 101.

Johnson, D.W. 1981. Tree hazards: recognition and reduction in recreation sites. USDA For. Serv., Tech. Rep. R2-1. For. Pest Manage., Lakewood, Colo.

Marx, H. 1976a. A tree hurts too. USDA For. Serv., Agric. Inf. Bull. 396.

Marx, H. 1976b. Rx for wounded trees. USDA For. Serv., Agric. Inf. Bull. 387.

May, C. and L. R. Schreiber. 1976. Pruning shade trees and repairing their injuries. USDA For. Serv. Home & Gard. Bull. 83.

Mills, L.J. and K. Russel. 1981. Detection and correction of hazard trees in Washington's recreation areas: a how-to guide for recreation site managers. State of Wash., Dep. Nat. Resour. Rep. 42. Olympia, Wash.

Phelps, W.R. and F.L. Czabator. 1978. Fusiform rust of southern pines. USDA For. Serv., For. Insect & Dis. Leafl. 26.

Phelps, W.R., A.G. Kais, and T.H. Nicholls. 1978. Brown-spot needle blight of pines. USDA For Serv., For. Insect and Dis. Leafl. 44.

Pirone, P.O. 1978. Diseases and pests of ornamental plants. 5th ed. John Wiley and Sons, New York, N.Y.

Robbins, K. 1984. Annosus root rot in eastern conifers. USDA For. Serv., For. Insect and Dis. Leafl. 76.

Scharpf, R.F. and F.G. Hawksworth. 1974. Mistletoes on hardwoods in the United States. USDA For. Serv., For. Pest Leafl. 147.

Shigo, A.L. 1984. The right treatments for troubled trees. Am. For. 90:13-16.

Small, D.M. 1979. The fascinating fungi. Am. For. 85:22-26.

Toole, E.R. 1959a. Decay after fire injury to southern bottom-land hardwoods. USDA For. Serv., Tech. Bull. 1189.

Toole, E.R. and G.M. Furnival. 1957. Progress of heart rot following fire in bottomland red oaks. J. For. 55:20-24.

USDA Forest Service. 1976. Trees need their skin too! USDA For. Serv. Pamphl. S.A. S.&P.F.-6. State and Priv. For., Southeast. Area, Atlanta, Ga.

Wagener, W.W. 1963. Judging hazard from native trees in California recreation areas: --a guide for professional foresters. USDA For. Serv. Res. Pap. PSW1., Pacific Southwest For. Range Exp. Stn., Berkeley, Calif.

Wallis, G.W., D.J. Morrison, and D.W. Ross. 1982. Tree hazards in recreation sites in British Columbia: management guidelines. Environment Canada, Can. For. Serv., Ottawa, Can.

Integrated Pest Management Concepts And Application In Wilderness And Natural Areas Management

by
Gerard D. Hertel, Garland N. Mason, and Robert C. Thatcher

ABSTRACT--Integrated pest management (IPM) based on ecological interrelationships can be practiced in wilderness and natural areas in the eastern United States. IPM technology dealing with the southern pine beetle and gypsy moth has advanced greatly over the past decade. Case studies with these two pests provide examples of how it might be applied in sensitive areas.

KEYWORDS: forest management strategies, insect impacts, wildland management, *Dendroctonus frontalis* Zimmermann, *Lymantria dispar* L.

Pest management is the component of forest management concerned with minimizing the negative effects of insects, diseases, weeds, and animals on forested land in an economically reasonable and biologically sound way. In the last two decades, foresters have made great progress in advancing from a crisis response to insect and disease problems to a more sophisticated ecologically sound approach. This modern approach includes monitoring of pest populations, host conditions, environmental influences, and pest-caused impacts to project damage events and consequences into the future. It enables more effective selection of economically and environmentally acceptable actions, including no action at all, and aids in assessment of followup needs through post-treatment evaluation. Understanding and consideration of biological, economic, social, and environmental processes provide the basis for integrated pest management (IPM). This paper describes the IPM concept and the possibilities for using this approach in eastern wilderness and natural areas threatened by the southern pine beetle, *Dendroctonus frontalis* Zimmermann, or the gypsy moth, *Lymantria dispar* L. USDA Forest Service Interim Directive No. 29-2324.04 provides guidelines for insect and disease control projects in such areas.

THE IPM APPROACH

As forests are set aside as wilderness and natural areas, a number of insect and disease problems must be kept in mind. These destructive agents may thrive in, and ultimately threaten the existence of, the very ecological setting we are trying to protect. Certain forest types and stand ages on particular sites are especially prone to pest attack. These circumstances dictate that managers of such areas recognize the potential for outbreaks, evaluate their possible effects, and make sound action decisions in a timely fashion. The manager must have reliable information to evaluate alternative means of maintaining pest-caused damage at tolerable levels (according to specific management objectives) (Waters and Stark 1980). These alternatives may include treatment tactics that are concerned with manipulating the forest or directly controlling target pest organisms. In either case, the manager must assess the influence of treatment on forest conditions, pest activity, management objectives, and environmental concerns. The benefit/costs of alternative actions must also be assessed. Emphasis in IPM is on information gathering and assessment, with a goal of selection options that are in harmony with management objectives. While the practices used in IPM often are quite intensive, they need not be. Less intrusive technologies can be applied to forests being managed for wilderness or natural areas.

IPM may be viewed as a means of maintaining destructive agents at tolerable levels by the planned use of a variety of preventive, suppressive, or regulatory tactics and strategies that are ecologically and economically efficient and socially acceptable. It is implicit that these actions be fully integrated into the total resource management process, which includes both planning and operations (Waters 1974).

THE COMPONENTS OF AN INTEGRATED PEST MANAGEMENT SYSTEM

IPM is directed at the entire forest ecosystem as a part of planned forest management (Fig. 1). IPM strategies should be supported by monitoring and prediction of forest, pest, and environmental conditions. These strategies must be based on knowledge gained from research and development activities, on-the-ground experience, and familiarity with management practices and constraints. Figure 1 further conceptualizes the basic components of IPM as they contribute to forest management. These components include: a) population changes that are associated with the rise and fall of pest outbreaks involving one or more closely associated pests, b) the dynamics of forest stand growth and development, c) biological and socioeconomic impacts of pest-caused damage on resource values and management objectives, and d) treatment strategies. The latter two components serve as direct input into benefit/cost determinations or other decisionmaking methods. Technology involved in these components provides the information needed for a complete pest management approach that ultimately can be incorporated into overall forest management.

Case Study: The Southern Pine Beetle

Southern pine forests contribute substantially to our Nation's needs for forest products. In the future, they will no doubt play an even more important role in the Nation's and region's economy. Many pest problems can affect the productivity of these forests (Hertel *et al.* 1984). To assure adequate resources for the future, forest managers must consider the potential impacts of such pests as the southern pine beetle (SPB) on all forest uses and, where possible, plan and manage to prevent or reduce pest-caused losses.

Periodic SPB outbreaks have been reported in the Southern United States since the late 1700's. They have significantly affected the management of wilderness areas, particularly in the West Gulf region in the last few years (Branham and Nettleton 1985, Warren 1985). Impacts on wilderness areas can be minimized by utilizing available IPM knowledge during the planning process and in the management strategy employed subsequent to wilderness establishment.

Anticipating problems--If forest conditions are favorable for SPB attack (old growth, high stand density, low tree vigor, poor drainage), most southern pine stands could ultimately be affected by the SPB. These factors are known to wilderness management planning teams. Stand hazard rating permits easy assessment of the poten-

APPLYING THE IPM CONCEPT

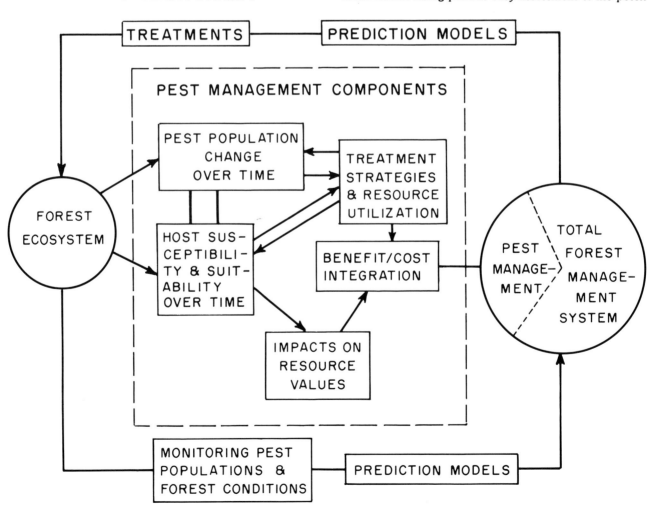

tial risk of infestation. There are now five geographic hazard-rating models available that cover the entire SPB range (Mason *et al.* 1985). These ratings help managers determine where SPB damage is most likely to occur and how much of the identified area is susceptible to beetle attack.

Stand growth models and SPB impact models have been combined so that forest changes and SPB effects can be projected over time. They show what the forests will be like with and without SPB attacks and the likely effects of various treatments (Hedden *et al.* 1985, Vasievich and Thompson 1985). In addition, there are two SPB information management or decision support programs that draw together a vast inventory of knowledge into computerized decisionmaking systems. These systems--the Southern Pine Beetle Decision Support System (Turnbow *et al.* 1983) and the Integrated Pest Management Decision Key (Anderson *et al.* 1982)--are presently available for use by managers or others interested in determining SPB impacts or needs for suppression. The use of simulation models together with stand hazard rating will help managers to determine a course of action. Managers, however, must address the following questions:
Decision Point 1:
1. Will SPB outbreaks affect achievement of my management goals?
2. Should I take action if an outbreak occurs?
3. Under what conditions should action be taken?

Anything that can be done to lower the SPB hazard of a forest will reduce the likelihood of significant losses and help maintain the stand in its present form. If management goals allow, hazard can be reduced by lowering stand density, selective thinning, or alteration of species composition to favor mixed pine/hardwood stands. Poorly stocked or cutover areas can be regenerated with more resistant longleaf or slash pines (Belanger and Malac 1980). In such operations, interactions with tree killing diseases such as annosus root rot, littleleaf disease, and fusiform rust should be considered (Anderson and Mistretta 1982).

Evaluating existing problems--The keys to minimizing losses are early detection and prompt action. High-hazard stands deserve first priority and more frequent observation because SPB infestations are most likely to occur there, and spot spread (infestation growth) will be most rapid.

Aerial surveillance should begin in March to June, depending on the geographic location (Billings and Doggett 1980, Billings and Ward 1984). If spots are located, the numbers of trees should be estimated and the potential for additional losses determined (Billings and Pase 1979). At this point, ground check priorities can be established using published procedures based on the number and size of trees and level of beetle activity. This is the time when a manager should further evaluate the effects of potential treatments on the attainment of management goals and potential problems with other pests (annosus root rot, *Ips* engraver beetles, black turpentine beetle) in the area.

Again, management constraints will affect these determinations.

Ground crews should examine reported infestations, identify the specific cause of tree mortality, and determine the potential for further damage in this or adjoining stands. Models are available for predicting rate of spot growth to determine additional tree losses expected over the next 30-90 day period (Billings and Hynum 1980, Feldman *et al.* 1985, Stephen and Lih 1985). Applying this approach to existing problem evaluation will provide information for additional decisionmaking involving:
Decision Point 2:
1. Should action be taken?
2. What kind of action should be taken?
3. When should it be implemented?
4. How will treatment affect tree losses?

Once an environmental assessment has been prepared and accepted, alternatives can be identified and the order of preference stipulated for specific management situations. The option selected should be the most appropriate one for the particular forest, the specific pest situation, and the defined management objectives. Four direct control options are currently available for stopping SPB spot spread: salvage removal, cut-and-leave, chemical control, and pile-and-burn. Each is described in detail by Swain and Remion (1981). Of course, taking no action might be the appropriate course under certain conditions. Another tactic currently under development is the use of the SPB's aggregating pheromone to prevent additional tree mortality (Payne *et al.* 1985).

If control is attempted, it is important to evaluate the effort to determine whether treatment was effective in preventing additional losses. The post-control evaluation will provide information needed to plan the following year's control program.

Case Study: The Gypsy Moth
The hardwood forests of the Northeast and South offer a very diverse forest community for a broad range of uses and users. Here, just as in southern pine forests, many insects and diseases can cause serious growth losses and tree mortality.

The gypsy moth, a defoliator introduced from Europe into Massachusetts in 1869, has caused many problems in the past and is of great concern to modern-day forest managers and landowners. This pest continues to be a threat to northeastern forests and is rapidly expanding its range South to include the hardwood forests of Delaware, Maryland, West Virginia, and Virginia. As with the SPB, technology is available to reduce losses caused by this destructive pest.

Anticipating problems--Techniques are available to identify hardwood stands where gypsy moth is most likely to occur (susceptible stands) and where mortality is most likely to be greatest (vulnerable stands) (Valentine and Houston 1979, Gansner and Herrick 1983). The distinction between susceptible and vulnerable must be made when developing any management approach for dealing with this pest.

Models are available to project stand changes over time with and without gypsy moth-caused mortality (Sheehan 1984). A stand succession model is being modified to include the effects of gypsy moth defoliation so that changes in stand conditions can be projected for hundreds of years (Shugart 1984).

Hazard-rating systems and stand projection models provide information that can aid wilderness and natural areas planners and managers in estimating and projecting impacts of gypsy moths in these sensitive areas. These tools can help in formulating management approaches that take into account the following questions:

Decision Point 1:

1. Will gypsy moths affect achievement of management goals?
2. If so, where, how and to what extent?
3. What, if anything, can we do about it?

During the planning stages, silvicultural actions may be considered to manipulate stands to reduce gypsy moth outbreaks (Gottschalk 1982). Silvicultural approaches include: 1) changing species composition (to lower susceptibility), and 2) identifying and removing stressed trees (to lower vulnerability). Techniques such a reducing the abundance of preferred tree species, protecting or encouraging conifers, or increasing stand diversity can be considered.

Evaluating existing problems--Unfortunately, time for advanced planning may be very limited. The pest may present an immediate threat, or an outbreak may be imminent. As with the SPB, approaches are available for evaluating the immediate threat to hardwood forests posed by a gypsy moth outbreak and for projecting the effects of this threat over the next several years.

Even when a gypsy moth problem already exists, hazard rating provides useful information for assessing the situation and making immediate decisions. With such information, managers can determine where to concentrate detection surveys. A well-designed early detection and monitoring program is a necessary prerequisite to any control effort.

Periodic observation flights should be conducted in sensitive areas to detect defoliation by the gypsy moth or other insects or other areawide forest problems at an early stage. There are many defoliators that can affect hardwood forests (Talerico 1978). If defoliation is detected, ground examination is needed to establish the cause, the potential impacts, and the proximity and threat to recreation areas, wildlife habitat, watersheds, and other ownerships.

Unlike the situation with SPB, aerial surveys are of limited value in detecting initial outbreaks of the gypsy moth. Gypsy moth problems cannot be detected from the air until major defoliation has already occurred, and, by then populations may be increasing at a rapid rate. Therefore, pheromone traps, egg mass surveys, and burlap bands should be employed to monitor population levels in a portion of the most susceptible areas (Eggan and Abrahamson 1983). Traps provide the first indication of gypsy moth activity in the area. Modified traps are being

developed that will improve estimates of area population levels in the near future. Egg mass estimates can be used to project expected defoliation (Gansner and Herrick 1984). Egg viability should be determined and early instar development monitored prior to any control action. The goal of any control program should be to maintain populations at a level below that which will cause significant impacts. The time and money spent on control should be weighed against the value of the resources being protected.

In evaluating the potential impacts of the existing or anticipated gypsy moth problems, it must be remembered that the impact on the forest may not always be negative or detrimental. In northeastern Pennsylvania, for example, most of the stands declined in stocking during the years when gypsy moth-caused tree mortality was the highest. After a few years, growth of the surviving trees had offset most of those losses, but species composition of the stands was appreciably changed (Gansner et al. 1984). Before the outbreak, oaks made up 50 sq. ft. of the basal area and 8 years later represented 40 sq. ft., a 20 percent reduction. After the first trees died, tree species less likely to be killed by the gypsy moth made up a greater proportion of the overall stocking in the residual stand.

After population level and the threat to surrounding forests has been determined, a second round of decisions should be made:

Decision Point 2:

1. Should action be taken?
2. What kind of action should be taken?

More control approaches exist for dealing with the gypsy moth than were described for the SPB (Table 1). The technique selected should be based on appropriateness to

Table 1. Control Options for the Gypsy Moth.

Approach	Chemical or Method	Operational (O) or Experimental (E)
Chemical sprays	Sevin	O
	Orthene	O
Growth regulator	Dimilin	O
Microbial sprays	B.t.	O
	Gypcheck	E
Sterility	Sterile male	E
	Inherited sterility	E
Pheromones	Trap out	E
	Confusion	E
Parasites	Release	E
No control		

the local situation and management objectives. Those currently recommended are effective for suppression or eradication in specific management situations; other techniques are still in the experimental stage. In an IPM approach, one or more of these techniques may be applied singly or in combination at specific locations or

IPM DECISION PROCESS FOR GYPSY MOTH

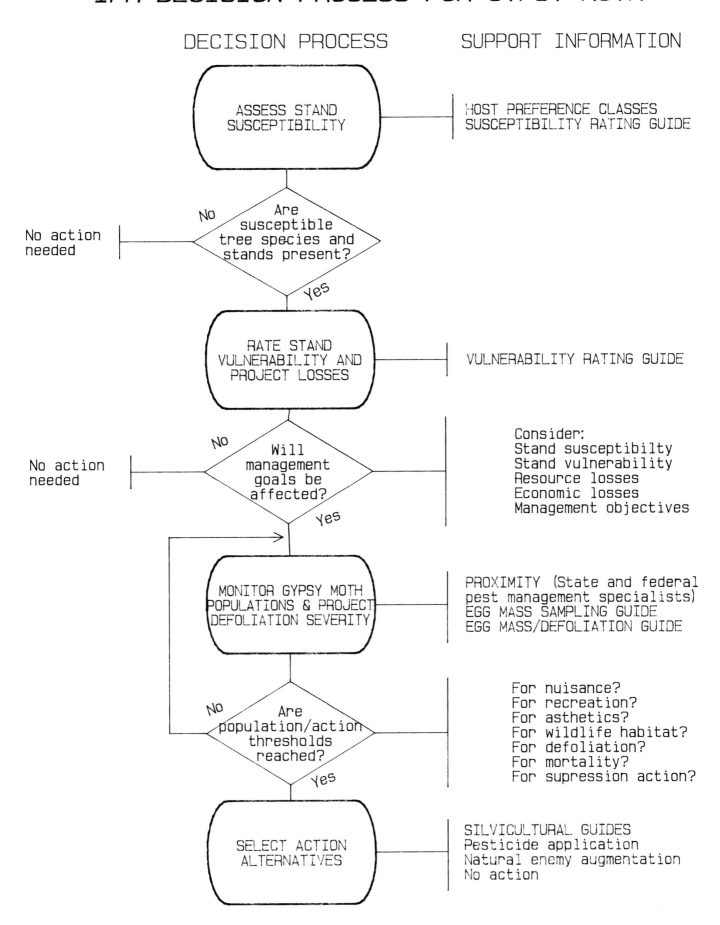

DECISION PROCESS

SUPPORT INFORMATION

ASSESS STAND SUSCEPTIBILITY

HOST PREFERENCE CLASSES
SUSCEPTIBILITY RATING GUIDE

Are susceptible tree species and stands present?
No — No action needed
Yes

RATE STAND VULNERABILITY AND PROJECT LOSSES

VULNERABILITY RATING GUIDE

Will management goals be affected?
No — No action needed
Yes

Consider:
Stand susceptibilty
Stand vulnerability
Resource losses
Economic losses
Management objectives

MONITOR GYPSY MOTH POPULATIONS & PROJECT DEFOLIATION SEVERITY

PROXIMITY (State and federal pest management specialists)
EGG MASS SAMPLING GUIDE
EGG MASS/DEFOLIATION GUIDE

Are population/action thresholds reached?
No
Yes

For nuisance?
For recreation?
For asthetics?
For wildlife habitat?
For defoliation?
For mortality?
For supression action?

SELECT ACTION ALTERNATIVES

SILVICULTURAL GUIDES
Pesticide application
Natural enemy augmentation
No action

142

over a broad area after all environmental aspects have been considered.

Any control program involving the gypsy moth should be followed by a post-treatment evaluation. The evaluation provides information that can be used to judge success or failure so that a more effective job can be done in the future.

GETTING TECHNICAL ASSISTANCE

Pests are just one of many concerns that confront resource managers, but occasionally, they can be a very major concern. Since managers often deal with these problems on an intermittent basis and today's technology is changing so rapidly, it is difficult to keep up-to-date and have access to the latest technology when it is most needed. A number of organizations offer assistance to landowners and land managers, including the Cooperative Extension Service, State forestry organizations, the USDA Forest Service, and others. Most natural and wilderness areas are publicly owned, and technical assistance in their management is available from the USDA Forest Service. Additional assistance is available from pest management specialists in State forestry organizations. The primary contacts are:

SOUTH: USDA Forest Service, Southern Region, Forest Pest Management, 1720 Peachtree Road, NW, Atlanta, GA 30367

NORTH: USDA Forest Service, Northeastern Area State and Private Forestry, Forest Pest Management, 370 Reed Road, Broomall, PA 19008

Pest management specialists at these locations are familiar with the latest technology through their contacts with Federal and university researchers. They also play a major role in large-scale field evaluations of experimentally proven techniques prior to the technology becoming operational.

DISCUSSION AND CONCLUSIONS

New or improved research information and the IPM concept have a place in the management of wilderness and natural areas. The approaches used in forests managed principally for timber may not be appropriate in wilderness, but many can be adapted for specific situations. Wilderness managers are encouraged to apply their best understanding of ecological interrelationships and the forest environment to management planning in their unique situation. Our interest here is to encourage managers to move from the more traditional crisis response to pest problems to the more selective application of ecologically based strategies. This approach requires, at a bare minimum, determination of the **potential** for a problem to develop and of its **ultimate** impact on

achievement of the organization's management objectives. Techniques for making sound decisions dealing with specific problems, monitoring the situation, and measuring success through followup evaluation also must be considered. The IPM technology for management of both the southern pine beetle and the gypsy moth has improved greatly over the past decade. By working through pest management specialists, managers can take advantage of current and developing technology to be more effective in the planning and management of wilderness and natural areas.

LITERATURE CITED

Anderson, R.L. R.P. Belanger, W.H. Hoffard, P.A. Mistretta, and R.J. Uhler. 1982. Integrated pest management decision key: a new decisionmaking tool for the forest manager. pp. 125-130. In J.W. Moser, Jr. (ed.). Proc. conference on microcomputers: a new tool for foresters. Soc. of Amer. For. SAF 82-05.

Anderson, R.L. and P.A. Mistretta. 1982. Management strategies for reducing losses caused by fusiform rust, annosus root rot, and littleleaf disease. USDA Agric. Handb. 597.

Belanger, R.P. and B.F. Malac. 1980. Silviculture can reduce losses from southern pine beetle. USDA Agric. Handb. 576.

Billings, R.F. and B.G. Hynum. 1980. Southern pine beetle. Guide for predicting timber losses from expanding spots in east Texas. Tex. For. Serv. Circ. 249.

Billings, R.F. and C. Doggett. 1980. An aerial observer's guide to recognizing and reporting southern pine beetle spots. USDA Agric. Handb. 560.

Billings, R.F. and H.A. Pase, III. 1979. (rev. 1983). A field guide for ground checking southern pine beetle spots. USDA Agric. Handb. 558.

Billings, R.F. and J.D. Ward. 1984. How to conduct a southern pine beetle aerial detection survey. Tex. For. Serv. Circ. 267.

Branham, S.J. and W.A. Nettleton. 1985. From wildwood to wilderness. Forests and People 35:18-23, 32-33.

Eggan, D.A. and L.P. Abrahamson. 1983. Estimating gypsy moth egg mass densities. Misc. Publ. No. 1 ESF83-002, State Univ. of New York, College Environ. Sci. and For.

Feldman, R.M, T.L. Wagner, P.J.H. Sharpe, and H. Wu. 1985. A methodology for biophysical modeling using TAMBEETLE as an example. pp. 195-201 In S.J. Branham and R.C. Thatcher (eds.). Proc. integrated pest management research symposium. USDA For. Serv., Gen. Tech. Rep. SO-56. South. For. Exp. Sta., New Orleans, La.

Gansner, D.A. and O.W. Herrick. 1983. Guides for estimating forest stand losses to gypsy moth. Northern J. Appl. For. 1:21-23.

Gansner, D.A. and O.W. Herrick. 1984. A guide for predicting gypsy moth defoliation. Northern J. Appl. For.

Gansner, D.A., O.W. Herrick, P.A. DeBald, and R.E. Acciavatti. 1984. Changes in forest condition associated with gypsy moth. J. For. 81:155-157.

Gottschalk, K.W. 1982. Silvicultural alternatives for coping with the gypsy moth. pp. 137-151. *In* Proc., Coping with the gypsy moth. The Penn. State Univ. Press.

Hedden, R.L. 1985. Simulation of southern pine beetle associated timber loss using CLEMBEETLE. pp. 288-291. *In* S.J. Branham and R.C. Thatcher (eds.). Proc., integrated pest management research symp., USDA For. Serv. Gen. Tech. Rep. SO-56., South. For. Exp. Sta., New Orleans, La.

Hertel, G.D., G.N. Mason, S.C. Cade, and R.C. Kucera. 1984. Strategies for reducing insect and disease losses. pp. 217-213. *In* Proc. symp. loblolly pine ecosystem (West Region). Miss. Coop. Ext. Serv., Ext. For. Dept., Miss. State Univ. Press.

Mason, G.N., P.L. Lorio, Jr., R.P. Belanger, and W.A. Nettleton. 1985. Rating the susceptibility of stands to southern pine beetle attack. USDA Agric. Handb. 645.

Payne, T.L., L.H. Kudon, C.W. Berisford, B.F. O'Donnell, and D.K. Walsh. 1985. Effects of frontalure in suppressing southern pine beetle spot growth under endemic and epidemic population levels. pp. 281-287. *In* S.J. Branham and R.C. Thatcher (eds.). Proc., integrated pest management research symp., USDA For. Serv. Gen. Tech. Rep. SO-56. South. For. Exp. Sta., New Orleans, La.

Sheehan, K.A. 1984. Development of forest-gypsy moth models. pp. 99-102. *In* Proc., National Gypsy Moth Review.

Shugart, H.H. 1984. A theory of forest dynamics. Springer-Verlag, New York, N.Y.

Stephen, F.M. and M. Lih. 1985. A *Dendroctonus frontalis* infestation growth model: organization, refinement, and utilization. pp.186-194, *In*

S.J. Branham and R.C. Thatcher, (eds.). Proc. integrated pest management research symp. USDA For. Serv. Gen. Tech. Rep. SO-56. South. For. Exp. Sta., New Orleans, Louis.

Swain, K.M., Sr. and M.C. Remion. 1981 (rev. 1983). Direct control methods for the southern pine beetle. USDA Agric. Handb. 575.

Talerico, R.L. 1978. Major hardwood defoliators of the eastern United States. USDA Home and Gard. Bull. 224.

Turnbow, R.H., Jr., L.C. Hu, E.J. Rykiel, R.N. Coulson, and D. Loh. 1983. Procedural guide for FERRET, the question analysis routine of the decision support system for southern pine beetle management. Tex. Agric. Exp. Stn., MP-1533, Tex. A&M Univ. College Station, Tex.

Valentine, H.T. and D.R. Houston. 1979. A discriminant function for identifying mixed-oak stand susceptibility to gypsy moth defoliation. For. Sci. 25:468-474.

Vasievich, J.M. and W.A. Thompson. 1985. ITEMS: An integrated method to project southern pine stand development. pp. 300-327. *In* S.J. Branham and R.C. Thatcher (eds.). Proc. integrated pest management research symp. USDA For. Serv.Gen. Tech. Rep. SO-56. South. For. Exp. Sta., New Orleans, La.

Warren, B.J. 1985. Why we need to control pine beetles in wilderness areas. For. Farmer 44:6-8.

Waters, W.E. 1974. Systems approach to managing bark beetles. 00. 11-14. Southern pine beetle symp., proc. Tex. A&M Univ. Press, College Station, Tex.

Waters, W.E. and R.W. Stark. 1980. Forest pest management: concept and reality. Annu. Rev. Entomol. 25:479-509.

4

An Introduction To Wilderness Management Issues

by
Larry N. Phillips, Richard N. Conner, and David L. Kulhavy

The 98th U.S. Congress added many new wilderness areas to the wilderness system in the United States. Most of these areas are located in the eastern United States. With each new area, many questions arise as to how these areas should be managed.

In October 1983, the University of Idaho at Moscow conducted the First National Wilderness Management Workshop. The theme of this workshop was "Taking Care of What We've Got." In his concluding remarks at the workshop, the Forest Chief, R. Max Peterson called for the Federal land management agencies to work with representatives of user groups to develop a Five-Year Wilderness Management Action Program, based on the wealth of ideas generated at the conference. He asked the College of Forestry, Wildlife, and Range Sciences of the University of Idaho to facilitate the process (Wilderness Research Center, University of Idaho Wilderness Management - A Five-Year Action Program, June, 1985).

First a national steering committee was formed to pull together the issues generated at the workshop. Then through broad public input, the committee developed a program of recommended actions dealing with major wilderness management issues. In June, 1985, the Wilderness Research Center of the University of Idaho published "A Five-Year Action Program" that features these five issues:

1. **Educating the Public.** Successful plans and programs for resource management are wholly dependent on public understanding and acceptance.

2. **Education and Training of Managers.** Many federal agency personnel lack adequate background and expertise in wilderness management to fulfill responsibilities implicit in the Wilderness act.

3. **Capacity and Concentrated Use.** Are visitors "loving wilderness to death?" Many areas clearly show signs of trampling, erosion and ecological damage.

4. **Interagency Coordination and Consistency.** Coordination and consistency within as well as among agencies (within the law's direction for each agency) is imperative, in managing nonconforming uses, authorized by prior use or by specific exemption by law; in dealing with areas with adjacent boundaries; and in sustaining the principles and philosophy of the Act.

5. **Wilderness Management Practices.** Wilderness by its very nature, requires a different approach than lands managed for other purposes, or even specifically for recreation. The perpetuation of the wilderness resource and its natural processes must come first.

The Management Issues section of this book as well as the total wilderness and natural areas symposium in Nacogdoches, specifically responded to the need to educate and inform managers and the public about wilderness management problems and management solutions. Although management issues are examined and discussed throughout this entire volume, selected special situations are examined in this section of the book.

One overriding management technique that must be considered for use in wilderness areas is prescribed fire. Numerous authors in this section of the book and other sections (Vegetation, Grasslands and Savannas, and Wildlife) stress the importance of fire. Fire is a natural part of wilderness. Papers in this section document the importance of fire in the longleaf pine bluestem ecological type, the Appalachian hardwood types, and the northeast mixed wood forests. However, prescribed fire has its problems when used as a management tool. Ever present is the risk of wildfire spreading to adjacent lands and the potential loss of life or property. Less serious are the problems caused by smoke including visibility problems for motorists and air quality. A timely solution to these problems creates a challenge for the wilderness manager who needs to manage his wilderness area as a fire climax ecosystem.

Several papers in this section address problems and challenges associated with management of oil, gas, and mineral extraction on wilderness areas. How do these activities affect the vegetation in wilderness and overall wilderness quality? A wilderness manager will need ingenuity and imagination to assure that the negative affects from such activities minimally affect wilderness quality.

Both air and water quality are very important aspects of wilderness management. Land use patterns around wilderness areas will be a major concern for the wilderness manager. He will have little direct control over pollutants that flow into his area from upstream. Likewise he will have little direct control over air pollution from nearby population centers and acid rain. These are potential problems the manager must be aware of and attempt to monitor and correct should they arise.

The wilderness manager will also be faced with problems and issues arising from the physical use of his areas by visitors. How much use can be permitted before the users begin to negatively affect the quality of wilderness? How can a manager limit use in a wilderness area?

The answers to these questions and many others focus attention to the title of this book: "Wilderness and Natural Areas in the Eastern United States: A Management Challenge." The management of wilderness type areas in the complex, industrialized, modern day world is indeed a challenge.

Wilderness Characteristics And Values

by
George D. Davis

ABSTRACT--This paper identifies and describes 25 wilderness values. Twenty-two are placed in five distinct categories which apply to all wilderness values: naturalness, ethical, psychological, recreational, and other issues. The three additional values apply only to certain wilderness areas. In conjunction with the wilderness attributes rating system, these 25 values, which are derived from legislative language and the literature, may be useful in wilderness resource decisionmaking.

KEYWORDS: wilderness values, aesthetics, recreation, mineral leasing, legislation.

The characteristics and values of wilderness cannot be described as precisely or even as dispassionately as one might describe a garden or an automobile. Wilderness is living, complex, and ever changing. In some respects its values depend on feelings and emotions. Despite the difficulties, as guardians and managers of this resource that can only shrink but never grow, we have a need to describe its characteristics and values so we may compare them to those of other uses competing for the same tract of land.

But how do we get a grasp on those characteristics and values that Robert Marshall (1930) described in this way: "The wilderness is . . . unique esthetically in that it stimulates not just the sense of sight, as does art, or the sense of sound, as does music, but all the senses which man has. The traveler wandering at evening to the shore of some wilderness lakelet senses through his sight the pink sunset sky and the delightful pattern which the deep bay makes along the spruce trees which rise from its shores; senses through his hearing the lapping of the water against the rocky shore and the evening song of the thrush; senses through his smell the scent of balsam and the marsh flowers at the water's edge; senses through his touch the gentle wind which blows on his forehead and the softness of the sphagnum beneath his feet. The wilderness is all of these senses harmonized with immensity into a form of beauty which to many human beings is the most perfect experience on earth."

Perhaps wilderness characteristics and values can only be communicated to those who believe in the sanctity and interdependency of all life rather than the dominance of the human race. Aldo Leopold (1949) put it succinctly, "Anyone who has to ask what is the value of wilderness, wouldn't understand the answer." Whether any of us fully understand the answer or not, I will summarize the characteristics and values stated or implied in the Wilderness Act and the literature. Millions upon millions of words have been written by such inspirational and eloquent authors as Brooks, Brower, Douglas, Emerson, Frome, Leopold, Muir, Olson, Stegner, Thoreau and Zahniser. To fully understand wilderness values one must feel what these authors wrote. To try to categorize and summarize their work and still convey their meaning has been the greatest lesson in humility I have ever faced.

Some, and perhaps most, of the following characteristics and values can be found in nonwilderness areas, such as large roadless tracts, but the latter are disappearing and cannot be relied on as the "*enduring*" resource described by Congress. At the start of each individual section of this paper, I quote the basis in the Wilderness Act for the characteristics and values to be described. Some are cited specifically, others implied.

Another approach to defining wilderness characteristics and values can be found at FSM 2321.11c. To my way of thinking, this section of the manual is overly simplistic, but it is easy to understand and is certainly easy to use. A much more comprehensive system for rating wilderness attributes (USDA 1977) was developed for use in the second roadless area review and evaluation, RARE II. This wilderness attributes rating system (WARS) includes individual ratings based on four factors required by the Wilderness Act--natural integrity, apparent naturalness, outstanding opportunities for solitude, and outstanding opportunities for primitive recreation. In addition, it provides for individual ratings of the four supplemental attributes specified in the Wilderness Act--outstanding ecological, geological, scenic, and cultural features. This rating system has the advantages of being tied directly to the

Wilderness Act, being used as part of the current National Forest land management planning process, and having already been applied to more than 2,500 potential wilderness areas.

The following description of wilderness characteristics and values is in no way intended to discredit WARS. It is meant to supplement the existing system by providing discussion that could well be used to enhance WARS. While more philosophic and, perhaps, subjective than WARS, it includes values inferred in the Wilderness Act and long accepted as wilderness values by the founders of the wilderness concept and the most respected writers in the wilderness field. It also recognizes that although attributes may reflect characteristics, they do not necessarily reflect all values. Although the approach used here may not be as scientific or as subject to measurement as WARS, that could well be its strength as well as its weakness.

NATURALNESS

Naturalness is, almost by definition, the basic characteristic of wilderness. The basis in the Wilderness Act for naturalness and the subcategories to be discussed under this section are indicated by underlining in the following quote from Section 2 of the Act.

DEFINITION OF WILDERNESS

(C) A wilderness, in contrast with those areas where man and his own works dominate the landscape, is hereby recognized as an area where *the earth and its community of life are untrammeled by man, where man himself is a visitor who does not remain.* An area of wilderness is further defined to mean in this Act an area of *undeveloped* Federal land *retaining its primeval character and influence, without permanent improvements or human habitation,* which is *protected and managed so as to preserve its natural conditions* and which (1) *generally appears to have been affected primarily by the forces of nature, with the imprint of man's work substantially unnoticeable;* (2) has outstanding opportunities for solitude or a primitive and unconfined type of recreation; (3) has at least five thousand acres of land or is of *sufficient size as to make practicable its preservation and use in an unimpaired condition*; and (4) may also contain ecological, geological, or other features of scientific, educational, scenic, or historical value.

It should be noted that such words as "generally" and "substantially" were included to accept ecological realities and avoid largely speculative arguments over purity.

Natural Ecological Processes

Natural ecological processes are allowed to run essentially free in a wilderness and as such they characterize wilderness. Both scientific and educational values (see Section III-E) flow from this characteristic. It is important to understand that these processes are not static; indeed, they are always changing toward complexity. They provide diversity and naturally evolving gene pools to partially offset those influences outside of wilderness that decrease diversity of the gene pool. The wilderness reservoir of ongoing natural processes provides us a savings account while elsewhere we tinker with nature's investments. "What we should be trying to do is to maintain all the natural ecological factors of an area and leave them as undisturbed as possible. The natural changes should be permitted to take place in a natural way. Only then does the (wilderness) habitat have full significance." (Murie, in Leydet, ed., 1963)

Native Flora and Fauna

A second indicator of wilderness naturalness is the existence of native flora and fauna. The ideal, of course, would be to have all species of flora and fauna that are native to the ecosystems of any given wilderness and to have no non-native species present. Neither of these two ideal situations is likely to exist, but the higher the percentage of native species still found and the fewer non-native species present, the greater the wilderness value.

Management directed toward reintroducing native species or eradicating non-native species could increase the value of a wilderness as long as its implementation does not reduce other wilderness values. To lose a native plant or animal species from a wilderness detracts greatly from the naturalness of the wilderness unless such a loss results from natural processes. Reintroduction, while sometimes possible, is often difficult and costly. Natural reintroduction is increasingly less common as the area around wilderness is developed and becomes an obstacle to the movement of some animal species and the dissemination of plant seeds. As our wilderness areas become more and more like isolated islands of wildness in a sea of development, natural reintroduction becomes less likely.

Wilderness is particularly important to certain wildlife species that compete with human economic activity or are extremely sensitive or vulnerable to human activity. Such species need wilderness sanctuaries and, equally important, well distributed sanctuaries. As Leopold (1949) wrote, "Relegating grizzlies to Alaska is about like relegating happiness to heaven: one may never get there."

Where wilderness harbors species that are either dependent on wilderness habitat, vulnerable to humans or human activity, or associated closely with wilderness in people's minds, the value of the wilderness is correspondingly greater. One of the most frequently expressed expectations of the wilderness visitor is to observe wildlife (Schoenfeld and Hendee 1978). Although I may not totally accept Crisler's (1958) comment that "Wilderness without wildlife is merely scenery," I do subscribe to Dr. C.H.D. Clarke's statement that "Wildlife is more than anything else, the hallmark of quality" (Temporary Study Commission on the Future of the Adirondacks, 1970). And quality, in terms of naturalness, is much of what wilderness is all about.

Natural Landscape

Another indicator of the naturalness characteristic is the physical setting or landscape. This indicator should not be confused with scenic quality. Landscape value relates to how little humans have physically modified it. For example, a terraced hillside, a plowed grassland, a drained wetland, or a bulldozer gouged mountainside would have far less wilderness value than an unmodified landscape.

Air and Water Quality

The quality of the air over the wilderness and the surface water within it indicate naturalness. Air or water pollution from human activities lowers the wilderness value. So-called natural pollution, such as decaying organic material from vegetation or wildlife, does not lower the wilderness value. Pollution that can be, and is likely to be, reduced should be considered separately from that which is likely to continue or increase.

Lack of Human Intrusion

The fewer visible human intrusions in an area, the higher its wilderness value. Old roads, cabins, mines, plowed fields, electronic sites, drill rigs, weeper dams, pipelines, compression stations, and such, reduce the naturalness of an area and, therefore, its wilderness value insofar as that value is measured by naturalness. The degree of reduction varies with the number of intrusions and their distribution within the wilderness. Certain limited historic artifacts may actually increase wilderness value when measured by other characteristics.

ETHICAL

Ethical considerations are a value of wilderness rather than a characteristic. Section 2(a) of the Wilderness Act states that it is the policy of Congress in establishing wilderness to secure this resource's benefits "for the American people of present and **future** generations . . ." The Congress, in the same section, also directs that these resources be administered ". . . in such a manner as will leave them unimpaired for **future** use and enjoyment as wilderness. . ." These are specific ethical references, others are implied by the very nature of wilderness and the concept of preservation in contrast to that of exploitation.

The ethical basis for wilderness and the use of an ethical basis for putting a value on wilderness is perhaps the most abstract of the five categories I have chosen to describe. It is certainly the most difficult to describe. Ethics deal with concepts of right and wrong; with morals and moral choices, particularly as made in relationship to others. It seems to me that the decision to leave a place alone for its own sake rather than to use it for economic and material benefit is in many respects an ethical decision; a decision that could be right or wrong, depending primarily on how frequently it is made and the needs of the society at the particular time and place.

Options for Future Generations

Most of us feel some obligation to generations yet unborn. Many of us, as our parents before us, work harder than we otherwise might so our children may have a "better" life. Some define "better" as an education, others as more material goods; still others expend extra energies in the hope of giving our children a legacy with some touchstones of the world we knew.

Thomas Jefferson believed one generation could not bind another. But we can leave them some choices, some options, some relics of an America that was. They have a right to that much, at least " . . . the right to find solitude somewhere, the right to see, and enjoy, and be inspired and renewed, somewhere, by those places where the hand of God has not been obscured by the industry of man" (Brower 1957). The value of wilderness is high for this indicator but can be lessened dramatically if some of the actions with irreversible impacts that the Wilderness Act provides for in Section 4 are implemented.

Humility

The environment can be viewed in different ways: the anthropocentric (man-centered) view and the ecocentric view of the interdependence of all living organisms and their physical environment. The former would see wilderness as principally a recreation resource while the latter would see it as a distinct resource. Since both the Congress and the Forest Service consider wilderness a distinct resource and one to be perpetuated for future generations, humility becomes an indicator of the ethical value of wilderness.

Humility merely recognizes that we do not have all the answers, that, as Brower (1957) put it, man needs wilderness "to find answers to questions that he has not yet learned how to ask." Muir felt people should feel "part of wild nature, kin to everything." Schweitzer felt that we should have reverence for all life. Humility acknowledges that we as a race have no inherent right to destroy. The Wilderness Act reaffirms our basic humility.

Humility implies respect. Leopold wrote: "In short, a land ethic changes the role of *Homo sapiens* from conqueror of the land community to plain member and citizen of it. It implies respect for his fellow members, and also respect for the community as such." (Leopold 1949). Wilderness that helps us become more humble and learn respect has a value.

Restraint

Another of the ethical values of wilderness is as a symbol of restraint.

"Our future, to a large degree, must be based on restraint; restraint of our rate of consumption, restraint in our life styles, restraint in the exercise of some of our rights and restraint in what we deem to be necessary. If we are not willing to set aside a limited number of the earth's complex systems which we have had the privilege of knowing and being a part of, our future on this planet is bleak. Exploiting every last niche because we feel a present day need for more resources is certainly short-sighted. If we as a society can't draw the line and say, 'Enough, this is what we must live with,' nature will soon do so for us. And when nature draws the line it will be too late to regain the standard of living we desire and there will be no flexibility left." (Davis 1980). Wilderness, with prohibitions on machines and the use of certain commodity resources, is of value as a small first step in proving we can do without.

Gene Pool Preservation

Much has been written about the need to preserve gene pools. We hear of miracle drugs that come from obscure plants and how the destruction of any gene pool at the species or variety level could withhold a much needed substance from us in the future. We read that over one billion dollars was spent last year on prescription drugs derived from the taxonomically higher plants alone. We read that even in this day of thousands of laboratory produced chemicals, the main ingredient in half of the prescriptions we buy is a naturally produced chemical.

In light of the above, perhaps the question is not about the value of gene pool preservation but rather why I include it as an ethical value instead of a scientific value. Simply stated, I, along with many others, find it amoral, and perhaps immoral, to totally destroy any species of plant or animal whether it has a value to humans today or even may have such a value--thus it is an ethical value of wilderness. Should others prefer to list it as a scientific or naturalness value, fine; the important thing is to remember to include gene pool preservation as a wilderness value.

PSYCHOLOGICAL

The psychological values of wilderness are almost as difficult to get a handle on as the ethical. The basis for the four psychological values I list, although implied throughout the Wilderness Act, are derived primarily from the word "contrast." Section 2(c) of the Act in defining wilderness says, "A wilderness, **in contrast with** those areas where man and his own works dominate the landscape . . . " (emphasis added). All four of these values imply serenity and a refinement of the sensory perceptions.

Contrast

The Outdoor Recreation Resources Review Commission (ORRRC) Study Report 3 concludes that "Much of the value of wilderness is in its contrast to the rest of the landscape." The report goes on to say:

"By standing toward a zenith in a scale of resources, wilderness gives definition to many other resources. Museums and concert halls are cultural edifices supported by society for comparable reasons: they are the places where one can go, if only on rare occasions, to measure the ordinary against the superlative and thereby retain perspective."(ORRRC 1962) Leopold wrote on the seeming contradiction between our desire to preserve American institutions and yet not make the connection of how equally important it is to preserve the American environment that produced these cherished institutions. Without this contrast how will we understand the basis for the American institutions and way of life whose preservation we hold so dear? Wilderness offers us individual liberties far beyond our workaday life in organized society. Although in many eastern cultures spiritual and aesthetic contrast can be self induced, the western mind seems to need external stimulus for such contrast. Perhaps, at least in the western world, the value of wilderness is proportionate to its difference from civilization.

Spiritual

An extensive amount of literature exists on the spiritual aspects of wilderness. In fact, in Section 2(b) of the 1975 amendment to the Wilderness Act (misnamed by many as the "Eastern Wilderness Act"), Congress specifically mentions "inspiration" as a wilderness value. There is little doubt that many people visit the wilderness to get their act back together, to find harmony with God's creation, to regain perspective. Christ, Mohammed, and many American Indian religious leaders fled to the wilderness, be it desert or mountaintop, to commune with God. Some wilderness areas contain formal religious sites; all possess inspirational potential.

In my limited literature search, three statements held special spiritual meaning to me. I repeat them here in the hope they help others understand this value of wilderness. "I was aware of a fusion with the country, an overwhelming sense of completion in which all my hopes and experiences seemed crystallized into one shining vision." (Olson 1963)

"The individual with any soul cannot live long in the presence of towering mountains or sweeping plains without getting a little of the high moral standard of Nature infused into his being." (Carhart 1920)

"I love music and all other art, but I do not attach such value to them as is generally done. I cannot, for example, recognize the values of those arts which require great technical value for their understanding. When I gaze at the star-strewn heavens and at the infinite beauty which confronts my eyes, they mean more to me than all human art can give me. That does not mean that I ignore the other values, but personally, in comparison with the infinite beauty of nature, I feel their unreality too intensely. Life is greater than all art." (Mahatma Gandhi, attributed)

Therapeutic

The therapeutic value of wilderness is also stressed in the literature and is closely allied with the spiritual value. Wilderness is described as a setting in which to find rejuvenation of the spirit, the body and the soul; a setting to gain new perspectives; a setting to rediscover human values.

Stegner believes wilderness is needed as "... a means of reassuring ourselves of our sanity as creatures, a part of the geography of hope" (ORRRC 1962). Olson found wilderness a place to find inspiration, insight, and personal peace. Marshall (1930) felt "wilderness furnishes perhaps the best opportunity for ... pure aesthetic rapture". Nash (1976) theorized that wilderness releases the right half of the brain, that half that holds the wild, holistic and creative part of our intelligence which is normally suppressed in our fast paced, structured world. Muir, as would be expected, waxed poetic about the therapeutic values of wilderness: "Nature's peace will flow into you as sunshine flows into trees. The winds will blow their own freshness into you and the storms their energy, while cares will drop off like autumn leaves" (Teale 1954). Some clinical psychologists and other medical professionals (e.g., Bernstein 1972, McKinley 1966, Benninger 1959, Thorstenson and Heaps 1973) believe strongly that wilderness can provide therapy to those emotionally run down or suffering from mental illness. Frome (1974) summed up the therapeutic value of wilderness rather well:

"Wilderness is a humanitarian resource, the basis of a more healthy social structure, a banner of hope to the ghetto dweller deprived of human dignity and boxed in by crowds, noise, litter, and concrete. How can human life be valued highly in a society shaped by destruction, despoliation, degradation, and exploitation of man by man? Wilderness is the alternative to waste and dissent that characterizes modern society. It restores belief in the environment, each other, and ourselves."

Vicarious

This is a value of wilderness enjoyed from a distance. It includes a variety of symbolic meanings attributed to wilderness, a feeling of solace, of reassurance that we have not conquered everything; had we already conquered everything, our wilderness discussions would be dealing only with history.

Many more hours are spent reading about wilderness, attending lectures, sharing photographs, watching television or movies with a wilderness setting or theme, and just plain daydreaming about wilderness than are actually spent in wilderness. These enjoyments and anticipations are very real values of wilderness. It is the existence of wilderness, not necessarily its use, that shows we as a society care--for the earth, for the future, and for our mental well being.

RECREATIONAL

The Wilderness Act specifies recreational opportunities as characteristic of wilderness, stating that wilderness "has outstanding opportunities for *solitude* or a *primitive and unconfined* type of *recreation*" (Section 2(c)). It also clearly considers recreation to be one of the values of wilderness in directing that wilderness "shall be adminis-

tered for the *use* and *enjoyment* of the American people" (Section 2(a)) and "wilderness areas shall be devoted to the public purposes of *recreational*, scenic, scientific, educational, conservation and historical use" (Section 4(b)). The 1975 amendment also specified "*physical and mental challenge*" as a specific value of wilderness (Section 2 (b)). (Emphasis added in all four quotes.)

Recreation, literally re-creation, is valuable in proportion to the degree with which it differs from, or contrasts with, the participant's routine life. For most of us, wilderness recreation therefore possesses extraordinarily high value. Despite frequent arguments from those who oppose wilderness preservation, wilderness recreation is available to practically all, whether rich or poor, young or old; and research statistics bear this out (e.g., Stankey 1972). Some claim that since the severely handicapped and the elderly can't enjoy wilderness, public lands should not be allocated to this use. W. Mitchell, a paraplegic wilderness advocate and user and former mayor of Crested Butte, Colorado, would surely dispute this. And so would one of my close Adirondack associates, Clarence Petty, now in his late-70s and still enjoying wilderness in New York and Alaska. I can still vividly recall Clarence, upon hearing the above argument, shaking his head and muttering that since an ankle injury made it impossible for him to ice skate anymore perhaps we should tear up all public skating rinks.

Primitive and Unconfined Recreation

Many forms of recreation can and do take place in wilderness. Some forms are enhanced by or even dependent on wilderness and others which may take place in wilderness are not enhanced by it. The former, such as backpacking, pack trains, canoeing, and quality hunting and fishing, are values of the wilderness resource, while the latter, such as tossing a frisbee, are not.

Primitive and unconfined recreation does not require vast acreages. Perhaps in the arid West size is important. Bob Marshall suggested that a wilderness should be large enough so it can't be crossed without spending a night out. That size was rather large for a man like Marshall, who was noted for covering 50, 60 or even 70 miles (80, 96, or 113 ha) a day with a pack on his back. But size should not be the only criterion in ranking this value; even Marshall wouldn't have covered many miles a day in a South Carolina pocosin swamp. Vegetation and topography are at least as important as size, as is the opportunity to escape schedules.

Solitude

The opportunities to find solitude and isolation are recognized as important wilderness values. Like the opportunity to find unconfined recreation discussed above, the opportunities to find solitude vary with size, topography, vegetation, and visitor use and distribution.

Wilderness "offers as important sanctuary into which one can withdraw, either temporarily or permanently, to find respite" (Hendee *et al.* 1978). The solitude one finds in such silence and isolation gives the freedom to cultivate one's own thoughts in one's own way. This value can often be enjoyed without a great deal of physical exertion. As we mature, we may measure the value of wilderness less in terms of miles per day or peaks ascended and more in terms of enjoying the opportunity to escape within ourselves and soaring in search of eternal truth or absolute beauty.

Mental and Physical Challenge

The spirit of adventure and the need to demonstrate self reliance help build and shape our individual character just as two centuries ago they helped build and shape our nation's character. Marshall called the opportunity for self sufficiency the "moral equivalent of war" (Marshall 1930). The challenge and the adventure that wilderness recreation epitomizes can become a motivator. The setting is there for fear and pain which we spend most of our life trying to eliminate, yet we may need to occasionally experience these emotions at a time and place of our choosing, for they were important factors in our very evolution.

OTHER VALUES

The Wilderness Act refers to other optional characteristics of wilderness in that it "... may also contain ecological, geological, or other features of scientific, educational, scenic, or historic value" (Section 2(c)). The values of such other characteristics are recognized in Section 2(a) by directing that these areas be administered "... for the *gathering* and *dissemination* of *information regarding their use as wilderness*;" and in Section 4(b) by devoting wilderness to the public purposes of recreational, *scenic, scientific, educational, conservation,* and *historical* use" (emphasis added).

Cultural

Although not specifically referred to in the Wilderness Act, the cultural values of wilderness cannot be denied. Some flow from inspiration, which is specifically mentioned as a wilderness value in the 1975 amendment; others helped form our national character and as such relate to historic values; and still others have resulted in the creative thinking that has enhanced the educational and scientific values of wilderness. But the cultural value of wilderness is more pervasive and needs to be considered separately from those values to which it contributes.

Culture includes tastes that satisfy our soul as well as our body. How much poorer we would be without the wilderness inspired art of Audubon, Bodmer, Catlin, Cole, Miller and Russell; the literature of Bartram, Cooper, Emerson, Irving, McPhee, Olson, Stegner, Thoreau and Twain; the photography of Adams, Hyde and Porter; and the music of Denver and Riordan. Perhaps the need for wilderness is as great for our soul and our creative potential as food, clothing and shelter are for our body.

In bringing out our individual talents, wilderness becomes not only a sustainer of human dignity and diversity but provides insurance against homogenization.

Wilderness is conducive to idiosyncracy; social and intellectual diversity; it provides a setting for us to learn, think, and increase our individual cultural development.

The "(a)bility to see the cultural value of wilderness boils down, in the last analysis, to a question of intellectual humility. The shallow-minded modern who has lost his rootage in the land assumes that he has already discovered what is important" (Leopold 1949).

Historical

The historical value of wilderness is closely allied with the cultural but is more definitive and easier to grasp. The remnants of what our pioneer forefathers faced may help us better understand how this new world became distinctly American rather than European. Wilderness "... has helped form our character and ... has certainly shaped our history as a people" (Stegner, in ORRRC 1962).

Wilderness areas can be thought of as living museums; yes, museums, for they are just as much so as those of natural history on which we spend millions of dollars each year. Each is a historical document just as much as those we keep under glass. Nash (1982) characterizes wilderness as the basic ingredient of American civilization. Leopold (1949) put it this way:

Wilderness is the raw material out of which man has hammered the artifact called civilization ... The rich diversity of the world's cultures reflects a corresponding diversity in the wilds that gave them birth ... This is a plea for the preservation of some tag-ends of wilderness, as museum pieces, for the edification of those who may one day wish to see, feel, or study the origins of their cultural inheritance.

Historians such as DeVoto, Nash, Stegner, Turner and Webb have all described the imprint of wilderness landscapes on the American mind. Perhaps Stegner was the most eloquent: "Something will have gone out of us as a people if we ever let the remaining wilderness be destroyed; if we permit the last virgin forests to be turned into comic books and plastic cigarette cases; ... " (Stegner, in ORRRC 1962).

Stegner added: "If the abstract dream of human liberty and human dignity became, in America, something more than an abstract dream, mark it down at least partially to the fact that we were in subtle ways subdued by what we conquered" (Stegner, in ORRRC 1961).

Educational

Educational values of wilderness range from providing a laboratory for study in the biological, physical, and social sciences to the casual identification of plant and animal species or learning survival skills. Both the casual or the formal observation of natural forces and the interrelationships of all life forms will aid our society in developing environmental understanding and responsibility. It may be a first step in reaching harmony between the needs of humans and the capabilities of the planet. It may help develop our sense of humility, a bedrock essential for practicing environmental responsibility.

Ordinarily, an individual's wilderness education evolves

from an interest in single ingredients--game, fish, birds, lichens, etc.--to an interest in the whole and the realization of the many interdependencies. This is, of course, ecology, which can then become the basis for so many decisions the individual makes outside the wilderness setting.

Scientific

We have discussed the importance of leisure time, solitude, and the wonders of the natural world to creative thinking in the arts. The same, of course, goes for the sciences. Imagine Newton settling down under the apple tree or Archimedes gingerly lowering his posterior into the hot bath! Many, and perhaps most, really new discoveries come as we let our minds run loose.

A more commonly mentioned scientific role for wilderness is that of benchmark laboratories that can be used as control or comparison areas for biological research of both academic and economic worth. Spurr (in Leydet 1963) and others have stressed the need for such areas in developing and testing basic ecological theory and concepts of community dynamics.

Each basic ecosystem needs its own control area, such as a wilderness, for comparative studies. As Leopold (1949) observed, "One cannot study the physiology of Montana in the Amazon." Leopold believed wilderness was important as a laboratory for the study of land health. He felt all available wild areas, large or small, had value as norms for land science.

Unfortunately, many ecosystems and physiographic features needed to illustrate natural history concepts are not represented in the wilderness system and, indeed, some no longer even exist (Davis 1980; USDA, Davis 1981; Davis 1984). For studies of some species of wide-ranging wildlife such as the grizzly bear and the wolf in their natural habitat, only wilderness is likely to provide us opportunities in the future. The same can be said of certain vegetative communities.

Wilderness is indeed, as Rod Nash (1976) said, a "national library." It has value as a creative, inspirational setting and an ecological benchmark for the biological, physical, and social sciences.

Scenic

The value of wilderness as a scenic resource varies with each area and with the beholder. I submit that all wilderness, where the natural processes are going on, is beautiful. I will not attempt to describe the value of beauty except to quote John Ruskin (1846), " . . . beautiful things are useful to men because they are beautiful, and for the sake of beauty only; and not to sell, or pawn, or in any other way turn into money."

Economic

The value of wilderness from an economic standpoint can, even if in crude ways, be quantified. These values accrue from recurring fees spent on outfitters and guides; monies pumped into local motels, restaurants, gas stations, and stores; and monies spent on equipment sales and rentals. The generally accepted travel cost method for valuing a recreation visitor-day has yielded an estimat-

ed value of $14.00 for each Colorado wilderness visitor-day (Walsh et al. 1982).

In addition to these recreationally oriented expenditures, wilderness has economic value for watershed protection and a host of other values. Results of recent research in Colorado (Walsh et al. 1982) indicate that the general population is willing to pay for the future option, vicarious, and bequest values inherent in preserving wilderness, as well as for its recreation value. In fact, the willingness to pay for these amenity values is approximately equal to the recreational value of wilderness. These research data are statistically accurate only for Colorado but they might be used as indicators nationwide until further research addresses the purely preservation value of wilderness nationwide.

VALUES OF INDIVIDUAL WILDERNESS

Individual wilderness areas often possess values very specific to them rather than generic to all wilderness such as those values discussed previously. This does not make these values any less important than those previously discussed; it may, in fact, make them more valuable because they are less common. Certainly these values should be incorporated into the evaluation criteria and the decision making process.

Wilderness Watersheds

From almost all aspects--ecological, recreational, water quality, solitude, et al.-- the preservation of entire drainages rather than sections of drainages is more feasible and valuable. Put another way, it is easier to administer the purposes of the Wilderness Act when the whole watershed is within the wilderness, and the purposes of the Wilderness Act are better met. This holds regardless of the drainage type, from first order, or unbranched, streams right on up through large many-branched rivers. The wilderness value of acreage with a watershed that is totally within a wilderness is higher than that of wilderness acreage in a watershed whose upstream area is not entirely wilderness.

Unique or Representative Ecosystems

At present only 81 of our nation's 233 basic ecosystems are adequately (2 or more examples) represented in the National Wilderness Preservation System (NWPS). Another 109 ecosystems are not represented in the NWPS at all (USDA, Davis 1981; Davis 1984). As scientific benchmarks or a legacy to future generations, it would seem that an extraordinarily high value should be attached to designated areas that contain ecosystems presently represented in two or fewer areas in the NWPS and to those potential wilderness areas with ecosystems presently represented in fewer than two areas in the NWPS.

The basic ecosystems of the United States are very broadly defined, primarily by physiographic region, climate and potential natural vegetation. Many small and unique ecosystems within these broad categories are also desirable as scientific benchmarks and should be considered along with the vital representation of the basic national ecosystems.

Proximity to Population Centers

Many values of wilderness--recreational, educational, contrast, therapeutic, *et al.*--are of increasing importance as they are more readily available to people. In this sense, wilderness close to large populations takes on an extra value, and greater management problems. This value should be recognized in the evaluation criteria of any analysis. It may also be necessary to recognize that some wilderness values (e.g., solitude, natural ecological processes) may be adversely affected by proximity to large populations unless carefully designed wilderness management programs, including controlled visitor distribution and use, are implemented.

As a point for discussion, I would suggest giving special recognition to this value for all areas within a 4-hour drive of a standard metropolitan statistical area (SMSA) of more than 100,000 people. The relative importance given this value might vary by both the number of areas and the total wilderness acreage within this distance and by the population and growth rate of the SMSA.

LITERATURE CITED

Bernstein, A. 1972. Wilderness as a therapeutic behavior setting. Therapeutic Rec. J. 6(4).

Brower, D.R. (ed.). 1957. Wildlands in our civilization. Sierra Club Bull. 42(6); June 1957.

Carhart, A.H. 1920. Recreation in the forests; Ame. For., Vol. 26.

Crisler, L. 1958. Arctic wild. Harper and Row New York.

Davis, G.D. 1980. The case for wilderness diversity. Ame. For. 86:(8).

Davis, G.D. 1984. Natural Diversity for Future Generations: The Role of Wilderness. pp. 141-154, In J.C. Cooley and J.H. Cooley, (eds.), Proceedings Natural Diversity in Forest Ecosystems Workshop, Institute of Ecology, University of Georgia.

Frome, M. 1974. Battle for the wilderness. Praeger Publ.

Hendee, J.C., G.H. Stankey and R.C. Lucas. 1978. Wilderness management; USDA For. Serv. Misc. Publ. 1365.

Leopold, A. 1949. A Sand County Almanac and sketches here and there. Oxford Univ. Press.

Leydet, F. (ed.). 1963. Tomorrow's Wilderness. Sierra Club.

Marshall, R. 1930. The problem of the wilderness. Sci. Mon. 5(30).

McKinley, D. 1966. Psychology of the wilderness. Mazama 48(13).

Menninger, K. 1959. Human Needs in Urban Society. Arch. Rec. 126(1).

Nash, R. 1982. Wilderness and the American mind. Yale Univ. Press.

Nash, R. 1976. Johnson Lecture at Northland College, Ashland, Wis.

Olson, S. 1963. Runes of the North. Alfred A. Knopf.

Outdoor Recreation Resources Review Commission. 1962. Wilderness and Recreation--A report on resources, values, and problems. Study Report 3, U.S. Govt. Printing Office.

Ruskin, J. 1846. Modern painters. Vol. II.

Schoenfeld, C.A., and J.C. Hendee. 1978. Wildlife management in wilderness. The Boxwood Press.

Stankey, G.H. 1971. Myths in wilderness decision-making. J. Soil and Water Conserv. 26(5).

Teale, E.W. 1954. The wilderness world of John Muir. Houghton Mifflin Co.

Temporary Study Commission on the Future of the Adirondacks. 1970. The future of the Adirondack Park. State of New York.

Thorstenson, C.T. and R.A. Heaps. 1973. Outdoor survival and its implications for rehabilitation. Ther. Rec. J. 7(1).

USDA, Forest Service. 1982. Memorandum and enclosure from George D. Davis to Chief (ref. 1920 and 2320); September 22, 1981 (enclosure revised February 20, 1982).

USDA, Forest Service, 1977. RARE II wilderness attribute rating system - A user's manual. mimeo.

Walsh, R.G., R.A. Gillman and J.B. Loomis. 1982. Wilderness resource economics: Recreation use and preservation values.

Indian Mounds Wilderness Area: Perceived Wilderness Qualities And Impacts Of Oil And Gas Development

by
Kent E. Evans

ABSTRACT--In October 1984, Congress established the 9,946 acre (4,025 ha) Indian Mounds Wilderness Area on the Sabine National Forest in east Texas. This area was recommended as nonwilderness following the RARE II effort by the Forest Service. Several citizens groups led a concerted effort to designate the wilderness in spite of considerable prior impacts, existing roads, and ongoing oil and gas development. Approximately, 85 percent of the area is subject to oil and gas drilling because of valid existing rights. A description of the wilderness values in the area was developed from the proponents views recorded in the media and through personal visits with local proponents. This description of the proponents perceived wilderness qualities depicts the area as a good example of an east Texas pine and mixed hardwood forest that is nearing maturity. The proponents feel that the area's contiguous stands of 50- to 60-year-old trees provide an adequate setting for pursuing their desired wilderness experiences--being alone, observing bird life, viewing large stands of trees free of clearcutting.

The impacts of oil and gas development on these perceived values were considered. Wilderness proponents favor intensive rehabilitation of disturbed areas to promote rapid recovery of the wilderness. Mitigation measures were suggested to protect the wilderness and promote rapid recovery within the constraints of State and Federal law and rights provided the mineral owner in his deed.

KEYWORDS: oil, gas, leases, wilderness.

On October 30, 1984, Public-Law 95-574,98 Stat. 3051, established the 9,946 acre (4,025 ha) Indian Mounds Wilderness Area. This area was one of five totaling 34,346 acres (13,900 ha) established on National Forest land in East Texas in 1984. The Indian Mounds Area was recommended as nonwilderness by the Forest Service following its Roadless Area Review and Evaluation (RARE II) process. However, several citizens groups in Texas led a concerted and successful effort to designate the area as wilderness.

A unique feature inside the Indian Mounds Wilderness, and the principal reason for this paper, is the presence of ongoing oil and gas development. This development is a valid existing right, specifically allowed in the legislation. The wilderness qualities that exist in the area are being impacted by an activity not usually associated with wilderness. Oil and gas development has the potential to permanently alter natural landforms, radically change soil fertility, and pollute surface and subsurface water sources. However, less severe damage can result when development is by a prudent oil company guided by a resource management team.

This paper identifies and describes wilderness qualities that are perceived in the area by proponents of the Indian Mound Wilderness. I will discuss mitigating the adverse oil and gas impacts to protect these perceived wilderness qualities.

INDIAN MOUNDS WILDERNESS AREA

The Indian Mounds Wilderness Area is located on the 104,000 acre (42,088 ha) Yellowpine Ranger District of the Sabine National Forest. The forest is in southeastern Texas, generally referred to as Deep East Texas. Houston is 180 miles (290 km) southwest of the forest; Dallas is 275 miles (443 km) to the northwest. The eastern boundary of the forest adjoins Toledo Bend Reservoir, which is the state boundary with Louisiana. Hemphill, the county seat of Sabine County is located 5 miles (8 km) west of the Indian Mounds Area.

The climate is characteristically hot and humid in the summer with a mean maximum July temperature of 93 degrees F. The majority of the 57-inch average annual rainfall comes in spring and fall. Heavy thunderstorms are common when fronts pass during these seasons. Winters are mild and short, with a mean minimum temperature in January of 39 degrees F. The growing season averages 240 days.

The wilderness is bisected by three major corridors: State Highway FM 3382, gravel Forest Service 115, and a 150-ft. (46 m) wide pipeline right-of-way. The roads carry an assortment of recreation, farm, oil-field, residential, and logging traffic. The largest contiguous acreage of this wilderness without a corridor is about 4,000 acres (1,620 ha). Two subdivisions and one marina adjoin the wilderness with about 30 residents in each area.

The Sabine National Forest is located in the pineywoods vegetation area of Texas (Gould 1975). Most of the wilderness is dominated by loblolly (*Pinus taeda L.*) and shortleaf pine (*P. echinata Mill*) approximately 50 years old. The wilderness, like most of east Texas, was heavily logged in the 1920's. The existing timber stand is the result of voluntary regeneration and 50 years of management by the Forest Service. About 1500 acres (610 ha) of the area are dominated by upland hardwoods, primarily red oak (*Quercus falcata vac. falcata Michx*), white oak (*Q. alba L.*), sweetgum (*Liquidamar styraciflua L.*) and hickory (*Carya tomentosa*). Bottomland hardwood stands containing water oak (*Q. nigra L.*), cherrybark oak (*Q. falcata var. pagodaefolia Ell.*), blackgum (*Nyssa sylvatica var. biflora*), and magnolia (*Magnolia grandiflora L.*) occur on about 300 acres (120 ha). Roughly 300 acres (120 ha) of the area are in pine regeneration area, having been logged within the past 10 years.

The wilderness wildlife populations are fairly typical of the Sabine National Forest. The list of known species include 259 birds (64 yearlong residents), 45 mammals, 87 reptiles and amphibians, and 88 fish. Two endangered bird species are known in the area, the bald eagle (*Haliaeetus leucocephalus*) and red-cockaded woodpecker (*Dendrocopus borealis*). The eagles are winter visitors to the Toledo Bend area. The woodpeckers have established one colony in a stand of mature shortleaf pine inside the wilderness. This birdlife is also found in other parts of the forest. The Yellowpine District has approximately 20 red-cockaded woodpecker colonies.

STATUS OF OIL AND GAS IN THE INDIAN MOUNDS AREA

The Sabine National Forest was purchased by the Federal Government from various private owners in the mid-1930's, and a variety of mineral ownerships exist under the Forest. Three basic mineral ownerships are found in the Indian Mounds Wilderness:

1. U.S. minerals--The mineral estate was purchased with the surface by the U.S.
2. Outstanding minerals--The mineral estate was severed from the surface estate prior to acquisition by the U.S.
3. Reserved minerals--The seller retained the mineral estate when he sold the surface estate to the U.S. In most cases, the minerals would revert to government ownership after a specified time period.

Surface activities by reserved mineral owners were made subject to the Rules and Regulations of the Secre-

tary of Agriculture of 1911. Surface activities on outstanding minerals in the area are regulated by State law, not Federal, since the mineral estate was severed prior to surface acquisition.

Approximately 60,000 acres (24,280 ha) of the Yellowpine District were purchased in 1936, from one landowner. About 9,600 acres (3,885 ha) of that purchase are in the wilderness. The deed conveying the land from that owner to the government reserved "all oil, gas and other valuable minerals by the vendor for 50 years, ending 01-01-85". The deed allowed the "full right to enter" and to prospect for and develop those minerals "on, in and under" those lands (Sabine Co., Texas, Deed records). Further stated in the deed was a provision that any oil or gas well in production on 01-01-85 would reserve a 1/2 mile (0.8 km) radius of mineral rights for another 5 years. The reserved acreage around each producing well would revert to U.S. ownership on 01-01-90, if the well went dry.

The drilling and exploration of reserved minerals in the Indian Mounds began several years prior to the designation of the new wilderness. The Indian Mound area was intensively prospected with approximately 120 miles (193 km) of shot-hole seismograph lines. By the time wilderness designation was finalized, the Indian Mounds had 18 wells drilled in it and several adjacent to it. By 01-01-85 producing wells reserved about 2750 acres (1,113 ha) inside the new wilderness area for future development by the reserved mineral owner.

Roughly 85 percent of the wilderness area is still available for oil and gas development (Table 1). The only area

OBJECTIVES

The objectives of this paper are to:
1. Describe the wilderness qualities perceived by proponents of the Indian Mounds Wilderness Area.
2. Identify which aspects of oil and gas development adversely impact those wilderness qualities.
3. Identify activities that can be mitigated within the constraints of relevant deeds and law.
4. Recommend management actions to protect the wilderness during oil and gas development.

PROCEDURES

Data were gathered in the following ways to meet the objectives of the study:
1. Literature was reviewed to describe wilderness qualities relevant to the Indian Mounds Wilderness Area.
2. Relevant deeds, laws, and Forest Service documents concerning oil and gas development by a reserved mineral owner in Texas were reviewed.
3. Local proponents of the Wilderness were interviewed to define their perceptions of the areas qualities.

These information sources were used to develop a rough description of the wilderness qualities that were perceived by proponents of the Indian Mounds Wilderness Area. The review also identified oil and gas activities that could be mitigated to protect existing wilderness qualities.

Table 1. Status of Mineral Ownership in the Indian Mounds Wilderness Area.

Status	Authority over Development	Acreage[1] 12-31-84	Acreage 1-1-85	% of Area 1-1-85
Reserved in perpetuity	D[2], Tx[3], SR[4]	2800	2800	28
Outstanding	Tx	2900	2900	29
Reserved subject to reversion	D, Tx, SR	3750	2750	28
U.S. ownership	US[5]			
Existing leases		500	500	5
No leases			1000	10

[1] Acreage estimates are pending title review by OGC.

[2] Deed of conveyance.

[3] State of Texas law.

[4] Secretary of Agriculture's Rules and Regulations of 1911.

[5] U.S. Government, leased prior to wilderness designation.

excluded from development currently is about 1500 acres (610 ha) of U.S. minerals which reverted to the government on 01-01-85. This land will not be leased. The existing U.S. leases, about 500 acres (202 ha), will not be released if they expire without development.

The discovery of oil and gas in the area suggests that all private mineral rights and existing U.S. leases will be developed. The challenge facing the Forest Service is to protect the wilderness values to the extent possible while oil and gas development proceeds.

Local proponents of the wilderness were visited personally to determine wilderness qualities they perceived. The conversations also helped verify which oil and gas activities were adverse to wilderness qualities.

These procedures employed a type of analytic inductive reasoning described and used by Bryan (1979). Bryan points out that strictly representative samples are not required for either the initial observation stage or the verification stage of research. A meaningful product can result from a description built around a relatively small sample.

Personal contacts were designed to avoid conflicts with U.S. Office of Management and Budget regulations on interviews and public involvement. Conversations with the local citizens were conducted in a very unstructured, casual format. The author selected citizens to visit based on their known support for the wilderness area. The visit was initiated by an offer to provide them with a look at a topographic map showing the boundaries of the wilderness and of the oil and gas development. As the features were explained, the citizens volunteered their views about the new wilderness area, oil and gas development, and the Forest Service. The visits lasted from 1 to 2 hours. The author made notes of the citizens comments after leaving. The author did not attempt to persuade or modify any of the views expressed during the conversations.

LITERATURE REVIEW

Wilderness Qualities in the Indian Mounds Area

To protect a wilderness during oil and gas development, a resource manager should have an understanding of which wilderness qualities are threatened. According to the Wilderness Act of 1964, a wilderness is an area that is untrammeled by man, has retained its primeval character and influence, and is without permanent improvements. In 1975, an amendment to the 1964 Wilderness Act was passed by Congress. This Act identified a need to add areas to the National Wilderness Preservation System, particularly in the East. The amendment allowed the consideration of roadless areas that would not normally fit the criteria given in the 1964 Act. This approach was legislated because of the limited area available in the East, the faster regenerative capacity to wilderness or near wilderness, and the need for wilderness close to populated areas (USDA Forest Service 1979).

The basic criteria for wilderness in the East were identical to those elsewhere except that consideration was given to areas that did not have more than one of the following:

1. More than 1/2 mile (0.8 km) of improved road for each 1,000 acres (405 ha).
2. More than 15% of area is in non-natural planted vegetation.
3. More than 20% of area has been harvested within past 10 years.
4. Area could contain a few dwellings if dwellings and access are obscured by natural features.

Using the RARE II process, the Forest Service concluded that the Indian Mounds area did not fulfill the criteria or intent of the 1975 amendment.

As prescribed by RARE II, the Forest Service inventoried and evaluated all land in East Texas for inclusion to the National Wilderness Preservation System. In 1978, a Forest Service evaluation team made up of Landscape Architects, Foresters, and Recreation Specialist rated the Indian Mounds Area using a system known as the

Wilderness Attribute Rating System. The evaluation covered about 14,000 acres (5,670 ha), including the core of the current 9,946 acre (4,025 ha) wilderness. By 1978, the team noted that the area had already experienced extreme impacts to its natural processes. The area had several roads through it, a 150-foot-wide pipeline right-of-way, and several utility rights-of-way. Prior influence was rated as "high" in the area because of these "physical developments" and "vegetation manipulation."

The most widespread prior influence on the area was logging. By 1930, the area had been intensively logged. Evidence of the past logging activity includes the old flattened grades of narrow-gauge railroads with their debris of rotted crossties, iron spikes, and occasional iron track. One long-time resident of the Indian Mounds area remembered the timber stand prior to 1930. He described the area south of Highway 83 east of Hemphill (currently in wilderness), as very different from the present. Before it was logged, the area was dominated by mature longleaf pine (*Pinus palustris Mill.*). Longleaf covered all the high ground. Loblolly pine and beech (*Fagus grandiflora Ehrh.*) were found down in the creek bottoms. He also recalled that the area had virtually no shrubs since it was burned every year or two by the people who ran livestock over the area (Luther Wood, pers. comm.). The presence of large open understory stands of mature longleaf pine resulted from hundreds of years of natural fire and/or regular burning by native Americans prior to the white man's settlement. The current stand of National Forest timber in the wilderness is the result of 50 years of management by the Forest Service.

The 1978 review further described the area as having a "very low" ability to provide solitude. The opportunity to experience primitive recreation was "low". The team rated ecological, geological, scenic or cultural value as "infrequent." The single significant ecological attribute was the presence of one red-cockaded woodpecker colony.

At the time of the evaluation the apparent naturalness of the area was rated "high" or "very high" impact rating because of mineral developments, vegetation manipulation and roads.

The 1978 review team and the RARE II process did not recommend the Indian Mounds as wilderness, and put it into a category for uses other than wilderness. These recommendations do not mean that the area was entirely void of wilderness qualities. The 1984 designation resulted because a different set of standards was applied by the citizens groups to recommend the area for wilderness. The citizens employed a liberalized concept of wilderness to include an area that would satisfy their purposes.

Forest Service recreation researchers have recognized that a new concept of wilderness is responsible for designation of new areas, particularly in the Southern and Eastern U.S. Hendee (1980) recognized that wilderness is evolving to a liberalized and expanded concept. Wilderness designations in the East, he points out, are notably different from western wilderness areas in such key attributes as size, naturalness, and solitude.

This liberalized concept of wilderness may explain a criterion for wilderness designation as a place where a specific wilderness experience can be pursued. Roggenbuck (1980) found that on both sides of the country wilderness visits were to enjoy scenery, learn about and experience nature, to face physical challenge, and to escape physical, social and mental stress.

Proponents View of Indian Mounds Wilderness Qualities: Media Records

Media records provide a good insight into the proponents views of wilderness in Texas. These citizens assembled a fact sheet (Citizens 1983) that characterized their perceived attributes of the Indian Mounds and other areas in the State. The media record also suggests that the citizens were motivated by a desire to halt Forest Service management activities such as clearcuts. Their proposed areas were described as beautiful, diverse, and distinctive and containing vanishing ecosystems, rare species, 22 champion trees, and numerous scenic vistas. Nonwilderness intrusions were recognized by the group as "roads and clearcuts by the USFS." The group noted that corridors existed and concluded that they were "needed for access to private land."

The single most visible leader of the citizens groups was Mr. Edward C. Fritz, Chairman of the Texas Committee on Natural Resources. His support for wilderness designation was strongly motivated by his desire to stop clearcutting by the Forest Service. The anticlearcutting motive was detected from most of his fellow proponents of the Indian Mounds designation. According to Mr. Fritz, "the principal purpose of a wilderness is to keep it from being clearcut" (Gunter 1983). He claims that Forest Service management would defraud our natural heritage and keep people from learning what the forests were like before they were so heavily clearcut. Forest Service management activities were labeled "Threats" to wilderness by Mr. Fritz. Specific concerns voiced by Mr. Fritz were that the Forest Service would: (1) clearcut every stand of available timber at the end of rotation, (2) grow pine on 94% of those regeneration areas, (3) burn almost all stands periodically to kill the hardwoods, and (4) lose species diversity including insects, herbs, microflora and fauna, as well as hardwood trees such as beech and magnolia (Fritz 1981).

Oil and gas development was not identified as a threat to wilderness, even though the citizens groups were aware of the potential for oil and gas development inside these proposed wilderness areas. "Since all minerals are privately owned or leased, exploration and production will continue unabated regardless of designation" (Citizens 1983).

No record was found of any effort by the citizens to halt future development by forcing minerals acquisition by the U.S. prior to wilderness designation. The wilderness legislation specifically noted that the administration of the area will be subject to valid existing rights (e.g., oil and gas). The Lone Star Chapter of the Sierra Club forwarded its desired wilderness management policy to the Forest Supervisor in a letter dated 11-12-84. Its desired management policy "in no way prevents or prohibits oil and gas drilling."

The National Forests in Texas hosted a RARE II re-evaluation workshop in Lufkin in 1983 to solicit citizen views for ranking 12 roadless areas into a priority list. This session provided another record of the wilderness proponents view of wilderness attributes present in the Indian Mounds. This gathering brought together representatives of the Sierra Club, the Texas Committee on Natural Resources, the Texas Parks and Wildlife Department, the Audubon Society, the East Texas Conservation Society, the USDA Forest Service, the Wilderness Society, the Governor's Office, the Texas Forest Service, the Deep East Texas Development Association, the Sportsmen's Club of Texas, and Texaco.

The working group compiled a list of the most important factors or criteria that should be considered when ranking the 12 roadless areas. Those factors in descending order of importance were:
(1) Uniqueness, (2) ecosystems, (3) soil and water, (4) size, (5) manageability, (6) wildlife, (7) succession, (8) aesthetics, (9) economics, (10) recoverability, (11) societal, and (12) lack of use.

The response of the working groups showed that they felt the Indian Mounds possessed natural attributes that merited protection of the area. After developing this list of factors, the group submitted a list that ranked the roadless areas for wilderness designation. The Indian Mounds area was ranked first or second by members of the Sierra Club, the Audubon Society, the Texas Committee on National Resources, and the East Texas Conservation Society.

Proponent's View of Indian Mounds Wilderness Qualities: Local Citizens

The author made personal visits to the homes of four local citizens who supported the Indian Mounds Wilderness Area. Three of the people are from families that had been in Sabine County for several generations. All of their responses reflected a deep appreciation for natural resources and for their county's forested heritage. They had strong feelings against timber companies that they feel are clearcutting every available acre of private land and managing for short-rotation pulp production. They also dislike Forest Service clearcuts even though the National Forests use a longer rotation favoring growth of larger trees than private companies.

Another significant factor surfaced in conversations with these local proponents of wilderness. These citizens want to capture and revive memories of their youth, back when the county had very few clearcuts. It was a time, according to them, when thousands of acres of Sabine County were contiguous forest stands with abundant hardwoods. Large pine regeneration areas were not a vivid part of their recollection. These citizens also remember a mature, bottomland hardwood forest that flanked the county line along the Sabine River. This forest had nature hardwood

trees and virtually no pine.

The citizens explained that this bottomland hardwood forest was permanently wiped out by a lake they did not want. Toledo Bend Reservoir, completed in 1968, has inundated the entire Sabine County frontage of the old river bottom. The lake is 80 miles (129 km) long, covering 181, 000 acres (73,250 ha). It flooded 31,000 acres (12,550 ha) of prime National Forest bottomland.

Most of the wilderness experiences sought by these citizens could have been satisfied in places outside the Indian Mounds Area 30 years ago. According to these citizens, it is now one of the only places left for their needs.

The author asked these citizens to describe the reasons why they went into the Indian Mounds Area and what they wanted to experience. A summary of their response follows:
1. To be alone.
2. To be in a quiet place away from city noises.
3. To enjoy the thick canopy and beauty of 50- to 60-year-old timber.
4. To view wildlife.
5. To view particular hardwoods (i.e.,hickory, beech magnolia, white oak, red oak).
6. To view specific forbs (e.g., yellow ladyslipper orchid *Cypripedium calceolus* L.).
7. To view and collect fossils.
8. To view and photograph landforms and plants within a 200-yard vista.
9. To show kids several thousand acres of forest that is 50 to 60 years old and contains natural processes of decay, regeneration, etc.
10. To see a large stand of timber dominated by hardwoods.
11. To escape all evidence of others.
12. To experience silence.
13. To listen to owls.
14. To refresh memories of youth (e.g., to experience a large uncut acreage of big trees along a creek).

These people all realize the imperfections of the area, especially when comparing the Indian Mounds to the Gila or Bob Marshall Wilderness Areas. But to experience the above mentioned items through the next several generations of their families, these citizens believed that wilderness designation was necessary.

DESCRIPTION OF PERCEIVED WILDERNESS QUALITIES

The media records and conversations with the Indian Mounds proponents allowed the following general description of the area's perceived wilderness qualities.
Apparent Naturalness
The single most important quality in the area is the presence of 50- to 60-year-old trees. Most of the experiences desired by the proponents required several thousand acres of mature or nearly mature trees. Such a tim-

ber stand is very close to their reference point in describing what natural east Texas is supposed to be. However, all of the proponents seemed to understand that this wilderness area had unnatural intrusions. They expect to seek out the natural, quiet, solitary places for satisfying specific wilderness experiences.

The existing stands of 50- to 60-year-old trees provide quiet places where they can experience solitude. The heavy underbrush and dense canopy in the area screen the users from most unnatural developments and from other users. For instance, an oil well is obscured from sight by the surrounding vegetation from less than 150 yards. In spite of surrounding noises, the proponents also view the area as a quiet place. The heavy growth in the area is an excellent sound insulator. Noises from the city, highway and lake are substantially muffled. Heavy traffic on roads through the area is usually not heard over one-half mile (0.8 km) through the woods.

The proponents also consider the streams in the area to be in a near-natural condition. Most of the streams are free-flowing and have no bridges or culverts in them. These streams host several uncommon plants such as the yellow ladyslipper orchid. These stream bottoms are key features in the enjoyment of the area because of the bottomland and hardwood species found there.

The wilderness area is partially bounded by a large, manmade lake, Toledo Bend Reservoir. The lake has caused such unnatural intrusions as: outboard motor noise, trash, and dramatic vegetation changes along the shoreline. One citizen noted these more subtle effects of the reservoir, as well as the unnatural increase in waterfowl and eagles to the area. The lake is seldom mentioned by the wilderness proponents as adversely affecting their wilderness experience.

Before oil and gas development accelerated, the most unnatural feature in the Indian Mounds was considered to be the Forest Service clearcuts. These areas are a visual contrast to surrounding uncut timber stands. The young regeneration areas are avoided by the group. The pine regeneration areas appear to be of a single pine species, and a single age. Young hardwoods in the stands are not as visible as the pine. These regeneration areas offer very few of the desired wilderness experiences expressed by the proponents. For instance, a visitor would have difficulty traveling or seeing through most regeneration areas because of the dense tangle of young stems. Most of the proponents believe that if they wait long enough-- perhaps 100 years--these pine areas will be replaced by hardwood.

Ecological/Scientific/Historical

Wilderness proponents see the area as a potential schoolroom for a demonstration of natural succession free of man's interference. They anticipate the existing forest will become a fairly stable population of trees. The possibility of insect or disease outbreaks is not adverse to their perception of wilderness. Pine mortality would be fairly well accepted by them as necessary to reach a natural balance of composition between pine and hardwood.

The wilderness is perceived as an island of natural ecological processes surrounded by forested land that is not natural. The difference between the ecologically balanced wilderness and the adjacent unbalanced land will become more obvious with time. Herein lies part of the scientific value of the wilderness, as perceived by the proponents. The area could be a study area for following vegetation changes after the release from Forest Service timber management activities.

The area does have two birds on the endangered species list: the bald eagle and the red-cockaded woodpecker. Wilderness proponents consider that both birds add to the desirability of the area. These birds are found in several places around the Yellowpine District.

Other ecological values frequently mentioned by the proponents are usually found in the 50- to 60-year-old timber stands in the Indian Mounds Area. For instance, viewing pileated woodpeckers (*Dryocopus pileatus*), squirrels, and listening to owls is most likely satisfied in timber more than 30 years old. The groups did not express an interest in activities that were satisfied only in a clearcut, or in a young pine regeneration area. Indeed, the proponents could view wildlife or collect fossils in a clearcut, but they preferred to do those activities in a mature or nearly mature forest.

Geologic/Cultural Values

The geologic and cultural values mentioned by the proponents would not be of national significance. But to some residents of east Texas, a few features are highly regarded. Traditional stories say that early settlers frequented several of the stony watering holes in the streams of the area. These areas contain remnants of old wagon trails crossing the streams, as well as worn areas where clothes washing may have occurred.

A few surface rock outcrops are also prized as sources of fossilized sea shells and sand dollars. These gravel areas are also along the streams.

Indian artifacts are not frequent in the area. No significant archeological sites have been recorded. The name "Indian Mounds" is a misnomer. It refers to some earthen humps now believed by archeologists to be a peculiar erosional or geologic feature. These humps are about one-half mile (0.8 km) outside the wilderness. The nearest verified Indian Mound is over 50 miles (80 km) from the wilderness.

Scenic Values

The area provides a key need expressed by all proponents of the wilderness. They all wanted to view large trees growing in contiguous stands across several thousand acres. The Indian Mounds area has an abundance of pine and hardwood that is near maturity. Trees with 24 to 30 inch diameters are common in the area. Several trees in the area are close to state champion sizes. One national champion, the littlehip hawthorn (*Crataegus spathulata Michx*) is about 200 yards outside the area.

Scenic values in the dense forest of east Texas are highly valued by the proponents. Their focus in viewing landforms, plants, or animals is generally within 200 yards. Long vistas are not possible because the dense vegetation closes off a long view and blocks out the scenery. Beauty that is close to the viewer, such as a delicate orchid, is more critical to these proponents than a panorama of the lake or its shoreline. A single, 2 foot waterfall along a free flowing stream is prized, and would warrant a half-mile (0.8 km) hike to enjoy it.

Proponents of this wilderness recognize its imperfections. They would not expect it to withstand a comparison test against the large unspoiled western areas such as the Bob Marshall or Gila Wilderness Areas. However, it contains the two basic ingredients necessary for their enjoyment: (1) free of future Forest Service clearcuts, (2) 50- to 60-year-old trees in large contiguous stands. These two qualities are prerequisites to their wilderness experience.

OIL AND GAS IMPACTS ON WILDERNESS QUALITIES

Oil and gas development generates impacts that are adverse to a wilderness experience. Drilling and development are accompanied by the use of heavy equipment, soil disturbance, and usually roads, to name a few of the associated unnatural conditions. Mitigating adverse impacts is an obvious goal of the resource manager.

One objective of this paper was to identify which oil and gas impacts adversely affect wilderness qualities in the Indian Mounds Area. Specific impacts mentioned by the local citizens are described below:

Noise--Traffic, seismograph blasting, well-pad construction, drilling rigs, road maintenance, pumpjacks, gas compressors, pipeline construction.

Visual--Traffic, equipment and facilities, landform changes, cleared rights-of-way, trash, erosional scars, vegetation changes.

Smells--Wastes in reserve pits on well-pads, tank battery wastes, exhausts from vehicles, compressors, drilling rigs, fumes following seismic blasts.

Contamination--Unknown adverse inputs to surface from drilling pit leaks, pipeline leaks, transport accidents, unknown subsurface inputs to water quality.

Crowding--Additional people and equipment present throughout area.

Wildlife threatened--Fewer natural acres because of occupancy and use, roaded areas provide easy access for violators.

MITIGATION MEASURES AND CONSTRAINTS ON FOREST SERVICE MANAGEMENT

Wilderness Management Implications

The passage of wilderness legislation that allows continued oil and gas development prompts us to question what mitigation measures are appropriate to impose on an activity that is specifically allowed. The Yellowpine District, uses an assortment of permit clauses, stipulations, and resource management plans to reduce natural resource damage. The Yellowpine's permit attachments were developed by District and Supervisor's staff and are on file in Hemphill.

Forest Service requirements conform with the authority provided by the deed of mineral conveyance and the relevant Secretary Rules and Regulations. Complications arise when the agency wishes to be more restrictive than state law permits for a surface owner. USDA's legal counsel has been very cognizant of rights possessed by mineral owners in Texas. Surface protection measures developed in other states, and their survival in courts of other states, does not ensure their support in a Texas court. That is why it is critical to the surface manager that he be fully aware of the constraints on his authority when dealing with mineral owners in Texas.

Texas law (Warren Petroleum Corp. v. Monzingo 157 Tex. 479, 3045. W. 2d 362 $BRTex. 1957$BR) has determined that the mineral interest is the dominant interest. Unless limited by the terms of the deed or lease, the mineral interest owner or his lessee has an implied easement to search for, develop, and produce oil and gas. The extent of the surface use is governed by key terms "reasonably necessary to carry out the purpose of the lease." Past case law in Texas has shown that a surface owner's right to sue for damages is limited to situations where (1) use of the surface is excessive or is not reasonably necessary to conduct oil and gas operations, (2) use is not for the benefit solely of minerals under the tract leased, or (3) use is contrary to the provision of the lease or statutes, ordinances, governmental rules or regulations.

Protecting wilderness qualities that rest on top of reserved or developed mineral deposits is difficult. Communication with and cooperation by the mineral operator becomes a key to successful wilderness management.

Currently, one oil company is operating in the Indian Mounds Wilderness Area. The author has discussed Forest Service wilderness management goals with that company. Both parties have identified ways to mute, soften, or blend in the oil and gas activities inside the wilderness. The company is willing to use reasonable methods of resource protection. The company has accepted operating permits that expand and clarify its responsibilities for surface protection beyond those mentioned in the deed of conveyance.

The company is concerned that the wilderness legislation may prompt more expensive site restoration than originally budgeted prior to drilling these wells. A small independent company relies on outside investors to fund the bulk of costs for exploration, development, and restoration. Investors rapidly lose interest in dry holes, leaving the company with an unwanted and unbudgeted expense. The company suggests that the Forest Service provide a cost estimate for restoration prior to well development.

The estimate would be used by the company to bill investors for restoration work before the well was drilled. Another alternative would be a bond collected by the agency and used for restoration later.

The current procedure on the Yellowpine for abandoning a well site is for the company to use dozers to reshape the general landform contours, waterbar roadways and remove aggregate surfacing. Soil compaction and instable grades require a ground cover, such as rye or bermuda grass that germinates on a harsh site and rapidly spreads to stabilize the watershed. These grasses do not persist once reforestation progresses in 3 to 5 years. In the wilderness, invading woody plants such as pine and sweetgum will establish naturally while the grasses are stabilizing the watershed.

Wilderness proponents understood the need to quickly stabilize and recover well sites. They did not like a 2.5 acre (1 ha) flat pad cut out of a sloping hill. Neither did they want it to take 75 years for it to recover. However, biodegradable erosion control netting, fertilizer application and temporary fencing were palatable methods to the proponents if they would stabilize the watershed and promote a speedy recovery.

As one local proponent explained it, a short-term intensive rehabilitation effort was okay if it meant their wilderness would be more natural because of the effort. According to him, the "concept of wilderness transcends an individuals lifetime or any one generation, . . . given time the impacts will heal . . . , it heals much faster in southeast Texas than out West."

Future wilderness management by the Forest Service should recognize that oil and gas development will continue. Potentially, 85 percent of the area could be developed. Trail systems should be postponed or diverted to avoid these potential development areas. Visitors to the area would benefit from interpretive signs that explain why the wilderness contains oil and gas development.

The author has proposed several wilderness management objectives concerning oil and gas development in the area (Table 2). These objectives can be com-

Table 2. Comparison of Preferred Actions by Mineral Operator vs. Wilderness Manager in Various Phases of Oil and Gas Development.

	Mineral Operator's Preferred Action	Forest Service Wilderness Management Objectives
Development phase activity		
Road construction	Meet FS standards when time permits construction. Use the shortest route possible.	Meet FS standards. Access by following corridors with least resource impact.
Traffic	Access sites from either end of existing roads to be closed in area. No gates. No limit on amount of traffic.	Limit access to one end of roads closed to public. Operator to gate all closed roads used to access wells. Limit traffic to authorized persons.
Well pad	Clear and utilize 2.5 acres per site.	Minimize site to 1.5 acres where feasible.
Production phase		
Facilities	Paint tanks silver to reduce heat gain and resulting evaporation.	Paint with earth tones to blend with background.
Pump jacks	Install gas powered engines.	Install quiet gas powered engines.
Pipelines	Clear 30' to 40' rights-of-way. Use shortest route. Trench through stream channels.	Minimize clearing to 20'. Follow existing corridors. Elevate pipes over stream channels and banks.
Rehabilitation phase		
Aggregate	Leave in place or recover for use on another project.	Remove.
Cut/fill slopes	Leave in place.	Reshape to previous contour of area. Use erosion control netting or terraces.
Vegetation	No reseeding. Volunteer plant recovery.	Prepare seed bed, seed a specified mixture, fertilize, mulch. Protect from grazing if needed.

pared with the preferred actions by a typical oil and gas operator. For instance, a typical operator would want to build a pipeline or road on the shortest route possible to cut down on construction costs. The wilderness manager would not want to create new openings in the forest. Therefore, the operator would need to build along a route, where feasible, that utilizes existing corridors.

SUMMARY

In October 1984, a 9,946 acre (4,025 ha) area of Sabine County, Texas, was added to the National Wilderness Preservation System. This acreage was intensively logged 60 years ago. Now, after 50 years of management by the Forest Service, the area is covered by quality stands of pine and hardwood trees. The Forest Service did not recommend this area for inclusion to the Wilderness System because of prior impacts evidenced through the area. However, several citizens groups felt that significant wilderness values are in the area. The citizens description of these wilderness qualities allowed the author to formulate a rough description of the wilderness qualities and experiences perceived in the Indian Mounds Wilderness Area.

According to the proponents of the Indian Mounds Wilderness, the area is representative of a natural east Texas forest ecosystem. Their perceived wilderness experience is tied directly to large acreages of uncut forest. The Indian Mounds fulfills their need for contiguous stands of large trees. The majority of its 9,946 acres (4,025 ha) of trees is the same age, 50 years old. The presence of several roads and a large pipeline right-of-way was not considered completely adverse to their wilderness experience. The primary threat to their experience was the forest management practice of clearcutting. They desired to designate the area as wilderness to remove it from standard Forest Service management. The proponents embraced the area as wilderness even though oil development was ongoing and could continue since most of the mineral rights in the area would never be in U.S. control.

Local citizens recognize, however, that many of their enjoyed experiences, such as quiet, solitude, clear streams and uncut timber are being seriously threatened by oil and gas development.

Adverse impacts from the mineral development include dust, noise, noxious smells, aesthetic degradation, crowding, and contamination. Most of these impacts are caused by normal oil field operations. Standard industry practices by the reserved mineral owner will continue as provided by state law, mineral deed, and the appropriate Secretary of Agriculture Rules.

The Forest Service in cooperation with a prudent oil company can mitigate some of the adverse impacts. Wilderness management objectives were proposed to guide future development in the area. Some of the recommended actions include minimizing work areas, prompt clean-up, utilizing existing corridors, and vigorous site rehabilitation. The key to successful wilderness management will be to stabilize disturbed areas and encourage rapid vegetation recovery. Oil and gas impacts will be obvious in the area for several generations, but eventually the favorable climate and vigorous vegetation of southeast Texas will allow the wilderness area to recover and obscure most of the adverse impacts of development.

LITERATURE CITED

Bryan, H.B. 1979. Conflict in the great outdoors: Toward understanding and managing for diverse sportsmen preferences. Social Studies No. 4. Univ. Alabama, Birmingham, Ala.

Citizens. 1983. Forest Section: Basic facts on East Texas Wilderness proposal. Handout.

Fritz, E.C. 1981. What's best for Texas forests?: Editorial. p. 15 In Houston Chronicle, March 3, 1981. Houston, Tex.

Gould, F.W. 1975. Texas plants - a checklist and ecological summary. Tex. Agric. Exp. Stn. Publ. MP-585 (rev.), Tex. A&M Univ., College Station, Tex.

Gunter, B. 1983. Annual wilderness pow wow planned. pp. 6-7. In This week entertainment, Houston, Tex.

Hendee, J.C. 1980. Principles of wilderness management applications for the east. pp. 44-57. In Vol. I. Wilderness management hand. USDA For. Serv. Region 8, Atlanta, Geor.

Roggenbuck, J.W. 1980. Wilderness user preferences: eastern and western areas. Mimeo on file, School of Forest Wildlife and Recreation Resources, VPI and SU, Blackburg, Virg.

USDA Forest Service. 1981. Oil and gas operations on national forest land subject to reserved and outstanding mineral rights: guidelines. Region 8, Atlanta, Geor.

USDA Forest Service. 1979. RARE II Press Kit. Final Environmental Statement, Washington, D.C.

USDA Forest Service. 1977. Sabine unit plan and final environmental impact statement. National Forests in Texas

Management Of Oil And Gas Exploration In Big Thicket National Preserve

by
James C. Woods

ABSTRACT--Legislative directives and regulatory requirements pertaining to the exercise of non-federal oil and gas rights within Big Thicket National Preserve have proven effective in reducing environmental impacts. Geophysical surveys and exploratory drilling operations can often result in severe and relatively long-term impacts if not professionally managed with due regard for natural resources. Impact mitigation techniques and alternative operational procedures afford land managers and industry reasonable and practical options to preserve and protect sensitive natural resources.

KEYWORDS: oil and gas impact, geophysical surveys, exploratory drilling, mitigation techniques.

The Big Thicket National Preserve (BTNP), established in 1974 as a unit of the National Park Service (NPS), is located in southeast Texas and comprises 12 management units totaling 34,217 ha within 7 counties (Fig. 1). The BTNP covers approximately 4% of a 9,000 km sq. area. Elevations range from sea level to 180 m, precipitation averages 132 cm annually (Trenchard 1977), and the climate is humid subtropical. The Big Thicket, known for its unique plant communities, is often referred to as a "biological crossroads." It is a transition zone between eastern deciduous forests, the longleaf pine-bluestem vegetative association, and coastal prairie. Eleven distinct vegetative types have been defined within BTNP (Watson 1979, Harcombe and Marks 1979).

Petroleum and forest products industries are the primary contributors to the region's economy. Although commercial timber harvesting is not allowed in the BTNP, oil and gas exploration and production activities continue. Historical records indicate that 133 exploratory oil/gas wells have been drilled within the boundaries of BTNP. Eighty-seven of the wells drilled were nonproductive and the sites were abandoned. Only 11 of the 46 productive oil and/or gas wells are operational at present. Approximately 272 km of geophysical survey operations have occurred in BTNP since 1976. Undoubtedly numerous additional geophysical surveys occurred on these lands prior to federal acquisition of the surface estate. Requests for permission to conduct oil and gas exploration in BTNP continue despite a depressed oil market and marginal chances of discovering an economically productive petroleum reserve.

Management of oil and gas operations to protect the unique ecological values of the area is the subject of this paper. I present here the basic policies and regulations

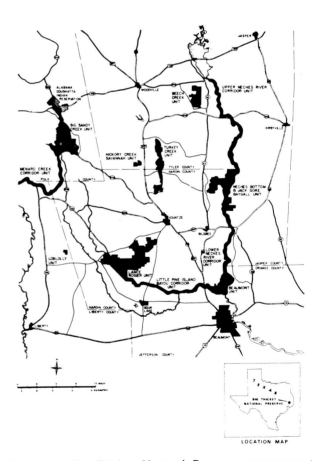

Figure 1. Big Thicket National Preserve management units.

developed to control such activity on NPS lands, identify typical environmental impacts, and discuss mitigation techniques to reduce such impacts.

MANAGEMENT GUIDELINES

Legislation and Executive Orders

The basic management philosophy of the NPS was originally presented in the "Organic Act" of 1916. The NPS was established and directed to regulate park use and promote enjoyment of parklands in a manner consistent with the conservation of park scenery, natural and historic objects, and wildlife by such means as will leave them unimpaired for future generations.

An act establishing a particular NPS unit states a specific intent for which that unit was created and infers a general philosophy by which the unit should be managed. The primary intent of Congress in establishing the BTNP (Public Law 93-439) was to: "assure the preservation, conservation, and protection of the natural, scenic, and recreational values of a significant portion of the Big Thicket area in the State of Texas and to provide for the enhancement and public enjoyment thereof."

The establishing legislation for BTNP also stipulated that the mineral estate in any property could not be acquired without the owners consent, unless usage of the property would be detrimental to the purposes of the act. Congress demonstrated its concern for oil and gas activities within BTNP by directing the NPS to promulgate specific rules and regulations to limit or control the use of federal lands and waters with respect to such activity. The resulting regulations promulgated and approved will be discussed below.

The primary legislative tool that a federal land manager must use to prevent or minimize damage to park resources is the National Environmental Policy Act of 1969 (NEPA). This legislative act requires careful consideration of the environmental effects of proposed federal actions. Permitting an oil and gas exploration or production operation on public land is indeed a federal action which must comply with the requirements and procedural provisions of NEPA. Detailed procedures in NEPA insure that adequate environmental information is available to public officials and members of the public before decisions are made and before actions are taken. The NEPA process must consider all applicable environmental legislation (i.e. Endangered Species Act, Archeological Resources Protection Act, Clean Water Act, etc. and Executive Orders (i.e. E.O. 11988, Floodplain Management; E.O. 11990, Protection of Wetlands, etc.).

Regulations

In response to the congressionally recognized need for regulation, and in furtherance of the statutory management responsibilities of the NPS, "Minerals Management Regulations" (Title 36, Code of Federal Regulations, Part 9b) pertaining to the exercise of non-federal oil and gas rights were promulgated in 1978. These regulations were designed to be in concert with the twin goals of allowing development of domestic energy sources while preserving the integrity of the lands and waters within units of the NPS. They were not directed toward elimina-

tion of oil and gas operations within units mandated to permit such activity.

Each operator requiring access on, across, or through NPS lands must file a plan of operations with the Superintendent of the affected unit, and no work will commence until the plan of operations is approved by the Regional Director. Within 60 days of receipt of any proposed plan of operations, the Regional Director must prepare an environmental assessment of the plan and must notify the operator of approval or rejection, or must notify the operator of necessary modifications before the plan of operations can be approved. The operator is responsible for compliance with approved procedures during operations and reclamation activities. In addition, a performance bond or cash deposit must be filed with the Secretary of Interior or his designee in an amount equal to the estimated cost of restoring or reclaiming federal lands damaged or destroyed as a result of operations, as set forth in the approved plan of operations. Upon completion of the reclamation requirements as defined by the plan of operations, the Superintendent then notifies the operator that the period of liability under the bond or security deposit is terminated. The NPS minerals management regulations have proven highly effective in terms of reducing environmental impacts.

State of Texas rules and regulations govern all phases of oil and gas operations, including exploration, development, production, and transportation. Additional state considerations involve safety and maintenance of environmental quality. Generally, state regulations address technical aspects of the various phases of oil and gas activities more specifically than the NPS regulations. The NPS regulations relative to those of the state are generally more concerned with natural, cultural and scenic resource protection. However, all State of Texas oil and gas regulations remain applicable within BTNP.

ENVIRONMENTAL IMPACTS AND MITIGATION TECHNIQUES

Geophysical Surveys

Subsurface geophysical exploration, to locate potential oil and gas reserves, is most often accomplished by using the indirect "seismic reflection" or acoustic method (Coffeen 1978). Explosive charges normally consisting of 9kg of 40-60% dynamite are placed at the bottom of holes drilled to a depth of 36-48 m below ground surface, and serially detonated to produce acoustic signals. The acoustic signals, or sound waves, propagated by each detonation penetrate the underlying geological strata and echo or reflect from these strata at differential rates. The reflected signals are received at the surface by geophones, instruments designed to detect vibrations passing through rock or soil. Geophones are placed a prescribed distance apart in a linear fashion similar to the explosive charges. The geophones transduce the

vibrations into electrical signals which are transmitted via cable to recording instruments. In some instances, radiotelemetry is employed to transmit the signals. The recorded data are then analyzed for mineral bearing formations.

Environmental impacts associated with geophysical surveys are often a direct result of mechanical equipment usage in the forest. Geophysical operators commonly use large all-terrain vehicles (ATVs) equipped with standard tractor-type tires for off-road operations. Such vehicles typically include an ARDCO Model K ATV equipped with a drilling apparatus, the same model configured as a water truck by replacing the drill apparatus with a 1,900 liter water tank, and an ARDCO Model L ATV used to transport additional equipment such as geophones, electrical cable, and explosives.

The severity of resource impact is largely dependent upon soil characteristics, vegetation community structure, topography, mobility and sensitivity of biota, equipment employed, and equipment operator performance. The use of large ATVs equipped with tractor-type tires often results in extensive rutting of frequently flooded, poorly drained, bottomland and swamp soils. There also exists a high potential for severe rutting of stream banks and soils in wetland baygall environments. Geophysical ATVs are capable of rutting saturated soils to a depth of 0.5 m. Upland sandy loam soils have a significantly lower rutting potential.

Understory trees and shrubs are commonly pushed over, uprooted, or crushed as an ATV traverses a dense forest. Although equipment operators attempt to avoid larger trees, damage often results from vehicles scraping them. Direct impact to trees and shrubs generally covers a swath 2.5m wide along the ATV path. Additional damage to vegetation and other resources occurs when vehicle operators use multiple paths.

Herbaceous vegetation in pine savannahs is apparently somewhat more resistant to vehicular impact when soils are relatively dry and rutting does not occur. Similarly, direct damage to vegetation in floodplain forests is low due to the paucity of shrubs, openness of the understory, and the relative ease of maneuvering equipment around large trees. However, soil moisture in this habitat type is abundant most of the year and thereby substantially increases the potential for indirect damage to vegetation due to ATV rutting. From a purely qualitative standpoint, as vegetation density and/or soil moisture increases, adverse environmental impact increases.

Impacts on fauna vary in severity with respect to species mobility, sensitivity, and tolerance level. Birds and other highly mobile animals will generally leave the immediate area due to the increased noise and the presence of humans and equipment. Due to the short duration of most geophysical surveys, they are likely to return following removal of the equipment. If operations are conducted during the breeding season, nest abandonment may occur. Jackson (1983) stated that breeding success or failure of Red-cockaded Woodpeckers (*Picoides borealis*) as it relates to unusual noise levels may be determined by the novelty and duration of the disturbance. If a new disturbance persists for more than a few minutes near colony areas after nesting activities are in progress, failure may result. Ground nesting species can be significantly impacted due to destruction of nests and dens by equipment. Less mobile taxa such as amphibians, reptiles, and invertebrates may be destroyed by the vehicles.

Water is commonly used during the drilling of shotholes at an average volume of 380 liters/hole. Operators prefer to secure water by pumping from surface water sources to an ATV equipped with a water tank. This action creates a limited demand on local surface water resources. However, the use of surface water could be a significant factor in more arid biotopes.

Mitigation of adverse environmental impact is accomplished by enforcing regulations and imposing specific operational standards. It is understood that all operators will comply with NPS regulations. Mandatory operational standards imposed upon geophysical operators in BTNP consist of the following: maximum ATV use of public roads and abandoned logging trails; ATVs are not permitted to cross major surface water courses; multiple ATV paths are prohibited; all combustion equipment must be properly equipped with conventional sound mufflers; no shotholes are permitted within 100m of major surface waters; strict avoidance of proposed or listed Federal and State of Texas threatened or endangered species; shotholes will be properly plugged below ground surface and backfilled above the plug with soil; injuries to trees are to be treated with a non-toxic pruning paint; vehicle ruts must be acceptably reclaimed; and all flagging and other debris is to be promptly removed from the area.

Further mitigation of impact can be accomplished by negotiating for selection of less damaging alternatives. For instance, if a geophysical survey line is proposed near a unit boundary, the operator may have the flexibility to relocate the survey line outside the boundary. Operators also have the flexibility to eliminate certain shotholes or to offset holes from the proposed seismic line to protect a fragile natural feature. If shotholes are eliminated, operators are allowed to manually lay geophones and cable on the surface to afford the acquisition of seismic data. In many instances operators specifically request permission to conduct a "cable-only" geophysical survey across BTNP lands in the interest of avoiding extensive "paperwork" requirements (i.e. plan of operations) and time delays. The park Superintendent has been delegated the authority to approve such operations. However, this alternative method is generally limited by the length of the proposed line. The majority of operators are highly reluctant to use this method if the geophysical line will exceed 1.6km. Finally, in sensitive environs, a "backpack auger" can be used to manually drill shotholes to a depth of 6m, thereby eliminating ATV impact. If this method is employed, dynamite charges should not exceed 2kg.

Exploratory Drilling

The most commonly used exploratory drilling technique is the hydraulic rotary method, often referred to as "wildcatting." The basic mechanics of rotary drilling are as follows: a string of drillpipe with a cutting bit is rotated; sections of drillpipe are added as drilling depth increases; and drilling fluid ("mud") is continuously circulated through the drillpipe, out nozzles in the bit, and back up to the surface to lubricate the bit, to remove ground up debris or "cuttings", and to maintain hydrostatic pressure in the hole (Moody 1961). The drilling equipment is collectively known as a "rig." A detailed discussion of essential component parts of a typical rig has been presented by Moody (1961).

Environmental impacts associated with exploratory drilling operations are most often related to site preparation, improper management of drilling muds, increased human activity and noise levels for extended periods of time, equipment malfunction, and operator negligence. If drilling operations are properly planned and professionally managed, long term detrimental impacts can be substantially reduced.

Site preparation alone causes severe damage to natural resources, and will result in a fairly long term impact. It includes total removal of vegetation, grading, filling, and leveling of the drilling area (well pad) and access route. Access road width will normally not exceed 9m. Road surface may be stabilized with material such as lumber, gravel, oyster shells, or crushed limestone. Lumber is most often used for such purpose in southeast Texas. Board roads and matting have proven highly satisfactory for the movement of heavy equipment into remote areas while causing minimal damage to the ground surface (EMANCO 1982).

Well pad size generally ranges from 1.3 to 2.0 ha. Approximately one half of the pad area is covered with a lumber mat. The drilling rig, mud and freshwater pumps, a pipe rack to hold reserve drill and casing pipe, supplies, and other auxiliary equipment will be located atop the mat. A water pit, a shale pit, a reserve (mud) pit are excavated in the remaining, unboarded portion of the pad. In addition, a peripheral ditch and earthen berm are constructed to collect and contain site runoff.

Site preparation activity results in the immediate loss of vegetation and wildlife habitat, and causes disruption of soil resources. Surface water runoff can be impeded and degradation of water quality can occur. It is imperative that a land manager carefully evaluate the natural resources of an area prior to approval of a particular drilling location and access route. Important items to consider when conducting a preliminary resource reconnaissance survey include, but are not limited to the following: vegetative type; soil characteristics; topography; wildlife; unique biota; threatened or endangered species; hydrology; and water quality. Abandoned logging trails and previously disturbed sites should be used wherever practical.

Well pads and access roads should be located on flat upland sites if possible, and clearing of vegetation should be kept to a minimum. Maximum utilization of flat terrain will reduce the amount of cut and fill required to produce a level pad and road surface. As noted for geophysical surveys, impacts related to drilling activities also magnify as soil moisture increases. Fountain (1984) determined that upland vegetal communities suffer far less impact (with respect to oil and gas drilling activities) than bottomland and wetland biotopes.

Most operators have the flexibility and technology to adjust the surface location of pads and roads to accommodate environmental concerns. Although vertical drilling is the least expensive and fastest method, directional drilling to 45 degrees from vertical is quite common and allows a certain flexibility in well site selection (USDI National Park Service 1977). Directional drilling should be considered to avoid critical wildlife areas and sensitive vegetation (Longly *et al.* 1978).

The actual drilling operation may take up to seven months to complete, depending upon depth of the well. Human activity and noise from machinery and vehicles continues to impact wildlife. During this phase of the operation, improper handling, storage and containment of drilling mud and additives can result in significant damage to natural resources. Drilling mud often consists of bentonite, barite, caustic soda, lime, chrome lignite/lignosulfonate, and diesel oil, plus bactericides and corrosion inhibitors.

Phytotoxic properties of various drilling mud compositions have been determined by Miller *et al.* (1980), and Miller and Pesaran (1980). Muds containing soluble salts and diesel oil hydrocarbons have the highest phytotoxic effect. Release of drilling muds into aquatic environs will increase specific conductance, pH, chloride concentration, total dissolved solids, total suspended solids, and turbidity.

Although not all forms of drilling mud are toxic, it is prudent to take appropriate precautions to prevent the escape of such substances into surrounding lands, waters, and substrata. The mud and shale pit must be of adequate size to contain the amount of fluid and cuttings generated during the drilling operation. Earthen berms should be constructed around each pit to prevent overflow during high rainfall or flood events. Pit bottoms should be lined with an impervious plastic material to prevent leakage of fluid into the substrata. It is also advisable to lay plastic below the board mat in case of accidental spillage. The perimeter moat encircling the well pad must be routinely monitored, and all site runoff collected should be pumped on an as-need basis to the reserve pit. Operators must also be instructed to immediately clean up any foreign substance spilled during the operation.

Eliminating the construction and use of mud and shale pits substantially reduces the potential for severe environmental impact. Large portable steel tanks can be used in lieu of pits to receive drill cuttings and excess drilling fluids. The solids and fluids can be stored in the tanks while drilling, and hauled out as necessary for off-site disposal. This mitigation technique affords maximum protection to subsurface strata, and considerably reduces overall pad size. This alternative method may soon become a standard operating procedure for exploratory drilling within BTNP.

The release of pollutants into adjacent environments during drilling operations is largely due to operator negligence. However, equipment malfunction can occasionally result in contamination of adjacent resources. The most damaging of all drilling accidents is a "blowout." A blowout can occur when hydrostatic pressure in the hole is no longer maintained by the mud. Uncontrolled flow results, pressure at the surface rapidly increases, and safety equipment (blowout preventer) fails to shut-in the well. If a blowout occurs, drilling mud can be broadcast over a considerable area. Operators must routinely inspect and test blowout preventers and other safety equipment to insure the devices are in proper working order.

Upon completion of the drilling and testing operations, the operator determines the productivity of the well. If the well is economically feasible, the site will be converted to a production location. Discussion of production impacts and mitigation techniques is beyond the scope of this paper. In the event that the well is non-productive, the operator is responsible for immediate reclamation of the site.

Basic provisions for reclamation include the following: plug and cap the well according to State of Texas regulations; remove all equipment, material and debris; properly dispose of all solid and liquid wastes; fill all pits, ditches, and excavations; grade the pad and road area to a contour similar to that which existed prior to the initiation of operations; and mark the well site with a permanent monument noting the operator, well name and number, and date of abandonment.

In the interest of providing operators with definable reclamation standards, BTNP developed specific reclamation guidelines and criteria. Operators are expected to comply with the requirements presented below prior to the release of liability.

During site preparation, a pre-operation soil test must be performed. Soil samples of the surface must be obtained from each quadrant of the pad prior to the removal of vegetation. Replicate samples are encouraged. Baseline analysis must include the following: pH; specific conductance; water soluble sodium (Na), calcium (Ca), magnesium (Mg), and chloride (Cl); and oil and grease. Values for Na, Ca, and Mg are used to calculate the sodium absorbtion ratio (SAR). Additional constituent ions may be analyzed at the operator's discretion. All analyses are to be performed using an adequate quality assurance program. All data are presented to the BTNP on a mg/km dry weight basis.

When reclamation of the site begins, proper removal and treatment of waste material contained in the mud and shale pit is of primary concern. All fluids and cuttings are to be removed from the pits and disposed of in the approved manner as presented in the plan of operations. The pits may be filled with soil only after inspection by BTNP personnel.

Following removal of the lumber mat, soil samples must be obtained from the surface and analyzed in the manner as prescribed above. Post-operation soil parameter values, except ph, must be at or below pre-operation valves. Soil ph may not exceed a one unit change. If post-operation valves do not satisfy these criteria, the operator must apply approved corrective actions. When appropriate soil parameter values are attained, the site contour is restored. The entire site will then provide an adequate seedbed for revegetation.

SUMMARY

Effectively meeting legislative mandates for preservation and protection of public resources becomes exceedingly difficult for a land manager charged with the responsibility of supervising oil and gas exploration activities. Geophysical surveys and exploratory drilling operations can often result in severe and relatively long-term impact if not professionally managed with due regard for natural resources.

Presented impact mitigation techniques and alternative operational procedures will acquaint land managers and industry with reasonable and practical options to protect sensitive natural resources. Many of the mitigation techniques discussed are in accordance with recommended drilling practices for protection of the environment as presented by the American Petroleum Institute (1975).

NPS minerals management regulations and additional guidelines developed by BTNP personnel have proven effective in reducing environmental impact associated with oil and gas exploration. Although a few operators take exception to the regulations and guidelines, it is important to note that the majority of operators demonstrate a strong desire and commitment to accommodate environmental concerns expressed by the NPS.

LITERATURE CITED

American Petroleum Institute. 1975. API recommended land drilling operating practices for protection of the environment. API Res. Pap. 52, API, Washington, D.C.

Coffeen, J.A. 1978. Seismic exploration fundamentals. PennWell Books, Tulsa, Okla.

EMANCO. 1982. Plan of operations for exploration/production wells, Lance Rosier Unit, Big Thicket National Preserve, Texas. Report to Regional Director, Southwest. Region, Natl. Park Serv., Santa Fe, New Mex.

Fountain, M.S. 1984. Impact of oil and gas drilling sites on the vegetation and soils of the Big Thicket National Preserve. Preliminary report to Division of Natural Resources Management, Southwest. Region, Natl. Park Serv., Santa Fe, New Mex.

Harcombe, P.A. and P.L. Marks. 1979. Forest vegetation of the Big Thicket National Preserve. Report to Office of Natural Sciences, Southwest. Region, Natl. Park Serv., Santa Fe, New Mex.

Jackson, J.A. 1983. Possible effects of excessive noise on Red-cockaded Woodpeckers. pp. 38-40. In D.A. Wood (ed.). Red-cockaded Woodpecker Symp. II Proc. Fla. Game and Fresh Water Fish Comm., U.S. Fish Wildl. Serv. and U.S. For. Serv.

Longly, W.L., R. Jackson, and B. Snyder. 1978. Managing oil and gas activities in coastal environments. U.S. Fish Wildl. Serv., Biol. Serv. Program. FWS/OBS - 78/54.

Miller, R.W., S. Honarvar, and B. Hunsaker. 1980. Effects of drilling fluids on soils and plants: I. Individual fluid components. J. Environ. Qual. 9:547-522.

Miller R.W., and P. Pesaran. 1980. Effects of drilling fluids on soils and plants: II. Complete drilling fluid mixtures. J. Environ. Qual. 9:552-556.

Moody, G.B. 1961. Petroleum exploration handbook. McGraw-Hill Book Company. New York, N.Y.

Trenchard, M.H. 1977. Baseline climatological data for the Big Thicket National Preserve. Report to the Office of Natural Sciences, Southwest Region, Natl. Park Serv., Santa Fe, New Mex.

USDI National Park Service. 1977. Synopsis of field technology for onshore oil and gas exploration and development. In Environmental Assessment, NPS minerals management regulations for nonfederal oil and gas rights, Appendix A:1-24. Natl. Park Serv., Denver Service Center, Denver, Colo.

Watson, G.E. 1979. Big Thicket plant ecology: an introduction. Big Thicket Mus. Publ. Series NO 5, Saratoga, Tex. 2nd Ed.

Air Resource and Wilderness Management Issues

by
Keith R. McLaughlin

ABSTRACT--Three issues arise in management of air resources in wilderness areas: (1) Class I vs. Class II wilderness areas, (2) institutional uncertainty, and (3) affirmative action. The USDA Forest Service, as a Federal Land Manager (FLM) is considering a 3-step strategy to meet its responsibilities defined in the Clean Air Act, the Resources Planning Act, and the Wilderness Act. The management of the air resource represents a different method of operation for the FLM. The air resource does not respect administrative boundaries, and the FLM is dependent upon Federal, State and local air quality regulatory agencies to attain air resource objectives.

KEYWORDS: Federal land manager, prevention of significant deterioration, air quality related values, limits of acceptable change, affirmative action, state implementation plan, Class I.

The Federal Land Manager (FLM) does not have direct control over potential effects of ambient air quality on wilderness. These potential effects can include impaired visibility to loss of vegetation vigor, reduced growth or mortality and acidification of terrestrial and aquatic ecosystems.

The role of the FLM in managing the air resource is specified in the Clean Air Act as amended in 1977 (PL95-95, 91 Stat. 685, as amended). This role is specific to only certain wilderness areas that are designated in the Act. However, when put in the context of the Wilderness Act of 1964 (PL88-577, 78 Stat. 890), and the Resources Planning Act of 1974 (PL93-378, 88 Stat. 476 as amended); the Forest Service role as FLM in the management of wilderness and air quality is greatly increased in complexity.

This paper identifies and discusses the issues and challenges of managing air quality in wilderness areas under Forest Service jurisdiction.

BACKGROUND

The Wilderness Act of 1964 directs that wilderness areas be managed in a manner that will leave these areas "unimpaired for future use and enjoyment as wilderness, and so as to provide the protection of these areas, the preservation of their wilderness character". Within the USDA Forest Service, Southern Region (Map 1), there are 59 wilderness areas managed by the Forest Service. These areas occupy approximately 4 percent (523,000 acres, or 211,660 ha) of the total National Forest acreage in the South.

The Clean Air Act designated Class I areas requiring special protection of air quality. Class I areas are international parks, national wilderness areas of over 5,000 acres (2,025 ha), and national memorial parks of over 6,000 acres (2,430 ha) existing on August 7, 1977. Nationally there are 156 Class I air quality areas. Eighty-eight areas are managed by the USDA Forest Service; 47 are managed by the USDI Park Service and 21 are managed by the USDI Fish and Wildlife Service. In the South, nine Class I areas in seven states (Map 1) are managed by the Forest Service.

Class I areas are protected through a permit system called the prevention of significant deterioration (PSD). This system is designed to protect areas of clean air, including those in Class II. It is administered by the States and requires protection of environmental values called air quality related values (AQRV) for Class I areas. The role of the FLM is specified as:
1) Designating AQRV.
2) Recommending denial of permits.
3) Recommending variance for permits.

The Resources Planning Act requires the Forest Service to recognize the fundamental need to protect and, when necessary, improve the quality of the air resource for National Forests. Therefore, since 1974, the Forest Service has had the responsibility to protect and improve the air resource for all lands that it manages. This responsibility in the context of the Clean Air Act and the Wilderness Act results in at least three major challenges or issues for wilderness management.

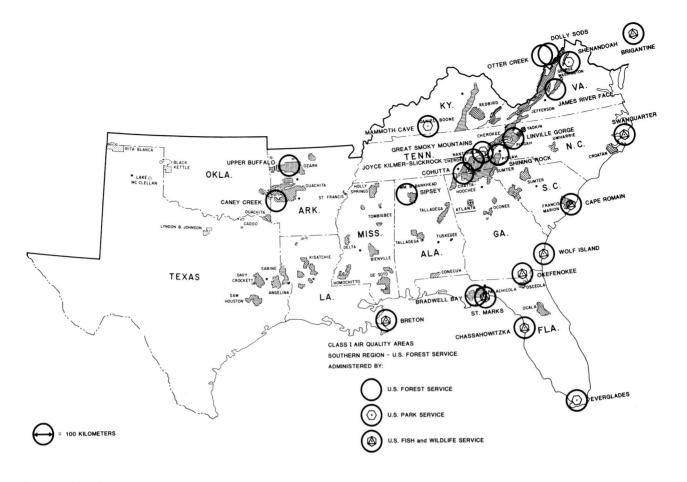

CLASS I AIR QUALITY AREAS
SOUTHERN REGION – U.S. FOREST SERVICE
ADMINISTERED BY:

- ⊖ U.S. FOREST SERVICE
- ⊙ U.S. PARK SERVICE
- ⊕ U.S. FISH and WILDLIFE SERVICE

⊖ = 100 KILOMETERS

1. Class I Wilderness Areas vs. Class II Wilderness Areas.
2. Institutional uncertainty.
3. Affirmative action.

CLASS I WILDERNESS AREAS VS. CLASS II WILDERNESS AREAS

There are three distinct differences between Class I wilderness areas and Class II wilderness areas. Class I areas are at least 5,000 acres (2,025 ha) in size, were in existence on August 7, 1977, and are administratively protected from new source pollution through a permit process (PSD) which requires FLM involvement..

The effects of a given air quality are the same whether a wilderness is Class I or Class II. Is the air resource for Class II wilderness less important than that for Class I wilderness? No! Within the context of the Wilderness Act of 1964 and the Resources Planning Act, all wilderness areas are managed by the Forest Service for the preservation of their wilderness character and the protection and, when necessary, the improvement of their air resource.

An example of this management is the Shining Rock Wilderness addition resulting from the 1984 North Carolina Wilderness Act (PL98-324, 98 Stat. 263). This Act added 5,100 acres (2,065 ha) to the Shining Rock Wilderness Area (Map 1). The addition is in Class II and

the original is in Class I. With the exception of PSD for the Class I portion, the management techniques and processes available for their management are the same. The PSD process is only initiated and the Forest Service FLM notified, however, when a new source is within 100-kilometers of the original Class I portion of the Shining Rock Wilderness Area (Map I).

INSTITUTIONAL UNCERTAINTY

The Clean Air Act requires that the FLM comply with the substantive and procedural requirements of State Implementation Plans for air resource management. The Clean Air Act also requires the FLM to protect the Air Quality Related Values for Class I areas from the effects of air pollution and to assure that the FLM land management practices do not violate National Ambient Air Quality Standards (NAAQS). The FLM is duty bound to accomplish these requirements in an "affirmative" manner. The Clean Air Act uses the term "shall" and the Senate report uses terms such as "aggressive" and "positive" in describing the manner in which the FLM is to accomplish their air resource management responsibilities (Connelly and Schwartz 1979). When there is uncertainty, the FLM is to err on side of the resources.

Other than the land management practices that the FLM applies, they have very little direct control over the quality and effects of the air resource. The existing Institutional processes and the dynamic nature of the air resource contribute to the uncertainty and complexity that the FLM must deal with in accomplishing their role in air resource and wilderness management. The FLM depends upon the States to adopt air resource management objectives to preserve the character of wilderness areas. For Class I wilderness areas the FLM uses the PSD permit process, which, by rule, is initiated when a proposed new source is located within 100-kilometers of the Class I areas and will emit certain levels of regulated pollutants. A process for notifying the FLM and for the FLM to evaluate and notify States of the effects of proposed new sources on Class II wilderness areas has yet to be formally defined. For both Class I and Class II areas, a process for notifying the FLM and for the FLM to evaluate cumulative effects of new sources that emit less than the threshholds for criterion pollutants has yet to be formally defined.

Scientific uncertainty about the dynamics and effects of the air resource upon ecosystems contributes to the institutional uncertainty. The air resource does not respect administrative boundaries or rules. Transport of pollutants is complex and poorly understood. Chemical reactions between pollutants and atmospheric conditions are highly variable. Synergistic effects of pollutants and other ecosystem stresses such as insects, disease, competition and drought are poorly understood.

The institutional and scientific uncertainty about the air resource results in the Forest Service FLM taking affirmative action by:
1. Working closely with and gaining the understanding of State and Federal air quality regulatory personnel about Forest Service air and wilderness management practices. The FLM has very little influence over the air resource for wilderness areas and is very dependent upon the Federal, State and local regulatory agencies to protect, and if necessary, improve the air resource.
2. Informing and gaining the understanding of the public, industry and Federal, state and local representatives about the effects of the air resource on wilderness areas.
3. Encouraging and supporting research to increase knowledge of effects air pollution has on forest ecosystems.
4. Identifying, inventorying and monitoring AQRV for wilderness areas.

AFFIRMATIVE ACTION

Despite the uncertainty of institutional and scientific knowledge, the Forest Service FLM is required to meet the intent of the Clean Air Act, the Resource Planning Act, and the Wilderness Act in an affirmative manner.

To meet the intent of these acts is to identify, inventory and monitor air quality related values. Sensitive receptors must be found and limits of acceptable change (LAC) must be designated. The Clean Air Act specifies visibility

as an AQRV. The Forest Service has identified additional AQRV; including flora, fauna, water, soil, visibility, cultural/archeological factors, geological features, and odor. On a local basis, sensitive receptors would need to be identified and the LAC for each receptor determined.

Considerations for selecting sensitive receptors for each AQRV are:
1. The relationship to the purpose(s) for which a wilderness area was established.
2. The ecological significance of the receptor (i.e., is it a good barometer for the trends in an ecosystem? Does it serve as a vital link in the food chain or is it of great commercial or scenic value?).
3. The managerial significance of the sensitive receptor (i.e., How easy is the receptor to monitor? How easy is it to identify the cause of any change in the sensitive receptor?).
4. The political significance of the sensitive receptor (i.e., a sensitive receptor should be the same sensitivity or more sensitive to air pollution than a rare and endangered plant or animal species, and the public needs to accept AQRV, sensitive receptors and their limits for acceptable change).

Another affirmative action method is through rule making, such as identifying a model and the minimum data needs for the model. The United States Environmental Protection Agency has purview over transport and deposition models. The FLM has purview over models for evaluating effects of the air resource on the forest ecosystem.

Recognizing the scientific uncertainty and the need to act affirmatively, the Forest Service is considering a strategy that utilizes models in the short-term, AQRV and limits for acceptable change in the mid- to long-term. Over the short-term, state-of-the art modeling that predicts chemical and physical sensitive receptors (i.e., pH of water) would be applied. In the mid-term, each Class I wilderness would be characterized to focus the selection of AQRV. Sensitive receptors for each AQRV would be selected using literature and available knowledge. Current condition of selected receptors or indicators would be determined. During the long-term, limits for acceptable change that are adequate to protect the wilderness resource would be developed. These limits for acceptable change would be quantitative measures of the forest ecosystem including visibility and would relate the impacts or effects of man caused air pollution to the natural processes associated with the ecosystem. In other words, the limits for acceptable change will recognize natural variation in the ecosystem, separate natural variation from man caused change and help to define whether the man caused change is adverse.

SUMMARY

Three issues surround the management of air resources in wilderness areas: (1) Class I vs. Class II designation, (2) institutional uncertainty, and (3) affirmative action. To meet the intent of legislation, the Forest Service manages for protecting and, if necessary, improving the air resource irrespective of whether wilderness or non wilderness. Institutional uncertainty is compounded by scientific uncertainty, and the management of the air resource represents a new or different way of operation for the FLM. The Forest Service is considering short-term, mid-term, and long-term strategies to meet the intent of affirmative action required by the Clean Air Act.

LITERATURE CITED

Clean Air Act Amendments of 1977. Act of August 7, 1977. (P.L. 95-95, 91 Stat. 685, as amended; 42 U.S.C. 7401, 7418, 7470, 7472, 7474, 7475, 7491, 7506, 7602).

Connolly, S. J. and Schwartz, J. H. 1979. Air quality related values and the Clean Air Act: Recommendations for air quality evaluation procedures. USDA For. Serv. Rocky Mtn. For. Range Exp. Stn. Res. Agreement No. 53-82 FT-9-101, Project Officer Douglas G. Fox.

Forest and Rangeland Renewable Resources Planning Act. Act of August 17, 1974. (P.L. 93-378, 88 Stat. 476: 16 U.S.C. 1601 (no North Carolina Wilderness Act of 1984. (P.L. 98-324, 98 Stat. 263).

Wilderness Act. Act of September 3, 1964 (P.L. 88-577, 78 Stat. 890; 16 U.S.C. 1121 (note), 1131-1136).

Water Resource And Wilderness Management Issues

by
Keith R. McLaughlin

ABSTRACT--Three water-resource issues in wilderness management are: (1) water quality, (2) water quantity and timing, and (3) riparian area and wetlands. The responsibilities of the Forest Service managers in addressing these issues are clearly mandated through legislation. To meet these responsibilities, the Forest Service manager is required to work with state and local water regulatory agencies.

KEYWORDS: riparian doctrine, appropriation doctrine, adjudication, succession, water quality parameters, instream flows, atmospheric deposition.

Demand for water in the Southern United States is expected to increase, causing conflicts over water use. Wilderness areas in the region will be affected by this increased demand and the resulting conflicts.

This paper identifies and discusses some of the issues and challenges of water-resource management in wilderness areas managed by the USDA Forest Service, Southern Region (See Map 1).

The mandate for the management of the water resource is clearly stated in many acts pertaining to the establishment and management of National Forests. However, the complexity of management is unusually great in the South due to the large amounts of private land within the boundaries of National Forests, public perception of wilderness areas, and the substantive procedural requirements resulting from the Clean Water Acts of 1972 and 1977.

BACKGROUND

National Forests in the South were originally established to attain favorable flows of water and to produce timber (Weeks Law of 1911). Congress, through the Multiple-Use Sustained-Yield Act of 1960 (P.L. 86-517), charged the Forest Service to manage the renewable surface resources of the National Forests for multiple-use

and sustained-yield. This Act is supplemental to the original purposes for National Forests. The renewable resources are outdoor recreation, range, timber, watershed, and wildlife and fish.

Through the Forest and Rangeland Renewable Resources Planning Act of 1974 (RPA), Congress designated the Forest Service as the nation's leader for forest and rangeland management. This Act recognized soil, water and air as the basic resources upon which all plant and animal life are dependent. It also reinforced Weeks Law and the Multiple-Use Sustained Yield Act for the protection and, when necessary, the improvement of the water resource.

The Wilderness Act of 1964 directs that the management of wilderness areas be in a manner that will leave these areas "unimpaired for future use and enjoyment as wilderness, and so as to provide the protection of these areas, the preservation of their wilderness character." These areas are perceived as "untrammeled by man." The water resource within these areas may be the ecological, scientific, educational or scenic feature for which the area was designated.

The Clean Water Act of 1977 established national goals for the quality of the water resource. One goal is to have all surface waters in the United States "fishable and swimmable" by 1983. This Act continued the requirement originally stated in the Federal Water Pollution Control Act of 1972--that all Federal agencies comply with Federal, State, interstate and local substantive and procedural requirements for control and abatement of wa-

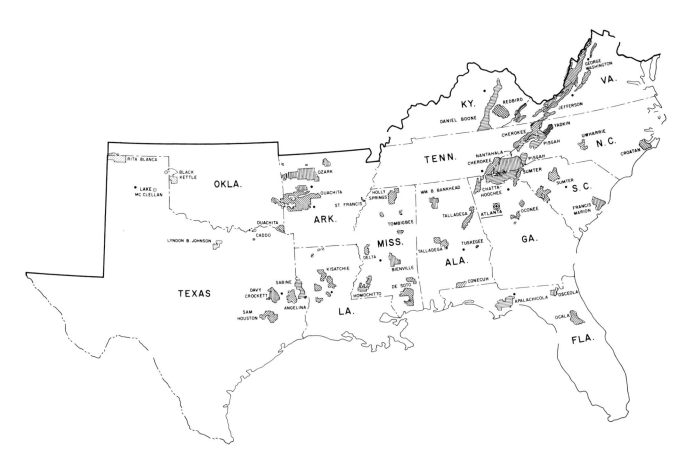

ter pollution.

The three issues or challenges for water-resource management in wilderness areas in the South are: (1) water quality, (2) water quantity and timing, and (3) riparian areas and wetlands.

WATER QUALITY

The perception of water quality by a wilderness user can be completely different from the actual water quality for the wilderness and thus result in a self-imposed health risk by the wilderness user.

There are five water quality characteristics: (1) physical, (2) chemical, (3) biological, (4) bacteriological, and (5) radiological. Each is described by a group of parameters, and all but the last are of major concern in wilderness areas. Some of the parameters describing the physical characteristic are quantity, timing, temperature, and dissolved oxygen. The chemical characteristic is described by parameters such as acidity and sodium and aluminum concentrations. The three most commonly used parameters to describe the bacteriological characteristic of water are Total Coliform, Fecal Coliform and Fecal Streptococcus. The biological characteristic is described by parameters such as species and number of microinvertebrates, fish, and plants.

If interpreted in the literal sense, the Wilderness Act of 1964 and Eastern Wilderness Act of 1975 could lead peo-

ple to perceive that the surface water in wilderness areas is safe to drink. Even under pristine conditions, the surface water in wilderness areas may not be safe to drink without treatment because of organisms like *Giardia* (Williams 1981). In fact, the surface water in some wilderness areas in the South is not safe to drink without some degree of treatment. The type and degree of treatment is dependent on: (1) physical and biological characteristics of the wilderness area, (2) land use prior to designation as a wilderness area, (3) location of the wilderness area in a watershed in relation to past and current types of land uses occurring in the watershed, and (4) occurrence and effects of atmospheric deposition in the wilderness area. These factors also determine if the quality of the water in the wilderness areas is "fishable and swimmable."

The Forest Service wilderness manager can influence water quality when the wilderness area is within a watershed that is entirely under Forest Service management and when atmospheric deposition is not significant. However, if the effective treatment of a water quality problem in a wilderness area requires the use of mechanical equipment (i.e., tractor), the control by the wilderness manager to remedy the problem is limited. When atmospheric deposition is significant or the wilderness area is located downstream from private land on which a water quality problem originates, the Forest Service manager is required to work through state and local agencies in order to attain water flows in the wilderness areas that are at least "fishable and swimmable."

QUANTITY AND TIMING

The quantity and timing of stream flows can be of concern. In the United States, there are two basic doctrines for allocating water. The Appropriation Doctrine is basically "first-in-time, first-in-right" and is predominantly used by States west of the Mississippi River. The Riparian Doctrine is predominantly used by states located east of the Mississippi River. Water rights obtained under the Riparian Doctrine stay with the property adjacent to the stream. Water cannot be transferred to another basin, and the upstream user cannot impair the quality, quantity or timing of water flows so as to be detrimental to the downstream user.

Each state is responsible for allocating the water occurring within its boundaries. The Forest Service is responsible for identifying its water needs in terms of quantity and timing and to obtain the water rights for its needs from the state. These needs are based on management goals and objectives. These goals and objectives can be the maintenance of channel integrity for the purposes of fish habitat, water quality, aesthetics, canoeing, and maintenance of riparian ecosystems. Techniques for quantifying the needed instream flows for various management goals and objectives are currently available.

In the management of wilderness areas, the Forest Service has responsibility for assuring that water entering and leaving the wilderness area is adequate in terms of quality, quantity, and timing for wilderness use and downstream uses. Unless machinery is required to remedy a water quality problem, the Forest Service manager has direct control over the quality of water contributed by the wilderness area. However, when the wilderness area is located downstream from private land, and water quantity, quality or timing is impaired for the purposes of wilderness, then the Forest Service manager needs to use state processes to enforce the water right for the wilderness area.

The Forest Service still needs to determine the instream flow needs and obtain the water rights for wilderness areas that it manages in the Southern Region. As the demand for water increases, the competition for water rights for wilderness areas is expected to increase. As competition increases, the need for adjudication of water rights by the State's is expected to increase and may even result in some modification of the Riparian Doctrine for allocating water (Edwards 1985).

RIPARIAN AREAS AND WETLANDS

Due to their unique values, the Forest Service is mandated to maintain or enhance riparian and wetland ecosystems (U.S. Water Resources Council 1978, USDA Forest Service 1982).

There are two management goals for wetlands and riparian areas located in wilderness areas managed by the USDA Forest Service, Southern Region. The first management goal for riparian areas and wetlands in wilderness areas is to permit plant succession to proceed to the climax species. This procession has implications on the unique values for these areas including the type and population of wildlife dependent upon these areas. Also, the amount and timing of instream flows to permit succession may be different than if the management goals and objectives for these areas were to maintain current conditions.

The second management goal is to permit debris falling into the stream to stay in the stream. This debris may be perceived as an adverse effect on aesthetics. However, it permits natural geomorphic processes to occur in the channel and enhances fisheries habitat.

The exceptions to these management goals for riparian areas and wetlands are when: (1) life and property downstream from the wilderness area are threatened, (2) water quality, quantity and timing are impaired so the water leaving the wilderness area cannot be used for downstream purposes, (3) the current condition of these areas is the reason for designation as wilderness, and (4) rare or endangered fauna or flora are present and depend upon the current condition of the area.

SUMMARY

Three issues for water management in wilderness areas in the South are: (1) water quality, (2) water quantity and timing, and (3) riparian areas and wetlands.

The Forest Service manager has direct control over the quality of water from the wilderness area, but must work with state and local agencies if the wilderness area is downstream from private land and activities on this land result in impaired water quality, quantity or timing for wilderness use. The Forest Service manager has the responsibility to quantify adequate instream flows for wilderness areas and to obtain the rights to those flows from the States. The current management goals for riparian areas and wetlands, in wilderness areas for the Southern Region is to let plant succession proceed to climax and leave any debris in the streams.

LITERATURE CITED

Clean Water Act of 1977. (P.L. 95-217, 33 U.S.C. 466 et. seg.).

Eastern Wilderness Act of 1975. (P.L. 93-622, 88 Stat. 2096; 16 U.S.C. 1132 (Note)).

Edwards, Greg. 1985. Proposed bills would alter Va. water policy. Roanoke Times and World News, July 25, 1985, p B9.

Federal Water Pollution Control Act of 1972. (P.L. 92-500, 86 Stat. 816, as amended; 33 U.S.C. 1251, et. seg.).

Forest and Rangeland Renewable Resources Planning Act of August 17, 1974. (P.L. 93-378, 88 Stat. 476; 16 U.S.C. 1601 (note) 1600-1614).

Multiple-Use Sustained Yield Act of 1960. (P.L. 86-517, 74 Stat. 215; 16 U.S.C. 528 (note) 528-531).

USDA Forest Service. 1982. National forest system land and resource management planning. 36 C.F.R. Part 219. 219.23 (f), 219.27 (a) (4), 219.27 (e). Fed. Reg. 47(190):43026-43052 (September 30, 1982).

U.S. Water Resources Council. 1978. Floodplain management guidelines for implementing E.O. 11988. 43 FR 6030. Fed. Reg. 43(29):6030-6055 (February 10, 1978. Vol. 43, No. 29).

Weeks Law of 1911 (36 Stat. 961 as amended; 16 U.S.C. 480, 500, 513-517, 517a, 519, 521, 552, 563).

Wilderness Act of 1964. (P.L. 88-477, 78 Stat. 890; 16 U.S.C. 1121 (note), 1131-1136).

Williams, O.R. 1981. *Giardia* and the waterborne transmission of giardiasis, a general review. USDA Forest Service WSDG Report, WSDG-TP-00003.

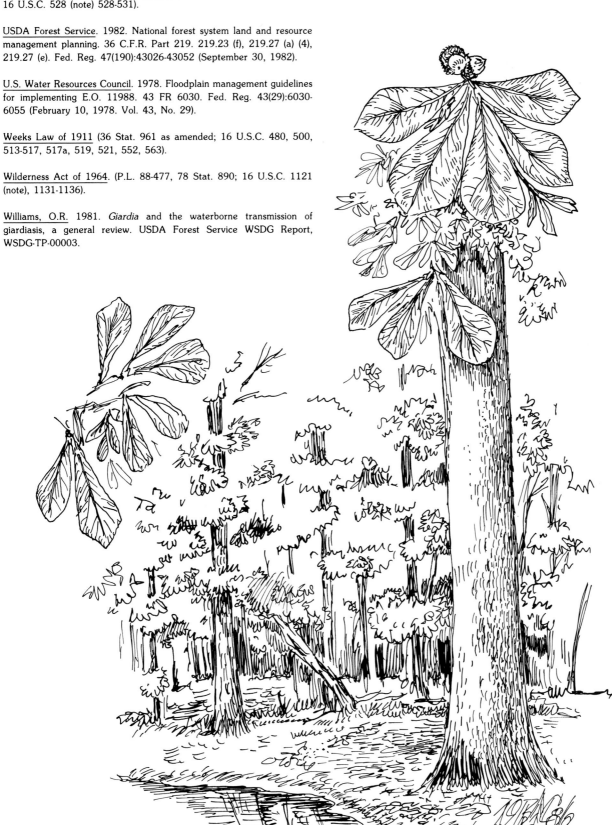

Influence Of Fire On The Longleaf Pine - Bluestem Range In The Big Thicket Region

by
Geraldine E. Watson

ABSTRACT--The diversity of the Big Thicket region of Southeast Texas is due largely to the influence of fire with different plant associations located according to their response to fires of varying frequency and intensity. Fire suppression by man in the last fifty years has caused many changes in the structure of vegetation associations. The restoration and preservation of the integrity of the diverse ecosystems of Southeast Texas by the use of applied fire is a subject of vital interest to managers of natural and wilderness preserves.

KEYWORDS: Big Thicket National Preserve, fire, longleaf pine.

THE BIG THICKET

The Big Thicket National Preserve was set aside because of the biological diversity of the area. Dr. Thomas Eisner, an eminent British scientist and ecologist at Cornell University, who, with his graduate students, has studied ecology on three continents, most of the United States and the Big Thicket in particular, wrote in Science Magazine: "The Thicket is ecologically unique not only to Texas, but to the entire North American expanse as well." The uniqueness of its diversity was further recognized when the Big Thicket was selected for inclusion in the international Man in the Biosphere Preserve program in 1981.

The reason for the diversity of the Big Thicket is a complexity of geographical location, geological and climatic history, and the occurrence of periodic wildfires.

Located where the mesic forests of the Southeastern United States meet the plains of the Central United States and the coastal prairies and marshes of the Gulf Coast, this land was laid as alluvial plain deposition during the Pleistocene Epoch. Fluctuating sea levels related to the glaciations of this epoch, repeated incursions and regressions of the Gulf of Mexico over the land, and the resultant erosion and deposition created the landforms and soil types which have remained relatively stable for the past five thousand years. Climate also has fluctuated with extremes of hot and cold, wet and dry, with only minor fluctuations in the past five thousand years. Since records have been kept, it appears that these cycles occur with severity each one hundred years with recurrences of decreased severity at seventy-five, fifty, twenty-five and ten year intervals. These cycles were extremely important in the determination of the vegetational zones of the Big Thicket region.

Equally important with weather in the location of vegetational communities was the topography. In general, the topography is gently undulating with relief more sharply dissected as the gradient rises to the north. Uplands have a thin (one meter average) layer of sand or sandy loam underlain by rock-like red clay plenthite. Rainfall on the uplands migrates downslope, seeping out in swales or at slope bases. Soil texture on the uplands is coarse, facilitating movement of moisture, while that of the swales is fine-textured, forming a poorly-permeable hardpan. Runoff through these swales is a very gradual surface sheet flow and water stands throughout the rainy season. These uplands form the divides of rivers and creeks.

Southeast Texas is a watershed for three major rivers: the Trinity, Neches and Sabine; a large creek: Village/Big Sandy; two bayous: Pine Island and Little Pine Island Bayous. Each river has numerous tributaries. Floodplains of the larger streams are deeply-filled valleys with varying terrace levels. These terraces have a ridge-and-swale topography, each being inundated according to terrace level and climate cycle. The upper terraces are seldom, if ever, flooded. Bluff lines of the floodplains have a beech-magnolia-loblolly pine (*Fagus grandifolia, Magnolia grandiflora,* and *Pinus taeda*) forest community which also occupies the ridges of the upper terraces. Seepage springs at the base of bluff slopes fill the swales, or old meander scars, creating acid swamps called "baygalls". Stream levee and point bar sand deposits on the

streamward edge of the upper terraces support xeric vegetation, as rainfall percolates quickly through the deep, porous sand, leaving the surface dry. The lower terraces are frequently flooded. Water-tolerant oaks and gums are on the ridges and cypress-tupelo sloughs fill the swales.

This moisture distribution is a determinant in "what grows where". Not just in positioning of xeric, mesic and hydric species, but in the positioning of species according to their tolerance for wildfire. This leads up to the topic of my paper: the importance of fire in the creation and maintenance of the vegetational communities of Southeast Texas.

FIRE AND THE BIG THICKET

The effects of fire on vegetation vary according to topography, wind speed and direction, humidity and flammability of material. The rapid migration of moisture from the uplands leaves them dry and the aridity decreases with downslope progression. Since lightning usually strikes the tallest objects, tall pines on the uplands draw lightning which ignites the pine straw and grasses about the tree bases. Longleaf pine (*Pinus palustris*) needles, and the native grasses of the longleaf pine-bluestem range are extremely flammable. A slight wind and the wildfire is on its way, burning downslope on the windward side until

stopped by water. A backfire (moving against the wind) will stop at seepage-saturated soil and duff of the lower slope forest or the standing water of a swale, but I have seen a head fire (moving with and by the wind), sweep across flat-woods sedge ponds. Since the fire on the downwind side of a slope will be a backfire, it will stop higher on the slope than a headfire. Also, a backfire usually stops at a shrub community where a headfire might sweep through it.

On extremely dry ridges or xeric sand deposits, grass and other flammable material will be sparse and only occasional wind-driven fires of high intensity will reach them. Semi-xeric species of oaks such as blackjack (*Quercus marilandica*), bluejack (*Quercus incana*), and post (*Quercus stellata*), as well as the less fire-tolerant shortleaf pine (*Pinus echinata*), can be found on these dry uplands. Most seedlings are killed during these occasional fires while the mature trees are spared. This prevents thickets from forming while allowing for perpetuation of the semi-xeric species. If, rarely, the mature trees are killed, they readily sprout from the charred stumps. Fire suppression on xeric sites results in accumulation of humus and moisture and cooling of the surface, thus preparing the site for the next successional stage.

Species which have evolved with the frequent fires of the uplands thrive under one-to-three-year burning intervals. Some even require fire to germinate seeds. I have seen plants (*Wahlenbergia emarginata* for instance), which have disappeared for many years suddenly appear in great abundance after a fire. Shrubs such as Arkansas blueberry (*Vaccinium arkansanum*), stagger bush (*Lyonia mariana*), and white azalea (*Rhododendron oblongifolium*), which tolerate and are even regenerated by fires of several years frequency, occupy a zone where moisture prevents too-frequent fires. The bearded grass pink orchid (*Calopogon barbatus*) was not known to be in Texas until a lightning fire burned a longleaf pine forest in the Kirby State Forest in Tyler County. Two plants appeared the following spring and the population increased after each burn. The same behavior has been observed after burning in Big Thicket National Preserve pinelands.

Many species are exterminated by crowding and shading. On uplands, fire has created a monoculture of fire-dependent longleaf pine trees with many species of fire-tolerant grasses and herbs. Wax myrtle (*Myrica cerifera*), yaupon (*Ilex vomitoria*), and other species become established during long wet periods and, with fire suppression, form dense thickets. These species contain waxes, oils, terpines and fats which are extremely volatile. During droughts, these thickets, densely hung with pine straw, literally explode when hit by wildfire, and everything, including the fire-tolerant, mature longleaf pines, can be destroyed. I have personally seen such fires.

During long, wet intervals, or with fire suppression, black gum (*Nyssa sylvatica*), white bay (*Magnolia virginiana*), and titi (*Cyrilla racemiflora*), invade savannah wetlands. With periodic fire, some will survive as widely-spaced arborescent forms. Without fire, the savannah will progress until these invaders have crowded and shaded out all the light-loving species of orchids, ferns and carnivorous plants and other rare and beautiful herbaceous species of this community. Laurel leaf oak (*Quercus laurifolia*), and willow oak (*Quercus phellos*), (locally called "pin oak") become established and an allelopathic factor prevents anything from growing beneath, so the savannah becomes what is locally called a "pinoak flat" with bare floor and water standing much of the year.

With long suppression of fire on longleaf pine uplands, the lower slope community (beech, magnolia and loblolly pine dominants with white oak (*Quercus alba*) and sugar maple (*Acer saccharum*) as subdominants), will migrate up slope and replace the longleaf pine association. On more xeric sites, an oak-hickory community will dominate.

Fire does not usually invade the mesic forests of the lower slopes and floodplains because the forest floor duff is normally damp and actually fire retarding. Fire scars at the base of hardwoods, especially beech, and the presence of "lightered" hardwood (blackened chunks of dense wood which resist decay), are evidence that fire does occur in lower forests during cycles of extreme drought; however, its progress is slow and low and does not kill mature trees. It does kill young seedlings and saplings, thus slowing, while not preventing, regeneration yet preventing thickets of hardwood species.

Infrequent fires in mesic forests could explain the presence of loblolly pine in the structure of hardwood forests. Since it requires sunlight to regenerate, the pine waits un-til the death of a mature, wide-spreading hardwood creates a patch of sunlight on the forest floor. The thick duff might then prevent pine from becoming established before the branches of the surrounding hardwood trees close in the opening in the canopy, so other pioneers: sweetgum (*Liquidambar styraciflua*), water oak (*Quercus nigra*), yaupon, ironwood (*Carpinus americana*), take over the opening. If fire bares the mineral soil, then pine gets a head start. This is all assuming that the openings occur on a ridge or slope which is not too wet for pine.

In Hardin and lower Tyler, Jasper, and Newton Counties, where topography is fairly level with poorly-developed drainage patterns, these moisture-related pyric zones are generally broad and poorly defined; yet they are readily apparent where the topography is more deeply dissected and where small spring branches dissect the swales. In the center of these wet depressions, farthest from the fire origin, a titi - redbay (*Persea borbonia*) - gallberry holly (*Ilex coreacea*) community grows tall and forms a canopy under which ferns, sphagnum moss, and many rare shade, acid and moisture-loving plants grow along the small branches. Lower shrubs border this canopied community because they bear the brunt of the fires and are reduced more often. Seldom do large forest trees become established here because during the rare cycles of severe drought, fire will sweep across the entire community and the shrubs will regenerate from sprouts and regain their dominance.

For all the reasons mentioned, very rarely does fire devastate an entire area, but instead it creates a mosaic pattern which is always changing with wind and weather, leaving browse and cover for wildlife and seed sources for non-pyric plants. Also, no species are rendered extinct by fire, but merely kept in the places in which they evolved.

Also, for all the above reasons, fire management must parallel the natural pattern as much as possible. Ignition should always be at the highest point of the proposed burn and allowed to progress and stop where it will. The creation of fire lanes to enable a crew to burn a certain number of acres in a given length of time, or to favor certain species, results in artificial communities and future problems. It also requires more time and personnel to manage.

The preceding discussion of pyric vegetational zones describes them under the natural, or pre-European man, order. During my lifetime of sixty years, I have watched drastic changes occurring in the vegetation of Southeast Texas. The rapidity with which a small tract of land I bought in 1956 has changed is an excellent example of the effects of fire suppression. The land was partly-open longleaf pine forest with some large loblolly pines at old fence lines. There were also some shortleaf pines. The larger longleaf pines were cut just prior to purchase. We attempted to keep the land open by removing the invading wax myrtle and yaupon by hand and burned it three times during the first five years. After being brush-hogged in 1963, it was allowed to grow up. Only the larger pines were left by the mowing.

The open areas were rapidly colonized by french mulberry (*Callicarpa americana*), yellow coneflowers (*Compositae* spp.), goldenrod (*Solidago canadensis*), and other weedy species. After two years, wax myrtle and yaupon had replaced the herbaceous species, and they were interspersed with loblolly pine, sweetgum and water oak seedlings. The tree species quickly gained dominance, forming an overhead canopy. The shrubs became sparse and "leggy", forming a middle canopy under which magnolia seedlings appeared. A few years after the magnolia appeared, beech seedlings came in. At the time of this writing, 1985, the loblolly pines, which came up when we acquired the property, are 36 cm diameter, the magnolias are 14 cm diameter and the beeches are 13 cm diameter. The older loblolly pines are being hit heavily by pine bark beetles. All the mature shortleaf pine died one at a time as the density and height of the understory grew. There has been no loss of the longleaf pines, but also no regeneration. Loblolly pine, sweetgum and water oak trees whose tops have been crowded out of the canopy or are strangled by vines, continue to die. The middle canopy of shrubs is being replaced by a mid canopy of american holly (*Ilex opaca*), and the beeches and magnolias. Some dogwood (*Cornus florida*) and red maple (*Acer rubrum*) have also come in.

In contrast, I recently had the opportunity to observe a longleaf pine stand belonging to Kirby Lumber Company, which I had last seen about twenty-five years or so ago. It has been managed by periodic burning during this time. Though it has been periodically harvested, it was the nearest thing to the virgin forests I remember from my childhood. The great diversity of grasses and wildflowers, the beauty of the ferns, mosses, orchids and azaleas in the little draws was so overwhelming that I had to go off to myself and shed a few tears and say a prayer of gratitude that at least one landowner in Southeast Texas had become enlightened.

When we view Southeast Texas of today and compare it with what we read about its appearance a hundred years ago, or even remember what much of it looked like fifty years ago, it becomes readily apparent that great changes have taken place. The National Park Service has watched this progression in the units of Big Thicket National Preserve for the past ten years and wondered what causes them. Are they part of the natural successional process? Should we do nothing? Should we do something? If so, what?

We know that most of these changes are due to the interference of man - directly and indirectly. An effort was made to select the least-altered areas for inclusion in the Preserve, but none of the units, with the possible exception of the Loblolly Unit, has "never known the saw or the ax". The most obvious changes are due to the over-manipulation by humans: subsistence utilization and commercial utilization.

For at least ten to fifteen thousand years, primitive man in Southeast Texas lived by hunting, fishing, gathering, and limited agriculture. There is no way we can compare conditions before their advent with those after, but the Indians apparently had learned to live in balance with, and become a part of, the natural order, as their culture was still thriving when Europeans appeared on the scene. They herded game by fire and fired fields preparatory to planting, so one can not say that pre-European-man fire frequency was solely dependent on lightning. There is evidence in literature that Indians burned in winter and lightning fires occurred largely in late summer.

The Indians practiced subsistence farming, but the European settlers came not to live comfortably off the land in harmony with the environment, but to seek their fortune and get rich off growing cotton, corn and tobacco on the virgin soils. Just as they had overused and abused the lands of the Eastern United States, so they did in Texas. Much of the Big Thicket area was spared intensive agriculture because of its poorly-drained acid soils; but the virgin upland pines were harvested for lumber and the fine white oaks of the slopes and stream terraces fed numerous barrel stave mills for the wine industry in France. Well-drained land was farmed, the rest was open range for cattle and was burned annually to encourage fresh grass for grazing. This was continued until closed-range laws were passed in the 1950's. The influence of grazing in keeping the land open and park-like has been largely ignored. There was an immediate explosion of vegetation in the units of Big Thicket National Preserve after grazing was removed. Quite obvious were the carpets of sugar maple seedlings in the Big Sandy Unit.

With the population increase and industrialization of Southeast Texas came a need for large water impoundments and real estate developments. Change continued with roads, drainage ditches, oil fields, etc., acting as barriers to fire when one did occur.

The most effective change came when the forest products industries, which control the vast majority of acreage in Southeast Texas, in the 1940's began converting natural woodlands to plantations of slash pine (*Pinus elliottii*). With much of the rural population moving to the industrialized Gulf Coast during World War II, fields were abandoned and were thickly colonized by loblolly pine. Since both slash and loblolly pine are not fire tolerant, a rigorous fire suppression policy was pursued. Such movies as Walt Disney's "Bambi", and the "Smokey the Bear" symbol, (portraying fire in the forest as a menace to wildlife, forest, people and property) reinforced the need to prevent fires at all cost.

Thirty to forty years of fire suppression resulted in a buildup of fuels -- forest floor duff, leaves and needles, fallen limbs, low flammable shrubbery, etc., with disastrous results. When a fire did start, whether by lightning, arson or carelessness, the heat was so intense that everything was literally destroyed. When natural fires are allowed to periodically consume fuels before they reach dangerous levels, they are characteristically a gentle creeping ground fire which deer, rabbits, etc., merely jump over. The roaring infernos so popular on movies and television are caused by fire suppression over lengthy periods.

Tree farming on incompatible surfaces created more problems than destructive wildfire, however. Natural pine/hardwood forests were converted to pine monocultures by poisoning hardwoods. Slash and loblolly pines were planted both on high, dry sandy surfaces and on floodplains. Longleaf pine thrives on these uplands because it is fire tolerant and has a long taproot which can penetrate the plenthite and obtain moisture and nutrients during droughts. On the other hand, slash and loblolly pines are not fire tolerant. They have a lateral root system which simply sits on top of the plenthite in a layer of sand and are severely stressed by drought. The floodplains and slopes where moisture-tolerant mixed pine/hardwood forests grow were also planted to dense stands of slash and loblolly. During periods of wet weather, these trees are also under stress. Under adverse conditions, nature, in the form of insects and disease, inevitably steps in and reduces the population density to that which available nutrients and moisture can sustain, thus altering species structure to one which can survive on that particular site. Fire is one of nature's most effective tools in restoring a healthy balance, providing thinning and some insect and disease control.

Some forest products industries, which were spending millions of dollars on chemical control -- pesticides, fungicides, herbicides, etc. -- soon realized that nature's remedy, fire, was not only economical and ecologically sound, but very effective, so they quietly and carefully began controlled burning in their forests. The National Park Service and U.S. Forest Service also came to this realization, but could not proceed without scientific justification, which has been very slow in coming. Bambi and Smokey the Bear did a good job--it will take time to re-educate the public to the necessity of a fire management program on public lands.

The Big Thicket National Preserve, which has a mandate to protect and preserve the plant and animal life of its units, has had to face the fact that, in many cases, it has to restore the natural integrity of a unit before it can preserve it. Much needs to be done in the way of restoring land contour where it has been altered by oil, timber, and real estate operations. Grazing of domestic livestock has been withdrawn and harvesting of timber has been discontinued, but the greatest challenge lies in restoring the original forest structure. Since all available evidence shows upland areas of Big Thicket to have been a longleaf pine - bluestem range habitat, and since there is voluminous literature which indicates that this habitat evolved and flourished under frequent fires for millennia, the Big Thicket National Preserve prepared a fire management program and has begun to implement it. Many barriers are presented to carrying out this program.

Due to the many restrictions placed on burning by various agencies, the Park Service is seldom allowed to burn when their fire ecologists and fire behaviorists think best. All the studies done to determine the natural frequencies, intensity and time to burn are thrown out as we are forced to burn, not where, when and how it is best for the Big Thicket National Preserve, but when it is deemed best by political agencies such as the Texas Air Control Board. Permits are issued to the petro-chemical industries to emit toxic substances which are proven carcinogens, into the air over the Beaumont-Port Arthur-Orange basin, but they forbid our burning when the north wind blows (the correct time for us to burn), for fear that wood smoke, which is relatively harmless, might find its way into this populated area. Since some plant communities depend on infrequent, hot fires during droughts, and there is no way we will be permitted to burn during that time, it appears that we will never be able to preserve the integrity of the diverse ecosystems which have caused the Big Thicket to be called the "Biological Crossroads of North America".

This paper is not intended to be a scientific treatise, but represents conclusions based on the observations and studies of one who, with generations of ancestors, has lived closely with the forests and streams of Southeast Texas. For those interested in pursuing the subject, the literature is replete with scientific data in support of fire management of the longleaf pine - bluestem range. It also represents my personal views and not the policies of the National Park Service by which I am employed.

The Role Of Fire In The Appalachian Hardwoods

by

Robert K. Strosnider

ABSTRACT--Fire has been a major factor in shaping the structure of the Appalachian forests. Indians used fire for agriculture, hunting and warfare, and its use since then was widespread up to the 1940's. Fire suppression and prevention are changing the effects of the past fire regime. The forest structure of the proposed Clifty Wilderness in the Daniel Boone National Forest is showing major changes.

KEYWORDS: fire history, hardwood forests, forest structure, fire suppression.

The role of fire in Appalachian hardwoods is complex, and its effects are difficult to isolate because fire was so common for so long. In addition, despite the importance of the region's forests, the effects of fire on them have not been well researched.

The region has a long history of occupancy by man. Man has influenced Appalachian forests for about 12,500 years. Human activities have included land clearing for agriculture and grazing as well as the use of forest products. This is an area where a major tree species, the American chestnut (*Castanea dentata*), as a result of man's activities, was effectively eliminated by an introduced disease. With this in mind let us begin by identifying some of what we do know about the area.

The Appalachian Mountain chain runs roughly northeast and southwest, stretching from northern Alabama to southern Quebec. It varies from less than 50 miles (80 km) to almost 700 miles (1,126 km) wide. The vegetation is very complex, ranging from subtropical forest representatives in its southern extremities to boreal forest representatives in the north and at high elevations in the south. Deciduous hardwood forests dominate due to a favorable climate and topography. The oak-hickory and cove forest types are found through the region: the oak-pine and white pine-hemlock types also are widely distributed.

The weather is mild and humid with a growing season which varies from about 150 to 250 days annually. The elevation ranges from less than 1,000 feet (304 m) to about 6,700 feet (2,042 m).

The average temperature decreases as you go north, as does the average rainfall which ranges from about 40 inches (102 cm) to 60 inches (152 cm) annually. The average intensity and frequency of lightning storms also decrease from south to north.

A climate of dry winters and wet summers is characteristic. Two to four weeks of drought usually occur during both spring and fall. During these periods the conditions of temperature and fuel are most conducive to fire. Spring droughts occur in late March or early April in the south and in late May or early June in the north. In the fall this period varies from mid September in the north to early December in the south.

Droughts can be prolonged, but the periods in spring and fall when serious burns can occur are usually brief. During these periods fires will occur if there is a source of ignition. One source is lightning. About two percent of the total annual number of fires result from lightning strikes.

HISTORY OF FIRE

Between 1960 and 1971 in the Great Smoky Mountain National Park and Cherokee National Forest an average of six lightning-ignited fires occurred per year per 1 million acres (0.4 million ha) (Barden and Woods 1974). "This frequency is greater than that of the Great Plains, Mississippi Basin, and northeast regions of the United States, but much less than that of western and extreme southeastern states where, on the average, lightning starts 20 or more fires per year per 400,000 hectares" (Schroeder and Buck 1970). Generally in the Appalachians, lightning fires have a low frequency of occurrence and are low intensity because the storm that generates the lightning is accompanied by rain. Barden and Woods (1974) also pointed out that over one half of the lightning fires occurred on the upper slopes but at elevations of 2,000 feet (610 m) above MSL and below. Although lightning has been and continues to be a source of fire ignition, man is by far the most important source.

A look at the historic role of the use of fire in the eastern United States and the Appalachians can provide insight into its role in the structure of present day forests. By far the most important source of fire is man. It generally is accepted that man has been present in the eastern United States for about 12,500 years. Settlement followed the retreat of the continental glacier. Man as a potential cause of fire was present long before recorded history, which generally began with the arrival of Europeans. The popular view of the forests of this area when colonists arrived was of a vast unbroken canopy so dense that sunlight seldom reached the ground. Based on some of the historical accounts found in journals of these settlers and explorers, we are told that Indians used fire as a tool for agriculture and hunting, and as a weapon of war.

The earliest records indicate that the countryside was parklike as a result of fire. Quoting early travelers, "Europeans were greatly impressed by the American wilderness. The upland regions of the eastern deciduous forest were typically described as being 'park like' in appearance: trees were well spaced, there was little understory growth or litter, and the forest floor was covered with tall grass. To this European eye this looked almost artificial, reminding him of the carefully managed parks at home. According to Captain John Smith these upland forests were so clear and open that one could gallop a horse through them." "Old fields, abandoned by Indian farmers were widely distributed throughout the East, often covering many acres" (Martin 1973).

As Europeans began to colonize America the use of fire as a tool for agriculture was continued. They brought with them a tradition of burning for clearing land and maintaining open areas once they had been cleared. This method continued in use well into the late 1930's and early 1940's. A report on forestry submitted to Congress by the Commissioner of Agriculture in 1882 and prepared by Franklin B. Hough said: "A frequent cause of disastrous fires in the woods is the mode of clearing land now generally followed by settlers. Of course, they must have recourse to fires in order to clear woodlands, but fire ought to be our servant, kept under continued control, not our master."

EFFECTS OF FIRE

What are the results of these centuries of fire in the Appalachian region? A definitive answer is not available. Natural fires in spring and fall were infrequent, and most appear to have been of low intensity (Komarek 1974). There are notable exceptions to this. Several disastrous fires have resulted during drought years, when there was an ample supply of fuel. Often the fuel consisted of logging debris. "The historical progression of logging and lumbering (was) from the early coastal settlements up the major river systems where transportation was easiest" ... "In most areas the story was essentially the same. Initial lumbering concentrated on the better softwoods -- white pine primarily. Westveld (1949) estimated that all virgin eastern white pine was cut by 1870, and by 1900 operations were beginning in second growth stands ... .Where pure stands predominated, clearcutting followed by extensive fire was common, and many of these areas regenerated to various mixtures of successional hardwoods. Better sites were converted eventually to hardwoods" (Blum 1975).

The forest structure is directly related to fire intensity, fire frequency and the time of the year at which a fire occurs. The following quote is most applicable to the northern Appalachians but reflects the vegetative succession well. From the 1882 Report on Forestry "Professor John W. Dawson, in describing the effect of forest fires and the process of reproduction as observed in Nova Scotia, and which are quite applicable to our forests throughout the Eastern and Northern states says: ... ,I may quote the views of Mr. Titus Smith secretary of the board of agriculture of Nova Scotia ---'If an acre or two be cut down in the midst of a forest and then neglected, it will soon be occupied by a growth similar to that which was cut down; but when timber ... is killed by fires ... at first a different growth springs up; at first a great number of herbs and shrubs, which did not grow on the land ... on most of the barren portions the blueberry appears ... ; great fields of red raspberries ... and wild red cherry appear soon after; but in a few years the raspberries and most of the herbage disappear and are followed by a growth of firs, yellow birch and poplar. When a succession of fires has occurred small shrubs occupy the barren ... in the course of ten or twelve years ... a thicket of small elder begin to grow, under the shelter of which fir, spruce ... and white birch spring up. When the ground is thoroughly shaded by a thicket 20 feet high, the species which originally occupied the ground begins to prevail ... and within 60 years the land will be generally covered with a young growth of the same kind that it produced of old."

Where there has been disturbance by fire, the succession of vegetation in other parts of the Appalachians has followed a similar pattern. Species of grass and other plants endemic to grasslands are still found in parts of the Appalachians. These plants " ... did not develop without a history of fire" (Komarek 1974). Indicative of a change in the fire regime is the change in the landscape as the early settlers knew it. It has changed from large areas of grass through which the buffalo were thought to range to tree species that seem to have a limited adaptation to fire.

Pitch pine (*Pinus ridgida*), which commonly occurs in the Appalachians, has serotinous cones. Some hardwoods, especially most oaks, will sprout profusely after one or two light fires. Pitch pine and shortleaf pine (*P. echinata*) saplings also sprout after fire. A yellow poplar (*Liriodendron tulipifera*) seed needs mineral soil for best

Figure 1. Mature oak stand with a sparse understory. Similar to descriptions of the eastern forests of pre-Colonial America.

germination and it will also remain viable in the leaf litter for up to 8 years. The grass balds that are found at high elevations may have been relics of a climatic change but now depend upon fire to keep them in the grass stage.

Based on the historical records in this region, fire appears to have exerted strong selection pressure, favoring the most fire-resistant or fire-dependent species.

Christensen (1978) stated that the larger upland oaks (*Quercus* spp.) and hickories (*Carya* spp.) are considerably more resistant to fire than the cove hardwoods such as yellow-poplar. Christensen also suggests that many hardwood species require major periodic disturbance for their long-term maintenance.

In general, information suggests that lightning-caused fires are fairly infrequent, are of relatively low intensity, and generally do not cover large areas. Until recently, fires either deliberately set or accidentally caused by man were intense and frequent and often covered large areas. There were major disruptions of the forest either by fire or weather disturbances throughout their history. As a result, hardwoods as well as pine species in the Appalachians have fire adaptations.

The historic reports of the use of fire by Indians and Europeans probably were based on observations in the heavily occupied areas of the east. It is reasonable to conclude, however, that in more remote areas there was similar treatment of the land.

The fire regime has been changed through major programs of modern man. Efforts in forest fire prevention and control appear to be setting the stage for less frequent but potentially more intense fires due to the buildup of fuels. It appears that overall potential disturbance to the ecosystem from such fires could be much more intense.

APPARENT TREND IN RED RIVER GORGE, KENTUCKY

For more than 10 years I have been observing Red River Gorge Geological Area (25,662 acres (10,385 ha), which was established as a special interest area in 1974 and a National Natural Landmark in 1976), which contains an area of about 13,000 acres (5,261 ha) known as the proposed Clifty Wilderness. During that period there has been a dramatic increase in the white pine component of the forest. This increase is most evident on ridges and on upper slopes. The most obvious cause is a major change in the fire regime as a result of Forest Service management.

The Red River Gorge Geological Area covers about 25,662 acres (10,385 ha) in Powell, Menifee, and Wolfe Counties on the Stanton Ranger District of the Daniel Boone National Forest in central eastern Kentucky. Elevation varies from about 700 feet (213 m) MSL to 1300 feet (396 m) MSL. Much of this area was heavily logged in the early 1900's. There is still evidence of railroad grades and splash dams on tributaries of the Red River. One major access road enters through a tunnel originally cut for railroad logging. Most of the area was logged prior to 1969. It is a mixed mesophytic forest dominated by maples (*Acer* spp.), buckeye (*Aesculus* spp.), beech (*Fagus grandifolia*), yellow poplar, oak and basswood (*Tilia americana*).

The 1974 Draft Environmental Impact Statement for the Red River Gorge Unit Plan states: "The Red River Gorge Unit supports an extremely complex and prolific plant community of many hundreds of individual botanical species. Species that range from remnant trees surviving from the pre-logging period to relic and even rare species of past epochs not presently known elsewhere are present in the Red River Gorge. The diversity of species can primarily be attributed to rather rapid changes in soil types throughout the area, and man-caused effects, past and present . . . . In addition to diversity of soils and man-caused features, factors of geography and slope also attribute to proliferation of existing plant life."

The ridges above the cliff lines and the upper slopes support pine and oak. Major components are Virginia pine (*Pinus virginiana*), pitch pine, shortleaf pine, scarlet oak (*Quercus coccinea*), chestnut oak (*Q. prinus*) and hickory (*Carya* spp). Generally the slopes below the cliff line support successional stages of a mixed mesophytic forest with mesic species as major components.

The history of fire in this area can be partly reconstructed from glimpses of the past. Recent archaeological excavations and carbon dating have indicated that man has occupied this area for at least 6,000 years. Remnants of burned leaves, uncovered during the excavation, indicate that fire has also been present in the area for the same period of time. Squash and sunflower seeds discovered at various archaeological sites throughout the area indicate that the occupants were engaged in farming.

Buffalo were known to range through parts of this area. The Red River Gorge is located on the eastern edge of the bluegrass and at the beginning of the mountains. Quoting again from Komarek (1974) "Braun (1950), writing on original conditions in the 'bluegrass' section of Kentucky, quoted from Daniel Boone (1784) as follows: . . . we found everywhere abundance of wild beasts of all sorts, through this vast forest. The bison (*Bison bison*) were more frequent than I have seen cattle in the settlements, browsing on the leaves of the cane, or cropping the herbage on those extensive plains, fearless, because ignorant of man and further: . . . where no cane grows there is an abundance of wild rye, clover and buffalograss, covering vast tracts of country, and affording excellent food for cattle . . . ." These species endemic to grasslands, not dense forests, certainly did not develop without a history of fire in the past.

Don Fig (pers. comm.) constructed a limited picture of the more recent fire history of this area. He determined that there was little information about fires prior to 1940. Generally they were large. Most of the fires occurred when local people burned to eliminate snakes and for agricultural purposes. Farms were found in the river and creek bottoms and above the cliff lines.

There have been no huge fires since the early 1940's. It is generally accepted that most of the area except for moist sites burned frequently before 1940. The forest was more open then than it is now. At present, there is a thick undergrowth of huckleberry (*Vaccinium* spp) and mountain laurel (*Kalmia latifolia*) with rhododendron (*Rhododendron maximum*) at lower elevations.

The Clifty section of the Red River Gorge Geological Area was recommended for wilderness by the Forest Service during the RARE II process. We are charged to manage it to protect its wilderness qualities. Fire has been one of the factors that shaped this area, but its role is being changed. In the 22 years from 1955 to 1977 there were six fires. The total acreage burned, under an aggressive fire suppression policy, was 25.5 acres (10.3 ha). The largest of these fires, which covered 15 acres (6.1 ha), occurred in 1972. Two fires were of unknown origin. The other four were man-caused. There were 12 years in which no fires occurred. In the seven years from 1978 to 1984, there were nine fires. All of them were man-caused and burned a total of 130 acres (53 ha). The largest of these fires was 75 acres (30 ha). There were two years when no fires occurred. Thus, numbers and sizes of fires have been increasing. These recent fires were low in intensity and resulted in loss of small shrubs and white pine

(*Pinus strobus*) in the understory. There are islands of white pine overstory scattered through the area, to provide a continuing seed source.

One result of aggresive fire suppression has been a significant increase of white pine in the understory. It is not now a major component in the upper canopy of the forest, but continued fire protection and the breakup of the aging oak stands on the ridges will change this situation.

There are some points to consider here:

1) Through management we have changed the fire regime in this area from a pattern of annual fires that burned over most of the area prior to 1940 to a recent pattern of smaller, infrequent fires.

2) Even though we are providing increased fire protection, fires have become more frequent and larger over the past seven years.

3) The composition of the forest of the proposed Clifty Wilderness is changing as a result of U. S. Forest Service management.

CONCLUSIONS

A look at the fire history of the Appalachians suggests that the structure of the present broadleaf hardwood forests was affected by fire and will be influenced by its absence or reduced occurrence. The questions to be asked are these: Are we managing wilderness and potential wilderness in a way that permits natural processes to dominate? Are we managing these areas in a way that protects the features that helped the areas to qualify as wilderness? Should we allow fire to continue to have its historic influence on the structure of wilderness in these broadleaved forests? Do we consider prehistoric and historic man a part of the natural system?

If wilderness management is the preservation of a natural system, what part should man play in that system? We could manage these areas to preserve them as they were at some point in time, such as when the first settlers saw them, or we could manage them in a way that removes many of the influences of man.

LITERATURE CITED

Barden, L.S. and F.W. Woods. 1974. Characteristics of lightning fires in southern Appalachian forests. Tall Timbers Fire Ecol. Conf. 13:345-361.

Blum, B.M. 1975. Regeneration and uneven-aged silviculture--the state of the art. p. 68 *In* Uneven-aged Silviculture in the United States. USDA For. Serv., Morgantown, West Va.

Braun, E.L. 1950. Deciduous forests of eastern North America. Hafner Publishing Company, New York, NY.

Christensen, N.L. 1978. Fire regimes in southeastern ecosystems. Proceedings of the conference - Fire Regimes and Ecosystem Properties; Pp. 112-136; Honolulu, Hawaii; December 11-15, 1978.

Komarek, E.V. 1974. Appalachian Mountains mesophytic forest and grasslands. Pp. 269-272 *In* Fire and ecosystems, T.P. Kozlowski and C.E. Ahgren, (eds.), Academic Press, New York, NY.

Martin, C. 1973. The Indian Historian. 6:23-26.

Schroeder, M.J. and C.C. Buck. 1970. Fire Weather. pp. 229 *In* USDA Handbook No. 36.

Westveld, R.H. 1949. Applied silviculture in the United States. John Wiley and Sons, Inc., New York, NY.

Don Fig is a Forestry Technician, Stanton Ranger District

Towards A Fire Management Strategy In Eastern Mixedwood Forest Conservation Areas

by

Ross W. Wein

ABSTRACT--Since the management goal of many conservation areas is to permit the ecosystem to function naturally with the full component of biotic influences, and since these areas are now only a remnant of former wilderness, the suppression or use of a powerful ecological factor such as fire deserves careful consideration before implementation. Fire has always been a natural part of the eastern mixedwood forest but the frequency of fire has varied widely, both spatially and temporally. Now that wilderness and other natural areas are small and scattered across the landscape in areas with inherently different fire frequencies, it is difficult to establish a unified policy regarding fire. Although the consequences of restricting fire from these ecosystems may not result in a significant build-up of fuel and more disastrous fires, as in western North America, there may be unacceptable consequences such as a decline in ecological diversity. Fire cannot be re-introduced into these areas unless specific goals are identified and unless evidence is provided to support the re-introduction. Fire managers are increasingly using computer-aided decision support systems and these can be useful in achieving wilderness goals.

KEYWORDS: ecological reserves, national parks, fire, eastern Canada.

Wilderness areas and natural areas in eastern North America are fragile in that they represent only a partial microcosm of the former wilderness and are subject to continuous pressures from surrounding intensively managed ecosystems. Also, many conservation areas have been greatly influenced by past human activity and when these conservation areas were protected by law they were in some ways an artifact of the real wilderness. Because ecological systems are dynamic, resource managers and researchers must recognize what variation is a result of human influences and what is a result of "natural processes". It is especially important to recognize points at which a specific ecosystem is signifying an irreversible change. For example, when biotic and abiotic influences are allowed to act "naturally", the combination of events may give unexpected results. There may be examples where a permanent change in ecosystems is less an unusual result than a reversion to presettlement period conditions. If ecosystem dynamics were better understood, we would better appreciate the natural range of ecosystem dynamics and these specific events would not be "surprises".

This paper brings together evidence of how fire influences the mixedwood forests of the northeastern United States and southeastern Canada but focuses more intensely on the Maritime Provinces and particularly on New Brunswick. Specifically, there is an attempt i) to establish the importance of fire in a "natural" eastern mixedwood forest region; ii) to describe the present range of conservation area types; iii) to provide some perspective of fire history in the larger conservation areas; iv) to present something of the present fire management policy and the consequences for conservation areas; and, finally iv) to suggest how fire can be re-introduced to conservation areas without violating the wilderness philosophy.

FIRE REGIMES IN THE MIXEDWOOD FOREST

The degree of aboriginal use of fire in eastern North America is far from clear, yet there is a general consensus that fire was utilized (Day 1953, Thompson and Smith 1970, Little 1974, Russell 1983). In these ecosystems fuel quantity was generally high and when the fuel periodically dried only an ignition source was needed to start a fire. Even without human activity, lightning provided the ignition. When Europeans settled eastern North America, trees were cut and land was cleared using fire, to facilitate European agriculture. Generally, early settlers gained little economically from the forest and hence land-clearing fires that escaped were of minor concern, unless settlements were threatened. As the human population grew and property values increased, more care with fire was exercised. Fire suppression activity continually strengthened even though it waxed and waned in response to the general economic climate. At the present time, fire detection and suppression equipment and techniques have become so effective that fire can be virtually eliminated from small natural areas, even from fire prone ecosystems if the area is readily accessible to machinery and personnel.

North American ecologists have long been aware that fire is a natural and important environmental factor in many ecosystems and the most rapid accumulation of knowledge, as evidenced by the large number of fire research papers and books that have been published, has occurred in the past decade.

Prehistoric frequencies for the mixedwood forest have been developed and long-term forest species dynamics have been described for areas in Maine (Anderson 1979), in Nova Scotia (Green 1976, 1981) and in New Brunswick (Burzynski 1984). Very briefly these studies indicate that fire was always present during the prehistoric period. Fire was particularly important between 2300 and 1500 yr B.P. and between 1200 and 430 yr B.P. but not more recently. In addition Green (1976, 1981) and Anderson (1979) found evidence that high quantities of charred particles were associated with major shifts to new vegetation types.

In reviewing the early historical record, it is important to realize that only the large fires which caused considerable damage were recorded. An example from the New Brunswick mixedwood forest was the Great Miramichi Fire of October 7, 1825 which was the largest recorded fire in North America. Ganong (1902) found references in the early literature to even larger fires at earlier dates. There were probably many years with many fires in the Nineteenth Century but records are scarce. More complete fire suppression records were maintained during the Twentieth Century so we know that widespread fires occurred in the years 1920-23, 1934, 1935, 1944, and 1947 (Wein and Moore 1977, 1979). The historical record also provides some evidence of the relative susceptibility of vegetation types to burning (Table 1). These data should be treated with caution because there is wide vari-

pression confounds the values, particularly since World War II, so that the mean annual burn should be adjusted upward. As examples of higher fire frequency areas, our research group has found jack pine landscapes with fire rotation periods of about 60 years (MacLean and Wein 1977) and blueberry barrens that can burn as frequently as once every five years.

CHARACTERISTICS OF OUR NATURAL AREAS

Throughout the eastern mixedwood forest there is a wide range of natural areas; these areas tend to be small parcels of land scattered across the landscape. Each area has a distinct history; each is at a different stage of development. Above all, it must be realized that each area is dynamic and will change over time. As an example of the range of natural areas in the eastern mixedwood forest, those of the Province of New Brunswick are presented because this is the area with which I am most familiar.

The Province of New Brunswick which is approximately 73,500 km sq in size, has Provincial Parks, Provincial Game Management Areas, and Provincial Game Refuges (Table 2), all of which afford only a limited degree of protection. Most of the approximately 60 Provincial Parks scattered throughout the Province are a few hectares in size although two are larger than 300 ha. The Provincial Game Management Areas are regulated with regard to hunting and trapping but this is the only reason to distinguish the area from other provincial land holdings. Two of these areas are over 80,000 ha in area and another six are larger than 10,000 ha. As for the Provincial Game Refuges, one is over 3,000 ha and one is just over 1,500 ha. No hunting or trapping is permitted but many other forms of land use are possible.

Federal legislation protects three National Bird Sanctuaries where no hunting is permitted. In addition, four National Wildlife Areas (only one of which is greater than 1,500 ha) affords some protection to wildlife species.

All of the above conservation areas permit some form of land use and cannot be construed to be wilderness by present-day definition. Only Ecological Reserves and National Parks relate closely to a wilderness designation; no other designations such as Wilderness Areas or Wild Rivers have been proclaimed. Ecological Reserves are seen as unique and/or representative areas which are to be protected from many forms of land use. They are to be managed according to a well documented management plan. At present there are seven areas protected under the Ecological Reserves Act but since these range in area from less than 10 to 50 ha, they are of limited value to persons desiring a wilderness experience. This leaves the two National Parks in the Province. Fundy National Park (over 20,000 ha) and Kouchibouguac National Park (over 22,000 ha) are located on the Bay of Fundy coast and the Atlantic Coast, respectively. It is in these parks that the only designation wilderness is found. I now wish to deal in

Table 1. Mean Annual Burn from 1931 to 1975 for All Fires over 20 ha in Size for the Major Vegetation Types of New Brunswick as Defined by Loucks (1959–60). (Adapted from Wein and Moore 1977).

Vegetation Type	Approximate Area ($\times 10^3$ ha)	Mean Annual Burn	
		ha	%
Red spruce-hemlock-pine	2591	5418	0.21
Sugar maple-yellow birch-fir	1655	2569	0.16
Coastal spruce-fir	197	253	0.13
Sugar maple-hemlock-pine	1005	731	0.07
Sugar maple-hemlock-pine	1202	480	0.04
Fir-pine-birch	522	68	0.01
Fir-pine-birch	99	2	T*
Sugar maple-ash	305	8	T

*T < 0.005%

ability in stages of stand development and stand type within each vegetation type, and the topographic discontinuity of fuel is not directly comparable. Fire sup-

Table 2. Partial List of Designated Conservation Areas in New Brunswick.

Designation	Name	Date of Establishment	Size (ha)
Provincial Parks (app. 60 in N.B.)	Mactaquc	1965	527
	New River Beach	1959	338
Provincial Game Management Areas	Plaster Rock-Renous		84,178
	Kedgwick		82,883
	Lepreau		24,347
	Canaan		22,534
	Burpee		19,685
	Mount Carleton		17,354
	Bantalor		15,281
	Becaguimac		11,137
	Tracadie River		3,885
Provincial Game Refuges	Utopia		3,108
	University of New Brunswick		1,554
	Fredericton		181
	Odell		155
	Wilson's Point		52
National Bird Sanctuaries	Machias Seal Island		1,036
	Grand Manan		78
	Aero Lake		78
National Wildlife Areas	Tintamarre		1,528
	Shepody		673
	Portage Island		440
	New Horton		104
Ecological Reserves	Blue Mtn. Red Pine	1976	50
	Cranberry Lake Red Oak	1978	47
	McCoy Brook Mixed Hardwood	1976	43
	Glazier Lake Mixed Hardwood	1976	40
	S. Kedgwick River Black Spruce	1978	30
	Lock Alva Red Spruce	1978	12
	Phillipstown Blue Heron Nesting Site	1978	8
National Parks	Kouchibouguac	1969	22,534
	Fundy	1938	20,591

more depth with the fire history of these areas because this is where fire management is necessary to perpetuate some ecosystems.

FIRE HISTORY IN MARITIME PROVINCES NATIONAL PARKS

There are five National Parks in the Maritime Provinces and each park has a particular fire history because of past human activity and because of the inherent climatic conditions which dictate the susceptibility of the fuels to fire.

Prince Edward Island National Park, located in the coastal zone, is largely unforested and has no record of fires since it was established in 1937.

Available records since Fundy National Park (New Brunswick) was established in 1947 suggest that only one small fire of 4-5 ha occurred in 1950 (Table 3). Wein and Moore (1977) suggested, on the basis of historic fire suppression records, that this general area probably has experienced fewer prehistoric fires than any other part of the Province.

Early fire records for Cape Breton Highlands National Park (Nova Scotia) have been summarized by Fraser (1955). Oral history suggests that significant fires occurred in 1845 and 1885; better documented fires occurred in 1921 (1500 ha) and 1936, which is the year that the park was established. The only significantly large fire that has occurred since that time was the 1947 Pleasant Bay fire which burned well over 3000 ha of which almost 2000 ha was within the park. Since that time small fires of a few hectares in size have been caused by humans although in 1975 a 14 ha fire was caused by lightning.

Kejimkujik National Park, located in Nova Scotia, has had more fires than Cape Breton Highlands National Park. During his travels in Nova Scotia at the turn of the century to evaluate timber resources, Smith (1801-02) was impressed with the destruction of timber by fire and wind storms. His tour did not pass through the park area but he frequently encountered burned areas along the coast where present-day fire frequencies are lower than in the park. An examination of the map produced by Fernow (1912) showed that both "recent burns" and "old burns and barrens" covered a large area of the landscape near the park (Wein and Moore 1979). The fire rotation period calculated from Fernow (1912) for the general vegetation type in this part of the Province was 110 years. An analysis of Nova Scotia fire records (1958-1975) showed no fires greater than 20 ha within the park boundaries but in the biophysical survey of Kejimkujik National Park, Gimbarzevsky (1975) noted that there was evidence that most of the park has burned sometime in the past. Forest stands had a mean age of less than 100 years with the oldest stands approaching 300 years. MacLean (1975) studied the Tobeatio Resource Management Area southwest of the park and found records of extensive fires in 1903, 1920, 1921, 1923 and 1927; in the past 25 years, eight fires burned over 4,000 ha and the Indians Field Fire of 1960 burned almost this total area. Since this park was established in 1968, there have been only a few small fires.

Kouchibougauc National Park located on the Atlantic Coast of New Brunswick, has had the greatest number of fires of all the Maritime National Parks. There have been a few lightning-ignited fires but most were from prescribed burning which was a common practice long before the park was established in 1969. Farmers traditionally burned roughland pasture in the spring to remove dead

Table 3. Fires over 0.5 ha in Size That Have Occurred in Maritime National Parks.

Fire Name & Location	Date	Size (ha)	Comments (Vegetation Type)
Fundy National Park (Established in 1947)			
Between Holey Brook and Broad River	?/?/50(L)*	4–5	
Cape Breton Highlands National Park (Established in 1936)			
Mica Hill Lake-7 miles west of Neil's Harbour	?/06/21	1500	Fraser (1955) suggests 160 ha.
Pleasant Bay	08/-?/47	3350	1875 ha in Park
Upper Brook Backland-Roper			
Brook section of North Ingonish	04/06/53	1	
Aubrey Stockley Wood Road-North Ingonish	13/07/54		
South Mountain Trail-5 miles off main road	02/06/57	1	
Fishing Cove River-between French &			
MacKenzie Mt. on road diversion	30/06/57	2	Slash on right-of-way
Presqu'lle-between Park entrance			
and Cape Rouge	20/08/61	1	
Barren Plain-south of tower,			
4 miles off road	05/07/75 (L)	14	
Kejimkujik National Park (Established in 1968)			
Big Dam Lake to Frozen Ocean Lake	1885	200 +	Mixed forest
Beaverskin Lake Area	1930	200 +	Softwood
Dennis Boot Lake Area	1931 (L)	200 +	Softwood
Joe Tom Bog on West River	1952 (L)	200 +	Bog and softwood
Mount Tom Brook	1973	4 +	Bog and mixedwood
Still Brook	1982	spot	Mixed forest
Kouchibouguac National Park (Established in 1969)			
Richibucto	11/09/32	60	
Kouchibouguac	10/06/33 (L)	80	
Kouchibouguac	29/05/34	330	
Fontaine Creek	04/06/34	350	
Point Sapin	24/10/47	130	
Point Sapin	27/10/47	60	
Point Sapin	30/10/56	80	
Point Sapin	01/09/57	140	
Point Sapin	15/09/57	190	
Sand dune-Calanders Beach	12/05/71	8–10	Dune vegetation
Rankin Brook	01/06/77	80	Young forest
North Richibucto Dune	14/06/80	10	Dune grass
Mocauque de Pointe-Sapin	09/05/81	12	Muskeg
Polly's Creek	29/05/82	24	Forest and old burn
Porter's Pond	14/07/82	36	Mixedwood
South Kouchibouguac Dunes	29/04/83	50	Dune grass
Polly's Creek	18/06/83	10	Mixedwood
Fontaine River	27/04/83	10	
Fontaine Group Campground	04/05/83	10	
North Richibucto Dune	30/09/84	25	Dune grass
Rankin Brook	09/06/84	42	Mixedwood
Northside of Kouchibouguac River	01/05/84	40	
Rankin Brook	09/06/84	50	

*(L) - Lightning caused. All other fires were ignited through human activity.

grass to stimulate new grass growth, and to kill invading shrubby species. Even vegetation on the coastal dunes is susceptible to low intensity early spring burns when the green proportion of the biomass is small. The provincial fire suppression records list fires of over 50 ha in size in the years 1932, 1933, 1934, 1947, 1956, and 1957. Of these, the 1934 fires burned over 600 ha and the 1957 fires burned over 300 ha. A general fire rotation period of 340 years has been calculated for the general vegetation type in which Kouchibouguac National Park is located (Wein and Moore 1977), based on the fire suppression records of 1931 to 1975. Since the park was established in 1969, many individual fires have occurred primarily in dune grass and shrub communities. Because of the long list of fires, only those exceeding 10 ha in size have been given in Table 3. In most years there are less than five fires of 0.5 to 10 ha in size with a similar number of fires that are less than 0.5 ha. The year 1983 was unusual in that more than 25 small fires were reported in grass and shrubby vegetation.

In general terms, almost all of the fires in the Maritime National Parks were caused by human activity. The fires were small, compared to fires in the more arid regions of western North America, but there is wide variability in fire size and number of fires from year to year. It is the large but widely spaced fires which show the power of this environmental force. As has already been indicated, the fuel is always available in the eastern mixedwood forest so fire frequency is a function of low moisture weather conditions. In general, fire cannot be ignored and therefore some form of fire policy is necessary.

PRESENT POLICY TOWARD FIRE

With the wide range of degrees of protection and jurisdiction, and the large number of small areas scattered across the landscape, it is difficult to establish a separate policy for each conservation area for concerns such as fire. In the Province of New Brunswick, for example, fires on any forested land fall under the Provincial Forest Fire Act and the provincial fire suppression organization attacks all unscheduled fires. Several large forest industries with private land holdings provide initial suppression of unscheduled fires but the Province takes responsibility on arrival at the fire. Federal government agencies with land holdings may contract with the Province for fire protection or may provide their own protection. Although fires are to be viewed as a natural agent in National Parks (Lohnes 1981), in practice the Maritime Provinces National Parks follow a fire exclusion policy.

FUTURE RESPONSES OF ECOSYSTEMS WITHOUT FIRE

It is problematic as to whether fire suppression will become more effective as natural areas are surrounded by more intensive land uses and the associated greater number of ignition sources, but let us assume that it is possible for fire to be virtually excluded from natural areas. What are the consequences?

A general understanding of forest dynamics and simple observations in our National Parks indicate that habitat diversity will decrease with complete fire exclusion unless some other force such as insect attack or wind storms play a significant role. When Maritime National Parks were established the areas included farmland, cutovers, and other manipulated ecosystems. Since the natural environmental conditions are conducive to forest development, short-term changes include the invasion of white spruce into old fields and shrub and tree invasion into areas such as blueberry barrens. It is also thought that in the longer term, disturbance-oriented tree genera such as *Populus*, *Alnus* and *Betula* will decline in abundance and even fire dependent genera such as *Pinus* will become less important.

Simulation models produced by El-Bayoumi *et al.* (1984) suggest that forest communities will maintain a mixed hardwood condition in more southern regions and on southern slopes in more northern regions of the mixedwood forest. To the north, and on northern exposures further to the south, there will be a tendency for fewer tree species to be successful over time. Since the life span of many of these trees is several centuries (estimated maximum ages are *Pinus strobus* - 450; *Picea rubens* - 400; *Tsuga canadensis* - 900+; *Acer saccharum* - 400; *Fagus grandifolia* - 400 (El-Bayoumi *et al.* 1984)), a forest community has the potential to dominate a site for centuries.

It should be mentioned that other forest influences will continue to operate to retain ecosystem diversity even if fire is virtually excluded. Gap stand dynamics will be obvious as individual trees or groups of trees mature and die; wind throw and insect attack could also provide open areas in the communities. The effectiveness of the spruce budworm to remove virtually all of the mature balsam fir and much of the mature spruce from Fundy and Cape Breton Highlands National Parks provide a dramatic example of changes in forest composition. The spruce budworm-fire hypothesis raised in Furyaev *et al.* (1983) suggests that insect-killed forests are more susceptible to fire spread. This has been a serious concern in recent years but weather patterns have not been conducive to widespread and serious fires.

RE-INTRODUCING FIRE TO THE WILDERNESS

For the person responsible for re-introducing fire to wilderness and natural areas, many of the above generalized fire rotation periods and generalized ecosystem responses provide only useful background. A manager must deal with a specific piece of landscape, to which must be applied a specific treatment, at a specific point in time. Thus, it is imperative that goals related to fire must be clearly formulated.

These goals must be in keeping with the wilderness concept and an individual's enjoyment of wilderness; in many cases the goal will be to avoid all forms of human interference. Goals such as the removal of fuel hazards, or the removal of insect-damaged stands by fire may be appropriate because this is a natural role of fire; however, if the conservation area is surrounded by high density urbanization, the expected high intensity fires may not be permitted. It may be necessary to remove fuels mechanically or to dedicate higher fire suppression resources to protect the area for decades until the fuel decomposes biologically. Goals related to fire will likely be focused on specific areas in order to maintain the diversity of ecosystems. For example, wilderness users are very aware that organisms are attuned to all ages of forests and this means that trees growing at the maximum rate have the same ecological value as trees which are very old or even dead. Thus fires could be used to provide diversity. Fires could also be used to return artifacts of past human intervention (such as selective tree cutting) to a more natural community composition. Fires should not be seen as destroying ecosystems so much as providing opportunities for other phases of ecosystem responses. Crawford (1985) provides such an example where prescribed burns have been used to improve habitat for moose.

Establishment of the goals probably requires less financial commitment than predicting the outcome of procedures put in place to reach these goals. To successfully reach goals, it is necessary to predict the outcome of each management treatment so as to avoid future difficulties that detract from the wilderness concept. The predictive approaches and the subsequent management procedures that are necessary have become exceedingly complex. Natural resource management will always be accompanied by uncertainty which requires the application of adaptive management (Holling 1978, Baskerville 1984) and powerful decision-support systems for its resolution (Keen and Morton 1978; Maloney and Potter 1983; Kourtz 1981, 1984).

Forest industries and government forestry agencies in Canada, as in the United States, are utilizing geographic information systems (termed Expert Systems) that could be relatively easily adapted to wilderness and natural areas. Park managers believe that geographical information should be used more widely (Lopoukhine 1983) because natural resource management is becoming more complicated as many competing pressures become highly interactive. The Maritime National Parks already have detailed computer data banks of biophysical information and this information is being retrieved when needed; for example, when an impact statement becomes necessary.

What is now needed is to convert this information into a dynamic and interactive form so that it can be available quickly as an aid to short-term decision making in fire management. For example, if an ignition point is detected, the fuel on that specific site combined with the predicted weather patterns and a fire behavior model can be used to predict the rate-of-spread of the fire across the landscape day-to-day. The predictions enable the fire manager to mobilize equipment and personnel efficiently according to the established goals for the ecosystem in the pathway of the fire (see Kourtz 1984).

There are two further aspects of these approaches that are especially important for the long-term management of wilderness areas. First, to make predictions it is necessary to have accurate spatial data banks. Much effort has been expended in the past with field surveys, aerial photography and more recently with satellite imagery, but also to have models which predict the response of ecosystem units for years, decades and even centuries into the future. Managers can look forward to having spatial data banks up-dated more and more easily and accurately as digital remote sensing techniques develop. Secondly, temporal dynamic models are needed to predict the response of ecosystem units for years, decades and even centuries into the future.

There are many temporal models of population dynamics but fewer models that explore long-term population dynamics in temporal and spacial dimensions. For example, it might be of interest to explore over time the population dynamics of an animal species that requires resources from a range of landscapes. More of these models will become available as wilderness managers develop goals and then seek quantitative predictions. Should predictions from these models be incompatible with stated goals, then fire management strategies can be implemented to rectify the perceived problems.

In closing I wish to mention that these management decision support systems are not incompatible with wilderness because these systems simply organize information and make it available quickly when a fire management decision is necessary. Wilderness goals remain and good fire management systems will aid in perpetuating wilderness for future generations.

ACKNOWLEDGEMENTS

I wish to recognize the financial support of our studies in National Parks in terms of equipment and operating grants from the Natural Sciences and Engineering Research Council of Canada, Parks Canada, and the University of New Brunswick Research Fund. Parks Canada personnel have been generous with their time in many ways while field research was conducted, and more recently they assisted in locating fire suppression records. S.J. Woodley, Acting Superintendent, Fundy National Park, kindly provided comments on the draft manuscript. Students who have contributed to the research include Jane (Speer) Hadley, Michael P. Burzynski, Mohamed A. El-

Bayoumi, Karen A. Kelly, David A. MacLean, Janice M. Moore and Peter A. Thomas. Dr. Hewlette Crawford kindly read this paper at the conference.

LITERATURE CITED

Anderson, R.A. 1979. A Holocene record of vegetation and fire at Upper South Branch Pond in northern Maine. M. Sci. Thesis, Univ. of Maine, Orono, Maine.

Baskerville, G.L. 1984. Adaptive management - wood availability and habitat availability. Canadian Forestry and Wildlife Management Symposium, Vancouver.

Burzynski, M.P. 1984. Prehistoric fires and vegetation changes as recorded in peat from New Brunswick bogs. M. Sc. Thesis, Univ. of New Brunswick, Fredericton.

Crawford, H. 1985. Moose in eastern wilderness--a role for prescribed fire. In D.L. Kulhavy and R.N. Conner (eds.), Wilderness and natural areas in the eastern United States: A management challenge. Stephen F. Austin State Univ., Nacogdoches, Tex.

Day, G.W. 1953. The Indian as an ecological factor in the northeastern forest. Ecology 34:329-346.

El-Bayoumi, M.A., H.H. Shugart, Jr. and R.W. Wein. 1984. Modelling succession of eastern Canadian mixedwood forest. Ecol. Model. 21:175-198.

Fernow, B.E. 1912. Forest conditions of Nova Scotia. Comm. Conserv. Can., Ottawa.

Fraser, A.T. 1955. History of forest fires in Cape Breton. pp. 45-46 In 1955 Annu. Meeting, Atlantic Section, Can. Institute of Forestry, Kentville, Nova Scotia.

Furyaev, V.V., R.W. Wein and D.A. MacLean. 1983. Fire influences in Abies-dominated forests. pp. 221-234. In R.W. Wein and D.A. MacLean (eds.). The role of fire in northern circumpolar ecosystems. SCOPE 18, John Wiley and Sons, Chichester, England.

Ganong, W.F. 1902. Great fires in New Brunswick. Bull. Nat. Hist. Soc. N.B. 20:434-435.

Gimbarzevsky, P. 1975. Biophysical survey of Kejimkujik National Park. Can. For. Serv., Info. Rep. FMR-X-81.

Green, D.B. 1976. Nova Scotia forest history - evidence from statistical analysis of pollen data. Ph.D. Diss., Dalhousie University, Halifax, Nova Scotia.

Green, D.G. 1981. Time series and postglacial forest ecology. Quat. Res. 15:265-277.

Holling, C.S. 1978. Adaptive environment assessment and management. John Wiley & Sons, New York.

Keen, P.G.W. and M.S.S. Morton. 1978. Decision support systems: an organizational perspective. Addison-Vesley Publ. Co. Inc., Reading, Mass.

Kourtz, P.H. 1981. Computer applications to daily forest fire management decision-making in southwestern Quebec. Intermountain Fire Council Meeting, Salt Lake City, Utah.

Kourtz, P.H. 1984. Decision-making for centralized forest fire management. For. Chron. 60:320-327.

Little, S. 1974. Effects of fire on temperate forests; northeastern United States. pp. 225-250. In T.T. Kozlowski and C.E. Ahlgren (eds.). Fire and ecosystems. Academic Press, N.Y.

Lohnes, D. 1981. Towards a new fire policy. Natural Res. Bull. (Spring 1981), Parks Canada, Ottawa.

Lopoukhine, N. 1983. Parks Canada in the boreal forest ecosystem (a pilgrim's progress). pp. 167-179. In R.W. Wein, R.R. Riewe and I.R. Methven (eds.). Resources and dynamics of the boreal zone. Assoc. Can. Univ. for Northern Studies, Ottawa.

MacLean, D.W. 1975. Tobeatic Resource Management Area conceptual plan. Dept. Environ., Can. For. Serv., and Nova Scotia Dep. Land and Forests.

MacLean, D.A. and R.W. Wein. 1977. Nutrient accumulation for postfire jack pine and hardwood succession patterns in New Brunswick. Can. J. For. Res. 7:562-578.

Maloney, J.E. and M.V. Potter. 1983. The fire management system-the fire management centre-preliminary results and design concepts. Can. For. Serv., Info. Rep. FF-X-45.

Russell, E.W.B. 1983. Indian-set fires in the forest of the northeastern United States. Ecology 64:78-88.

Smith, T., Jr. 1801-02. A natural resources survey of Nova Scotia in 1801-1802. Notes transcribed from Public Archives of Nova Scotia. Vol. 380.

Thompson, D.Q. and R.H. Smith. 1970. The forest primeval in the northeast - a great myth. Tall Timbers Fire Ecol. Conf. 10:255-265.

Wein, R.W. and J.M. Moore. 1977. Fire history and rotations in the Acadian Forest of New Brunswick. Can. J. For. Res. 7:285-294.

Wein, R.W. and J.M. Moore. 1979. Fire history and recent fire rotation periods in the Nova Scotia Acadian Forest. Can. J. For. Res. 9:166-178.

"An area of wilderness is . . . an area of undeveloped Federal land retaining its primeval character and influence, . . . which is protected and managed so as to preserve its natural conditions and which . . . has outstanding opportunities for solitude or a primitive and unconfined type of recreation . . . "

This definition clearly indicates that while "naturalness" is essential, there is also an intended purpose and an intended use of such areas. These are much better defined in the "Eastern Wilderness Act" of January 3, 1975, which says that:

" . . . areas in the eastern half of the United States (shall) be . . . designated . . . in order to preserve . . . an enduring resource of wilderness which shall be managed to promote and perpetuate the wilderness character of the land **and its specific values of solitude, physical and mental challenge, scientific study, inspiration, and primitive recreation** . . . "(Underscoring provided.)

Even this better guidance left me somewhat unsatisfied, as how, for example, could a wilderness manager assure the retention of "primeval character and influence" in "mini-wilderness" areas, some of which are no larger than 1,100 acres (445 ha)? How could a wilderness manager provide a place for "physical and mental challenge" in small wilderness areas that are within sight and sound and smell of major highways, private lands, and residential and industrial development; and how could a wilderness manager provide opportunities for "solitude" and "inspiration" where high levels of day use are already firmly established without imposing very costly and highly unpopular systems for rationing use? While I could readily understand that a person who was standing up to his armpits in a 1,100 acre (445 ha) swamp full of alligators could find "physical and mental challenge," it was difficult for me to understand how a wilderness manager could evoke these feelings on a forested area that could be crossed on a well marked trail in an hour, or be jogged across in less than 20 minutes.

I carried these questions into a number of meetings, and once suggested--and only half in jest--that in small wilderness areas we should probably obliterate all trails, should remove all references to any included features in guide books, and should replace any physiographic or topographic aids on all hiking maps with a blank area and the simple statement that, "This designated wilderness area is unknown territory."

I was thoroughly convinced, however, that wilderness character and values would not happen nor continue to occur by accident or neglect--but that they could only occur through very careful and deliberate management actions.

A major conceptual breakthrough occurred for me in March of 1976 when the Department of the Interior officially notified the Senate Subcommittee on Parks and Recreation that it was planning to recognize three types of wilderness. The statement is as follows:

"Within the diversity of National Park System wilderness lands, three general types of wilderness or three wilderness zones can be identified because of their location, size or other factors affecting remoteness, and their volume of use."

"Some areas of wilderness have no constructed trails or facilities of any kind, may be extremely rugged, remote, and appeal primarily to the expert wilderness explorer or the scientist. This type of wilderness receives infrequent use and could be referred to as zone III since it is normally the most remote of the three wilderness zones."

"Other areas of wilderness have constructed trails but are a considerable distance away from access roads. These areas require several days to several weeks to visit and therefore appeal to those with the equipment, experience and time needed to make such a trip. This type of wilderness receives light use and could be referred to as zone II."

"Still other areas of wilderness have a number of constructed trails and are within a short distance of access roads. These areas typically appeal to novices or families with young children and are used primarily for a few hours to a day or two. This type of wilderness receives moderate to frequent use, requires the highest degree of management and maintenance of the three, and could be referred to as zone I."

An earlier memorandum had already noted that all of the proposed wilderness in Shenandoah would be of the last type.

Although the thought proved bothersome to some people, I felt comfortable with the idea that heavy day use could continue to occur along established travel corridors within the park's designated wilderness areas so long as "solitude" could be easily found elsewhere within the area, and so long as overnight use could be sufficiently well dispersed to keep its social and resource impacts within acceptable limits.

Sometime earlier, and expanding upon explicit instructions from Senator Frank Church, Nat Reed, the Assistant Secretary of Interior for Fish and Wildlife and Parks, had published a set of guidelines which spoke to the issues of management philosophy and appropriate facilities within designated wilderness areas. The guidelines formalize the "minimum tool" concept--stating that:

"The manager should use the minimum tool, equipment or structure necessary to successfully, safely and economically accomplish the objective. When establishing the minimum tool and equipment necessary for a management need within wilderness areas economic factors should be considered the least important of the three criteria. The chosen tool or equipment should be the one that least degrades wilderness values temporarily or permanently."

These guidelines listed a number of tools, equipment, structures, and practices that are acceptable within wilderness areas if they are determined to be "reasonably necessary"--using the words of Senator Church--"to serve the purposes of the wilderness area (as opposed to (being) simply for the comfort and convenience of park visitors)."

On November 10, 1975, National Park Service Director Gary Everhardt reiterated these instructions during a wilderness hearing before the House Subcommittee on National Parks and Recreation, and added a number of important trail management guidelines--saying that:

"Trail management is critical to providing for use that does not diminish the wilderness resource through which the trails pass. Trail location, maintenance, and use are all vital elements. An essential aspect of wilderness management is flexibility to change use patterns as necessary to protect resources and to achieve other management objectives. This may include closing some trails and constructing new ones at new locations within wilderness . . . Trails intended for foot travel only will maintained, generally, to a width sufficient for persons to walk single-file. Trails intended for combined foot and horse travel, or for horse travel only, will be maintained to a width sufficient for horses and their riders to travel single-file . . . .Trail bridges are permitted at stream crossings if the crossing, without a bridge, would be unsafe during the normal period of use. Signs are provided only where necessary for visitor safety, management, or resource protection. Interpretive information may be provided before the visitor enters the wilderness, but interpretive exhibits or devices will not be placed in wilderness. Along a wilderness trail there will be no facilities designed merely for the convenience of visitors such as dinking fountains, flush toilets, benches, or picnic tables."

He also noted that:

" . . . wilderness perpetuation requires constant monitoring of man's influences on natural processes and life systems, and responsive, careful management."With these various guidelines in hand, we were ready in October 1976 when the Congress designated nearly 80,000 acres (32,380 ha) of Shenandoah National Park--in three areas and 11 separate parcels--as components of the National Wilderness Preservation System--the three areas being roughly 3,000, 32,000, 41,000 acres in size. Excepting only the wilderness areas in the Everglades and the Okefenokee swamp in the south, and the Boundary Waters Canoe Area and Isle Royale in the far north, this makes the designated wilderness area in Shenandoah--as small as it may be--by far the largest in eastern America.

We recognized, through its relatively small size, its already established levels and patterns of visitor use, and the presence of immediately adjacent nonconforming land use activities, that our wilderness area was not of the highest order--and immediately adopted a "non-degradation" policy. We said that "while our wilderness area is not supreme, we will **not** allow its primeval character, and its opportunities for solitude, inspiration, and physical and mental challenges to decline. Furthermore, we will strive, and might be able, to improve its overall quality."

During the next 18 months we implemented the wilderness designation. Included in this activity was the removal of an included trail shelter; the installation of bear-proof concrete trail sign posts at each trail junction; and the removal of all other signs, to include those which

had identified springs or water developments. We removed all man-made water developments, except for those that were constructed prior to 1930 by former inhabitants, and which we considered to be cultural resource remnants. We closed and back-sloped all borrow and dump sites; and removed much of the fence wire and "non-historic" trash and debris located near the included fire roads. These roads were then "put to bed." This involved the filling of uphill drainage ditches, the physical removal of shallow culverts, and the cutting of water bars to restore natural drainage; and the permanent blockage of the roads to prevent further vehicular access. All such work was performed in a manner that allowed horseback use to be continued. Each former road was re-designated as a horse or foot trail, and all maps and publications were revised to accommodate these changes. These and other actions, to include the removal of fire tower and an overhead powerline, and the transference of a number of special access permits to other administrative roads, also allowed us to designate an additional 560 acres (227 ha) of potential wilderness as wilderness through publication of a Federal Register notice on September 1, 1978.

We also began a series of studies about the then current level and type of visitor use by area and by trail; entertained a study by the University of West Virginia into the desires and expectations of overnight backcountry users; and began an inventory of the heavily impacted use areas so the progress and results of our backcountry and wilderness planning could be monitored and evaluated. With regard to the overnight backcountry user study, we were very pleased to find a very high level of user satisfaction with our backcountry management regulations, as their descending order of preferences were:

1. to find solitude while camping,
2. to select their own personal campsite,
3. to enjoy solitude while hiking,
4. to camp where there is no evidence of previous use,
5. to have campfires, (which we do not permit)
6. to meet other backpackers,
7. to contact park personnel,
8. to make use of permanent shelters, and
9. to stay in developed campsites.

At the same time, efforts were begun to reduce the volume of non-wilderness use within designated wilderness areas. There was no reason, for example, for us to continue to accommodate park visitors who were seeking a simple outdoors experience inside of a designated wilderness area **if** this use could be readily transferred elsewhere. To try to do so, we reduced our foot trail standards within wilderness areas to single-file width, and allowed downfall and branches to remain in place if they could be safely crossed or ducked under by a person carrying a backpack. Obstructions were left on wilderness horse trails if they could be safely crossed by a horse and rider-- and if they did not, in themselves, create a drainage or other maintenance problem. Troublesome trail access routes leading into wilderness areas were abandoned and obliterated, as were redundant parallel trails and short spur trails within wilderness areas. These latter actions were intended, also, to encourage "bushwhacking" and to permit personal discoveries of special view points, waterfalls, and other "secret places." Park trails and trailhead parking areas leading into wilderness areas were given new and non-specific names to discourage casual, destination-oriented visitor use. At the same time, we removed most references to specific wilderness destinations from park informational materials, hiking maps, and trail signs.

In order to entice non-wilderness use away from wilderness areas, efforts were made in park literature and on hiking maps to focus attention on trails and destination points in non-wilderness areas. Plans were made for parking areas leading to non-wilderness areas to be enlarged, new trail systems in non-wilderness areas were designed, and signing was altered accordingly. All persons who applied for backcountry permits and who did not have specific areas or destinations in mind were encouraged, through suggestion, to utilize lesser-used non-wilderness areas.

We then tried to reduce the intensity of adjacent uses that might have a discordant effect upon the character of designated wilderness areas. An example was our removal of a nearby trail shelter to reduce the attractiveness of that area to use by boisterous, and often illegal, teenage gatherings.

Our current efforts are directed toward a better understanding of our park wildlife, and toward the discovery and correction of any possible negative interactions with our wilderness users. We are monitoring visitor use impacts, with special emphasis on sensitive environmental areas, and in heavy-use areas. We hope, through our continuing management actions, to be able to continue to accommodate a high level of use without unacceptable impacts upon our natural and wilderness resources, and to do so with a minimum of regulations and use limits.

All of these ideas and activities have been incorporated into the park's overall General Management Plan.

The result of these various activities--and following approximately 8 years of testing--is that we now have management plans and programs in place that are well related to our wilderness objectives, and are well accepted by our full spectrum of National Park visitors.

Can Wilderness Remain Untrammeled Without Restricting Use? A Case History Of Management In Shining Rock Wilderness

by

Paul J. Wright

ABSTRACT--When Shining Rock Wilderness was designated in 1964, managers had no idea that use would exceed projections by nearly 500%. Heavy use caused physical and social impacts, and efforts to monitor and manage use patterns were begun.

KEYWORDS: wilderness, distribution of use, indirect management, volunteer rangers, Shining Rock.

The 13,400-acre (5,423 ha) Shining Rock Wilderness in western North Carolina was established with the passage of the Wilderness Act of 1964 (P.L. 88-577). The area was expanded to 18,500 acres (7,490 ha) in 1984 with the addition of recommended RARE II lands. In two decades, annual use has increased from 2,800 recreation visitor days (RVD) to 120,000 RVD. This increase was due, in part, to some early concepts of wilderness management that succeeded beyond anyone's expectations.

The initial Wilderness Management Plan drafted in 1964 focused on strategies to promote visits, including construction of a road from the Blue Ridge Parkway to the Wilderness boundary at Ivestor Gap in 1966. Fortunately, this road was terminated 2 miles (3.2 km) short of the boundary, at Black Balsam. It presently is the entry portal for over half of all visitors to Shining Rock. Traffic on the Blue Ridge Parkway increased nearly 200% between 1964 and 1984, and the segment serving the Black Balsam Road carries over 1 million vehicles annually.

Early Forest Service planners noted that few campers used the Shining Rock Area, and assumed that Scouts and other outdoor-oriented youth groups would be the major users in the future. Hiking, horseback riding, and fishing were expected to increase, while hunting would decline due to transition to a mature forest habitat. Intensive public information efforts, such as promotional brochures and maps, were planned to encourage use. Furthermore, a new network of trails was to be developed to assist and encourage use of the Wilderness. Projections of future use in this initial plan reached 24,500 RVD by the year 2000. This figure was exceeded within 10 years of designation.

Agency planners of this era also failed to anticipate the "outdoor boom" of the late 1960's through the mid 70's.

Based on historical trends, their estimates were probably realistic at the time. However, a survey conducted by the Bureau of Outdoor Recreation in 1965 showed that 9.9 million Americans hiked or backpacked, while a Heritage Conservation and Recreation Service (HCRS) survey revealed that 28.1 million were participating by 1977 (Spencer *et al.* 1980). This threefold growth in one decade was a common phenomenon nationwide. And areas that the public thought of as "wilderness", regardless of designation, were absolutely magnetic in their attraction of these new outdoor enthusiasts.

Land managers turned to controls that promised immediate relief from the unexpected flood of visitors. Wilderness Entry Permits were commonplace by the early seventies, and use rationing was applied to the "saturated" wilderness areas of the Far West. This regulatory approach helped somewhat to stem the rapid increase in physical resource impacts. A growing population of wilderness users came to accept reservations and use rationing as a means to preserve the wilderness they sought to enjoy (Fazio and Gilbert 1974). The mandatory permit system was initiated in Shining Rock in 1974 to develop a data base for management decisions and to provide a contact point to inform wilderness users of regulations and appropriate backcountry behavior.

THE SECOND DECADE

A growing body of wilderness "professionals" recognized that enforcement-oriented direct management techniques were contradictory to the philosophical qualities of wilderness: freedom of choice and lack of managerial constraints (Stankey 1971, 1973; Gilbert *et al.* 1972; Lucas 1973, 1982; Peterson 1974; Stankey *et al.*

1974; Stankey and Baden 1977; Bradley 1979; Roggenbuck and Berrier 1980). Managers and researchers also grappled with the questions of physical and social carrying capacity, especially in areas perceived as overcrowded. The National Forest Management Act directed that wilderness plans would:

"Provide for limiting and distributing visitor use of specific portions in accord with periodic estimates of the maximum levels of use that allow natural processes to operate freely and that do not impair the values for which wilderness areas were created" (U.S. Fed. Register 1979).

Unfortunately, as recently as 1980, 85% of all National Forest wilderness areas had not established carrying capacity. At the same time, managers of 73% of these areas indicated that use appeared to exceed capacity at some time during the year. Shining Rock was, and is, typical of this situation. It operates under an estimated carrying capacity of 56,100 RVD/yr., but actual use is approximately twice that.

Numbers *per se* are not the only indicators of overcrowding. Uneven distribution of use in time and space increases the potential for unacceptable social and physical impacts (Roggenbuck and Berrier 1980). Furthermore, user behavior is more critical than sheer numbers. In Shining Rock, 35% of the trail system--or less than 0.02% of the total land base--accommodates 85% of the use. Five of the seven primary trails converge on one point: Shining Rock Gap. Sixty-five percent of all visitors to the Wilderness were observed in 1978 to pass through the Gap, and over half of all overnight visitors camped at or near this spot (Roggenbuck et al. 1979). As Saunders (1985) points out, over 2200 square meters of this camp spot were denuded in 1979; it was the largest single backcountry camp in the Appalachian's Balsam Mountains.

The 1978 VPI&SU survey in Shining Rock revealed that visitors to the area were predominantly young, educated males with a slightly more rural and blue collar component than typical wilderness users (Roggenbuck *et al.* 1979). They came in small groups, usually of four or less, and about half remained at least one night. About half their time was spent hiking on trails in the area. Keeping in mind that half the overnight users stayed at Shining Rock Gap, it is understandable that over 60% of the users felt that devegetation and fire rings were a problem, and that 30% felt they were a major problem. The predominant problem voiced by all visitors to Shining Rock was litter, closely followed by the presence of too many people in certain locations. Typically, these users encountered five other groups per day, including one large group (over 6 people). They generally camped within sight or sound of at least one other group. Although overall satisfaction with the wilderness experience was

good, respondents indicated that slight increases in encounter levels or numbers of nearby campers would sharply decrease their satisfaction. Nearly all agreed that there were not too many regulations, and about half felt that controls on use were currently needed. Interestingly, nearly two-thirds of these visitors expressed a need for more information on heavily used areas and times of year.

Apparently, the problem was not the total number of users, but where they congregated, and how they behaved. Users tended to be tolerant of higher use levels than resource managers predicted, and sensitive to environmental conditions. And most importantly, users were receptive to information. As Bradley (1979) observed, inappropriate wilderness behavior is done "more out of ignorance and lack of sensitivity than from malicious destructiveness."

With this picture of the social makeup of Shining Rock, researchers from VPI&SU came back the following season to see what could be done to modify patterns of use (Roggenbuck and Berrier 1980). It was thought that a program to inform and educate wilderness visitors would be instrumental in dispersing use, since Shining Rock visitors, like many other wilderness users, had a limited knowledge of the alternatives available to them (Lime and Lucas 1977, Hendee et al. 1978, Hulbert and Higgins 1977). Furthermore, few wilderness and backcountry users actively seek out information from land managers when planning their trip (Schomaker 1975, Fazio and Bramlette 1977, Taylor and MacKay 1978, Krumpe 1979).

Very little experimentation had been conducted heretofore on redistributing wilderness campers. Most studies had been directed at hiking. The configuration of the trail system in Shining Rock--like the spokes of a wheel--suggested little could be done to change the way that people negotiated the terrain. It was also felt that changing a campsite location would require less behavioral change than altering a route selection. Therefore, the emphasis would be on campsite selection. This was all the more important, since supporting research indicated that wilderness users were more sensitive to contacts with others at campsites than on the trail (Stankey 1973, Hendee et al. 1978).

Researchers had to select the style, mode, source and channel of communication that offered the greatest prospect for success. The informational message was selected over instructional or motivational messages, since camper preferences had already been established (Roggenbuck et al. 1979). Shining Rock users were looking for alternatives. To increase the receptiveness and effectiveness of the message, it was felt that it should be delivered by an "outdoor professional", such as a uniformed ranger, with follow-up written material.

This research revealed that personal contacts were most effective with inexperienced campers and small groups. However, contacts had to be made early in the day, or near the trailhead, to be significantly more effective than a brochure and map alone. During this study, up to 30% of the overnight campers were reported to have selected alternative sites over periods when no information was available. Acceptance of both verbal and written information seemed to be very high. Unexpectedly, the advantage of verbal contacts over written information in dispersing use was not statistically significant. This result may have been due, in part, to the demonstrated desire of Shining Rock users to locate alternative sites to Shining Rock Gap.

Since this study demonstrated the feasibility of dispersing use and suggested additional opportunities for behavioral modification, through instruction, the Pisgah Ranger District discontinued its permit program in 1982 in favor of a wilderness ranger system. The permit system had been fairly successful in documenting numbers of users, but a failure in terms of imparting any sort of message regarding wilderness behavior.

Four volunteer rangers have been recruited each year since 1982. For the first 2 years, they worked at litter clean-up, fire ring disposal, trail maintenance, and visitor contact. The emphasis of contacts was informational, with some discussion of appropriate wilderness behavior--the "No trace" ethic.

In 1984, a VPI&SU researcher studied visitor perceptions of volunteer ranger contacts and the effectiveness of contacts in reducing site impacts within the wilderness (Irwin 1985). Some of the results of this study reinforced Roggenbuck et al. (1979), in that visitors were generally satisfied with their experience. Of particular interest is the change in perception of litter problems. Seventy-three percent agreed that there was little trailside litter, and 80% said there was little campsite litter. This is a drastic departure from the 1978 survey, in which 83% of respondents viewed litter as a problem. In 1978, 87% also felt that wilderness conditions were the same or worse than on previous visits. By contrast, in 1984 over 80% of return users indicated that litter conditions were at least the same or better.

On the other hand, more respondents felt that fire rings and damaged trees were a growing problem--over half said it was about the same as in previous visits while about one quarter indicated there were more fire rings and damaged trees. There may be a correlation between visitor dispersal and proliferation of fire rings. Visitor attitudes also play a part. Removing fire rings and preserving dead standing wood were the two least acceptable aspects of the "No Trace" camping techniques promoted by the volunteer rangers.

The role the volunteer wilderness rangers played in achieving the reported changes in site conditions in Shining Rock is not entirely clear. Visitors indicated they felt unthreatened by contact with the rangers, and largely accepted that their information could be helpful. However, it remains to be seen if the techniques and attitudes presented to visitors over the last 3 years will truly become a way of life in the wilderness. The lack of litter and the grass growing in Shining Rock Gap are certainly encouraging signs.

THOUGHTS FOR THE FUTURE

Shining Rock Wilderness may be thought of as passing through adolescence. The past two decades were characterized by a lot of experimentation, testing of limits, and emerging awareness of the role of wilderness in the greater National Forest system. We must keep the fundamental charter of the Wilderness Act in mind: "Wilderness areas . . . shall be administered for the use and enjoyment of the American people in such manner as will leave them unimpaired for future use and enjoyment as wilderness, and so as to provide for the protection of these areas, the preservation of their wilderness character, and for the gathering and dissemination of information regarding their use and enjoyment as wilderness . . . "(PL88-577).

Clearly, wilderness is a resource for "use and enjoyment." But it is also one to be preserved, and left unimpaired by such use and enjoyment. Towards that end Hendee (1985), suggests five management principles:
(1) Be biocentric--manage to preserve the physical resource upon which the wilderness experience is dependent.
(2) Do only what is necessary--allow natural processes to predominate.
(3) Apply the nondegradation concept--do not accept human impact as inevitable and unavoidable.
(4) Involve the public--as stewards of the public trust, work to make wilderness what the American public wants it to be.
(5) Use minimum tools--remain light-handed in your management approach. Do not over-regulate.

These principles, together with the basic direction contained in the Act, suggest that as Shining Rock moves toward maturity, two unresolved problems remain:
(1) Levels of use--although total use has not been as serious a situation as distribution and behavior, it threatens to compromise the opportunity for solitude over time.
(2) Type of experience--primitive and unconfined recreation use, involving mental and physical challenge, should be the predominant activity in the wilderness.

Management objectives that may help resolve these problems include:
(1) Identify users whose experience does not depend on unique physical conditions within the wilderness.
(2) Redirect such users to nonwilderness areas.
(3) Increase the degree of mental and physical challenge encountered by users of the wilderness.
(4) Restore and protect areas where past use has degraded the wilderness resource.

Management actions that may work towards meeting these objectives include:
(1) Conduct further research to determine how to identify nonwilderness-dependent users, and how to influence their selection of an off-site alternative.
(2) Inventory and identify off-site opportunities.
(3) Lower trail, sign and map standards at and within wilderness boundary.
(4) Emphasize wilderness conditions that would be perceived as negative by potential users, such as frequent rainfall, lack of signs, poor trails, toxic plants, noxious insects and reptiles . . . and so on.
(5) Improve access to nonwilderness "backcountry".
(6) Intensify informational campaign directed at users and potential users. Seek to educate these people in unique properties of and practices in wilderness.

While this "laundry list" is not complete, it should provide some sense of purpose and direction as present and future wilderness managers work towards fulfilling the potential of Shining Rock. It can, and must, be an area where the physical and social values mandated by Congress are retained, without undue restrictions on the freedom and enjoyment of the wilderness visitor. It can remain untrammeled, without confining use.

LITERATURE CITED

Bradley, J. 1979. Human approach to reducing wildland impacts. Rec. Impacts on Wildlands, Seattle, Wash. pp. 222-226.

Fazio, J.R., and D.L. Gilbert. 1974. Mandatory wilderness permits: some indications of success. J. For. 72: 753-756.

Fazio, J.R. and W.W. Bramlette. 1977. Communicating with the wilderness user. Final Rep. to PNW Reg. Comm., For., Wildlife and Range Exp. Stn., Univ. of Idaho, Moscow, Idaho.

Gilbert, C.B., G.L. Peterson and D.W. Lime. 1972. Toward a model of travel behavior in the Boundary Waters Canoe Area. Environ. and Behav. 4:131-157.

Hendee, J.C., G.H. Stankey and R.C. Lucas. 1978. Wilderness Management. USDA For. Serv. Misc. Publ. 1365, Washington, D.C.

Hendee, J.C. 1986. Wilderness: Legal, social, philosophical and management perspectives. Wilderness and Natural Areas in the Eastern U.S.: A Management Challenge. D.L. Kulhavy and R.N. Conner (eds.). Center for Applied Studies, School of Forestry, SFASU, Nacogdoches, TX.

Hulbert, J.H. and F.J. Higgins. 1977. Boundary Waters Canoe Area visitor distribution system. J. For. 75:338-340.

Irwin, K.M. 1985. Wilderness visitor response to ranger educational contacts at trailheads. Unpubl. Master Thesis (draft), VPI&SU, Blacksburg, Virginia.

Krumpe, E.E. 1979. Redistributing backcountry use by a behaviorally based communications device. Unpubl. Ph.D. Diss., Colorado State Univ., Ft. Collins, Colo.

Lime, D.W. and R.C. Lucas. 1977. Good information improves the wilderness experience. Naturalist 28:4 pp.

Lucas, R.L. 1973. Wilderness: A management framework. J. Soil Water Conserv. 28(4):150-154.

Lucas, R.L. 1982. Recreation Regulations - When are they needed? J. For. 80:148-151.

Peterson, G.L. 1974. Evaluating the quality of the wilderness and environment: Congruence between perceptions and aspirations. Environ. and Behav. 6:169-193.

Roggenbuck, J.W., W.N. Timm and A.E. Watson. 1979. Visitor perception of the recreation carrying capacity of three wilderness areas in North Carolina. Unpubl. rep. on file at Dep. of For., VPI&SU, Blacksburg, Va.

Roggenbuck, J.W. and D.L. Berrier. 1980. The effectiveness of information on dispersing Wilderness Campers. Unpubl. rep. on file at Dep. of For., VPI&SU, Blacksburg, Va.

Saunders, P.R. 1986. Shining Rock Wilderness: Impacts of dispersed use. In D.L. Kulhavy and R.N. Conner (eds.). Wilderness and Natural Areas in Eastern United States: A management challenge. Center for Applied Studies, School of Forestry, Stephen F. Austin State Univ., Nacogdoches, TX.

Spencer, E.L., H.E. Echelberger, R.E. Leonard and C. Evans. 1980. Trends in hiking and backcountry use. USDA For. Serv. Tech. Rep. NE-57.

Stankey, G.H. 1971. The perception of wilderness carrying capacity: A geographic study in natural resource management. Ph.D. Diss. Mich. State Univ., Ann Arbor, Mich.

Stankey, G.H. 1973. Visitor perception of wilderness recreation carrying capacity. USDA For. Serv. Res. Pap. INT-192.

Stankey, G.H., R.L. Lucas and D.W. Lime. 1974. Patterns of wilderness use as related to congestion and solitude. Annu. Mtg. Assn. Am. Geogr., Seattle, Wash.

Stankey, G.H. and J. Baden. 1977. Rationing wilderness use methods, problems and guidelines. USDA For. Serv. Res. Pap. INT-192.

Schomaker, J.H. 1975. Effect of selected information on dispersal of wilderness recreationists. Unpubl. Ph.D. Diss., Colorado State Univ., Ft. Collins, Colo.

Taylor, D.T. and R.D. MacKay. 1978. Backcountry information and education recommendations. AMC, Res. Dep.

The Wilderness Manager And The Mass Media

by
Thomas M. Webb, Jr.

ABSTRACT--Successful Wilderness/Land Management will depend largely on the manager's ability to guide the affected public's perception of the activity. It is imperative that managers with this responsibility improve on and increase utilization of the mass media.

KEYWORDS: mass media, news reporters.

Wilderness management is a relatively new, if not newborn, addition to the responsibilities of land managers here in the East. Like many other new ideas or programs, wilderness management is a highly controversial, sometimes volatile, issue. And like many other controversies, this one is often intensified by lack of understanding fueled by the dissemination of misinformation and half-truths. If everyone can agree with this idea, then it stands to reason that part of the wilderness manager's job is to diffuse controversy through the dissemination of accurate, factual information concerning the issue. We, as public land managers have a story to tell about our activities and we should remember this: If you don't tell it, someone else is apt to tell it for you. And that someone else may be your worst adversary and very adept at slanting the story to your detriment.

An extremely effective way to get information out is by one-on-one contact. But I think you will all agree that you do not have the time or resources to reach a great many publics via this route. However, I would encourage managers to contact influential people in their local areas when possible.

The mass media--television, radio, and newspapers--offer alternatives to direct contact. They are efficient for conveying simple messages to large numbers of people. These media are used extensively and artfully by vocal critics of public land management. It behooves the wilderness manager to increase and improve upon his or her use of the same media if the affected publics are going to have benefit of the true story. This is not to say that criticism will disappear; it may even heighten. However, I have and will continue to believe that the truth will come out in the end. The affected public will have the opportunity to discern for themselves.

Over the past few years I have had the opportunity to make some observations about working with the media.

These are not new or unusual, but sometimes it is beneficial to review the old and usual.

(A) Reading Jack Anderson's news column about the latest bunglings of government or watching "20/20"'s Jeraldo Rivera barge into offices of unalerted and unwilling interviewees causes a deep inner feeling of being all alone when you suddenly learn a mass media team wants you to grant an interview on a controversial subject. Well, strange as it may seem, not all media people are "gremlins." In fact, most are pretty decent folk with a job to do just like most of your other contacts. A few may be thorns in your side, but you will quickly be able to recognize these and deal with them accordingly.

(B) Media crews prefer to deal with managers rather than public relations specialists. This can be attributed to the "I'd rather hear it from the horse's mouth" syndrome.

(C) News people often develop a distrust when their request for an interview is denied. Think back to the last time you watched "20/20" or "60 Minutes" when the reporter stated "X was contacted but refused to be interviewed." The viewer or reader is left with the distinct impression that the refusal to be interviewed indicates all is not right and that the individual must have something to hide.

(D) Relating to a news reporter is much easier than relating to a group of your peers. In an interview about your business or profession, you have the luxury of knowing more about the subject than the interviewer knows.

RECOMMENDATIONS

These observations have evolved for me over the past few years and after several opportunities to meet and deal with media people. From these I have formulated a few recommendations:

1. Make an effort to get to know and establish a working relationship with your local media. Try to become familiar with their deadline dates and times.

2. Be alert to situations and happenings within your agency or area that are of local, regional, or national interest. Contact your media representatives and get the word out.

3. If you are contacted by the media concerning a news item and a request for an interview, try to accommodate--even on short notice. This type of cooperation and response builds a good rapport. Remember, you are dealing with a very powerful force. The better and stronger your working relationship is with the media, the better you will fare.

4. Always be honest with your media contacts. Nothing will destroy your rapport quicker or deadlier than to lie to your media contact. If you do not know the answer to a particular question, there is no better answer than, "I really don't know the answer to that, but I can find out and get back with you." Then follow-up. Find the answer and relate it to your media contact as soon as possible.

5. If you experience a development in your organization that is likely to be controversial and you would like to have some control over how this development is related to the public, remember that the best defense is a good offense. The public response is usually greatest to the initial release or series of releases. Often, releases can and should be orchestrated so that cooperating agencies and educational or other organizations produce carefully planned series of releases on the topic.

Natural resource managers have traditionally operated somewhat in a vacuum as far as public relations are concerned. This tradition is no longer a valid alternative. Your success as a wilderness manager and natural resource manager will depend heavily on how well you are able to keep your public informed.

5

Visitor Needs And User Impact

by
H. Ken Cordell, Michael H. Legg, and Karen E. Cathey

The intent of Congress in establishing a National Wilderness System was to protect areas of federal land where there were outstanding opportunities for solitude and the imprint of man's presence was essentially unnoticeable. However, as wilderness use has increased the opportunities for solitude in a pristine environment is often threatened by the presence and impact of large numbers of visitors. The papers in this section deal with management issues generated by users that affect the recreational carrying capacity of wilderness areas.

The carrying capacity of a wilderness area can be divided into three major components:
1. The capacity of the resource to bear the impact of recreational activity;
2. The users attitudes and perceptions of wilderness and the manner in which these affect visitor behavior; and
3. The management regulations and activities that affect visitor behavior.

All of the above combine to determine the quality of the wilderness recreation experience received by the visitor.

The impacts users have on the natural resources of a wilderness area vary greatly. Often the attraction of crowds to a popular site within a wilderness area causes damage to the actual experience the area was established to protect. The most common problems involve compaction of soil, alteration of vegetation, and pollution of water. What was once a sloping grassy meadow may become a bare eroded hillside due to overuse by campers or injudicious grazing of livestock. Beyond the vegetative damage from an occasional escaped campfire is the destruction that occurs as users collect firewood. The pollution of wilderness streams and lakes by visitors has led to disease problems such as Giardiasis.

Solutions to user impacts include: dispersion and limitation of use, closure of heavily impacted areas for restoration, and increased maintenance to rejuvenate impacted areas. Other solutions include the manipulation of user behavior through educational programs on minimum impact camping and wilderness courtesy.

The users perceptions and attitudes concerning wilderness are largely influenced by previous experience and education. Those that are familiar with information concerning visitor impact seem to be more perceptive of the changes that are occurring due to wilderness use and are more conducive to management practices and regulations to control the damage. The effectiveness of management through information depends upon clear definition of desired wilderness conditions. Attitudes formed by visiting one wilderness area may not be appropriate in another. Educational efforts must be tailored to the resources and visitors of each area. Personal contacts with users have been shown repeatedly to be the most valuable form of contact available in accomplishing management goals.

Management practices are perhaps the most important component of wilderness carrying capacity. Managers, through their decisions on factors such as the initial selection, the extent of site maintenance, and the amount of visitor regulations, affect not only the quality of each wilderness recreation experience but the overall quality of experiences available.

The changes that have occurred in Wilderness use over the past several years, not only in number of users, but in the technology affecting wilderness camping supplies have forced managers to become more aware of visitor behavior patterns. The decreasing size of wilderness areas, especially those in the highly populated eastern half of the U.S., will also force reconsideration of management techniques and emphasize the importance of good communications with users.

Perhaps the most important consensus from the papers in this section was that wilderness users have demonstrated an amazing willingness to modify their behavior in order to protect the resource and the quality of their own recreation experience when regulations are clear and well explained.

MANAGEMENT IMPLICATIONS

Our interpretation of the principal implications of the papers presented in this section follow:
1. Permits and rationing measures can successfully reduce resource impacts and such measures will for the most part be acceptable to users.
2. The diversity of physical settings represented by the

National Wilderness Preservation System probably results in a diversity of personal expectations and experiences and thus may create a need for diverse management practices.

3. Impact monitoring and strategies to alleviate impacts are necessary for an integrated, effective wilderness management program.

4. Camping use should be targeted to wilderness sites that have the most resistance to human impact. Impact resistance classification methodology is needed.

5. Information should be used as a management tool to affect dispersal of users. Effectiveness of management with information depends on clear definition of desired wilderness conditions, and potential redistribution of impacts should be considered.

6. Classification of wilderness areas by use density will likely prove more useful for managing and for applying research findings than the previously used east-west dichotomy.

7. Development and other conversions of forest land should consider their impacts on the availability of roadless areas as Wilderness System candidates or as substitute sites for wilderness experiences.

Eastern/Western Wilderness Use And Users

by
Franklin E. Boteler

ABSTRACT--The National Wilderness Preservation System has significantly changed during the last ten years. During 1984 a large amount of acreage was added to the system. New wilderness units are smaller and more heavily used. In recent years wilderness use has leveled off. Research conducted to date reveals few differences between eastern and western wilderness visitors. The value of drawing a dichotomy between eastern and western wilderness use is questionable.

KEYWORDS: wilderness users, wilderness use.

The definition of America, its cultural values and heritage, has been patterned by a wilderness tradition (Nash 1973). Indeed, noted historian Frederick Jackson Turner argued that the presence of an untamed frontier was a prerequisite to the formation of our capitalistic democracy. For Turner (1920), the character and culture of a people are shaped by their environment.

In this technological, information-age society such seminal ideals have been articulated in the designation of the National Wilderness Preservation System (P.L. 88-577). A concern with wilderness management naturally followed this organizational structuring of primitive lands into a system. Interest in management of the system has generated a considerable amount of scientific investigations.

In 1978 the results of this scientific effort was synthesized with the publication of *Wilderness Management* by Hendee, Stankey, and Lucas (1978). The text centers upon concerns with the National Wilderness Preservation System (NWPS) as it existed in 1977. At that time the NWPS was typified by relatively large wilderness units in the west.

Since that time many units have been added to the NWPS. However, it is widely recognized that these new wilderness units are different than the "instant wilderness" designated in 1964. In particular, resolution of the Alaska Native Claims Settlement Act (P.L. 92-203), passage of the so called Eastern Wilderness Act (P.L. 93-622), and the recent designation of many new wilderness areas have done much to change the image of what constitutes a typical wilderness area.

GROWTH OF THE NWPS

Following resolution of the release clause controversy, Congress designated many new wilderness units during 1984. "Fully one-third of all the designated wilderness in the lower forty-eight was enacted in just one year--1984" (Scott 1984). Twenty-one bills were passed into law classifying 6,819,917 acres (2,760,020 ha) as wilderness in the contiguous 48 states (Table 1). The number of USDA Forest Service units increased from 165 to 329.

The new wilderness units are smaller in size than their predecessors (Table 2). In 1983 the mean size of eastern wilderness units was 9700 acres (3,925 ha). The 1984 eastern additions had an average size of 8895 acres (3,600 ha). Likewise, in 1983 the mean size of western wilderness units was 111,553 acres (45,146 ha). The 1984 additions averaged 45,076. Clearly, many smaller wilderness units have been added to the NWPS since the research was synthesized by Hendee *et al.* (1978).

EVOLVING PATTERNS OF WILDERNESS USE

During the 1960's and 1970's visitation to National Forest Wilderness greatly increased. "From 1965 to 1975, visitor days (the new unit of measure) increased 66 percent while visits probably nearly doubled (data gaps prevent precise calculations). Population grew only about 10 percent in the period" (Hendee *et al.* 1978, pp. 307).

However, recently wilderness visitation has dropped off. Van Doren (1984) reports a leveling-off of dispersed recreation demand and the USDA Forest Service recorded a decrease of 1,248,800 visitor days on wilderness units during fiscal year 1983.

In spite of the recent leveling-off of wilderness visitation, the density of use has increased. In 1975 the mean visitor days/acre of eastern wilderness was 1.33. By 1983 it had increased to 1.75. For western wilderness areas mean visitor days/acre in 1975 was 0.40. In 1983 it was 0.72. In particular, many of the eastern wilderness areas support higher densities of use (Table 3).

EASTERN/WESTERN WILDERNESS USERS

The possibility of broad-range, significant differences between eastern and western wilderness has been a source of academic debate for the last several years. Most experts agree that the resource setting is different. Eastern areas are generally smaller, closer to major metropolitan areas, dominated by hardwood forest, and more likely to be in proximity to non-conforming uses (Cermak 1976, Tim 1980). However, debate continues regarding possible differences between eastern and western wilderness users.

In Tables 4 and 5 the patterns of use and socioeconomic descriptors of eastern wilderness users are compared to western wilderness visitors. Publications by Lime (1976) and Hendee et al. (1978) summarize the results from many studies of western wilderness users. Henwood's (1977) thesis discusses the characteristics of wilderness visitors in three areas of Western Canada--Banff, Mt. Assiniboine, and Waterloo Lakes.

Table 1.   Wilderness Bills Enacted in the 98th Congress (USFS Holdings).

Title	Act	Acres
Western wilderness:		
Lee Metcalf Wilderness Act	P.L. 98-140	253,000
Irish Wilderness Act	P.L. 98-289	16,500
Oregon Wilderness Act	P.L. 98-358	852,962
Washington Wilderness Act	P.L. 98-339	1,021,933
Arizona Wilderness Act	P.L. 98-406	767,390
California Wilderness Act	P.L. 98-425	1,778,782
Utah Wilderness Act	P.L. 98-428	749,550
Wyoming Wilderness Act	P.L. 98-550	884,129
Texas Wilderness Act	P.L. 98-574	34,346
San Juan Wilderness Act	P.L. 98-603	20
		6,358,612
Eastern wilderness:		
Wisconsin Wilderness Act	P.L. 98-321	24,339
Vermont Wilderness Act	P.L. 98-322	41,260
New Hampshire Wilderness Act	P.L. 98-323	77,000
North Carolina Wilderness Act	P.L. 98-324	68,750
Florida Wilderness Act	P.L. 98-430	49,150
Arkansas Wilderness Act	P.L. 98-508	91,103
Georgia Wilderness Act	P.L. 98-514	14,439
Mississippi Wilderness Act	P.L. 98-515	5,500
Tennessee Wilderness Act	P.L. 98-578	24,942
Pennsylvania Wilderness Act	P.L. 98-585	9,705
Virginia Wilderness Act	P.L. 98-592	55,984
		462,172

Source: USFS 1985.

Table 2. New National Forest Wilderness Units Established from September 30, 1983 to October 30, 1984.

Unit	National Forest	Region	State	Acres
Porcupine Lake	Cheguaneon	9	WI	4,235
Headwaters	Nicolet	9	WI	20,104
Total				24,339
Breadloaf	Green Mtn	9	VT	21,480
Big Branch	Green Mtn	9	VT	6,720
Peru Peak	Green Mtn	9	VT	6,920
George D. Aiken	Green Mtn	9	VT	5,060
Total				41,260
Pemigewasset	White Mtn	9	NH	45,000
Sandwich Range	White Mtn	9	NH	25,000
Total				77,000
Birdhead Mountains	Uwarrie	8	NC	4,790
Catfish Lake	Croatan	8	NC	7,600
Middle Prong	Pisgah	8	NC	7,900
Pocosin	Croatan	8	NC	11,000
Pond Pine	Croatan	8	NC	1,860
Sheep Ridge	Croatan	8	NC	9,540
Southern Nantahala	Nantahala	8	NC	10,900
Total				68,750
Mud Swamp	Apalachicola	8	FL	1,170
Big Gum Swamp	Apalachicola	8	FL	7,800
Alexander Springs	Ocala	8	FL	7,700
Juniper Prairie	Ocala	8	FL	13,260
Little Lake George	Ocala	8	FL	2,500
Billies Bay	Ocala	8	FL	3,120
Total				49,150
Black Fork Mtn	Ouachita	8	AR	7,568
Dry Creek	Ouachita	8	AR	6,310
Poteau Mtn	Ouachita	8	AR	10,884
Flatside	Ouachita	8	AR	10,105
Hurricane Creek	Ozark	8	AR	15,177
Richland Creek	Ozark	8	AR	11,822
East Fork	Ozark	8	AR	10,777
Leatherwood	Ozark	8	AR	16,956
Total				91,103
Black Creek	DeSoto	8	MISS	4,560
Leaf	DeSoto	8	MISS	940
Total				5,500
Allegheny Islands	Allegheny	9	PA	368
Hickory Creek	Allegheny	9	PA	9,337
Total				9,705
Big Frog	Cherokee	8	TN	5,055
Citico Creek	Cherokee	8	TN	16,000
Bald River Gorge	Cherokee	8	TN	3,887
Total				24,859
Beartown	Jefferson	8	VA	6,375
Kimberling Creek	Jefferson	8	VA	5,580
Lewis Fork	Jefferson	8	VA	5,730
Little Dry Run	Jefferson	8	VA	3,400
Little Wilson Creek	Jefferson	8	VA	3,855
Mountain Lake	Jefferson	8	VA	8,253
Peters Mtn	Jefferson	8	VA	3,326
Thunder Ridge	Jefferson	8	VA	2,450
Ramseys Draft	Jefferson	8	VA	6,725
Saint Mary's	Jefferson	8	VA	10,090
Total				55,984

Table 3. *Use Levels in Eastern Wilderness Areas for 1983.*

Wilderness Area	Visitor Days	Acreage	Visitor Days per Acre
Alabama:			
Sipsey	13,000	12,726	1.02
Cheaha	5,600	6,780	.83
Arkansas:			
Caney Creek	11,500	14,344	.80
Upper Buffalo	2,200	10,242	.21
Florida:			
Bradwell Bay	1,300	23,432	.06
Georgia:			
Cohutta	71,500	32,307	2.21
Ellicott Rock	400	181	2.21
Kentucky:			
Beaver Creek	2,600	4,791	.54
Louisiana:			
Kisatchie Hills	6,300	8,700	.72
New Hampshire:			
Great Gulf	24,900	5,552	4.48
Presidential	10,400	20,380	.51
North Carolina:			
Ellicott Rock	500	342	1.46
Joyce Kilmer	47,400	10,201	4.65
Linville Gorge	72,900	7,575	9.62
Shining Rock	123,700	13,350	9.27
South Carolina:			
Ellicott Rock	6,900	2,809	2.46
Hell Hold Bay	100	1,980	.05
Little Wambaw Swamp	800	5,000	.16
Wambaw Creek	1,100	1,640	.67
Wambaw Swamp	700	5,100	.14
Tennessee:			
Joyce Kilmer	6,100	3,832	1.59
Gee Creek	9,100	2,493	3.65
Cohutta	3,400	1,795	1.89
Vermont:			
Bristol Cliffs	800	3,738	.21
Lye Brook	3,700	14,600	.25
Virginia:			
James River Face	4,400	8,703	.51
West Virginia:			
Dolly Sods	23,100	10,215	2.26
Otter Creek	16,600	20,000	.83
Cranberry	18,300	35,864	.51
Laurel Fork North	2,000	6,055	.33
Laurel Fork South	1,500	5,997	.25

Source: USDA Forest Service, 1983.

Results from studies involving eastern wilderness users are cited by principal authors in Tables 4 and 5. Bowley (1979) surveyed backcountry users in Allegheny National Forest, Pennsylvania. Leonard (1978) and Godin (1977) worked with wilderness users in New Hampshire. Plumley (1978) researched users of the Long Trail in Vermont. Murray (1974) analyzed hikers on the southern portion of the Appalachian Trail. Echelberger and Moeller (1977)

Table 4. Patterns of Use in Eastern and Western Wilderness Areas.

Use Characteristic	Western Wilderness			Eastern Wilderness
	Lime*	Hendee et al.*	Henwood*	Study by author*
Geographic distribution of use	Uneven among and within areas	Uneven among and within areas	Uneven among and within areas	Bratton—use uneven within areas Leonard—use concentrated at access points Plumley—uneven use within areas
Seasonal pattern of use	Use concentrated in summer weekends	Weekend peaking occurs on smaller areas close to metropolitan areas	Use concentrated in summer Weekend peaking common	Bowley—2/3 of summer use is weekend peaking Bratton—use evenly distributed from March to October Leonard—during peak season use is uniform Plumley—use uniform during peak season
Length of stay	2.5 Days avg. for overngtrs.	2.9 Average for overnight	Banff–4.7 days Mt. Assis–2.7 WL–1.6 days	Bowley—65% of users on 2–3 day hikes Bratton—2.5 days Godin—63% 2 nights or less Leonard—1.99 days average Murray—2.5 days average Tim—1.8 × for LG 1.9 × for SR 2.3 × for JKS
Day/overnight		About 50% day users		Bowley 45% day users Tim—53% day use in LG 63% day use in SP 28.9% day use in JKS
Party size		65% of use by 2–4 people/party	Banff—2.9 peop/party Mt. Assis–2.7 peop/party WL—3.5 peop/party	Bowley—40% of use by 2–4 person parties Bratton—2.8 people/party Cannon—47% of use 2 people/party 19% of use 3 peop/party Leonard—2.96 $\bar{x}$ party size Plumley—42% of use 2 peop parties Tim—LG $\bar{x}$ 4.9 peop/party SR $\bar{x}$ 4.6 peop/party JKS $\bar{x}$ 3.4 peop/party

*References are cited in literature cited.

Abbreviations: Mt. Assis (Mount Assiniboine, Can), WL (Waterloo Lakes, Can), LG (Linville Gorge, NC), SR (Shining Rock, NC), JKS (Joyce Kilmer-Slickrock, NC).

identified characteristics of visitors to the Cranberry Wilderness in West Virginia. And Tim (1980) list information about users in the Linville Gorge, Shining Rock, and Joyce Kilmer-Slickrock Wilderness Areas in North Carolina.

From reviewing the studies in Tables 4 and 5 the following preliminary observations can be drawn:
1) Use is unevenly distributed within and among most wilderness areas. Concentrated use is most often found at principal access points and well known areas.
2) Most wilderness areas experience a summer peak-use season. Weekend peaking is more likely to occur in western areas. Eastern areas may experience relatively uniform summer use.
3) The average length of overnight stay in most wilderness areas ranges from 2-4 days. Eastern users may spend slightly less time.
4) About 50% of wilderness users are day users.

5) The average party size in all wilderness areas ranges from 2-4 people with most parties composed of 3 individuals.
6) The majority of wilderness users come from metropolitan areas in proximity to the wilderness areas.
7) Young adult males (age 30) compose the most abundant using group.
8) The majority of wilderness users have a college education.

A theme which emerges from these preliminary observations is that there appears to be few clear distinctions between western and eastern wilderness users in regard to their use patterns and socioeconomic descriptors. In an empirically based study comparing wilderness users, Tim (1980) found few differences between eastern and western wilderness visitors. She advises that there may be individual differences in users distinct to each wilderness area which overshadow east/west generalizations.

Table 5. Characteristics of Eastern and Western Wilderness Users.

Characteristic	Western Wilderness		Eastern Wilderness
	Lime*	Hendee et al.*	Study by author*
Age	Young adults most common no single age group a majority	All age groups well represented. Large portions of young adults and children	Bowley—44% of users 16–24. Murray—young adults more common but age groups 16–44 evenly distributed. Tim—LG $\bar{x}$ age 28.7, SR $\bar{x}$ age 30.8, JKS $\bar{x}$ age 29.1
Occupation		High education level most distinguishing characteristic. College students and professionals	Echelberger—36% of users professional and technical workers 64% high school or less. Murray—80% have college background. Tim—LG 15.1 yrs., SR 14.7 yrs, JKS 15.2 yrs
Gender		25% Are females	Echelberger—32% females. Murray—25% females. Tim—LG 22% female, SR 15.6% female, JKS 25.3% female
Home residence		Overwhelming majority from region near wilderness. Hail from urban area but have rural background	Bowley—46% of use from metropolitan areas. Leonard—users from metropolitan areas close by. Murray—most users from large towns or cities. Even distribution between rural/urban background. Plumley—long distance hikers from out of state, short distance from local areas

*References are cited in literature cited.
Abbreviations: Mt. Assis (Mount Assiniboine, Can), WL (Waterloo Lakes, Can), LG (Linville Gorge, NC), SR (Shining Rock, NC), JKS (Joyce Kilmer-Slickrock, NC).

CONCLUSIONS

The changing character of the NWPS during the last ten years presents managers with additional challenges. New wilderness units designated on National Forests are smaller and heavier used. The portion of USDA Forest Service land designated as wilderness has grown to 19% and includes many wilderness units in the east.

In spite of the temptation to draw broad generalizations contrasting eastern and western wilderness, the scientific literature to date has revealed few distinct differences between eastern and western wilderness users. Although much work remains to be done concerning this issue, there is a possibility that individual differences between users of each wilderness area overshadow any east/west dichotomy.

It is suggested that a classification of wilderness areas by use density may prove to be more heuristic than an eastern-western dichotomy. By developing management prescriptions for various use density levels occurring on wilderness areas (e.g., gt 3.0 visitor days/acre, 2.0-3.0 visitor days/acre, 1.0-2.0 visitor days/acre, ...), managerial experience and the scientific literature could be combined into a system of knowledge that is more responsive to the situations each wilderness area presents.

ACKNOWLEDGMENTS

I would like to express my gratitude to Ed Bloedel, USDA Forest Service, Washington D.C., for his generous supply of recent wilderness use data.

LITERATURE CITED

Bowley, C.S. 1979. Motives, management preferences, and perceptions of crowding of backcountry hiking trails users in the Allegheny National Forest of Pennsylvania. M.S. Thesis. Pennsylvania State Univ.

Cermack, R.W. 1976. Wilderness in the East: problems for research. pp. 52-59. In Proc. Southern States Recreation Research Applications Workshop. USDA For. Serv. Gen. Tech. Rep. SE-9.

Echelberger, H.E. and G.H. Moeller. 1977. Use and users of the Cranberry Backcountry in West Virginia: insights for eastern backcountry management. USDA For. Serv. Res. Pap. NE-363.

Godin, V. and R. Leonard. 1977. Permit compliance in eastern wilderness: preliminary results. USDA For. Serv. Res. Note NE-238.

Hendee, J.C., G.H. Stankey, and R.C. Lucas. 1978. Wilderness Management. USDA For. Serv. Misc. Publ. No. 1365.

Henwood, W.D. 1977. Backcountry recreation management in the alpine and subalpine zones of the Rocky Mountains, Alberta. M.S. Thesis, Univ. of Guelph.

Leonard, R.E., H.E. Echelberger, and M. Schnitzer. 1978. Use characteristics of the Great Gulf Wilderness. USDA For. Serv. Res. Pap. NE-428.

Lime, D.W. 1976. Wilderness use and users: a summary of research. In Proc. 54th Annual Winter Meeting, Allegheny Section, Society of American Foresters. Dover, Del.

Murray, J.B. 1974. Appalachian Trail users in the southern national forests: their characteristics, attitudes, and management preferences. USDA For. Serv. Res. Pap. SE-116.

Nash, R. 1973. Wilderness and the American mind. (Rev. Ed.). Yale Univ. Press. New Haven, Conn.

Plumley, H.J., H.T. Peet, and R.E. Leonard. 1978. Records of backcountry use can assist trail managers. USDA For. Serv. Res. Pap. NE-414.

Scott, D.W. 1984. The National Wilderness Preservation System-its place in natural area protection. Natural Areas J. 4:6-10.

Tim, W. 1980. A comparison of the carrying capacity perceptions of eastern and western wilderness users. M.S. Thesis. Virginia Polytechnic Institute and State Univ., Blacksburg, Va.

Turner, F. 1920. The significance of the frontier in American history. In The Turner Thesis. G.R. Taylor (ed.). D.C. Heath and Company, Boston, Mass.

Van Doren, C. (co-editor with M. Clawson). 1984. Statistics on outdoor recreation. Resources for the Future. Washington, D.C.

Identifying Wilderness Management Issues Through An Interactive Process

by
William J. McLaughlin and Edwin E. Krumpe

ABSTRACT--A process obtaining broad public input and consensus on wilderness management issues conducted from 1983-1985 is outlined. The diverse groups involved, the details of the process used, and the results of the effort are reported. Challenges and future needs in wilderness management are discussed.

KEYWORDS: wilderness, wilderness management issues, wilderness action program, nominal group process.

The First National Wilderness Management Workshop took place in October, 1983. It was conducted under the auspices of the Wilderness Research Center of the University of Idaho and in cooperation with the Bureau of Land Management, the U.S. Fish and Wildlife Service, the U.S. Forest Service and the National Park Service.

The goal of that workshop was to focus **on** and bring attention to wilderness management as opposed to the wilderness allocation issue. It seemed about time. After all, wilderness has been a reality since September 3, 1964, when that "Great Texan," Lyndon B. Johnson, signed the Wilderness Act of 1964 (PL 88-577).

It seemed only reasonable that some 20 years later we begin focusing our effort on the responsibility of managing one of our nation's most precious resources. Like everyone, we would like to think we were first -- but that is really not the case. Individuals like Bob Lucas, Dave Lime, John Hendee, George Stankey, Ned Fritz (here in Texas), Michael Frome, numerous conservation interest groups, and managers themselves had sounded the bell about the need for wilderness management long before we came along.

But we felt our goal to refocus was timely and needed in these times of budget cuts and our society's renewed commodity orientation. The Idaho conference entitled "Taking Care of What We've Got" was only meant to be a beginning. And that it has been. Since that time there has been a renewed interest in wilderness -- a regional conference like this one is a good example. This summer the National Wilderness Research Conference July 23-26, in Fort Collins, Colorado, entitled "Learning to Preserve," and in 1987 the fourth World Wilderness Congress, will further continue all of our efforts to better understand wilderness as a national and international resource -- no matter where it is located.

Perhaps the one thing I remember most from the Moscow conference was the revitalized spirit of those in attendance. As one participant said, "It's great to know there are hundreds of managers and people like me -- people who really do believe in wilderness and its values!" It is this very commitment to wilderness and its management that we had hoped to kindle and tap.

Now that I have discussed the rekindling of a renewed commitment to wilderness, let me address the *energy and ideas that were tapped* and *the results* of the Idaho workshop and conclude with *what needs to be done* according to many of the diverse interests associated with wilderness across the United States. Before I address these topics, let me make one point -- nothing really will be accomplished in the area of wilderness management unless we join hands with all those interested in wilderness, whether we agree with them or not -- moving forward must be our goal.

TAPPING THE ENERGY

At the Idaho workshop, just like at this conference, perhaps the greatest resource was not the many fine speakers, but rather the collective ideas and energy the participants brought to focus on wilderness and the management of it. To tap this energy, we utilized the "nominal group process" to identify the key issues facing wilderness management in the next five years. This process is a scientifically proven method for small groups to identify and prioritize a list of concerns in a short time. Developed by Andre L. Delbecq (1975), the process is designed to allow every participant to express their own ideas, to hear the reasoning behind other people's ideas, and to prioritize those ideas without being dominated by vocal and argumentative persons. The key to the process is the group facilitator whose purpose is to impartially moderate each phase, keep the group on schedule, and record the results of each step. All workshop participants were assigned to a nominal group of 10 to 15 persons.

The 38 working groups were preselected based on data collected on the workshop registration form. In general, groups consisting of a maximum of ten persons contained representatives from the U.S. Forest Service, Bureau of Land Management, National Park Service, U.S. Fish and Wildlife Service, universities, conservation groups, wilderness users (wilderness outfitters and guides, National Outdoor Leadership School, Wilderness Education Association, unaffiliated citizens), other traditional forest client groups (timber, mining, grazing), and another category that consisted of state and Canadian natural resource agency personnel. The goal of structuring the groups was to encourage interaction about wilderness management across diverse value systems, institutions, and geographic areas.

The actual steps of the nominal group process that were used are as follows:
1. Each individual silently generated their own list of issues facing wilderness management over the next five years.
2. Beginning with each participant's most important issue, a composite group list was made by soliciting one issue from each person in turn until all issues were listed.
3. After all issues were listed, each issue was briefly discussed to clarify its meaning.
4. Individually, each person selected what he/she considered the seven most important issues on the group's

composite list and then ranked them by distributing from one to seven points among the top seven issues.
5. Finally, a composite group rating for the issues was developed by combining the individual ratings.

In two and one-half hours everyone had participated in generating over 1,000 separate ideas. Following the workshop, a content analysis of these 1,000 revealed 152 common issues that could be ranked into a prioritized list of the key issues facing wilderness management in the next five years (Frome 1985). This list is displayed on Table 1.

Table 1. 1983 Wilderness Management Workshop Participants' Rank Order of Critical Wilderness Management Issues to be Addressed Over the Next Five Years. (n = 380)[1]

Issue Title	Total Score
Need for increased funding	340
Educate public on wilderness values	272
Effectiveness of methods to educate the public	271
Limits of acceptable change	239
Training	208
Non-conforming prior uses	200
Carrying capacity methods	189
Consistency in interagency management	143
Outfitted vs. non-outfitted allocation	142
Biocentric vs. anthropocentric management	139
Need to manage overused areas	138
Planned ignition	136
Visitor freedom through minimum regulations	131
Keeping the Wilderness Act philosophy in gov't.	109
Management plans	109
Educate users on low impact techniques	107
Identifying use & user capacity	105
Ecological monitoring	105
Public support for management	101
User impacts on physical/biological/social attributes	97
Consistency in interagency policy	93
Recognizing the non-recreation values of wilderness	90
Buffer zones	89
Restoration/rehabilitation	86
Social/biological interaction	85
Wilderness in the context of a larger recreation system	85
Use allocation	83
Educate managers	82
Protection from outside threats	82
Career ladder	81
Permits & quotas	80
Wilderness features and their value	80
Physical resource carrying capacity	77
Fees	76
Maintaining natural processes in the wilderness	73
External threats	73
Threatened & endangered species	70
Wildlife & human conflicts	70
Managing with limited funding	70
Line item funding	69
Physical, biological & social carrying capacity	69
Management standards	68

[1]This table contains the results of the 380 persons attending the First National Wilderness Workshop. Divided into 38 working groups, they identified and listed a total of 1,000 issues. Following group discussions all the participants selected their own critical, or foremost, issues. They prioritized those issues by allocating points: from the highest priority, receiving 7 points, down to the lowest, receiving 1 point.

RESULTS OF THE WORKSHOP

The energy and interest tapped in generating the list of management issues was not to die with the close of the workshop. In his closing comments, Forest Service Chief Max Peterson called upon the four federal agencies to join in the formation of a national steering committee that would also include representatives of industry and wilderness user groups. The purpose would be to develop a National Wilderness Management Action Program that defines the issues facing wilderness management in the next five years and recommends actions to address them (Frome 1985).

The national steering committee made up of representatives from recreation, preservation, commercial, commodity production, state resource management agencies and the four federal wilderness management agencies defined its purpose to be the development of a National Wilderness Preservation System Management Action Program that identified and defined the issues facing wilderness management in the next five years and recommended solutions. To accomplish this formidable task, they developed four goals to guide their work.

Goal 1 - Involve all four federal wilderness management agencies in developing the management action program.

Goal 2 - Involve the interested public, including conservation, preservation, wildlife management, outfitter, and recreation-user groups, as well as appropriate resource industries, in developing and implementing the management action program.

Goal 3 - Utilize the critical wilderness management issues and potential management actions developed by participants of the National Wilderness Management Workshop and continue their involvement in developing the action program.

Goal 4 - Make the Management Action Program available to agencies, interest groups, workshop participants and other relevant publics.

Starting with the issues displayed in Table 1, the committee settled upon five broad umbrella issue categories: (1) educating the public, (2) education and training of managers, (3) capacity and concentrated use, (4) interagency coordination and consistency, and (5) acceptable wilderness management practices. The committee drew upon the material generated at the workshop to recommend several actions for each of the five broad categories. Their goal was that the recommended actions should be brief and specific, attainable within a time frame of five years or less, expressed as actions rather than statements of policy, and above all, feasible to accomplish.

The committee discussed at length whether to include "funding" as an issue category. Funding received very high scores at the workshop. The committee reasoned that funding is an ever-present problem in all areas of resource management. Rather than focusing on the lack of funds, it was decided to concentrate on what actions should be done if the money were available. Their rationale was that a sound program of recommended actions should serve as a strong base to seek adequate funding. Furthermore, the committee decided the action plan would not deal with allocation of additional wilderness areas. Allocation is a separate political issue and the action plan would continue the focus of the workshop, "taking care of what we've got." Finally, they agreed that additional legislation would not be proposed. Existing legislation and directives to protect and perpetuate wilderness are broad and clear. To be feasible and timely, the actions must be things that can be done right now.

The committee met on two occasions. A two-day workshop served as the format of the meetings. University of Idaho Wilderness Research Center personnel were used as meeting facilitators. After several committee drafts, numerous phone calls and letters back and forth, a draft for public comment was developed.

The steering committee's draft action program was distributed to all workshop participants and to others interested in wilderness management. Over 700 copies were sent out and more than 200 individuals took the time and effort to respond. Although we welcomed public involvement, tabulating and summarizing the 1600 individual comments we received was a formidable task. Almost 100 pages of summarized comments were produced for detailed consideration by the steering committee. Their publication, WILDERNESS MANAGEMENT--A FIVE-YEAR ACTION PROGRAM (Krumpe 1985), has now been published and made widely available to the public. Out of the 23 actions that were recommended under the five broad categories, the steering committee chose the following five as the most important:

* Examine existing wilderness education techniques and evaluate their effectiveness. Be sure wilderness education material defines the wilderness resource and its values.

* Institute and revitalize comprehensive in-service wilderness management training, focused on the value of the wilderness resource, wilderness ethics, and low-impact camping, utilizing both agency and nonagency expertise.

* Identify, monitor, and publicly report internal and external threats to wilderness values from whatever source, whether overuse, acid rain, other forms of degraded air quality, visual or sound impairments.

* Manage indigenous plant and animal communities to sustain natural processes, assuring that levels of human use are compatible rather than detrimental, with emphasis on preserving endangered and threatened species, as required by law.

* Conduct workshops and other programs, nationally, regionally, and locally, as cooperative ventures of agencies, educational institutions, and interest groups in order to share ideas, concerns, and techniques relating to wilderness management.

WHAT NEEDS TO BE DONE

Obviously much remains to be done to ensure effective and responsible management of our priceless wilderness heritage. In this paper we have outlined a process whereby broad public involvement was brought to focus on the problems and issues facing wilderness management. The key to success is that the actions recommended are to be undertaken cooperatively by federal wilderness management agencies, the public, the private sector, and nonprofit organizations.

This conference on wilderness and nature preservation in the East is a fine example of how agencies and institutions can cooperate to begin to accomplish the last-mentioned action above, to cooperate in conducting workshops and other programs nationally and regionally. Throughout the 23 actions are items that no single agency or organization should be responsible for undertaking. Rather, all those interested in wilderness management can play a role and do their part to help accomplish the recommended actions. The challenge is to get on with the cooperative management of wilderness. We must settle for no less if we are to achieve our long-term goal of efficient, effective wilderness management.

LITERATURE CITED

Delbecq, A.L., A.H. Van deVen and D.H. Gustafson. 1975. Group techniques for program planning: A guide to nominal group and Delphi processes. Scott, Foresman & Co., Glenview, Ill.

Frome, M. 1985. Issues in wilderness management. Westview Press, Boulder, Colo.

Krumpe, E. 1985. Wilderness management - a five-year action program. University of Idaho Wilderness Research Center. Moscow, Id.

User Perception Of Backcountry Management Policies At Great Smoky Mountains National Park

by

John H. Burde and Kevin A. Curran

ABSTRACT--Visitors to the backcountry at Great Smoky Mountains National Park strongly support rationing by permit. They also favor retention of shelters and bridges in the backcountry even though shelters are in a run-down condition. Litter is the major backcountry maintenance problem. Compliance with backcountry policies is high. Actual use, however, is 18 percent lower than indicated from permit data. Backcountry visitors to the Smokies today are older and more experienced. Backpacking trips are similar to ten years previous in trip length and group size. Groups are more likely to be peer groups rather than families.

KEYWORDS: Great Smoky Mountains National Park, backcountry use, user characteristics, trip characteristics, permit system, litter.

Management policies at the agency level are the result of an evolutionary process. Initially, they are created to meet a management need, but as time passes these policies become more refined, being altered by legislation, agency regulation, executive orders, and secretarial orders (Daugherty 1978). Policies exhibit a wide latitude in application in a field situation such as a national park. This is especially true in the National Park Service where agency guidelines are quite limited (National Park Service 1978), as compared, for example, to the voluminous Forest Service or Bureau of Land Management Handbooks.

Within this framework, specific management policies are developed at the park level to meet local management problems. They have evolved based on the needs of resource protection, visitor safety, and, to a certain extent, public input.

Individual park policies do not necessarily evolve to a state identical to that desired by the visitor. Frequently, they result from what Lucas (1982) calls the bandwagon effect, i.e., adopting what is currently fashionable. Policies often reflect ease of management rather than an optimum visitor experience. Regulations may be adopted that minimize management and/or staff costs rather than optimizing the visitor's enjoyment. Research has shown that manager and visitor perceptions are often widely divergent (Peterson 1974).

Great Smoky Mountains National Park (GSMNP) is similar to other areas within the National Park System in terms of policy formulation. Policies currently in place have evolved over years of management experience. The basis of backcountry management is the Wilderness Act of 1964 though the area has not been officially designated

as a unit of the National Wilderness Preservation System.

National Park Service (NPS) staff responsible for backcountry management at GSMNP were concerned how visitors to the backcountry perceived management policies in use. It had been ten years since the last formal study of backcountry users had been conducted. During the summer of 1983 a comprehensive survey of backcountry users was undertaken to determine if attitudes towards the park's backcountry management policies had changed and, if so, how. The objectives of the study were: (1) to describe the perceptions of management policies in use in the backcountry at Great Smoky Mountains National Park by backpackers and day hikers, (2) to assess changes in those perceptions over the previous decade, and (3) to describe the characteristics of the backcountry user at the Smokies.

PREVIOUS WORK

There have been numerous studies of backcountry users conducted throughout the United States in the recent past. These studies have been summarized in Hendee *et al.* (1978). There has been, however, only one study that describes backcountry use in the Great Smoky Mountains, a study conducted during the summer of 1972 by Marsh (1973) who analyzed hiker attitudes and characteristics. Another study that is useful for comparison purposes is a survey of Appalachian Trail users on national forests of the southeast (Murray 1974). These two studies will be used as the bases for assessing change in the decade of 1973 to 1983.

The management policies addressed in the 1983 study were as follows: (1) use rationing, (2) restrictions on camping locations, (3) provision of shelters and other structures, (4) trail and structure maintenance, and (5) litter.

Use Rationing

Many backcountry areas in the east require a permit for entry though some are voluntary. Where use pressures are heavy, a mandatory permit may be necessary. In such cases, there are several alternative methods of distribution: by advance reservation, lottery, queuing, price and merit (Stankey and Baden 1977), the most common being advance reservation or queuing (first come - first serve). GSMNP instituted a mandatory permit system in 1972, available by advance reservation or by queuing (GSMNP 1982b).

Restrictions on Camping Locations.

There are several alternative systems for restricting camping locations. These include allowing camping only within designated areas (Big Bend, Grand Teton, Denali), allowing camping at designated sites only (Great Smoky Mountains, Yellowstone, Glacier), or allowing unrestricted camping (most USFS backcountry areas). The intensity of use in an area determines which alternative is appropriate; the greater the use pressure, the more restrictions are required. Additional restrictions may be warranted, such as limiting the number of nights per site (Hendee *et al.* 1978). At GSMNP, camping is allowed at designated sites only. These sites include designated campsites and developed shelters and may be used only three consecutive nights, campsite shelters for only one (GSMNP 1982b).

Provision of Shelters and Other Structures

Shelters are common in many backcountry areas but information on visitor perceptions of shelters are limited. A study in the northwest (Hendee *et al.* 1968) suggests that backcountry visitors favor retaining shelters. A survey of shelter users at GSMNP showed that three-fourths of them preferred shelters to tents (Marsh 1973). Despite this, many shelters have been removed as inappropriate for wilderness (Hendee *et al.* 1978). The authors stress that the remainder should be phased out.

The policy at GSMNP is, however, to retain the shelter. The General Management Plan (1982a) states: "Trail shelters will be retained except where environmental deterioration is severe or where contemporary need is lowest. The schedule of actions concerning individual shelters will be determined in consultation with advisory groups. Visitor input is also desirable."

Another question is whether sanitation facilities should be provided. Hendee *et al.* (1968) found that more than one-half of the visitors to wilderness areas in Oregon and Washington favored toilets. In a study of nine western wilderness areas, Lucas (1980) found 30 to 45 percent of visitors found outhouses undesirable except the Desolation Wilderness in California where 66 percent viewed outhouses as undesirable. The policy at GSMNP was to provide backcountry sanitation facilities essential to public health and appropriate to wilderness status (GSMNP 1982a). However, subsequent to publishing the General Management Plan, toilets are being removed. Tables and grills are not provided in the backcountry.

Trail and Structure Maintenance

The degree to which the trails and associated structures are maintained in the backcountry largely determines the amount and type of use that will occur. Well maintained trails with bridges over most stream crossings will tend to attract use. Unmaintained trails discourage all but the hardiest hikers and can be used as an indirect means to reduce use in certain areas (Lucas 1982).

Marsh (1973) found that trails at GSMNP were perceived to be in good condition. The Great Smoky Mountains National Park General Management Plan (1982a) states the backcountry trails within the park will continue to be maintained although no standards are noted. Bridges will be constructed and maintained at hazardous stream crossings.

Litter

Most backcountry management regimes stress the removal of litter by the slogan "pack-it-in, pack-it-out." The presence of litter is the single most annoying problem encountered during backcountry experiences (Muth and Clark 1978). Litter is characterized as a careless action that can be remedied by persuasion, education, and if need be, rule enforcement (Hendee *et al.* 1978). At GSMNP minimal effort is made concerning litter. Only a brief note is provided visitors in backcountry literature.

METHODOLOGY

Backcountry users, both backpackers and day hikers, were interviewed on site during the summer of 1983. The backcountry, defined as any point more than one mile from a public road within the park, was subdivided into eight zones based on typical access: Cades Cove, Elkmont, Deep Creek, Cataloochee, Mount LeConte-Newfound Gap, Cosby, Smokemont, and Abrams Creek. Using data from the park's Backcountry Office, each zone was sampled at a rate proportional to use. Specific sample sites within each zone were randomly selected. Backpackers were interviewed at backcountry campsites and shelters; day hikers at popular destination points and along trails. The apparent leader of each group was interviewed using a personally administered questionnaire. Total sample size for backpackers was 128 groups (418 individuals). The Backcountry Office recorded 25,482 backcountry visits during the sample period, resulting in a sampling intensity of approximately 1.6 percent.

In addition 108 day hiker groups totalling 367 persons were interviewed. Since the park has no record of backcountry day use, no estimate of day use sampling intensity is feasible.

RESULTS

Permit System

Use of the backcountry in the Smokies was substantially reduced with the institution of a permit system beginning in June, 1972. Marsh's study (1973), conducted during this change in policy, showed substantial opposition to use restriction. Less than one-half of the respondents in his survey approved of such restrictions; almost one-fourth were strongly opposed.

In the intervening ten years, support for the permit system has grown substantially. Almost 95 percent of the respondents in 1983 study recognized the necessity of the permit system; 89 percent felt the opportunity to make a reservation for a backcountry site was a positive aspect of park services.

Knowledge of the permit system has been widely disseminated. Nearly 94 percent of backpackers knew of the system prior to arrival.

Even though visitors knew of the system and generally supported its use, there was some question as to how backpackers actually followed permit procedures. The number of backpackers encountered each night in the backcountry was compared to the number of users who had actually acquired a permit for that site on that particular date. Of 67 days of interviewing, only 13 days showed more campers present than had obtained permits. Conversely, on 31 days there were fewer campers present than had obtained permits; on 23 days, the observed number of campers equalled the number of campers obtaining permits. The campers without permits represents an eight percent increase in use as recorded in the park's Backcountry Office. Conversely, campers who had permits but were not present represented a 26 percent decrease in use. Overall, actual use is 18 percent lower than park records would indicate.

Campsite Restrictions

Currently backpackers in the Smokies must stay at designated campsites or shelters. More than 80 percent of the respondents would prefer more freedom to select a campsite. Backcountry rangers, however, report almost no evidence of people camping outside designated sites. Also, though the Smokies limit the number of consecutive nights, 82 percent of backpackers interviewed reported this had no effect on their visit.

Shelters

A major policy question in the Smokies backcountry is the condition of the park's shelters. In 1973, Marsh found that only 16 percent of shelter users found some type of maintenance problem; in 1983 that figure had risen to 51 percent. The maintenance problems noted (and percent of respondents) were litter within the shelter (23 percent), human waste problems (5 percent), rodents (9 percent), leaking roofs (3 percent) and improper maintenance such as graffiti and broken fencing (17 percent). Users also noted overcrowding (3 percent) and unfriendly acquaintances at shelters (2 percent). Despite all the apparent problems, the retention of shelters is overwhelmingly supported by visitors.

The park's Resource Management staff felt that due to the rundown condition of the shelters, the structures should be removed. Users and management on this issue were almost totally polarized.

Removal of sanitation facilities from the Smokies backcountry is nearly complete. This change in policy is strongly supported by visitors (77 percent). When asked if sanitation facilities detract from the visitor's experience, 57 percent stated pit toilets detracted; 73 percent stated chemical toilets did so as well. Murray (1974) found similar results on the Appalachian Trail when 58 percent of the hikers rejected the presence of toilets.

Conversely, most backcountry visitors favor retaining bridges. Stankey (1973) noted that in a study of four wilderness areas, 66 percent of visitors favored having bridges. In the Smokies, 61 percent of backpackers favored bridges as did 69 percent of the day hikers.

Litter

Stankey (1973) found litter to be a substantial problem in the backcountry, a problem more severe than encountering too many people. In the Smokies more than 82 percent of the backpackers noticed litter on their trip; 90 percent of them felt it detracted from their experience.

Further, 63 percent of the day hikers also noticed litter; 93 percent felt their experience was diminished by it.

User Characteristics

Age--The typical backcountry user in 1983 was somewhat older than in previous research. The mean age of users in 1983 was 31.3; it was 26.3 in 1973 (Marsh 1973). A comparison is shown in Table 1.

Sex--Backcountry users remain predominately male. Survey results showed that 89 percent were male, a figure quite similar to Marsh's result of 92 percent male. To the contrary, Murray (1974) found only 70 percent male in her study on national forest lands.

Years of Hiking Experience

The data suggest that users of the Smokies backcountry are more experienced than in the past (Table 2). The mean years of experience was 9.4 years.

Backpackers had visited the Smokies an average of 6.2 times previously. However, more than one-third were on their first trip to the Smokies (Table 3).

Trip Length

Most hikers in 1983 were on short trips. More than one-half of the hiking groups were on trips of three nights or less. On the other hand, 5 percent were on trip of 10 days or more. The mean was 4.5 days. The distribution of trip length is shown in Table 4. Marsh (1973) also found a mean trip length of 4.5 days.

Party Size

The average number of people in the group has declined slightly due, probably, to subsequent restrictions on group size. In 1983, the average group was 3.3 persons; in 1973, Marsh found the average group was 3.8 persons. Most groups in 1983 were 2 to 4 persons, but 16 percent were individuals traveling alone (Table 5).

Hiking Companions

In 1973, Marsh found that more than one-half of the hiking parties in the Smokies were families. By 1983, that figure was only 40 percent. There were substantial increases in individuals hiking alone and peer groups (Table 6).

Hiker vs Horse Use

The conflict between hikers and horsemen has been consistently apparent. Marsh (1973) noted that 60 percent of hikers objected to horses using hiking trails. Murray (1974) found similar results. In 1983, 60 percent of hikers stated they noticed horses; of that number, 70 percent stated the encounter detracted from their experience.

The Day Hiker

There have been no previous studies on day hikers in the Smokies or in nearby areas. Since such users are not required to have a permit, no information is available from that source nor does the park routinely collect data on day users in any other form.

The following paragraphs briefly describes the day hiker in the Smokies backcountry for the summer of 1983.

Most day hikers stay outside the park in private accommodations (64 percent) as opposed to NPS campgrounds

Table 1. Comparison of Age of Respondents.

	16–17	18–21	22–35	36–50	51 +	16–18	19–24	25–34	35–44	45–54	55–64	65 +
Burde and Curran (1985)	5	14	53	23	6							
Marsh (1973)	7	15	43	28	7							
Burde and Curran (1985)						8	27	32	19	9	4	1
Murray (1974)						20	27	20	16	9	4	2

Table 2. Comparison in Years of Hiking Experience.

	0–1	2–5	6–10	11–20	20 +
Burde and Curran (1985)	9	30	34	20	7
Marsh (1973)	12	42	25	12	9
Murray (1975)	29	29	19	10	13

Table 3. Distribution of Previous Trips to the Smokies, 1983.

Previous Trips	Percent
None	34
1	13
2	11
3–5	13
6–10	14
11 +	14

Table 4. Distribution of Trip Length, 1983.

Number of Days	Percent
1	18
2	18
3	15
4	9
5	11
6–10	25
10 or more	5
Mean	4.5

Table 5. Distribution of Party Size, 1983.

Number of People	Percent
1	16
2	38
3	15
4	13
5–6	5
7–8	10
9	4

Table 6. Preferred Hiking Company.

	Percent	
Preference	Burde and Curran 1985	Marsh 1973
Alone	16	7
Peer Group	44	35
Family	40	57

(36 percent). More than one-third are visiting the park for three days or less. One of six is a local resident. Only 26 percent reported that they were on their first visit to the park. Almost 40 percent reported they visit several times per year.

Day hikers were generally in groups of three or less (64 percent); 7 percent of the day hiker groups exceeded the backpacker groups size limit of eight. For most of the day hiking groups (58 percent), only one day hike was taken during the current visit. Another 37 percent took one or two additional hikes.

Only 13 percent discussed their hike with NPS staff prior to their hike; only 5 percent contacted a ranger in the backcountry. Fortunately, less than 10 percent of the day hikers could be considered novices. Day hikers were slightly older than backpackers, 35.7 years vs. 31.4.

CONCLUSIONS

Backpackers and day hikers generally support management policies in use in the backcountry at Great Smoky Mountains National Park. This support was not apparent at the outset of the institution of the permit system, but has grown substantially over the years.

Backcountry rationing has succeeded in reducing crowding as well as physical impact over the past decade. During that time, for example the amount of bare soil at campsites along the Appalachian Trail within the park has actually declined (Burde and Renfro 1985). It appears that current policy has successfully lowered use levels below the physical carrying capacity of the backcountry. Further research to determine social carrying capacity in the Smokies backcountry is definitely warranted, before the appropriateness of current use levels can be discussed.

The perceptions of the remaining policies discussed above have remained remarkably constant over the decade. Acceptance of restrictions and perceptions of problems have changed little.

The major backcountry management problem today in the Smokies is litter. Litter was the most widely mentioned problem by visitors. Litter is most common at campsites and shelters. It destroys the aesthetic experience for most visitors, and frequently results in physical problems such as rodent infestation. A more enlightened management approach to litter is needed.

Backcountry users in 1983 were slightly older and more experienced than in previous studies. This may foretell a decline in backcountry use in coming years.

The characteristics of backcountry use have remained constant over the decade. One may conclude that politics have "homogenized" the experience. However, the availability of permits almost every day of the year, at any time of day, and the lack of constraints of visitor activities, suggest that the policies in place are doing what they were intended without undue hardship on the visitor.

More information on the day hiker specifically and day use in general should be a research priority of the park. Dayhikers are a user group whose wants and needs have only been peripherally addressed.

LITERATURE CITED

Burde, J.H. and J.R. Renfro. 1985. Incidence and intensity of trail impacts on the Appalachian Trail in Great Smoky Mts. National Park. (In preparation) Uplands Research Lab, Great Smoky Mts. Natl. Park.

Daugherty, G. 1978. Notes from orientation to NPS operations. Horace M. Albright Training Center, Grand Canyon National Park. Grand Canyon, Ariz.

Great Smoky Mountains National Park. 1982a. General Management Plan.

Great Smoky Mountains National Park. 1982b. Great Smoky Mts. Trail Map. Unpaged pamphlet.

Hendee, J.C., W.R. Catton, Jr., L.D. Marlow, and C.F. Brockman. 1968. Wilderness users in the Pacific Northwest - Their characteristics, values, and management preferences. USDA For. Serv. Pac. Northwest For. Range Exp. Stn. PNW-61.

Hendee, J.C., G. Stankey, and R. Lucas. 1978. Wilderness management. USDA For. Serv. Misc. Publ. 1365.

Lucas, R.C. 1980. Use patterns and visitor characteristics, attitudes and preferences in nine wilderness and other roadless areas. USDA For. Serv. Intermountain For. Range Exp. Stn. INT-253.

Lucas, R.C. 1982. Recreation regulations - When are they needed? J. For. 80:148-151.

Marsh, G.G. 1973. Hikers in the Gr. Smoky Mts. National Park - Their attitudes, characteristics and implications for management. M.S. Thesis. Univ. of Tennessee, Knoxville, Tenn.

Murray, J.B. 1974. Appalachian Trail users in the southern national forests: Their characteristics, attitudes, and management preference. USDA For. Serv., Southeast. Exp. Stn. SE-116.

Muth, R.M. and R.N. Clark. 1978. Public participation in wilderness and backcountry litter control. USDA For. Serv. Pac. Northwest For. Range Exp. Stn. PNW-75.

National Park Service. 1978. Management policies.

Peterson, G.L. 1974. A comparison of the sentiments and perceptions of wilderness managers and canoeists in the Boundary Waters Canoe Area. J. Leisure Res. 6:194-206.

Stankey, G.H. 1973. Visitor perception of wilderness carrying capacity. USDA For. Serv. Intermountain For. Range Exp. Stn. INT-142.

Stankey, G.H. and J. Baden. 1977. rationing wilderness use: Methods, problems, and guidelines. USDA For. Serv. Intermountain For. Range Exp. Stn. INT-192.

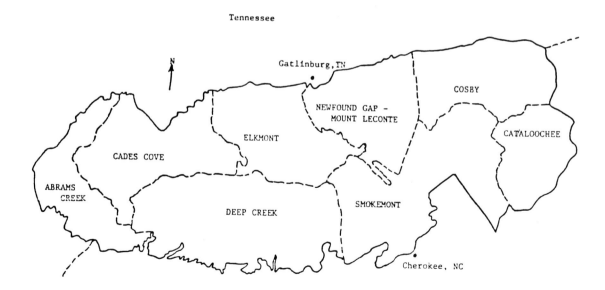

Great Smoky Mountains National Park Backcountry Sampling Zones

Recreational Resource Impacts: Visitor Perceptions And Management Responses

by
Jeffrey L. Marion and David W. Lime

ABSTRACT--Research findings from a nationwide survey of river recreationists indicate that visitors have limited perceptions of resource impacts, such as vegetation and soil damage, but are perceptive of impacts resulting from depreciative behavior by other recreationists, such as litter and improperly disposed human waste. Wildland managers are nevertheless responsible for maintaining environmental quality and integrity. Impact assessment and monitoring systems offer managers an objective approach to identify the nature and severity of resource impacts, and a number of management strategies can be applied to minimize further impacts.

KEYWORDS: visitor attitudes, impact assessment, impact monitoring, impact management strategies.

Deciding how much and what kinds of recreation use are acceptable for an area requires definitions of what constitutes acceptable environmental change or damage. At some point, resource administrators must decide how much and what types of resource impacts are acceptable before management intervention is required. Such decisions often are influenced by legal and administrative policies, but usually they are guided by professional judgement. Understanding how recreationists define resource quality and how they feel about environmental impacts that may be occurring also can help resource planners and managers assess the seriousness of such problems.

This paper briefly reviews recreationists' perceptions of recreational impacts and presents pertinent research findings from a nationwide study of river recreationists. These findings include visitor's perceptions of impact occurrence, the kinds of impacts noticed, and whether more management controls are necessary to protect wildland environments. Potential management responses to resource impact problems also are discussed, including the need for objective impact assessment and monitoring systems and the selection of general impact management strategies.

RECREATIONISTS' PERCEPTIONS OF RECREATIONAL IMPACTS

Review of Past Research

Studies of recreationists' perceptions of resource impacts are scarce and inconclusive. However, Lucas' review of such research at the 1978 Conference on

Recreational Impacts on Wildlands provides an excellent synthesis of what is known and not known about this aspect of recreation resource management (Lucas 1979). Other recent reports of research on perception of recreational impact build on this knowledge base (Nieman and Futrell 1979, Anderson 1981, 1983, Knudson and Curry 1981, Knopf 1982, Roggenbuck et al. 1982, Anderson and Brown 1984). Most studies have been conducted in designated wilderness or wildland environments, but their implications apply to other areas. For example, previous research has found that:

1. Recreationists generally have limited perception of the normal wear and tear impacts that occur at recreation sites (e.g. trails and campsites) and do not find such impacts particularly disturbing.

2. Recreationists are more sensitive to direct impacts of other recreationists (such as the occurrence of litter, horse manure, human waste, malicious damage to vegetation and rocks) than they are to wear and tear impacts. Such impacts are attributed to the presence of previous recreationists whose unacceptable behavior mars their experience.

3. Recreationists and resource administrators relate to resource change in different ways. Managers generally are more aware of and sensitive to both wear and tear impacts and the effects of human misbehavior than are recreationists. Managers are fairly consistent in their response to impacts; recreationists generally display a wider range of feelings about what is not acceptable and what should be done about it.

4. Perceptions of recreationists about acceptable change probably will vary in degree but not in kind among recreational settings. In road access campgrounds and pic-

nic areas, for instance, what is perceived as an acceptable impact may be considered as inappropriate in wilderness. However, the relative importance of various types of impacts, once identified, probably would be about the same regardless of setting. Further study would clarify relationships.

Recent Studies of River Recreationists

An ongoing study by the USDA Forest Service's North Central Forest Experiment Station describes the characteristics, preferences, and use patterns of recreationists visiting a variety of river settings (Lime et al. 1980, Knopf and Lime 1984). Visitors are interviewed as they enter or exit the river. Later, a sample of those interviewed onsite are mailed a questionnaire. About 250 questionnaires are returned per river, representing an average response rate of almost 75 percent among all rivers studied. More than 65 river segments nationwide and two in Europe have been studied since 1977.

As part of this study, recreationists were asked to rate the degree to which a list of possible problems existed on the river (Knopf 1982). Among 50 items, the only wear and tear impacts to appear in the top 15 problems were water pollution and steambank erosion (a slight to very serious problem for about one-fourth of the respondents). Litter surfaced as the number one problem, but the other most mentioned ones were too few toilet and drinking water facilities, insufficient information, navigation difficulties, insect bites, and seeing too many people.

More indepth probing focused on the visitors' perceptions of the kinds of environmental impacts occurring on the rivers and what, if anything, resource administrators should do about such impacts.

Are impacts occurring?-- Among 40 river segments studied between 1979 and 1984, 23 percent of the respondents thought the river environment was being damaged by recreational use. The variation in perceived seriousness of such impacts among rivers ranged from a low of 6 percent for commercially outfitted respondents on the Snake River (south of Teton National Park, Wyoming) in 1984, to a high of 49 percent for respondents interviewed in 1979 on the Upper Delaware National Scenic and Recreational River in the Northeast.

Among selected eastern rivers east of the Mississippi River, a wide range in impact perception is found between wildland rivers and non-wildland rivers (Table 1). By wildland rivers we mean settings in which bank and onshore development is minimal or is not readily apparent to river travelers. Access points are few. By non-wildland settings we mean where bank and shoreline activities (roads, railroads, small communities, and buildings) are readily visible to the river traveler and access points are numerous, giving the travelers more of a feeling of human intervention.

Although responses were varied, an average of 32 percent of non-wildland river visitors felt river environments were being damaged compared to 21 percent of wildland river visitors. This may indicate that environmental damage is greater or more obvious on non-

Table 1. Response of Eastern River Visitors to Both Wildland and Non-Wildland Settings to "Do you feel the river environment is being damaged by recreational use?" (1979–1984 Data)

	Environment Is Being Damaged	
	Number	Percent
Eastern Rivers in Wildland Settings		
Withlacoochee (FL)	45	34
Suwanee (FL)	56	30
Ichetucknee (FL)	56	25
Juniper Springs (FL)	56	24
Upper St. Croix (MN-WI)	152	21
New (WV)	63	20
Alexander Springs (FL)	41	19
Blackwater (FL)	39	18
Indian (MI)	33	14
Ocoee (TN)	33	13
TOTALS	574	21
Eastern Rivers in Non-Wildland Settings		
Upper Delaware (PA-NY)	111	49
Farmington (CT)	81	33
Housatonic (CT)	60	25
Lower St. Croix (MN-WI)	36	18
TOTALS	288	32
All 40 Study Rivers		
Eastern	862	24
Western	1215	22
TOTALS	2077	23

wildland rivers. If one hypothesizes that visitors to wild rivers are more demanding in their standards (they certainly would not be expected to be less demanding), our findings suggest an even wider range in actual impact conditions.

No significant difference in response was found between the eastern and western rivers studied (Table 1). *What kinds of environmental impacts were identified?--* Those respondents who thought environmental damage was occurring were asked to report what kinds they had seen. An open-ended, free-response format was used so respondents could identify concerns that truly left an impression and may have disrupted their experience and so specific impacts at each river could be differentiated.

Various damages were reported. Among the 14 eastern rivers studied, the most frequently cited specific impacts to the resource itself were soil damage, disturbance to fish and wildlife and/or their habitats, vegetation damage, and water pollution (Table 2). The predominant impact left by past visitors was litter, with human waste a distant second. Of course, had we been able to distinguish the specific concerns from some of the general categories (such as general deterioration, pollution, overuse/people pressures, and general loss to the recreational experience), our measure of the seriousness of selected problems might have been more precise. Other concerns, although few in number, can give resource administrators on some rivers increased clues about possible problems.

Table 2. For Those Who Feel the River Environment Is Being Damaged by Recreational Use, What Kinds of Damage Do They See? (14 Eastern River Segments, 1978–1984)

Kinds of Damage	Times Mentioned	
	Number	Percent
Normal Wear and Tear, General Deterioration of the Resource		
General resource deterioration	333	27
Soil damage/erosion	111	9
Disturbance to wildlife/fish habitat	83	7
Pollution (unspecified)	79	6
Vegetation damage	63	5
Overuse/people pressures	45	4
Water pollution	28	2
General campsite deterioration	14	1
Depreciative Behavior by Other Recreationists		
Litter	301	24
General loss to recreation experience	70	6
Human waste	54	4
Campfire scars/misuse	13	1
Abuse of facilities/vandalism	12	1
Noise pollution	12	1
Poor facility maintenance	7	1
Excessive firewood cut	6	1
Presence of development/commercialism	4	1
Graffiti	3	1
Total number of responses	1,238	100.0
Total number of visitors who feel the environment is being damaged	897	

Note: Respondents can report more than one damage. Therefore, the total number of responses exceed the total number of visitors who feel the environment is being damaged.

Are more controls needed to prevent environmental damage?-- Among the 40 river segments studied, at least as many respondents who felt damage was occurring also felt management controls should be increased to prevent further environmental change (Tables 1 and 3). Among the 14 eastern rivers only on the Farmington River was the percentage feeling this way lower. In contrast, on the Ocoee and Suwanee Rivers the percentage of visitors feeling increased controls were necessary was much greater. Again, little difference in response was found between eastern and western rivers.

MANAGEMENT IMPLICATIONS

Many visitors have limited experience with natural environments so it is not surprising that resource impacts such as vegetative trampling, soil erosion, and tree damage and removal (except when extensive or severe) appear to go unnoticed by most visitors. Most are not trained in the biological sciences nor do they typically return to the same recreational sites often enough to notice site deterioration. But they do appear to notice litter, perhaps because of extensive anti-litter educational campaigns in both urban and recreational environments, and improperly disposed human waste, perhaps because it is so unattractive.

New visitors to an area generally have limited expectations regarding environmental quality and may simply accept what they find (Schreyer and Roggenbuck 1978, Schreyer and Lime 1984). Many repeat visitors may learn to both accept and expect increasingly deteriorated conditions. These visitors are capable of *adapting* to deteriorating recreation environments. Adaptation, in this sense, works to an ultimate disadvantage in maintaining high quality recreation environments. Dustin *et al.* (1982) contends that recreationists are able to adjust to the negative elements of heavily used recreation resources without experiencing losses of satisfaction. Visitors who are sensitive to such environmental changes and do not adjust are *displaced* from the resource or alter their use patterns accordingly. The views of those who no longer use the resource are therefore not represented in surveys such as ours.

For these reasons (limited knowledge and adaptation or displacement of visitors) we believe that wildland managers cannot rely heavily on visitors' perceptions of resource impacts. Instead, we suggest that resource impact concerns should be based predominantly on legal and professional obligations. Wilderness, defined in Section 2(c) of the Wilderness Act, is an area "protected and managed

Table 3. Response of Eastern River Visitors to Both Wildland and Non-Wildland Settings to "Do you feel more controls are needed to prevent the river environment from being damaged by recreational use?" (1979–1984 Data).

	Controls needed to prevent damage	
	Number	Percent
Eastern Rivers in Wildland Settings		
Suwanee (FL)	77	43
Withlacooche (FL)	52	38
Ichetucknee (FL)	63	29
Juniper Springs (FL)	64	29
Alexander Springs (FL)	58	28
New (WV)	82	27
Upper St. Croix (MN-WI)	182	26
Ocoee (TN)	63	26
Blackwater (FL)	50	24
Indian (MI)	46	20
Totals	737	30
Eastern Rivers in Non-Wildland Settings		
Upper Delaware (PA-NY)	124	56
Lower St. Croix (MN-WI)	59	45
Farmington (CT)	88	37
Housatonic (CT)	77	33
Totals	348	42
All 40 Study Rivers		
Eastern	1085	33
Western	1554	29
Totals	2639	31

so as to preserve its natural conditions and which generally appears to have been affected primarily by the forces of nature, with the imprint of man's work substantially unnoticeable.'' This legal definition indicates that wilderness was intended to be land largely unmodified by man and where man's impact was and should continue to be minimal. Congress clearly intended wilderness areas to be managed in such a way that recreational use would not significantly impair the resource.

Wildland managers also have a professional obligation to not become caught up in the adaptation-to-deterioration process, becoming complacent with increasingly impacted "wilderness" conditions. Future generations should have the right to experience "wilderness" areas at least as pristine and natural as they were upon their designation. Therefore, in areas where wildland visitors are not sensitive to deteriorating resource conditions, managers have a responsibility to not simply serve popular tastes but to elevate them (Dustin *et al.* 1982). This involves increasing visitors' awareness of recreational impacts and promoting conduct consistent with the preservation of environmental quality and integrity.

IMPACT ASSESSMENT AND MONITORING

In addition to visitor education and in order to manage effectively, wildland managers must assess and monitor resource impacts caused by recreational use. This is necessary if managers are to maintain environmental quality and integrity over long periods and preclude the adaptation and displacement processes just described. In the past, managers often have relied on intuitive judgements to assess resource change. This was perhaps appropriate when visitor use was low. But, increasing wilderness visitation, particularly in the east where wildland areas are near large cities, calls for more objective impact assessment and monitoring methods.

Several impact assessment systems have been developed and applied on both campsites (Cole 1983a, Marion 1985) and trails (Cole 1983b). Their use enables managers to keep standardized records of conditions even though individual managers may come and go. Trends can be detected and evaluated through periodic comparisons of present and past impact assessments. Similarly, managers also can evaluate the success or failure of specific resource protection measures, as required by the National Forest Management Act of 1978.

Additional advantages of impact assessment and monitoring systems include their ability to detect deteriorating resource use areas. This allows managers to implement appropriate actions *before* severe or irreversible impacts occur. Impact assessment data also may suggest what programs and actions are needed to achieve resource-related management objectives.

Campsites, which are the primary focus of visitor activity in many wildland areas, have had considerable management attention. Researchers have identified numerous biophysical impacts associated with concentrated use, including trampling and loss of ground vegetation, shrubs, tree seedlings and saplings; erosion of surface litter and humus; exposure, erosion, and compaction of soil; and exposure of tree roots and damage to tree trunks (Settergren 1977, Cole 1982, Marion 1984).

Campsite impact assessment systems differ greatly in the types of information collected, accuracy, and ease of application. Among the first developed was an easily-applied condition class system based on visual criteria (Frissell 1978). This system requires the matching of campsite conditions with a set of five use-related site descriptions.

In contrast, a combined inventory and impact assessment system by Moorhead and Schreiner (1976) requires over 40 biophysical and management-related measurements at each site. This system is similar to one developed by Hendee *et al.* (1976) for inventorying dispersed recreation sites. Both systems use edge-punch cards and needle-sorting methods for recording, storing, and retrieving basic site information.

Multiple parameter impact assessment systems developed by Parsons and MacLeod (1980), Cole (1983a), and Marion (1985) offer perhaps the best mix of accuracy, meaningful information, and ease of application for most purposes. These systems generally use eight to 10 impact parameters, each with three to five impact ratings to assess the severity of impact. Among the impact parameters often included are: 1) campsite area; 2) barren core area; 3) vegetation loss; 4) tree damage; 5) root exposure; 6) shoreline disturbance; 7) number of access trails; 8) cleanliness; and 9) extent of campsite development. An overall mean value, computed from individual parameter ratings, represents each campsite's "impact class." Further descriptive and evaluative information concerning assessment systems can be found in Cole (1983a).

These multiple parameter impact assessment systems should be modified for each area in which they are applied. To be effective, these systems must differentiate and accurately assess the selected resource impacts within a given wildland area. This requires adapting each impact parameter's rating classes (defining the severity of impact) to match the range of conditions present in the area. Failure to do this typically results in an uneven distribution of sites among impact rating categories thus weakening the ability of a system to differentiate between lightly, moderately, and heavily impacted sites (Marion 1985). For example, if 90 percent of the campsites for an area fell into the "severe" impact category for vegetation loss, this could mean that the category was defined too broadly, this including moderately as well as heavily impacted sites. Furthermore, sites within the category could greatly deteriorate or improve over time without detection by the impact assessment system.

Procedures developed by Marion (1985) can aid managers in the development and calibration of these multiple parameter systems. As part of a multi-year cooperative research agreement between the USDA Forest Service's North Central Forest Experiment Station and the Mid-Atlantic Region of the National Park Service, these procedures currently are being applied in the development of separate campsite monitoring systems for two eastern park units: the Delaware Water Gap National Recreation Area in eastern Pennsylvania and the New River Gorge National River in West Virginia. Resource conditions for selected impact parameters are being measured on a representative sample of campsites in each of these areas. These measurements will be summarized and used to develop impact rating descriptors for each impact parameter so they evenly differentiate among the conditions present in each area. The use of microcomputers for storing, evaluating, and summarizing impact assessment and monitoring data also will be evaluated.

The Wilderness Research Center at the University of Idaho is currently conducting a study to identify and evaluate potential indicators to detect human-caused change in wilderness conditions. This study will provide valuable information for wildland managers nationwide concerning the selection of soil, vegetation, wildlife, water, and air indicators for wilderness monitoring programs.

The Center is also investigating the potential application of portable field microcomputers for campsite monitoring data storage and evaluation. At Oregon State University, Manfredo and Hester (1983) have developed a microcomputer based system for storing and analyzing campsite inventory data.

IMPACT MANAGEMENT STRATEGIES

Information from impact assessment and monitoring systems can help managers select, apply, and evaluate impact management strategies. However, before selecting an appropriate resource protection measure, managers should first reconcile resource impact problems(s) with the management objectives for the area. In particular, managers should understand the underlying **causes** of the problem so these may be addressed directly. Next, managers should consider all solutions to the resource impact problem(s). Often a combination of actions will most effectively control resource impacts.

Campsites

Due to their concentrated use, campsites typically present wildland managers with the most challenging resource impact problems. Visitors spend a significant amount of their time at campsites and their perception of wildland environments are influenced by the condition of these sites. Key management strategies and methods for minimizing campsite impacts are presented in Table 4 and discussed below:

Visitor dispersal, a traditional impact management strategy, involves the distribution of visitor use over as

large an area as possible to avoid severe impacts at any given site. Ideally, visitors should be directed away from heavily used areas and encouraged or required to camp on sites with little or no previous use (Cole and Dalle-Molle 1982). However, campsite impact studies have documented significant impacts with only initial or light use (less than 12 nights/year) while the rate of additional damage diminishes rapidly with increasing use levels (Merriam et al. 1973, Cole and Fichtler 1983, Marion and Merriam 1985).

These findings suggest that visitor dispersal will not minimize impacts. In many environments studied, failure to accomplish a high degree of dispersal would result in a significantly larger total area of resource alteration. Educating visitors to select impact-resistant sites such as grassy meadows, open forests, and sandbars, and to adopt minimum impact camping techniques, should increase the effectiveness of this strategy.

A strategy involving some form of **visitor concentration** would be more effective in areas receiving moderate to heavy visitor use. This strategy is designed to minimize impacts by encouraging or requiring visitors to camp on a limited number of well-established sites. Managers can then concentrate use on the most damage resistant sites thus avoiding and protecting

Table 4. A Framework of Management Strategies and Methods to Minimize Campsite Impacts.

General Management Strategies	Methods to Implement Strategies
Visitor dispersal	Encourage or require visitors to camp on sites with little or no previous use.
	Educate visitors to select impact resistant sites.
	Educate visitors on minimum impact camping techniques.
	Limit length of stay to 1 or 2 nights/campsite.
Visitor concentration	Encourage or require visitors to camp on well-established sites.
	Select and promote the use of impact resistant sites.
	Educate visitors on minimum impact camping techniques.
Site management	Implement a rehabilitation program for open sites to minimize extent and severity of impacts.
	Improvement/maintenance of essential use areas, closure of non-essential use areas.
	Plantings of trees, shrubs, and grasses.
	Temporary or permanent site closure.
Use limitations	Limit amount of use.
	Limit group size.
	Limit length of stay in area.

fragile, easily-damaged areas. Because the damage done does not increase in direct proportion to the amount of visitor use, this strategy will minimize the total area affected by visitor use and will not greatly increase many types of impacts at any given site.

This strategy may be implemented by encouraging visitors to select and use moderately impacted sites and to avoid, where possible, lightly and severely impacted sites (Cole and Benedict 1983). Where use is particularly heavy, such as in northeastern Minnesota's Boundary Waters Canoe Area Wilderness (BWCAW), managers may need to require visitors to use designated campsites. Such regulations are not unduly restrictive to visitors, provided the number and location of sites are matched to visitor numbers and use patterns (Peterson and Lime 1980). Campsite solitude also may be ensured by selecting sites away from main travel routes and out of sight and sound of each other, wherever possible.

An alternate strategy, which does not involve the visitor, is **management of the site itself**. Impacts on some heavily used sites may necessitate additional management attention. One option is temporary closure to allow natural or assisted rehabilitation. However, research generally has found impact rates to far exceed recover rates, suggesting that campsite rest-rotation schemes will not be effective (Thorud and Frissell 1976, Cole and Ranz 1983, Marion 1984).

Managers in the BWCAW have implemented an alternate site management approach: a rehabilitation and maintenance program for open campsites (Marion and Sober 1987). The goal is to keep campsites open and in good condition through the reduction of both the area and severity of impact at each site. Concentrating on areas of heavy use, field crews close non-essential portions of sites and shorelines, level selected onsite tenting areas to prohibit the development of offsite tenting areas, and plant trees, shrubs and grasses. Only native materials and species are used and every effort is made to ensure that rehabilitation work is visually and ecologically less obstrusive than the original problem.

The final impact management strategy is the **restriction of visitor use**, by limiting the number of visitors, group size, or lengths of stay. Again, research on the general use/impact relationship suggests that limiting use will not reduce impacts unless nearly all use is curtailed. However, some studies have indicated that a few impacts, such as campsite size, amount of exposed soil, and exposed tree roots, continue to increase significantly with increasing use levels (Cole 1982, Marion and Merriam 1985). More research is needed to fully document these relationships before use limitation can be justified as an impact minimization strategy.

CONCLUSION

In the early 1900's wildland resources were abundant. Today we have a limited wildland resource base and

increasing recreational demands. Wildland management efforts have intensified to meet these new demands. To some extent the alteration of natural conditions in recreational areas is inevitable. However, proper management is essential if the wildland qualities of naturalness and limited human-related impacts are to be maintained. The value society places on wildland environments lies in their continued "naturalness." Recreational impacts, if not monitored and controlled, will compromise the inherent value of wilderness and ultimately reduce the quality of recreational experiences.

With increasing wildland recreation pressures in the future, managers will need to cope with resulting resource impacts. Objective and standardized impact assessment and monitoring systems will be indispensable. Effective resource protection measures will involve the careful integration of a variety of visitor and resource management strategies and methods. Limited resource manipulation, in the form of campsite and trail maintenance and rehabilitation programs, also may aid resource administrators in the restoration and minimization of recreational impacts.

LITERATURE CITED

Anderson, D.H. 1981. The effect of user experience on displacement. pp. 272-279. In J.W. Frazier and B.J. Epstein (eds.). Proc. Appl. Geogr. Conf., Vol. 4, Dep. Geogr. SUNY, Binghamton, N.Y.

Anderson, D.H. 1983. Displacement: one consequence of not meeting people's needs. pp. 31-37. In Research in forest productivity, use, and pest control. USDA For. Serv., Northeast. For. Exp. Stn., Gen. Tech. Rep. NE-90.

Anderson, D.H. and P.J. Brown. 1984. The displacement process in recreation. J. Leisure Res. 16:61-73.

Cole, D.N. 1982. Wilderness campsite impacts: effect of amount of use. USDA For. Serv., Intermountain For. Exp. Stn., Res. Pap. INT-284.

Cole, D.N. 1983a. Monitoring the condition of wilderness campsites. USDA For. Serv., Intermountain For. Exp. Stn., Res. Pap. INT-284.

Cole, D.N. 1983b. Assessing and monitoring backcountry trail conditions. USDA For. Serv., Intermountain For. Exp. Stn., Res. Pap. INT-303.

Cole, D.N. and B. Ranz. 1983. Temporary campsite closures in the Selway-Bitterroot Wilderness. J. For. 81:729-732.

Cole, D.N. and J. Benedict. 1983. Wilderness campsite selection - what should users be told? Park Sci. 3:5-7.

Cole, D.N. and J. Dalle-Molle. 1982. Strategies and practical techniques for managing backcountry campfire impacts. USDA, For. Serv., Intermountain For. Exp. Stn., Gen. Tech. Rep. INT-135.

Cole, D.N. and R.K. Fichtler. 1983. Campsite impact on three western wilderness areas. Environ. Manage. 7:275-288.

Dustin, D.I., L.H. McAvoy, and J.H. Schultz. 1982. Stewards of access - Custodians of Choice. Burgess Publ. Co., Minneapolis, Minn.

Frissell, S.S. 1978. Judging recreation impacts on wilderness campsites. J. For. 76:481-483.

Hendee, J.D., R.N. Clark, M.L. Hogans, D. Wood, and R.W. Kock. 1976. Code-a-site: a system for inventory of dispersed recreational sites in roaded areas, backcountry, and wilderness. USDA For. Serv., Pac. Northwest For. Exp. Stn., Res. Pap. PNW-209.

Knopf, R.C. 1982. Management problems in river recreation: what floaters are telling us. Naturalist 33:12-17.

Knopf, R.C. and D.W. Lime. 1984. A recreation manager's guide to understanding river use and users. USDA For. Serv., North Central For. Exp. Stn., Gen. Tech. Rep. WO-38.

Knudson, D.M. and E.B. Curry. 1981. Campers' perceptions of site deterioration and crowding. J. For. 79:92-94.

Lime, D.W., R.C. Knopf, and G.L. Peterson. 1980. The national river recreation study: growing new data base with exciting potential. pp. 1-8. In Some recent products of river recreation research. USDA For. Serv., North Central For. Exp. Stn., Gen. Tech. Rep. NC-63.

Lucas, R.C. 1979. Perceptions of non-motorized recreational impacts: a review of research findings. pp. 24-31. In Ruth Ittner and others (eds.). Recreational Impact on Wildlands, Conf. Proc. Oct. 27-29, 1978. USDA For. Serv., R-6 Portland, Ore.

Manfredo, M.J. and A. Hester. 1983. A microcomputer based campsite data system. pp. 731-734. In: J.F. Bell, T. Atterbury (eds.). Renewable Resource Inventories for Monitoring Changes in Trends, An International Conference. Aug. 15-19, 1983. Ore. State Univ., College of Forestry, Corvallis, Ore.

Marion, J.L. 1984. Ecological changes resulting from recreational use: a study of backcountry campsites in the Boundary Waters Canoe Area Wilderness, Minnesota. Ph.D. diss. Univ. of Minnesota, St. Paul, Minn.

Marion, J.L. 1985. Campsite impact assessment systems: application, evaluation, and development. In 1984 River Recreation Symposium, Conf. Proc. Oct. 31 - Nov. 3. Baton Rouge, La. Lousiana State Univ., Baton Rouge, La.

Marion, J.L. and L.C. Merriam. 1985. Recreational impacts on well-established campsites in the Boundary Waters Canoe Area Wilderness. Univ. of Minnesota Stn. Bull. AD-SB-2502, Agric. Exp. Stn., St. Paul, Minn.

Marion, J.L. and T. Sober. 1987. Wilderness campsite management in the Boundary Waters Canoe Area Wilderness. North. J. App. For. (in press).

Merriam, L.C. et al. 1973. Newly developed campsites in the Boundary Waters Canoe Area - a study of five year's use. Univ. Minn. Agric. Exp. Stn., Stn. Bull. 511, St. Paul, Minn.

Moorhead, B.B. and E.L. Schreiner. 1976. Management studies of human impact at backcountry campsites in Olympic National Park, Washington. In Proc. First Conf. on Sci. Res. in the National Parks. 2:1273-1278.

Nieman, T.J. and J.L. Futrell. 1979. Projecting the visual carrying capacity of recreation areas. p. 420-427. In Proc. of Our National Landscape. USDA For. Serv., Pacific Southwest For. Exp. Stn., Gen. Tech. Rep. PSW-35.

Parsons, D.J. and S.A. MacLeod. 1980. Measuring impacts of wilderness use. Parks 5:8-11.

Peterson, G.L. and D.W. Lime. 1980. Recreation policy analysis in wilderness management: a case study of the Quetico-Superior. pp. 4-13. In J.W. Fisher and B.J. Epstein (eds.). Proc. Third Annual Appl. Geogr. Conf., Dep. Geogr. SUNY, Binghamton, NY, and Dep. Geogr., Kent State Univ., Kent, Ohio.

Roggenbuck, J.W., A.E. Watson, and G.H. Stankey. 1982. Wilderness management in the Southern Appalachians. South. J. Appl. For. 6:146-152.

Schreyer, R. and D.W. Lime. 1984. A novice isn't necessarily a novice - the influence of experience use history on subjective perceptions of recreation participation. Leisure Sci. 6:131-149.

Schreyer, R. and J.W. Roggenbuck. 1978. The influence of experience expectations on crowding perceptions and social-psychological carrying capacities. Leisure Sci. 1:373-394.

Settergren, D.C. 1977. Impacts of river recreation use on streambank soils and vegetation -- state of the knowledge. pp. 55-59. In River Recreation and Management, Conf. Proc. USDA For. Serv., North Central For. Exp. Stn., Gen. Tech. Rep. NC-28.

Thorud, D.B. and S.S. Frissell. 1976. Time changes in soil density following compaction under an oak forest. Univ. Minn. Dep. For. Resources, For. Res. Note No. 257,

Providing Information For Management Purposes

by
Joseph W. Roggenbuck and Alan E. Watson

ABSTRACT--Providing information to wilderness users is a lighthanded management strategy that permits freedom of choice in wilderness. Information also meets the mandates of the Wilderness Act. Empirical research indicates that simple written brochures can disperse wilderness users, enhance opportunities for solitude, and reduce site impacts, but personalized information contacts are generally more effective. Effectiveness in modifying behavior is influenced by relevancy and detail of information, format and channel of presentation, timing, and the extent to which the target audience actually receives the message.

KEYWORDS: information, education, use redistribution, site impacts, communication, brochures, wilderness rangers, knowledge, attitudes, behavior.

Management of wilderness in the Eastern United States is becoming an increasingly important function of federal resource management agencies, particularly the USDA Forest Service. The 98th Congress designated 52 new Forest Service wildernesses east of the 100th meridian during 1983-84; this is more than had been created between 1964 and 1982. While most of the public's attention and resource agencies' efforts in recent years have focused on the allocation process, wilderness designation itself does not assure protection. A variety of uses, outside influences, and legal mandates make the management of wilderness necessary. This is particularly true in the East where areas tend to be small, visitation levels high, and past or current incompatible uses exist within or adjacent to designated areas. Indeed, management may be the greater challenge, for the allocation process will eventually be complete (Hendee 1974). From that time forward, management will be necessary to meet changing wilderness demands on a static resource base.

Management's responsibility is to maintain, enhance where necessary, and provide those wilderness values that the American public expects from its wilderness resource. These values, as institutionalized in the Wilderness Act (Public Law 88-577) and reaffirmed in the so-called Eastern Wilderness Act (Public Law 93-622), are primarily the protection of areas that "generally appear to have been affected primarily by the forces of nature, with the imprint of man's work substantially unnoticeable;" and the provision of "outstanding opportunities for solitude or a primitive and unconfined type of recreation." These values of naturalness, solitude, and freedom, spontaneity, and escape run deep in the American consciousness, and

have consistently been important in studies of wilderness users (Stankey 1973, Hendee et al. 1978, Lucas 1980, and Roggenbuck et al. 1982).

Managing for these values is particularly challenging, for many recreation management strategies are inappropriate in wilderness. For example, site manipulation, site hardening and facility development to mitigate resource impacts appear to violate the mandate for naturalness. Other strategies which might provide the wilderness user with opportunities for solitude under conditions of even relatively high use, such as assigned departure times, places, travel routes and campsites, seem incompatible with the mandate for freedom and unconfined recreation. Visitor management is necessary, but that management must be lighthanded and unobtrusive (Lucas 1980, 1982). Management strategies must assure naturalness, maintain opportunities for solitude, and retain freedom at levels not found at less primitive outdoor recreation settings.

The purpose of our paper is to suggest that providing information to wilderness users is both an appropriate and an effective management tool to accomplish wilderness management objectives. We then make suggestions on how information might be packaged to increase its effectiveness. Finally, we describe some pitfalls that a manager should avoid when implementing an information management program.

WHAT IS INFORMATION FOR MANAGEMENT?

236

As is the case with any management strategy, providing information requires that management objectives clearly and specifically state the conditions to be maintained or achieved within wilderness. Providing information on wilderness site characteristics might help people attain the experiences they seek, avoid disappointments from expectations not met, and separate user groups seeking to participate in conflicting and incompatible activities. Information might be used to direct potential wilderness users seeking experiences not dependent on wilderness to more appropriate areas outside designated wilderness. Informing visitors of heavily and lightly used zones and times within a wilderness might better redistribute use throughout the area or through time, and provide increased opportunities for solitude. Instructing actual or potential wilderness users on "leave-no-trace" wilderness use practices might increase knowledge and skill levels, change behavior, and reduce site impacts. Finally, through effective communication, managers might gain the cooperation of wilderness users in management programs (e.g. litter clean-up, trail maintenance). This seems especially important during times of tight budgetary and personnel ceilings.

IS INFORMATION FOR MANAGEMENT APPROPRIATE IN WILDERNESS?

When selecting any management tool, the manager must ask if the strategy under consideration violates the mandates of the Wilderness Act or the values contained therein. When considering the implementation of an information program, the manager must be particularly concerned about freedom, exploration, and spontaneity. Does information restrict freedom and individual decision making to unacceptable levels? Does it destroy the sense of exploration and discovery so important in wilderness?

The text of the Wilderness Act, philosophical papers by wilderness scholars, and opinions of wilderness users all suggest that information is an ideal wilderness management strategy. The Wilderness Act (Public Law 88-577) explicitly mandates the provision of information to visitors when it states that wilderness areas "shall be administered . . . in such manner . . . so as to provide . . . for gathering and dissemination of information regarding their use and enjoyment as wilderness." No wilderness law has since rescinded that mandate.

Wilderness scholars have consistently labelled information as a lighthanded management tool (Gilbert *et al.* 1972, Hendee *et al.* 1978, Fazio 1979, Lucas 1982). They have done so because they view information as unobtrusive and non-authoritarian. With information, the wilderness visitor retains freedom of choice; he can choose to respond or not to respond. With this approach the manager becomes a helpful guide rather than one who restricts or regulates (Lucas 1981).

Research findings through time and throughout the country have consistently shown that a majority of wilderness users want information. Stankey (1973) found that about 60% of his respondents in the Boundary Waters Canoe Area, Bob Marshall Wilderness, Bridger Wilderness, and High Unitas Primitive Area favored maps and information pamphlets. About 85% of the Bob Marshall respondents and two-thirds of the users of the other three study areas supported the presence of rangers in the backcountry. Lucas (1980) found that almost everyone in his study of nine wilderness and backcountry areas in the West thought good maps and guidebooks were desirable. Only 4 to 15 percent of the visitors to the nine areas thought wilderness rangers were undesirable. Roggenbuck *et al.* (1982) found that about 90% of Linville Gorge, Shining Rock, and Joyce Kilmer/Slickrock wilderness users in North Carolina supported better information on use. Finally, wilderness users who have been given informational brochures have thought such distribution of information was a good idea and should be continued (Lime and Lucas 1977, Berrier 1980, Lucas 1981).

Recently, however, Irwin (1985) questioned whether informational contacts, especially by wilderness rangers at trailheads or inside the area, permit *psychological* freedom, and conducted a more in-depth look at visitor response to information. He wondered whether wilderness users really felt free to ignore a wilderness ranger's request for use dispersal. He also wondered if wilderness users had a sense of "being watched" after rangers provided trailhead messages on low impact camping. He found that about 60% of Shining Rock Wilderness visitors felt that their trailhead ranger contact with its low impact camping message was slightly, quite, or extremely lighthanded; only 4% thought it was heavyhanded. Between 70% and 80% liked the contact because it permitted their questions to be answered correctly and permitted them to learn the proper way to use the wilderness. Between 80% and 90% liked the contact because it demonstrated that the Forest Service cared about the wilderness, because the Forest Service should teach appropriate wilderness use practices, and because by following the ranger's suggestions they could continue to freely use the wilderness. Only about 6% disliked the contact because they felt they would be penalized if they didn't follow the ranger's suggestions. Fewer than 5% did not like it because they wanted to be left alone, they felt they had to give up their favorite ways of camping, they had to delay the start of their trip, or they felt they were being watched the whole trip. Only 1.6% felt it took away their freedom.

IS INFORMATION AN EFFECTIVE MANAGEMENT STRATEGY?

While there is general consensus that the use of information is an appropriate management tool, there is considerable debate about its effectiveness. While many wilderness managers use information and education, they disagree both across and within agencies on its effectiveness (Godin and Leonard 1979, Bury and Fish 1980, Washburne and Cole 1983). If any generalization can be made, it is that managers tend to implement lighthanded strategies like information to *prevent* overuse and impacts, and adopt heavyhanded strategies to *manage existing* overuse problems (Irwin 1985). The majority of managers in the Cole and Washburne study (1983) did, however, feel that a personal contact with the visitor was the most effective technique to improve visitor camping practices and use dispersal.

The amount of empirical research on the effectiveness of information in solving wilderness management problems is limited. What does exist generally addresses only one of the many uses of information: the use of information to disperse use through time or space within an area (e.g. see Schomaker 1975, Lime and Lucas 1977, Canon *et al.* 1979, Lucas 1981, Roggenbuck and Berrier 1981, 1982, and Krumpe and Brown 1982). Success has been mixed, and appears to depend on the purposes for which the information was used, the sources of the information, amount of information given, the timing of the message transfer, the channel used to communicate the information, and characteristics of the target audience and situation.

Inter-area Redistribution of Use

An example of the use of information to potentially shift use from high use to lightly used areas is the USDA Forest Service's Recreation Opportunity Guide (ROG) (USDA Forest Service 1979). The guide assists the public in choosing settings that meet their needs. It is generally placed at national forest headquarters, visitor centers, and/or district ranger offices. It typically is a loose-leaf notebook that describes recreation facilities and opportunities within a national forest and/or district. The general public, either alone or with the help of a Forest Service receptionist, uses the guide to make better recreation choices.

The authors are unaware of any systematic evaluation of ROG or any other informational program to alter use across areas. Such an evaluation is a high priority research need. Researchers and managers need to determine if forest visitors actually use ROG, if ROG's indexing system permits people to find preferred recreation sites with ease and accuracy, if people actually change their behavior and visit a different site, if behavioral changes result in more satisfying experiences, if shifts from high use areas to lightly used areas can be accomplished, and if shifts in use from formal wilderness to nondesignated backcountry are possible.

Intra-area Redistribution of Use

As has already been indicated, much has been learned on the ability of information to disperse use from areas of concentrated use to zones of light use within a wilderness. Our own research indicates that information can be very effective for this purpose.

The Shining Rock camper study.-- In 1979 we worked with Forest Service managers in Shining Rock Wilderness in North Carolina to use information to disperse campers from a heavily used, half-acre meadow called Shining Rock Gap. The heavy concentration of campers had caused physical and biological impacts judged unacceptable. Also, previous research has indicated that approximately 54 percent of Shining Rock overnight users believed a lack of privacy in campsites was a problem (Roggenbuck *et al.* 1979). Our specific purposes were to determine the relative advantage of information treatments, (a brochure alone and a brochure plus personal contact), and to identify the influence of user and situational characteristics upon the success of each informational treatment. (For complete details of the study, see Roggenbuck and Berrier 1981, 1982).

Our informational brochure contained a short narrative describing damage caused by concentrated use and the benefits of use dispersal in protecting wilderness resources and maintaining solitude. The brochure also contained a map of five more lightly used camping areas within one mile of the Gap, and a description of their location and characteristics (distance to campsite from the Gap, trail difficulty, visibility from trail, distance from water, number of campsites, view, wind protection, campsite screening, vegetation, and amount of use).

Both information treatments were effective in dispersing camping groups from Shining Rock Gap. The percentage of camping use that occurred at Shining Rock Gap dropped from 62% (control) to 44% during the brochure alone treatment, and from 62% to 33% during the brochure plus personal contact treatment. Both of these changes were statistically significant.

The difference in the relative effectiveness of the two informational treatments was not statistically significant, and this surprised us. Previous research had suggested that personalized contacts were much more effective in increasing knowledge of wilderness ethics than a brochure alone (Fazio 1979). Upon closer analysis of our data, we noticed much higher variation in visitor response to the brochure-plus-ranger contact than to the brochure alone. Certain groups were much more likely to disperse under the ranger-contact treatment (i.e. groups lacking previous experience in the area, lacking formal organization, arriving at the meadow more than three hours before dark, and in medium size groups).

Influences on success of information programs

Our research indicates that simple information can cause substantial changes in where people camp in the backcountry. An average of 6.9 groups camped each night in the Shining Rock Gap under the control condition; this dropped to 2.7 and 2.6 groups under the brochure-alone and the brochure-plus-contact treatments, respectively. Whether or not this reduction is "good enough" depends on management objectives and standards for the area, and these are managerial judgments. We can, however, on the basis of our own research and that of others make suggestions on how to increase the effectiveness of information.

Managers who use information should take every step possible to assure that their intended audiences get the messages. Lucas (1981) had little success in the use of informational brochures aimed at redistributing use among trailheads on the Stevensville Ranger District of the Selway-Bitterroot Wilderness. In probing the reasons why, he discovered that fewer than half of his study participants had actually received the brochure. Of those who had the brochure, 77% had received it from trailhead dispersal boxes. Only 12% obtained the brochure from the ranger station, national forest office, or regional office. Fazio (1979) also found that few wilderness users received information on wilderness management, personal safety and equipment in wilderness, and biophysical aspects of the land from such mass media sources as television and newspapers. This was the case even though he had run a half-hour videotape on a local television station and had published a feature story on the topic in an area newspaper. For information to be effective, we must target the message at our clientele groups, and present it at places where they will receive it (Robertson 1982).

Information provided must also be relevant and detailed enough to permit the receiver to carry out the suggested behavior. For example, Schomaker (1975) gave wilderness hikers information at trailheads about the amount of use of the various trails in the Rawah Wilderness. He found little change in trail selection behavior, and suggested that his program might have been more successful had he provided more information about alternate trails than just use levels. Several researchers have followed his suggestion (e.g. Lime and Lucas 1977, Canon *et al.* 1979, Krumpe and Brown 1982, and Roggenbuck and Berrier 1982) and have had considerable success. Lucas (1981) has noted that detailed information is necessary if people are to have enough confidence in a message to change familiar behaviors.

People must also have confidence in the accuracy of

the information provided (Lucas 1981). In our own research, we have worked with the resource agencies and have identified them as a co-author of the informational messages. In personal contacts, our research assistants have worn agency volunteer vests, and our brochures have indicated agency support. We think this has increased our credibility and our success. We note, however, that agency authorship of brochures does not necessarily assure accuracy or receiver's perceptions of accuracy. In Lucas' study (1981), respondents had little faith in the trail use information provided because these data were based on trail registers. Visitors were apparently right; trail registration levels were low and may not have accurately reflected reality.

Krumpe and McLaughlin (1982), Krumpe and Brown (1982) and Watson and Roggenbuck (1985) have suggested that the way information is presented can enhance its effectiveness. Krumpe and Brown (1982) recognized that people use a sequential decision-making strategy to choose recreation sites. They do this by first eliminating potential sites on the basis of their most important criterion attributes, and then proceed to less important variables until the choice is made. Given this, the authors provided descriptions of lightly used trails in Yellowstone National Park in a decision-tree format. Visitors were asked questions and provided information on trails with streams, mountain peaks, lakes, or off-trail, cross-country travel. Once a decision was made on selection of one of these four trail types, several more questions and increased information about more detailed setting aspects led to a final decision. The authors found that 37% of the respondents in their experimental group (i.e. the group received information) compared to 14% of the control group took one of the lightly-used trails. Watson and Roggenbuck (1985) believe that use dispersal might have been even greater had Krumpe and Brown permitted respondents to use their own decision-making criteria in their own preferred sequence. Such a strategy is possible through employment of "user-friendly" microcomputer-based decision aids.

Communication theorists (e.g. Bettinghaus 1968) have suggested that oral communication is often more effective than written communication for messages that are not complex. This is most likely to be true when the persuasive effect of the oral communication is dependent on the recipient's perception of the credibility of the source. While our own work has shown that written brochures can be effective, most research in park and wilderness settings indicates that oral and face-to-face communication is more effective. For example, Fazio (1979) found that a brochure did not significantly increase knowledge of wilderness management and use practices, but that a slide-tape program on the subject and trailhead contacts with rangers did. In our study described earlier, ranger contacts were more effective than a brochure alone for novice users and for medium-size (3-6 people) user groups. Finally, Oliver *et al.* (1985) have recently reported that a brochure-plus-contact was significantly more effective than a brochure alone in reducing litter and tree damage in a forested car campground.

Timing of message transfer is vitally important. Generally, the earlier in the decision-making process that recreationists receive information, the more likely that they will change their behavior. Often this means that the contact must be made before visitors arrive at the site. For example, both Schomaker (1975) and Lucas (1981) have suggested that their lack of success at redistributing use from one trailhead to another was because their study participants didn't receive information until they had arrived at the trailhead. By that time they were apparently highly committed to a travel route. When Lime and Lucas (1977) mailed information early in the spring of the year to individuals who had visited the Boundary Waters Canoe Area the previous year, they found they influenced the choice of entry point, route, or time of subsequent visits of about a third of their study participants. Of these, most followed the information and visited more lightly used areas. However, not all contacts have to be made before arrival on-site. Our own research indicates that trailhead contacts or in-camp contacts are early enough to alter camping practices (Oliver *et al.* 1985) or camping location (Roggenbuck and Berrier 1981, 1982).

Characteristics of the individuals and user groups toward whom information is directed also influence its effectiveness. Research has consistently shown that wilderness visitors without previous experience in the area are more influenced than experienced visitors (Lime and Lucas 1977, Krumpe and Brown 1982, and Roggenbuck and Berrier 1982). Roggenbuck and Berrier (1982) reported that both a brochure and a brochure-plus-contact was effective in dispersing small (1 or 2 person) camping groups in Shining Rock Wilderness, the brochure plus contact was more effective than the brochure alone for medium size (3-6 people) groups, and neither informational channel was effective in dispersing large groups. Time of group arrival at the trailhead or at the high use meadow campsite also influenced the effectiveness of informational treatments in the Roggenbuck and Berrier study (1982). Late arriving visitors were less likely to disperse. We also note that virtually all the reports of successful alteration of wilderness behavior change due to information involve day or overnight wilderness hikers. We wonder if informational programs would be as effective with user groups like hunters that are more goal-oriented.

Finally, we have found in our own research that visitor response to individual rangers varied considerably across time. Even though they were highly trained, our rangers may not have always been able to maintain high performance levels. Also, we have noted the need to know the influence of varying rapport levels established between contact rangers and the visiting public, and whether effectiveness varies by sex, personality, and experience of the rangers (Roggenbuck and Berrier 1982). Irwin (1985), however, has recently examined visitor response to three trailhead rangers and found no difference in visitor perceived freedom and the perceived lighthandness of the contact on the basis of sex or experience level of the rangers.

Information to Reduce Impact Behavior

Many resource managers believe that wilderness users typically do not commit malicious acts to harm the wilderness environment or wilderness experience. Instead, problem behaviors are generally unintentional and the result of ignorance of proper behavior (Godin and Leonard 1979, Bradley 1979, and Hart 1980). Hendee *et al.* (1978) have classified problem behaviors as illegal actions, careless actions, unskilled actions, uninformed actions, and unavoidable impacts. Of these, they believe unskilled actions to be the most numerous, and they believe information-education to be ideally suited to reducing careless, unskilled, and uninformed actions.

Surprisingly few rigorous studies have been conducted to determine if written or oral information actually reduces impacts in the backcountry. Both Hart (1980) and Bradley (1979) report that trailhead and in-area ranger contacts did reduce such impacts as littering and tree damage in their wildernesses, but their observations lacked a control group and systematic data collection. Irwin (1985) reported that, after a trailhead contact, 100% of his respondents in Shining Rock Wilderness agreed they should pack out all littering; between 90% and 99% agreed they should bury human wastes, pack out leftover food, bathe away from a stream, not make excessive noise, wash dishes away from a stream, and not cut living trees or bushes. Approximately three-fourths of the study subjects agreed that they should remove all traces of their fire ring and not cut standing dead trees or bushes. However, such attitudes do not necessarily result in equivalent low impact behavior, and Irwin's study design does not permit us to know with any degree of certainty that low impact attitudes and behavior were due to the trailhead contacts.

Implementing an Information Program - Some Cautions.-- Empirical research and managerial experience indicate that information can change visitor behavior while still retaining freedom in wilderness. Before implementing an information program, the manager needs to specify in management objectives the desired conditions within wilderness. Only with the statement of specific objectives can the manager judge whether information is appropriate and whether a program, once implemented, is effective. For example, information can disperse use throughout a wilderness area, thus reducing contacts between users and increasing opportunities for solitude. But completely even distribution of use throughout an area probably is not desirable. People vary in their definitions of what is solitude, and areas differ in their susceptibility to ecological impacts. Managers may want to maintain some zones in wilderness where virtually no one goes. Such areas would exist for those who have the most sensitive definitions of solitude.

Secondly, a well-planned use dispersal program considers potential impacts on the dispersal sites. Research indicates that recreation site impacts occur under conditions of light use (Wagar 1964, Frissell and Duncan 1965, Merriam and Smith 1974, Cole 1982). Thus, a use redistribution program might increase opportunities for solitude at the cost of an increase in area of site impacts (Cole 1981). To avoid the undesirable impacts, Cole (1983) has recommended that wilderness campers be directed to durable and moderately impacted sites. Campers should be dispersed to pristine sites only when they employ low-impact-camping techniques, and select resistant sites with little or no repeat use.

Finally, care needs to be taken lest information attract users who are not seeking wilderness-dependent experiences. This problem might best be avoided by a comprehensive regional information management program. Information would be provided on regional attractions across the entire spectrum of outdoor recreation settings. Information on wildernesses in the region would emphasize their wilderness qualities (Hendee *et al.* 1978). For example, the lack of facilities, the presence of biting insects, and the ruggedness of the terrain would receive as much coverage as the area's fishing opportunities. Such an approach would likely protect wilderness, provide realistic expectations, match experiences with expectations, and provide the broadest array of human benefits.

LITERATURE CITED

Berrier, D.L. 1980. The effectiveness of information on dispersing wilderness campers. Unpublished M.S. Thesis, Dep. of Forestry, Virginia Polytech. Inst. and State Univ., Blacksburg, Vir.

Bettinghaus, E.P. 1968. Persuasive Communication. Holt, Rinehart and Winston, New York, N.Y.

Bradley, J. 1979. A human approach to reducing wildland impacts. pp. 222-226. *In* R. Ittner *et al.* (eds.). Recreational Impact on Wildlands. USDA For. Serv. and USDI National Park Serv. R-6-001-1979.

Bury, R.L. and C.B. Fish. 1980. Controlling wilderness recreation. What managers think and do. J. Soil Water Conserv. 35:90-93.

Canon, L.K., S. Adler, and R.E. Leonard. 1979. Factors affecting dispersion of backcountry campers. USDA For. Serv. Res. Note NE-276.

Cole, D.N. 1981. Managing ecological impacts at wilderness campsites. An evaluation of techniques. J. For. 79:86-89.

Cole, D.N. 1982. Wilderness campsite impacts: Effect of amount of use. USDA For. Serv. Res. Pap. INT-284.

Cole, D.N. 1983. Wilderness campsite selection - What should users be told? Park Sci. 3:5-7.

Frissell, S.S. and D.P. Duncan. 1965. Campsite preference and deterioration. J. For. 63:256-260.

Fazio, J.R. 1979. Communicating with the wilderness user. Univ. Idaho, Coll. For., Wildl. and Range Sci. Bull. 28.

Gilbert, C.G., G.L. Peterson, and D.W. Lime. 1972. Toward a model of travel behavior in the Boundary Waters Canoe Area. Environ. and Behav. 4:131-157.

Godin, V.B. and R.E. Leonard. 1979. Management problems in designated wilderness areas. J. Soil Water Conserv. 34:141-143.

Hart, P. 1980. New backcountry ethic: leave no trace. Am. For. 86:38-41, 51-54.

Hendee, J.C. 1974. A scientist's view on some current wilderness management issues. West. Wildlands 1:27-32.

Hendee, J.C., G.H. Stankey, and R.C. Lucas. 1978. Wilderness management. USDA For. Serv. Misc. Publ. 1365.

Irwin, K.M. 1985. Wilderness visitor response to ranger educational contacts at trailheads. Unpublished M.S. Thesis, Dep. of Forestry, Virginia Polytech. Inst. and State Univ., Blacksburg, Vir.

Krumpe, E.E. and P.J. Brown. 1982. Redistributing backcountry use through information related to recreation experiences. J. For. 80:360-362, 364.

Krumpe, E.E. and W.J. McLaughlin. 1982. A model of recreationists' decisionmaking process. pp. 94-99 *In* Forest and River Recreation: Research Update. Univ. Minn. Agric. Exp. Stn. Misc. Publ. 18 St. Paul, Minn.

Lime, D.W. and R.C. Lucas. 1977. Good information improves the wilderness experience. Naturalist 28:18-20.

Lucas, R.C. 1980. Use patterns and visitor characteristics, attitudes, and preferences in nine wilderness and other roadless areas. USDA For. Serv. Res. Pap. INT-253.

Lucas, R.C. 1981. Redistributing wilderness use through information supplied to visitors. USDA For. Serv. Res. Pap. INT-277.

Lucas, R.C. 1982. Recreation regulations-When are they needed? J. For. 80:148-151.

Merriam, L.C., Jr. and C.K. Smith. 1974. Visitor impact on newly developed campsites in the Boundary Waters Canoe Area. J. For. 72:627-630.

Oliver, S.S., J.W. Roggenbuck, and A.E. Watson. 1985. Education to reduce impacts in forest campgrounds. J. For. 83:234-236.

Robertson, R.D. 1982. Visitor knowledge affects visitor behavior. pp. 49-51. *In* Forest and River Recreation: Research Update. Univ. Minn. Agric. Exp. Stn. Misc. Publ. 18., St. Paul, Minn.

Roggenbuck, J.W. and D.L. Berrier. 1981. Communications to disperse wilderness campers. J. For. 79:295-297.

Roggenbuck, J.W. and D.L. Berrier. 1982. A comparison of the effectiveness of two communication strategies in dispersing wilderness campers. J. Leisure Res. 14:77-89.

Roggenbuck, J.W., W.N. Timm, and A.E. Watson. 1979. Visitor perception of the recreation carrying capacity of three wilderness areas in North Carolina. Dep. of Forestry, Virginia Polytech. Inst. and State Univ., Blacksburg, Vir.

Roggenbuck, J.W., A.E. Watson, and G.H. Stankey. 1982. Wilderness management in the Southern Appalachians. South. J. Appl. For. 6:147-152.

Schomaker, J.H. 1975. Effect of selected information on dispersal of wilderness recreationists. Ph.D. diss. Colo. State Univ., Fort Collins, Colo.

Stankey, G.H. 1973. Visitor perception of wilderness recreation carrying capacity. USDA For. Serv. Res. Pap. INT-142.

USDA Forest Service. 1979. Recreation Opportunity Guide Manual. U.S. Government Printing Office. 796-058/32.

Wagar, J.A. 1964. The carrying capacity of wildlands for recreation.

For. Sci. Monogr. No. 7, Society of American Foresters, Washington, D.C.

Washburne, R.F. and D.N. Cole. 1983. Problems and practices in wilderness management; A survey of managers. USDA For. Serv. Res. Pap. INT-304.

Watson, A.E. and J.W. Roggenbuck. 1985. The use of microcomputers for presenting recreation site information. pp 9-14. In Proc.: Presented Papers, 1984 Southeastern Recreation Res. Conf. Inst. for Behavioral Research, Univ. Georgia, Athens, Ga.

Recreation In Eastern Wilderness: Do We Know What The Visitors Expect?

by

Alan E. Watson and Joseph W. Roggenbuck

ABSTRACT--Increased wilderness acreage in the East means increased numbers of wilderness managers. A very relevant question is to ask what we know about the expectations of visitors to Eastern wilderness areas. While it appears that visitors to Eastern areas do not expect different physical and managerial attributes and psychological experiences, differences within the East related to unique land form and ecosystem types may need further investigation.

KEYWORDS: perceptions, expectations, motivations, physical attributes, social/psychological experiences, managerial attributes.

In 1984, there was a new surge in supply of classified wilderness. Over 8 million acres (3.2 million ha) were classified as wilderness in that one year alone (Davis 1984a). Teamed with this, there were five additions to the National Wild and Scenic River System (Davis 1984b).

These newly classified areas on the primitive end of the recreation spectrum were not confined to the West. The Au Sable/Pere Marquette National River was established in Michigan and over 500,000 acres (202,350 ha) of new wilderness were designated in the two eastern regions of the Forest Service.

Along with this sudden increase in wilderness acreage was an accompanying increase in the number of wilderness managers. The question we would like to address now is "Do we know what visitors to wilderness in the East really demand, or expect? What should we strive to be providing?" Special interest is in newly classified wilderness and newly charged wilderness managers. Managers need to know what is expected of them, and of the site, by the visitors to wilderness in the East.

MANAGERS' PERCEPTIONS OF WILDERNESS VISITORS' EXPECTATIONS

Hendee and Harris (1970) suggested that proper management of wilderness depends upon the ability of managers to perceive user preferences and to satisfy them. In their assessment of how well 56 Forest Service wilderness managers in Oregon and Washington could estimate users' opinions there appears some justification for current concerns about how accurately managers of new wilderness can anticipate visitor expectations. In this 1970 study, managers underestimated user support of "reasonable" measures of behavior control. Users also evaluated facility development (trail surfacing, fireplaces, tables, and outhouses) in the wilderness as much less desirable than managers expected them to. On many other issues, however, managers expected visitors to exhibit more purist ideals than they did. Exposure to purist philosophies of very vocal environmental groups may have contributed to managers overestimating the extent of purist ideals among typical users and underestimating those who had very neutral opinions on many management issues.

Peterson (1974) also found some differences between what wilderness managers and visitors thought were acceptable. In a comparison of responses from 17 Boundary Waters Canoe Area managers and 127 visitors it was found that managers may be more permissive of some activities that visitors reject as inappropriate. Visitors were more demanding of "natural purity" than managers were. The managers also perceived more diverse motivations for visitors coming to the BWCA than actually existed.

Wellman and others (1982) provided additional insight into how accurately managers can predict motivations of visitors to primitive recreation areas. In this case, 36 managers of Shenandoah backcountry and wilderness were relatively accurate in their estimations of visitor motivations. However, they significantly underestimated the importance of scenery and nature, physical exercise, security, meeting/observing new people, reflection on personal values, and creativity. Managers of this primitive recreation area, however, predicted visitor motivations much better than managers of a more developed recreation area (Wellman et al. 1982).

These findings suggest that managers of wilderness

must be very careful in assuming an understanding of what the visitors expect when they visit. While managers of some areas appear to be able to predict a substantial number of visitor motivations accurately, there remain some very important reasons for visiting that may be significantly underestimated.

EFFECTS OF WILDERNESS CLASSIFICATION ON DEMAND

It may be expected that newly classified wilderness will present a special problem to managers trying to predict visitor expectations. Recent research suggests that the commonly held belief that use and users change considerably when an area becomes designated "wilderness" may be an inaccurate belief.

Shomaker and Glasford (1982) found that roadless area and wilderness area visitors in northern Idaho and eastern Oregon were very similar in their preferences for various aspects of the primitive recreation experience. In this comparison of responses from 186 Eagle Cap Wilderness visitors and 126 Selkirk backcountry area visitors, it was found that visitors to these two areas, with somewhat different use classifications, had very similar attitudes towards appropriate development levels and interparty encounters. This suggests that what contributes to enjoyable recreation experiences for visitors of backcountry may not be significantly different from when it becomes wilderness. Or if changes occur, they may be only temporary.

McCool (1985) provided quantitative support for the premise that use may not always change as a result of a wilderness designation effect. In the Rattlesnake National Recreation Area and Wilderness Area, near Missoula, Montana, use levels and activity patterns were documented before and after wilderness designation. While not offering conclusive evidence, for at least one area in Montana, McCool has documented a lack of the suspected designation effect. Total numbers of users actually went down, though the characteristics of the users remained relatively the same with the exception of group size. After wilderness designation, average group size was significantly smaller.

WHAT IS EXPECTED?

A substantial amount of research on what influences individuals to visit wilderness has occurred in the West. Concern about applicability of this research to perceived unique Eastern situations has led to comparable research in Eastern wilderness in recent years.

One might expect visitors of Eastern Wilderness to be in search of something somewhat different from visitors to areas in the West. These areas in the East are generally

smaller, more impacted, closer to population centers, and more heavily used (Hendee 1980). Investigative work by Roggenbuck (1980) provided very convincing evidence that visitors to areas in the East are not seeking anything different than visitors to areas in the West. User preference has been investigated for both regions of the country with some consistent findings regarding preferences for physical and managerial attributes and social/psychological benefits attributed to a visit to an area.

Physical Attributes Expected

Wilderness visitors, East and West, expect, and receive satisfaction from, opportunities to view scenery (Shafer and Meitz 1969, Echelberger and Moeller 1977, Haas 1979, Lucas 1980, Roggenbuck 1980). Providing visitors to wilderness with opportunities to experience undisturbed nature, another expectation of the physical environment

(Glock and Selzynick 1962, Catton and Hendee 1968, Roggenbuck 1980), may be a difficult task for managers. Presence of litter, destruction of vegetation, and presence of fire rings detract from wilderness recreation experiences (Roggenbuck 1980). Principal elements of the physical environment which visitors value particularly high in a wilderness experience are water, wildlife, and panoramic views of nature (Roggenbuck 1980).

Social/Psychological Experiences Expected

A low number of social encounters is generally expected by wilderness visitors (Glock and Selzynick 1962,

Echelberger and Moeller 1977, Lucas 1980, Roggenbuck 1980, Roggenbuck et al. 1982). Social encounters at campsites have been found to be less acceptable than those along trails, for example, and encountering several small groups is more acceptable than encountering one very large group of hikers. Additional experiences commonly expected are escape (Glock and Selzynick 1962, Catton and Hendee 1968, Roggenbuck 1980) and exercise/physical fitness (Roggenbuck 1980). Risk, coping with the primitive environment, and social recognition are experiences not commonly demanded by wilderness visitors (Roggenbuck 1980).

Managerial Attributes Expected

In the past, wilderness visitors have indicated reluctance to support restrictive use or rationing of the wilderness resource (Catton and Hendee 1968, Lucas 1980, Roggenbuck et al. 1982). Support for low-keyed regulations and light handed approaches to solve overuse or physical impact problems, however, was apparent (Hay 1974, Lucas 1980, Roggenbuck et al. 1982). Visitors emphasize taking the minimum management action necessary to ensure an enduring resource.

AN ALTERNATIVE TO THE EAST-WEST DICHOTOMY

From these research reports it appears that across the National Wilderness Preservation System, both East and West, visitors are expecting similar physical and managerial attributes and social/psychological benefits. One note of caution surfaces in review of this literature to draw this conclusion. When we examine characteristics of the areas in which much of this previous wilderness visitor motivation research was conducted we find a predominance of a single type of study area. Of specific interest are those studies in which conclusions were made regarding a comparison of motivations of users of eastern and western "mountain wilderness" areas. Wilderness visitor motivation researchers may have unknowingly overlooked a more useful dichotomy (trichotomy?) of landform or ecosystem types in efforts to disprove the commonly discussed dichotomy of East and West.

Roggenbuck (1980) compared user expectations for visitors to Linville Gorge, Shining Rock, Joyce Kilmer/Slickrock, and Shenandoah Wilderness in the East to Indian Peaks Primitive Area in Montana, and Desolation Wilderness in California. Echelberger and Moeller (1977) cited user preferences for visitors to Cranberry Backcountry in the Appalachian region of the East. Comparing mountain wilderness visitors in the East to mountain wilderness visitors in the West to draw conclusions about similarities of preferences of Eastern and Western wilderness visitors, seems something like comparing the specific gravity of Eastern White Pine to that of Western White Pine in order to draw conclusions about similarities between all species of conifers, nationwide.

The predominance of data collection in mountain wilderness leads to hypotheses regarding similarity of expectations for visitors to mountain wilderness. Working within this particular landform, or ecosystem type, we might safely say that we have visitors desiring similar attributes and management practices in mountain wilderness in the East and the West.

Kerr (1980) pointed out the uniqueness of our wilderness units in the East by classifying them into ecosystem (landform) types. We have mountain, waterbased (lake and swamp), and island wilderness. We might even add to this new landform or ecosystem types with the new additions. There have been unique additions such as that in Texas which may not have been represented previously in the East. Previous East-West comparisons did not specifically compare expectations of visitors to all ecosystem types in the East to all ecosystem types in the West. We do not appear to even have done that locally in the East.

In the West we have mountain and desert wilderness. Beaulieu and Schreyer (1984) recently found that factors critical in selecting a specific wilderness environment for a visit are likely to vary depending upon, in part, the type of environment involved. While scenic views and escape are cited among reasons for visiting the western deserts, exploring, adventure, experiencing freedom, and just having fun are also frequently cited (Hillier 1982).

CONCLUSIONS

It appears likely that managers underestimate the acceptance by visitors for some behavior control measures. Managers may overestimate the predominance of purist ideals and they often cannot accurately anticipate visitor perception of appropriate activities in wilderness. We can also expect that designation of new wilderness will not create extreme changes in what motivates visitors to visit and activities in which they participate. In using previous research to anticipate what will be desired from specific management areas, there is some risk involved. In past comparisons of user demands from East to West, there has been a predominance of comparable areas used. Some of the unique areas which we have classified as wilderness in the East precludes the possibility of assuming we currently know what is demanded by visitors to these areas. In refuting between-region differences, Roggenbuck (1980) cited greater within-region differences than between-region differences. Comparing nonrepresentative units of a heterogeneous collection of wilderness areas provides little insight into demand for the range of wilderness areas existing in the East.

IMPLICATIONS

In contacts with key wilderness resource management personnel, previous comparisons of users of eastern and western areas are commonly cited. The belief now is that visitors to eastern and western wilderness are expecting similar types of physical and managerial attributes and personal experiences. In our efforts to explore similarities and differences along the East-West geographical location dichotomy, we may have slighted wilderness categorizations which will aid more in understanding and projecting changes in user expectations. In particular, the very unique ecosystem types and landforms of eastern wilderness may imply some differences in motivations, or demands, which we have not yet determined. A concentration on within-region differences may be a more productive pursuit in the future than between-region differences. Or, examination of between-region differences should include representation across the diversity of wilderness in the East and the West.

Current Forest Service planning philosophy is to provide diversity of recreation settings in order to meet a diversity of demands. This diversity of demands originates from recognition of very personalized definitions of recreation quality. The National Wilderness Preservation System has evolved into a set of very diverse physical settings. With this diversity of physical attributes we would expect to find a diversity of personal experiences expected and experienced and the possibility of diverse management practices. Research efforts toward a better understanding of motivations for visitation to unique eastern wilderness areas seems a necessary step in deciding upon appropriate management actions.

LITERATURE CITED

Beaulieu, J.T. and R. Schreyer. 1984. Choices of wilderness environments-differences between real and hypothetical choice situations. Paper presented at the Recreation Choice Behavior Symp., Missoula, Mont., March 21-23.

Catton, W.R. and J.C. Hendee. 1968. Wilderness users-what do they think? Am. For. Sept.:29-31, 61.

Davis, J.A. 1984a. Millions of acres in 20 states win wilderness protection. Congr. Q. Weekly Rep. 42:2667-2669.

Davis, J.A. 1984b. Congress expanding scenic river system. Congr. Q. Weekly Rep. 42:2985, 2988-2989.

Echelberger, H.E. and G.H. Moeller. 1977. Use and users of the Cran-berry Backcountry in West Virginia; insights for eastern backcountry management. USDA For. Serv. Res. Pap. NE-363.

Glock, C.Y. and G. Selzynick. 1962. The wilderness vacationist. pp. 126-162. In Wilderness and Recreation-A Report on Resources, Values and Problems. A report to the Outdoor Recreation Resources Review Commission. Study Report 3, Univ. Calif. Berkeley, Berkeley, Calif.

Haas, G.E. 1979. User preferences for recreation experience opportunities and physical resource attributes in three Colorado wilderness areas. Ph.D. Diss., Colorado State Univ., Ft. Collins, Colo.

Hay, E. 1974. Wilderness experiment: it's working. Am. For. 80:26-29.

Hendee, J.C. and R.W. Harris. 1970. Foresters' perceptions of wilderness user attitudes and preferences. J. For. 68:759-762.

Hendee, J.C. 1980. Principles of wilderness management: applications for the East. In Proceedings, Wilderness Management Symposium, USDA For. Serv. Knoxville, Tenn.

Hillier, G.E. 1982. California desert: playground in paradise. Your Public Land 32:16-19.

Kerr, R. 1980. Diversity within the wilderness system: a visitor's perspective. In Proc., Wilderness Management Symp., USDA For. Serv. Knoxville, Tenn.

Lucas, R.C. 1980. Use patterns and visitor characteristics, attitudes and preferences in nine wilderness and other roadless areas. USDA For. Serv. Res. Pap. INT-253.

McCool, S.F. 1985. Does wilderness designation lead to increased recreational use? J. For. 83:39-41.

Peterson, F.L. 1974. A comparison of the sentiments and perceptions of wilderness managers and canoeists in the Boundary Waters Canoe Area. J. Leisure Res. 6:194-206.

Roggenbuck, J.W. 1980. Wilderness user preferences-eastern and western areas. In Proc., Wilderness Management Symp., USDA For. Serv. Knoxville, Tenn.

Roggenbuck, J.W., A.E. Watson, and G.H. Stankey. 1982. Wilderness management in the Southern Appalachians. South. J. Appl. For. 6:147-152.

Shafer, E.L., Jr. and J. Meitz. 1969. Aesthetic and emotional experiences rate high with northeast wilderness hikers. Environ. and Behav. 1:187-197.

Shomaker, J.H. and T.R. Glasford. 1982. Backcountry as an alternative to wilderness? F. For. 80:358-360, 364.

Wellman, J.C., M.S. Dawson and J.W. Roggenbuck. 1982. Park managers' predictions of the motivations of visitors to two National Park Service areas. J. Leisure Res. 14:1-15.

Identification Of Visitor Subgroup Differences To Facilitate Management Decisions

by
Cary D. McDonald and William E. Hammitt

ABSTRACT--Recent increase in the use of wildland recreation resources has created a challenging problem for managers of these areas. They are responsible for the protection of the resource and the provision of quality recreation experiences. The increase in use has led to problems such as crowding, conflicts, and resource impacts in wildland areas. These problems have prompted a need to obtain information on visitors. Often this information is summarized in such a manner that does not identify various subpopulations. This paper identifies an example of such subgroups and determines how they differed with respect to their support for various management actions. The subgroups identified were based upon the visitor being with an outfitted or a nonoutfitted group. The two groups differed significantly in their support for four management actions: 1) visitor services, 2) visitor facilities, 3) visitor protection, and 4) visitor use restrictions. Identification of subgroups should help recreation resource managers implement certain actions after identifying the diverse needs and preferences of these subgroups. A sound management plan must identify these subgroups and specify how and if the diverse needs of each will be met. Clearly, the call for management action from each will be different.

KEYWORDS: river recreation, visitor preferences, management actions, outfitted use, Wild and Scenic Rivers Act, quality experiences, subgroup differences.

The recreational use of our nation's rivers has increased dramatically during the past two decades, and the upward trend is likely to continue (Knopf and Lime 1984). The need for strong management of river recreation became clear during this period as problems of water quality, visitor conflicts, crowding, visitor safety, and resource impacts emerged (USDA 1977, Lewis 1977). Furthermore, visitors have expressed preferences for the development of certain services and facilities which may not be in the best interest of the river environment or appropriate under legal designation and current management philosophy.

This paper briefly identifies some legal mandates pertaining to wildland river management and identifies visitor preferences for certain management actions. Also, differences with respect to these management actions between commercial outfitted visitors and nonoutfitted visitors are examined. Implications of these findings for wildland river management are then discussed.

WILDLAND RIVER MANAGEMENT

Traditionally, river management has been absent from the majority of wildland rivers that flow through wilderness areas or other natural areas. For purposes of this paper wildland river connotes a river setting in which the influence of man is minimal, maintenance of a natural condition exists, and few river access points are available. Increasing use has required management intervention and increased management activity. As a result, an increase at controlling or influencing visitor behavior on many previously "unmanaged" wildland rivers has occurred.

While increasing use has created new and exciting opportunities to serve the recreating public, it has also created many difficult management problems. Managers responsible for administering river recreation resources have been increasingly challenged to meet a diverse set of visitor needs and at the same time maintain a sense of a quality recreation experience, often defined in terms of visitor satisfaction (Heberlein 1977). Furthermore, legal designation requires a commitment by recreation resource managers to resource protection *and* at the same time a commitment to maintain a quality recreation experience for the visitor.

Legal Constraints of Wildland River Management
Legal constraints for wildland river management, at the National level, are imposed by the Wilderness Act of 1964 (Public Law 88-577), the 1975 "Eastern Wilderness Act" (Public Law 93-622), and the Wild and Scenic Rivers Act (Public Law 90-542) for many of the rivers that flow through wilderness or wildland areas. Several addi-

tional federal laws have implications for the management of wildland rivers but will not be addressed in this paper (e.g. National Environmental Policy Act, Public Law 91-190). Several rivers not under the jurisdiction of the Wilderness Act, the Eastern Wilderness Act, or the Wild and Scenic Rivers Act are under similar jurisdiction imposed by state governments under specific state wild and scenic river legislation. In fact, 25 states have a designated state wild and scenic rivers program (Knudson 1984). Furthermore, many rivers are not legally bound by specific legislation but are managed to maintain their natural character (e.g. Big South Fork of the Cumberland River, National Park Service, Oneida, Tennessee).

Wilderness Act-Legislation pertaining to the management of river environments in designated wilderness areas can be referenced to the 1964 Wilderness Act. Section 2(c) of the Act defines wilderness as an area "protected and managed so as to preserve its natural conditions and which generally appears to have been affected primarily by the forces of nature, with the imprint of man's work substantially unnoticed." This legal definition mandates the management of rivers within the boundaries of classified wilderness areas to be managed to such a manner that the "naturalness" of the river environment be maintained. Some of the more popular wildland rivers are in designated wilderness areas (e.g. Middle Fork Salmon River, River of No Return Wilderness Area, Idaho).

Wild and Scenic Rivers Act-The Wild and Scenic Rivers Act is aimed specifically for river management. The Act states that " . . . certain select rivers of the Nation, which, with their immediate environment, possess outstandingly remarkable scenic, recreational, geologic, fish and wildlife, historic, cultural and other similar values, shall be preserved in free-flowing condition, and that they and their immediate environments shall be protected for the benefit and enjoyment of present and future generations." Here again, the element of management to maintain the "naturalness" of the river environment is evident.

Three river classifications are defined in the Wild and Scenic Rivers Act:

1. Wild River Areas--those rivers or sections that are free of impounds and generally inaccessible except by trail, with watersheds or shorelines essentially primitive and unpolluted;
2. Scenic River Areas--those rivers or sections of rivers that are free of impounds, with shorelines or watersheds still largely primitive and shorelines largely undeveloped, but accessible in places by roads;
3. Recreational River Areas--those rivers or sections of rivers that are readily accessible by road or railroad, that may have some development along their shorelines, and that may have undergone some impoundment or diversion in the past.

All rivers in the Wild and Scenic River System, regardless of classification, are to be managed in such a manner to preserve and protect the river system for the benefit and enjoyment of the public.

Quality Recreation Experiences

With increasing use of a resource comes the management challenge of managing the resource in the most efficient way possible while still maintaining the quality of the recreation experience. The provision of quality recreation experiences is widely accepted as the overriding goal of recreation planning and management (Driver and Brown 1978, Dustin and McAvoy 1981, Jubenville 1976, Knudson 1984). The quality experience in wildland environments is dependent upon the "naturalness" of the recreation resource and the ability of the "naturalness" to satisfy certain needs. It is the satisfaction of those needs by which quality experiences are measured (Heberlein 1977). Development of certain services and facilities which impact the "naturalness" of the resource pose a direct threat to the quality of the recreation experience.

Understanding Wildland River Visitors

In recent years several research endeavors have centered around wildland river research with much of the effort directed at identifying and understanding the visitors. In fact, the U.S. Forest Service's North Central Forest Experiment Station has a river recreation research unit. This unit has produced several documents pertaining to river recreation in recent years which include a proceedings from a management and research symposium on river recreation (USDA 1977), an annotated bibliography on river recreation (Anderson *et al.* 1978), a collection of recent research papers on river recreation research (USDA 1981) and a guide to understanding river use and users (Knopf and Lime 1984).

A brief review of wildland recreation research has involved the identification of motivations for river recreation (Schreyer and Roggenbuck 1978, Knopf *et al.* 1983), the influence of past visitor experience on visitor preferences (Hammitt and McDonald 1983, Schreyer *et al.* 1984), visitor impacts (Knopf 1982), and carrying capacity (Heberlein and Vaske 1977, Shelby 1980, Hammitt *et al.* 1984).

One of the needs identified by the North Central Forest Experiment Station's River Recreation Project was to be able to differentiate or segment river recreation user groups into meaningful typologies that better reflect the diversity of people using rivers for recreation (North Central Forest Experiment Station 1983). Research has shown that within specific populations of recreationists, substantial diversity among individuals can exist in terms of experiences sought (Driver 1976). The basic tenet is that various user groups hold differing views on management actions. Knopf and Lime (1984) examined outfitted and nonoutfitted visitor preferences for various management actions on California's Kings River. Their findings indicated that several differences regarding preferences for various management actions were evident between the two subgroups. Nonoutfitted visitors were consistently more opposed to the management actions.

Obtaining this type of information is extremely valuable to river managers for planning and management purposes. Not only is the information important to resource

248

planners and managers, but required. The legislative branch of government has mandated the collection and use of such information for decision making (e.g. 1974 Forest and Rangeland Renewable Resources Planning Act).

In order for managers to facilitate the planning and implementation of management actions a need to understand the visitor and the different subgroups is essential. Managers are often put in the position of deciding between or among alternative management actions. With the increased importance of public input to the planning process, visitors provide valuable information to the manager. In many instances managers have had to justify their decision to the visiting public. Therefore, the more known about the visitor, the more likely managers can make wise decisions regarding management actions that would protect the wildland resource *and* the quality of the visitor experience.

Managers require information on visitor characteristics and preferences in order to develop effective management plans. Quite often visitor information is summarized in such a manner that does not identify various subgroups within the sample. Summary data are usually based upon the aggregate sample. Because some subgroups may be discriminated against by certain management actions, it becomes important to identify subgroup differences pertaining to their support or opposition to specific management actions. Identification of these subgroup differences can potentially assist management in meeting the diverse needs of various subgroups within their limitations and realization that not all needs can be satisfied. However, identification of subgroup differences will help managers identify which group or groups are being impacted. This paper attempts to identify such subgroup differences related to preferences for management actions among users of a wildland river.

METHODS

Study Area

The Big South Fork National River and Recreation Area, under jurisdiction of the National Park Service, located in north-central Tennessee served as the study area. The river segment between Burnt Mill Bridge and Leatherwood Ford was the particular river stretch of the Big South Fork of the Cumberland River studied. The distance of this river stretch is about 11 miles (18 km) with an average drop of about 20 feet (6.1 m) per mile (km). No river access points are located between Burnt Mill Bridge and Leatherwood Ford. The scenery is exceptional as the river winds through the Big South Fork Gorge area with massive sandstone cliffs, little or no sign of people, and no development. Even though the river is not a member of the Wild and Scenic Rivers System, it is managed within those guidelines to maintain its "naturalness" and

can be classified as a "wild river" under the Act's classification procedure. The river is managed for the wildland-like characteristics stressing solitude and a natural setting. This river is one of the few remaining free flowing rivers located in the southeastern part of the country. The difficulty of this river stretch, according to the American Whitewater Association, has a Class III and IV rating.

Sampling

Sampling was conducted during the Spring of 1984. Individuals were contacted at Leatherwood Ford, the most popular take-out location. An attempt was made to contact all individuals 14 years of age and older as they departed from the river. On selected sampling days individuals were contacted between 1:00 p.m. and 8:00 p.m. Although sampling was limited to a seven week period on weekends between March 31 and May 19, the greatest amount of use occurs during this time so additional sampling was not considered to be needed. Still, the brief sampling period may bias the representativeness of the sample.

Instruments

Each individual contacted was requested to complete a "River Use Survey Form" which took one to two minutes to complete. Individuals were approached by an interviewer as they came off the river and were asked to complete the survey form. Four hundred two visitors completed the form. The main purpose of this form was to obtain the names and addresses of visitors. Also, these forms were used to select a representative sample of river visitors. This sample was selected from the contact forms based upon a sampling fraction of two-thirds. It was determined that this sampling fraction would yield enough cases for data analysis. Two hundred sixty-eight of the 402 visitors contacted were selected by this method and sent a survey packet one month after their visit. In addition to a 12-page questionnaire, the survey packet contained a cover letter explaining the purpose of the study, assuring confidentiality, and stressing the importance of a reply, and a stamped-addressed return envelope. Three follow-up reminders were used. An 88.6 percent response rate was obtained.

A section of the questionnaire was designed to obtain visitor preferences for a variety of management actions. Twenty-five management actions, representing four underlying dimensions, were examined to determine visitor support or opposition for each. Respondents rated each management action on a 5-point Likert scale labeled: 1=Strongly Oppose, 2=Oppose, 3=Neither Support Nor Oppose, 4=Support, and 5=Strongly Support. These 25 management actions were combined into four composite variables representing the underlying dimensions of visitor services, visitor facilities, visitor protection/enforcement, and visitor use restrictions.

RESULTS AND DISCUSSION

Management Actions Supported By Visitors

The 25 management actions, grouped by the underlying dimension each represents, are presented in Table 1. Two visitor services were supported by a major-

Table 1. Ratings of 25 Management Actions by Respondents.

Management Action	Average[1]	Support[2] (%)	Oppose[3] (%)
Visitor services			
Provide more information (signs, displays) at put-in and take-out points	3.3	44	16
Post signs along the river warning and advising of hazards and rapids	2.4	22	53
Post distance markers along the river	2.4	22	53
Post information signs along the roads to direct people to river access points	3.5	53	14
Provide garbage containers	3.9	76	8
Visitor facilities			
Improve landing areas at put-in and take-out points	3.5	50	8
Provide more parking at put-in and take-out points	3.2	36	16
Improve existing roads to put-in and take-out points	3.4	47	12
Provide toilet facilities at put-in and take-out points	3.8	73	8
Provide campsites at put-in and take-in points	3.1	42	26
Visitor protection/enforcement			
Require people to carry out their own trash	4.5	90	4
Designate certain areas along the river for lunch stops	2.5	24	50
Provide more patrols to assist river users	2.8	19	31
Be more aggressive in the enforcement of safety rules and regulations	3.1	30	21
Prohibit primitive camping along the river	3.2	12	64
Prohibit the use of cans, bottles, and other throw away containers	3.4	51	25
Visitor use restrictions			
Charge a fee to use the river	2.2	18	64
Issue free permits through a mail reservation system	3.2	50	30
Issue a limited number of permits on a first-come first-serve basis	2.8	42	41
Issue a limited number of permits on a drawing or lottery basis	2.2	14	66
Limit the size of groups floating the river	3.2	52	25
Achieve better spacing by assigning the time of day to begin trip	3.3	53	25
Allow 20 minutes between groups entering the river	2.9	32	30
Allow 30 minutes between groups entering the river	3.1	34	27
Allow use to continue without controls	3.0	34	39

[1] Rating Scale: 1 = Strongly Oppose, 2 = Oppose, 3 = Neither Support Nor Oppose, 4 = Support, and 5 = Strongly Support.

[2] Percentage represents the sum of those respondents who rated the item as Strongly Support or Support.

[3] Percentage represents the sum of those respondents who rated the item as Strongly Oppose or Oppose.

ity of visitors. Three of every four respondents supported "provide garbage containers" while over one-half of the respondents, 53 percent, supported "post information signs along the roads to direct people to river access points." These services have little affect upon the naturalness of the river environment itself. On the other hand, 53 percent of the visitors opposed two actions that would indicate the influence of man while on the river, "post signs along the river warning and advising of hazards and rapids" and "post distance markers along the river." These results may indicate visitors are aware, to a certain extent, what services would be appropriate to maintain the condition of "naturalness."

Two visitor facilities were supported by a majority of visitors. One of every two visitors, 50 percent, supported "improve landing areas at put-in and take-out points." Seventy-three percent of the visitors supported "provide toilet facilities at put-in and take-out points." Again, these facilities would be located at access points and not along the river so that the river segments between access points would exhibit little influence by man. A level of "naturalness" along the river would be maintained.

Ninety percent of the visitors supported "require people to carry out their own trash" indicating a sense of responsibility on their behalf toward protecting the wildland environment. Furthermore, they may feel that garbage containers are acceptable at access points but not along the river between access points. A majority of visitors, 51 percent, supported "prohibit the use of cans, bottles, and other throw away containers." One of ever two visitors, 50 percent, opposed "designate certain areas along the river for lunch stops." Perhaps, visitors feel this measure would disrupt the "naturalness" along the river. Sixty-four percent of the visitors opposed "prohibit primitive camping along the river." Possibly, visitors feel primitive camping is in line with the notion of recreational use of wildlands.

The management actions regarding limiting visitor use received mixed reactions from the visitors. Three of the nine use limitations were supported by visitors. About one-half of the visitors supported "issue free permits through a mail reservation system," "limit the size of groups floating the river," and "achieve better spacing by assigning the time of day to begin trip." Nearly two of every three visitors, 64 percent, opposed "charge an entrance fee," while 66 percent of the visitors opposed "issue a limited number of permits on a drawing or lottery basis." Support and opposition for the remaining management actions were almost evenly divided.

Subgroups of Visitor Use

Two subgroups of visitor use were identified: outfitted visitors, visitors with equipment and guide provided by a commercial outfitter, and nonoutfitted visitors, visitors without the services of a commercial outfitter. A majority of visitors contacted were with an outfitter. Of the 233 respondents, 138 (59 percent) were with a commercial outfitter and 95 (41 percent) were nonoutfitted.

Four Underlying Management Action Dimensions

The four underlying management action dimensions identified by respondents were: 1) Visitor Services, 2) Visitor Facilities, 3) Visitor Protection/Enforcement, and 4) Visitor Use Restrictions. No management action was supported or opposed by a majority of visitors (Table 2).

Table 2. Ratings of the Four Underlying Management Action Dimensions by Respondents.

Management Action	Average[1]	Support[2] (%)	Oppose[3] (%)
Visitor services	3.1	31.5	20.7
Visitor facilities	3.4	45.9	9.4
Visitor protection and enforcement	3.1	25.8	12.0
Visitor use restrictions	2.9	6.9	20.8

[1] Rating Scale: 1 = Strongly Oppose, 2 = Oppose, 3 = Neither Support Nor Oppose, 4 = Support, and 5 = Strongly Support.

[2] Percentage represents the sum of those respondents who rated the item as Strongly Support or Support.

[3] Percentage represents the sum of those respondents who rated the item as Strongly Oppose or Oppose.

The management action receiving the greatest support was "visitor facilities." Almost one-half of the visitors, 46 percent, supported the action while nine percent opposed it. Due to the current lack of some facilities at the river (e.g. restroom facilities, adequate parking facilities) this finding was anticipated. Only seven percent of the visitors supported "visitor use restrictions." Surprisingly, about one of every five visitors, 21 percent, opposed this action. The majority of visitors, 72 percent, neither supported nor opposed "visitor use restrictions."

Subgroup Differences Between Outfitted and Nonoutfitted Visitors

Even though there was not strong support or opposition for the management actions, support for each action significantly differed between outfitted and nonoutfitted visitors (Table 3). Outfitted visitors were more likely than nonoutfitted visitors to support management actions which would provide visitor services, visitor protection/enforcement, and visitor use restrictions. On the other hand, nonoutfitted visitors supported visitor facilities to a greater degree than outfitted visitors. This

was not expected. One would think outfitted visitors would support visitor facilities to a greater degree than nonoutfitted visitors. One explanation for this finding could be that outfitted visitors arrived by "shuttle bus" and did not have to be concerned with parking facilities. For nonoutfitted visitors, parking was definitely a real concern and management actions addressing this concern were supported more strongly by nonoutfitted visitors.

Nonoutfitted visitors were also more likely to oppose management actions which did not protect the resource or inhibited a certain level of individual choice and freedom of behavior. Overall, outfitted visitors were more likely to support management actions than nonoutfitted visitors.

MANAGEMENT IMPLICATIONS

The legal mandates that have jurisdiction over many of the nation's wildlands stress the importance of resource protection while at the same time indicate the importance of visitor enjoyment. This paradox has created an almost impossible challenge for wildland managers. Wildland managers are confronted with an attempt to manage the resource and the visitor in the most efficient way possible under these constraints. If wildland, including rivers, are to maintain their integrity, then certain management directions are necessary.

Wildland recreation resource managers must realize that they cannot satisfy the needs of all visitors. Their primary responsibility should be resource protection. Those visitor needs dependent upon the "naturalness" of the resource (e.g. solitude, experiencing nature) should be most prominent. If wildland recreation resource managers are to maintain the integrity of the resource then some visitor needs will have to be foregone. Perhaps, visitors who's needs not dependent upon the wildland environment should be encouraged to go elsewhere or supplied with information and education materials that stress the importance of the wildland resource to satisfy only those needs that are highly dependent upon that resource.

Those visitors desiring development in terms of facilities and services should go to areas where this development has occurred rather than encouraging wildland managers to implement such actions. Implementation of visitor use restrictions should be stressed to the visitor because these restrictions not only protect the resource but also maintain a level of quality visitor experiences that are dependent upon that resource. Safety is always a concern for resource managers. However, a safety shield should not be imposed in wildland areas. For wildland areas provide one of the few remaining resources where an individual can take risks and increase self-confidence. Implementation of safety restrictions will reduce the quality experience for the risk-taking individual.

In order for wildland resource managers to facilitate implementation of specific management actions an understanding of the diversity among visitor preferences is es-

Table 3. Results of Student's t-Test of Mean Differences between Outfitted and Nonoutfitted Visitors with Respect to Management Actions.

Management Action	Nonoutfitted			Outfitted			Student's t-Value	Prob.
	Average[1]	Support[2] (%)	Oppose[3] (%)	Average[1]	Support[2] (%)	Oppose[3] (%)		
Visitor services	2.96	27.7	24.5	3.21	34.1	18.1	−2.48	0.014
Visitor facilities	3.59	60.0	10.5	3.32	36.2	8.7	3.09	0.002
Visitor protection and enforcement	2.89	16.8	21.1	3.24	31.9	5.8	−4.81	0.001
Visitor use restrictions	2.65	4.2	34.7	3.02	8.8	11.0	−5.30	0.001

[1]Rating Scale: 1 = Strongly Oppose, 2 = Oppose, 3 = Neither Support Nor Oppose, 4 = Support, and 5 = Strongly Support.

[2]Percentage represents the sum of those respondents who rated the item as Strongly Support or Support.

[3]Percentage represents the sum of those respondents who rated the item as Strongly Oppose or Oppose.

sential. Identification of subgroups should help managers better implement certain policies. Certain management actions may need to be accompanied by information addressed to a particular subgroup. Information could be targeted toward one of the subgroups that opposed a particular management action. This information could include an explanation of the management action in an attempt to justify the decision. A sound management plan must identify these subgroups and specify how and if the diverse needs of each will be met. Clearly, the call for management action from each will be different.

LITERATURE CITED

Anderson, D.H., E.C. Leatherberry and D.W. Lime. 1978. An annotated bibliography on river recreation. USDA For. Serv. GTR NC-41. North Cent. For. Exp. Stn., St. Paul, MN. 62p.

Driver, B.L. 1976. Toward a better understanding of the social benefits of outdoor recreation participation. pp. 163-189. In Proceedings of the Southern States Recreation Research Applications Workshop. USDA For. Serv. GTR SE-9. Southeast For. Exp. Stn., Asheville, NC. 302p.

Driver, B.L. and P.J. Brown. 1978. The opportunity spectrum concept and behavioral information in outdoor recreation resource supply inventories: a rationale. pp. 24-32. In Proceedings, Integrated Inventory of Renewable Natural Resources Workshop. USDA For. Serv. GTR RM-55. Rocky Mtn. For. and Range Exp. Stn., Ft. Collins, CO.

Dustin, D.I. and L.H. McAvoy. 1981. The decline and fall of quality recreation opportunities and environments? Environ. Ethics 4:49-57.

Hammitt, W.E. and C.D. McDonald. 1983. Past on-site experience and its relationship to managing river recreation resources. For. Sci. 29:262-266.

Hammitt, W.E., C.D. McDonald, and F.P. Noe. 1984. Use levels and encounters: important variables of perceived crowding among nonspecialized recreationists. J. Leisure Res. 16:1-8.

Heberlein, T. 1977. Density, crowding, and satisfaction: sociological studies for determining carrying capacities. In River Recreation Management and Research Symposium. USDA For. Serv. GTR NC-28.

North Cent. For. Exp. Stn., St. Paul, MN.

Heberlein, T. and J. Vaske. 1977. Crowding and visitor conflict on the Bois Brule River. Univ. Wisconsin, Water Resources Center, Tech. Rep. Wisc. WRC-77-04, Madison, Wisc. 100p.

Jubenville, A. 1976. Outdoor recreation planning. W.B. Saunders, Philadelphia, Penn. 399p.

Knopf, R.C. 1982. Management problems in river recreation: what floaters are telling us. Naturalist 33:12-17.

Knopf, R.C. and D.W. Lime. 1984. A river manager's guide to understanding river use and users. USDA For. Serv. GTR WO-38. North Cent. For. Exp. Stn., St. Paul, MN. 37p.

Knopf, R.C., G.L. Peterson, and E.C. Leatherberry. 1983. Motives for recreational river floating: relative consistency across settings. Leisure Sci. 5:231-255.

Knudson, D.M. 1984. Outdoor recreation. Second Edition. Macmillan Publishing Company, New York, NY. 655p.

Lewis, J.H. 1977. TVA's role in river-oriented recreation. pp. 139-141. In River Recreation Management and Research Symposium. USDA For. Serv. GTR NC-28. North Cent. For. Exp. Stn., St. Paul, MN.

North Central Forest Experiment Station. 1983. River recreation management research: a problem analysis. USDA For. Serv. North Cent. For. Exp. Stn., St. Paul, Minn.

Schreyer, R. and J. Roggenbuck. 1978. The influence of experience expectations on crowding perceptions and social-psychological carrying capacities. Leisure Sci. 1:373-394.

Schreyer, R., D.W. Lime, and D.R. Williams. 1984. Characterizing the influence of past experience on recreation behavior. J. Leisure Res. 16:34-50.

Shelby, B. 1980. Crowding models for backcountry recreation. Land Eco. 56:43-55.

USDA. 1977. River recreation management and research. USDA For. Serv. GTR NC28. North Cent. For. Exp. Stn., St. Paul, MN. 455p.

USDA. 1981. Some recent products of river recreation research. USDA For. Serv. GTR NC-63. North Cent. For. Exp.Stn., St. Paul, MN. 61p.

Resource Impacts Of Recreation On Wilderness

by
William E. Hammitt

ABSTRACT--Disturbance to natural areas as a result of dispersed recreational use has typically been defined as resource or ecological impact. Because wildland recreation managers are responsible for maintaining the quality of wildland recreation resources, they are concerned with understanding the type, rate, amount, and pattern of undesirable changes occurring in natural areas as a result of recreational use. This paper provides an overview of: (1) types of resource impacts, (2) rates of impact occurrence, (3) amount of resource degradation, and (4) patterns of disturbance, resulting from dispersed recreation in wildland areas.

KEYWORDS: recreational impacts, ecological impacts, recreational carrying capacity, resource degradation.

Recreational use of wildland areas has increased dramatically in recent decades (Hendee *et al.* 1978). Along with this increase in recreational use has come human disturbances and degradation to the natural conditions of wildland areas. Recreation resource managers are understandably concerned with these ecological impacts because they are responsible for maintaining the quality of recreational resources. This is particularly true for designated wilderness areas and national parks where a major goal is preservation of natural conditions. To deal effectively with the problem of resource impacts in wildland recreation areas, resource managers need to understand the dynamics of recreational disturbances in sufficient detail to determine what kind and how much change is occurring and is acceptable (Cole and Schreiner 1981).

TYPES OF IMPACTS

Ecological impacts are best considered in view of the major resource components of natural environments. Soil, vegetation, water, and wildlife are potentially affected by wildland recreation. Figure 1 illustrates the interrelationships of these four resources and associated impacts.
Soil
The major factor causing adverse impacts on soil resources is human trampling. Trampling results in the destruction of the organic matter layer, the compaction of the upper 6 to 8 in. of the soil profile, and a resulting decrease in the infiltration rate of water. Manning (1979)

describes these distinct but related effects through a seven-step soil impact cycle.

The initial impact involves the scuffing away of leaf litter. Leaf litter readily pulverizes when trampled, causing it to be easily scuffed and eroded off-site by wind and water erosion forces. The second step, involving the loss of organic matter from the upper soil horizons, is caused by the loss of leaf litter in step one. Third is compaction of the soil and reduction in macroporosity; trampling on the soil surface forces individual soil particles into closer proximity and reduces pore space. The fourth, fifth, and sixth steps in the cycle are directly caused by reduced soil macroporosity. Reduction in the larger pore spaces means the soil is less permeable to air and water. With less water permeating the soil, plus a reduction in infiltration rate, there is more surface runoff. This leads to the final step, an increase in soil erosion. Sheet erosion can be quite severe on sloping recreation sites, particularly hiking trails. Removal of surface litter, compaction and truncation of surface soils, and erosion forces can combine to result in a loss of 2 to 9 in. of soil on recreational sites and up to several feet on some horse and foot trails (Settergren and Cole 1970).
Vegetation
The ground cover vegetation of a forest site is usually the first and best indicator of site deterioration. Trampling rapidly affects the herbaceous ground cover through the crushing, breakage, and bruising of stems, leaves, and flower stalks. Loss of ground cover vegetation and leaf litter results in a compacted, bare soil area, which is unconducive to reproduction and regeneration of most flora. The shrub layer is more resistant to recreational use than the ground cover, but the shrub layer usually suffers

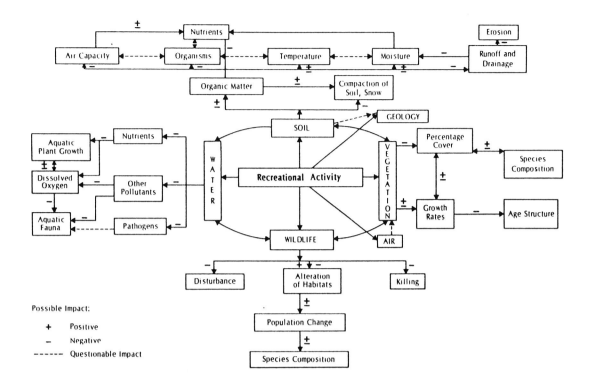

Figure 1. Recreational impact interrelationships for the four major resource components of natural areas. (Source: Wall and Wright 1977).

from trampling which destroys the seedlings. Shrubs often are deliberately removed when a site is cleared for camping. The main impacts to trees occur from mechanical damage such as ax scars, lantern burn scars, and nails in trees; and from loss of growth vigor because of compacted soils.

Water

Recreational impact to water resources falls primarily into two categories: nutrient and waste inputs, and health hazards. Nutrient inputs and waste deposits are particularly important in lake systems. In 1969 it was estimated that one ton of phosphate, 9 tons of sodium chloride, and 13 tons of nitrogen were deposited in the lakes of the Boundary Waters Canoe Area (Merriam et al. 1973). The same study reported solid waste deposits of three pounds of bottles, cans, and unburnables per user.

Water quality is a major concern with springs and small streams. Coliform bacteria counts above approved health standards have been recorded in some backcountry areas, but the major source of bacteria has usually been from animal sources rather than humans. Giardia and other human diseases are an obvious management concern in backcountry areas where drinking water is untreated.

Wildlife

The impacts of recreational use on wildlife are the least understood of the four resource components being considered. The research that has been conducted indicates that recreational use can cause a reduction in animal habitat, lead to displacement of certain species, and cause alteration in behavioral patterns of some wildlife (Ream 1980). The response to disturbance depends upon the species' feeding and breeding characteristics; the type, degree, and length of the disturbance; and the season and weather conditions (Stace-Smith 1975). Animal dependence on garbage dumps and food at campsites alters the feeding and travel patterns of these organisms and is a common impact at many recreational areas. Panhandler bears can be a serious problem for recreation managers since the alteration of their feeding habits can lead to human injury and property damage.

RATES OF IMPACT

A major concern in wildland recreation management is the rapid rate at which many of the ecological impacts occur. Perhaps more alarming is the rapid rate at which the impacts occur under even low to moderate levels of visitor use.

Several studies have documented the temporal pattern of impacts. Merriam and Smith (1974), in a five year study of campsites in the Boundary Waters Canoe Area, found that soil compaction, infiltration rate, and leaf litter impacts appeared to reach a maximum in two years. After this, soil compaction did not increase significantly. Researchers have found a similar response with respect to ground cover vegetation (LaPage 1967, Liddle 1975, Cole 1982).

Although ground cover vegetation tends to deteriorate rapidly under recreation use, there is also a successional change caused by the initial site impact. While the more succulent and ephemeral species are heavily impacted, more resistant species, such as grasses, tend to prosper after the initial impact. Light trampling and site wear can actually stimulate growth, especially among resilient vegetatively reproducing species (Bates 1935, Liddle 1975). However, with increased use even the most resilient grasses will decline eventually until the ground is bare (Liddle 1975).

The intensity of use is closely associated with the temporal rate of site deterioration. Frissell and Duncan (1965) found that the impact zone of campsites in the Boundary Waters Canoe Area of Minnesota lost an average of 80 percent of the ground cover vegetation with 0 to 30 days per season of use. Sites used 61 to 90 days per season lost 87 percent of their ground cover. Cole (1982) shows similar results, implying that most of the disturbance which is likely to occur on wilderness campsites can result from use of the site only a limited number of times per year. Of 20 types of ecological change measured by Cole (1982), only seven were more pronounced on heavily used sites.

Finally, the rate of site recovery should be considered. While impacted areas deteriorate quite rapidly, their recovery is much slower. Several studies have shown that six to 12, or more, years are needed for the soil to become uncompacted (Orr 1960, Thorud and Frissell 1976, Legg and Schneider 1977). At a backcountry lake in Kings Canyon National Park, California, Parsons and DeBenedetti (1979) found that after 15 years of closure, soil compaction had returned to assumed pre-use values, but the depth of soil organic horizons and accumulation of woody fuels had not. With ground cover vegetation at least three to four years are required to re-establish a good cover. Ranz (1979), on closed campsites in the Selway-Bitterroot Wilderness, Montana, found that the ground cover increased significantly over a five year period, but the species composition was closer to that of a suburban lawn than of undisturbed wilderness. Thus, with the general rate of ecological impacts being two to three years and the rate of recovery being four to 12 years, recreation resource managers often find the periodic resting and rotating of impacted sites infeasible (Cole 1981).

AMOUNT OF RESOURCE IMPACTED

While resource impacts in natural areas used for wildland recreation may be severe at locations of concentrated use, large portions of these natural areas remain unused in the physical sense and therefore maintain a relatively undisturbed state (Manning 1979). Ward and

Berg (1973) demonstrated the limited spatial impact of soil compaction associated with hiking trails when they revealed that all effects of soil compaction disappeared at a distance of 4.5 feet (1.4 m) from the trail's center. In the Eagle Cap Wilderness, Oregon, vegetation impacts associated with trail use occur along 58.8 miles (94.7 km) of trail in a zone approximately 13.2 feet (4 m) wide; 0.3 percent of the entire wilderness area (Cole 1981). Similarly, there are about 336 backcountry campsites with an estimated mean radius of site disturbance equal to 49.5 feet (15 m). This area/extent of campsite alteration is 0.2 percent of the total area. Thus, only 0.5 percent of Eagle Cap Wilderness is directly impacted by recreation use.

Because ecological impacts of wildland recreation areas tend to be zonal--to occur in popular and functional use zones--rather than being distributed uniformly, it is useful to study the "patterns of occurrence" of impacts.

ZONES AND PATTERNS OF IMPACT

Zonation and pattern occurrences of recreational impacts are determined by the sensitivity to disturbance of resource areas and habitats. Most wildland areas are comprised of a variety of environmental conditions that having different tolerance limits and sensitivity to impacts. Some coastal, alpine and wetland areas are examples of recreational ecosystems that are sensitive to vegetation and soil trampling, and other impacts. Within these ecosystems, there is also considerable difference in the sensitivity of specific habitats and zones. In many recreation areas the environmental conditions of the resource are a far better predictor of impact than amount of visitor use.

Sensitive Areas and Habitats

Recreation resource managers readily recognize that certain areas and habitats are more sensitive to recreational impacts than others. Areas with poorly drained soils, succulent herbaceous vegetation, high rainfall, steep slopes, and severe weather conditions are particularly sensitive.

At the community and habitat level, patterns of impact sensitivity may be operating at a fairly small scale. That is, adjacent plant communities may show quite distinctively different levels of impact while experiencing similar amounts of use. Trail erosion work in the Great Smoky Mountains National Park indicates that higher elevation communities are the most erosion sensitive (Bratton 1977, Bratton et al. 1979). Grassy balds and the red spruce-Fraser fir forest are the most sensitive, while lower elevation xeric oak and pine forests are the most resistant. Mesic cover hardwood forests have intermediate resistance (Table 1).

Certain zones or sections of recreation areas differ in impact sensitivity even at the species level. Areas containing rare and endangered plants and high-density animal populations are particularly sensitive areas. These

Table 1. The Sensitivity of Major Forest Types to
Soil Erosion on Trails, Great Smoky Mountains
National Park. (Source: Bratton 1977).

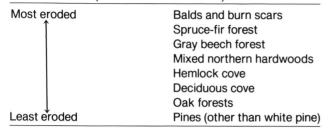

Most eroded	Balds and burn scars
↑	Spruce-fir forest
	Gray beech forest
	Mixed northern hardwoods
	Hemlock cove
	Deciduous cove
↓	Oak forests
Least eroded	Pines (other than white pine)

areas and habitats need to be mapped and zoned according to their sensitivities (Figure 2).

Spatial Patterns of Impacts

Perhaps the most distinctive feature of recreation site deterioration is the spatial pattern in which it occurs. As noted earlier, visitor use of recreation areas is spatial, often restricted to travel and destination locales. Likewise, ecological impacts tend to be restricted to a linear and nodal arrangement that corresponds to visitor use patterns. Initial impact areas often will expand progressively into larger impact areas over time and in various patterns.

Forest type:

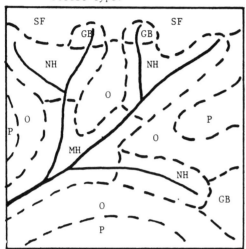

SF – Spruce-fir GB – Beech O – Oak
NH – Northern hardwoods P – Pine
MH – Mesic hardwoods
Solid line is stream system

Probability of trail, soil erosion:

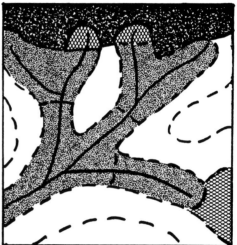

Black – Highly prone to erosion
Cross-hatch – Problems likely
Gray – Mild erosion problems possible
White – Erosion usually minor problem

Bear population densities:

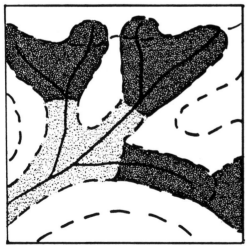

Dark gray – High bear densities in
June
Lighter gray – Moderate densities

Concentrated flowering displays:

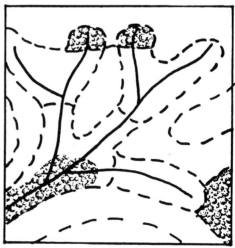

Shaded areas – Concentrated vernal
flowering displays

Figure 2. An idealized resource mosaic showing impact zones sensitivity for a mountainous area. Mapping of habitats and zones sensitive to recreational impacts allow for better placement of backcountry campsites. (Source: Bratton 1977).

A five year study of backcountry campsites in the Boundary Waters Canoe Area indicated that the majority of sites underwent a significant expansion in the area of bare ground. Ten campsites expanded their area by more than 50 percent; four more than doubled in size (Merriam *et al.* 1973). Perhaps more striking than the site expansion were the spatial patterns in which the expansion developed. The clearing of underbrush and rearrangement of campsite facilities commonly led to the development of linear sites and even satellite sites (Figure 3).

SUMMARY

Resource impacts as a result of recreational use in natural areas are a major concern for wildland recreation managers. Recreational use in these areas, when unmanaged, may result in degradation of the soil, vegetation, water, and wildlife components beyond acceptable limits. However, before resource impacts can be managed within acceptable limits, managers must have a basic understanding of the types and rates at which impacts occur, and of the sensitivity of various habitats to impacts. While various parameters of use and resource interactions must be considered when managing recreation-caused impacts, this paper was limited to addressing four basic areas: the types of resource impacts that occur, the rate at which they occur, the amount of resource influenced, and the pattern of occurrence of impacts.

The majority of soil and vegetation impacts occur within the first two years of use. Recovery, through the resting of sites, requires an average of 8-12 years. This rate of impact to recovery ratio has lead many resource managers to question the wisdom of "resting and rotating" backcountry campsites, as it tends to disperse the impact problem over a larger area.

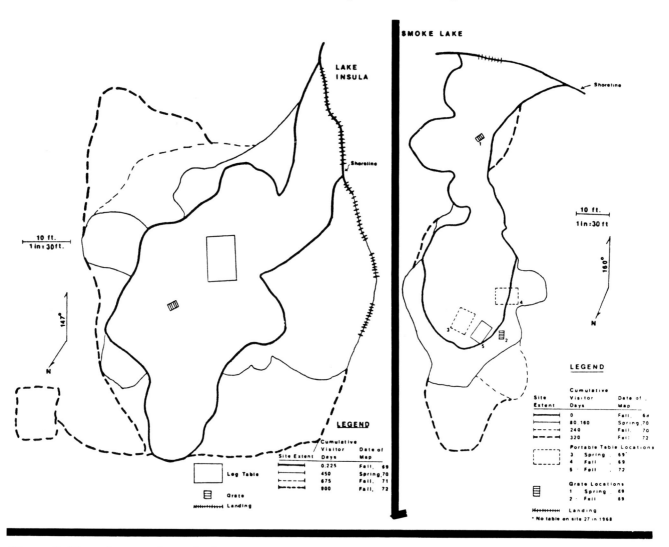

Figure 3. Through years of use, backcountry campsites commonly expand in size, with linear and satellite sites being two common patterns of site boundary expansion. (Source: Merriam *et al.* 1973).

Although recreational use in natural areas can lead to non-vegetated, soil compacted sites within a relatively short period of use, the zones of impact tend to involve a small portion of most natural areas. Certain zones and habitats are definitely more sensitive to use and are impacted more readily than others. It is recommended that natural areas to be used for wildland recreation be mapped for habitats and zones that are impact prone and that use be encouraged in areas whose inherent properties make them more resistant to change.

NOTE:

This paper is based on the forthcoming book (1987): WILDLAND RECREATION: ECOLOGY AND MANAGEMENT, by William E. Hammitt and David N. Cole, John Wiley & Sons, Inc.

LITERATURE CITED

Bates, G.H. 1935. The vegetation of footpaths, sidewalks, cart-tracks and gateways. J. Ecol. 23:470-487.

Bratton, S.P. 1977. Visitor Management. Unpublished report. Uplands Field Lab., Great Smoky Mountains National Park, Gatlinburg, Tenn.

Bratton, S.P., M.G. Hickler, and J.H. Graves. 1979. Trail erosion patterns in Great Smoky Mountains National Park. Environ. Manage. 3:431-445.

Cole, D.N. 1981. Vegetational changes associated with recreational use and fire suppression in the Eagle Cap Wilderness, Oregon: Some management implications. Biol. Conserv. 20:245-270.

Cole, D.N. 1982. Wilderness campsite impacts: Effects of amount of use. USDA For. Serv. Res. Pap. INT-248, Intermt. For. and Range Exp. Stn., Ogden, Utah.

Cole, D.N. and E.G.S. Schreiner. 1981. Impacts of backcountry recreation: Site management and rehabilitation--an annotated bibliography. USDA For. Serv. Gen. Tech. Rep. INT-122.

Frissell, S.S., Jr., and D.P. Duncan. 1965. Campsite preference and deterioration in the Quetico-Superior Canoe Country. J. For. 63:256-260.

Hendee, J.C., G.H. Stankey, and R.C. Lucas. 1978. Wilderness Management. USDA For. Serv. Misc. Pub. No. 1365. Washington, D.C.

LaPage, W.F. 1967. Some observations on campground trampling and ground cover response. USDA For. Serv. Res. Pap. NE-68.

Legg, M.H. and G. Schneider. 1977. Soil deterioration on campsites: Northern forest types. Soil Sci. Soc. Am. J. 41:427-441.

Liddle, M.J. 1975. A selective review of the ecological effects of human trampling on natural environments. Biol. Conserv. 7:17-34.

Manning, R.E. 1979. Impacts of recreation on riparian soils and vegetation. Water Res. Bull. 15:30-43.

Merriam, L.C., Jr. and C.K. Smith. 1974. Visitor impact on newly developed campsites in the Boundary Waters Canoe Area. J. For. 72:627-630.

Merriam, L.C., Jr., C.K. Smith, D.E. Miller and Others. 1973. Newly developed campsites in the Boundary Waters Canoe Area: A study of five years use. Univ. Minn. Agric. Exp. Stn. Bull. No. 511.

Orr, H.R. 1960. Design and layout of recreation facilities. pp 23-28 In USDA For. Serv., Recreation symp. proc., Northeast. For. Serv. Exp. Stn., Broomall, Pa.

Parsons, D.J. and S.H. DeBenedetti. 1979. Wilderness protection in the High Sierra: Effects of a 15-year closure. pp. 1313-1317. In R.M. Linn (ed.). Proc. First Conf. on Scientific Research in the National Parks, USDA Natl. Park Serv., Trans. and Proc. Ser. 5, Washington, D.C.

Ranz, B. 1979. Closing wilderness campsites: Visitor use problems and ecological recovery in the Selway-Bitterroot Wilderness, Montana. Unpublished M.S. thesis. Univ. Montana, Missoula, Mont.

Ream, C.H. 1980. Impacts of backcountry recreationists on wildlife: an annotated bibliography. USDA For. Serv. Gen. Tech. Rep. INT-81, Intermt. For. Range Exp. Stn., Ogden, Utah.

Settergren, C.D. and D.M. Cole. 1970. Recreation effects on soil and vegetation in the Missouri Ozarks. J. For. 68:231-234.

Stace-Smith, R. 1975. The misuse of snowmobiles against wildlife in Canada. Nat. Can. 4:3-8.

Thorud, D.V. and S.S. Frissell. 1976. Time changes in soil density following compaction under an oak forest. Minn. For. Res. Note 257, Univ. Minn., For. Dep., St. Paul, Minn.

Wall, G. and C. Wright. 1977. The environmental impact of outdoor recreation. Dep. Geogr. Publ. Ser. 11, Univ. Waterloo, Ontario, Canada.

Ward, R.M. and R.C. Berg. 1973. Soil compaction and recreational use. Professional Geogr. 25:369-372.

Shining Rock Wilderness: Impacts of Dispersed Use

by

Paul Richard Saunders

ABSTRACT--Shining Rock Wilderness, Pisgah National Forest, is located in the Balsam Mountains of North Carolina, an area which underwent severe anthropogenic ecological changes prior to national forest and wilderness designation. Effects of dispersed recreational use on campsites were measured in spruce-fir communities. Campsites from Shining Rock Wilderness were found to have more disturbance than similar spruce-fir campsites in the Balsam Mountains and Southern Appalachian Mountains. Implications for management are discussed.

KEYWORDS: *Abies fraseri, Picea rubens*, soil compaction, soil erosion, species cover, exotic species, tree vigor.

Shining Rock Wilderness (SRW) is within the Blasam Mountains of North Carolina. Elevations in SRW range from 1067 to 1838 meters. Red spruce-Fraser fir (*Picea rubens-Abies fraseri*, scientific nomenclature for vascular flora follows Radford *et al.* 1968) was the major vegetation type until logging from 1918 to 1927 and catastrophic fires of 2000 to 10,000 hectares in 1925, 1939, 1941, and 1942 destroyed much of the remaining forests and regeneration (Korstian 1937, Forest Service 1970). Today spruce-fir stands are a minor component in SRW compared to grassy balds (dominated by *Danthonia compressa*, heath balds (dominated by *Rhododendron catawbiense, Kalmia latifolia, Vaccinium* spp. and other shrubs), and stands of fire cherry (*Prunus pensylvanica*), yellow birch (*Betula lutea*), and beech (*Fagus grandifolia*) (Ramseur 1960, Sanders 1981).

SRW now encompasses 7490 hectares of Pisgah National Forest following the 1984 North Carolina Wilderness Act additions (Forest Service 1980, Wright 1985). Use estimates range from 130,000 to 257,000 recreation visitor days or a minimum of 17 visitor days per hectare (Roggenbuck and Berrier 1981, Wright 1985), making this one of the most heavily used wilderness areas in the country. The number of visits in 1984 was 64,020; over 8 per hectare (Wright 1985). Use in SRW is not evenly distributed; 75 percent of users pass through Shining Rock Gap (SRG) and 53 percent camp in or near SRG (Roggenbuck *et al.* 1979). Average length of stay was 24.4 hours in 1984, down from 31.0 hours in 1983 (Wright 1985).

The purpose of this paper is to describe the impacts of dispersed recreational use on the spruce-fir stands of SRW. This will be accomplished by describing the campsites within spruce-fir stands, comparing these campsites to those in the remainder of the Balsam Mountains, and comparing SRW campsites to those in other Southern Appalachian Mountain spruce-fir stands. Management implications will be discussed.

METHODOLOGY

Campsites throughout Southern Appalachian spruce-fir stands were identified and sampled beginning in 1976. Data collection at each campsite were based on four relocatable transects 3 meters wide begun at the center of the site and of sufficient length (10-75 meters) to terminate within the forest beyond the zone of obvious human use. Shrub, herb, and ground layer species presence and percent cover were measured at one-half meter intervals perpendicular to a line down the center of the transect. Tree species, diameter at breast height, and increment cores were collected from 1 x 3 meter quadrats in each transect.

Stands without evidence of human use were sampled using a series of random 10 x 10 meter quadrats for overstory trees, and 2 x 2 meter nested quadrats for shrub, herb, and ground layer species and cover. Sampling procedures permitted comparisons between disturbed and undisturbed stands.

RESULTS

Logging and subsequent fires essentially destroyed all continuous spruce-fir stands within SRW and the Balsam

Mountains. Their original extent was reduced from about 3125 hectares to 614 hectares; 19.6 percent of the original area (Saunders 1979). Their extent in SRW may not exceed 200 hectares, but these stands are popular camping sites. Scattered groups of trees or small stands may be found on Cold Mountain, Stairs Mountain, Shining Rock, Shining Rock Gap, Dog Loser Knob, and along Shining Rock Ledge.

Campsites within SRW spruce-fir (except one) occupy an average of 283 square meters with an inner bare zone (devoid of vegetation cover) of 78 square meters (27.9 percent). The exception is SRG campsite. It is on the south side of the gap in a stand of spruce, fir, beech, birch, and rhododendron with trees 20-70 years old. Essentially the entire stand of about one hectare has been disturbed by campers. The campsite core occupies 4231 square meters; the bare zone is 2290 square meters (54.1 percent). Firewood at this site is scarce; most trees are limbed and scarred. Understory herbs and shrubs are infrequent and usually at the base of trees, rhododendrons, or rocks. During the almost daily orographic thunderstorms from May through August, surface runoff on the average 6 percent slope carries forest litter and soil into SRG.

Campsites throughout the Balsam Mountains averaged 314 square meters with a bare zone of 71 square meters (22.6 percent). In all spruce-fir stands from Mt. Rogers in Virginia through eastern Tennessee and western North Carolina, campsites occupied an average of 581 square meters with a bare zone of 163 square meters (28.1 percent) (Saunders 1979). SRG campsite was the largest found; Mt. Chapman in the Great Smoky Mountains, the second largest, was 1855 square meters smaller.

Common tree species in SRW campsites included *A. fraseri, P. rubens, F. grandifolia, B. lutea,* and *P. pensylvanica.* Shrubs were *R. catawbiense,* and *Vaccinium erythrocarpum.* Common herbs were *Athyrium asplenioides, Luzula acuminata, Angelica triquinata, Houstonia serpyllifolia, Aster divaricatus* var. *chlorolepis, A. acuminatus, Viola* spp., *Plantago lanceolata,* and *Poa* spp. Ground cover was usually bare soil, roots, rock, duff and bryophytes.

In contrast, other campsites in Southern Appalachian spruce-fir usually also had *Rubus canadensis* and *Sorbus americana* in the shrub layer, and *Saxifraga michauxii, Oxalis acetosella,* and *Dryopteris campyloptera* in the herb layer. The absence of these species in SRW campsites is probably due to trampling by campers since they are present in undisturbed SRW stands (Saunders 1979).

DISCUSSION

Campsite conditions in SRW were comparable in size and extent of bare zone to those in the Balsam Mountains

and other Southern Appalachain spruce-fir forests. The exception is SRG campsite, the largest campsite found. If the portion of this campsite within the grassy, unforested gap were included, the total impact area would increase two or threefold.

SRG is a significant topographic feature for several reasons. From the gap one may view and access the white quartz rock outcrops for which the wilderness is named. All but two of the seven main trails intersect in the gap due to topographic limitations. The gap is also within a one day hike of all SRW entrances. A high proportion of hikers in SRW pass through SRG and stay overnight in the gap, accounting for the poor condition of SRG campsite.

This high use level has also reduced the social experience; 54 percent of overnight users felt a lack of privacy in campsites (Roggenbuck *et al.* 1979). High use levels and lack of screening vegetation are no doubt causal factors. I interviewed a user who had hiked and camped in Shining Rock nine years earlier, just after wilderness designation on September 3, 1964. He recalled no other visitors and smaller, vegetated campsites (Davis 1976). In one decade soils have been compacted, vegetation trampled away, firewood depleted, and overland flow of soil and duff frequent. Conditions are worst at SRG campsite.

IMPLICATIONS

Continued high use of SRW can be expected to cause further campsite deterioration. These conditions are contradictory to the intent of wilderness legislation. Several of the expected problems are discussed below.

Forest trees can be expected to show reduced growth rates and vigor. These results have been documented in other spruce-fir areas (Saunders 1979). Continued soil compaction and erosion, scuffed roots, and bole damage by campers and firewood gathers are the main causes. Both spruce and fir have thin bark and are susceptible to heart rots. Fir often suffer broken boles during windstorms. Both trees are shallow rooted and easily windthrown.

Exotic species present within SRW can be expected to continue invading campsites (*Poa annua, P. pratensis, Plantago lanceolata*, and *Taraxacum officinale*). While they may provide some ground cover and reduce duff and soil erosion, they contradict the wilderness concept and indicate severe disturbance. They successfully outcompete native spruce-fir herbaceous species, none of which are adapted to these kinds of human impacts.

Campsites can be expected to increase in size. Causal factors include pressure for firewood (users have been observed cutting live trees), reduced tree vigor and their subsequent death, more instances of heart rot, and windthrow as openings in the forest canopy enlarge. Enlarged campsites with a reduced forest canopy will alter the microenvironment of the forest floor, light will reach

the floor, and a better habitat will exist for invading exotic species.

Soil erosion will become an increasing problem. Annual precipitation in the Balsam Mountains ranges from 152 centimeters at Mt. Pisgah (1573 meters) on the east side, to 193 centimeters at Richland Balsam (1921 meters) on the west side (Hardy and Hardy 1971). Reduced forest canopy, reduced shrub and herb species cover, and reduced forest duff leave the soil unprotected. Trampling compacts the soil, reducing pore space for water infiltration. The catastrophic fires four decades earlier destroyed the organic horizons and damaged the upper mineral horizons, causing the expanse of grass and heath balds (Sanders 1981, Saunders *et al.* 1983). Thin soil horizons developed since the fires are susceptible to trampling and erosion. Soil erosion will reduce the ability of these sites to support vegetation and recover from use.

Finally there is the problem of human and packstock waste disposal, and drinking water contamination. SRG is served by a spring southeast and below the gap. The potential for overland soil and waste flow, or groundwater infiltration about tree roots is obvious. Shallow waste burial in 5-30 centimeter holes in comparable spruce-fir and meadow sites in Montana did not kill bacteria after three years (Temple *et al.* 1980, 1982). The over 68,900 annual recreation visitor days of camping in SRG pose a threat to the purity of this spring. Other water sources in SRW are also threatened.

SUMMARY

Shining Rock Wilderness has one of the highest use levels on a per hectare basis of any wilderness. Heavy use has impacted campsites within the spruce-fir zone of this wilderness on a level comparable to that in other spruce-fir forests in the Southern Appalachian Mountains. The heaviest impact has been at Shining Rock Gap campsite where over one-half of all overnight visits occur. Heavy use levels have resulted in tree damage, reduced species presence, reduced species cover, and overland soil and duff erosion.

Future effects of continued high use probably include reduced tree growth rates and vigor, increased exotic species presence, enlarged campsites, increased soil erosion, and decreased water quality. Consequently, there is a need for change in management direction. Recreational use, especially campsites, should be placed in habitats less susceptible to degradation from current high use. Closing and rehabilitating severely deteriorated sites should be a high priority. Development of a plan to monitor and assess the effects of use would quantify existing site conditions and rates of deterioration, as well as lead to the formulation of management solutions. Improving the integrity of the wilderness environment, and educating, limiting, or redirecting wilderness users would improve the quality of the wilderness experience.

ACKNOWLEDGMENTS

This is scientific paper 7136, Agriculture Research Center, Washington State University, Pullman, Washington, Project 0596.

LITERATURE CITED

Davis, J. 1976. Carolina Hiking Club. Asheville, North Carolina. Personal Communication.

Forest Service. 1970. History of the Shining Rock Wilderness Area. Pisgah National Forest, Pisgah Forest, North Carolina

Forest Service. 1980. Land areas of the national forest system. USDA, For. Serv. Washington, D.C. FS-360. 77p.

Hardy, A.V. and J.D. Hardy. 1971. Weather and climate in North Carolina. North Carolina Agric. Exp. Stn. Raleigh, North Carolina. Bull. 396 (rev.). 48p.

Korstian, C.F. 1937. Perpetuation of spruce on cut-over and burned land in the higher southern Appalachian Mountains. Ecol. Monogr. 7:125-167.

Radford, A.E., H.E. Ahles, and C.R. Bell. 1968. Manual of the vascular flora of the Carolinas. Univ. North Carolina Press, Chapel Hill, North Carolina. 1183p.

Ramseur, G.S. 1960. The vascular flora of high mountain communities of the Southern Appalachians. J. Elisha Mitchell Sci. Soc. 76:82-112.

Roggenbuck, J.W., W.N. Timm, and A.E. Watson. 1979. Visitor perception of the recreation carrying capacity of three wilderness areas in North Carolina. Dep. For., Virginia Poly. Inst. and State Univ., Blacksburg, VA 303p.

Roggenbuck, J.W. and D.L. Berrier. 1981. Communications to disperse wilderness campers. J. For. 79:295-297.

Sanders, B. 1981. Prescribed burning for golden eagle habitat management. pp. 88-95. *In*, P.R. Saunders (ed.). Status and Management of Southern Appalachian Mountain Balds: Proc.of a Workshop. Southern Appalachian Research/Resource Management Cooperative. Western Carolina Univ., Cullowhee, North Carolina. pp. 88-95.

Saunders, P.R. 1979. Vegetational impact of human disturbance on the spruce-fir forests of the Southern Appalachian Mountains. Ph.D. Diss. Duke Univ. Durham, North Carolina. 177p.

Saunders, P. R., G. A. Smathers, and G. S. Ramseur. 1983. Secondary succession of a spruce-fir burn in the Plott Balsam Mountains, North Carolina. Castanea. 48:41-47.

Temple, K. L., A. K. Camper, and G. A. McFeters. 1980. Survival of two entrobacteria in feces buried in soil under field conditions. Appl. Environ. Microbiol. 40:794-797.

Temple, K. L., A. K. Camper, and R. C. Lucas. 1982. Potential health hazard from human wastes in wilderness. Soil Water Conserv. 37:357-359.

Wright, Paul. 1985. Recreation Assistant. Pisgah Ranger District, Pisgah National Forest, Pisgah Forest, North Carolina. Personal Communication.

Emerging Patterns In The Distribution Of Roadless Forested Areas In The Midsouth

by

Victor A. Rudis

ABSTRACT--Of the roughly 100 million acres (40.5 million ha) of forest land in the Midsouth, roadless forested areas comprise some 23 million acres (9.3 million ha). Although much of the acreage is on bottomland sites (7 million acres, or 2.8 million ha) and areas with rugged terrain or steep slopes (4 million acres, or 1.6 million ha), half of the acreage is on upland sites with level-to-rolling terrain. This paper discusses the distribution of roadless forested areas by location, stand characteristics, and proximity to population centers. Roadless timberland areas are clustered around selected landforms. Current patterns suggest trends toward greater representation in hardwood forest types, public ownership, and sawtimber stands. Data were obtained from a 1975-84 survey of Midsouth timberland.

KEYWORDS: wilderness, remote forests, forest inventories, mapping, primitive areas.

For many years numbers of people hiking and camping in remote or roadless areas have been increasing (Spencer *et al.* 1980). Crowding is anticipated in roadless areas near metropolitan areas, thereby increasing the demand for these areas, particularly in the eastern United States (Cordell and Hendee 1982). Coupled with increased demand for roadless areas is a declining supply that has resulted from accelerated roadbuilding since World War II (Irland and Rumpf 1980). Pressures for intensified multiple-use management of public as well as private roadless areas are likely to lead to a major decrease in primitive recreation opportunities (Cordell and Hendee 1982).

The USDA Forest Service's Forest Inventory and Analysis (FIA) Units have been conducting statewide timber surveys since the 1930's to assess private as well as public forest resources in the United States. A geographically extensive data base has been prepared to assist in these timber assessments. In response to requirements that they address multiresource values, the Forest Service has begun to assemble comparable information on nontimber attributes of forested land. Efforts are underway by FIA units to record objective characteristics that help to describe specific recreation, wildlife, range, and watershed values of forested land (Labau 1984). Although such characteristics do not translate directly into wilderness or recreational values, they should prove useful as bases for regional assessments.

Distance from roads is such a characteristic. Forests distant from roads are, by definition, remote--a chief criterion for wilderness or primitive recreational opportunity designation (USDA Forest Service, undated). Roadless forested areas also provide key habitat for black bears and other wildlife in need of seclusion. The relatively small designated wilderness areas common in the eastern United States may not support some raptorial and mammalian species that have extensive home ranges. Presence of extensive areas of similar habitat outside designated wilderness areas is a key ingredient in the survival of these species. As a limited resource, roadless forested areas should be monitored to ensure that an adequate supply remains for the future.

In this paper, existing data on roadless forested areas in the Midsouth Region (Alabama, Arkansas, Louisiana, Mississippi, eastern Oklahoma, Tennessee, and eastern Texas) are summarized. Inventory years range from 1975 for eastern Texas to 1984 for Louisiana. Information is presented on the location, kinds of vegetation, stand size, and ownership characteristics of roadless forested areas. Limitations associated with existing data are also described.

METHODS

The Southern Forest Experiment Station's FIA Unit established a system of permanent sample plots located systematically at the intersection of perpendicular grid lines spaced at 3-mile (4.8 km) intervals throughout the Midsouth. Plot locations were transferred to aerial photos, and all plots were visited on the ground to verify conditions. Detailed measurements were made at all plot locations classified as timberland (at least 1 acre, or 0.4 ha in forest cover, 120 feet (36.6 m) in width, capable of producing crops of industrial wood, and not withdrawn from timber utilization by statute or administrative regulation). Forest resource information was obtained for some 17,000 plots throughout the seven states surveyed. Survey details are described in FIA field manuals (FIA Research Work Unit 1985).

In 1974, additional criteria were added to survey procedures to address timber availability, including distance of the plot from the nearest road. Although not intended as an aid in determining wilderness or primitive recreation opportunities of forested stands, this measure does provide an estimate of remoteness.

For all states, distance from roads was measured from the plot center to the nearest all-weather road (improved and maintained) or unimproved road. Unimproved roads were considered only if they were currently truck operable or could be made so with minimum improvement such as removal of blown down trees.

(The reader should note that due to changes in photo quality and interpretation between 1974 and 1984, and recent emphasis on this measure as an estimate of remoteness, timberland area 1/2 mile (0.8 km) or more from roads may be slightly overestimated, particularly for surveys prior to 1981).

RESULTS AND DISCUSSION

Timberland in the Midsouth Region occupies 98.5 million acres. Of this area, 75.8 million acres are less than 1/2 mile from roads, 16.1 million acres are 1/2 to 1 mile, 6.0 million acres are 1 to 3 miles, and 0.6 million acres are more than 3 miles. The total of 22.7 million acres (23% of the Region's 98.5 million acres) 1/2 mile or more from roads are considered in this report as roadless. Timberland is distributed unevenly among the seven states, with most acreage in Alabama (22%) and the least acreage in Oklahoma (4%) (Fig. 1). Timberland 1/2 mile (0.8 km) or more from roads is found in every state, with the largest acreage in Arkansas (21%) and the least acreage in Oklahoma (6%).

Of the 98.5 million acres (40 million ha) of timberland in the Midsouth, 66.2 million acres (26.8 million ha)

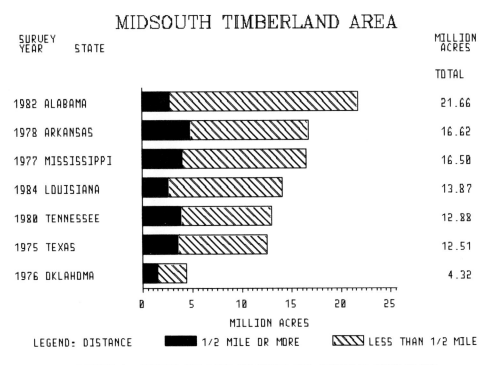

FIGURE 1. TIMBERLAND AREA BY STATE AND DISTANCE FROM ROADS.

MIDSOUTH STATES REGION

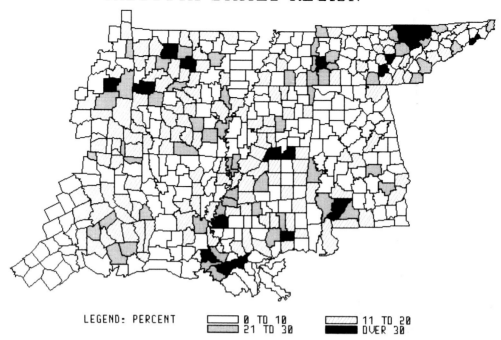

LEGEND: PERCENT

| 0 TO 10 | 11 TO 20 |
| 21 TO 30 | OVER 30 |

PERCENT ROADLESS TIMBERLAND AREA PER LAND AREA BY COUNTY

(67%) are classified physiographically (physiographic class is defined according to its suitability for growing pines, upland hardwoods, and bottomland hardwoods. Pine physiographic class is favored where pines and upland hardwoods are present) as pine sites (Table 1). Upland hardwood sites, 14.0 million acres (5.7 million ha) (14%), are found chiefly in the northern portions of the Region. Bottomland sites, 18.3 million acres (7.4 million ha) (19%), are concentrated in the lower Mississippi River Floodplain, but are also found in widely scattered locations throughout the Region (Fig. 2).

Of the areas classified as roadless, 12.0 million acres (4.9 million ha) (53%) are pine sites, 4.0 million acres (1.6 million ha) (17%) are upland hardwood sites and 6.8 million acres (2.8 million ha) (30%) are bottomland sites. Roadless timberland areas are illustrated in Fig. 3 by physiographic class. As one might expect, roadless timberland areas are often found in swamps and in areas with steep terrain (slopes greater than 20 percent) where road building is difficult (Table 1). Half of the roadless acreage, 12.2 million acres (4.9 million ha), however, is found on upland hardwood or pine sites with level-to-rolling terrain. Because such areas are more suited to a wide variety of land uses, one can expect this acreage to diminish more rapidly with time than other roadless timberland areas.

The largest clusters of roadless timberland areas are in bottomlands along the paths of major rivers, in the mountainous areas of Arkansas and Tennessee, and in the loess or bluff hills bordering the Mississippi River Floodplain (Major landforms are described by Nelson and Zillgitt (1969)). Clusters indicate areas where wildlife in need of seclusion may be abundant, and areas where the potential for primitive recreation opportunities is greatest.

However, overall recreation value may be low, as clusters are isolated from metropolitan areas (see Cordell and Hendee 1982, p.72), or represent suitable environments for a limited number of activities.

Acreage by forest type, ownership, and stand size class is summarized in Tables 2, 3, and 4. Differences between roadless and roaded areas are significant (P (larger Chi-square) lt 0.005). Roadless areas are more frequent in oak-gum-cypress and elm-ash-cottonwood forest types, in sawtimber stands, and among public land-holding agencies. Roaded areas are more frequent in longleaf-slash and loblolly-shortleaf forest types, in sapling and seedling stands, and among non-industrial private landowners.

CONCLUSIONS

The most recent forest surveys show that roadless areas represent less than one-fourth of the timberland in the Midsouth. Some of the roadless areas may not be developed soon, such as the clustered acreage of bottomland hardwoods and many of the upland hardwood or pine sites with rough terrain. These clusters represent areas that may contain and continue to retain wilderness potential for the near future. As such, they provide buffers against encroachment of dissimilar land uses for nearby designated or proposed wilderness areas.

Roadless timberland areas are significantly different from roaded areas, not only in terms of location and physiography, but in terms of forest type, ownership, and stand size as well. Undoubtedly the patterns, or "trends" suggested by the data--more hardwood forest types, more public owners, and more sawtimber stands--in roadless vs.

Table 1.   Midsouth Timberland Area by Physiographic Class, Slope Class, and Distance from Roads.

Physiographic class and slope class	All Timberland		1/2 Mile or More		Less than 1/2 Mile	
	Million Acres	Percent	Million Acres	Percent	Million Acres	Percent
Pine						
Greater than 20%	8.74	8.9	2.16	9.5	6.58	8.7
20% or less	57.50	58.4	9.82	43.2	47.68	62.9
Total	66.23	67.2	11.97	52.7	54.26	71.6
Upland hardwood						
Greater than 20%	4.53	4.6	1.55	6.8	2.99	3.9
20% or less	9.44	9.6	2.40	10.6	7.04	9.3
Total	13.97	14.2	3.95	17.4	10.02	13.2
Bottomland hardwood	18.31	18.6	6.79	29.9	11.52	15.2
Total	98.53	100.0	22.71	100.0	75.82	100.0

Table 2.   Midsouth Timberland Area by Forest Type and Distance from Roads.

			Distance from Roads			
	All Timberland		1/2 Mile or More		Less Than 1/2 Mile	
Forest Type	Million Acres	Percent	Million Acres	Percent	Million Acres	Percent
Longleaf-slash	3.74	3.8	0.42	1.9	3.32	4.4
Loblolly-shortleaf	25.15	25.5	3.94	17.4	21.21	28.0
Oak-pine	17.61	17.9	3.35	14.7	14.26	18.8
Oak-hickory	34.88	35.4	8.42	37.1	26.46	34.9
Oak-gum-cypress	15.63	15.9	5.94	26.2	9.69	12.8
Elm-ash-cottonwood	1.38	1.4	0.59	2.6	0.79	1.0
Other[1]	0.14	0.1	0.05	0.2	0.09	0.0
Total	98.53	100.0	22.71	100.0	75.82	100.0

[1] White pine-hemlock, sugar maple-beech-birch, and nontyped (nonstocked) stands.

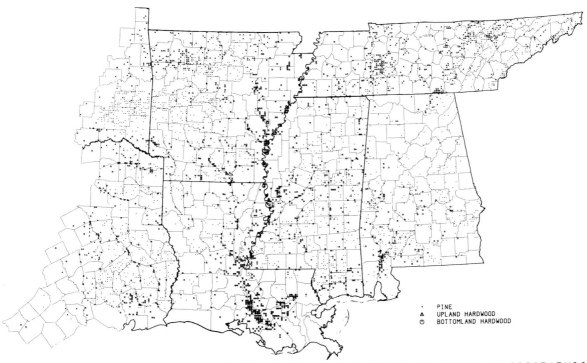

FIGURE 2. MIDSOUTH TIMBERLAND 1/2 MILE OR MORE FROM ROADS BY PHYSIOGRAPHIC CLASS.

- PINE
△ UPLAND HARDWOOD
⊙ BOTTOMLAND HARDWOOD

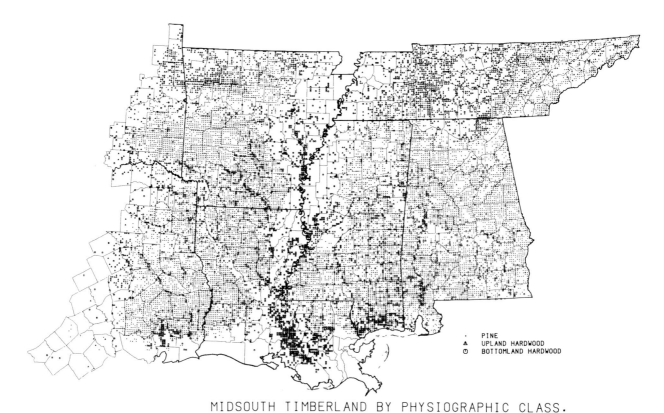

MIDSOUTH TIMBERLAND BY PHYSIOGRAPHIC CLASS.

· PINE
△ UPLAND HARDWOOD
⊕ BOTTOMLAND HARDWOOD

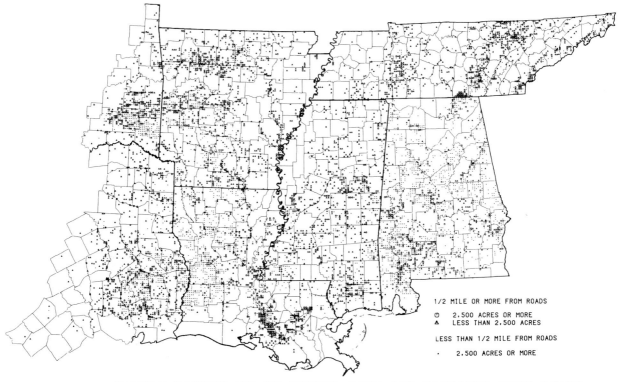

1/2 MILE OR MORE FROM ROADS
⊕ 2,500 ACRES OR MORE
△ LESS THAN 2,500 ACRES

LESS THAN 1/2 MILE FROM ROADS
· 2,500 ACRES OR MORE

REMOTE TIMBERLAND BY FOREST SIZE AND DISTANCE FROM ROADS.

Table 3. Midsouth Timberland Area by Ownership Class and Distance from Roads.

| | All Timberland | | Distance from Roads | | | |
| | | | 1/2 Mile or More | | Less Than 1/2 Mile | |
Ownership Class	Million Acres	Percent	Million Acres	Percent	Million Acres	Percent
National Forest	6.31	6.4	2.18	9.6	4.13	5.4
Other public	3.51	3.6	1.25	5.5	2.26	3.0
Forest industry	21.38	21.7	4.96	21.8	16.42	21.7
Other private	67.33	68.3	14.33	63.1	53.00	69.9
Total	98.53	100.0	22.71	100.0	75.82	100.0

Table 4. Midsouth Timberland Area by Stand Size Class and Distance from Roads.

| | All Timberland | | Distance from Roads | | | |
| | | | 1/2 Mile or More | | Less Than 1/2 Mile | |
Size Class	Million Acres	Percent	Million Acres	Percent	Million Acres	Percent
Nonstocked	1.50	1.5	0.32	1.5	1.15	1.5
Sapling/seedling	24.30	24.7	4.22	18.6	20.09	26.5
Poletimber	29.93	30.4	6.78	29.9	23.15	30.5
Sawtimber	42.79	43.4	11.36	50.0	31.43	41.5
Total	98.53	100.0	22.71	100.0	75.82	100.0

roaded timberland areas will continue. Conversion of some roaded areas to roadless areas can be expected, however, as abandoned farm and logging roads revert to forest cover.

Roadless areas represent a limited range of resources, are unevenly distributed and eventually may be restricted to a few sections of the Region. Planned development of these sections for timber management, wildlife, agriculture, human settlement, or recreation should be evaluated in terms of how such development will affect the regional supply and isolation of roadless areas.

LITERATURE CITED

Cordell, H.K. and J.C. Hendee. 1982. Renewable resources recreation in the United States: supply, demand, and critical policy issues. Amer. For. Assoc., Washington, D.C.

Forest Inventory and Analysis Research Work Unit. 1985. Forest Survey Inventory Work Plan. USDA For. Serv., Southern Forest Exp. Stn., Starkville, Miss.

Irland, L.C. and T. Rumpf. 1980. Trends in land and water available for outdoor recreation. pp. 77-87. In Proc. 1980 National Outdoor Recreation Trends Symp. Volume 1. USDA For. Serv. Gen. Tech. Rep. NE-57.

Labau, V.J. 1984. A review of non-timber data collection and information reported by the Forest Inventory and Analysis Projects in the United States. pp 59-63, 153-165. In E. Schlatterer and H.G. Lund (eds.). Proc. of the inventory integration workshop, Portland Ore., October 15-19, 1984. Washington, D.C., USDA For. Serv. Range and Timber Management Staffs.

Nelson, T.C. and M.W. Zillgitt. 1969. A forest atlas of the South. USDA For. Serv., South. For. Exp. Stn., New Orleans, La. and Southeast. For. Exp. Stn., Asheville, North Car.

Spencer, E.L., H.E. Echelberger, R.E. Leonard, and C. Evans. 1980. Trends in hiking and backcountry use. pp. 195-198. In Proc. 1980 National Outdoor Recreation Trends Symp., Volume 1. USDA For. Serv. Gen. Tech. Rep. NE-57.

USDA Forest Service. (undated). ROS Users Guide. Washington, D.C.

273

Management Of Plant Communities In Wilderness Areas

by
Jack D. McCullough

Before a vegetation management plan for a wilderness area can be developed, one must understand that a plant community is a dynamic assemblage of species and cannot be preserved in the same manner that one would preserve a historical site. The presence and abundance of plant species in the community are dictated by variations in soils, moisture, nutrients, competition, insect infestation, and many other complex environmental interactions. The preservation of a plant community would essentially involve controlling those parameters as well as the complicated successional forces that created that community.

One would assume a major objective would be to simply maintain any type of vegetation in the wilderness. This would encompass techniques which prevent catastrophic destruction of vegetation, such as uncontrolled wildfire, insect epidemics, plant disease, and livestock grazing. In addition to these events, wilderness managers will have to contend with the pressure from private companies and government agencies that will want to open the wilderness for oil exploration, strip mining, hunting, water impoundments, logging, and other commercial activities.

An additional objective in the vegetation management plan might include the preservation of certain dominant species in the forest ecosystem, such as the longleaf pine (*Pinus palustris*) or dwarf palmetto (*Sabal minor*) in the Upland Island Wilderness in eastern Texas. This approach would allow successional changes to occur which might permit the dominant woody species to survive, but some understory and herbaceous species might disappear.

Finally, management objectives might include the preservation of plant communities characteristic of certain successional stages. This might include preservation of a climax forest in order to present a vegetational aspect which the early American pioneers might have witnessed. On the other hand, there may be a desire to preserve a subclimax stage, such as a pitcher plant bog where successional changes are occurring rapidly. Management practices would be quite different in those two cases and preservation techniques, particularly in the case of subclimax communities, would only be applied in appropriate areas.

Many conservationists oppose man's efforts to manage wilderness areas. This includes control of fire, insects, and disease. Certainly, in a completely natural setting this would be possible. But wilderness areas in the eastern United States are relatively small areas. Uncontrolled fire or epidemics of insects in those small areas would be catastrophic, and it might require 100 to 200 years for the area, once decimated, to recover. At best, the wilderness area is only a partially natural setting. The wilderness will be visited by man whose imprint hopefully will be minimal, but the areas are surrounded by forests and other lands that are intensively managed by man. The influence of surrounding land use activities on wilderness areas, and the impact of wilderness on those same areas must be considered, and almost demand management procedures. Even the atmosphere in the wilderness is influenced by air pollution from cities and industries hundreds of miles away. Wilderness vegetation is not in a completely natural environment and some management by man would therefore be necessary. However, vegetation management practices should consist merely of those actions that are necessary to achieve one or more of the objectives.

Once the objectives have been established for preservation of vegetation in the wilderness, experienced plant ecologists should be consulted: first, so that a thorough understanding of the ecology of each plant community might be obtained, and secondly, so that appropriate management practices might be developed to maintain conditions necessary to preserve those communities.

However, management practices should not be left entirely to the professionals. The wishes of a concerned public must be implemented in the management plan as much as possible.

Vegetation Of The Roy E. Larsen Sandylands Sanctuary, Hardin Co., Texas

by

J. A. Matos and D. C. Rudolph

ABSTRACT--The vascular flora of the Roy E. Larsen Sandylands Sanctuary, located in the Big Thicket region of Texas, was analyzed during a 16 month period. Five hundred forty-four species in 105 families were collected. Distribution of species by habitat was noted and the percentage of introduced plant species in each habitat was included in the analysis. In addition, eight woody plant communities were analyzed on the preserve representing each of the major plant communities. Uplands on the Sanctuary are receiving intensive management at the present time in the form of: (a) the systematic removal of the introduced species, *Pinus elliotti* and (b) prescribed burns.

KEYWORDS: Big Thicket, floodplain, baygall, uplands, transition forest, endemic, disturbed areas.

The Roy E. Larsen Sandylands Sanctuary is a 920.4 ha preserve located in Hardin County, Texas, and is owned and managed by the Texas Nature Conservancy. The Sanctuary was established when 865.2 ha were donated to the Nature Conservancy in 1977 by Temple-EasTex and Time, Inc. An additional 16.2 ha were later donated by Gulf State Utilities. Since the completion of this study, a 39 ha addition has been donated to the Sanctuary by Sun Oil Co. The area has been managed as a natural area by the Nature Conservancy since 1977. There is one main nature trail through the Sanctuary with three branch trails. All nature trails are in the southern half of the Sanctuary; therefore, much of the area is inaccessible to the public.

The Sanctuary is located in Hardin County (Fig. 1, which is included in the East Texas Forest Region or Piney Woods of Texas (Correll and Johnston 1970). The area is generally considered to be part of the Big Thicket region of east Texas. The Big Thicket has been described as a floristically diverse area, located at the ecotone between the eastern deciduous forests and the drier savannah and prairie regions to the west (Watson 1979). The Roy E. Larsen Sandylands Sanctuary is located in the "upper" Big Thicket region of McLeod (1972), that is, the area of the Big Thicket where *Fagus grandifolia* (beech) occurs. The Sanctuary is approximately halfway between the towns of Kountze and Silsbee in Hardin County. The study area is bisected by the 95 degrees 15'W longitude while 30 degrees 20'N and 30 degrees 25'N latitude enclose it. Village Creek forms the western boundary of the Sanctuary. Village Creek is a major tributary of the

Neches River, and flows in a south southeasterly direction.

Elevation in the preserve varies from just above sea level on Village Creek to a maximum of 18.3 m on the highest sand ridge.

Hardin County has a generally mild climate with temperatures averaging 19.5 degrees C. Rainfall averages 132 cm per year, and is in general, evenly distributed throughout the year. There is usually slightly more rainfall in the spring (April and May) and again in mid-winter (December), and usually slightly less in the late summer (Carr 1967).

The Sanctuary displays several of the habitat features commonly found in the Big Thicket (Watson 1979). There is an extensive floodplain forest, a transition area between the floodplain and the dry sandy uplands, and extensive baygall areas (Fig. 1). In addition, there were two, and are at present three upland ponds in the preserve. These ponds are of the type that Watson (1979) describes as an early successional stage in the formation of baygalls and are populated with an abundance of hydrophytes.

The Sanctuary has several areas of disturbance. Three rights-of-way traverse the preserve and are maintained by utilities, private oil and gas concerns, and the Santa Fe Railroad. These rights-of-way are regularly cleared of woody vegetation. There are several active natural gas wells, and an old county dump site at the north end of the Sanctuary.

Most of the upland areas of the preserve were cut and replanted in *Pinus elliottii* (slash pine) in the early 1960's. The upland areas dominated by slash pine are currently being selectively cut to remove all but the occasional indi-

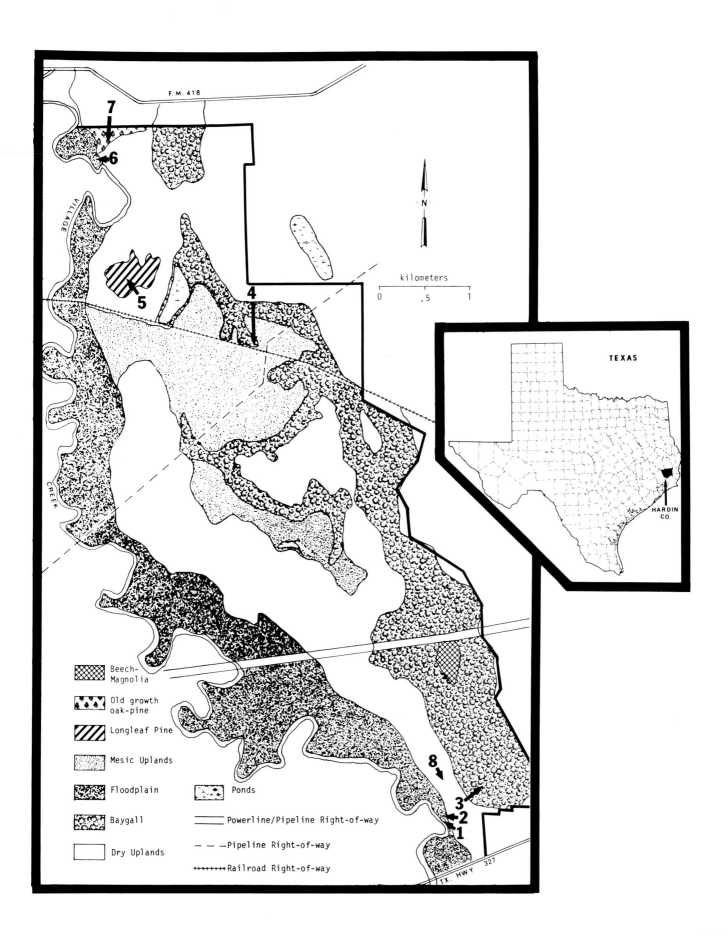

F.M. 418

7

6

VILLAGE

CREEK

N

kilometers

0   .5   1

5

4

TEXAS

HARDIN CO.

Beech-Magnolia

Old growth oak-pine

Longleaf Pine

Mesic Uplands

Floodplain

Baygall

Dry Uplands

Ponds

Powerline/Pipeline Right-of-way

— — —Pipeline Right-of-way

++++++Railroad Right-of-way

8

3

2

1

TX. HWY. 327

vidual of this introduced species from the preserve.

Floodplain and baygall areas had been selectively cut periodically prior to the stewardship of the Nature Conservancy.

METHODS

A. Woody Community Analyses.

Eight study areas were selected as representative of the forest types found in the various communities within the preserve. Woody communities analyzed included: the floodplain forest at a typical floodplain site (Stand 1) and in a very wet area (Stand 2); baygalls of two types, the typical mature baygall (Stand 3) and a sphagnum bog (Stand 4); the arid sandy uplands in a longleaf pine forest (Stand 5), a slightly more mesic upland site (Stand 6), and in an arid, open area (Stand 8); and the slope or transition forest (Stand 7). Upland areas which had been planted in *Pinus elliottii* were not included in the woody sites analyzed.

Stands were analyzed using 35 to 75 contiguous 5m X 5m plots arranged in two belt transects. In the analysis of Stand 1, 75 plots were used. Stand 2 was analyzed using only 35 plots and stands 3-8 were analyzed using 50 plots each.

Shrubs, trees, and vines were recorded and measured in each plot for all plants with a diameter at breast height greater than 0.5 cm. Density, frequency, basal area, and importance values were determined. Importance value is equal to the sum of the relative density, relative basal area, and relative frequency (Daubermire 1968).

B. Species List

Field collections were generally made at two week intervals between February 1982 and June 1983. Collections were made throughout the entire preserve at each interval. Within the Angiospermae, normally, only flowering individuals were collected, exceptions being some of the tree species as well as *Sabal minor* and *Arundinaria gigantea*. All specimens are deposited in the Stephen F. Austin State University Herbarium (ASTC) in Nacogdoches, Texas. Taxonomic nomenclature follows Correll and Johnston (1970) except in the case of *Eleocharis elongata* where nomenclature follows Godfrey and Wooten (1979).

RESULTS AND DISCUSSION

A. Woody Community Analysis

Tables 1-8 are the results for the eight woody stands analyzed in the preserve. Fig. 1 shows the location within the preserve of the stands. Stands within each community, i.e., floodplain, baygalls, uplands, and transition, will be discussed together.

Stands 1 and 2, Floodplain Forest Near Village Creek (Tables 1 and 2)- Stand 1 corresponds to the Floodplain

Hardwood Forest type of Marks & Harcombe (1981). A shallow litter layer, usually less than 1 cm thick, accumulated during the summer, fall, and winter in the floodplain stands. The litter layer was washed away during the spring flooding of Village Creek. No sign of human disturbance was evident, although in Stand 2 several wind thrown trees were observed.

Stand 1 had the greatest number of woody species of the areas analyzed in this study. It was an open forest with a sparse understory. The canopy was composed of *Quercus* spp., *Liquidambar styraciflua*, and *Nyssa sylvatica* with a few *Carya aquatica* and *Ilex opaca*. The mid-layer was composed of *Carpinus caroliniana*, *Halesia diptera* and *Ilex decidua*. A few seedlings of overstory trees were observed, primarily *Crataegus marshallii* and *Ilex opaca*. Other species observed in the area, but not included in the transect, were *Morus rubra* and *Quercus prinus*.

Backswamps, meader scars, and other depressions give the floodplain added diversity (Mahler 1979, Marks and Harcombe 1981), one of these intermittent drainages was the site for Stand 2. Stand 2 was at the base of the bluff bordering the floodplain of Village Creek, in a low area where standing water was usually present.

The overstory in Stand 2 was composed of *Nyssa aquatica*, *Liquidambar styraciflua*, *Fraxinus pensylvanica*, *Taxodium distichum*, and *Acer rubrum*. The midstory was composed of *Itea virginica*, *Styrax americana*, *Cornus racemosa*, and transgressives of overstory trees. The herbaceous layer was composed primarily of *Onoclea sensibilis*. Seedlings observed were of *Taxodium distichum* and *Liquidambar styraciflua*.

Stands 3 and 4, Baygalls (Tables 3 and 4)- Stand 3 was an example of a Wetland Baygall Shrub Thicket (Marks and Harcombe 1981). Water was observed standing in the baygall approximately eight (late winter, spring, and early summer) of the 16 months of this study. The overstory was composed of *Nyssa sylvatica*, *Quercus laurifolia*, *Q. nigra*, and *Pinus taeda*. The midstory was made up of *Acer rubrum* and small individuals of *Liquidambar styraciflua*, while the understory was dominated by *Cyrilla racemiflora* and *Ilex vomitoria*. There was a sparse herbaceous layer. Where there was no free standing water, the floor of the baygall was carpeted with *Sphagnum* spp. *Magnolia virginiana* was observed in the area but not included in the transect.

Stand 4 was an extensive sphagnum bog where water, as deep as 40 cm, stood during all but the driest months of the year. The sphagnum carpet was interrupted by mounds made of *Nyssa sylvatica*, *Taxodium distichum*, and *Cyrilla racemiflora* roots; these mounds provided a non-submerged substrate for seedlings. Trees were, in general, small, seemingly stunted individuals. There was a low overstory of *N. sylvatica*, *T. distichum*, and a few *Pinus taeda*. The midstory was composed of *C. racemiflora* and transgressives of the overstory trees. Numerous *N. sylvatica* and occasional *P. taeda* seedlings were observed, almost all of which were on the root

Table 1. Stand 1. Floodplain Forest Near Village Creek

Species	Plots N = 75	Frequency %	Relative Frequency %	No. of Stems	Density No./m²	Relative Density %	Basal Area cm²/m²	Relative Basal Area %	Importance Value
Carpinus caroliniana	45	60.0	19.9	59	0.031	18.2	6.525	14.4	52.4
Quercus nigra	18	24.0	8.0	22	0.012	6.8	13.150	28.9	43.7
Vitis rotundifolia	40	53.3	17.7	78	0.040	24.0	0.356	.8	42.5
Liquidambar styraciflua	14	18.7	6.2	24	0.013	7.4	10.823	23.8	37.4
Ilex decidua	15	20.0	6.6	32	0.017	9.9	0.508	1.1	17.6
Carya aquatica	10	13.3	4.4	11	0.006	3.4	3.041	6.7	14.5
Halesia diptera	16	21.3	7.1	18	0.010	5.5	0.347	.8	13.4
Acer rubrum	3	4.0	1.3	6	0.003	1.9	2.385	5.2	8.4
Berchemia scandens	8	10.7	3.5	12	0.006	3.7	0.462	1.0	8.3
Campsis radicans	9	12.0	4.0	10	0.005	3.1	0.148	.3	7.4
Pinus taeda	1	1.3	.4	2	0.001	.6	2.684	5.9	7.0
Nyssa sylvatica	5	6.7	2.2	7	0.004	2.2	1.142	2.5	6.9
Ilex opaca	4	5.3	1.8	4	0.002	1.2	1.411	3.1	6.1
Rhus toxicodendron	7	9.3	3.1	7	0.004	2.2	0.046	.1	5.4
Viburnum dentatum	6	8.0	2.7	7	0.004	2.2	0.003	<.1	4.8
Bignonia capreolata	6	8.0	2.7	6	0.003	1.9	0.005	<.1	4.5
Taxodium distichum	1	1.3	.4	1	0.001	.3	1.047	2.3	3.1
Ulmus alata	3	4.0	1.3	3	0.002	.9	0.289	.6	2.9
Ilex vomitoria	3	4.0	1.3	4	0.002	1.2	0.091	.2	2.8
Betula nigra	1	1.3	.4	1	0.001	.3	0.774	1.7	2.5
Celtis laevigata	2	2.7	.9	2	0.001	.6	0.113	.3	1.8
Ulmus americana	2	2.7	.9	2	0.001	.6	0.013	<.1	1.5
Smilax rotundifolia	2	2.7	.9	2	0.001	.6	0.003	<.1	1.5
Bumelia lanuginosa	1	1.3	.4	1	0.001	.3	0.094	.2	1.0
Quercus laurifolia	1	1.3	.4	1	0.001	.3	0.007	<.1	.8
Sebastiana fruticosa	1	1.3	.4	1	0.001	.3	0.005	<.1	.8
Crataegus marshallii	1	1.3	.4	1	0.001	.3	0.001	<.1	.8
Vitis cinerea	1	1.3	.4	1	0.001	.3	0.001	<.1	.8
Total			99.7	325	0.172	100.2	45.474	99.9	300.6

Table 2. Stand 2. Floodplain Forest in a Wet Area.

Species	Plots N = 35	Frequency %	Relative Frequency %	No. of Stems	Density No./m²	Relative Density %	Basal Area cm²/m²	Relative Basal Area %	Importance Value
Nyssa aquatica	31	88.6	24.2	77	0.088	29.0	80.285	84.7	137.8
Liquidambar styraciflua	30	85.7	23.4	75	0.086	28.2	4.878	5.1	56.8
Fraxinus pensylvanica	22	62.9	17.2	43	0.049	16.2	1.319	1.4	34.8
Taxodium distichum	12	34.3	9.4	15	0.017	5.6	5.121	5.4	20.4
Acer rubrum	5	14.3	3.9	11	0.012	4.1	1.475	1.6	9.6
Rhus toxicodendron	2	5.7	1.6	13	0.015	4.9	0.048	.1	6.5
Itea virginica	4	11.4	3.1	6	0.007	2.3	0.006	<.1	5.4
Quercus lyrata	4	11.4	3.1	4	0.004	1.5	0.576	.6	5.2
Carpinus caroliniana	4	11.4	3.1	4	0.004	1.5	0.112	.1	4.7
Cornus racemosa	3	8.6	2.3	4	0.004	1.5	0.065	.1	3.9
Betula nigra	2	5.7	1.6	2	0.002	.8	0.736	.8	3.1
Ulmus americana	2	5.7	1.6	2	0.002	.8	0.026	<.1	2.3
Vitis lincecumii	1	2.9	.8	3	0.004	1.1	0.008	<.1	1.9
Planera aquatica	1	2.9	.8	2	0.002	.8	0.016	<.1	1.6
Quercus laurifolia	1	2.9	.8	1	0.001	.4	0.090	.1	1.3
Styrax americana	1	2.9	.8	1	0.001	.4	0.015	<.1	1.2
Crataegus opaca	1	2.9	.8	1	0.001	.4	0.023	<.1	1.2
Carya aquatica	1	2.9	.8	1	0.001	.4	0.023	<.1	1.2
Ulmus alata	1	2.9	.8	1	0.001	.4	0.003	<.1	1.2
Total			100.1	266	0.301	100.3	94.825	100.0	300.1

Table 3. Stand 3. Baygall.

Species	Plots N = 50	Frequency %	Relative Frequency %	No. of Stems	Density No./m²	Relative Density %	Basal Area cm²/m²	Relative Basal Area %	Importance Value
Cyrilla racemiflora	47	94.0	23.4	234	0.187	49.0	1.647	2.7	75.0
Nyssa sylvatica	38	76.0	18.9	74	0.059	15.5	17.663	28.8	63.2
Quercus laurifolia	38	76.0	18.9	62	0.050	13.0	18.392	30.0	61.9
Liquidambar styraciflua	26	52.0	12.9	42	0.034	8.8	6.222	10.2	31.9
Pinus taeda	8	16.0	4.0	13	0.010	2.7	10.462	17.1	23.8
Acer rubrum	22	44.0	11.0	28	0.022	5.9	1.018	1.7	18.5
Quercus nigra	3	6.0	1.5	3	0.002	.6	5.652	9.2	11.4
Ilex opaca	7	14.0	3.5	9	0.007	1.9	0.050	.1	5.4
Vaccinium elliottii	4	8.0	2.0	4	0.003	.8	0.003	<.1	2.8
Myrica cerifera	3	6.0	1.5	3	0.002	.6	0.010	<.1	2.1
Magnolia virginiana	2	4.0	1.0	3	0.002	.6	0.101	.2	1.8
Ilex vomitoria	1	2.0	.5	1	0.001	.2	0.023	<.1	.8
Ilex coriacea	1	2.0	.5	1	0.001	.2	0.002	<.1	.7
Styrax americana	1	2.0	.5	1	0.001	.2	0.002	<.1	.7
Total			100.1	478	0.381	100.0	61.247	100.0	300.0

Table 4. Stand 4. Baygall, Sphagnum Bog.

Species	Plots N = 25	Frequency %	Relative Frequency %	No. of Stems	Density No./m²	Relative Density %	Basal Area cm²/m²	Relative Basal Area %	Importance Value
Nyssa sylvatica	26	52.0	22.0	205	0.164	32.0	10.940	57.5	111.5
Cyrilla racemiflora	25	50.0	21.2	260	0.208	40.6	2.739	14.4	76.1
Taxodium distichum	21	42.0	17.8	99	0.079	15.4	3.955	20.8	54.0
Myrica cerifera	19	38.0	16.1	34	0.027	5.3	0.170	.9	22.3
Pinus taeda	6	12.0	5.1	6	0.005	.9	1.162	6.1	12.1
Ilex coriacea	7	14.0	5.9	14	0.011	2.2	0.038	.2	8.3
Lyonia ligustrina	5	10.0	4.2	6	0.005	.9	0.004	<.1	5.2
Myrica heterophylla	3	6.0	2.5	7	0.006	1.1	0.004	<.1	3.7
Persea borbonia	3	6.0	2.5	5	0.004	.8	0.019	.1	3.4
Smilax laurifolia	1	2.0	.9	3	0.002	.5	0.007	<.1	1.4
Ilex opaca	1	2.0	.9	1	0.001	.2	0.002	<.1	1.0
Itea virginica	1	2.0	.9	1	0.001	.2	0.001	<.1	1.0
Total			100.0	641	0.513	100.1	19.041	100.0	300.0

mounds. There appeared to have been no recent disturbance in the baygalls.

Stands 5, 7, and 8, Uplands (Tables 5, 7, 8). Stand 5, the vegetational type described by Marks and Harcombe (1981) as a Sandhill Pine Forest, was located on deep sandy soil. This longleaf pine stand escaped the general cutting of timber from upland areas in the early 1960's. This was an open, mature, *Pinus palustris* forest of fairly even age.

The overstory was exclusively of *Pinus palustris*, while the sparse midstory was dominated by *Quercus incana*. The herbaceous layer was dominated by grasses. Both seedlings and saplings of *P. palustris* and *P. taeda* were observed in the stand, although no mature trees of *P. taeda* occurred in the immediate study area.

Stand 7 was an example of an Upland Pine Forest (Marks and Harcombe 1981). It was, generally, a dry upland area, but there were some low, mesic areas. Stand 7 appeared less disturbed than most of the upland areas on the preserve. The diversity of woody species in this area was high compared to other upland areas. This increased diversity was probably partially due to the presence of the mesic areas where species such as *Quercus alba* and *Magnolia grandiflora* occurred.

The open overstory of Stand 7 was composed primarily of *Pinus. taeda* and *P. palustris*. The understory was made up of *Quercus incana, Carya texana,* and *Ilex vomitoria*. The well-developed herbaceous layer was a mix of grasses and forbs. Seedlings of *P. palustris, P. taeda,* and *C. texana* were evident in the area.

Stand 8 was located in a dry, deep sand, upland area. The arid sandy uplands of the preserve, located on high terraces of Village Creek, have been described by Watson (1979) as the best example of the oak-farkleberry plant association in the Big Thicket.

Stand 8 consisted of an extremely sparse *Quercus incana, Vaccinium arborium* overstory, with a diverse herbaceous layer. Scattered individuals of *Pinus elliottii* and *Carya texana* were noted. Seedlings of *P. taeda, P. palustris,* and *P. elliottii* were observed in the stand.

Table 5. Stand 5. Longleaf Pine Uplands.

Species	Plots N = 50	Frequency %	Relative Frequency %	No. of Stems	Density No./m²	Relative Density %	Basal Area cm²/m²	Relative Basal Area %	Importance Value
Pinus palustris	31	62.0	33.3	48	0.038	16.8	19.999	92.2	142.4
Quercus incana	49	98.0	52.7	208	0.166	73.0	1.593	7.3	133.0
Pinus taeda	11	22.0	11.8	27	0.022	9.5	0.092	.4	21.7
Bumelia lanuginosa	1	2.0	1.1	1	0.001	.4	0.006	<.1	1.5
Vaccinium arboreum	1	2.0	1.1	1	0.001	.4	0.002	<.1	1.4
Total			100.0	285	0.228	100.1	21.692	99.9	300.0

Table 7. Stand 7. Old Growth Dry Uplands.

Species	Plots N = 50	Frequency %	Relative Frequency %	No. Of Stems	Density No./m²	Relative Density %	Basal Area cm²/m²	Relative Basal Area %	Importance Value
Quercus incana	42	84.0	28.0	133	0.106	44.8	3.198	16.9	89.7
Pinus taeda	27	54.0	18.0	52	0.042	17.5	6.635	35.1	70.6
Pinus palustris	9	18.0	6.0	10	0.008	3.4	5.005	26.5	35.9
Carya texana	22	44.0	14.7	35	0.028	11.8	1.102	5.8	32.3
Ilex vomitoria	11	22.0	7.3	15	0.013	5.1	0.157	.8	13.2
Bumelia lanuginosa	8	16.0	5.3	12	0.010	4.0	0.164	.9	10.2
Liquidambar styraciflua	4	8.0	2.7	5	0.004	1.7	1.020	5.4	9.8
Vaccinium arboreum	4	8.0	2.7	9	0.007	3.0	0.413	2.2	7.9
Quercus alba	4	8.0	2.7	5	0.004	1.7	0.003	<.1	4.4
Ilex decidua	4	8.0	2.7	4	0.003	1.4	0.046	.2	4.3
Quercus marilandica	1	2.0	.7	1	0.001	.3	0.528	2.8	3.8
Pinus elliottii	1	2.0	.7	1	0.001	.3	0.492	2.6	3.6
Quercus stellata	2	4.0	1.3	4	0.003	1.4	0.070	4	3.1
Viburnum dentatum	3	6.0	2.0	3	0.002	1.0	0.002	<.1	3.0
Asimina parviflora	2	4.0	1.3	2	0.002	.7	0.002	<.1	2.0
Quercus phellos	1	2.0	.7	1	0.001	.3	0.051	.3	1.3
Ilex opaca	1	2.0	.7	1	0.001	.3	0.001	<.1	1.0
Vaccinium elliotti	1	2.0	.7	1	0.001	.3	0.001	<.1	1.0
Bignonia capreolata	1	2.0	.7	1	0.001	.3	0.001	<.1	1.0
Magnolia grandiflora	1	2.0	.7	1	0.001	.3	0.001	<.1	1.0
Rhus toxicodendron	1	2.0	.7	1	0.001	.3	0.001	<.1	1.0
Total			100.3	297	0.240	99.9	18.893	99.9	300.1

Table 8. Stand 8. Dry Sandy Uplands.

Species	Plots N = 50	Frequency %	Relative Frequency %	No. of Stems	Density No./m²	Relative Density %	Basal Area cm²/m²	Relative Basal Area %	Importance Value
Quercus incana	42	84.0	39.3	128	0.102	47.6	1.761	25.7	112.5
Vaccinium arboreum	16	32.0	15.0	79	0.063	29.4	0.533	7.8	52.1
Pinus elliottii	19	38.0	17.8	23	0.018	8.6	1.736	25.3	51.6
Carya texana	7	14.0	6.5	8	0.006	3.0	1.405	20.5	30.0
Quercus stellata	12	24.0	11.2	16	0.013	6.0	0.784	11.4	28.6
Bumelia lanuginosa	6	12.0	5.6	10	0.009	3.7	0.214	3.1	12.4
Pinus taeda	1	2.0	.9	1	0.001	.4	0.362	5.3	6.6
Pinus palustris	1	2.0	.9	1	0.001	.4	0.063	.9	2.2
Asimina parviflora	1	2.0	.9	1	0.001	.4	0.002	<.1	1.3
Ilex vomitoria	1	2.0	.9	1	0.001	.4	0.001	<.1	1.3
Rhus toxicodendron	1	2.0	.9	1	0.001	.4	0.002	<.1	1.3
Total			99.9	269	0.215	100.3	6.862	100.0	299.9

Stand 6, Transition Forest (Table 6)- Stand 6 was an open, mesic transition area well above the floodplain of Village Creek. This forest is an example of the Lower Slope Hardwood Pine Forest vegetation type of Marks and Harcombe (1981). There was a dense overstory dominated by *Quercus nigra*, with a few individuals of *Q. lyrata* and *Pinus taeda*. Thus, the ground was, for the

burning. In the spring of 1985, numerous populations of *Phlox nivalis*, not previously recorded, were observed in the newly disturbed uplands.

Eight additional species collected on the preserve are endemic to Texas, they are: *Loeflingia squarrosa* (Caryophyllaceae), *Evax candida, Heliathus debilis, Palafoxia reverchonii, Thelesperma flavodiscum*

Table 6.   Stand 6. Transition Forest.

Species	Plots N = 50	Frequency %	Relative Frequency %	No. of Stems	Density No./m²	Relative Density %	Basal Area cm²/m²	Relative Basal Area %	Importance Value
Carpinus caroliniana	48	96.0	30.8	106	0.085	42.6	6.787	13.6	86.9
Quercus nigra	16	32.0	10.3	20	0.016	8.0	16.842	33.6	51.9
Liquidambar styraciflua	16	32.0	10.3	30	0.024	12.1	10.692	21.4	43.7
Pinus taeda	6	12.0	3.9	6	0.005	2.4	8.846	17.7	23.9
Ilex decidua	12	24.0	7.7	17	0.014	6.8	0.250	.5	15.0
Ilex vomitoria	11	22.0	7.1	17	0.014	6.8	0.083	.2	14.1
Viburnum dentatum	11	22.0	7.1	16	0.013	6.4	0.043	.1	13.6
Ostrya virginiana	9	18.0	5.8	10	0.008	4.0	0.294	.6	10.4
Quercus lyrata	2	4.0	1.3	2	0.002	.8	3.545	7.1	9.2
Ilex opaca	3	6.0	1.9	3	0.002	1.2	0.117	.2	3.4
Bignonia capreolata	3	6.0	1.9	3	0.002	1.2	0.021	<.1	3.2
Vitis rotundifolia	3	6.0	1.9	3	0.002	1.2	0.006	<.1	3.1
Betula nigra	2	4.0	1.3	2	0.002	.8	0.460	.9	3.0
Acer rubrum	1	2.0	.6	1	0.001	.4	0.814	1.6	2.7
Fraxinus pensylvanica	2	4.0	1.3	2	0.002	.8	0.147	.3	2.4
Nyssa sylvatica	1	2.0	.6	1	0.001	.4	0.643	1.3	2.3
Taxodium distichum	2	4.0	1.3	2	0.002	.8	0.086	.2	2.3
Ulmus americana	1	2.0	.6	1	0.001	.4	0.277	.6	1.6
Carya aquatica	1	2.0	.6	1	0.001	.4	0.076	.2	1.2
Chionanthus virginica	1	2.0	.6	1	0.001	.4	0.010	<.1	1.1
Ilex coriacea	1	2.0	.6	1	0.001	.4	0.010	<.1	1.1
Vitis palmata	1	2.0	.6	1	0.001	.4	0.010	<.1	1.1
Vaccinium arboreum	1	2.0	.6	1	0.001	.4	0.006	<.1	1.1
Vaccinium elliottii	1	2.0	.6	1	0.001	.4	0.001	<.1	1.0
Crataegus marshallii	1	2.0	.6	1	0.001	.4	0.001	<.1	1.0
Total			99.9	249	0.203	99.9	50.067	100.1	300.3

most part, bare of herbaceous vegetation. There was a light litter layer usually less than 4 cm deep, and no evidence of disturbance. The midstory was dominated by *Carpinus caroliniana, Liquidambar styraciflua*, and *Ilex opaca*. Individuals of *Fagus grandifolia* were observed near the transect.

B. Species List

The vascular plant survey resulted in 922 field collected specimens including voucher specimens of 105 families, 327 genera, and 544 species. Families with the greatest number of representatives are Compositae (65 species), Gramineae (64 species), Leguminosae (37 species), Cyperaceae (25 species), and Euphorbiaceae (19 species).

At the time of this study, *Phlox nivalis* (Polemoniaceae), a southeast Texas endemic, occurred as several small, scattered populations in the dry pine uplands at the north end of the preserve. This species is considered threatened according to the Texas Organization for Endangered Species (1983). Since June 1983, the uplands have been modified by removal of *Pinus elliottii* and controlled

(Compositae); *Astragalus leptocarpus, Lupinus subcarnosus*, and *Petalostemum griseum* (Leguminosae).

Ten additional species are endemic to portions of Texas and Louisiana. They are: *Amsonia glaberrima* (Apocynaceae); *Polanisia erosa* (Capparidaceae); *Silene subciliata* (Caryophyllaceae); *Tradescantia reverchonii* (Commelinaceae); *Aster pratensis, Berlandiera X betonicifolia, Erigeron traversii, Hymenopappus artemisiaefolius, Liatris acidota*, and *Silphium gracile* (Compositeae). One species, *Streptanthus hyacinthoides* (Cruciferae), is endemic to Texas and Oklahoma, found only in sandy oak woods.

Other interesting collections were *Eleocharis elongata* (Cyperaceae), which has not previously been reported in Texas, and *Cuphea carthangesis* (Lythraceae), which has a wide distribution from South America to North Carolina, but only occurs in southeast Hardin County in Texas (Correll and Johnston 1970). An additional nine species collected in the preserve are peripheral, and of restricted distribution in Texas, or are considered rare in Texas by either the Texas Organization for Endangered Species

(1983) or Correll and Johnston (1970). *Carex albolutescens, C. tenax, Psilocarya nitens, Rhynchospora filifolia* (Cyperaceae); and *Proserpinaca pectinata* (Haloragaceae) are all eastern coastal plain species which reach the westernmost edge of their ranges in Texas. *Scleria triglomerata* (Cyperaceae), *Lycopus rubellus* (Labiatae), *Tipularia discolor* (Orchidaceae), and *Pyrus arbutifolia* (Rosaceae) are eastern species which extend only into east Texas.

Table 9 gives the number of families and species collected and observed in each of the major habitats found

McWorter for the help and insight he gave us during this project.

LITERATURE CITED

Carr, J.T. 1967. The climate and physiography of Texas. Texas Water Development Board Report 53. Tex. Water Dev. Board, Austin, Tex.

Correll, D.S. and M.C. Johnston. 1970. Manual of the vascular plants of Texas. Tex. Res. Foundation, Renner, Tex.

Table 9. Number of Native and Introduced Taxa Collected or Noted in Each of the Major Habitats of the Roy E. Larsen Sandylands Preserve.

Habitat	Number of Families	Total Number of Species	Number of Introduced Species	Percent Introduced Species
Floodplain	59	108	4	3.7%
Transition	38	63	1	1.6%
Baygall	60	118	1	0.8%
Uplands	62	208	3	1.4%
Disturbed areas	69	224	38	17.0%
Total	106	546	46	8.4%

on the preserve. Designation as introduced, follows Correll and Johnston (1970). A listing of all species collected on the preserve can be found in Matos and Rudolph (1985).

MANAGEMENT CONSIDERATIONS

Upland areas on the preserve have received the greatest amount of disturbance due to the logging operations and replanting that occurred during the 1960's. The upland areas are at present undergoing intensive management as the *Pinus elliottii* are removed to allow native species regeneration. Fire management of upland areas has been initiated and the continuation of this form of management is planned. The sandy upland community includes most of the plant species which are rare, threatened, endemic, or are at the edge of their ranges, that are found on the preserve. These species are, in general, found in areas which were historically dominated by *P. palustrus*, and in the *Quercus incana, Vaccinium arborium* community.

At present no management is planned in any of the other communities of the preserve, with the exception of long range plans to remove *Sapium sebiferum* from the floodplain. This weedy introduced species occurrs at low densities in the floodplain at this time.

ACKNOWLEDGEMENTS

This study was funded in part by the Texas Nature Conservancy. The authors wish to thank Mr. Ike

Daubermire, R. 1968. Plant communities--a textbook of synecology. Harper and Row, New York, New York.

Godfrey, R.K. and J.W. Wooten. 1979. Aquatic and wetland plants of southeastern United States: Monocotyledons. Univ. of Georgia Press, Athens, Ga.

McLeod, C.A. 1972. The Big Thicket forest of Eastern Texas, a brief historical, botanical and ecological report. Sam Houston State Univ. Press, Huntsville, Tex.

Mahler, C.L. 1979. An analysis of floodplain vegetation of the lower Neches drainage, southeast Texas, with some considerations on the use of regression and correlation in plant synecology. Ph.D. Diss., Correll Univ., Ithaca, New York.

Marks, P.L. and P.A. Harcombe. 1981. Forest vegetation of the Big Thicket, southeast Texas. Ecol. Monogr. 51:287-305.

Matos, J.A. and D.C. Rudolph. 1985. The vegetation of the Roy E. Larsen Sandylands Sanctuary in the Big Thicket of Texas. Castanea (*in press*).

Texas Organization for Endangered Species. 1983. Endangered, threatened, and watch lists of plants of Texas. Texas Organization for Endangered Species Publ. 3 (first revision). Tex. Organ. for Endangered Species, Austin, Tex.

Watson, G. 1979. Big Thicket plant ecology, an introduction, 2nd ed. Big Thicket Mus. Publ. Ser. No. 5, Saratoga, Tex.

Floristic Composition And Management Of East Texas Pitcher Plant Bogs

by
Elray S. Nixon and John R. Ward

ABSTRACT--Six pitcher plant bog sites in eastern Texas were visited every two weeks from March to November to determine floristic composition. Certain soil characteristics were also determined. The six bogs contained 203 taxa representing 55 families. The mean number of taxa present is 103 with numbers per community ranging from 88 to 116. Plant families with greatest representation are Poaceae (30 taxa), Cyperaceae (26 taxa), and Asteraceae (23 taxa). Indices of similarity indicate that the bogs are quite similar with values ranging from 55 to 78. The management of bogs is discussed in general.

KEYWORDS: *Sarracenia alata*, springs, seepages, fire, soil characteristics.

Pitcher plant bogs, so named because pitcher plants (*Sarracenia* spp.) are a noticeable and interesting component (Folkerts 1982), are fairly common in eastern Texas, especially in the southeastern portion. They are characterized by a variety of plant species, many of which are restricted to this habitat type and many of which produce beautiful flowers and leaves at various times during the growing season. Thus, this assemblage of plants is quite distinct.

Pitcher plant bogs in eastern Texas are usually associated with sandy uplands underlain by impermeable layers of clays developed from tuffaceous and pyroclastic materials. Water percolates downward through the sandy soils to the impermeable clays and then laterally surfacing on the lower slopes of hills. Lateral water movement is usually slow and continuous being little affected by fluctuations in precipitation.

Information is scarce concerning bogs in eastern Texas. Rowell (1949) and Kral (1955) are among the first to describe bogs vegetationally. Rowell (1949) discussed the vegetational composition of a sphagnum bog in Robertson County in southwestern east Texas and Kral (1955) floristically described and compared two hillside bogs in northeastern Texas. Only the Robertson County bog contained *Sarracenia alata*. Although focusing on net aerial primary production, Lodwick (1975) presents some information on the floristics of three west central east Texas peat bogs in Anderson County. More recently, Ajilvsgi (1979) mentions some of the more noticeable species, including *S. alata*, inhabiting wet, acid bogs in the Big Thicket of southeastern Texas. The present study was performed to help characterize east Texas bogs.

METHODS

Study Sites

Soils and Climate--Two geologic formations of greatest importance associated with east Texas pitcher plant bogs are the Willis and Catahoula. The Catahoula is the oldest, originating during the Miocene Epoch of the Tertiary Period. The Willis Formation, which usually overlies the Catahoula, is of Pleistocene origin during the Quaternary Period. The Willis sands essentially provide the water source and the Catahoula clays the impermeable layer causing lateral movement of water. Soils of the pitcher plant areas are generally considered to be wet alfisols.

The more upland sandy sites associated with pitcher plant bogs are usually savannah-like with pines dominating the overstory. Shrubs and small hardwood trees occur occasionally throughout the sites. Pines present are mostly longleaf (*Pinus palustris*), with shortleaf (*P. echinata*), slash (*P. elliottii*) and loblolly (*P. taeda*) also present. Little bluestem grass (*Schizachyrium scoparium*) is a common herbaceous layer component.

Larkin and Bomar (1983) place the eastern third of Texas within a Subtropical Humid region most noted for its warm summers. Average annual precipitation at the study site areas is about 119 cm. Average monthly precipitation at these sites is fairly evenly distributed, ranging from about 8 to 11 cm with slight highs occurring during April, May and December. Average annual low temperature is 12 degrees C, while average annual high temperature is 26 degrees C.

Location and Description--The six pitcher plant bog sites are generally located along the Angelina-Jasper county line, with three bogs located in Angelina County and three in Jasper County. The two westernmost bogs are within the Upland Island wilderness area just south of Zavalla, Texas. The remaining four extend eastward within the Angelina National Forest to near Sam Rayburn Reservoir. With the exception of communities 2 and 3, the sites are some distance apart. Communities 2 and 3 are actually part of the same bog but a road transects the site causing the upper portion to pond. Thus, the habitats are somewhat different.

The pitcher plant bogs studied by us are generally of two types. Spatulate shaped simibasins with seepages and springs occurring on three sides and drained on the lower side by small streams, and single slopes with springs and seepages drained by small creeks. Three bogs, communities 1, 2 and 3 are designated basin bogs and three (communities 4, 5 and 6) as slope bogs. The basin bogs are generally characterized by having fringe, marshy areas composed primarily of herbaceous heliophytes which grade into central areas consisting of shrubs and small trees. Shrubs are usually more prevalent on the wooded margins. Slope bogs are generally marshy with scattered individuals, patches or rows of shrubs and trees. Shrubs and trees occurring on these six sites are oftentimes broadleaved evergreens; pines occur occasionally. Vines are common and frequently dominate portions of the canopy. All six bogs contain sphagnum moss. Communities 1 and 4 contain outcrops of rock (Catahoula mudstone). Aspect for the bog communities is west, south and southwest with slope ranging from 5 to 30%. None are considered savannah bogs, which are characterized by little relief.

Techniques--To determine floristic content of the six pitcher plant bogs, plants were collected, as they flowered, beginning in March and ending the last of October. Bogs were sampled every two weeks. Soil samples from the upper 15 cm of the soil were also taken. Soils were analyzed by the Stephen F. Austin State University Soil

Testing Laboratory. Exchangeable ions were determined by atomic absorption spectrophotometry, organic matter content by loss on ignition and textural class by the hydrometer method.

Species richness, presence and index of similarity were used to determine the extent of floristic similarity among the six communities. Species richness is defined as the number of species present in a community, whereas presence is defined as the percentage of occurrence of species in communities of different size (Daubenmire 1968). It should be noted, however, that the communities were generally of similar size. Sorensen's index of similarity was used to compare communities following the formula IS = (2C/A+B)X100, where C is the number of species in common to the two communities, A is the total number of species in community A, and B is the total number of species in community B.

Scientific nomenclature follows Correll and Johnston (1970) and Gould (1975).

RESULTS

Soils

Soils are generally similar among the six bog sites (Table 1). Community 4, a hillside bog, has the highest pH (5.3) and contains higher concentrations of exchangeable Ca and Mg. The pH ranged from 4.3 to 4.7 at the other five sites. Organic matter content ranged from 2.2% to 5.8%. Texturally, soils are clays or sandy clay loams.

Plants

Plants began flowering in the pitcher plant bogs in March. The number of taxa flowering increased in April and May and then remained fairly constant through July. A peak flowering period occurred during August and September.

A total of 203 taxa, representing 118 genera and 55 families, was recorded for the six bog sites. The mean number of taxa for the six bog communities is 103, ranging from 88 taxa at community 5 to 116 at community 1. Four bogs had over 100 taxa present.

Species that are present in five or more bogs are presented in Table 2. Plant families with the greatest representation are Poaceae (30 taxa), Cyperaceae (26 taxa) and Asteraceae (23 taxa). Other families have less than eight representatives. Insectivorous species of four genera are present--*Sarracenia* (pitcher plants), *Drosera* (sundews), *Pinguicula* (Butterworts), and *Utricularia* (bladderworts).

Indices of similarity indicate that the bogs are vegetationally similar (Fig. 1). Indices averaged 65.5 and ranged from 55 to 78. As might be expected, communities 2 and 3, which are next to each other, are most similar (IS = 78). When averaged within, slope and basin communities displayed the same average index of similarity (IS = 68 for each group). Average similarities between slope and basin communities is slightly lower (IS

Table 1. Soil Characteristics (Upper 15 cm) of Six Pitcher Plant Bog Sites.

Site	pH	Exchangeable Ions (ppm)				OM %	Sand %	Silt %	Clay %	Texture Class
		P	K	Ca	Mg					
Basin communities										
Community 1	4.6	4	30	372	85	2.3	60	16	24	Sandy clay loam
Community 2	4.6	4	32	254	72	5.8	26	24	50	Clay
Community 3	4.7	4	31	200	63	5.3	22	32	46	Clay
Slope communities										
Community 4	5.3	1	76	670	283	4.0	60	15	25	Sandy clay loam
Community 5	4.6	3	8	146	38	2.2	20	16	64	Clay
Community 6	4.3	4	19	150	48	5.5	22	20	58	Clay

Table 2. List of Species in the Six Bogs with Presence[1] Values Greater Than 80 Percent.

Ferns
   Osmunda cinnamomea

Angiosperms
  Trees
    Acer rubrum
    Magnolia virginiana
    Persea borbonia
  Shrubs
    Ascyrum hypericoides
    Ascyrum stans
    Myrica heterophylla
    Pyrus arbutifolia
    Rhus vernix
    Rubus louisianus
    Vaccinium arkansanum
    Viburnum nudum
  Woody vines
    Gelsemium sempervirens
    Smilax laurifolia
  Herbs
    Agalinis purpurea
    Aletris aurea
    Aster dumosus
    Calopogon pulchellus
    Carex glaucescens
    Centella asiatica
    Coreopsis linifolia

Herbs (cont.)
   Drosera capillaris
   Eleocharis tuburculosa
   Eriocaulon decangulare
   Eriocaulon texensis
   Eryngium integrifolium
   Eupatorium leucolepis
   Eupatorium rotundifolium
   Fuirena squarrosa
   Helianthus angustifolius
   Heterotheca graminifolia
   Hypoxis hirsuta
   Liatris pycnostachya
   Lobelia reverchonii
   Marshallia tenuifolia
   Paspalum floridanum
   Pinguicula pumila
   Pogonia ophioglossoides
   Polygala mariana
   Polygala ramosa
   Ptilimnium capillaceum
   Rhexia mariana
   Sarracenia alata
   Scutellaria integrifolia
   Spiranthes vernalis
   Utricularia cornuta
   Viola primulifolia
   Xyris ambigua

[1] Presence is defined as the percentage of occurrence of species in communities of dissimilar size.

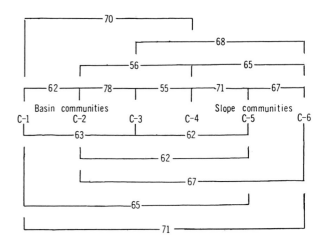

Figure 1. Community coefficients of similarity of six pitcher plant bogs in eastern Texas.

= 64). Basin communities have a slightly higher species richness, averaging 106 taxa. Slope communities averaged 98. Species in common among the six bogs ranged from 54 to 80.

DISCUSSION

Soils

Pitcher plant bog soils of the Gulf Coast Plain are typically sands, loamy sands or sandy loams (Pullen and Plummer 1964, Folkerts 1982). Thus, the high clay

content of eastern Texas bog soils is of interest. Hillside bog sites in eastern Texas are usually characterized by having a few inches of sand overlying the more impermeable clay. Because we sampled to a depth of 15 cm, we sampled both the sand and clay layers resulting in a higher clay content.

Organic matter content varies among bogs, depending on the type of bog and sample location. In eastern Texas, both Rowell (1949a, 1949b) and Kral (1955) indicated high amounts of organic matter in various portions of the bogs they studied. Organic matter content in bogs we studied was not high (2.2 to 5.8%). Generally, organic matter accumulation is small in Gulf Coast bogs due to frequent fires (Folkerts 1982). The bogs we studied have been subjected to fire and, in addition, are hillside which could result in less accumulation of organic materials.

Pitcher plant bogs are generally acid bogs. Soils usually range in pH from 3.5 to 5.0 (Schnell 1982, Folkerts 1982). The bog soils of our study generally fall within this range. Acidity evidently results from activity of mineral components of the soil as well as from organic acids (Folkerts 1982).

Nutrient content, in regard to those analyzed in our study, is generally low in pitcher plant bog soils (Plummer 1963, Schnell 1982). However, Eleutarius and Jones (1969), upon examining bog soils in Mississippi, did not find deficiencies in N, P or K. East Texas bog soils do not appear to be deficient, any more than other acid east Texas soils in regard to P, K, Ca and Mg. Soils of a mesic beech forest in east Texas have 50 ppm Ca, 4 ppm P, 28 ppm K, and 10 ppm Mg (Nixon et al. 1980b). Wet, creek branch soils have 207 ppm Ca, 45 ppm K and 96 ppm Mg (Nixon et al. 1980a). Our bog soils averaged 295 ppm Ca, 3 ppm P, 33 ppm K, and 98 ppm Mg.

Plants

After the initial flowering flush in March and April, the number of plants flowering remains somewhat constant from May through July. A peak flowering period occurs during August and September. Eleuterius and Jones (1969) noted peak flowering periods during June and August in southern Mississippi bogs. Lodwick (1975) indicates that peak production periods occur during spring and fall in west central east Texas bogs.

Although number of taxa inhabiting bogs varies considerably, depending on size, type, degree of disturbance, etc., some comparisons can be made. We recorded 203 taxa, representing 118 genera and 55 families, for the six east Texas bogs. Lodwick (1975), in his work with eastern Texas bogs, presents a partial listing of bog species. Eighty-one percent of the families, 63% of the genera, and 45% of the species that Lodwick (1975) lists, are present in bogs of our study. The two hillside bogs Kral (1955) studied in eastern Texas have 44% of their species in common with bogs we sampled. Eleuterius and Jones (1969) list 271 taxa, representing 134 genera and 63 families, occurring in south Mississippi bogs. Eighty-seven percent of the families, 65% of the genera, and 44% of the species located in our six east Texas bogs occur in the Mississippi bogs. Therefore, floristic composition of east Texas bogs is somewhat similar to those eastward.

There also appears to be some consistency in regard to plant families with greatest representation. The Poaceae (30 taxa), Cyperaceae (26 taxa) and Asteraceae (23 taxa) contained the largest number of bog species in eastern Texas. Most represented plant families in south Mississippi bogs were Asteraceae (54 taxa), Poaceae (27 taxa), and Cyperaceae (27 taxa) (Eleuterius and Jones 1969). The Liliaceae and Orchidaceae families have 11 and 10 taxa, respectively, in Mississippi. In South Carolina pine savannahs, which at times have *Sarracenia* species present, the Asteraceae (29 taxa), Poaceae (12 taxa), Cyperaceae (12 taxa), and Orchidaceae (10 taxa) families are most represented based on number of species (Gaddy 1982).

MANAGEMENT

In general, pitcher plant bog species are heliophytes which are capable of tolerating fire and water saturated soils (Pullen and Plummer 1964). Plant succession on bog sites appears to be towards a sedge-woody species community (Eleuterius and Jones 1969). Therefore, factors which result in the retardation of shrub, tree and woody vine growth, in the maintenance of soil acidity coupled with low nutrient levels (to inhibit the invasion of competing species), in the sustaining of anaerobic soil conditions and in the sustenance of periodic fire, are important in arresting succession (Folkerts 1982). The most important of these factors seems to be fire. Its absence, regardless of other situations, results in the eventual elimination of bog species (Folkerts 1982).

Because natural fires (and fires possibly caused by native peoples) have arrested succession in the past, authors refer to pitcher plant communities as a "fire type" vegetation (Eleuterius and Jones 1969) or as fire subclimax or fire disclimax (Folkerts 1982). They could also be called a fire climax community. The key to a fire climax is fire frequency (Barbour et al. 1980). Fires every 5 - 10 years will generally select against woody invaders.

Fire results in a number of favorable conditions for bog maintenance. Not only does fire eliminate woody and other competitors, it also releases some nutrients bound up in organic matter (Pullen and Plummer 1964, Schnell 1982). There is some question, however, as to the overall benefit of fire in regard to nutrient release. Both N and K volatilize and thus may not increase in availability following fires. The addition of N-P-K to bog sites by Eleuterius and Jones (1969) did not increase production. It should also be noted that loss of organic matter by burning may result in a concomitant loss of cation exchange capacity that characterizes organic matter (Barbour et al. 1980).

Schnell (1982) feels that the primary value of fire in regard to *Sarracenia* is release from competition and that the most significant competitive factor is shade. Eleuterius and Jones (1969) compared an unburned bog, dominated by sedges, with one which had been recently burned. *Sarracenia* plants growing in the burned bog were more vigorous, having larger leaves and rhizomes than those on the unburned site. Fire increased both productivity and species richness. Schnell (1982) was also able to observe the effects of clearing on *Sarracenia*. Those growing in dense brush grew poorly, except in rare small openings, whereas the effects of clearing resulted in an exuberant growth release of *Sarracenia* and an increase in seedling activity. In summary, to maintain pitcher plant bogs in wilderness areas, it is extremely important that we understand the vital role that fire plays in maintaining this ecosystem.

The maintenance of a high moisture level in bogs is also critical. Ditches as shallow as 2 dm can cause drying of surface soils in savannah type bogs. The plowing of fire lanes to restrict fires to bogs may thus be hazardous to bog species. Other damaging factors include over collecting and destruction of bog plants by grazing and trampling. In addition, heavy livestock usage on some adjacent upland longleaf pine sites could contribute to a decline in percolation and seepage due to soil compaction. Also, clearcutting of uplands associated with bog sites could result in erosional soil movement onto bog sites, eliminating many species and changing habitat conditions. Pitcher plant bogs are extremely fragile systems.

There is concern in regard to conservation and preservation of pitcher plant bogs throughout the eastern United States. Not a whole lot of effort has been put forth. Pullen and Plummer (1964) indicate that many bog sites have been drained, cleared and burned for pasture as well as other uses. Eastern Texas is no exception. On the other hand, many pitcher plant bogs are being preserved and maintained in eastern Texas. They are present in some of our wilderness areas, in the Big Thicket National Preserve, and in Nature Conservancy holdings. Some are fenced or otherwise preserved in our National Forests and on private land. Thus, many are presently preserved as a part of eastern Texas' natural heritage.

LITERATURE CITED

Ajilvsgi, G. 1979. Wild flowers of the Big Thicket, east Texas, and western Louisiana. Tex. A&M Univ. Press, College Station, Tex.

Barbour, M.G., J.H. Burk and W.K. Pitts. 1980. Terrestrial plant ecology. The Benjamin/Cummings Publishing Company, Inc., Menlo Park, Calif.

Correll, D.S. and M.C. Johnston. 1970. Manual of the vascular plants of Texas. Univ. Tex. at Dallas, Richardson, Tex.

Daubenmire, R. 1968. Plant Communities - a textbook of plant synecology. Harper and Row, Publishers, New York, New York.

Eleuterius, L.N. and S.B. Jones, Jr. 1969. A floristic and ecological study of pitcher plant bogs in south Mississippi. Rhodora 71:29-34.

Folkerts, G.W. 1982. The Gulf Coast pitcher plant bogs. Am. Sci. 70:261-267.

Gaddy, L.L. 1982. The floristics of three South Carolina pine savannahs. Castanea 47:393-402.

Gould, F.W. 1975. The grasses of Texas. Tex. A&M Univ. Press, College Station, Tex.

Kral, R. 1955. A floristic comparison of two hillside bog localities in northeastern Texas. Field and Lab. 23:47-69.

Larkin, T.J. and G.W. Bomar. 1983. Climatic atlas of Texas. Tex. Dep. of Water Res., Austin, Tex.

Lodwick, L.N. 1975. Net aerial primary production of three east Texas bogs. Master's Thesis, Baylor University, Waco, Tex.

Nixon, E.S., J.W. Higgins, P.L. Blanchette and F.A. Roth. 1980a. Woody vegetation of a wet creek branch in east Texas. Tex. J. Sci. 32:337-341.

Nixon, E.S., K.L. Marietta, R.O. Littlejohn and H.B. Weyland. 1980b. Woody vegetation of an American beech (*Fagus grandifolia*) community in eastern Texas. Castanea 45:171-180.

Plummer, G.L. 1963. Soils of the pitcher plant habitats in the Georgia Coastal Plain. Ecology 44:727-734.

Pullen, T. Jr., and G.L. Plummer. 1964. Floristic changes within pitcher plant habitats in Georgia. Rhodora 66:375-381.

Rowell, C.M., Jr. 1949a. A preliminary report on the floral composition of a *Sphagnum* bog in Robertson County. Tex. J. Sci. 1:50-53.

Rowell, C.M., Jr. 1949b. Floral composition of a *Sphagnum* bog in Robertson County, Texas. Master's Thesis, Tex. A&M Univ., College Station, Tex.

Schnell, D.E. 1982. Effects of simultaneous draining and brush cutting on a Sarracenia L. population in a southeastern North Carolina pocosin. Castanea 47:248-260.

Vegetal Development On Abandoned Oil/Gas Drilling Sites In The Big Thicket National Preserve

by
Michael S. Fountain

ABSTRACT--Examination of vegetational development on 32 abandoned oil/gas drilling sites indicated that on most dry and abandoned sites the initial floristic composition was dominated by loblolly pine. Evidence indicated that these virtually pure stands of pine will maintain this dominance in the absence of continued disturbance. Data from sites that were in production indicated that secondary succession was inhibited by materials used to stabilize the operational portions of the drilling pads. Evidence of other management problems, such as rapid invasion of Chinese tallowtree on bottomland sites and remnants of ditches, berms, and pits, were also discussed.

KEYWORDS: secondary succession, importance values, species diversity, similarity coefficients, vegetative types, East Texas.

The Big Thicket National Preserve was established through enactment of Public Law 93-439 on October 11, 1974. This legislation was passed to "assure the preservation, conservation, and protection of the natural, scenic, and recreational values of a significant portion of the Big Thicket area in the State of Texas and to provide for the enhancement and public enjoyment thereof."

Pressure to obtain passage of this act stemmed from a longterm effort by several groups and many individuals. It was felt that the uniqueness of the Big Thicket region would be lost forever unless a significant portion could be permanently set aside. The historical record of this fight for the Thicket has been well documented by Cozine (1976) and by Watson (1979). The various units that comprise the present National Preserve total 84,550 acres (34,217 ha). This total, while seemingly large, is in reality a relatively small portion of the area originally included in various descriptions of the Big Thicket (McLeod 1971 and Parks and Cory 1936). However, the present boundaries do include representative samples that reflect the biological associations that were unique or endemic to the region.

In addition to establishing the Preserve, Public Law 93-439 also stipulated that "mineral estate in any property, and existing easements for public utilities, pipelines, or railroads cannot be acquired without the consent of the owner, unless it is determined that such property or estate is subject to or threatened with uses detrimental to the purposes and objectives of the establishment act." As a consequence, oil and gas exploration and extraction activities are allowed and have continued to the present (USDI National Park Service 1982) under strict supervision. The Secretary of the Interior and the National Park Service have developed rules and regulations, published in the *Federal Register* (Vol. 43, No. 237 Friday, December 8, 1978), that have been deemed necessary and appropriate to control oil and gas exploration and extraction. These regulations require that comprehensive plans regarding a proposed activity be submitted prior to initiation of any activity and they also require the posting of a bond to ensure compliance with the regulations.

OBJECTIVE AND METHODOLOGY

Information provided by administrators of the Preserve indicated that 133 drill sites have been located within Preserve boundaries. The objective of this project was to make a determination of the impact of actual drilling operations on the vegetation of the Big Thicket National Preserve. This evaluation was made on the basis of the potential vegetative types present in the area as defined by Harcombe and Marks (1979). Their classification described eleven types: upland pine (UP), wetland pine savannah (WPS), sandhill pine (SHP), upper slope pine oak (USPO), midslope oak pine (MSOP), lower slope hardwood pine (LSHP), flatland hardwood (FH), floodplain hardwood pine (SFF), floodplain hardwood (RFF), cypress-tupelo (CT), and acid baygall (BG). Due to space limitations, this paper will examine general trends in all types and then focus specifically on the documentation of the relative recovery rate (successional stage) following completion of drilling and abandonment of six of these types.

At each selected well location, a circular plot (0.1 hectare) was established (radius of 17.83 meters) within the disturbed area and also in an adjacent undisturbed area (control plot). The bearing and distance from the pad plot to the control plot were measured and used to calculate the X and Y coordinates for the control plot. The plot center of both plots was permanently marked. Each woody stem that had a minimum diameter of 10.0 cm at breast height (1.3 m above groundline) was recorded by dbh and species.

The shrub component and individual stems of tree species that were between 1.0 and 9.9 cm at 1.3 m were tallied by diameter and species on a smaller (0.01 ha; radius = 5.64 m) concentric plot with the same center as the plot utilized to sample the tree component. Where clumps of stems occurred, notations as to which stems comprised the clump were made.

Effort was made to locate each control plot in a topographical position similar to the impacted area while attempting to ensure that it had not been adversely affected by the operations on the pad. This consideration was critical to the analysis of the data since no pre-drilling vegetative data are available for the impacted areas. In order to assess the relative recovery rate of the vegetation on the impacted areas, quantitative measures of the plant associations on both the control and pad plots were calculated. For the tree component (stems greater than 10 cm dbh), an importance value for each species was calculated for each plot and for the combined control plots for each vegetative type. This importance value was the sum of a species' relative density and relative dominance where:

relative density = stem count for species i/total stem count of all species times 100;
relative dominance = basal area for species i/total basal area for all species times 100.

An importance value was calculated for each shrub

species that was also the sum of a species' relative density and relative dominance; a maximum score possible for a species was 200.00.

A coefficient of similarity between pad plots and average values for respective control plots and between each pair of control and pad plots was utilized as an indication of the relative rate of recovery toward a natural state. These coefficients of community similarity were computed using Jaccard's coefficient as suggested by Cox (1980) utilizing the formula C = 2w/a + b, where
w= the sum of the lower of the two quantitative values for species shared by the two communities; a = sum of all values for first community; and b = sum of all values for second community.

Additionally, these coefficients of community similarity were computed using only the presence of each species. A maximum value of 1.00 is theoretically possible in both applications if the communities have exactly the same composition. However, Cox (1980) also stated that replicate samples of the same community usually show coefficients of only about 0.85.

RESULTS

None of the pad plots illustrated a very high coefficient of community for either the tree or shrub component using average importance value data for each type. The highest similarities were found between pads that had been abandoned in the wetland pine savannah and midslope oak pine types (Table 1). These data indicated that as soil moisture increased, the degree of similarity between the pad plots and the average for control plots decreased. This apparent trend was indicated by both tree and shrub data. Average coefficients of community calculated using both importance values and species presence data between the control and pad plot at each sample location for each vegetative type did not reflect the same trend of decreasing similarity as soil moisture increased (Table 2).

Species diversity (combined richness and evenness) and species richness were also calculated (Pielou 1977) to aid in the assessment of the degree of recovery of a site following abandonment. Average diversity values for the tree component for control plots in seven of the vegetative types were fairly high (range from .732 to .882), while the remaining two were moderately high (Table 3). Diversity values for the shrub component on control plots were generally lower than for the tree component. In addition, all but the baygall and wetland pine savannah types had richness values for the overstory component between 8.0 and 11.0. However, these same average diversity and richness measures for the overstory component on the pad plots reflect much lower values. The average diversity value of the overstory was less than half that of the control plots within a vegetative type in all but one type.

Table 1. Average Coefficients of Community by Vegetative Type for Tree and Shrub Data between Each Plot and Average Values for Each Vegetative Type.

Vegetation Type[1]	Coefficient of Similarity	
	Tree Component	Shrub Component
SHP	0.356	0.571
WPS	0.585	0.378
USPO	0.287	0.076
MSOP	0.490	0.295
LSHP	0.302	0.117
SFF	0.266	0.049
RFF	0.277	0.106
FH	0.184	0.204
BG	0.082	0.194

Table 2. Average Coefficients of Community by Vegetative Type for Tree and Shrub Data between Each Pair of Control and Pad Plots Calculated from Importance Value Data and from Presence Data.

Vegetation Type	Coefficients of Similarity			
	Tree Component		Shrub Component	
	Imp. Val.	Presence	Imp. Val.	Presence
SHP	0.356	0.462	0.571	0.400
WPS	0.586	0.571	0.462	0.310
USPO	0.301	0.273	0.067	0.159
MSOP	0.504	0.607	0.442	0.167
LSHP	0.289	0.211	0.126	0.252
SFF	0.199	0.277	0.096	0.154
RFF	0.214	0.320	0.069	0.119
FH	0.191	0.482	0.127	0.184
BG	0.082	0.283	0.171	0.190

Table 3. Average Species Diversity and Richness Values for the Tree Component for Each Vegetative Type.

Vegetative Type	Average Diversity		Average Richness	
	Pads	Controls	Pads	Controls
SHP	0.332	0.806	3.00	9.00
WPS	0.074	0.490	2.00	5.00
USPO	0.216	0.818	3.20	9.80
MSOP	0.849	0.882	10.00	13.00
LSHP	0.142	0.843	2.00	9.86
SFF	0.295	0.880	4.50	9.50
RFF	0.407	0.732	4.67	8.33
FH	0.329	0.861	6.40	10.20
BG	0.323	0.452	3.67	4.67

Table 4. Average Species Diversity and Richness Values for the Shrub Component for Each Vegetative Type.

Vegetative Type	Average Diversity		Average Richness	
	Pads	Controls	Pads	Controls
SHP	0.539	0.471	5.00	5.00
WPS	0.211	0.565	2.50	4.00
USPO	0.425	0.596	4.20	6.40
MSOP	0.827	0.452	9.00	3.00
LSHP	0.384	0.625	4.51	5.71
SFF	0.684	0.716	6.50	7.00
RFF	0.549	0.337	4.67	3.50
FH	0.611	0.541	7.00	4.40
BG	0.237	0.299	3.00	3.00

The general trends just discussed do provide valuable insight into the vegetal development on abandoned drilling sites. More detailed evidence of secondary succession on these disturbed sites can be garnered from inspection of the data from specific vegetative types. Data from six types, including two upland and four bottomland types, are included in this report.

Two locations were sampled in the wetland pine savannah type: one was abandoned in November, 1955 and the other was abandoned in August, 1970. Thus the vegetation present on the pad plots had developed over 28 and 13 growing seasons, respectively. The overstory on the 1970 plot was composed entirely of loblolly pine (Pinus taeda) saplings, while the understory was principally loblolly pine, southern bayberry (Myrica cerifera), and sweetgum (Liquidambar styraciflua). This pad area was still undergoing the establishment process since the shade intolerant pine was dominating both the shrub and overstory canopies. The overstory on the 1955 disturbed area was also dominated by loblolly pine but did contain sweetgum and blackgum (Nyssa sylvatica). The shrub component on this older pad contained only transgressives of these latter two species. The dense overstory of pine virtually precludes further establishment of intolerant species except in small openings created by natural thinning. Given that the biological maturity of loblolly pine is approximately 150+ years (Harlow et al. 1979), it is reasonable to assume that both of these disturbed areas will continue to remain as virtually pure stands of pine for more than a century, barring further disturbance. Successional theories based on initial floristic composition and differential longevity proposed by Egler (1954) and expounded by Monk (1983) support this hypothesis.

The only pad area sampled in the sandhill pine type was abandoned in October, 1972. After twelve growing seasons, the overstory was dominated by loblolly pine (IV = 151.24) with shortleaf pine (Pinus echinata) and longleaf pine (Pinus palustris) as secondary species (IV = 26.45 and IV = 22.31, respectively). Species diversity on the pad plot was less than half of the diversity value on the control plot. The shrub layer was dominated by the same three species (with longleaf and shortleaf reversing their order). Post oak (Quercus stellata) was also present. The coefficient of community similarity calculated from importance values, between the pad and control plots, was only 0.356 and 0.571 for the overstory and shrub components, respectively. The disturbed area, therefore, had not yet returned to the same species composition as the surrounding stand. All of the species, except post oak, found on the pad area are considered as intolerant of shade and as pioneer species. All three pine species were present in the surrounding stands and, due to seeding characteristics, are the woody plants expected to dominate the early phases of succession. The control plot contained twelve species (in both components combined); most of which are classified as intermediate to tolerant species. Several oak and holly (Ilex spp.) species present in the adjacent stands should eventually establish themselves on the pad area as their seeds are distributed by various bird or mammal species. However, one can assume that barring future disturbance, the pad area will be dominated by a mixture of the three pine species.

Five abandoned drilling sites were sampled in the flatland hardwood type. This type was found on low, wide, and interdistributary flats. The vegetation on these flats was quite variable, but was usually dominated by one or more of several oak species; including swamp chestnut oak (Quercus michauxii), laurel oak (Quercus laurifolia), and willow oak (Quercus phellos). Loblolly pine did occur sporadically throughout this type. The understory commonly was dominated by palmetto (Sabal minor). The oldest site sampled was abandoned in July 1929; the most recently abandoned site included was completed in October, 1966. The primary dominant species on all five pad sites was loblolly pine. The 1929 site, after 55 growing seasons, remained a dense stand of pine with only a few other species maintaining their presence. Water oak (Quercus nigra), sweetgum, yaupon (Ilex vomitoria), and southern bayberry all were found on the disturbed site and their collective importance should increase over time. The other four sites exhibited a higher species richness in the combined shrub and canopy layers than did this plot. Following Egler's theory, these sites should be dominated for a long period by loblolly pine but with other species increasing in importance over time. The species composition of the vegetation on the pad plots did indicate that these disturbed areas will eventually resemble the surrounding stands. Palmetto, a key indicator of this type was abundant on all pad areas.

The lower slope hardwood pine type was sampled on six dry, abandoned sites. The oldest location sampled was abandoned in December, 1951 and the most recent was abandoned in June, 1976. The control plots on these locations had a high average diversity (0.843) and high average species richness (9.86). Species diversity was low on all six pad areas (ranging from 0.000 to 0.328). The number of species per pad plot varied from one to four. The dominant species on all but one area was loblolly pine (importance values ranged from 155.16 to 200.00). The one plot not dominated by loblolly pine was an almost pure stand of sweetgum, which is also an intolerant species that produces a large amount of wind-disseminated seed. Its seeding habits are very similar to those of the native pines. Loblolly pine was the principal dominant in the shrub layer on this plot. Only three of the pad plots contained any oak stems; two contained only shrub-sized stems. Red maple (Acer rubrum) was also found on only three plots, all were present only in the shrub component. Neither American beech (Fagus grandifolia) nor southern magnolia (Magnolia grandiflora) were present on any of the impacted areas. These latter two species are utilized as the indicator species for this type (Harcombe and Marks 1979) and were listed as the primary constituents of the climax forest vegetation dominating much of southeastern Texas (Quarterman and Keever 1962). These six pad areas appear to be maintaining the pattern described for the three previous types; that is, if pines were present in the stands adjacent to the disturbed area, then pines rapidly invaded the site.

All of the well sites included in the analysis of the four vegetative types just described were dry and abandoned locations; they were never in active production. Over sixty-five percent of the drilling sites within Preserve boundaries were dry and abandoned. The remainder were once producing wells or are still in production and pose different management problems.

In order to sustain heavy traffic on the pad, it was commonly necessary to stabilize the soil surface by adding foreign materials. The most common method of stabilization was the addition of crushed shell. The pads that were treated in this manner and then abandoned, are re-vegetating extremely slow. A good example of this was provided by examination of two pad areas cleared in the lower slope hardwood pine type in the Lance Rosier unit. One location was dry and abandoned in June, 1976; the other was a producing gas well for several years and then abandoned in January, 1975. There was a difference of only one growing season between these plots but the vegetation that had developed was markedly different. The overstory on the site that was dry and abandoned was now a pure stand of loblolly pine saplings (avg. dia. =12.8 cm; avg. no. of stems per ha = 520). The understory or shrub component consisted of seven species, including several intermediate to tolerant hardwoods such as American holly (Ilex opaca), red maple, and southern red oak (Quercus falcata). The site that was a producing gas well contained only two woody species, neither of which are tree species (baccharis (Baccharis halimifolia) and southern bayberry). Other sites, that received similar treatment in all vegetative types, reflect this same problem.

Two additional management problems of vital concern were indicated by examination of plots within the wetland baygall and floodplain hardwood types. Baygalls occur in depressional areas where water stands for much of the year. The overstory dominates are laurel oak (Quercus laurifolia) or blackgum. Sweetbay (Magnolia virginiana) and red maple are common overstory associates; black titi (Cyrilla racemiflora) and gallberry holly (Ilex coriacea) are dominants in the shrub layer (Harcombe and Marks 1979). Loblolly pine would not normally be found within this type. However, all three pad plots sampled contained loblolly pine; it was the dominant overstory species on two of the plots even though it did not occur on any of the control plots. During the construction process, the pad was usually elevated slightly to provide drainage from the pad. This well drained, flat, exposed seedbed was ideal for wind-blown seeds of loblolly pine. The only pad area where loblolly was not dominant was located in a very wet site where a board platform was utilized as the operational pad and when abandoned, the platform was left in place. This situation cannot arise in the future due to current regulations requiring the removal of such structures.

Two of the plots in the baygall type and four of the six plots in the floodplain hardwood type provide evidence of an additional hindrance to natural vegetative development. Chinese tallowtree (Sapium sebiferum), an escaped ornamental species, ranked as first or second in importance on these plots. The aggressiveness of this species in invading disturbed sites appears to be greater than any native species. The longterm impact on vegetal development is not known since very little scientific data on the ecology of this species exists. Its aggressiveness was further illustrated by its presence on three of the control plots; it was the fourth ranking species in the overstory on two plots.

MANAGEMENT IMPLICATIONS

Field inspection and quantitative analysis of vegetative data indicated that three major physical factors of the drilling sites inhibit natural revegetation: residual stabilization materials (crushed shell), remnants of, or complete berms around the site or reserve pit area, and disruption of natural water flow. Current regulations are designed to eliminate future occurrences of these three types of problems. These regulations require operators to remove residues from reserve pits and then backfill. The site must be re-contoured, as much as feasible, to the conditions prevalent prior to disturbance. Additionally, any foreign materials applied for stabilization must be removed. If these regulations are enforced, then vegetal development should proceed naturally, following similar patterns to those described in this report.

Resource managers within the National Park Service can utilize the data from this project to aid in the formulation of management criteria for those disturbed sites, and to aid in future management of oil/gas activities. The data illustrate that on most sites, where a pine seed source is nearby, pines should dominate for a long period of time. A decision must then be made whether to attempt to modify this pine dominance or allow it to continue.

If pine dominance is desired, such as in the sandhill pine or wetland pine savannah types, then perhaps the use of prescribed fire should be initiated to reduce hardwood invasion. If hardwood dominance is preferred, such as would be the case in the lower slope hardwood pine and flatland hardwood types, then several possible strategies are apparent. One is to restrict fires if possible and allow natural succession to occur. This will be a painfully slow process since the pine overstory has an expected lifespan in excess of 150 years. On the positive side,

these virtually pure stands of pines do increase overall diversity of vegetative types within a particular unit and may actually increase wildlife diversity by juxtiposing a mixture of age and species types within the unit. Eventually, these stands could provide suitable habitat for endangered species such as the Red-cockaded Woodpecker(Picoides borealis).

A second strategy would be to attempt to increase hardwood invasion by creating small openings or by selective thinning around understory hardwoods. Removal of pines in small patches and subsequent planting of tolerant hardwoods or underplanting of hardwoods do not appear to be feasible alternatives, primarily due to an extreme degree of transplanting shock (Johnson 1980). The rate of replacement of these pure pine stands with hardwoods will possibly be increased due to southern pine beetle activity. Many of these stands will eventually reach the stage where they will be classified as high hazard stands due to high density and their occurrence on lower slopes or flats.

On those sites where crushed shell was utilized to stabilize the pad areas, managers are faced with the decision of re-clearing the site of vegetation and removal of the foreign materials. In many cases, this would be beneficial since vegetal development has been restricted greatly. This decision must be based on site by site examination.

SUMMARY

Thirty-two well locations were investigated. General trends in vegetal development were examined across all vegetative types in which drilling occurred and specific data were presented for vegetative types. In general, the rate of succession appears to be inhibited as available soil moisture increases. Much of this inhibitory action is created by the rapid invasion of pine species, on sites where pine is not normally dominant, to the extent that they virtually eliminate other woody species in the initial establishment process. This low diversity of the initial floristic composition is then compounded with the longevity of these pine species which creates a situation where the pine is expected to dominate for perhaps a century or more.

Several additional problems inhibiting natural succession were also highlighted and management implications were discussed. These discussions illustrate that continued research into vegetal development following drilling activities is needed in order to more pointedly direct the decision making process.

LITERATURE CITED

Cox, G.W. 1980. Laboratory manual of general ecology, 4th ed. W.C. Brown Company, Dubuque, Iowa.

Cozine, J.J., Jr. 1976. Assault of a wilderness: the Big Thicket of East Texas. Ph.D. diss. Tex. A&M Univ., College Station, Tex.

Egler, F.E. 1954. Vegetation science concepts. I. Initial floristic composition - a factor in old-field vegetation development. Vegetatio 4:412-417.

Harcombe, P.A. and P.L. Marks. 1979. Forest vegetation of the Big Thicket National Preserve. Report to Office of Natural Sciences, Southwest. Region Natl. Park Serv., Santa Fe, New Mex.

Harlow, W.M, E.S. Harrar and F.M. White. 1979. Textbook of Dendrology. 6th ed. McGraw-Hill, New York, N.Y.

Johnson, P. 1980. Oak planting in mid-south uplands hardwoods: problems and prospects. pp. 74-87. In Proc. Mid-South Upland Hardwood Symp. for the Practicing Forester and Land Manager. USDA For. Serv. Tech. Publ. SA-TP12.

McLeod, C.A. 1971. The Big Thicket forest of east Texas. Tex. J. Sci. 23:221-233.

Monk, C.D. 1983. Relationship of life forms and diversity in old-field succession. Bull. Torrey Bot. Club. 110:449-453.

Parks, H.B. and V.L. Cory. 1936. Biological survey of East Texas Big Thicket Area. Tex. Acad. Sci.

Pielou, E.C. 1977. 2nd Ed. Mathematical ecology. John Wiley and Sons, Inc., New York, N.Y.

Quarterman, E. and C. Keever. 1962. Southern mixed hardwood forest: climax in the southeastern coastal plain, U.S.A. Ecol. Monogr. 32:167-185.

USDI National Park Service. 1982. Resources management plan and environmental assessment: Big Thicket National Preserve. Southwest. Region Natl. Park Serv. Office of Natural Resources.

Watson, G.E. 1979. Big Thicket plant ecology: an introduction. Big Thicket Museum Publ. Ser. No. 5, Saratoga, Tex. 2nd Ed.

Twenty-Seven Years Of Over-Browsing: Implications To White-Tailed Deer Management On Wilderness Areas

by
James C. Kroll, William D. Goodrum and Pamela J. Behrman

ABSTRACT--In 1957, deer-cattle and cattle exclosures were established near Lufkin, TX. Two sets of these exclosures, one in bottomland and the other in an upland mixed pine-hardwood forest, were relocated in 1984. Examination of the overstory and subcanopy woody plant communities of each revealed that prolonged exposure to over-browsing had substantial impact on community structure and composition. This was particularly evident in the subcanopy component. The upland deer-cattle exclosure had significantly higher species diversity (Hs), richness (R), and equitability (J') than the cattle exclosure or control. Total canopy cover (%C) was significantly higher for both deer-cattle and cattle exclosures than for the control. Bottomland exclosures showed similar results. Hs , R, and J' were significantly higher for both deer-cattle and cattle exclosures than for the control. Total woody cover was also significantly higher. Implications of these findings to management of white-tails on wilderness areas is discussed. Deer and livestock clearly have the potential to have a significant impact on the vegetative composition of the forest. Population irruptions are seldom controlled by either the environment or predators; although, predators can have a dampening effect in some cases. Sport hunting, supplemented by removals, by professional wildlife managers should be used early on to attain a dynamic equilibrium between deer populations and their habitat.

KEYWORDS:white-tailed deer, population ecology, habitat, wilderness, *Odocoileus virginianus*, population irruptions, over-browsing, over-population.

The white-tailed deer (*Odocoileus virginianus*) is probably the most popular big game animal in North America (Kroll 1981). Numbering only about 500,000 animals at the of turn this century (Seton 1909, Trefethen 1975), white-tails have responded dramatically to protection and scientific management. Today, there are approximately 15 million white-tails in North America (McCabe and McCabe 1984); yet, in spite of its popularity, the white-tailed deer remains one of the most poorly managed game species (Kroll 1981). Socio-political pressures throughout the white-tail's range have produced deer herds with abnormally skewed sex and age ratios and population levels dangerously close to carrying capacity. For example, Texas alone has an estimated 3.9 million animals (C.K. Winkler pers. comm.), with an annual harvest of only 300,000 (7.7%) deer. However, annual recruitment rate for the Texas herd is 30-40% (G. Boydston pers. comm.). Consequently, much of the available Texas deer range is at or near saturation (G. Spencer pers. comm.). Population irruptions which exceed carrying capacity are known to adversely affect habitat quality (Matschke *et al.* 1984, McCullough 1984).

Herein, we report on the impact of twenty-seven years of over-population on two southern forest communities, and discuss implications to wilderness management.

BACKGROUND

In 1957, the Texas Forest Service and the Southern Pine Lumber Company erected eight pairs of deer-cattle and cattle exclosures near Lufkin, Texas, in an effort to determine impact of deer and cattle foraging on forest regeneration. After four years of exclusion, woody study plants increased 296% in height and 764% (by weight) in browse production in the deer-cattle exclosure. Plants within the cattle exclosure increased in height by 95% and browse production increased by 176% (Lay 1961).

In 1984, we re-located three of these exclosures at Boggy Slough Hunting and Fishing Club (Trinity Co., Tex.). The remaining five structures were apparently destroyed prior to 1984 by logging activities. One of the three existing exclosures was in such poor condition, with poorly defined boundaries, that we decided to not include it in this study. Consequently, the two remaining exclosures represent a case history study of the impact of longterm deer over-population on upland mixed pine-hardwood and bottomland forest communities.

STUDY AREA

Boggy Slough Hunting and Fishing Club (Temple-EasTex, Inc.) is located about 15 km West of Lufkin, Texas (Houston and Trinity Cos.). Boggy Slough contains approximately 6,455 ha of pure pine, mixed pine-hardwood, and bottomland hardwood stands. Pure pine and mixed pine-hardwood stands were managed on an uneven-age, selection system until 1980, after which an even-age management strategy was adopted. Average deer population densities are high (1979 = 1 deer/6 ha) due to intensive protection programs, involving a bucks only harvest system. Doe harvest was not begun in earnest until 1981. A 3 m high, deer-proof fence was erected in 1979 in an attempt to maintain control over the genetic composition of the herd.

Vegetation

Vegetation was previously described by Kroll *et al.* (1979). Upland vegetation is primarily loblolly (*Pinus taeda*)-shortleaf (*P. echinata*) pine-hardwoods, while hardwoods dominate lowland areas. Average basal area (BA) is 9.6+/-0.3 (SE) m squared/ha for pines and 5.5+/-0.2m squared/ha for hardwoods. White oak (*Quercus alba*), southern red oak (*Q. falcata*), and willow oak (*Q. phellos*) comprise most of the hardwoods with an average BA of 3.3+/-0.2m squared/ha. Overstory stem density averages 176 stems/ha (pine and hardwood); however, some areas contain up to 198 stems/ha (pure pine). Overstory and midstory (subdominant) cover for the entire area is moderate at 45+/-4% and 48+/-4%, respectively. Average understory cover is low at 14+/-3%. Stand ages range from 5 to 81 years with an average of 49+/-3 years. Approximately 70% of the area is comprised of mixed pine-hardwood, with 16% and 14% of the area in pure hardwood and pure pine, respectively.

Topography

Land surface ranges from nearly level along bottomlands to gently rolling hills. Elevations range 57-105 m above mean sea level. Small permanent and intermittent streams are abundant throughout the area, usually supplying adequate free water to deer. The Neches River lies along the eastern boundary of Boggy Slough.

Grazing

Cattle and hogs were given free-range until about 1964, at which time grazing was officially discontinued on the area. However, free-ranging animals, especially hogs, remained on the area for several years. Feral horses and burros were also present until 1982. At this time, only feral hogs remain on the range.

METHODS

Upland exclosures were located in a predominantly loblolly pine stand. Bottomland exclosures were located adjacent to Cochina Creek. Deer-cattle exclosures measured 100 x 100 ft (30.5 m x 30.5 m), and were constructed of treated pine posts spaced 10 ft. (3 m) apart with 9 ft. (2.7 m) net wire fencing attached. Cattle exclosures measured 208 x 208 ft. (63.4 x 63.4 m), and were constructed of standard four strand barbed wire fencing. Spacing of posts was also 10 ft. (3 m). At the time of study, much of the net wire had been removed from the bottom 4 ft. (1.2 m) of the upland deer-cattle exclosure, and both cattle exclosures were in poor repair. Fences were repaired for future studies in 1985.

Due to the difference in size of the two exclosure types, we randomly selected a 0.1 ha area from each cattle exclosure. An adjacent unfenced area of equal size was also selected as a control. Control areas were subjected to both livestock and deer foraging during the study period.

A systematic sampling system was used to measure vegetative parameters relating to the subcanopy vegetation. A total of 16 circular sample plots were measured in each exclosure. Sample plots were 3 m in radius, with plot centers located at intersections of 6.1 x 6.1 m grid. Woody plant species present, and numbers of individuals for each plant species were recorded for each plot. In addition, a standardized method was developed (Kroll and Legg, unpubl.) to measure total canopy (overstory=subcanopy) cover. A 35 mm camera, outfitted with a 50 mm lens, was placed on the ground surface at plot center with the lens pointing upward. Subsequently, Kodalith R film was exposed for 1/2-second at f5.6. Kodalith film is an orthochromatic film that produces high contrast images. Photographs were taken only on full sun days, between 1100-1300 h. After development, Kodalith (Fig. 1) negatives were density analyzed using a Linear

Figure 1. Positive print of a Kodalith negative used to measure woody canopy cover (%C) in exclosures and control areas. Negatives were subsequently density sliced using a Linear Measurements Set (LMS), Apple IIe and LMS software.

Measurement Set R (LMS) density slicer (Measuronics CorporationR), and area occupied by canopy vegetation (=% cover, %C) computed using an Apple IIeR microcomputer and LMS supplied software.

Overstory trees within exclosures were already present when the exclosures were erected. However, we recorded the number of species (R) and number of trees (N)

present, as well as, tree heights (TH) and diameters (TD) at breast heights (1.4 m) for all trees within each exclosure and control area.

Species diversity (Hs) and and equitability (J') were calculated using standard information theory (Shannon and Weaver 1963). Statistical comparisons of vegetative parameters (vis. Hs, J', R, N, TH, TD, and %C) were conducted using oneway analysis of variance and Duncan's multiple range test (Nie *et al.* 1975). Data were tested for normality, prior to the ANOVA, using the Kolmogorov-Smirnov goodness-of-fit test. The 0.05 *a*-level was used throughout statistical tests.

RESULTS AND DISCUSSION

Exclosure Studies

Observations of both upland and bottomland exclosure sets suggested substantial differences in woody plant community composition and structure. Deer-cattle and cattle exclosures appeared as forested "island" communities within each forest type (Figs. 2 and 3). Vegetative analyses confirmed these initial observations.

Upland Exclosures--Upland exclosures were established in a young seedling-sapling seral stage pine plantation, primarily to determine impact of browsing on pine regeneration. Impact of both deer and cattle foraging on overstory composition was striking, and manifested by the species composition and density of this vegetative component (Tables 1 and 2). The control area had more tree species (R=4), higher diversity (Hs=1.019), and equitability (J'=0.742) than either deer-cattle or cattle exclosures. The deer-cattle exclosure had only one species (viz., *P. taeda*) occupying the canopy, while the cattle exclosure had two pines (*P. taeda* and *P. echinata*). Consequently, deer-cattle and cattle exclosures contained 206.3% and 287.5%, respectively greater overstory pine densities than the control. Tree heights for the three treatment types were not significantly different; however, trees within the cattle exclosure did have significantly (P lt 0.05) smaller TD than trees within the deer-cattle exclosure and control area. This was probably due more to random variation in stocking density than treatment effects.

Subcanopy (midstory + understory), woody vegetation also showed considerable differences with treatment type. The deer-cattle exclosure had significantly higher species richness (R), diversity (Hs), and equitability (J') than the cattle exclosure or control area (Tables 2 and 3). We also ranked woody, understory plants by palatability (Lay 1967). The deer-cattle exclosure contained one more preferred (first or second choice) browse species than the control, and two more than the cattle exclosure. Total vegetative cover (%C) was significantly higher for both deer-cattle (59.6+/-3.6%) and cattle (59.2+/-3.3%) exclosures than for the control (46.8+/-3.4%). As a result, herbaceous understory vegetation was less dense in exclosures than the control.

Figure 2. Upland exclosures and control area were strikingly different in appearance. Pictured are (A) deer-cattle exclosure, (B) cattle exclosure, and (C) control area.

Bottomland Exclosures--Bottomland exclusion areas showed reversed trends to those observed in upland areas (Tables 4-6). Although overstory species diversity and equitability were similar for all treatments, the cattle exclosure and control area contained higher total number of plants (N) and total number of species (R) (Table 5) than did the deer-cattle exclosure (Table 4). Hs was slightly higher in the two exclosure types than in the control. Overstory trees were generally taller in the cattle exclosure and control area, while TD was greater in the deer-cattle exclosure. It is not surprising that these trees were shorter, with greater diameters, than those in the other two treatment types, since lower densities usually produce shorter, more robust trees.

Densities of understory woody vegetation (N) were significantly higher in the deer-cattle exclosure than either cattle exclosure or control area (Table 5 and 6); while Hs and R were significantly higher for both deer-cattle and cattle exclosures. J' was not significantly different for any treatment. The control area contained only two understory woody species (Table 6). Further, palatability rankings showed that the control area was devoid of either first or second choice browse plants (Table 6). The cattle exclosure had two less preferred browse species than the deer-cattle exclosure. Browse plants within both the control and cattle exclosure showed heavy utilization (Fig. 4), with more than 70% utilization. Seventy percent or greater utilization is indicative of a heavy deer stocking (Lay 1967). Total vegetative cover (%C) was significantly higher for both cattle and deer-cattle exclosures (Table 5).

Figure 3. Examination of bottomland treatments showed similar results to those for upland plots. Pictured are (A) deer-cattle exclosure, (B) cattle exclosure, and (C) control area.

Table 1. Overstory Tree Species Occurring on Upland Plots at Boggy Slough Hunting and Fishing Club (Trinity Co., TX).

Tree Species	Number (%) by Treatment Type		
	Deer-Cattle Exclosure	Cattle Exclosure	Control
Liquidambar styraciflua	—	—	1(3.8)
Pinus echinata	—	3(6.5)	5(19.2)
P. taeda	33(100)	43(93.5)	16(61.5)
Quercus falcata	—	—	4(15.4)
Total individuals	33	46	26
Total species	1	2	4
H_s	—	0.241	1.029
J'	—	0.348	0.742

Table 2. Comparisons of Vegetative Parameters for Upland Plots at Boggy Slough Hunting and Fishing Club (Trinity Co., TX).

Vegetative Parameter	Type of Treatment		
	Deer-Cattle Exclosure	Cattle Exclosure	Control
Overstory			
Average tree height (m)	24.5±0.8	23.7±0.7	24.0±0.5
Average D.B.H. (cm)	30.0±2.0	24.1±1.3	28.2±2.3
Number of trees	33	46	26
Number of species	1	2	4
H_s	—	0.241	1.029
J'	—	0.348	0.742
Subcanopy[1]			
Total number of plants (N)	27$_a$	23$_a$	28$_a$
Total number of species (R)	11	8$_a$	8$_a$
H_s	2.260	1.505$_a$	1.747$_a$
J'	0.942	0.724$_a$	0.840$_a$
Cover (%C)	59.6±3.6$_a$	59.2±3.3$_a$	46.8±3.4

[1] Variables with the same subscript denote homogeneous subsets; = 0.05.

High canopy screening, especially in the bottomland deer-cattle exclosure, resulted in very low herbaceous density (cf., Fig.3).

Table 3. Subcanopy Woody Species Occurring on Upland Plots at Boggy Slough Hunting and Fishing Club (Trinity Co., TX).

| Woody Species[1] | Number (%) by Treatment Type | | |
	Deer-Cattle Exclosure	Cattle Exclosure	Control
Berchemia scandens*	—	1(4.3)	3(10.7)
Callicarpa americana*	—	1(4.3)	8(28.6)
Carya tomentosa	2(7.4)	—	—
Cornus florida*	5(18.5)	—	—
Ilex decidua*	1(3.7)	—	—
I. opaca	2(7.4)	2(8.7)	2(7.1)
I. vomitoria*	3(11.1)	1(4.3)	—
Liquidambar styraciflua	4(14.8)	2(8.7)	—
Myrica cerifera	—	13(56.5)	9(32.1)
P. taeda	2(7.4)	—	—
Pinus echinata	1( )	—	1(3.6)
Quercus phellos*	1(3.7)	—	—
Symplocos tinctoria*	—	—	3(10.7)
Ulmus alata*	2(7.4)	—	1(3.6)
Vaccinium arboreum	—	2(8.7)	—
Vitis rotundifolia*	4(14.8)	1(4.3)	1(3.6)
Total preferred Browse plants	6	4	5

[1] Species marked with an asterisk are preferred (1st or 2nd choice) browse plants. Herbaceous understory, especially grasses, are less abundant within exclosures (Kroll unpubl.).

Table 4. Overstory Tree Species Occurring on Bottomland Plots at Boggy Slough Hunting and Fishing Club (Trinity Co., TX).

| Tree Species | Number (%) by Treatment Type | | |
	Deer-Cattle Exclosure	Cattle Exclosure	Control
Carpinus caroliniana	—	1(4.2)	—
Carya cordiformis	—	1(4.2)	—
C. ovata	1(7.1)	—	1(5.0)
C. tomentosa	1(7.1)	—	1(5.0)
Celtis laevigata	—	—	1(5.0)
Fraxinus pennsylvanica	2(14.3)	—	1(5.0)
F. americana	—	2(8.3)	—
Liquidambar styraciflua	5(35.7)	7(29.2)	12(60.0)
Nyssa sylvatica	—	1(4.2)	—
Quercus falcata	3(21.4)	1(4.2)	—
Q. falcata var. pagodaefolia	—	—	1(5.0)
Q. michauxi	1(7.1)	—	1(5.0)
Q. nigra	1(7.1)	—	1(5.0)
Tilia americana	—	—	1(5.0)
Ulmus americana	—	2(8.3)	—
U. alata	—	1(4.2)	1(5.0)
U. crassifolia	1(7.1)	1(4.2)	—
Total individuals	14	17	20
Total species	7	9	9
H_s	1.730	1.869	1.505
J'	0.889	0.851	0.685

Comparisons of Upland and Bottomland Exclosures--It is interesting that the upland study area, especially in the overstory, often showed reversed trends from the bottomland study area. In both cases, heavy foraging by both deer and cattle seemed to have greatly influenced forest structure and composition. Excessive browsing in the upland area seemed to enhance overall species diversity for the overstory. We assume that this is due to heavy predation on pine regeneration, allowing invasion by more shade tolerant hardwood species (*L. styraciflua* and *Q. falcata*). Both species inhabiting the canopy (subdominant)

Table 5. Comparisons of Vegetative Parameters for Bottomland Plots at North Boggy Slough Hunting and Fishing Club (Trinity Co., TX).

| Vegetative Parameter | Type of Plot | | |
	Deer-Cattle Exclosure	Cattle Exclosure	Control
Overstory			
Average Tree Height (m)	22.1±1.9	23.2±1.8	24.2±1.8
Average D.B.H. (cm)	41.4±6.1	37.8±3.3	35.3±3.0
Total Number of Trees	14	17	20
Total Number of Species	7	9	9
H_s	1.730	1.869	1.505
J'	0.889	0.851	0.685
Subcanopy[1]			
Total Number of Plants (N)	24	7$_a$	3$_a$
Total Number of Species (R)	6$_a$	5$_a$	2
H_s	1.491$_a$	1.550$_a$	0.636
J'	0.832	0.963	0.918
Cover (%C)	68.5±2.4a	60.6±3.8$_a$	42.6±3.6

[1] Variables with the same subscript represent homogenous subsets; = 0.05.

Table 6. Subcanopy Woody Vegetation Occurring on Bottomland Plots at Boggy Slough Hunting and Fishing Club (Trinity Co., TX).

| Woody Species[1] | Number (%) by Treatment Type | | |
	Deer-Cattle Exclosure	Cattle Exclosure	Control
Carpinus caroliniana	11(45.8)	—	1(33.3)
Celtis laevigata*	2(8.3)	—	—
Diospyros virginiana	—	1(14.3)	—
Ilex decidua*	2(8.3)	—	—
I. opaca	—	1(14.3)	—
Liquidambar stryaciflua	—	—	2(66.7)
Quercus nigra*	1(4.2)	1(14.3)	—
Ulmus americana*	3(12.5)	—	—
U. crassifolia*	5(20.8)	2(28.6)	—
U. rubra*	—	2(28.6)	—
Total preferred Browse species	5	3	0

[1] Species marked with an asterisk represent preferred (1st or 2nd choice) browse species (Lay 1967).

of the control area were classified as a low choice browse by Lay (1967). However, we are uncertain at this time whether or not this is the correct interpretation, since initial species composition of the overstory was not reported by Lay (1959, 1961). These trees were less than 30 years of age, and were probably available for browsing at the time of exclosure establishment.

Overstory trees within bottomland areas were in excess of 80 years of age; hence, these trees were well established prior to erection of exclosures. Interpretations on the impact of browsing on these individuals would be questionable at best. However, trees within the deer-cattle exclosure were fewer and more robust than those in the cattle exclosure or control area. Enhanced growth could have been the result of several confounding factors, and will not be discussed at this time.

We feel that during the twenty-seven year study period, deer and cattle browsing have a profound influence on subcanopy plant composition and structure for both upland and bottomland study areas. That these differences can be attributed to predation on certain woody plant species, is evidenced by the fewer numbers of preferred browse species in cattle exclosures and control areas. Since some of these species are seedling and sapling hardwood trees, the climax forest resulting on each treatment type will be much different for exclosures than controls. In light of these findings, the white-tailed deer, and to some

Figure 4. Greenbriar *Smilax* spp., showing extremely heavy utilization in excess of 70%. Lay (1967) indicated that 70% or higher utilization is characteristic of heavy deer stocking.

extent domestic livestock, must be considered as a significant agent to forest succession. Implications to wilderness management will be discussed below.

WHITE-TAILED DEER MANAGEMENT ON WILDERNESS AREAS

Background

White-tailed Deer Population Ecology--White-tails are generally considered to be K-strategists (McCullough 1979); meaning that they maximize competitiveness, and that population processes are strongly density dependent (MacArthur and Wilson 1967, Pianka 1970, 1972 and Stubbs 1977). However, as McCullough (1979) pointed out, pure r- and K-strategists rarely exist in nature since both r- and K-selective forces operate on any population. It is commonly thought that K-strategists produce fewer offsprings and provide greater parental care. This is certainly the case with white-tails. Females (does) usually have only one or two offspring per year, and spend a great deal of time (six months or more) attending their fawns. However, does are known to live up to 20 years (Hayne 1984), producing at least one fawn per year after the yearling age class. Hence over a period of years, the white-tail doe has a reproductive potential of at least 19 fawns.

White-tailed-Habitat-Environment Complex--White-tailed deer probably inhabited the pristine forest in great numbers during pre-Columbian times. Several predators, as well as, aboriginal man depended heavily on white-tails for subsistence (McCabe and McCabe 1984, Mech 1984). Population estimates are highly variable, but are generally considered to have been from 14 to 34 million (Seton 1909, 1929, McCabe and McCabe 1984). Much of the difficulty in estimating deer populations prior to the 1500's, probably results from the dynamic and unpredictable nature of the habitat-environment complex.

Although occurring throughout succession, white-tails are predominantly a subclimax species (Leopold 1950). Population biology is closely tied to periodic habitat disturbances. The American Indian was well aware that deer were a subclimax species, responding to both natural and man-caused disturbances. For example, indians of several tribes regularly used fire to set back forest succession (Stewart 1951, Allen 1970, Trefethen 1970); while Truett and Lay (1984) presented several historical records of large scale, natural disturbances (i.e., tornadoes, hurricanes, and ice storms) in east Texas and Louisiana.

McCullough (1979) presented an excellent empirical model to white-tail population dynamics, which can give insight into pre-Columbian deer-habitat interactions. White-tail populations do not respond immediately to the positive effects of disturbance--there is a time lag effect (Fig. 5). Population irruptions basically occur under two situations, 1) creation of new habitat by some form of disturbance, and 2) introduction of a population into an unoccupied range. We feel that sudden protection afforded to previously heavily exploited herds produces an effect similar to introduction. At first, recruitment rate is quite high, producing a growth rate, even in K-adapted species, which is exponential in nature. At the same time, the population is approaching K, natural successional processes, coupled with negative habitat exploitation effects, are reducing K. The stage is therefore set for population over-shoot. Habitat conditions deteriorate to a point where the population crashes to a level well below K. There is then a subsequent recovery period for both the habitat and the population. However, since the population crashes well below K, the habitat recovers at a faster rate than the population. The cycle is then repeated. Additional habitat disturbances during this recovery period further confound the model, although these stochastic processes can be included in any model. Hence, from a historical perspective, white-tailed deer have probably experienced countless population irruptions and crashes in response to a changing environment, reaching an equilibrium only on a broad geographical scale. McCullough (1979) eloquently noted that:

"It is theoretically possible to achieve an equilibrium state between vegetation and deer in which succession is halted, with the subsequent deer population at a higher level than it was prior to the creation of new habitat. However, such an equilibrium is difficult to achieve, particularly if rate of succession is rapid. If the deer population is increasing at the same time K carrying capacity is decreasing because of succession, achieving equilibrium at the intercept of these two variables with opposite signs is unlikely, even with management."

Role of Predators--There is considerable confusion in regard to the role of predators in white-tail population ecology. Although wolves are considered to be the major historical predator, coyotes, bobcats, and mountain lions are more common throughout the white-tail's present range (Hornocker 1970, Cook *et al.* 1971, Beasom 1974, Mech 1984). Elaborately contrived theories (Rasmussen 1941, Leopold 1943) have been established which often over-state the impact of these predators on some deer species (Caughley 1978); yet, serious population reductions by predators are more the exception than the rule (Mech 1984). Predators more commonly exert a dampening effect on white-tail populations (McCullough 1979, Mech 1984). Although Mech (1984) noted several localized cases where wolves over exploited deer populations. McCullough (1979) reported that neither predation by wolves nor by aboriginal man tracked normal population age structure. Wolves, and probably other predators, usually select individuals that are very young, very old, or infirm (Pimlott *et al.* 1969, Mech and Frenzel 1971, Mech and Karns 1977, Fritts and Mech 1981). Evidence from archeological sites (Smith 1975, Elder 1965) suggest that aboriginal man harvested mostly prime animals in the younger age classes. Hence, prior to the coming of Europeans to North America, predators and primitive hunters with a few localized exceptions, probably had little influence on deer populations. Modern sport hunting, on the other hand, tends to produce harvests which track population age structure (cf., Fig. 6). Therefore, overall impact of sport hunting on white-tail populations should be greater than for either predators or primitive hunting. Unfortunately, this is rarely the case.

Sport Hunting--The greatest problem faced by white-tail managers today is the sport hunter (Kroll 1981). Theoretically, harvest strategies can be implemented

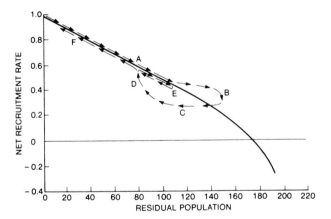

Figure 5. Observed recruitment rates (smoothed) compared with equilibrium rate for white-tailed deer of the George Reserve in Michigan over time, showing time lag. Time intervals are: (A) initial population growth rate following introduction and experimental population growth (1928-1931,1975-1980); (B) initial population overshoot (1932-35,1981-1982); (C) decline in growth rate due to vegetation damage (1936-1946); (D) recovery rate due to population reduction and vegetation recovery; (E) subsequent population increase with observed rate and equilibrium rate comparable (1947-1967); and (F) recent population with observed rate comparable to equilibrium rate (1968-1974). Equilibrium was achieved by balancing harvest with recruitment. (taken from McCullough 1979).

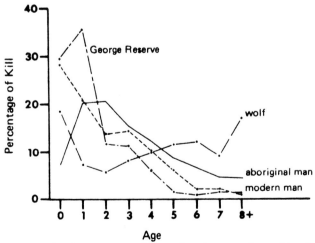

Figure 6. Comparison of age distribution of combined deer kills by wolves, aboriginal man, recent hunters, and the George Reserve deer herd, Michigan (taken from McCullough 1979).

which either, 1) approach a maximum sustained yield harvest (MSY) or 2) maintain population at or below carrying capacity. However, it is often difficult to achieve population goals using sport hunting. Several factors confound the issue, among which are socio-political pressures, hunter bias, and physical constraints inherent to sport hunting itself (McCullough 1979, Matschke *et al.* 1984, Kroll 1981). Annual recruitment rates for most deer herds are about 30-40%, yet harvest rates seldom approach recruitment (Teer *et al.* 1965, Matschke *et al.* 1984). Harvest goals are rarely achieved even when hunter attitudes favor increased removal of females. Hunter access is often a major physical constraint to harvest. White (1968) and Kroll (1985) found that hunters do not venture far from a road or trail. Hence, hunting pressure is unevenly distributed over large areas, producing patchy, often locally dense, deer populations.

Wilderness White-tail Management

In considering white-tailed deer management on wilderness areas, one basic question arises: Can white-tailed deer populations reach a dynamic equilibrium with the habitat-predator-environment complex?

We have maintained population density records (spotlight and track counts) on Boggy Slough since 1969 (Fig. 7). It is appropriate to examine Boggy Slough as a limited wilderness model because: 1) Boggy Slough is a large (ca., 6,500 ha) area of diverse habitat types and uneven-age stands, 2) little timber harvesting operations occurred prior to 1981, 3) bottomland habitats are near climax while uplands were at mid-succession, and 4) there was minimal antlerless harvest prior to 1980. Since its establishment in

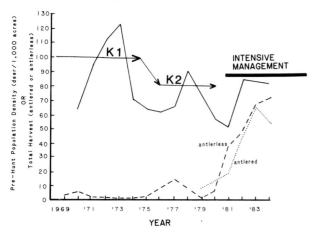

Figure 7. Population and harvest history of Boggy Slough Hunting and Fishing Club (Houston and Trinity Cos., TX). The population experienced an over-shoot of carrying capacity (K1) in 1973; then declined rapidly (1974-1976), during which the carrying capacity (along with possible succession) was lowered (K2). Recovery and over-shoot again occurred in 1978, followed by another decline. In 1981, an intensive management program, involving both increased removals of antlerless deer and regular timber harvests, was initiated in an attempt to produce a maximum sustained yield. At this time, the population appears to be dampened by these strategies.

the late 1930's, Boggy Slough deer populations have exhibited several "boom-crash" cycles. Lay (1958) reported population crashes for Boggy Slough as early as 1957, and suggested that such crashes had occurred several times over the previous 20 years. In 1973, the population reached a peak density of 125 deer/1,000 ac. Over the next three years, the deer population crashed to a low of 62 deer/1,000 ac., a 50.4% decrease. Using Adams' (1976) carrying capacity model for the mixed pine-hardwood forest type, we estimated carrying capacity for this period to be 100 deer/1,000 ac. Yet, subsequent recovery of the population during 1976-78 maximized at only 90 deer/1,000 ac., apparently over-shooting K. Hence, carrying capacity of the range had decreased. We feel that the reduction in carrying capacity was due to normal successional processes and/or deterioration of the habitat by previous over-browsing. The exclosure study reported herein, gives evidence that previous over-shoots of carrying capacity were responsible for habitat degradation. White-tailed deer had not only adversely affected their own habitat quality, but had also apparently altered the structure and composition of the forest. It is also interesting to note that predators apparently had little dampening effect on the deer population.

In 1980, a commitment was made to control population growth by substantially increasing antlerless harvest. In addition, timber management was converted to an even-age system in order to conform to corporate management policy, as well as, increase forage production. The area was hunted almost daily throughout the fall (1980-81) season, yet harvest goals were not achieved. Hunters were placed in permanent stands, located on green food plots (clover and cereal grain). Although deer used these food plots on a regular basis before the deer season, heavy hunting pressure during the first ten days of the season caused deer to shift activity patterns and home ranges (Kroll 1985). In subsequent years, antlerless harvest quotas were only achieved by implementing a system involving rotation of hunting areas and times. These extraordinary methods were apparently effective in achieving harvest goals, and in dampening population oscillation (fig. 7). It is at this point that Boggy Slough becomes an inappropriate wilderness model. It is one thing to achieve population control on a privately owned, intensively managed property; however, it is quite a different thing to control deer numbers through public sport hunting, especially for wilderness areas.

Recommendations

In establishing a wilderness area, especially one of a small size (2,000 ha), it should be decided early on whether or not white-tailed deer populations should be controlled. At this time, only three management tools are available to the wilderness manager; prescribed fire, grazing, and sport hunting. Since controlled burns are generally detrimental to hardwood species, this management practice should be limited to upland habitats. Consideration should be given to positive white-tail population responses *prior* to implementation of a burning program. Grazing, as this study suggests, also has potential to produce damaging effects. Care should be taken not to exceed range carrying capacity for domestic livestock. It should be understood that deer and cattle foraging are additive, *not* compensatory.

Public sport hunting can be an excellent white-tail management tool on wilderness areas, however, one serious question arises; whether or not sport hunting alone will effectively dampen population irruptions. A public education program, aimed at both hunters and non-hunters, appears to offer the best solution to the problem. We recommend that an educational program be developed which stresses the following points:
1) white-tailed deer can alter forest composition and structure;
2) antlerless harvest is necessary on wilderness areas, and
3) wilderness areas provide quality, rather than quantity, deer hunting opportunities.

Most newly established wilderness areas contain early succession stage forest communities, and low deer population densities. Since white-tails are subclimax animals, there is immediate potential for population irruption. Such irruptions are more likely to occur with initially low populations, than at high densities. We recommend periodic examination of the understory plant community and utilization/availability relationships similar to those proposed by Lay (1967). When necessary, sport hunting removals should be supplemented with population reductions by professional wildlife managers. We feel that trapping and other capture methods will be much too expensive and ineffective in controlling wilderness white-tail populations.

ACKNOWLEDGMENTS

The authors wish to extend special appreciation to Dr. Harry Jacobson, who was the initial driving force behind this work.

LITERATURE CITED

Adams, D.J. 1976. A computer model for deer-forage-timber interactions in the loblolly-shortleaf pine-hardwoods ecosystem of east Texas. MSF Thesis. Stephen F. Austin St. Univ., Nacogdoches, Tex.

Allen, D.L. 1970. Historical perspective. *In* Land use and wildlife resources. pp. 1-28. compiled by, Comm. Agric. Land use and Wildl. Resour., Div. Biol. and Agric., Nat. Res. Council. Washington, D.C., Nat. Acad. Sci.

Beasom, S.L. 1974. Relationships between predator removal and white-tailed deer net productivity. J. Wildl. Manage. 38:854-859.

Caughley, G. 1978. Analysis of Vertebrate Populations. John Wiley & Sons, N.Y.

Cook, R.S., M. White, D.O. Trainer, and W.C. Glazener. 1971. Mortality of young white-tailed deer fawns in South Texas. J. Wildl. Manage. 35:47-56.

Elder, W.H. 1956. Primeval deer hunting pressures revealed by remains from American Indian middens. J. Wildl. Manage. 29:366-370.

Fritts, S.H. and L.D. Mech. 1981. Dynamics, movements, and feeding ecology of a newly protected wolf population in northwestern Minnesota. Wildl. Monogr. 80. Washington, D.C. The Wildl. Soc.

Hayne, D.W. 1984. Population dynamics and analysis. pp. 203-210. *In* L.K. Halls (ed.) White-tailed Deer Ecology and Management. Stackpole Books, Harrisburg, Penn.

Hornocker, M.G. 1970. An analysis of mountain lion predation upon mule deer and elk in the Idaho primitive area. Wildl. Monogr. 21. Washington, D.C. The Wildl. Soc.

Kroll, J.C., R.E. Zaiglin, and G. Garza. 1979. Multivariate analysis of summer white-tailed deer habitat in east Texas. Abs. 2nd SE Deer Study Group. Starkville, Miss.

Kroll, J.C. 1981. Hunting--An American tradition. pp. 12-13. *In* The American Hunter. (April).

Kroll, J.C. 1985. Buck Sanctuaries: Trophy Hunting's Great Discovery (Part I). pp. 34-38, 75. *In* North American Whitetail (July).

Lay, D.W. 1958. Extensive Deer Range Survey. East Texas Deer Study. Job Completions Rept. P-R Proj. W-80-R-1 (Job 5). Texas Parks & Wildl. Dept.

Lay, D.W. 1959. Deer and Cattle Exclosures. East Texas Deer Study. Job Completions Rept. P-R Proj. No. W-80-R-2 (Job 1). Texas Parks & Wildl. Dept.

Lay, D.W. 1961. Deer and Cattle Exclosures. East Texas Deer Study. Job Completions Rept. P-R Proj. No. W-80-R-2 (Job 1). Tex. Parks & Wildl. Dept.

Lay, D.W. 1967. Deer range appraisal in eastern Texas. J. Wildl. Manage. 31:426-432.

Leopold, A.S. 1943. Wisconsin's deer problem. Wis. Conserv. Bull. 8:1-11.

Leopold, A.S. 1950. Deer in relation to plant succession. Trans. N. Amer. Natur. Resour. Conf. 15:571-580.

MacArthur, R.H. and E.O. Wilson. 1967. The Theory of Island Biography. Monogr. Pop. Biol., Princeton Univ. Press, Princeton, N. J.

Matschke, G.H., K.A. Fagerstone, F.A. Hayes, W. Parker, R.F. Harlow, V.F. Nettles, and D.O. Trainer. 1984. Population Influences. pp. 169-188. *In* L.K. Halls (ed.) White-tailed Deer Ecology and Management. Stackpole Books, Harrisburg, Penn.

McCabe, R.E. and T.R. McCabe. 1984. Of Slings and Arrows: An Historical Retrospection. pp. 19-72. *In* L.K. Halls (ed.) White-tailed Deer Ecology and Management. Stackpole Books, Harrisburg, Penn.

McCullough, D.R. 1979. The George Reserve Deer Herd: population ecology of a K-selected species. Univ. Mich. Press, Ann Arbor, Mich.

McCullough, D.R. 1984. Lessons from the George Reserve, Michigan. pp. 211-242. *In* L.K. Halls (ed.) White-tailed Deer Ecology and Management. Stackpole Books, Harrisburg, Penn.

Mech, L.D. and L.D. Frenzel, Jr. An analysis of the age, sex, and condition of deer killed by wolves in northeastern Minnesota. pp. 35-51. *In* L.C. Mech and L.D. Frenzel, Jr. (eds.). Ecological Studies of the timber wolf in northeastern Minnesota. Res. Pap. NC-52. USDA Forest Serv., N. Cent. For. Exp. Stn., St. Paul, Minn.

Mech, L.D., L.D. Frenzel,Jr., and P.D. Karns. 1977. Role of the wolf in a deer decline in the Superior National Forest. Res. Pap. NC-148. USDA For. Serv., N. Cent. For. Exp. Stn., St. Paul, Minn.

Mech, L.D. 1984. Predators and Predation. pp. 189-200. *In* L.K. Halls (ed.). White-tailed Deer Ecology and Management. Stackpole Books, Harrisburg, Penn.

Nie, H.H., C.H. Hull, J.C. Jenkins, K. Steinbrenner, and D. Bent. 1975. Statistical Package for the Social Sciences. 2nd ed. McGraw-Hill. New York, N.Y.

Pianka, E.R. 1970. On r- and K-selection. Amer. Nat. 104:592-597.

Pianka, E.R. 1972. r- and K-selection or b and d selection: Amer. Nat. 106:581-588.

Pimlott, D.H., J.H. Shannon, and G.B. Kokensoky. 1969. The ecology of the timber wolf in Algonquin Provincial Park. Wildl. Res. Rept. No. 87. Ontario Dept. Lands and For., Ottawa.

Rasmussen, D.I. 1941. Biotic communities of the Kaibab Plateau, Arizona. Ecol. Monogr. 3:229-275.

Seton, E.T. 1909. Life Histories of Northern Mammals. Vol. I. Chas. Scribner's Sons, New York.

Seton, E.T. 1929. Lives of Game Animals. Vol. III, Part I. Doubleday, Doran and Co., Inc. Garden City, N.Y.

Shannon, C.E. and W. Weaver. 1963. The mathematical theory of Communication. Univ. Ill. Press, Urbana, Ill.

Smith, B.D. 1975. Middle Mississippi exploitation of animal populations. Mus. Anthro. Pap. 57. Univ. Mich. Press, Ann Arbor, Mich.

Stewart, O.C. 1951. Burning and natural vegation in the United States. Georgia. Rev. 41:317-320.

Stubbs, M. 1977. Density dependence in the life-cycles of animals and its importance in K- and r-selected stragegies. J. Anim. Ecology. 46:677-688.

Teer, J.G., J.W. Thomas, and E.A. Walker. 1965. Ecology and Management of the White-tailed Deer in the Llano Basin of Texas. Wildl. Monogr. 15. The Wildl. Soc., Washington, D.C.

Trefethen, J.B. 1970. The return of the white-tailed deer. Amer. His. 21:97-103.

Trefethen, J.B. 1975. An American Crusade for Wildlife. Winchester Press, New York, N.Y.

Truett, J.C.K. and D.W. Lay. 1984. Land of Bears and Honey. A Natural History of East Texas. Univ. Tex. Press, Austin, Tex.

White, D.L. 1968. The New Hampshire hunter and his harvest. pp. 113-173. *In* H.R. Siegler (ed.). The White-tailed Deer of New Hampshire. Surv. Rept. 10. New Hamp. Fish & Game Dept., Concord, N.H.

Floristic Aspects Of The Upland Island Wilderness Area In East Texas

by
John R. Ward

ABSTRACT--The plot method of vegetation analysis was used to describe the woody vegetation of the Upland Island wilderness area in eastern Texas. Topographically defined habitat types include dry upland, mesic upland, mesic creekbottom, and river bottomland forests. Field collections resulted in 464 taxa, referable to 95 families and 257 genera. Problems of management and vegetational succession are discussed in general.

KEYWORDS: bogs, bottomland forest, community ordination, pine forest, pitcher plants, vegetational succession, Upland Island Wilderness.

The National Wilderness Preserve System was established in 1964 to protect areas in their natural condition. Most potential wilderness areas in the eastern United States are second growth forests, which are reforested with new composition (Wright 1974). This description applies to the newly designated Upland Island Wilderness area in eastern Texas (formerly known as the Graham Creek area). Under designation of wilderness, however, the area must be managed to maintain its primitive character (Wilderness Act 1964). This paper describes the woody vegetation as it exists today at Upland Island with problems of management and vegetational succession discussed in general.

The Upland Island Wilderness is positioned on the West-Gulf Coastal Plain (Fenneman 1938) of the United States on Pleistocene to late Tertiary surfaces (Arbingast et al. 1967). This corresponds closely with Braun's (1950) Southeastern Evergreen Forest Region characterized by pines and hardwoods, with longleaf pine the dominant species. Regional treatments place the wilderness in the Pineywoods Vegetational Area of Texas (Gould 1975a). The site is located along the Angelina-Jasper county line, bordered on the south by the Neches River.

The eastern third of Texas has a subtropical humid climate that is most noted for warm summers. Annual precipitation is 117-122 cm, with an average annual temperature of 19 degrees C (Larkin and Bomar 1983). Elevations within the wilderness area range from 31-91 meters above sea level.

METHODS AND PROCEDURES

To describe the woody vegetation of Upland Island as it exists today, the landscape was divided first according to major habitat types, and second according to species composition. High altitude color infrared photography was used to delineate pine, pine-hardwood, and hardwood stands by differences of color and shade. A vegetation map was produced by copying the stands, creeks, and ponds first to transparencies and then to topographical maps. Representative areas were ground-proofed by extensive field reconnaissance.

A total of ten communities was selected for analysis based on topographic position and vegetation. The woody vegetation of each site was analyzed by the plot method consisting of 100 contiguous, 5 meter square plots, situated in belt transects, for a total sample area of 0.25 ha. The names and diameters of all woody species with a diameter-at-breast height (dbh) of 1/2 cm or greater, were recorded for each plot. From these data, frequency, density, and basal area were calculated for each species recorded at each community. Dominance, as used in this study, is based on importance value. An importance value for each species was calculated as the sum of relative frequency, relative density, and relative basal area. The importance values in turn were used to organize composition tables for each community sampled and to determine community similarity coefficients (Cox 1980). A polar community ordination was also established, following the techniques set forth by Cox (1980), and based on variation in community composition. Coefficients of dissimilarity (0.85 - coefficient of similarity) were used in this procedure. Species diversity is a product of species richness, the number of species in a community, and species evenness, the distribution of individuals among the species (Barbour et al. 1980). Data obtained were used to compute species diversity, employing the Shannon-Weiner Diversity Index (Shannon and Weaver 1949).

A species checklist was compiled for all woody and herbaceous species encountered during the course of the study. Special attention was given to two hillside pitcher plant seeps, one open and grassy in appearance and the other mostly wooded. Voucher specimens were placed in the Stephen F. Austin State University Herbarium. Scientific nomenclature follows that of Correll and Johnston (1970) and Gould (1975b).

RESULTS

Ordination is the process of arranging samples in relation to one or more gradients or axes of variation (Whittaker 1967). A polar ordination, representing degree of difference between the ten communities sampled, is graphically presented in Fig. 1. The communities tend to

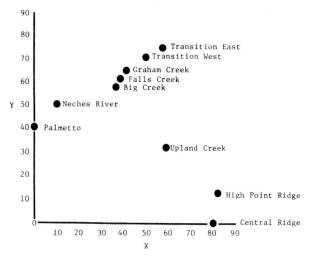

Figure 1. Polar ordination of plant communities of Upland Island.

cluster into four general groups, with the Upland Creek as a separate entity. End communities selected for the first or X axis, represent the extreme ends of the moisture gradient at Upland Island based on species compositions and environmental characteristics. Decreasing hydrophytism is exhibited along this axis moving from the seasonally inundated palmetto flat to the dry, longleaf uplands.

Community Descriptions

The community designated Upland Creek is positioned in the ordination between the mesic and dry upland stands (Fig. 1). The community is dominated by longleaf pine (*Pinus palustris*), and codominants are species with high importance values in the mesic creekbottoms. A general lack of the more moist, level areas along the Upland Creek allows for the extension of prescribed fire to creekside. Codominants include blackgum (*Nyssa sylvatica*) and sweetgum (*Liquidambar styraciflua*). The major shrub species are azalea (*Rhododendron* spp.) and wax myrtle (*Myrica cerifera*).

Composition tables were combined for the remaining communities according to habitat type.

Dry Uplands--Longleaf pine forests are found primarily in the most xeric environments and those subject to prescribed burning. At Upland Island, these communities occur on ridge tops and upper slopes. An average density of only 1.53 plants per plot reflects the openness of the park-like forests. Longleaf pine is by far the dominant species with loblolly pine (*Pinus taeda*) having the second highest importance value (Table 1). However, all individ-

Table 1. Relative Frequency, Density, Basal Area and Importance Values of Dominant Trees and Shrubs of Upland Ridge Tops.

Species	Rel. Freq. %	Rel. Dens. %	Rel. B.A. %	I.V.*
Pinus palustris	54	46	99.00	199
Pinus taeda	14	17	.16	31
Myrica cerifera	7	13	.10	20
Callicarpa americana	8	12	.10	20
Rhus copallina	5	4	.02	9

*Sum of relative frequency, relative density and relative basal area.

uals of loblolly pine had dbh's of less than 10 cm. Occasional hardwoods include sandjack oak (*Quercus incana*), blackjack oak (*Q. marilandica*), post oak (*Q. stellata*), sweetgum, and flowering dogwood (*Cornus florida*). The most important shrubs are wax myrtle, american beautyberry (*Callicarpa americana*), and flameleaf sumac (*Rhus copallina*). Sample plots contained only eighteen species. The species diversity index of 2.05 was the lowest of the habitat types sampled.

The coarse sands of the ridge tops vary in depth and are underlain by a less permeable clay or bentonite layer, which impedes the downward movement of water (Stephenson 1980). The water, moving horizontally along the clay substratum, surfaces on the sides of the hills or gullies creating seepage slopes or beginnings of a small upland stream (Ajilvsgi 1979). Greater than 20 seepages were noted at Upland Island, five of which contained pitcher plants (*Sarracenia alata*). Another interesting feature of the upland ridges is the occurrence of three ponds, each of which differs in community physiognomy.

Mesic Uplands--Mesic upland communities (transition forests) exist on gentle slopes between the dry, longleaf pine uplands and mesic creekbottoms. The mesic conditions result in a much greater species richness compared to dry uplands. Fifty-two species were encountered with loblolly pine, sweetgum, and southern red oak (*Quercus falcata*) as the dominants (Table 2). Common

Table 2. Relative Frequency, Density, Basal Area and Importance Values of Dominant Trees and Shrubs of Transition Areas.

Species	Rel. Freq. %	Rel. Dens. %	Rel. B.A. %	I.V.*
Pinus taeda	10	10	64	84
Liquidambar styraciflua	12	21	7	40
Quercus falcata	10	8	12	30
Quercus stellata	7	8	4	19
Nyssa sylvatica	7	6	2	15

*Sum of relative frequency, relative density and relative basal area.

associates in the overstory were post oak, blackgum, and shortleaf pine (*Pinus echinata*). The most important understory species are farkleberry (*Vaccinium arboreum*), yaupon (*Ilex vomitoria*), american beautyberry, and flowering dogwood. The 9.8 plants per plot was the highest number recorded of the habitat types.

Mesic Creekbottoms--Mesic creekbottoms at Upland Island are dominated by American hornbeam (*Carpinus caroliniana*), loblolly pine, sweetgum, and water oak (*Quercus nigra*) (Table 3). Vines are a conspicuous component of the creekbottom forests, as evidenced by the high frequency and density of muscadine grape (*Vitis rotundifolia*) (Table 3). Prevalent understory species, in

Table 3. Relative Frequency, Density, Basal Area and Importance Values of Dominant Trees, Shrubs and Vines of Creek Bottoms in the Study Area.

Species	Rel. Freq. %	Rel. Dens. %	Rel. B.A. %	I.V.*
Carpinus caroliniana	12	15	5.00	32
Pinus taeda	2	2	22.00	26
Liquidambar styraciflua	7	6	12.00	25
Quercus nigra	3	2	15.00	20
Vitis rotundifolia	9	9	.48	19

*Sum of relative frequency, relative density and relative basal area.

addition to American hornbeam, are two-winged silverbell (*Halesia diptera*), deciduous holly (*Ilex decidua*), sweetleaf (*Symplocos tinctoria*), and flowering dogwood. American beech (*Fagus grandiflora) and eastern hophornbeam (Ostrya virginiana*) are locally important at Big Creek. Density averaged 5.89 plants per plot.

Neches Riverbottom--The Neches River floodplain consists of alternating intermittent creeks, sloughs, flats, and ridges. Sample plots included these landforms. The principal woody species are willow oak (*Quercus phellos*), deciduous holly, American hornbeam, and sweetgum (Table 4). In addition to willow oak and sweetgum, important

Table 4. Relative Frequency, Density, Basal Area and Importance Values of Dominant Trees, Shrubs and Vines of the Neches River Floodplain.

Species	Rel. Freq. %	Rel. Dens. %	Rel. B.A. %	I.V.*
Quercus phellos	14	10	56.00	80
Ilex decidua	18	27	2.00	47
Carpinus caroliniana	8	16	1.00	25
Liquidambar styraciflua	4	2	18.00	24
Rhus toxicodendron	9	12	.20	21

*Sum of relative frequency, relative density and relative basal area.

overstory species include southern red oak, baldcypress (*Taxodium distichum*), overcup oak (*Quercus lyrata*), ashes (*Fraxinus* spp.), and loblolly pine. The understory consists chiefly of deciduous holly, American hornbeam, hawthorns (*Crataegus* spp.), and sebastian bush (*Sebastiana fruticosa*). Poison ivy (*Rhus toxicodendron*) is the most prevalent vine. Two large oxbow lakes in the riverbottom are characterized by many large baldcypress trees. Other species associated with the oxbows are swamp privet (*Forestiera acuminata*), water elm (*Planera aquatica*), common persimmon (*Diospyros virginiana*), and overcup oak. An average density of 7 plants per plot was recorded for the Neches River floodplain.

Field Collections

Topographical relief and resultant soil moisture is generally regarded as the primary factor governing the distribution of woody species in east Texas. This is well illustrated at the Upland Island wilderness area where landforms range from dry, upland ridges to river floodplains. The wide range of habitat types provides excellent representation of east Texas flora. The flowering plants and ferns of Texas are incorporated into 174 families (Correll and Johnston 1970). Field collections documented a total of 95 families occurring in the wilderness area. This represents 55% of the number of families in Texas and approximately 67% of those occurring in eastern Texas.

A total of 464 species was found, referable to 257 genera. The sunflower family (Asteraceae), with 36 genera and 57 species, and the grass family (Poaceae), with 25 genera and 63 species, contained the greatest number of taxa at Upland Island.

Indications were made for those species considered to be infrequent or rare according to Correll and Johnston (1970). Twenty-nine species were listed as "infrequent", sixteen species as "rare", and one species was considered to be "very rare." The majority of these plants were in the sunflower, grass, and sedge (Cyperaceae) families.

DISCUSSION

The Upland Island wilderness area exemplifies the diversity of habitat occurring in eastern Texas. The widely different forest communities provide excellent opportunities for education, research, and recreation. The present day forest composition reflects to varying degrees man's influence. The 1964 Wilderness Act, however, states that wilderness must be managed to maintain its primitive character (Wilderness Act 1964). Wright (1974), while considering the scarcity of true wilderness, believed that designated wilderness areas should be managed to reestablish natural regimes. At Upland Island, management objectives may require only that exploitation be curtailed. Natural processes would then be permitted to determine the forest composition.

The role of fire in maintaining certain habitats has been the focus of much study. Pitcher plant bogs depend on fire not only to eliminate competitors, but to release nutrients bound up in organic matter as a result of previous growth (Eleutarius and Jones 1969). Folkerts (1982) reports that bogs in a natural or nearly natural condition are now very rare. The preservation of bogs at Upland Island may require some management to insure that burning occurs periodically. Also, grazing and trampling by livestock has been shown to cause major changes in the composition of bog flora (Pullen and Plummer 1964). The prescribed use of fire to maintain small select habitats or rare species should not disrupt large scale natural processes, which would be allowed to proceed within the Upland Island ecosystem.

A knowledge of successional relations provides insight to long-term changes in vegetation upon the restoration of natural regimes. Virtually all evaluations of the climax concept are based on studies of modern vegetation (Wright 1974). The close proximity to a Neches riverbottom virgin forest described by Nixon *et al.* (1977) provides opportunity for comparison to the Upland Island riverbottom forest. According to the authors, the virgin forest may be climax.

The mesic upland forests were dominated by loblolly pine and sweetgum. According to some authors (Edminston 1963, Monk 1965), the predominance of loblolly pine and sweetgum is indicative of fire or cutting. There is a consensus that forests such as these, in time, will revert to mixed forests containing much less pine.

Successional status of longleaf pine forests is less clear than that of mesic forests. Many authors conclude that fire is essential to maintain longleaf pine (e.g. Chapman 1932, Heyward 1939, Boyer 1979). Under the natural regime, an increase in such hardwoods as sandjack oak, blackjack oak, and flowering dogwood would be expected. According to Wahlenberg (1946), these species were common understory associates in original stands of longleaf pine.

The deep sandy soils of dry uplands are a major factor in determining the species which occupy these sites. The short hydroperiod is compounded in eastern Texas by the occurrence of the "summer drought" (Ward 1984). Marks and Harcombe (1981) considered deep sandy soils on the coastal plain too dry (or infertile) to support closed hardwood forest. This is supported by Ward (1984), who found an average density of only 4.42 plants per 5 meter square plot in unburned dry upland communities in southeast Texas. Marks and Harcombe (1981) found that some longleaf stands that exist in southeast Texas today without fire management are not vigorously being invaded by hardwoods. The authors reported that the problem of postfire succession, from longleaf to hardwoods, may be mostly restricted to well-drained upland sites, with excessively-drained sites (such as Upland Island ridge tops) excluded.

With the exclusion of prescribed fire, a trend toward hardwood dominance is expected on lower slopes now dominated by longleaf pine at Upland Island. The presence of man will increase the frequency of fires above the low numbers caused by lightning. These fires, and the drier soil regime, may provide conditions which are favorable for the maintenance of longleaf pine on the ridge tops.

ACKNOWLEDGMENTS

This study was supported by National Science Foundation Grant SPI 8004098.

LITERATURE CITED

Ajilvsgi, G. 1979. Wildflowers of the Big Thicket. Tex. A&M Univ. Press, College Station, Tex.

Arbingast, S.A., L.G. Kennamer, R.H. Ryan, J.R. Buchanan, W.L. Hezlep, L.T. Ellis, T.G. Jordan, C.T. Granger, and C.P. Zlatkovich. 1967. Atlas of Texas. Bureau of Business Res. Univ. of Tex., Austin, Tex.

Barbour, M.G., J.H. Burk and W.D. Pitts. 1980. Terrestrial plant ecology. Benjamin/Cummings, Menlo Park, Calif.

Boyer, W.D. 1979. Regenerating the natural longleaf pine forest. J. For. 77:572-775.

Braun, E.L. 1950. Deciduous forests of eastern North America. The Blakiston Co., Philadelphia, Penn.

Chapman, H.H. 1932. Is the longleaf pine type a climax? Ecology 13:328-334.

Correll, D.S. and M.C. Johnston. 1970. Manual of the vascular plants of Texas. Tex. Res. Found. Renner, Tex.

Cox, G.W. 1980. Laboratory manual of general ecology. William C. Brown Co., Dubuque, Iowa.

Edminston, J.A. 1963. The ecology of the Florida pine flatwoods. Ph.D. thesis. Univ. Florida, Gainesville, Fla.

Eleutarius, L.N. and S.B. Jones, Jr. 1969. A floristic and ecological study of pitcher plant bogs in south Mississippi. Rhodora 71:29-34.

Fenneman, N.M. 1938. Physiography of eastern United States. McGraw-Hill Book Co., New York, NY

Folkerts, G.W. 1982. The Gulf Coast pitcher plant bogs. Am. Sci. 70:260-267.

Gould, F.W. 1975a. Texas plants--a checklist and ecological summary. Tex. Agric. Exp. Stn. MP-585/revised. Tex. A&M Univ., College Station, Tex.

Gould, F.W. 1975b. The grasses of Texas. Tex. A&M Univ. Press, College Station, Tex.

Heyward, F. 1939. The relation of fire to stand composition of longleaf pine forests. Ecology 20:287-304.

Larkin, T.J. and G.W. Bomar. 1983. Climatic Atlas of Texas. Tex. Dep. Water Resour. LP-192. Austin, Tex.

Marks, P.L. and P.A. Harcombe. 1981. Forest vegetation of the Big Thicket, southeast Texas. Ecol. Monogr. 51:287-305.

Monk, C.D. 1965. Southern mixed hardwood forest of north central Florida. Ecol. Monogr. 32:335.

Nixon, E.S., R.L. Willett and P.W. Cox. 1977. Woody vegetation of a virgin forest in an eastern Texas riverbottom. Castanea 42:227-236.

Pullen, T.M., Jr. and G.L. Plummer. 1964. Floristic changes within pitcher plant habitats in Georgia. Rhodora 66:375-381.

Shannon, C.E. and W. Weaver. 1949. The mathematical theory of communication. Univ. Ill. Press, Urbana, Ill.

Stephenson, C. 1980. An ecological investigation of Graham Creek, a proposed wilderness area. Geology Section, p. V-1 through V-13. Natl. Sci. Found. Grant SPI 8004098.

Wahlenberg, H.G. 1946. Longleaf pine. Charles L. Pack Forestry Foundation, Washington, D.C.

Ward, J.R. 1984. Woody vegetation of the dry uplands in east Texas. Masters Thesis, Stephen F. Austin State University, Nacogdoches, Tex.

Whittaker, R.H. 1967. Gradient analyses of vegetation. Biol. Rev. 42:207-264.

Wilderness Act (PL 88-577). 1964.

Wright, H.E., Jr. 1974. Landscape development, forest fires, and wilderness management. Science 186:487-495.

Bottomland Hardwoods: Ecology, Management, And Preservation

by
Jim Neal and Jeff Haskins

ABSTRACT--A myriad of abiotic and biotic factors interact to influence the vegetational composition of the southeastern bottomlands. Bottomland vegetation communities are often associated with distinct physiographic features of alluvial river floodplains. Management techniques to maximize such resources as wildlife, timber, and recreation are well documented. However, management of bottomlands for wilderness or natural area features is less well known. Research is needed to establish appropriate management strategies for wilderness and natural areas. Preservation of relatively intact bottomland ecosystems is also a major need.

KEYWORDS: bottomland hardwood forests, management, wilderness and natural areas, vegetation communities, floodplain physiography, preservation.

The diversity of the bottomland hardwood ecosystem of the southeastern United States is a direct result of a number of abiotic factors including climate, physiography and topography, soils and their parent geological materials, hydrological regime, and land use. Water is the primary driving force for the entire system (Wharton et al. 1982). Overbank flooding in alluvial river floodplains produces the prominent physiographic features and associated vegetational types of bottomlands (Putnam et al. 1960).

Besides the biological resources of the bottomlands, a number of other values are obtained from these floodplain systems (Jahn 1978, Wharton 1980). These values often provide incentives that make management of the resource a worthwhile pursuit.

Traditional management of bottomlands has been directed toward harvesting or improving the timber, wildlife, and recreational potential. Other management options involve the conversion of bottomland hardwood forests to other land use categories. Bottomlands also can be managed for wilderness or natural attributes. Only a small amount of the bottomland area of the Southeast is managed for these attributes. Often other values or resources can be enhanced under wilderness and natural area management.

The basic needs of bottomland systems, beside proper management, are research and preservation. Priority should be given to applied research and long-range monitoring studies. Bottomland hardwoods are among the most threatened ecosystems in the United States (Sternitzke 1976, Frayer et al. 1983), and a number of measures must be utilized to protect this diminishing resource.

TOPOGRAPHY AND FLOODPLAIN PHYSIOGRAPHY

Bottomland hardwood forests occur on the floodplains of large creeks and rivers in the southeastern United States. These forests are primarily found in the lower Piedmont, lower Mississippi River Valley, and southern Coastal Plain from Virginia to eastern Texas and Oklahoma (Fig. 1). The largest extant area of bottomland forests occurs in the lower Mississippi Valley Delta and its tributaries.

The complexities of the hydrological regime, climate, soils, and physiography/topography have produced a complex mosaic of zones and associations in the bottomland hardwood ecosystem (Wharton et al. 1982). The timing and duration of inundation (i.e. hydroperiod) and the deposition of silts, sands, and clays on the alluvial floodplains are primarily responsible for the origin, character, and maintenance of floodplains and their vegetational aspect (Wharton et al. 1982).

Active rivers and streams of the Southeast constantly meander across the floodplain as a means of accommodating slope (Wharton et al. 1982). Meandering streams cut their banks and form new land, the point bar, on the opposite bank immediately downstream (Fig. 2). With additional cutting and deposition, the point bar increases in elevation and becomes a front. When a stream or river undergoes overbank flooding, suspended sand and sediments are deposited as a natural levee, ridge, or first bottom (Putnam et al. 1960). Over time, a number of well-drained, parallel ridges, separated by intervening swales, are formed. The natural levees slope gradually landward to flats or backswamps, which include low ridges and shallow depressions or sloughs (nearly filled channels of former water courses). Flats are composed of fine clays and silts laid down in slackwater areas that have poor surface drainage. Other minor features of floodplains include scour channels (small waterways formed during flooding as water seeks shortcuts), hammocks (islands produced by erosion within scour channels), and minibasins (shallow depressions between tree bases) (Wharton et al. 1982).

In contrast to these gradual erosional and depositional changes, rivers also form physiographic features by abrupt changes (Putnam et al. 1960). Often during heavy flooding, a river may shorten its course by cutting across a sharp meander bend to produce an oxbow lake. In addition, within most of the floodplains of major southeastern rivers, second and, sometimes third bottoms are found. These bottoms or terraces were produced in earlier geological time and have older, better differentiated soils than the first bottoms. The bottoms of smaller, fast-moving rivers and large creeks usually have lighter soils and

rolling topography. Generally, these site conditions parallel those of second bottoms of large rivers (Putnam et al. 1960).

Differences in relief within the floodplain are slight and variable. A low ridge is usually no more than 1 to 4.5 meters below a front and no more than 0.3 to 3 meters above a flat (Putnam et al. 1960). Within slackwater areas, differences in relief may be almost indistinguishable. In South Carolina, second bottoms lie 1.5 to 3 meters above the modern floodplain and 1.5 to 6 meters below the third bottoms (Gagliano and Thom 1967).

ECOLOGICAL RELATIONSHIPS

Vegetationally, the southeastern bottomlands are within the Outer Coastal Plain Forest, the Southeastern Mixed Forest, and Prairie Parkland Provinces (Bailey 1980). Various terms have been utilized to describe the bottomland forests (Table 1).

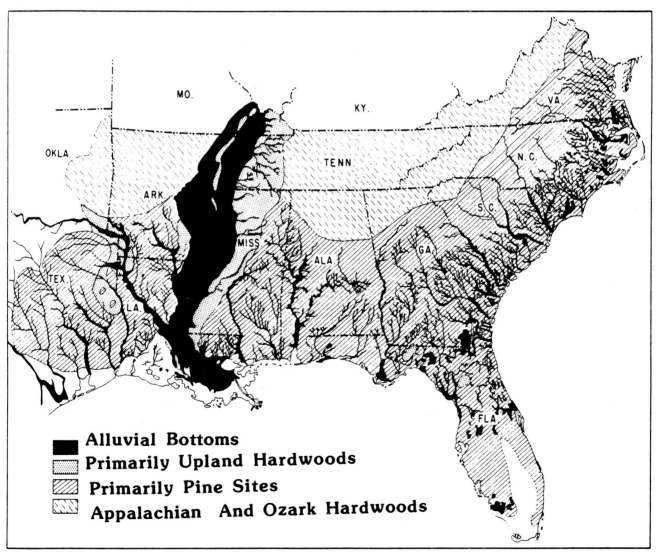

Figure 1. Bottomland Hardwood Forests of the Southeast U. S. (after Putnam et al. 1960).

The species and plant community composition of bottomlands are profoundly influenced by the physiographic features and soil types of floodplains. As previously mentioned, the driving force of floodplain formation is water; principally the frequency, timing, and duration of flooding.

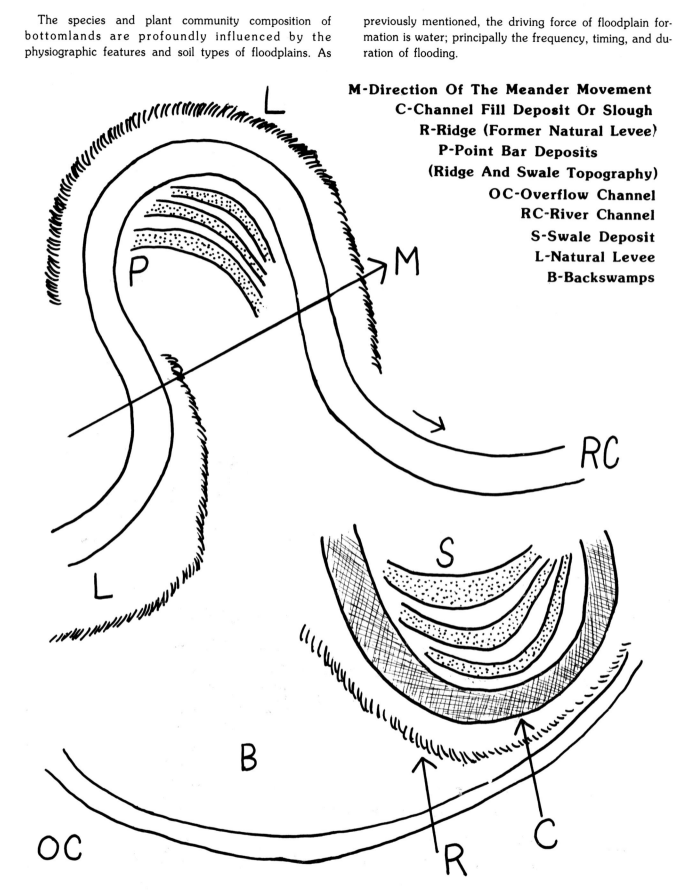

M-Direction Of The Meander Movement
C-Channel Fill Deposit Or Slough
R-Ridge (Former Natural Levee)
P-Point Bar Deposits
(Ridge And Swale Topography)
OC-Overflow Channel
RC-River Channel
S-Swale Deposit
L-Natural Levee
B-Backswamps

Figure 2. Idealized Alluvial Floodplain. (after Wharton *et al.* 1982).

Table 1. Terms Utilized to Describe Bottomland Hardwood Forests.

Bottomland hardwood forests	Various authors
Forested palustrine wetlands	Cowardin *et al.* (1979)
Forested estuarine wetlands	Cowardin *et al.* (1979)
Swamps and deep swamps	Various authors
Overflow bottomlands	Various authors
Seasonally flooded basins and flats	Shaw And Fredine (1956)
Oak-Gum-Cypress forests	U.S. Forest Service
Elm-Ash-Cottonwood forests	Various "Status And Trends" Surveys
Wetland hardwoods	Boyce And Cost (1974)
Stream margin forests	U.S. Forest Service Resource Bulletins
Floodplain forests	Various authors
Riparian forests	Various authors
Cold-deciduous Alluvial forests	Driscoll *et al.* (1984)
Lowland hardwood forests	Samson (1979)

Complex but distinct vegetational associations characterize these flood-plain features (Fig. 3 and Table 2). As an area changes through the action of the river and/or through ecological succession, the plant communities also change.

River channels are vegetated with a diverse group of aquatic herbaceous plants. The point bars are dominated by pioneer species, such as black willow (*Salix nigra*) and eastern cottonwood (*Populus deltoides*) which occur on mineral soils saturated for up to 40 percent of the year (Larson *et al.* 1981). The well-drained, better developed soils of the natural levees are dominated by a number of communities and species (Table 2). The major portion of the floodplain, within the coastal alluvial plain, is located on low flats and terraces (Wharton *et al.* 1982). The low terraces, which are dominated by several community types (Table 2), are seasonally inundated for one to two months of the growing season, and the soils are saturated for about 22% of the year (Larson *et al.* 1981). The flats (backswamps) are poorly to very poorly drained with soils saturated from 22% to 40% of the year. The less poorly drained flats and swales are dominated by a variety of community types (Table 2), and the wettest sites are typically dominated by the overcup oak (*Quercus lyrata*) - water hickory (*Carya aquatica*) forest type (Fig. 3). The

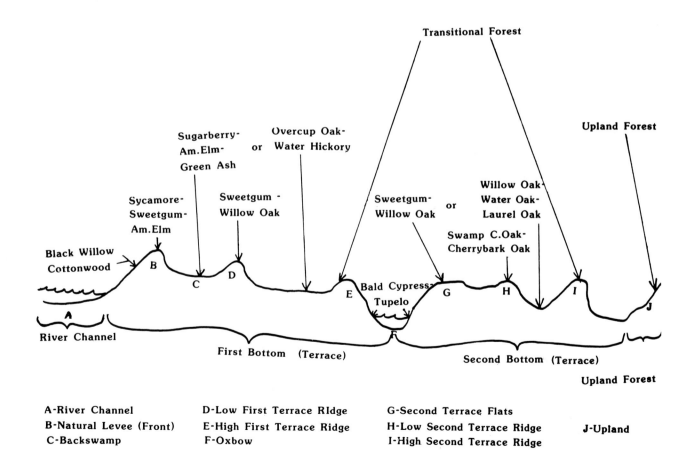

A-River Channel   D-Low First Terrace Ridge   G-Second Terrace Flats
B-Natural Levee (Front)   E-High First Terrace Ridge   H-Low Second Terrace Ridge   J-Upland
C-Backswamp   F-Oxbow   I-High Second Terrace Ridge

Figure 3. Alluvial Floodplain Topography and Plant Community Types. (after Wharton *et al.* 1982).

Table 2. Bottomland Hardwood Forest Types and Associated Topographic Occurrence/Floodplain Setting in the Southeast[1].

Forest type	Topographic occurrence/ floodplain setting
Wetland Pine or Pine-Oak Types	
Loblolly Pine-Hardwood (SAF#82)[2]	Creek Bottoms, Second Bottoms, Ridges
Longleaf Pine-Slash Pine (SAF#83)	Fire Excluded, Successional Flatwoods
Slash Pine (SAF#84)	Fire Excluded, Successional Flatwoods
Slash Pine-Hardwood (SAF#85)	Poorly Drained Depressions And Sloughs
Cabbage Palmetto-Slash Pine (SAF#86)	Hammocks and Flatwoods
Pond Pine (SAF#98)	Poorly Drained Depressions And Flats
Slash Pine-Swamp Tupelo (SAF#99)	Flatwoods And Depressions
South Florida Slash Pine (SAF#111)	Sub-climax, Flatwoods And Hammocks
Transition Hardwood Type	
Lower Slope Hardwood-Pine	Smaller Creek Bottoms, Second Bottom Ridges, Coves, Branches Or Creek Heads, And Slope Forests
Yellow Poplar (SAF#57)	
Yellow Poplar-White Oak-Northern Red Oak (SAF#59)	
Sweetgum-Yellow Popular (SAF#87)	
Beech-Southern Magnolia (SAF#90)	
Early Succession Bottomland Hardwood Types	
River Birch-Sycamore (SAF#61)	Natural Levees
Silver Maple-American Elm (SAF#62)	Natural Levees
Cottonwood (SAF#63)	Point Bars
Sycamore-Sweetgum-American Elm (SAF#94)	Natural Levees
Black Willow (SAF#95)	Point Bars
Later Succession Bottomland Hardwood Types	
Willow Oak-Water Oak-Laurel Oak (SAF#88)	Second Terrace Flats
Live Oak (SAF#89)	Fronts and Hammocks
Swamp Chestnut Oak-Cherrybark Oak (SAF#91)	Highest First Bottom Ridges And Low Second Bottom Terraces
Sweetgum-Willow Oak (SAF#92)	First Bottom Ridges
Sugarberry-American Elm-Green Ash (SAF#93)	Backswamps Or First Terrace Flats
Overcup Oak-Water Hickory (SAF#96)	Poorly Drained Floodplain Flats
Flatland Hardwood (Swamp Chestnut Oak-Willow Oak-Laurel Oak)	Flats in S.E. Texas
Cedar Elm-Sugarberry-Willow Oak	Bottomland Flats In Central Texas
Sugarberry-Hawthorne	Streamside Woodlands In Tidally Influenced Areas
Swamp Forest Types	
Atlantic White-Cedar (SAF#97)	Successional, Wet Soil Of Stream Swamps
Pondcypress (SAF#100)	Poorly Drained Blackwater Flatwoods
Baldcypress (SAF#101)	Oxbows, Swales, Flats, Sloughs, Backswamps
Baldcypress-Water Tupelo (SAF#102)	Oxbows, Swales, Flats, Sloughs, Backswamps
Water Tupelo (SAF#103)	Oxbows, Swales, Flats, Sloughs, Backswamps
Sweetbay-Swamp Tupelo (SAF#104)	Branch Heads, Small Creeks, Pocosins, Tidal Forests
Shrub Swamp Types	
Water Elm-Swamp Privet Flat	Swales, Sloughs, Floodplain Depressions
Shrub Swamp/Beaver Pond Complex (Buttonbush, Alder, Water Elm, Western May Haw, etc.)	Sloughs, Seeps, Beaver Ponds, Floodplain Depressions

[1] *Sources:* Eyre (1980), Putnam *et al.* (1960), Wharton *et al.* (1982).
[2] SAF-Society of American Foresters, Forest Type

wettest, most poorly drained oxbows, flats, sloughs, beaver ponds, and backswamps have saturated soils throughout the growing season with occasional fall drawdowns, and are dominated by forest and shrub swamps (Table 2). The highest floodplain elevations include the levees and terraces of the second and third bottoms and highest terraces of the first bottoms. The soils are saturated from 2% to 12.5% of the growing season (Wharton *et al.* 1982), and dominated by transitional forest types (Table 2). Creek bottoms also are typically dominated by transitional communities.

The bottomlands of the southeastern United States support a significant number of rare and endangered species (state and federal) or species of special concern. In fact, these bottomlands were (or are) the last refuge of the eastern cougar (*Felis concolor*), Bachman's warbler (*Vermivora bachmanii*), and the Ivory-billed Woodpecker (*Campephilus principalis*). Bottomlands also contain good populations of a number of game species, such as the wood duck (*Aix sponsa*), mallard (*Anas platyrhynchos*), wild turkey (*Meleagris gallopavo*), white-tailed deer

(*Odocoileus virginianus*), and gray squirrel (*Sciurus carolinensis*). A large number of other game and non-game animal species and a significant portion of the southeastern flora are found in the bottomland ecosystem.

MANAGEMENT OF BOTTOMLAND ECOSYSTEMS

Alluvial floodplains of the Southeast provide at least five basic categories of values to society: 1) biological/ecological resource values (previously discussed), 2) water resource values, 3) life support values, 4) cultural resource values, and 5) cultivated resource values (Jahn 1978, Wharton 1980) (Table 3). Value does not necessarily imply economic or personal reward. However, in several cases, bottomlands do provide incentives that make management of the system a worthwhile pursuit. Bottomlands are primarily managed for 1) water resources, 2) crop production, 3) livestock production, 4) timber production, 5) recreational resources, 6) wildlife and fishery resources, and 7) natural and wilderness values (Table 4).

Water Resources
Management of floodplain systems for water resources usually involves the construction of water control structures (i.e. dams, etc.) and the subsequent conversion of riverine systems to slackwater lakes or the conversion of meandering rivers to straight channels. This management usually involves the loss of bottomland hardwoods and makes other forms of management less viable.

Crop Production
Management of floodplain systems for crops requires the conversion of bottomland forests to a managed agricultural system. Most other management goals cannot be realized under this system, and often a variety of chemicals harmful to the aquatic system are introduced with cropland management. An increasing number of hectares of bottomland forests have been converted to croplands in the last 20 years. Conversion of forests for soybean production has been particularly severe in the lower Mississippi River Delta.

Livestock Production
Livestock grazing is a much used management option in the southeastern bottomlands and in riparian zones throughout the country. It does not prevent the exercise of most other management options and is permissible under certain forms of wilderness and natural area management. However, when grazing is utilized, bottomland systems often are degraded for other uses as a result of soil compaction, erosion, and destruction of vegetation.

Timber Production
The actual type of silvicultural system utilized to manage timber resources (Table 4) depends on several factors: 1) present species composition (size, age, and vigor), 2) requirements of the desired species, 3) whether other functions, such as wildlife resources, are being managed, 4) economic return to be realized and the immediacy of the need, and 5) the presence of managerial constraints (USDA Forest Service 1973, Dickson 1978). Timber management, especially to improve the species composition, may be appropriate under certain types of natural area management.

Recreational Resources
Non-consumptive recreational use is compatible with other management options, including wilderness area management (Table 4). Often, the recreational use of wilderness areas must be limited to prevent degradation of the natural features of the area (Hendee *et al.* 1978, Stankey *et al.* 1985). Recreational use is sometimes discouraged or prohibited in certain particularly sensitive

Table 3. Environmental Functions and Values of Bottomland Hardwood Forests.[1]

I. Biological resource values
  - Approximately 35 plant communities
  - Plant and animal species of special concern
  - Wintering and breeding waterfowl populations
  - Numerous game species (squirrels, rabbits, deer, turkey, etc.)
  - Diverse non-game wildlife populations
  - Furbearers
  - Migratory corridors

II. Water resource values
  A. Water quantity
    - Management of high water pulse (i.e., flooding)
  B. Water quality
    - Lessen soil erosion and scour
    - Filter for pollutants: pesticides, phosphorus, nitrogen, and fecal coliform bacteria
    - "Sink" for cesium, oil, heavy metals, fly ash, etc.

III. Life support values
  A. Floodplain productivity
    - Among most productive ecosystems in S.E. and U.S. resulting from heavy input of nutrients and subsequent decomposition
  B. Inland aquatic productivity
    - Micro- and macro-invertebrate diversity
    - Fish (feeding and spawning)
    - Aquatic plants
  C. Estuarine productivity
    - Breeding and nursery habitat
    - Contributing nutrients to estuary
    - Stabilizing hydrological conditions

IV. Cultural resource values
  - Archaeological and historical features
  - Hunting, fishing, boating, bird watching, and nature study
  - Wilderness and natural areas
  - Open space
  - Scientific study
  - Outdoor education
  - Food for man

V. Cultivated resource values
  - Major source of hardwood timber
  - Supports most productive agricultural lands in south
  - Livestock grazing
  - Hay production
  - Aquaculture

[1]*Source:* Jahn (1978) and Wharton (1980).

Table 4. Management Options for Bottomland Hardwoods.

I. Water resources
    A. Recreation
    B. Water supply
    C. Flood control
II. Cropland production
    A. Soybeans
    B. Other field crops
    C. Hay
III. Livestock production
IV. Timber production
    A. Selection system: individual and group
    B. Shelterwood system
    C. Seed-tree system
    D. Clearcutting
    E. High-grading
V. Recreational resources
    A. Non-consumptive (nature study, birdwatching, camping and canoeing)
    B. Consumptive—wildlife and fishery oriented (hunting, fishing and boating)
    C. Consumptive—other (woodcutting and ORV use)
VI. Wildlife and fishery resources
    A. Aquaculture
    B. Water management (green-tree reservoirs and moist soil management)
    C. Habitat manipulations (creation of wetlands and edge)
    D. Selective timber harvest
VII. Wilderness and natural values

areas or in areas devoted to scientific research. Consumptive recreational use is not always permitted in natural and wilderness areas, but is appropriate or even necessary (i.e., to control deer populations) under certain conditions. Woodcutting and off-the-road-vehicle use are detrimental in many cases and are not appropriate in natural areas.

Wildlife and Fishery Resources

Management of wildlife resources in bottomlands often utilizes techniques of habitat manipulation which may not be permissible in wilderness or natural areas. Techniques, such as the creation of green-tree reservoirs (Fredrickson and Taylor 1982) and wetland habitats to benefit waterfowl and other wetland species, are examples. Wildlife management activities are usually compatible with other management schemes, and less active management and management of wilderness-dependent species are appropriate in natural areas.

Wilderness and Natural Values

Management of an area for wilderness or natural attributes requires a great deal of flexibility, depending upon the particular type of area being managed and the management entity of the area. Wilderness area management is guided by provisions of the Wilderness Acts (Public Laws 88-577 and 93-622). In Research Natural Areas, emphasis is given to scientific research and the establishment of monitoring programs to document change (Federal Committee on Ecological Reserves 1977).

A number of agencies/groups maintain or manage areas for natural conditions, but without the rigidity of the Wilderness and Research Natural Area designations. Examples of areas managed for natural conditions include preserves of The Nature Conservancy and National Audubon Society. Management options and principles for wilderness and natural areas are listed in Table 5.

RESEARCH PRIORITIES

In order to properly manage bottomland ecosystems, one of the highest priority needs is for research (Table 6). Priority should be given to research that is primarily goal-oriented (determining actions necessary to produce change) rather than consequence-oriented (detecting the results of change) (Lyon 1978), that is principally management oriented, and that can be utilized in long-range monitoring studies designed to measure change over time. Natural and wilderness sites are particularly valuable for research study areas because they can be utilized as experimental controls (Anderson 1983), are relatively stable units, are useful in understanding basic ecosystem processes, and are especially useful in monitoring change.

PRESERVATION

All our attempts at management and research are for naught, however, unless we have natural areas on which to practice our trade. Existing wilderness and natural areas in the bottomland zone of the Southeast are very limited. Of a total of nearly 253,000 ha of wilderness and 17,000 ha of Research Natural Areas in the Southeast, a large percentage is found in a few areas (nearly 14,200 ha of Research Natural Areas and over 141,650 ha of wilderness are in Okefenokee National Wildlife Refuge), and only a very small portion of the above total is actually in bottomland hardwoods. Only three percent of the total bottomland area in eastern Texas and 13 percent in the lower Mississippi River Delta, where concerted efforts have recently been made to acquire lands, are in public ownership (U.S. Fish and Wildlife Service 1985).

The bottomland ecosystem has suffered precipitous declines in area since original settlement by the Europeans. The loss has accelerated since the turn of the century and has been especially severe in the last 30 years. From the 1950's to 1970's, there has been a net loss of 2.43 million ha of palustrine, forested wetlands (Frayer et al. 1983). Losses in the southeastern U.S. have been particularly sharp with declines over 63 percent from the original bottomland area. From the mid-60's to mid-70's, the lower Mississippi River Delta bottomlands declined at a rate of 105,222 ha annually (Sternitzke 1976). Further declines are predicted for the future.

Table 5. Management Options for Bottomland Ecosystem Wilderness and Natural Areas.

1. Keep bottomlands in hardwoods!
2. Maintain mature stands of hardwoods (Dickson 1978)
3. Limited timber harvest (selection cuts for timber stand improvement)
4. Retain wildlife corridors between wilderness/natural areas and other forested or wetland units (Dickson 1978)
5. Retain snags for wildlife
6. Priority management for key, wilderness-dependent, or special species
7. Protect special concern species, endangered species, colonial waterbirds, and other wildlife from harassment
8. Define sensitive areas or areas containing sensitive species
9. Eliminate grazing
10. Define limits of acceptable change or carrying capacity of bottomland communities (Stankey *et al.* 1985; Hendee *et al.* 1978)
11. Control of noxious or exotic species
12. Maintenance of key successional stages by minimum impact methods
13. Active revegetation of disturbed areas
14. Reintroduction of extirpated species (with caution and after careful study)
15. Creation/enhancement of wetlands
16. Erect nesting, perching, and roosting structures
17. Establish research programs
18. Establish long-term monitoring program
19. Control natural forces only as allowed by law

Table 6. Research Needs in Bottomlands of the Southeast.[1]

1. Baseline inventories (physical and biological)
2. Vegetative community analysis and classification
3. Correlation of plant community data with physical and faunal parameters
4. Role of natural disturbances in influencing community structure
5. Effect of various management treatments on bottomlands and biota
6. Impact of beavers on bottomland forests (Hair *et al.* 1978)
7. Methods of reestablishing natural communities and stream systems
8. Abiotic-biotic interactions in bottomlands
9. Pre- and post-impoundment studies on the impact of reduced flows on downstream bottomland habitats
10. Snag ecology (Conner 1978)
11. Population trends of fauna by community type
12. Energy flow and nutrient cycling

[1]*Sources:* Anderson (1983) and Patton (1977).

The principal reasons for the destruction of bottomland forests are a result of conversion to croplands and reservoirs. Within the lower Mississippi River Delta, losses have primarily resulted from conversion to croplands devoted to the production of soybeans. In eastern Texas

and Oklahoma, the losses have primarily been a result of conversion of riverine areas to slack-water reservoirs. In Texas, over 263,000 surface ha of lakes have been constructed in the eastern portion of the state.

To halt this decline, many methods are needed to preserve as much as possible of the remaining bottomland hardwood forests (Table 7). These methods vary from

Table 7. Methods of Preservation of Southeastern Bottomlands.

A. Voluntary protection agreements through natural area registries, etc.
B. Protection by zoning
C. Protection by existing regulatory programs
D. Leases by conservation agencies/groups, hunting clubs, etc.
E. Perpetual easments
   1. Scenic easments
   2. Non-development easments
   3. Non-development easments with management rights
F. One of above options with right-of-first-refusal to purchase
G. Fee acquisition by conservation agency/group
H. Wild and scenic river designation

voluntary agreements that can be terminated at any time by either a landowner or conservation entity, to fee acquisition by a government entity or conservation group. Wild or scenic river designation by Congress provides further protection by prohibiting reservoir construction along protected stream or river segments. Major preservation efforts by the Nature Conservancy (Blair 1981), the U.S. Fish and Wildlife Service (U.S. Fish and Wildlife Service 1985), and a number of states, most notably Florida and Mississippi, have been initiated in recent years. Increased efforts by these and other entities are needed in the future.

SUMMARY

1. Bottomland forests occur on the floodplains of the lower Piedmont, lower Mississippi River Valley, and Coastal Plain of the southeastern United States. The timing and duration of flooding and the deposition of suspended materials on these floodplains are primarily responsible for the formation and maintenance of floodplains and their vegetational aspects. Distinct vegetational communities are associated with specific physiographic features of the floodplain.
2. Alluvial floodplains are primarily managed for water resources, crop production, livestock production, timber production, recreational resources, wildlife and fishery resources, and natural and wilderness values. Some of these management options are incompatible with wilderness and natural area management, while other options are compatible with the maintenance of natural values.
3. Research is one of the high priority needs required for

proper management of bottomland systems. Research should be primarily goal-oriented, management-oriented, and designed to monitor long-term change.

4. The bottomland ecosystem is one of the most threatened in the United States, primarily as a result of conversion to croplands and reservoirs. Preservation of representative bottomland hardwood areas is another priority need in the southeastern United States.

LITERATURE CITED

Anderson, D. 1983. Research goals for natural areas. Nat. Areas J. 3:27-32.

Bailey, R.G. 1980. Description of the ecoregions of the United States. USDA For. Serv., Misc. Publ. 1391.

Blair, W.D. 1981. The Conservancy's Richard King Mellon Grant: great expectations. The Nature Conservancy News 312:4-5.

Boyce, S.G. and N.D. Cost. 1974. Timber potentials in the wetland hardwoods. pp. 131-151, In N.C. Blount (ed.). Water resources, utilization and conservation in the environment. Taylor Printing Co., Reynolds, Ga.

Conner, R.N. 1978. Snag management for cavity nesting birds. pp. 120-128. In R.M. DeGraaf (tech. coord.), Proc. workshop: Management of southern forests for nongame birds, Jan. 24-26, 1978; Atlanta, Ga., USDA For. Serv. Tech. Rep. SE-14, Southeast. For. Exp. Stn., Asheville, NC.

Cowardin, L.M., V. Carter, F.C. Golet, and E.T. LaRoe. 1979. Classification of wetlands and deepwater habitats of the United States. U.S. Fish Wildl. Serv., Office of Biological Services, FWS/OBS-79/31, Washington, D.C.

Dickson, J.G. 1978. Forest bird communities of the bottomland hardwoods. pp. 66-73. In R.M. DeGraaf (tech. coord.), Proc. workshop: Management of Southern forests for nongame birds, Jan. 24-26, 1978; Atlanta, GA., USDA For. Serv. Gen. Tech. Rep. SE-14, Southeast. For. Exp. Stn., Asheville, NC.

Driscoll, R.S., D.L. Merkel, D.L. Radloff, D.E. Snyder, and J.S. Hagihara. 1984. An ecological land classification framework for the United States. USDA For. Serv., Misc. Publ. 1439, Washington, D.C.

Eyre, F.H. (ed.). 1980. Forest cover types of the United States and Canada. Society of American Foresters, Washington, D.C.

Federal Committee on Ecological Reserves. 1977. A directory of Research Natural Areas on federal lands of the United States of America. USDA For. Serv., Washington, D.C.

Frayer, W.E., T.J. Monahan, D.C. Bowden, and F.A. Graybill. 1983. Status and trends of wetlands and deepwater habitats in the conterminous United States, 1950's to 1970's. Dep. of Forest and Wood Sciences, Colorado State Univ., Ft. Collins, Colo.

Fredrickson, L.H. and T.S. Taylor. 1982. Management of seasonally flooded impoundments for wildlife. U.S. Fish Wildl. Serv., Resour. Publ. 148, Washington, D.C.

Gagliano, S.M. and B.G. Thom. 1967. Deweyville Terrace, Gulf and Atlantic Coasts. pp. 23-41. In Tech. Rep. 39. Bull. 1, La. State Univ. Studies, Baton Rouge, La.

Hair, J.D., G.T. Hepp, L.M. Luckett, K.P. Reese, and D.K. Woodward. 1978. Beaver pond ecosystems and their relationships to multi-use

natural resources management. pp. 80-92. In R.R. Johnson and J.F. McCormick (tech. coords.), Strategies for protection and management of floodplain wetlands and other riparian ecosystems. Proc. Symp. Dec. 11-13, 1978; Callaway Gardens, GA, USDA For. Serv. Gen. Tech. Rep. WO-12, Washington, D.C.

Hendee, J.C., G.H. Stankey, and R.G. Lucas. 1978. Wilderness management. USDA For. Serv., Misc. Publ. 1365, Washington, D.C.

Jahn, L.R. 1978. Values of riparian habitats to natural ecosystems. pp. 157-160. In R.R. Johnson and J.F. McCormick (tech. coords), Strategies for protection and management of floodplain wetlands and other riparian ecosystems, Proc. Symp. Dec. 11-13, 1978; Callaway Gardens, Ga., USDA For. Serv. Gen. Tech. Rep. WO-12, Washington, D.C.

Larson, J.S., M.S. Bedinger, C.F. Bryan, S. Brown, R.T. Huffman, E.L. Miller, D.G. Rhodes, and B.A. Touchet. 1981. Transition from wetlands to uplands in southeastern bottomland hardwood forests. pp. 225-273. In J.R. Clark and J. Benforado (eds.), Wetlands of bottomland hardwood forests. Proc. of a workshop on bottomland hardwood forest wetlands of the southeastern United States held at Lake Lanier, Ga., June 1-5, 1980; Developments in agricultural and managed-forest ecology, Vol. 11. Elsevier Scientific Publishing Company, New York.

Lyon, L.J. 1978. Information requirements for wildlife management. pp. 45-52. In H.G. Lund, et al. (tech. coords.), Integrated inventories of renewable natural resources: proc. of the workshop, Jan. 8-12, 1978; Tucson, Ariz., USDA For. Serv. Gen. Tech. Rep. RM-55, Rocky Mt. For. and Range Exp. Stn., Ft. Collins, Colo.

Patton, D.R. 1977. Riparian research needs. pp. 80-82. In R.R. Johnson and D.A. Jones (tech. coords.), Importance, preservation and management of riparian habitat: a symposium. July 9, 1977, Tucson, Ariz., USDA For. Serv. Gen. Tech. Rep. RM-43, Rocky Mt. For. Range Exp. Stn., Ft. Collins, Colo.

Putnam, J.A., G.M. Furnival and J.S. McKnight. 1960. Management and inventory of southern hardwoods. USDA For. Serv. Agric. Handb. 181, Washington, D.C.

Samson, F.B. 1979. Lowland hardwood bird communities. pp. 49-66. In R.M DeGraaf (tech. coord.). Proc. workshop: management of northcentral and northeastern forests for nongame birds. Jan. 23-25, 1979, Minneapolis, Minn., USDA For. Serv. Gen. Tech. Rep. NC-51, North Cent. For. Exp. Stn., St. Paul, Minn.

Shaw, S.P. and C.G. Fredine. 1956. Wetlands of the United States. U.S. Fish Wildl. Serv., Circ. 39, Washington, D.C.

Stankey, G.H., D.N. Cole, R.C. Lucas, M.E. Petersen, and S.S. Frissel. 1985. The limits of acceptable change (lac) system for wilderness planning. USDA For. Serv., Gen. Tech. Rep. INT-176, Intermt. For. and Range Exp. Stn., Ogden, Utah.

Sternitzke, H.S. 1976. Impact of changing land use on Delta hardwood forests. J. For. 74:25-27.

USDA Forest Service. 1973. Silvicultural systems for the major forest types of the United States. USDA Handb. 445, Washington, D.C.

U.S. Fish and Wildlife Service. 1985. Texas bottomland hardwood preservation program. Albuquerque, NM.

Wharton, C.H. 1980. Values and functions of bottomland hardwoods. Trans. N. Am. Wildl. and Nat. Resour. Conf. 45:341-353.

Wharton, C.H., W.M. Kitchens, and T.W. Sipe. 1982. The ecology of bottomland hardwood swamps of the southeast: a community profile. U.S. Fish Wildl. Serv., Office of Biological Services, FWS/OBS-81/37, Washington, D.C.

Water Yield And Quality From Undisturbed Forested Watersheds In East Texas

by
W.H. Blackburn and J.C. Wood

ABSTRACT--Three small forested watersheds in East Texas were monitored from 1980 through 1984 for water quality and yield. Water yields ranged from 0.48 to 1.4 ha-cm/yr with a mean of 0.87 ha-cm/yr. Mean annual sediment loss was 48.6 kg/ha, and ranged from 4.8 to 184.0 kg/ha. Mean nitrate nitrogen, total filtered nitrogen, and total phosphorus losses were 6.9, 124.2, and 14.1 g/ha/yr, respectively. Losses, however, ranged from 2.0 to 14.3 g/ha/yr for nitrate nitrogen; from 50.7 to 243.8 g/ha/yr for total filtered nitrogen; and from 4.8 to 33.0 g/ha/yr for total phosphorus. These data represent expected water yields and quality from wilderness areas in East Texas. Water quality from wilderness areas can generally be expected to be of a high quality and not to exceed values presented in this paper.

KEYWORDS: sediment, nitrogen, phosphorus, clearcut, wilderness.

Undisturbed forest watersheds or wilderness areas are a primary source of high quality water, and sediment and nutrients seldom present a water quality problem. Forest vegetation, together with litter and ground cover, provide maximum protection to the soil surface and minimize the amount of mineral soil exposed to the erosive forces of raindrop impact and overland flow. Although the water quality from undisturbed forests is generally good, intense rainfall events may result in substantial sediment and nutrient losses. This paper provides water yield and quality data for undisturbed forests in East Texas.

METHODS

Study Site

The three study watersheds are located in Southwest Cherokee County in East Texas. The watersheds range in size from 2.61 to 2.66 ha and are located within a 1.6 kilometer radius of each other. The area is characterized by rolling topography with numerous drainages. Slopes range from 4% near the ridges to as much as 25% for short distances near stream channels. The study site experiences long, warm summers and relatively short, mild winters. Mean annual temperature is 19 degrees C with an average frost-free season of 264 days. Annual precipitation of 107 cm is fairly well distributed throughout the year (USDC 1980). Major vegetation is shortleaf pine (*Pinus echinata*) and mixed hardwoods dominated primarily by oak species. The area had been previously managed under a selective cutting system, with the last harvest occurring in 1972.

Soils were developed from marine deposited sediments of the Queen City Sand geologic formation. The predominant soil series are the Cuthbert and Kirvin, which comprise 78% of the soils found on the watersheds. These soils are classified as clayey, mixed thermic typic Hapludults. The Kirvin series dominates the upper slopes and the Cuthbert, the side slopes.

Methods

Precipitation was measured by a network of 14 standard and 2 recording rain gauges. Stormflow volumes were measured with 0.91 m H-flumes equipped with FW-1 type water level recorders. A Coshocton wheel sampler was used to collect a composite water sample. The day following each runoff event, a subsample was taken from a throughly-mixed collection of runoff from each watershed. Suspended sediment was determined by vacuum filtering each subsample through 0.45 micron filters, oven drying at 60 degrees C, and weighing. Suspended sediment loss from each event was calculated by multiplying sediment concentration by the volume of stormflow and dividing by the watershed area to convert to losses per hectare.

Coarse sediment was collected in a 1.7 m x 0.9 m x 0.2 m concrete drop box located at the front of the flume approach section. The sediment volume was determined after each storm and a sub-sample was oven-dried at 105 degrees C, weighed, and multiplied by the sediment volume. The total sediment deposited by each storm was divided by watershed area and expressed in kg/ha. Total sediment loss is the sum of suspended sediment and coarse sediment loss.

Samples collected for nitrogen and phosphorus were

frozen until analyzed for nitrates, total nitrogen, and total phosphorus, using a Technicon AutoAnalyzer II. Total nitrogen and nitrate samples were vacuum filtered through a 0.45 micron filter prior to analysis. Nitrates were analyzed by the cadmium reduction method (APHA *et al.* 1976). Total nitrogen, which includes organic and ammonia nitrogen, was measured using the ammonia/salicylate complex method after digestion with a salt/acid catalyst mixture (APHA *et al.* 1976). Total phosphorus was analyzed unfiltered. Total phosphorus samples were digested using the persulfate digestion method and concentrations were determined by the ascorbic acid reduction method (APHA *et al.* 1976).

A 10% inventory was made of the dominant and co-dominant trees and woody stems greater than 2.5 cm diameter breast height (dbh), using 0.04 ha circular plots. Ground cover was measured by point sampling (Levy and Madden 1933) at 20 cm intervals, along a series of 20 m transects. Surface cover was classified as litter, vegetation, rock, or mineral soil. If mineral soil was exposed, it was recorded as no erosion, sheet or rill erosion, or deposition.

RESULTS

Watershed Condition

Pine volumes on the three forest watersheds averaged 159,855 m cubed/ha for sawlogs and 239 m cubed/ha for pulpwood (Table 1). Hardwood sawlogs and pulpwood were relatively sparse and volumes averaged only 13,142 m cubed/ha and 117 m cubed/ha, respectively. The number of stems in the 2.5-12.7 cm dbh category were uniform among the watersheds and averaged 689 stems/ha.

Understory woody stems less than 2.5 cm in diameter are listed in Table 2. The number of pine seedlings averaged 10,209 stems/ha. Hardwoods, shrubs, and vines averaged 22,485, 14,581, and 26,536 stems/ha, respectively for the three watersheds.

Litter covered an average of 95.1% of the watersheds (Table 3). Rill and sheet erosion were evident on only 0.03% of the exposed mineral soil; thus the remaining soil was considered to be in stable condition.

Water Yield

Water yields ranged from 0.48 to 1.4 ha-cm/yr with a mean of 0.87 ha-cm/yr (Table 4). Runoff, as a percent of annual precipitation, averaged 2% for the five year period. A single storm on May 15, 1980 produced 75% of the total runoff for that year. The May 15th storm also resulted in the highest peak discharge rate of 11.5 ha-cm/hr (0.32 m cubed/s).

Water Quality

Sediment--The five year mean sediment loss was 48.6 kg/ha/yr and ranged from 4.8 to 184.0 kg/ha/yr. The May 15, 1980 storm was the primary source of sediment loss during 1980. Total sediment export from this one storm averaged 180.3 kg/ha, which represented 98% of the total sediment loss for the year.

Table 1. Tree Volumes and Stems/ha for the Undisturbed Watersheds, Alto, Texas, June 1980.

Watershed No.	Pine Sawlogs m³/ha	Pine Pulpwood m³/ha	Hardwoods Sawlogs m³/ha	Hardwoods Pulpwood m³/ha	Stems (dbh 2.5–12.7 cm)/ha Total
1	162,655	233	4,666	117	549
2	120,198	152	34,759	170	783
3	196,713	332	-0-	63	736
Mean	159,855	239	13,142	117	689

Table 2. Understory Woody Vegetation (Stems < 2.5 cm dbh/ha), for the Undisturbed Watersheds, Alto, Texas, June 1980.

Vegetation	Watershed No. 1	2	3	Mean
Pine				
Loblolly & Shortleaf pine	7,311	3,606	19,711	10,209
Hardwoods				
Total	26,577	19,241	21,637	22,485
Shrubs				
Total	17,315	13,881	12,548	14,581
Vines				
Total	23,169	17,315	39,125	26,536

Table 3. Ground Surface Condition (%) of the Undisturbed Watersheds, Alto, Texas, June 1980.

Surface Condition	Watershed No. 1	2	3	Mean
Litter	95.4	95.0	95.0	95.1
Rock	0.0	0.1	0.3	0.1
Mineral soil	2.6	3.4	3.7	3.2
Erosion				
Rill	0.1	0.0	0.0	0.0
Sheet	0.0	0.0	0.0	0.0
Deposition	0.0	0.0	0.0	0.0
Tree	0.8	0.3	0.4	0.5
Shrub	0.3	0.2	0.2	0.2
Grass	0.7	0.8	0.3	0.6
Forb	0.2	0.2	0.1	0.2
Moss	0.0	0.1	0.0	0.0

Table 4. Annual Precipitation, Water Yield and Quality from Three Undisturbed Forested Watersheds with Means for All Years Combined, Alto, Texas, 1980–1984.

Hydrologic Parameter	Year 1980	1981	1982	1983	1984	Mean
Precipitation cm	79.1	129.8	114.1	118.1	114.1	111.0
Water yield ha-cm/yr	1.40	1.05	0.48	0.86	0.56	0.87
Sediment kg/ha/yr	184.0	32.8	5.1	4.8	16.3	48.6
Nitrate g/ha/yr	12.5	3.1	2.5	2.0	14.3	6.9
Total nitrogen g/ha/yr	243.8	174.7	50.7	76.8	74.9	124.2
Total phosphorus g/ha/yr	33.0	15.3	4.8	6.3	11.3	14.1

Nutrients--Nitrate losses ranged from 2.0 to 14.3 g/ha/yr with an average of 6.9 g/ha/yr. Total nitrogen loss averaged 124.2 g/ha/yr and varied from 50.7 to 243.8 g/ha/yr. Total phosphorus loss ranged from 4.8 to 33.0 g/ha/yr and averaged 14.1 g/ha/yr. The intense rainstorm of May 15, 1980 was again responsible for 79%, 72%, and 90% of the nitrate, total nitrogen, and total phosphorus loss for the year, respectively.

DISCUSSION

Water yields from three undisturbed forest watersheds in East Texas were low and represented only 2 percent of the total precipitation. Of the precipitation falling on a mature forest, from 10 to 30 percent is intercepted by the forest canopy and lost to evaporation (Rogerson 1967). In most cases, the rain reaching the forest floor filters through the litter covered surface and infiltrates into the soil. Under certain circumstances of prolonged rainfall, such as the May 15, 1980 storm, the soil becomes saturated, the infiltration rate is reduced and overland flow occurs. Pierce (1967) found evidence of overland flow occurring over accumulated leaf debris and laterally at the interface of humus and/or litter layers and the mineral surface. Nonetheless, contribution to streamflow is primarily the result of subsurface flow (Hursch 1944, Whipkey 1967).

Sediment and nutrient losses from the three undisturbed forested watersheds were low, and well below tolerable levels. The natural sediment loss from undisturbed forests varies with location, soils, geology, vegetation, watershed size, and season. Research in the southeast has demonstrated that natural erosion rates from undisturbed forest range from a trace to 717 kg/ha/yr (Schrieber *et al.* 1980, Beasley 1982, Yoho 1980). Schrieber *et al.* (1976) found that nutrient losses from five undisturbed forests in northern Mississippi were less than the input from precipitation. Individual storm sediment and nutrient losses may occasionally be elevated due to the periodic flushing of sediment and nutrients which have collected in the stream channel. As evidenced by the May 15, 1980 storm, the potential for large sediment and nutrient losses from undisturbed forests exists under intense rainfall and high antecedent soil moisture conditions.

Research has demonstrated that properly applied silvicultural practices will not adversely impact the high water quality from undisturbed forests. Three additional forested watersheds in the same study area were clearcut and site prepared by roller chopping in the latter part of 1980 (Blackburn *et al.* 1985). Sediment and nutrient losses were similar to those from the undisturbed forest watersheds, while at the same time water yields were increased two-fold (Table 5).

Table 5.   Annual Precipitation, Water Yield and Water Quality from Three Clearcut Forest Watershed Sites Prepared by Roller Chopping with Means for All Years Combined, Alto, Texas, 1981–1984.

	1981	1982	1983	1984	Mean
Precipitation cm	129.8	114.1	118.1	114.1	119.0
Water yield ha-cm/yr	3.35	1.43	1.80	1.42	2.0
Sediment kg/ha/yr	25.1	5.5	5.4	16.3	13.1
Nitrate g/ha/yr	79.7	5.0	7.7	31.4	30.5
Total nitrogen g/ha/yr	670.5	117.2	168.7	204.4	290.2
Total phosphorus g/ha/yr	38.8	9.1	12.6	14.7	18.8

MANAGEMENT CONSIDERATIONS

Data presented in this paper represents expected water yields and quality from undisturbed forested watersheds in East Texas. These data also provide a baseline for water yield and quality from wilderness areas. Generally, wilderness areas can be expected to yield high quality water not to exceed values presented in this paper. This is especially true when state-of-the-art forest activities and site preparation methods are applied, and water quality, similar to that from undisturbed forest, can be maintained and water yields increased. Wilderness area managers should be aware of the potential for increased stream channel erosion by increased visitor activity, and for natural or man's activities, such as southern pine beetle or wild fires, that have the potential to temporarily increase water yields and quality above baseline values.

ACKNOWLEDGMENTS

Special acknowledgement is given to Mark G. DeHaven, Andrew T. Weichert, Patricia M. Fazio and T.K. Hunter for their assistance in the collection and analysis of research data. The financial support of the U.S. Forest Service, Texas Forestry Association, Office of Water Research and Technology and Texas Water Resources Institute is appreciated.

LITERATURE CITED

American Public Health Assoc., American Water Works Assoc., Water Pollution Control Federation. 1976. Standard Methods for the Examination of Water and Wastewater. Fourteenth Edition. American Public Health Assoc., Washington, D.C.

Beasley, R.S. 1982. Water quality in south Arkansas forests. *In.* Proc. Environmentally Sound Water and Soil Management, Irrig. and Drainage Div. of the Am. Soc. Civil Eng., Orlando, Florida.

Blackburn, W.H., J.C. Wood and M.G. DeHaven. 1985. Forest harvesting and site preparation impacts on stormflow and water quality in East Texas. Proc. of Forestry and Water Quality: Midsouth Symposium, Little Rock, AK.

Hursch, C.R. 1944. Report of sub-committee on subsurface flow. Amer. Geophys. Union Trans., Part V, 743-746.

Levy, E.B. and E.A. Madden. 1933. The point method of pasture analysis. New Zealand J. Agr. 43:267-279.

Pierce, R.S. 1967. Evidence of overland flow on forest watersheds. pp. 247-253. *In* W.E. Sopper and H.W. Lull (eds.). International Symp. on For. Hydrology. Pergamon Press, Elmsford, New York.

Rogerson, T.T. 1967. Throughfall in pole-sized loblolly pine as affected by stand density. pp. 187-190 *In* W.E. Sopper and H.W. Lull (eds.). International Symp. on For. Hydrology. Pergamon Press, Elmsford, New York.

Schrieber, J.D., P.D. Duffy and D.C. McClurkin. 1976. Dissolved nutrient losses in storm runoff from five southern pine watersheds. J. Environ. Qual. 5:201-205.

Schrieber, J.D., P.D. Duffy and D.C. McClurkin. 1980. Aqueous- and sediment-phase nitrogen yields from five southern pine watersheds. Soil Sci. Soc. Am. J. 44:401-407.

USDC, NOAA. 1980. Climatological Data, Texas. 85(13).

Whipkey, R.Z. 1967. Theory and mechanics of subsurface streamflow. pp. 255-260. *In* W.E. Sopper and H.W. Lull (eds.). International Symp. on For. Hydrology. Pergamon Press, Elmsford, New York.

Yoho, N.S. 1980. Forest management and sediment production in the South - a review. So. J. Appl. For. 4:27-36.

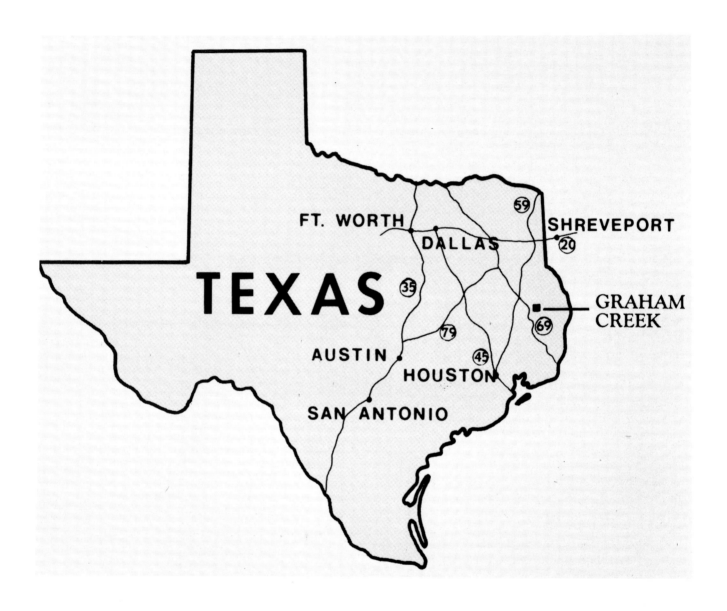

Limnological Aspects Of Upland Island: A Wilderness Area In East Texas

Jennifer A. Sidnell, Clarence W. Reed, and Jack D. McCullough

ABSTRACT--In 1980, a physico-chemical and biological investigation of the major streams and ponds in the Upland Island Area was conducted. Falls, Graham, and Cypress Creeks were found to be the most sensitive habitats with good water quality and diverse aquatic communities. All streams had low primary productivity rates and had detrital based food chains. Oxygen concentrations were marginal because of abundant leaf litter, and flow rates were critical for diverse benthic communities. Reduction of leaf litter, stream side vegetation, and formation of trails in the watersheds would probably have serious consequences on streams. Management to prevent erosion and sedimentation is recommended.

KEYWORDS: wilderness, streams, ponds, water quality, benthic macroinvertebrates, plankton, fish.

In 1980, an ecological study was conducted on the Upland Island Area (also known as the Graham Creek Area), a 3,650 ha tract of pine-hardwood forest located in the Angelina National Forest in eastern Texas. Subsequent to that investigation, the United States Congress has designated the Upland Island Area as a wilderness. That wilderness area is within the Southern Evergreen Forest formation (Tharp 1926), or region (Braun 1950), characterized by pines and hardwoods, with longleaf pine the dominant species. Also, within this region, are the floodplains of various rivers. The Neches River forms the southern boundary of the wilderness area and is part of the Bottomland Forest formation characterized by Bray (1906) as a typical mesophytic formation of the South Atlantic (Austroriparian) type. The purpose of this research was to evaluate the major aquatic ecosystems within the Upland Island Wilderness and to identify the more sensitive streams. Recommendations for preservation management are also given.

DESCRIPTION OF COLLECTION SITES

Eight collecting sites were selected within the wilderness area (Fig. 1). Station 1 was located on Oil Well Creek which flows through a beech-magnolia community. The collecting site was a pool, in water less than one meter deep. Station 2 was on Big Creek, also in a pool area less than one meter deep. Vegetation surrounding the area was predominantly beech and magnolia trees. Station 3 was in an acid bog surrounded by sweetgum trees. At the deepest point, the bog was 1.5 meters deep,

and measured 60 meters long and 50 meters wide. Station 4 was a swamp area, with pine and sweetgum predominating. A dense canopy of vegetation supplied a deep layer of leaf litter on the bottom of the pond. Station 5 was located midway along Falls Creek in a pool area. Surrounding vegetation was predominantly pine and hardwood species. Station 6 was located in a pool on Graham Creek in a heavily forested, palmetto, bottomland area. Station 7 was located in a pool and a riffle area on Cypress Creek. Cypress, pine, and hardwoods dominated the canopy over the creek. Station 8 was located in a shallow pond with a sparse stand of pines along the shoreline. A few shrubs grew in the shallow area within the pond, and thick mats of sphagnum moss grew along the margin.

METHODS AND MATERIALS

Physico-Chemical Methods

All water samples for chemical analysis were collected just below the surface and stored in darkness on ice for transport to the laboratory. Stream flow rates, water temperature, dissolved oxygen, carbon dioxide, and alkalinity were determined in the field, using a Yellow Spring Oxygen and Temperature meter, model 54, and procedures reported in *Standard Methods* (APHA 1980). Calcium and sodium were analyzed using a Beckman Flame Spectrophotometer, model B, while iron, sulfate, orthophosphate, total phosphorus, nitrate, nitrite, ammonium, and color (true and apparent) were determined using colorimetric methods (APHA 1980). Optical density was

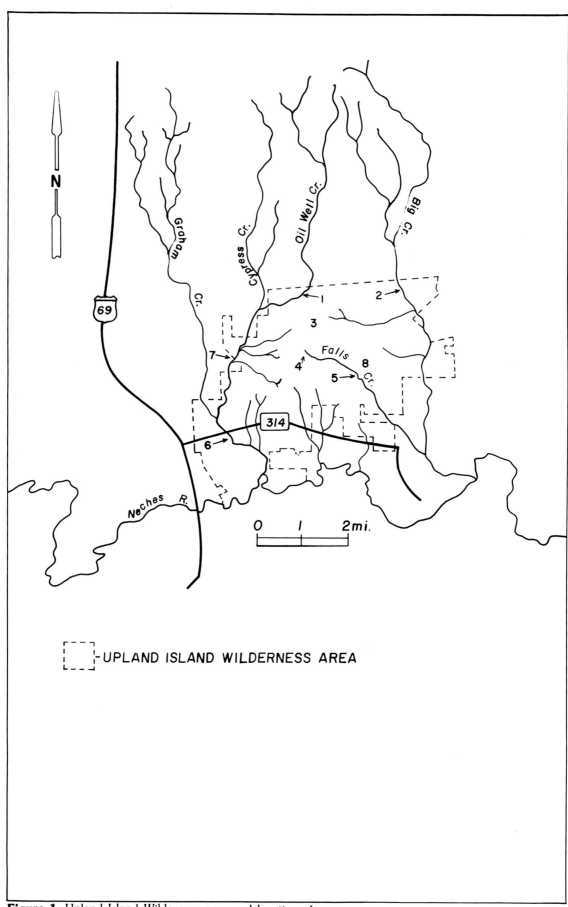

Figure 1. Upland Island Wilderness area and location of collecting sites.

determined using a Bausch and Lomb Spectrophotometer, model 70. Biochemical oxygen demand (BOD) was determined after samples were incubated five days in a Lab-Line incubator and using a Yellow Springs BOD oxygen probe and oxygen meter (APHA 1980). Turbidity was determined using a Hach Turbidimeter, model 2100A, and total suspended solids (TSS) were determined gravimetrically using a Mettler Analytical Balance, model H10. Chloride concentrations were analyzed by the mercuric nitrate method, and phytoplankton chlorophyll a concentrations were determined using a Turner Flourometer, model 110 (APHA 1980). Total Kjeldahl nitrogen was determined by a method reported by the EPA (1971).

Benthic Community Methods

Five grabs were collected along a transect at each site using an Ekman Dredge, and a wash bucket with a No. 30 screen bottom (0.59mm). Identifications were made using Edmondson (1959), Mason (1973), Hobbs (1976), Merritt (1978), and Pennak (1978). Species diversity was computed using Shannon's equation (Shannon and Weaver 1963). Benthic productivity was determined using a method reported by Menzie (1980).

Plankton Methods

Zooplankton were collected by pouring a known volume of water through a No. 20 plankton net. Samples were preserved and populations were estimated using methods reported by Lind (1979). Organisms were identified using Pennak (1978) and Edmondson (1959). Phytoplankton were collected by centrifuging one liter of water from each site in a Foerst Plankton Centrifuge. Population estimates were done using methods in Lind (1979), and identification of algal species were based on keys from Whitford and Schumacher (1973) and Patrick (1966). Periphyton productivity was done using an artificial substrate technique (APHA 1980).

Fish Collection and Coliform Bacteria Methods

Fish were seined from each creek and a list of taxa compiled. Identification of fish were based on keys from Eddy and Underhill (1980). Samples for coliform analysis were collected in sterilized 250 ml erlynmeyer flasks and stoppered with cotton plugs. *Standard Methods* procedures were used (APHA 1980), and values were reported in MPN/100, or the most probable number of coliform bacteria per 100 mililiters of water.

RESULTS AND DISCUSSION

The results of chemical and biological data suggest that the streams fall into two categories: Falls, Graham, and Cypress Creeks were found to be the most sensitive ecological areas, while Oil Well Creek and Big Creek were found to be more stressed habitats. The ponds were also stressed, ephemeral, bodies of water, but were none the less important in the forest ecosystem.

Streams

Table 1 reflects slightly stressful conditions in several of the streams. Dissolved oxygen values, while not anoxic, occasionally fell below 5 mg/L, which can be stressful to some aquatic organisms. Those concentrations were due to an abundance of decaying leaf litter on the stream bottom. While the benthic oxygen demand was high, the oxygen demand of organisms suspended in the water column

Table 1. Physicochemical Means for All Stream Stations Sampled in the Upland Island Area during the Summer of 1980.

Parameter	Station				
	1	2	5	6	7
O^2	4.5	5.4	5.9	5.4	4.2
Temp ($^{\circ}$C)	23.7	24.5	23.5	25.1	25.3
CO_2	21.6	32.8	18.0	15.6	24.4
HCO_3 alk.	43.8	31.7	40.3	67.7	24.4
pH	6.7	6.5	6.5	6.8	6.6
Turbidity (NTU's)	21.8	20.0	16.3	23.3	28.2
Ca	0.2	0.2	trace	trace	trace
Na	17.3	22.8	11.0	26.9	17.3
Cl	15.8	24.3	11.0	29.5	17.7
Fe	2.42	1.64	2.17	1.45	2.55
SO_4	28.4	59.4	17.8	39.1	33.6
PO_4	0.36	0.12	0.14	0.25	0.25
Total phos.	0.64	0.38	0.41	0.51	0.62
NO_3-N	0.03	0.01	0.01	0.04	0.02
NO_2-N	0.06	0.03	0.04	0.05	0.05
NH_4-N	1.37	1.18	1.03	1.40	1.49
Total Kjeldahl nitrogen	3.05	3.87	3.78	3.39	5.04
Chlorophyll a (ug/L)	1.3	1.7	trace	1.2	0.8
BOD	1.7	1.1	1.4	1.2	1.4
Total suspended solids	55.6	22.3	12.6	34.1	92.1
Flow rate (CMS)	0.02	0.02	0.09	0.23	0.04
Conductivity (micromhos)	133	186	49	251	135
App. color (cu)	98	95	79	76	117
True color (cu)	64	61	61	64	68

Parameters are expressed in mg/L unless otherwise indicated.

(BOD) was relatively low. Coliform bacteria numbers (Table 2) were somewhat elevated, but those values probably originated from soils and from wildlife fecal input. Nitrogen and phosphorous concentrations were relatively high, probably because of decaying leaf litter, but shading from the heavy forest canopy greatly limited phytoplankton and periphyton density. In addition, turbidity and color

Table 2. Coliform Counts (MPN) for Stream Stations Sampled in the Upland Island Area during the Summer of 1980.

Date	Station				
	1	2	5	6	7
May 28, 1980	1400	1800	5300	1400	2100
June 11, 1980	666	1246	1263	966	710

values were somewhat elevated, further restricting algal populations in the streams. The color values were partly due to dissolved organic matter from decaying vegetation, but also to relatively high iron concentrations. East Texas streams, generally, have high iron values because of the soils in this region. Generally, the streams were found to contain soft, slightly acid water with low sulfate, chloride, and sodium concentrations.

Benthic macroinvertebrates, because of their relatively low mobility, are good indicators in water quality studies. Mayflies, caddisflies, and stoneflies in high numbers, indicate good water quality, whereas the dominance of more pollution tolerant organisms, such as oligochaetes and chironomids, reflect stressful conditions. Figure 2 would suggest Oil Well creek and Big Creek were the most stressful environments. Graham and Cypress creeks were considerably less stressed, and benthic indicators in Falls Creek reflected very little stress. The mean benthic species diversity indices (Table 3) supports those observations. Oil Well and Big Creeks had the lowest benthic diversity. Dissolved oxygen values were near stressful levels in all the streams, but flow rates seemed to be the important difference between streams. Gaufin (1973) reports that flow rate is a very important factor in the survival of aquatic insects when exposed to lower oxygen concentra-

Table 3. Species Diversity and Redundancy of the Stream Benthos Sampled at the Upland Island Area during the Summer of 1980.

Date		Station				
		1	2	5	6	7
May 28	d	1.44	0.0	1.59	2.00	2.54
	r	<.01	0.0	0.28	0.08	0.07
June 11	d	0.0	1.56	1.54	2.29	1.55
	r	0.0	0.69	0.40	<.01	<.01
June 25	d	1.00	0.92	1.91	1.73	2.34
	r	<.01	<.01	0.21	0.49	0.14
July 9	d	0.0	1.00	—	1.76	1.58
	r	0.0	<.01	—	0.48	<.01
July 23	d	1.50	—	—	1.97	1.32
	r	0.60	—	—	<.01	0.35
Mean	d	0.79	0.87	1.68	1.95	1.87

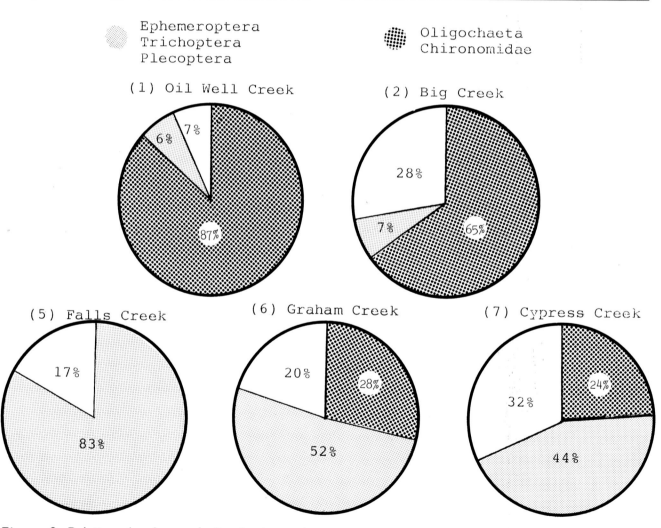

Figure 2. Relative abundance of oligochaetes and chironomids; ephemeropterans, trichopterans, and plecopterans; and other taxa collected at five streams in the Upland Island Area.

tions. Insects are able to tolerate lower oxygen levels in increased flow rates, and both Oil Well and Big Creeks had the lowest rates. Benthic standing crop and productivity were relatively low in all the streams, but Oil Well and Big Creeks had the lowest (Table 4).

Blancher (1984) reports that in the zooplankton community, cladocera and copepods generally predominate in less euthrophic habitats, while rotifers dominate in more euthropic waters. Again, Oil Well and Big Creeks had the larger numbers of rotifers (Fig. 3 and Table 5-6).

Phytoplankton populations were relatively low, as reflected by phytoplankton chlorophyll *a* values and by cell counts (Table 7). Shading, color, and turbidity were probably the limiting factors. Diatom species of *Navicula*, *Nitzschia*, *Synedra*, and *Melosira* were frequent and indicated stressful conditions. However, that impact was lessened somewhat by the presence of clean water indicators *Cyclotella*, *Pinnularia*, *Surirella*, *Achnanthes*, *Cymbella*, and *Frustulia* (Fig. 4). The periphyton community was very similar to the phytoplankton (Table 8), in fact, much of the phytoplankton probably came from the

Table 4. Organisms per m^2, mg. wet wt./m^2 (parentheses) and Productivity of the Benthic Macroinvertebrates Collected from Streams in the Upland Island Area during the Summer of 1980.

Date	Station				
	1	2	5	6	7
May 28	473	43	869	165	89
	(524)	(83)	(1686)	(243)	(186)
June 11	9	164	1376	172	22
	(18)	(229)	(2534)	(5830)	(11494)
July 9	34	18	—	86	9
	(26)	(11)	—	(479)	(11)
July 23	138	—	—	96	58
	(292)	—	—	(891)	(103)
Mean	134	63	843	126	287
	(184)	(87)	(1493)	(1535)	(2450)
Productivity	0.76	0.13	2.89	1.21	0.35

Table 6. The Occurrence of Zooplankton at Collecting Sites in the Upland Island Area during the Summer of 1980.

Genus	Station							
	1	2	3	4	5	6	7	8
Copepoda								
Canthocamptus				X	X	X		
Cyclops			X	X				X
Ectocylops	X	X		X				X
Eucyclops	X	X	X		X	X	X	
Paracyclops				X				
Cladocera								
Alona			X		X		X	
Bosmina	X	X		X		X		X
Ceriodaphnia			X					X
Chydoras			X					X
Daphnia		X		X				X
Macrothrix			X					
Scapholeberis	X	X	X	X	X	X		X
Rotifera								
Asplancha			X	X				
Brachionus	X	X	X					
Keratella	X	X	X	X	X	X	X	X
Lecane	X			X		X	X	
Manfredium			X					
Platyias				X				
Rotaria	X	X			X	X	X	X
Testudinella				X				

Table 5. Organisms per Liter and Relative Abundance (%) of Copepods, Cladocerans, and Rotifers Collected from All Stations in the Upland Island Area during the Summer of 1980.

		Station							
		1	2	3	4	5	6	7	8
May 28	Copepods	37	36	34	72	89	84	53	
	Cladocerans	27	40	48	22	8	8	20	
	Rotifers	36	24	18	6	3	8	27	
	Orgs/liter	2	2	240	500	53	42	3	
June 11	Copepods	72	62			90	53	66	
	Cladocerans	20	20			8	30	29	
	Rotifers	8	18			2	17	6	
	Orgs/liter	3	5			8	18	2	
June 25	Copepods	78	67			83	90	70	
	Cladocerans	17	20			11	4	22	
	Rotifers	5	13			6	6	8	
	Orgs/liter	2	7			18	12	2	
July 9	Copepods	61	67			82	57	60	44
	Cladocerans	17	22			5	29	30	18
	Rotifers	22	11			13	14	10	38
	Orgs/liter	18	7			26	30	4	123
July 23	Copepods	81					92	96	
	Cladocerans	7					6	1	
	Rotifers	12					2	3	
	Orgs/liter	35					16	32	

periphyton community. Periphyton primary productivity was relatively low (Table 9). Mean productivity values ranged from 54 to 186 mg Carbon/m squared/day. Wetzel (1979) suggests that values between 50 and 300 mg C/m squared/day represent very low production (Oligotrophic conditions). Since phytoplankton and periphyton production were low, the importance of the abundant leaf litter in the streams is apparent. All of the streams had detrital based food chains, rather than grazing food chains. Leaf litter input is absolutely vital in these stream ecosystems.

Table 7.   Organisms per Liter of Phytoplankton Collected from All Stations at the Upland Island Area during the Summer of 1980.

	Station							
	1	2	3	4	5	6	7	8
May 28	260	400	2200	2200	480	360	280	
June 11	130	720			170	540	320	
June 25	120	1020			210	190	140	
July 9	2680	1180			420	400	500	3220
July 23	3240					850	1180	

Table 8.   Relative Abundance (%) of Diatoms Collected from Periphyton Samples on June 11, 1980 in the Upland Island Area.

	Station				
Genus	1	2	5	6	7
Achnanthes	4.6	2.5	3.5		2.9
Capartogramma			0.9	0.8	
Cocconeis	0.8	0.8			1.0
Cyclotella	3.1				
Cymbella	13.0	5.8	1.7	3.0	5.7
Diploneis	2.3			3.0	
Eunotia	11.5	25.8	7.0	7.3	12.4
Frustulia	6.2	2.5	6.1	4.5	3.8
Gomphonema	1.5	4.2	0.9	5.3	2.9
Gyrosigma	0.8				1.0
Melosira	2.3	1.7	1.7	0.8	1.9
Navicula	14.6	7.5	20.0	17.2	24.8
Neidium					1.9
Nitzschia	8.5	15.8	12.2	37.1	20.0
Pinnularia	6.9	7.5	13.9	5.3	7.6
Rhopalodia	3.1		1.7	0.8	1.9
Stauroneis	6.9	1.7	2.6	2.3	1.9
Surirella	5.4	5.0	4.3	7.3	6.5
Synedra	8.5	19.2	23.5	4.5	3.8

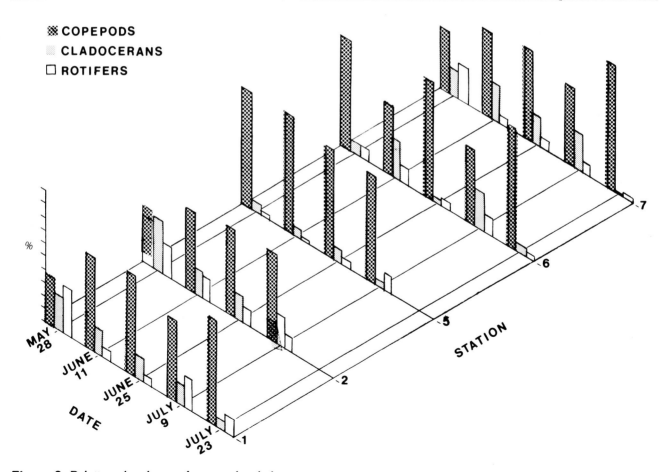

Figure 3. Relative abundance of copepods, cladocerans, and rotifers in the zooplankton of streams sampled in the Upland Island Area.

A relatively diverse fish community was found in all of the streams (Table 10). The assemblage of fish is typical of unpolluted East Texas streams, but are species that can tolerate less than 5 mg/L of dissolved oxygen for short periods of time.

Ponds

All of the ponds were found to be temporary and very environmentally stressed, aquatic habitats. Dissolved oxygen values were often less than 5 mg/L and dropped to as low as 1.1 mg/L. The pH at station 8 was 4.9, possibly because of the sphagnum moss beds. Station 4 had 95.7% oligochaetes and chironomids and station 8 had 89.4%. Zooplankton and phytoplankton populations were abundant (Table 6 and Table 7). The phytoplankton collected from the ponds were dominated by desmids *Eustrum, Desmidium* and *Xanthidium*, genera associated with acid water (Table 11). Station 3 was highly stressed (3.5 mg/L of oxygen) due to the dense mat of leaf litter, and the phytoplankton there was dominated by a small *Chlorella*-like alga, indicating organically polluted conditions. Stressful conditions at station 8 were reflected by the dominance of *Stigeoclonium*, an alga also associated with polluted water.

Management Recommendations

Falls, Graham, and Cypress Creeks were found to be sensitive aquatic habitats, and those areas would be most vulnerable to disturbance by man. Removal of vegetation from streamside on any of the streams or from any of the tributaries would be especially detrimental, since all the streams in the Upland Island Area have detrital based food chains. Falls Creek is the most environmentally sensitive of the habitats studied. It is an area of considerable aesthetic appeal, with lush, dense, vegetation along the

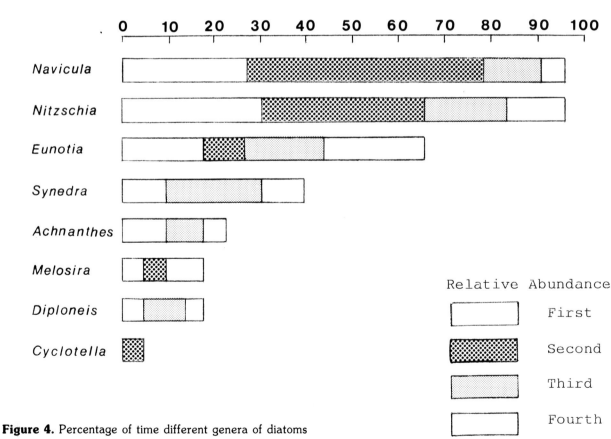

Figure 4. Percentage of time different genera of diatoms were first, second, third, or fourth in abundance in plankton samples collected from streams in the Upland Island Area. Only those genera that were first or second in abundance at least once are listed.

334

stream, and a thick canopy over the stream bed. The deep shading there resulted in cooler water compared with the other streams, thus higher oxygen values. Falls Creek and Cypress Creek were the only streams with populations of stoneflies (Plecoptera), which were indicators of good water quality and require high oxygen concentrations. The Falls Creek area is very remote, and the streamside vegetation provides an extensive wildlife habitat, supporting diverse avian, mammal, reptile, and amphibian communities. Certainly no seining or specimen collecting should be permitted. Human intervention should be kept at a minimum in the three sensitive areas. Trails created by the use, the cutting of trees, shrubs, or herbaceous vegetation, or the reduction in leaf litter near those streams will increase erosion and greatly disrupt biotic communities by increased sedimentation. No water removal from the streams should be permitted because of low discharge rates. Camping activity should be restricted

to the higher elevations. No wastewater from man's activities should be allowed to enter any of the watersheds, because of the low discharge rates and because the streams are stressed to a degree by leaf litter.

The temporary ponds, while ephemeral and highly stressed bodies of water, are nevertheless quite important in the forest ecosystem. They support diverse amphibian and reptilian populations. In addition, a variety of birds and mammals were observed to feed on prey, in, and attracted to the ponds, and the ponds supplied a source of drinking water for them. Not only did many invertebrates complete their life cycles in those ponds, the rare Hillard's Toothpick Grasshopper (*Achurum hilliardi*) was found in the grasses and sedges which surround low wetlands in the Upland Island Area.

Because of their very shallow depth, the greatest danger to the ponds is filling in by sedimentation through erosion. Proper vegetation management and other erosion preventative measures must be practiced in the immediate vicinity of the marshes and temporary ponds.

Table 9. Primary Productivity, mg Ash-Free wt/m²/day, Dry Weight (g/m²), and Ash-Free wt [g/m²] of Periphyton from Stream Stations Sampled at the Upland Island Area in the Summer of 1980.

Date	Station 1	2	5	6	7
June 11	238.1	182.2	309.9	213.2	98.9
	(32.7)	(28.2)	(33.6)	(33.2)	(13.0)
	[3.3]	[2.6]	[4.3]	[3.0]	[1.4]
July 9	150.8	49.2	377.7	149.2	261.9
	(44.3)	(41.1)	(36.2)	(39.6)	(28.3)
	[5.1]	[1.7]	[12.9]	[5.0]	[8.8]
July 9	351.6	66.6			300.0
	(45.3)	(65.7)	SL	SL	(29.0)
	[11.8]	[2.2]			[10.1]
Mean	246.8	99.3	343.8	181.2	220.3
	(40.8)	(45.1)	(35.0)	(36.4)	(23.4)
	[6.7]	[2.1]	[8.6]	[4.0]	[6.8]

SL—sampler lost.

LITERATURE CITED

American Public Health Association. 1980. Standard methods for the examination of water and wastewater. 12th ed. APHA, New York, New York.

Blancher, E.C. 1984. Zooplankton-trophic state relationships in some north and central Florida lakes. Hydrobiologia 109: 251-263.

Braun, E.L. 1950. Deciduous forests of eastern North America. The Blankiston Company, Philadelphia, Penn.

Bray, W.L. 1906. Distribution and adaptation of the vegetation of Texas. Univ. Tex. Bull. 82.

Eddy, S. and J.C. Underhill. 1980. How to know the fresh-water fishes. Wm. C. Brown Company Publishers, Dubuque, Iowa.

Table 10. The Occurrence of Fish Species at Collection Sites in the Upland Island Area during the Summer of 1980.

Species	Station 1	2	5	6	7
Esox americanus redfin pickerel		X			
Phenacobius mirabilis suckermouth minnow		X	X		
Opsopoeodus emiliae pugnose minnow		X			
Notropis venustus blacktail shiner				X	
Notropis umbratilis redfin shiner	X	X			X
Erimyzon oblongus creek chubsucker	X	X			
Ictalurus melas black bullhead				X	
Fundulus notatus blackstripe topminnow	X		X		
Fundulus olivaceus blackspotted topminnow					X
Gambusia affinis mosquitofish		X	X	X	X
Centrarchus macropterus flier				X	
Chaenobryttus gulosus warmouth			X		
Lepomis megalotis longear sunfish	X	X	X	X	X
Lepomis macrochirus Bluegill			X		

Table 11. Relative Abundance (%) of Non-Diatom Phytoplankters Collected in the Upland Island Area during the Summer of 1980.

Genus	Station[1] 3	4	8
Ankistrodesmus	10.9		
Chlorella-like		83.3	
Closterium	4.7		
Desmidium	18.8		
Dinobryon			37.4
Euastrum	38.3		
Euglena		3.7	
Oscillatoria	2.3	0.9	9.4
Pleurotaenium	3.1		
Spirogyra	3.9		
Staurastrum	0.8		
Stigeoclonium			52.3
Xanthidium	17.2		

[1] Stations 3 and 4 collected May 28, 1980, station 8 collected July 9, 1980.

Edmondson, W.T. (ed.). 1959. Freshwater biology, 2nd ed. John Wiley and Sons, New York, New York.

Environmental Protection Agency. 1971. Methods for chemical analysis of water and wastes. 16020-07/71.USEPA, Cincinnati, Ohio.

Gaufin, A.R. 1973. Water quality requirements of aquatic insects. Project 18050FLS. EPA, Corvallis, Oregon.

Hobbs, H.H. 1976. Creyfishes (Astacidae) of North and Middle America. EPA Water Pollution Control Research Series 10850 ELD05/72.

Lind, O.T. 1979. Handbook of common methods of limnology. 2nd ed. C.V. Mosby, St. Louis, Mo.

Mason, W.T. 1973. An introduction to the identification of chironomid larvae. EPA.

Menzie, C.A. 1980. A note on the Hynes Methods of estimating secondary production. Limnol. Oceanogr. 25:770-773.

Merritt, R.W. and K.W. Cummins (eds.). 1978. An introduction to the aquatic insects of North America. Kendall/Hunt, Iowa.

Patrick, R. 1966. Diatoms of the United States. The Academy of Natural Sciences of Philadelphia, Philadelphia, Penn.

Pennak, R.W. 1978. Fresh-water invertebrates of the United States. 2nd ed. John Wiley and Sons, New York, New York.

Shannon, C.D. and W. Weaver. 1963. The mathematical theory of communication. Univ. Illinois Press, Urbana, Ill.

Tharp, B.C. 1926. Structure of Texas vegetation east of the 98th meridian. Univ. Tex. Bull. 2606.

Wetzel, R.G. 1979. Limnology. W.B. Saunders Co. Philadelphia, Penn.

Whitford, L.A. and G.J. Schumacher. 1973. A manual of freshwater algae. Sparks Press, Raleigh, NC.

Grasslands And Savannahs: Ecology, Preservation Status And Management

by
Fred E. Smeins

Grassland and savannah communities occur throughout the eastern forests of North America, and on the western forest margin there are extensive savannahs and tallgrass prairies that give way to the central grassland region. Within the forest, these communities are the result of local interactions of biotic history, geology, soils, topography, herbivory, fire, drainage regime or anthropogenic factors. These enclaves often exhibit floral, faunal and physiognomic properties that make them biologically distinct. The western border of the forest likewise has prairies and savannahs that are the result of interaction of the above identified factors, and in addition, weather fluctuations and decreased precipitation to the west contribute to their features.

Savannahs and grasslands that occur within the forest have been greatly altered or destroyed since the time of European settlement by changing fire frequency, intensity and timing, altering drainage regimes, conversion to cropland, overgrazing, use as settlement sites and a host of other impacts. The western forest margin has suffered the same fate primarily because it is the breadbasket region of the nation and has been nearly totally converted from natural to manmade landscapes. The net result is that only a few isolated remnants remain of these endangered biotic communities. The purpose of this section is to bring attention to the kinds of eastern grasslands and savannahs, document the current status of preservation, and identify management problems and policies unique to these areas. Unfortunately, most of these communities do not occur within federal lands and certainly not within wilderness areas. Most occur on private lands or are under the jurisdiction of private conservation groups. Their location, isolation and diverse ownership pattern make management a difficult proposition.

The theme of the papers in this section is to provide an overview of the general ecology, preservation status and management problems associated with eastern grasslands and savannahs. The first paper deals with the preservation status of the True Prairie and identifies some ecological concepts relevant to management of prairie preserves (Risser). This is followed by a series of papers on specific kinds of savannahs and grasslands. The first evaluates the oak-hickory savannahs which form the forest-grassland transition (Johnson). The grasslands of Missouri are discussed and the longterm experience gained from management of these tallgrass prairie remnants is provided (Toney). The extensive mosaic of grasslands and savannahs of east central Texas is reviewed and problems of preservation and management are presented (Smeins and Diamond). Throughout the forest are many small isolated barrens, prairies and associated communities that are exceedingly difficult to preserve, and if preserved, to manage (Deselm). The once extensive fire-dependent savannahs of the southeastern United States are addressed and their endangered status emphasized (Frost, Walker and Peet). The New Jersey pine barrens represent a variety of communities and a plan for a statewide approach to maintain these ecosystems is presented (Collins, Roman and Good). The last paper deals with the role of private organizations, and in some cases their interaction with the federal government, to preserve and manage these endangered biotic communities (Boner).

The result is a cross-section of views on where these communities occur, how much of the various types exist under some sort of preservation, the need for additional acquisition and preservation, and perhaps, most importantly, problems and solutions encountered in management of these systems.

Preservation Status Of True Prairie Grasslands And Ecological Concepts Relevant To Management Of Prairie Preserves

by

Paul G. Risser

ABSTRACT--The tallgrass prairie is particularly amenable to natural area designation and management, because there are a number of significant protected sites and considerable information exists to understand this ecosystem, but additional preservation is needed and interesting management questions remain. The status of tallgrass preservation is described. While the concepts of succession and edge heterogeneity have been recognized in managing prairies, newer ideas now also appear to be important, e.g., disturbance, size and shape, and spatial arrangement on the landscape. In addition, management strategies need to more explicitly embrace other attributes, in particular, the fauna and the capacity to retain soil and nutrients.

KEYWORDS: true prairie, tallgrass prairie, natural areas, prairie preservation, grassland management, ecological considerations.

There are two major points that I wish to address. The first is a summary of the degree to which the United States has been successful in establishing preserves of tallgrass prairie. Here, the discussion will involve the total amounts of preserved prairie and the distribution among States, vegetation types, and sizes of prairies. Second, I will discuss some ecological ideas which should play a greater role in the development of grassland preserve management approaches.

PRESERVATION STATUS OF THE TRUE PRAIRIE

The presettlement true prairie or tallgrass prairie covered a large area in the central United States (Kuchler 1964), but the area has been dramatically reduced because of land use changes. Although this reduction has been severe, there are significant areas of tallgrass prairie remaining in the Flint Hills of eastern Kansas and northeastern Oklahoma. Elsewhere, tallgrass prairie remains only in specifically preserved areas.

Preservation of the remaining tallgrass prairie has been the objective of many organizations. Partly because of this diverse effort, it is difficult to determine the actual amount of tallgrass prairie that has been preserved. That is, preservation has been actively pursued on a national scale by several federal agencies and, for example, The Nature Conservancy; at the state scale by numerous state game and fish, as well as natural resource agencies; and at the local scale by organizations with special interest in

a particular prairie. The actual definition of what constitutes a tallgrass prairie varies among preservation efforts, as does the accuracy with which the acreages are known.

The Nature Conservancy maintains a data base of lands which are owned or controlled by the organization (information on the size of each preserve graciously provided by J. Prince, The Nature Conservancy, Arlington, VA.). This is perhaps the most comprehensive data base on the preservation of tallgrass prairies, and a summary of these lands by state is presented in Table 1. As indicated, almost 44,920 ha are distributed among preserves in 14 states. The largest tract occurs in Nebraska and, as

Table 1. Summary of Nature Conservancy Preserves Containing Tallgrass Prairie in Each State.

State	Hectares	(Acres)	Percent
Illinois	787	(1,969)	1.8
Indiana	186	(460)	0.4
Iowa	1,350	(3,337)	3.0
Kansas	4,405	(10,884)	9.8
Michigan	37	(91)	0.0
Minnesota	6,998	(17,291)	15.6
Missouri	2,569	(6,349)	5.7
Nebraska	22,430	(55,548)	50.2
North Dakota	757	(1,870)	1.7
Ohio	340	(839)	0.8
Oklahoma	16	(40)	0.0
South Dakota	3,257	(8,049)	7.3
Texas	781	(1,931)	1.8
Wisconsin	788	(1,946)	1.8
Total	44,761	(110,604)	99.9

will be discussed later, much of this area consists of Bluestem Prairie and Nebraska Sandhill Prairie. The acres listed in Table 1, are the acres in each Nature Conservancy preserve that contains tallgrass prairie--not the actual number of acres of tallgrass prairie. The Nature Conservancy does not have data on the acres of each vegetation type in all its preserves.

From other sources of data, I have compiled a more complete list of preserved tallgrass prairies (Table 2). This list includes The Nature Conservancy prairies of Table 1, but also notes additional prairie in the indicated states. Here, the total is about 105,600 ha. These additional areas are likely to be primarily tallgrass prairie, but because accurately mapped data using the same definitional criteria are not available for all the sites, again this is a maximum estimate of tallgrass prairie.

The Nature Conservancy classifies vegetation according to the categories of Kuchler (1964), and Table 3 summarizes these preserves according to these vegetation types. As noted earlier, a large proportion (48.6 percent) occurs as a mixture of Nebraska Sandhills Prairie and Bluestem Prairie. Bluestem Prairie (39.2 percent) consti-

tutes the next largest category, with a total of 16,766 ha. Thus, preservation efforts by The Nature Conservancy in

Table 2. Summary of Preserves Containing Tallgrass Prairie in Each State.

State	Hectares	(Acres)	Percent
*Iowa	1,852	(4,577)	1.8
Illinois	797	(1,969)	0.8
Indiana	186	(460)	0.2
*Kansas	11,732	(28,990)	11.1
Michigan	39	(91)	0.0
*Minnesota	18,212	(45,000)	17.2
*Missouri	4,557	(11,260)	4.3
*Nebraska	35,426	(87,536)	33.5
*North Dakota	2,318	(5,727)	2.2
Ohio	340	(839)	0.3
*Oklahoma	18,244	(45,080)	17.3
South Dakota	3,257	(8,049)	3.1
*Texas	7,956	(19,660)	7.5
Wisconsin	788	(1,946)	0.7
Total	105,704	(261,184)	100.0

*States which include areas with protected prairies in addition to those protected by the Nature Conservancy.

Figure 1. Railroad prairie remnant near Tonti, Illinois. (Photograph by P. G. Risser)

Table 3. Summary of Vegetation Types in Preserves Containing Tallgrass Prairies Protected by the Nature Conservancy.

Kuchler Vegetation Type	Hectares	(Acres)	Percent	Number
Blackland Prairie	16	(40)	0.0	1
Bluestem Prairie	16,766	(41,430)	39.2	96
Bluestem-Grama Prairie	337	(833)	0.8	3
Bluestem-Sacahuista Prairie	1,403	(3,467)	3.3	1
Juniper-Oak Savanna	1,038	(2,565)	2.4	2
Mosaic of Bluestem and Savanna	743	(1,835)	1.7	7
Nebraska Sandhills Prairie and Bluestem Prairie	20,821	(51,447)	48.6	2
Oak Savanna	1,136	(2,806)	2.7	14
Sandsage Bluestem Prairie	525	(1,298)	1.2	1
Wheatgrass-Bluestem-Needlegrass	25	(62)	0.0	2
Total	42,810	(105,783)	99.9	129

the general region of the true prairie have successfully protected significant amounts of two major grassland types and smaller amounts of other vegetation types.

As will be discussed under the topic of ecological concepts, the size of the grassland preserve is important for long-term integrity and for maintaining maximum biological diversity. In Table 4, the sizes of the protected grasslands are compared. This analysis includes the 129 preserves controlled by The Nature Conservancy and the 32 additional ones for which I have obtained descriptions from the various states. As Table 4 demonstrates, almost half of the preserves containing tallgrass prairie are less than 100 acres (40.5 ha) in size. Realizing that these are sizes of preserves, not sizes of actual prairies, indicates that most of the preserved prairies are small in size. On the other hand, there are 22 preserves which are 405 ha or larger in size.

In summary, there are preserves which total over 100,000 ha in which tallgrass prairie is a major component. Many of these preserves are relatively small, but 22 are larger than 405 ha. The Bluestem Prairie and the Nebraska Sandhills Prairie are the two largest categories of vegetation types which have been preserved. Eleven states have preserved 810 ha or more of tallgrass prairie, though this estimate is not completely accurate, because the acreages describe the size of preserves rather than the acres of prairie.

The success in preserving tallgrass prairie is significant. Future preservation efforts should continue, and emphasis should be placed on large preserves and on those which contain a variety of vegetation types. Furthermore, it would be desirable to develop a comprehensive data base which contains information about the specific amounts of each vegetation type within the preserves. Only with such a data base, will it be possible to describe confidently the success of preserving the tallgrass prairie.

ECOLOGICAL CONCEPTS RELATED TO MANAGEMENT OF PRAIRIE PRESERVES

Table 4. Size Class Distribution of Preserves with Protected Tailgrass Prairies.

Acres in Preserve (ha)	Number of Preserves	Accumulated Percent
0–99 (0–40)	72	44.7
100–199 (41–80)	27	61.5
200–299 (81–121)	19	73.3
300–399 (122–161)	2	74.5
400–499 (162–202)	5	77.6
500–999 (203–404)	14	86.3
1,000–4,999 (405–2,024)	16	96.3
5,000 or more (>2,025)	6	100.0
Total	161	

Much is known about the ecology of the tallgrass prairie (Risser *et al.* 1981), but existing ecological theory is not always invoked during the development of management plans for tallgrass prairie preserves. In the following sections, I will suggest that management plans must recognize the most current ecological principles and, also, that prairie preserves are appropriate locations on which to develop a better understanding of grassland ecology.

1. Patches

As more is learned about grasslands, the importance of spatial heterogeneity becomes more obvious. Indeed, spatial heterogeneity is now recognized as a fundamental component of ecosystems (Achouri and Gifford 1984, Risser *et al.* 1984). Earlier discussions about patches in the tallgrass prairie focused on the role of small disturbances in maintaining plant species diversity (Platt 1975). While the role patches play in enhancing plant species diversity remains an important issue (Collins and Uno 1983), it is now clear that many animal species also depend upon heterogeneous vegetation. This spatial pattern requirement is true for mammals, birds, and invertebrates (Risser *et al.* 1981). Thus, management plans should include special attention to maintaining patches in various successional stages, and vegetation with a diverse array of structures. Obviously, such a management scheme requires more effort because uniform treatments are usually more cost effective than treatments requiring spatial patterns.

This notion of patches can be examined in the context of prairie burning. Controlled burning has been used for many years as a management tool for maintaining grasslands, especially where the climate would otherwise support woody vegetation. Also, some adventive species can be controlled by burning treatments. Table 5 is an example of directions for managing prairies with burning, and this information is included in a completely commercial publication to be read by a lay person considering the establishment of a prairie. However, scientific studies have provided sufficient information that the prairie now can be managed much more precisely (Towne and Owensby 1984, Schacht and Stubbendieck 1985). By examining the summary in Table 6, it is clear that a manager could select the species composition by carefully controlling the burning schedule in relation to the plant species phenology. Furthermore, judicious grazing may increase the patchiness and species diversity of the prairie (Penfound 1964). Therefore, burning and grazing regimes should be planned much more precisely and should be conducted in reference to a detailed plan of which species will be enhanced.

2. Landscape

Most management plans for a prairie focus on the prairie itself. However, the prairie is an integral part of an interacting landscape. Even prairies which appear to be isolated and surrounded by relatively sterile agricultural cropland still have interactions with the surrounding landscape (Risser *et al.* 1984). These interactions may involve habitat requirements for species which, for example, depend upon a nearby riparian forest or stock pond. Thus, considering the entirety of the fauna of the grassland may demand that adjacent areas be considered. Future management for prairie may include management easements on adjacent habitats.

Admittedly, this landscape concept is new and, therefore, not well developed. A reasonable first step would be to consider the species known to inhabit a prairie preserve. If the life cycle requirements demand access to habitats not on the prairie, then the manager may wish to ensure that these adjacent habitats are maintained. If a certain species does not occur on the preserve, yet it might be expected as part of the prairie fauna, then perhaps the adjacent areas could be managed to provide the habitat requirements.

3. Wildlife Habitat

As indicated from the preceding section, management of the grassland should focus on the animal species as well as the plant species (Jackson 1972). Although it might be argued that animals are routinely considered in management approaches, I believe that too little attention has been paid toward developing innovative management schemes to enhance wildlife habitat on prairie preserves (Stenseth and Hansson 1981). It is more convenient to manage for plants because plants are easier than animals to find and census. However, animal species are important components of the prairie ecosystem and those management approaches successful for plants may not be

Table 5. Guidelines for Burning Prairies (LaFayette Home Nursery, Inc., LaFayette, Illinois, 1985).

Late Fall or Winter Burning of Grasslands
Advantages
    Generally better weather for burning
    Grasses and forbs are erect for burning
    Dryer vegetation and hotter fire
    Weed seed destruction is maximized
    Allows longer growing season subsequent year
Disadvantages
    Loss of moisture from soil during winter
    Deeper soil freezing
    Loss of winter cover for animals
    Loss of some prairie seed
    Open habitat for some alien forbs

Early Spring Burning of Grasslands
Advantages
    Winter cover left for animals
    Less soil water lost during winter
    More snow moisture retained
    Longer growing season
    Head start for prairie seeds
Disadvantages
    Less predictable weather for burning
    Cooler fire because vegetation matted
    Less control of weeds

Late Spring Burning of Grasslands
Advantages
    Winter cover left for animals
    Less soil water lost during winter and spring
    More snow moisture retained
    Weather somewhat more stable
    Significant destruction of weeds and woody vegetation
Disadvantages
    Later start for plant growth
    Less hot fire because of matted vegetation
    Temporary weakening of spring flora
    Some disturbance of cover for birds and mammals

Table 6. Long-term Annual Burning of the Tallgrass Prairies (Towne and Owensby, 1984).

Late Spring Burn
    Increase grass production
    Increase *Andropogon gerardi*
    Increase *Sorghastrum nutans*

Winter, Early and Mid-Spring Burn
    Reduced herbage production
    Favored other species

Early and Mid-Spring Burn
    Increase *Andropogon scoparius*

Early Spring and Winter Burn
    Increase forb and sedges

Unburned
    Mulch buildup
    Increase *Poa pratensis*
    Increase tree species
    Reduce grass production

successful for animals. As an example, R. and J. Graber of the Illinois Natural History Survey compared the grassland birds in Illinois over a 20-year period. They found that though there had been some decrease in the total amount of grassland, the decrease in prairie birds ranged from about 80 to 95 percent. This dramatic decrease in bird populations was probably attributable to many factors, but the authors believe the small size and isolation of the remaining grasslands probably were the greatest contributors to the decrease in population numbers of grassland birds.

Much has been written about the relationship between size of area and the maintenance of species and genetic diversity (Simberloff and Abele 1976, Strong et al. 1984, Schaffer and Samson 1985). This literature was initially interpreted as indicating that nature preserves should be large and that greater species diversity would be proportional, in a non-linear manner, to the size of the preserve. However, a closer examination of these ideas as applied to terrestrial situations, did not substantiate this contention. Indeed, there are data sets which suggest that a greater number of species could be maintained on smaller, connected preserves. The optimum strategy undoubtedly depends upon the species in question, the characteristics of the intervening habitat, and the diversity of the habitat in the preserves. Clearly, the point is that grassland management strategies must be developed after careful examination of the species requirements vis-'a-vis the prairie preserve and the surrounding landscape.

One further example will indicate the interconnectedness of the preceding concepts. Grassland preserves in Illinois are routinely burned to control woody plant species. Since this control is more effective with late spring burns, the grasslands are usually burned in April to mid-May. Unfortunately, burning at this time is not optimum for several grassland bird species which have begun to nest; however, one could easily argue that if the grassland is not burned and is, therefore, converted to shrubland, these grassland birds would not find the required habitat. A more precise approach would be to burn parts of the prairie at different times or to burn only parts of the prairie, depending upon bird nesting habitats.

The point can be further explored by considering the life cycle of the aphid, *Rhopalsiphum cerasifolis*, which has a complicated life cycle described by D. Voegtlin of the Illinois Natural History Survey. The aphid requires two very different hosts in reasonable proximity. It overwinters as eggs on chokecherry, *Prunus virginiana*, and the winged adults live on species *Scirpus*. Thus, when all Illinois prairie was burned in the spring to control chokecherry (without much success because of subsequent sprouting), the aphid was lost from the prairie. Again, one cannot manage simultaneously for all species, especially when life cycle requirements are different and require reciprocal management approaches. However, by knowing the life cycle of the prairie species and the habitat requirements of the resident fauna, management schemes can be developed so that trade-offs are made

knowingly and can be adjusted over the years to maintain the greatest diversity.

4. Integrated Pest Management

Integrated pest management has developed over the past 10 years in various cropping systems. In essence, the techniques involve judicious application of chemicals as necessary, but also the management of crops and adjacent habitats so that natural predators assist in the control of crop pests (Rabb *et al.* 1976). Adventive weeds are a continuing, indeed escalating, problem on prairie preserves. For example, in making this point, J. Schwegman of the Illinois Department of Conservation developed a list of problem weedy species in the prairie preserves of Illinois (Table 7). Although weeds may be controlled by

Table 7. Serious Alien Invading Species of Illinois Prairies (J. Schwegman, Illinois Dep. Cons., Springfield).

Purple loosestrife (*Lythrum salicaria*)
White sweet clover (*Melilotus alba*)
Crown vetch (*Coronilla varia*)
Multiflora rose (*Rosa multiflora*)
Autumn olive (*Elaeagnus umbellata*)
Giant teasel (*Dipsacus laciniatus*)
Kudzu (*Pueraria lobata*)
Tall fescue (*Festuca elatior*)
Giant foxtail (*Setaria faberi*)
Black locust (*Robinia pseudoacacia*)
Loosestrife (*Lysimachia nummularia*)
Silver poplar (*Populus alba*)
Sericea lespedeza (*Lespedeza cuneata*)

burning or mowing, chemicals are a common management technique on rangelands (Lym and Messersmith 1985) and sometimes even in natural areas.

It would appear that integrated pest management or, more precisely, biological control of adventive plant species, would be a very appropriate approach to be investigated by those who manage prairie preserves. The task is not simple, since it requires a careful analysis of the natural predators or diseases, and then an attempt to rear or encourage the natural biological controls of the pest species. In many cases, this will entail habitat management for the control species. A few documented successes will certainly encourage others to undertake the necessary research effort needed to develop practical management strategies.

5. Soil and Water Conservation

Probably no objective is upheld so ubiquitously as the benefits of soil and water conservation. The ability of prairies to retain soil and water is widely known (Williams *et al.* 1984) though it may be quite variable within a grassland (Springer and Gifford 1980, Archouri and Gifford 1984). Justification of prairie preserves frequently depends primarily upon emotional issues or rather vague arguments about genetic diversity. The role prairie preserves play in controlling soil and water losses can be quantified. Furthermore, the monetary benefits of this process can be calculated. While one would never want to argue the need for prairie preserves only on the basis of economic value, grasslands do contribute to the economically valuable, ecological processes of a region. Some representative examples of these contributions may be useful in developing powerful rationales for expanding the prairie preserves of this Nation.

SUMMARY

Although not representing a significant portion of the original prairie, there are a number of preserves containing examples of the tallgrass prairie. These preserves contain approximately 105,000 ha and are distributed among 14 midwestern states. Many of the prairies are small in size, though accurate data are not available on the amount of tallgrass prairie in each preserve.

Several concepts in grassland ecology could be more fully incorporated into management schemes for prairie preserves. For example, burning regimes can be fine-tuned to manipulate phenological cohorts of species and to enhance various vertebrate and invertebrate species of wildlife. The landscape setting of the prairie can also be considered, especially in relation to the habitat requirements of wide ranging species which depend, in part, upon the grassland preserves. Integrated pest management techniques should be a challenging, but rewarding, approach to the biological control of alien species. Finally, the value of prairie preserves can be more explicitly stated, and the control of water and soil losses is a prime candidate for such a calculation of value.

LITERATURE CITED

Achouri, M. and G.F. Gifford. 1984. Spatial and seasonal variability of field measured infiltration rates on a rangeland site in Utah. J. Range Manage. 37:451-455.

Collins, S.L. and G.E. Uno. 1983. The effect of early spring burning on vegetation in buffalo wallows. Bull. Torrey Bot. Gard. 110:474-481.

Jackson, A.S. 1972. Quail management handbook for west Texas rolling plains. Texas Parks and Wildlife Bull. 48.

Kuchler, A.A. 1964. Potential natural vegetation of the conterminous United States. Am. Geogr. Soc. Special Publ. 36. New York, N.Y.

Lym, R.G. and C.G. Messersmith. 1985. Leafy spurge control with herbicides in North Dakota: 20-year summary. J. Range Manage. 38:149-154.

Penfound, W.T. 1964. The relation of grazing to plant succession in the tallgrass prairie. J. Range Manage. 5:256-260.

Platt, W.J. 1975. The colonization and formation of equilibrium plant species associations on badger disturbances in a tall-grass prairie. Ecol. Mongr. 45:285-305.

Rabb, R.L., R.E. Stinner, and R. van den Bosch. 1976. Conservation augmentation of natural enemies. pp. 233-254. In D.B. Huffaker and P.S. Messenger, (eds.). Theory and practice of biological control. Academic Press, New York, N.Y.

Risser, P.G., E.C. Birney, H.D. Blocker, W.S. May, W.J. Parton, and J.A. Wiens. 1981. The true prairie ecosystem. Hutchinson and Ross, Publishers, Stroudsburgh, Penn.

Risser, P.G., J.R. Karr, and R.T.T. Forman. 1984. Landscape ecology: directions and approaches. Illinois Natural His. Surv. Special Publ. No. 2. Champaign, Ill.

Schacht, W. and J. Stubbendieck. 1985. Prescribed burning in the loess hills mixed prairie of southern Nebraska. J. Range Manage. 38:45-51.

Schaffer, M.L. and F.B. Samson. 1985. Population size and extinction: a note on determining critical population sizes. Am. Nat. 125:144-151.

Simberloff, D.A. and L.G. Abele. 1976. Island biogeography theory and conservation practice. Science 191:285-286.

Springer, P.E. and G.F. Gifford. 1980. Spatial variability of rangeland infiltration rates. Water Res. Bull. 16:550-552.

Stenseth, N.C. and L. Hansson. 1981. The importance of population dynamics in heterogeneous landscapes: management of vertebrate pests and some other animals. Agro-ecosystems 7:187-221.

Strong, D.R., Jr., D. Simberloff, L.G. Abele, and A.B. Thistle (eds.). 1984. Ecological communities: conceptual issues and evidence. Princeton Univ. Press, Princeton, New Jersey.

Towne, G. and C. Owensby. 1984. Long-term effects of annual burning at different dates in ungrazed Kansas tallgrass prairie. J. Range Manage. 37:392-397.

Williams, J.R., R.G. Menzel, and G.A. Coleman. 1984. Prediction of sediment yield from southern plains grasslands with the universal soil loss equation. J. Range Manage. 37:295-297.

Oak-Hickory Savannahs And Transition Zones: Preservation Status And Management Problems

by
Forrest L. Johnson

ABSTRACT--The oak-hickory savannahs and transition zones occupy a broad band between the deciduous forest and the grasslands from Texas to Minnesota. Much of the original vegetation of the prairie-forest transition has been changed since settlement, primarily as a result of agricultural practices and fire suppression. Most of the original oak savannah in the Cross Timbers region, Wisconsin, and Minnesota has been converted to forest. Much of the prairie-forest mosaic in Missouri, Iowa, and Illinois is now farmland. Federal and state resource-management specialists are aware of the problem of vegetation change induced by fire suppression, and are beginning to use management techniques such as prescribed burning to preserve and restore some areas of transition zone vegetation to presettlement conditions.

KEYWORDS: eastern deciduous forest, tallgrass prairie, fire, prescribed burning, Oklahoma, Kansas.

The transition zone between the eastern deciduous forest and the western grasslands covers a broad band, stretching from Texas to Minnesota (Kuchler 1964). Vegetation types and species are very different from place to place in the transition zone, but much of the area is (or was) savannah or woodland and many of the tree species are oaks.

The transition zone is represented in south Texas by mesquite-live oak savannah. This area is dominated by *Prosopis juliflora, Quercus fusiformis,* and species of *Andropogon.* The Texas portion of the transition zone was described by Gould (1975).

In central Texas, other species of oaks come into the savannah, and in places the mesquite is replaced by junipers. Typical tree species in this area are live oak, post oak (*Q. stellata*), blackjack (*Q. marilandica*), Texas red oak (*Q. texana*), rock cedar (*Juniperus ashei*), and eastern red-cedar (*J. virginiana*). Johnson (1982) gave a quantitative description of two rock cedar-live oak sites near Temple.

The Cross Timbers or post oak-blackjack type, consisting of savannah in places and thickets of small trees in other places, is found from north central Texas, across Oklahoma, and into southern Kansas. This vegetation type is usually dominated by post oak, blackjack, or black hickory (*Carya texana*). The Cross Timbers vegetation type has been described in its various aspects by several authors (Bruner 1931, Dyksterhuis 1948, Rice and Penfound 1959, Johnson and Risser 1975).

From northeastern Oklahoma, through eastern Kansas, northern Missouri, southern Iowa, and most of Illinois, the transition zone is/was represented by a mosaic of oak-

Figure 1. Oak-bluestem savannah in central Oklahoma. A large fire scar visible on the blackjack *Quercus marilandica* in the center. Other plants prominent in the photograph are post oak *Q. stellata*, sumac *Rhus glabra*, and little bluestem *Andropogon scoparius*. (Photograph by Forrest Johnson)

hickory forest and tallgrass prairie. In Wisconsin and Minnesota, the prairie-forest border is a combination of several forest types and oak savannah.

The complex assemblage of vegetation types in the prairie-forest transition zone is thought to be a result of a number of factors including climate, topography, soils, fire, and human activity. For example, Gleason (1913) attributed the mosaic of forest and prairie in Illinois to fires driven by the prevailing southwesterly winds. Forest stands tended to be on the northeast side of fire barriers, such as bodies of water. Native Americans apparently made extensive use of fire for several thousand years throughout North America (Pyne 1982). Several authors have considered the recent increase of forests at the expense of savannahs in the Midwest to be a result of fire suppression after settlement (Cottam 1949, Beilmann and Brenner 1951, Rice and Penfound 1959, Johnson and Risser 1975, White 1983). Buck (1964) and Crockett (1964) found the distribution of grassland and forest to be correlated with geological formations and soil types in the Wichita Mountains of Oklahoma. Climatic factors have a very important influence on the distribution of vegetation, but the effect of climate is somewhat modified by soils and topography (Walter 1973).

PRESERVATION STATUS

Much of the transition zone vegetation remains, but most of it has been changed to some extent from the presettlement condition. Fire suppression, grazing, clearing, and plowing of land for agricultural uses have taken their toll of the original vegetation, especially the oak savannahs. Oak savannah occupied a much larger area before white settlement than it does at present, especially in the central and northern part of the transition zone. This is documented by comparison of present vegetation with nineteenth century land survey records in a number of places (Cottam 1949, Curtis 1959, White 1983) and other evidence (Beilmann and Brenner 1951, Rice and Penfound 1959, Johnson and Risser 1975). The oak savannahs of Wisconsin were originally dominated by bur oak (Q. macrocarpa) and prairie grasses, but have largely been replaced by white oak (Q. alba) dominated forest (Cottam 1949). A site in Minnesota, described by White (1983), was originally bur oak-northern pin oak (Q. ellipsoidalis) savannah, but has become a dense northern pin oak forest.

Oak savannahs in southern and central Texas may cover most of their original area, although they may have been modified by fire suppression and grazing. Cedar and mesquite may have increased where they were originally present and invaded where they were absent. Oaks and cedars probably increased in the rock cedar-live oak vegetation type of central Texas after the area was settled (Johnson 1982). The oak savannahs further north in Oklahoma (Rice and Penfound 1959), Missouri (Beilmann and Brenner 1951), Wisconsin (Curtis 1959), and Minnesota (White 1983) have mostly been converted to forest as a result of fire suppression.

The mosaic of tallgrass prairie and oak-hickory forest which extended across eastern Kansas, northern Missouri, southern Iowa, and most of Illinois has been changed a great deal. Most of the forest component of the moasic either has been cut over for timber or cleared for farming. Nearly all of the prairie component of the area has been converted to agricultural crops, principally wheat, corn, and soybeans.

Numerous small areas and a few large areas of transition zone vegetation receive at least some protection from exploitation through their status as wildlife refuges, state parks, and other public lands. A few large military bases, such as Fort Hood in Texas and Fort Sill in Oklahoma, have areas of relatively undisturbed vegetation. Part of the Wichita Mountains Wildlife Refuge in Oklahoma is officially designated wilderness under the Wilderness Act. Other major federal lands with transition zone vegetation are Chickasaw National Recreation Area, Caddo National Grassland, and Lyndon B. Johnson (LBJ) National Grassland.

MANAGEMENT PROBLEMS

Fire suppression was routinely practiced for many years in the belief that all fires were detrimental to natural ecosystems. During this time, much of the savannah vegetation in the transition zone was converted to forest. Conversion of savannah to forest is apparently much easier than reversing the process and converting forest to savannah. Studies in central Minnesota, which involved several years of annual burning in a northern pin oak forest in an attempt to convert it back to savannah, were only partially successful (White 1983), because trees larger than 25 cm dbh were unaffected by the fires. The same problem may be found further south. In central Oklahoma, a late winter fire was much more intense in a savannah than in an adjacent forest, resulting in a much lower kill rate for the small woody vegetation in the forest (Johnson and Risser 1975).

Resource managers have come to realize that fire is not always detrimental to ecosystems, and in some cases can have a beneficial effect (Heinselman 1978). Prescribed burning has become a useful tool for vegetation management on public lands. Some examples of vegetation management practices in Oklahoma and Texas are given below.

In the Wichita Mountain Wildlife Refuge, approximately 10,000 ha of the 24,000 ha refuge is burned on a 10 year cycle for grazing improvement and control of red cedar. Burning gives good control of red cedar, since it is easily killed by fire when small, and does not sprout from underground parts. There is still some invasion of post oak, blackjack, and coralberry (Symphoricarpos orbiculatus) into the grassland because these species are vigorous sprouters after fire. A shorter fire return interval might give better control of sprouting species.

At Caddo National Grassland, 0 to 475 ha of the 7200 ha area is burned each year, depending on the occurrence of suitable fire weather in the November to April period. Woody vegetation encroaching on the grassland consists mostly of cedar, winged elm (*Ulmus alata*), and common persimmon (*Diospyros virginiana*). Burning controls cedar well, but is only fair for elm and persimmon. Fire seems to have little effect on the small areas of post oak in the grassland. Chemical control of vegetation is practiced only in a few special areas.

LBJ National Grassland is further west than Caddo, and woody vegetation is less of a problem. Some invasion of cedar and plum (*Prunus* spp.) into grassland occurs, and is managed by a combination of burning, mowing, and herbicides. Chickasaw National Recreation Area also has the problem of cedar and other woody plants invading grasslands and savannahs, and a prescribed burning program is planned for the near future.

CONCLUSIONS

The natural vegetation of the prairie-forest transition has undergone considerable change since settlement as a result of farming, grazing, logging, fire suppression, and other human activities. Some reasonably large areas of the transition zone (with the exception of the mosaic type in Missouri, Iowa, and Illinois) have been preserved. Fire suppression has changed most of the original savannah to forest. Better understanding of ecosystem processes is bringing about better management practices which will probably result in the restoration of some of the original savannah vegetation on public lands.

LITERATURE CITED

Beilmann, A.P. and Brenner, L.G. 1951. The recent intrusion of forests in the Ozarks. Ann. Missouri Bot. Gard. 38:261-282.

Buck, P. 1964. Relationships of the woody vegetation of the Wichita Mountains Wildlife Refuge to geological formations and soil types Ecology 45:336-344.

Bruner, W.E. 1931. The vegetation of Oklahoma. Ecol. Monogr. 1:99-188.

Cottam, G. 1949. The phytosociology of an oak woods in southwestern Wisconsin. Ecology 30:271-287.

Crockett, J.J. 1964. Influence of soils and parent materials on grasslands of the Wichita Mountains Wildlife Refuge, Oklahoma. Ecology 45:326-335.

Curtis, J.T. 1959. The vegetation of Wisconsin. Univ. Wisconsin Press, Madison, Wisconsin.

Dyksterhuis, E.J. 1948. The vegetation of the Western Cross Timbers. Ecol. Monogr. 18:325-376.

Gould, F.W. 1975. Texas plants--a checklist and ecological summary. Tex. A&M Univ., Tex. Agric. Exp. Stn. MP-588/rev., College Station, Tex.

Gleason, H.A. 1913. The relation of forest distribution and prairie fires in the middle west. Torreya 13:173-181.

Heinselman, M.L. 1978. Fire in wilderness ecosystems. pp. 248-278. *In* J.C. Hendee, G.H. Stankey, and R.C. Lucas, (eds.). Wilderness management. USDA For. Serv. Misc. Publ. No. 1365. U.S. Govt. Printing Office, Washington, D.C.

Johnson, F.L. 1982. Effects of tank training activities on botanical features at Fort Hood, Texas. Southwest. Nat. 27:309-314.

Johnson, F.L. and Risser, P.G. 1975. A quantitative comparison between an oak forest and an oak savannah in central Oklahoma. Southwest. Nat. 20:75-84.

Kuchler, A.W. 1964. Potential natural vegetation of the conterminous United States. Am. Geogr. Soc. Spec. Publ. No. 36, New York.

Pyne, S.J. 1982. Fire in America: A cultural history of wildland and rural fire. Princeton Univ. Press, Princeton, N.J.

Rice, E.L. and W.T. Penfound. 1959. The upland forests of Oklahoma. Ecology 40:593-608.

Walter, H. 1973. Vegetation of the earth. Springer-Verlag. New York, N.Y.

White, A.A. 1983. The effects of thirteen years of annual prescribed burning on a *Quercus ellipsoidalis* community in Minnesota. Ecology 64:1081-1085.

Fire-Dependent Savannas And Prairies Of The Southeast: Original Extent, Preservation Status And Management Problems

by
Cecil C. Frost, Joan Walker and Robert K. Peet

ABSTRACT--A diverse mosaic of pine savannas and grasslands once extended along the Coastal Plain from southeastern Virginia to Texas and south Florida. Of numerous distinctive types, most could be subsumed under longleaf or slash pine savanna, canebrakes, and moist prairies. In addition, in south Florida, a large region is dominated by slash pine rocklands, cypress savannas, and marl prairies. Probably less than 10% remains of the area once occupied by grasslands. Principal environmental gradients determining natural grassland vegetation on flat lower Coastal Plain terraces are fire frequency and depth to water table. Frequency of fire required to maintain community types may range from 1 to gt 30 years. Consideration in size and design of areas to be perpetuated should include practical fire-management policies. Most insectivorous plants, and many rare species and endemics, occur in moist savannas where optimum position on a complex environmental stress gradient and high fire frequency can produce species density in excess of 40/square m, the highest reported from North America. Similar conditions often exist along ecotones where dryer savannas meet wetlands. Of serious concern, is the management practice of plowing fire lines between uplands to be burned and adjacent wetland, truncating the vegetation gradient above the ecotone. Highest priority should be given to protection and restoration of species-rich, moist savannas--the most threatened of southeastern grasslands.

KEYWORDS: savannas, *Pinus palustris*, presettlement vegetation, fire ecology, diversity.

The natural vegetation of the southeastern United States once included a rich and varied pattern of savanna and prairie, interspersed among woodland and forest over a vast region from Virginia to Texas. Distribution of vegetation types was controlled by moisture characteristics related to topography, and by fire. Removal of fire as a primary determinant of the pattern of natural vegetation has led to sweeping changes. Where not actually converted to agriculture or other uses, former savanna and woodland have succeeded to the mesophytic forests of loblolly pine and hardwoods characteristic of the region today. The processes of change can still be seen throughout the South.

The high frequency of fire required to maintain some communities has not generally been recognized. There is accumulating evidence that a variety of savanna types require nearly annual or biennial fire. Among these are the moist savannas with spectacular floral displays, especially of orchids and insectivorous plants. The high degree of endemism and specialization of this flora suggests an evolutionary antiquity that is not widely appreciated. Because of their requirement for frequent fire, moist and mesic savannas of a number of substantially different kinds are endangered and in need of protection and study.

NATURAL GRASSLANDS OF THE SOUTHEASTERN COASTAL PLAIN

In this treatment of natural grasslands, we are concerned with a variety of vegetation types characterized by conspicuous herb strata and a dependence on fire. Communities in this group have been variously designated prairie, meadow, marsh, and savanna. Use of these terms has never been consistent and clarification is in order.

Marsh includes emergent wetland vegetation dominated by graminoids, and is applied to types along the salinity gradient from those dominated by predominantly freshwater species like *Typha latifolia* to true halophytes such as *Spartina alterniflora*. For our purposes, marshes are included only when intermixed with coastal prairie or where grading into savanna. Using the water regime modifiers in Cowardin *et al.* (1979), we distinguish between marsh and wet prairie at the interface between semipermanently flooded (surface water persists throughout the growing season in most years) or wetter for marsh, and seasonally flooded (surface water present for extended periods but absent by the end of the season in most years) or drier for prairie or savanna.

Figure 1. Moist longleaf pine savannas of Mississippi coastal meadows provide the most spectacular displays of insectivorous plants, orchids, grasses and other savanna flora remaining to be seen in the South. Species richness is greatest on sites burned annually or biennially, with average density of 25 species per 0.25 square m (Sandhill Crane National Wildlife Refuge, Jackson Co.).

In the United States, 'prairie' is used exclusively for natural treeless grasslands, while meadow carries the connotation of a small, intimate opening surrounded by trees, as in the mountain meadows of the western states. 'Meadow' is applied to mowed grassland as well as certain natural situations, such as the longleaf pine savannas of coastal Mississippi, Alabama, and Louisiana.

Savanna is a New World term, acquired by the Spanish from Taino, the language of an extinct group of Arawak Indians of the Greater Antilles and Bahamas. The original meaning was in fact a flat, treeless plain, essentially synonymous with prairie, and was correctly used as such by the Spanish in Florida and by Bartram (1791) in his numerous descriptions of prairie openings in the virgin longleaf pine savannas of North Florida. In modern use, however, savanna is usually applied to grassland with scattered trees. Walter (1979) implies that trees in savannas are very widely scattered; Vankat (1979) specifies tree cover lt 30%. In the southeastern U.S., however, savanna has been used wherever community structure is bilayered with pine canopy and well-developed

herbaceous understory, with the consequence that the term is frequently applied to communities with tree cover values that elsewhere would be called woodland or even forest.

For consistency in future work in the South, we propose the following working definition which seems to circumscribe the concept as used here.

Savanna: vegetation which is essentially bilayered, with tree cover less than 30%, graminoids usually prominent, and the herb layer the best developed statum: or with tree cover up to 50% and a nearly continuous herb layer. The focus of this report will center largely on savanna vegetation.

Canebrake, an additional grassland type, is widespread in the region. *Arundinaria gigantea* is sometimes an important component of moist savannas and prairies, but the term canebrake is usually reserved for situations where height and density of stems retard growth of competing species. The canebrake community is a fire-dependent type transitional between savanna and wetlands like pocosin, bay-gall, bay forest, or swamp forest. Since it may alternate with these types with changes in fire regime on the same soil, canebrake is better treated with pocosin and swamp vegetation rather than savanna or prairie.

The term 'bog' has been broadly applied to any wet, miry place, but usually carries the connotations of wet peat soil and shrubby vegetation. The only true ombrotrophic bogs in the Southeast are the evergreen shrub bogs called pocosins, which reach their greatest development on lower terraces of the Atlantic states from Virginia to Florida. The designation 'bog' is not used by locals in the South, who know better, but has been misapplied, mostly by ecologists, to a variety of situations, including small, wet meadows and fens in the Appalachians, wet prairie openings in longleaf pine savanna (e.g. 'upland grass-sedge bog', Wells and Shunk 1928), and any place where pitcher plants are found (see Folkerts 1982).

PRESETTLEMENT VEGETATION

Figure 2 illustrates the original extent of major fire-dependent communities in the Southeast. Boundaries are based on material in Sudworth (1913), Harper (1906, 1911, 1913, 1914), Lockett (1876), Wahlenburg (1946), Ashe (1894), Parrott (1967), Medici (1969), Gunderson et al. (1983), Schantz and Zon (1924), Lewis et al. (1974), Kuchler (1949), Little (1971), numerous other sources and field observations.

Longleaf Pine/Wiregrass and Bluestem Savannas

Longleaf, one of the most fire-adapted trees in the eastern United States, is taken as an indicator of the primary range of presettlement fire vegetation (Fig. 2). This is because it is one of two widespread species (longleaf pine and wiregrass Aristida stricta) believed to

facilitate fire by production of highly flammable litter (Wells and Shunk 1931), and because it is not known to persist in the absence of fire.

Most of the several hundred members of the species-rich graminoid-forb layer, characteristic of pine savannas, are shade-intolerant and many disappear within a few years of fire exclusion. On all but the driest sites, 10 to 20 years of fire suppression leads to virtually irrevocable conversion from fire communities to non-pyrophytic shrubland or forest. A fire regime sufficient to maintain establishment of longleaf pine and recruitment into the canopy always entails maintenance of a flammable herb layer. It is assumed, then, that some kind of savanna vegetation formerly occurred wherever remnant longleaf pine canopy trees are still found or formerly were present.

Lands covered with longleaf pine had declined to less than 1/6 their original extent by 1946 (Wahlenberg), and have continued to decrease. The era of effective fire suppression, beginning around 1920, and establishment of extensive pine plantations, dating from the late 1940's, have essentially precluded the possibility of southeastern savanna and prairie as unmanaged vegetation. Perpetuation of any pyrophytic community in the Southeast is now a management decision.

Bluestem (Andropogon spp.) was the understory dominant on the uplands over large areas in central and southern Alabama, Mississippi, Louisiana, and East Texas, and wiregrass (Aristida stricta) was dominant in parts of

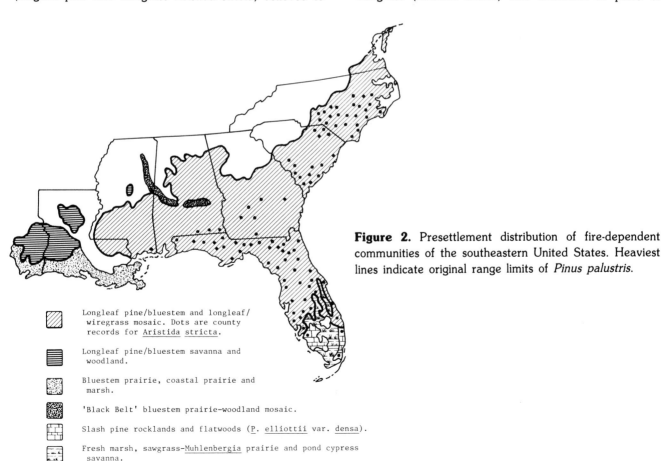

Figure 2. Presettlement distribution of fire-dependent communities of the southeastern United States. Heaviest lines indicate original range limits of Pinus palustris.

Longleaf pine/bluestem and longleaf/wiregrass mosaic. Dots are county records for Aristida stricta.

Longleaf pine/bluestem savanna and woodland.

Bluestem prairie, coastal prairie and marsh.

'Black Belt' bluestem prairie-woodland mosaic.

Slash pine rocklands and flatwoods (P. elliottii var. densa).

Fresh marsh, sawgrass-Muhlenbergia prairie and pond cypress savanna.

Florida, Georgia, and the Carolinas. The role of bluestems on the Atlantic slope, however, has been obscured by longer and more intensive land use. There are only small remnants of bluestem savanna in these states, mostly on fine-textured soils. While wiregrass was probably more abundant in presettlement savannas than indicated by existing county records (Fig. 2), bluestem savanna and woodland was also widespread. A pine-bluestem belt may have extended from the Gulf states, north to Virginia, along upper Coastal Plain terraces, while lower terraces supported a complicated mosaic of pine-bluestem, pine-wiregrass, and other types. In view of differential elimination of savanna types, it would seem inappropriate to categorize most of the original savanna vegetation of the Atlantic Coastal Plain as longleaf-wiregrass as has sometimes been suggested. Although longleaf-bluestem once dominated a large area of the Atlantic Coastal Plain, it is now virtually extinct as a community in this region.

The Black Belt is a narrow zone of calcareous soils in central Alabama and adjacent Mississippi. It was described as prairie-like by early settlers and was conspicuously more fertile than neighboring piedmont clay and acid coastal plain soils. Consequently, it was developed rapidly, beginning in the early 1800's, subsequently depleted by cotton farming, and had largely reverted to pasture and old fields by the time of Harper's investigations (1913). From his descriptions, however, and examination of General Land Office Survey records from the period 1820 to 1834 (Caddell *et al.* 1981), it seems likely that the Black Belt was a mosaic of patches of bluestem prairie (species composition unknown) in savanna and woodland of shortleaf pine (*P. echinata*), blackjack oak (*Q. marylandica*), and post oak (*Q. stellata*), perhaps similar to shortleaf pinelands and post oak savanna in east Texas.

ECOLOGY OF COASTAL PLAIN GRASSLANDS

There is a remarkable paucity of ecological literature dealing specifically with savannas. Most of what is available must be gleaned from studies focusing on silviculture of longleaf pine, range management, and in descriptive reports of regional vegetation.

Previous classifications of savanna vegetation have used only broad types based largely on physiognomy, edaphic factors, and moisture regime. Examples include longleaf pine-bluestem savanna, longleaf pine-wiregrass savanna, xeric sandhills, and upland grass-sedge bog (Wells 1928, Garren 1943, Christensen 1979, Walker 1985). No detailed regional classification of pyrophytic vegetation in the Southeast is available.

Understanding the variation in vegetation of southeastern savannas will depend upon examination of their distribution along critical environmental gradients. Among the more salient gradients are moisture, from communities of dry sands and clays through mesic, wet-mesic, and hydric

prairies; soil texture from coarse sand to loams and clay, and the gradient from mineral to organic soil. Also critical, are the gradients of fire frequency and intensity.

Species Richness and Community Structure

Mesic, coastal plain savannas can be extraordinarily species-rich communities. Frequently burned sites often have in excess of 30 species per square meter, making these communities the richest in North America, at least at small size scales. The herb flora includes numerous species of orchids and other showy wildflowers, and the most diverse assemblage of carnivorous plants to be found in the world. Savannas and their ecotones provide habitats for a remarkably high number of threatened and endangered species. In North Carolina, for example, 19 species, listed as endangered, threatened, or rare in the state (Sutter *et al.* 1983) are found in mesic savanna communities.

It is well-known that both site moisture status and fire frequency are critical for maintenance of rich savanna communities (Wells and Shunk 1928, Lemon 1949, Kologiski 1977, Peet *et al.* 1983, Walker and Peet 1983). A study of savannas in the Green Swamp of North Carolina showed that maximum diversity was found on annually burned sites of intermediate moisture conditions and with fine to medium-textured soils (Walker and Peet 1983, Walker 1985). Both drainage of adjacent lands and reduction of fire frequency to less than once every year or two can be expected to depress richness.

Understanding factors that affect species extinctions requires a sound understanding of the biology of component species (Terborgh 1974, Shaffer 1981, Terborgh and Winter 1980). While describing species biology of the many savanna species is a formidable research problem, focus on the processes that control the success of infrequent or rare species might secondarily ensure success of populations of common ones, as well as that of community structure as a whole (Shaffer 1981).

Fire Ecology

The timing and frequency of fire has particular relevance to grassland preservation. Winter fires (Jan.-Feb.) have long been standard practice for control burns. The natural lightning cycle of the region, however, is a strong indicator that summer fires were the norm long before emigration of man into the region during the Wisconsin glacial period.

Summer fires are hotter than winter burns and affect vegetation differently. Below-ground carbohydrate reserves of woody species are lowest in summer. Hence, repeated summer burns represent cumulative stress, which eventually leads to high mortality of woody plants (Chalkin 1952, Langdon 1971). Annual winter fires had little effect on resprouting or elimination of the understory on 73 permanent plots in the Everglades (Taylor and Herndon 1981), while a series of hot summer fires has been shown to eliminate persistent understory species like sweetgum and bayberry (Lotti 1956).

Effects of season of burn on productivity and floristics of savannas have largely been studied in relation to range grasses. Little is known of relative effects of fire on forbs. In one case, significantly more legumes were found on plots burned with backing fires (Cushwa *et al.* 1966). Backing fires may maintain heat for a longer time and hotter temperatures may occur closer to ground. Headfires move rapidly and reach their greatest temperatures at higher levels above ground--1 to 4 feet (0.3 to 1.2 m) in one study (Davis and Martin 1960).

One area of limited investigation is the increase in probability of fire with litter buildup in various kinds of pyrophytic vegetation. Veno (1976) suggests that probability of fire increases with time since last fire in *Pinus clausa*/scrub oak stands. Lemon (1949), however, noted apparent equilibrium between litter accumulation and decomposition after about 5 years in wiregrass-*Sporobolus curtissii* savanna, suggesting a levelling-off of flammability after the initial increase.

While the natural role of fire in the Southeast has gained wide appreciation among foresters, range scientists, and ecologists, it has until recently been regarded as a form of disturbance. It is clear, however, that there is a continuum of situations with regard to fire and natural vegetation. At one extreme are mesic, beech-magnolia forests in which fire is a random hazard, normally absent, but always with the possibility that a fire could occur at a time of critical leaf moisture, initiating a destructive crown fire. At the other extreme, are species-rich, mesic savannas which may actually require fire on a nearly annual basis. In the first instance, fire is clearly a disturbance in the classical sense. In the second, it is vital to stability of the community.

MANAGEMENT PROBLEMS AND THREATS TO DIVERSITY: MANAGEMENT RECOMMENDATIONS

Remnant savanna and prairie is threatened by innumerable processes related to increasing domestication of the landscape and intensive utilization of woodland. These include fire exclusion or reduction in frequency, drainage, urbanization, conversion to agriculture or pine plantation, and semipermanent marring of the landscape by vehicles, fire plows, and logging equipment.

The most serious problem facing remaining, high quality savanna ecosystems is maintenance of something approximating a natural fire regime. Most prescribed fire on public and private lands in the South is done in the name of hazard reduction and control of hardwood understory (Lewis *et al.* 1974, Vogl 1973). Frequency and intensity of fire adequate to reduce fire hazard may not be sufficient to prevent conversion of some pyrophytic communities to non-pyrophytic types. This is particularly true of vegetation on moist or fertile soils. The Leon sand, which supports rich savanna flora when burned at intervals of 1-3 years, is often rapidly taken over by a thick shrub layer or invaded by loblolly, slash, or pond pine when the interval is reduced to 5 years or longer. Rever-

sal of hardwood invasion may require a series of hot, summer burns, if it is possible at all.

One problem that should be addressed at the regional planning level is the practice on some national forests of declaring all mesic or wet mesic soils 'loblolly sites' or 'slash pine sites', while longleaf savanna is maintained only on drier soils. Under natural fire regimes, many such moist areas are burned frequently enough to support species-rich, longleaf pine savannas. Similarly, because of their greater fertility, mesic longleaf pine-bluestem communities have suffered much more from site conversion than longleaf-wiregrass.

Impact of Air Pollution on Site Fertility and Species Richness

A subtle threat to diversity, difficult to document, may be the increase in atmospheric precipitation of nutrients as a result of human activities. It has been shown that highest species richness occurs on sites of relatively low productivity (Al-Mufti *et al.* 1977, Peet *et al.* 1983). When fertility is increased, productivity is increased and sites tend to become dominated by a few robust species, leading to exclusion of smaller species and reduction in diversity. Inadvertent fertilization of naturally oligotrophic communities may occur as a result of smokestack output from burning fossil fuels, fixation of nutrients by automobile engines, and deflation of fine nutrient dust from fertilized agricultural fields. The expected impact of fertilization on savannas might be increased dominance by bunch grasses and more rapid invasion by shrubs and saplings. This might require a corresponding increase in fire frequency to maintain the same diversity.

Impacts of Grazing by Domestic Livestock

The response of grassland species to stresses such as grazing and fire is closely linked to their evolutionary history (Naveh and Whittaker 1980). In long grazed grassland, diversity often drops when grazing is excluded. Southeastern savannas, however, appear to have evolved with fire as the principal selective agent, but with little grazing. Consequently, introduction of grazing now leads to decreased species diversity.

Effects of grazing by cattle on the hundreds of savanna species, other than principal range grasses, have been little studied. Cattle on open range may consume 70 to 80% of aboveground production in the first year after a burn (Pearson and Cutshall 1984). Effects on botanical composition is sparsely documented, but two mechanisms implicated in loss of native species are selection for protein-rich forbs and elimination of disturbance-intolerant species. Stoddard and Komarek (1941) noted disappearance of many native legumes when moderate grazing was introduced, and *Tripsacum dactyloides* (gamma grass) was eliminated from a site grazed by cattle within 2 years (Komarek 1965). Where the primary management objective is preservation of diversity and original floristic composition, it seems clear that grazing by cattle should be excluded.

Impacts of Vehicles, Logging Equipment and Fire Plows

User impacts include off-road vehicles, collecting of rare plants, and simple trampling. The sum of these effects, however, seems at present to be much lower than surface damage by fire plows and logging equipment.

Effects of physical disturbance on upper soil horizons is known for only a few species. Wiregrass is greatly reduced by heavy equipment used in surface preparation and is difficult to reestablish once eliminated. Simply plowing and resting a grazed wiregrass stand may suffice to convert it to bluestem (Carter and Hughes 1974). Little is known of the effects of site preparation and soil disturbances on the hundreds of other savanna species.

Semipermanent marring of the soilscape is a cumulative problem. On public and private lands, where silviculture is an objective secondary to preservation of wildlife habitat, natural diversity, or scientific, recreational, or aesthetic values, it is questionable whether present timber harvest techniques can prevent significant resource degradation. Each episode of timber harvest usually entails an increment of surface degradation.

Wheel ruts pool water, and are invaded by more hydrophytic species than those naturally occurring on the site, while wheel ridges are colonized by more xerophytic species. Erosional and aesthetic considerations aside, heavily rutted soils are useless for many ecological studies dealing with soil processes, forest succession, floristics, nutrient cycling, hydrology, fire ecology, and the like.

Integrity of topography, soil structure, and soil horizonation are significant elements of natural diversity, but have seldom been included as management objectives in forest plans. Some flat-lying soils of the Coastal Plain have been in place without significant erosion for periods of up to 10 million years (Daniels *et al.* 1971). These ancient soils have been little studied, and undisturbed soil sequences are becoming a rarity.

Cumulative effects of fire plow lines warrant serious concern because of certain fire control practices. On national forests and other managed lands, the most serious management problem today, other than too infrequent burning, is placement of fire plow lines in the moist transition area between uplands and wetlands. This zone is critical habitat for many of the rarest savanna species. In the natural situation, fire often burned wetlands or ran down the moisture gradient until it ran out of dry fuel. This kept critical zones of moist, mineral soil open for savanna species which require moist soil but cannot tolerate shading.

Current practice of prescribed fire often places fire lines directly along these narrow bands, resulting in systematic destruction of rare plants and habitat. Or, where the fire line is placed too far up the moisture gradient, shrubs move up to the line, eliminating the fire-maintained moist zone. Further, there is a tendency once shrubs have grown, for operators to place the line for the next fire even further up the moisture gradient to keep fire away from the shrubs.

The consequences of this practice are evident from the consideration of a single species: two of only three known

major sites for an endangered species, *Lysimachia asperulaefolia* (rough-leaved loosestrife), are found in a national forest. In both cases, the habitat has been nearly destroyed by the method of placement of fire lines.

Design Considerations for Savanna and Prairie Natural Areas

Since fire is essential for maintenance of species diversity in savanna and prairie, boundaries should be acquired that may be readily defended during prescription burning. Complete, natural units of flammable vegetation should be included in natural area boundaries. As a worst case, consider a boundary which runs through pocosin on deep peat. If adjacent landowners do not want their portions of the same wetland burned, a major and expensive effort would be required to control fire at the boundary.

The chance of extinction of species increases with the distance of islands of natural habitat from each other, and is greater in smaller than in larger 'islands'. Savannas today, largely persist in the landscape as islands surrounded by other natural vegetation types (e.g., pocosins) or by artificial communities such as pine plantations or cultivated fields.

Based on an application of island biogeographic concepts, a number of general recommendations for design of nature preserves have been made (Diamond and May 1976, Diamond 1975, Wilson and Willis 1975). They specify that reserves should be large, and they should either be close enough to each other to facilitate dispersal of component species, or be connected by protected corridors of habitats that facilitate species movements. Both requirements pose large problems in the case of savanna vegetation already dissected into small areas, separated by more-or-less permanently altered areas of non-pyrophytic vegetation.

Management Recommendations for Remnant Grasslands on Public Lands and Natural Area Preserves

When any natural community containing grassland is acquired, immediate efforts should be undertaken to determine past fire history. This may include field examination for conspicuous age classes of shrubs and saplings dating from recent fires, as well as examination of historical records and consultation with long-term residents. Unless a fire plan which mimics the original natural fire regime is devised and implemented, 'protection' of a natural area may lead to loss of diversity, succession to common woody species, and extinction of savanna flora.

Since there have been but a few quantitative studies on effects of fire frequency, intensity, and season of burn on maintenance of diversity in savannas (Lemon 1949, 1967, Walker and Peet 1983, Evans and Platt 1984, Davis and Platt 1984), no clear guidelines exist and managers should be encouraged to use cautious experimentation. As a minimum, it is necessary to watch for overtopping and competitive exclusion of smaller species by more robust species. Competition should be reduced by burning as often as necessary to retain all of the native flora.

Loss of species diversity from small, isolated preserves

(predicted by the equilibrium theory of island biogeography) and potential extinction of species cut off from migration corridors during periods of climatic change, present critical long-term problems. There must be considerable duplication and overlap in habitat preserves. Indeed, we may see the day when species may be 'migrated' by hand from one preserve to another along a climatic gradient if extinction is to be prevented.

Research Needs and Protection Priorities

Basic inventories, which are critical to ensure protection of the full range of savanna diversity, have not been completed for any of the southeastern states. Subsequent to inventory work, studies in different savanna systems will be needed to assess the appropriate fire regime for each type. Studies of species biology, particularly of rare and endangered species and of certain community dominants are badly needed.

Protection priority should be given to sites subject to rapid mesophytic succession in the absence of fire (these include the most species-rich, mesic and moist savannas); sites that have an uninterrupted fire history; sites with concentrations of rare or endemic species; and sites with diversity of soil types, hydrologic regimes, and topographic situations.

STATUS OF REMNANT SAVANNA AND PRAIRIE VEGETATION

Since listing and classification of plant communities in the South is in the early stages of development, no inventory exists of natural areas with examples of savanna. The following state-by-state account is a brief survey of kinds of native grasslands, and an indication of preservation status of remnants. Many have only recently been acquired for protection and managers have inherited communities in a variety of conditions. The list is necessarily incomplete, but may be considered glimpses into the diversity of original natural vegetation.

Texas

In the portion of East Texas covered by this report, there are only three protected examples of pyrophytic vegetation. The tiny Marysee Prairie is a rare, 6 acre remnant of coastal prairie where needed management by fire is limited by adjacent housing development.

The Roy E. Larsen Sandylands sanctuary is a Nature Conservancy preserve of 880 ha (2,178 acres). About 1/3 is xeric, riparian, sand ridge, a longleaf pine/dry savanna habitat once common throughout the South. Only a small stand of longleaf remains but there is an unusual concentration of rare xerophytic savanna herbs.

Hickory Creek Savanna in the Big Thicket contains three communities at present: forest, bluestem savanna, and moist, clay-based longleaf pine/mixed graminoid-forb savanna. It has been shown that the forest area was also savanna until reduced fire frequency in the 1950's allowed invasion by trees. Persistence of the other two savanna

communities has been related to edaphic factors (Streng and Harcombe 1982). The site is presently receiving restorative management with prescribed fire.

Louisiana

There are two calcareous prairies in north central Louisiana bearing floristic affinities with western tallgrass prairies, and probably with the original prairie openings of the Black Belt of Mississippi and Alabama. Substantial remnants of longleaf pine-bluestem savanna may be seen on various units of the Kisatchie National Forest where management with prescribed fire has been carried on for research purposes for many years by range scientists at the Southern Forest Experiment Station in Pineville.

Some 57,800 ha (142,846 acres) of coastal marsh and prairie, distributed along a continuous salinity gradient from mesic prairie ridges through fresh, brackish, and euhaline marsh occur within the Sabine National Wildlife Refuge. Year-long grazing by cattle constitutes significant disturbance, but the marshes are managed with fire, and effects of old canals on fresh water drainage and salt water intrusion are being controlled. Virtually nothing is known to remain of coastal pine meadows in the southeastern corner of the state or the several types of coastal and upland prairie described by Lockett (1876) to have occupied nearly the whole of southwestern Louisiana.

Mississippi

Open, moist, longleaf pine savannas form the matrix for a mosaic of wet, species-rich prairies that probably once stretched, almost unbroken, along the Pamlico Terrace from eastern Louisiana to northern Florida. The spectacular 'coastal meadows' of the Pamlico Terrace in Mississippi (Fig. 1) are among the most species-rich and are certainly the most geographically extensive of the remaining savanna lands of the southeast. Long spared because of poor drainage, infertility, and the frequent fires which swept the region, these important and extensive communities are now faced with urban and industrial development. The only protected examples occur on the Sandhill Crane NW Refuge, where their existence may be threatened by future management for sandhill cranes, including plowing, seeding, or impoundment.

Buttercup Flats, a Nature Conservancy preserve in Hancock Co., is a 28 ha (70 acre) remnant of species-rich, moist, longleaf pine savanna of a type which must have once been common on moist slopes and swales in rolling, coastal plain lands inland from the Pamlico Terrace.

Alabama

There are no protected examples of coastal meadows in Alabama. An excellent example remains, however, on the state line between Alabama and Mississippi near Grand Bay. At this location, is found a virgin prairie with a mile-long gradient, seemingly perfectly continuous, from open prairie with species density up to 40/square m, through pond cypress savanna to brackish and salt marsh (Norquist 1984). Inland from the Pamlico Terrace, as in Mississippi, small patches of moist, savanna vegetation still occur on hillside seepage areas, but none are protected.

Only in Alabama and Georgia, did longleaf pine-bluestem communities overlap substantially onto Piedmont soils. In fact, a map of the presettlement extent of longleaf pine (Harper 1928) indicates pyrophytic vegetation to cover nearly 3/4 of the state. The highest elevation longleaf pine grasslands were discovered by Mohr (1901) at elevations up to 610 m (2,000 ft) in the mountains of Alabama and Georgia. These appear to have been longleaf pine-bluestem communities maintained by topoedaphic factors and fire on steep, dry, south-facing slopes. No protected remnant of this interesting grassland type is known to exist. Similarly, in the rest of the state, most of the original longleaf pine-bluestem and wiregrass savanna has been converted to loblolly and slash pine plantation. Neither is there any known, undisturbed remnant of the Black Belt prairie-woodland mosaic.

Georgia

Over 2/3 of Georgia included lands which supported fire communities in at least part of the landscape. Of large areas of longleaf pine on the Piedmont, upper and lower Coastal Plain, only small amounts remain.

Remnants of high elevation longleaf pine/savanna or woodland exist unprotected on Pine Mountain (Bartow Co.). There are a few moist, pond cypress savannas on the Coastal Plain and small, species-rich, moist savannas in swales of the Tifton upland and Tallahassee Hills (Wharton 1978). Two magnificent remnants of virgin longleaf pine/wiregrass savanna are protected near Thomasville, each of about 325 ha (800 acres).

Florida

Grasslands of the Florida peninsula have received the widest spectrum of protection of any southern state. The singular, limestone based types of South Florida are particularly well represented. Slash pine rocklands, vast expanses of sawgrass (*Cladium jamaicense*)-*Muhlenbergia filipes* marl prairie, and pond cypress savanna are preserved in Everglades National Park and Big Cypress National Preserve. These are managed for preservation of natural communities, and studies are being carried out on effects of hydrology, fire frequency and season of burn (e.g., Taylor and Herndon 1981, Gunderson *et al.* 1983).

Somewhat similar conditions exist in central and northern Florida where tens of thousands of small, oval prairies lie in shallow solution pans in limestone, interspersed in slash pine and longleaf pine 'flatwoods' (woodland and savanna). Three national forests, Apalachicola, Osceola, and Ocala contain a diversity of savannas managed with fire. In addition, the state of Florida has an excellent system of state preserves (including Payne's Prairie), state forests, wildlife management areas, and state parks, many of which contain examples of marsh, prairie, and savanna (Gleason 1984).

Five Nature Conservancy preserves in Florida contain a variety of grasslands. These include the 2,465 ha (6,090 acre) Whitell-Ordway Kissimmee Prairie in Okeechobee Co. and the 1,200 ha (2,947 acre) Putnam Prairie in Putnam Co.

South Carolina

On the 60 ha (150 acre) Barataria Island Nature Conservancy preserve, there is a rare example of longleaf pine savanna with maritime influence. The preserve has small patches of longleaf, as well as live oak (*Q. virginiana*) and cabbage palm (*Sabal palmetto*). The Conservancy's Tillman Sand Ridge is an example of xeric longleaf pine/turkey oak/wiregrass savanna, while more mesic types are found on Cheraw National Wildlife Refuge and Cheraw State Park. The park is managed as pine plantation, however, and stand density is mostly that of forest, not savanna.

Additional sites with longleaf pine/wiregrass vegetation exist in Francis Marion National Forest, where small areas of mesic savanna persist in ecotones between upland pine sites and pocosins. A number of privately owned, mesic savannas ranging in size from lt 20 ha to gt 81 ha are scattered throughout the Coastal Plain (Gaddy 1982). Included, are the Scottswood Savanna (30 ha, Williamsburg Co.), Okeetee Savanna (81 ha, Jasper Co.), Summerville Savanna (20 ha, Dorchester Co.), Bates Hill Plantation Savanna and woodlands (Georgetown Co.), and Socastee Savanna (Horry Co.).

North Carolina

There are good examples of the most xeric types of longleaf pine savanna on sand ridges in the Bladen Lakes State Forest, and covering low sand rims of selected bay lakes, like Singletary Lake in the southeastern part of the state. Extensive areas of upland longleaf pine/wiregrass, as well as smaller remnants of longleaf/mixed graminoid savanna, are extant in the Sandhills Game Lands (Moore Co.), Holly Shelter Game Lands (Pender Co.), Weymouth Woods State Natural Area (Moore Co.), and the Croatan National Forest. Mesic to wet savanna is found in seepage areas in the sandhills and in low savannas of the Green Swamp.

The 4,850 ha (12,000 acre) Green Swamp preserve owned by the Nature Conservancy has a number of small, moist savannas with a long history of annual burning. The best remaining examples of species-rich, mesic savanna on the Atlantic coast are Big Island Savanna (corporate ownership) and Lanier Quarry savanna (mixed private ownership). A number of sites, variously designated sinks, depressions, and bays in Brunswick and New Hanover Counties also support savanna communities. Of particular interest are bluestem communities found in several small clay-based bays.

Virginia

Only tiny remnants of former savanna remain in North Carolina north of the Roanoke River, and essentially none remain in southeastern Virginia where perhaps several hundred square miles of longleaf pine savanna and woodland existed at the time of settlement. Restoration attempts, however, have begun on the 120 ha (300 acre) Blackwater Ecological Preserve in Isle of Wight Co., where there are remnant longleaf pine and scattered individuals of savanna herbs, many disjunct from southern populations by more than 200 km.

Despite a much longer period of land use by Europeans, the Southeast contains a greater diversity of unspoiled grassland remnants than the Midwest. The landscape mosaic, including swamp forests, steep slopes, sterile sand ridges, acid soils, and shrub bogs has fortunately not lent itself to uniform treatment with the plow. Many sites are small, hidden in obscure places, and partially overgrown, but if action is taken soon, there is still time and sufficient remnants to allow protection of almost the full spectrum of rich savanna and prairie communities of the South.

LITERATURE CITED

Al-Mufti, M.M., C.L. Sydes, S.B. Furness, J.P. Grime and S.R. Band. 1977. A quantitative analysis of shoot phenology and dominance in herbaceous vegetation. J. Ecol. 65:759-791.

Ashe, W.W. 1894. The forests, forest lands and forest products of eastern North Carolina. Josephus Daniels, State Printer, Raleigh, NC.

Bartram, W. 1955. 1791. Travels through North and South Carolina, Georgia, East and West Florida. Dover Pubs., New York.

Caddell, G.M., A. Woodrick and M.C. Hill. 1981. Biocultural studies in the Gainesville Lake area. Univ. of Alabama. Off. of Archaeological Res. Rept. No. 14.

Carter, C.W. and R.H. Hughes. 1974. Longleaf-slash pine wiregrass range. In C.E. Lewis (ed.) Range resources of the South. Univ. of Georgia. Coastal Plain Exp. Sta. Bull. N.S. 9, Tifton, Ga.

Chalkin, L.F. 1952. Annual summer fires kill hardwood rootstocks. USDA For. Serv. Southeastern For. Exp. Sta. Res. Note 19.

Christensen, N.L. 1979. The xeric sandhill and savanna ecosystems of the southeastern Atlantic Coastal Plain, USA. Veroff. Geobot. Inst. ETH, Stiftung Rubel, Zurich 68. Heft, 246-262.

Cowardin, L.M., V. Carter, F.C. Golet and E.T. LaRoe. 1979. Classification of wetlands and deepwater habitats of the United States. US Fish and Wildlife Serv. Pub. FWS/OBS-79/31. Washington, DC.

Cushwa, C.T., E.V. Bender and R.W. Cooper. 1966. The response of herbaceous vegetation to prescribed burning. USDA For. Serv. Southeastern For. Exp. Sta. Res. Note SE-53.

Daniels, R.B., E.E. Gamble and W.H. Wheeler. 1971. Stability of coastal plain surfaces. Southeastern Geol. 13:61-75.

Davis, L.S. and R.E. Martin. 1960. Time-temperature relationships of test head fires and backfires. USDA For. Serv. Southeastern For. Exp. Sta. Res. Note 148.

Davis, M. and W.J. Platt. 1984. Effects of season of burn upon flowering phenologies of the tribe Astereae (Compositae) in the ground cover of longleaf pine forests, Wakulla County, Florida. Bull. Ecol. Soc. Am. 65:202 (abstract).

Diamond, J.M. 1975. The island dilemma: lessons of modern biogeographic studies for the design of nature preserves. Biol. Conserv. 7:129-146.

Diamond, J.M. and R.M. May. 1976. Island biogeography and the design of natural reserves. pp. 163-186. In R.M May, (ed.). Theoretical Ecology. W.B. Saunders, Philadelphia, Penn.

Evans, G.W. and W.J. Platt. 1984. Responses of C3 and C4 grasses to variations in fire regimes in pine savannas of the southeastern United States. Bull. Ecol. Soc. Am. 65:180 (abstract).

Folkerts, G.W. 1982. The Gulf Coast pitcher plant bogs. Am. Sci. 70:260-267.

Gaddy, L.L. 1982. The floristics of three South Carolina pine savannas. Castanea 47:393-404.

Garren, K.H. 1943. Effects of fire on vegetation of the southeastern United States. Bot. Rev. 9:617-654.

Gleason, P.A., ed. 1984. Environments of South Florida, present and past. 2nd ed. Miami Geol. Soc. Coral Gables, Fl.

Gunderson, L., D. Taylor and J. Craig. 1983. Fire effects on flowering and fruiting patterns of understory plants in pinelands of Everglades National Park. NPS South Florida Res. Cen. Rept. SFRC-83/04. Homestead, Fl.

Harper, R.M. 1906. A phytogeographical sketch of the Altamaha Grit Region of the Coastal Plain of Georgia. Ann. N.Y. Acad. Sci. 17:1-415.

Harper, R.M. 1911. The relation of climax vegetation to islands and peninsulas. Bull. Torrey Bot. Club 38:515-525.

Harper, R.M. 1913. Economic botany of Alabama. Geol. Surv. of Ala. Monogr. 8. Vol. 1, University, Ala.

Harper, R.M. 1914. Geography and vegetation of northern Florida. pp. 163-437. In Sixth Ann. Rept. Fl. Geol. Surv.

Harper, R.M. 1928. Economic Botany of Alabama. Part 2. Geol. Surv. Ala. University, Ala.

Kologiski, R.L. 1977. The phytosociology of the Green Swamp, North Carolina. NC Agr. Exp. Sta. Tech. Bull. 250. Raleigh, No. Car.

Komarek, E.V. 1965. Fire ecology-grasslands and man. Proc. Tall Timbers Fire Ecol. Conf. 4:169-220.

Kuchler, A.W. 1964. Potential natural vegetation of the United States. Am. Geographical Soc. (map).

Langdon, O.G. 1971. Effects of prescribed burning on timber species in the southeastern Coastal Plain. pp. 34-44. In Proc. prescribed burning symp. Southeastern For. Exp. Sta., Asheville, No. Car.

Lemon, O.C. 1949. Successional responses of herbs in the longleaf-slash pine forest after fire. Ecology 30:135-145.

Lemon, O.C. 1967. Effects of fire on herbs of the southeastern United States and central Africa. Proc. Tall Timbers Fire Ecol. Conf. 6:112-127.

Lewis, C.E., H.E. Grelan, L.D. White and C.W. Carter. 1974. Range resources of the South. Univ. Ga. Coastal Plain Expt. Sta. Bull. N.S. 9. Tifton, Ga.

Little, E.L., Jr. 1971. Atlas of United States trees. Vol. 1. USDA For. Serv. Misc. Pub. 1146, Washington, DC.

Lockett, S. 1969 (1876). Louisiana as it is. A geographical and topographic description of the state. L.C. Post (ed.) LSU Press, Baton Rouge, La.

Lotti, T. 1956. Eliminating understory hardwoods with summer prescribed fires in coastal plain loblolly pine stands. J. For. 54:191-192.

Medici, G., ed. 1969. World atlas of agriculture. Istituto Geographico De Agostini, Novara, Italy.

Mohr, C. 1901. Plant life of Alabama. Brown Print. Co., Montgomery, Ala.

Naveh, Z. and R.H. Whittaker. 1980. Structure and floristic diversity of shrublands and woodlands in northern Israel and other Mediterranean areas. Vegetatio 41:171-190.

Norquist, H.C. 1984. A comparative study of the soils and vegetation of savannas in Mississippi. M.S. Thesis. Mississippi State Univ., Miss.

Parrott, R.T. 1967. A study of wiregrass (*Aristida stricta* Michx). with particular reference to fire. M.A. Thesis, Duke Univ., Durham, No. Car.

Pearson, H.A. and J.R. Cutshall. 1984. Southern forest range management. pp. 36-52. *In* N.E. Linnartz and M.K. Johnson. (eds.), Agroforestry in the southern United States. La. Agr. Exp. Sta. and La. Coop. Ext. Serv. Baton Rouge, La.

Peet, R.K., D.C. Glenn-Lewin and J.W. Wolf. 1983. Prediction of man's impact on plant species diversity. pp. 41-54. *In*. W. Holzner, M.J.A. Werger and I. Ikusima (eds.). Man's impact on vegetation. Junk, The Hague.

Shaffer, M.L. 1981. Minimum population sizes for species conservation. BioScience 31:196-201.

Shantz, H.L. and R. Zon. 1924. Natural vegetation. pp. 1-29. *In* O.E. Baker (ed.). 1936. Atlas of American agriculture. Part 4. U.S. Govt. Print. Off. Washington, DC.

Stoddard, H.L. and E.V. Komarek. 1941. The carrying capacity of southeastern quail lands. Trans. N. Am. Wildl. Conf. 6:477-484.

Streng, D.R. and P.A. Harcombe. 1982. Why don't East Texas savannas grow up to forest? Am. Midland Nat. 108:278-294.

Sudworth, G.B. 1913. Forest atlas: geographic distribution of North American trees, Part 1. Pines. USDA For. Serv., Washington, DC.

Sutter, R.D., L. Mansberg, and J. Moore. 1983. Endangered, threatened and rare plant species of North Carolina: a revised list. ASB Bull. 30:153-163.

Taylor, D.L. and A. Herndon. 1981. Impact of 22 years of fire on understory hardwood shrubs in slash pine communities within Everglades National Park. NPS So. Fl. Res. Ctr. Rept. T-640. Homestead, Fl.

Terborgh, J. 1974. Preservation of natural diversity: the problem of extinction prone species. BioScience 24:715-722.

Terborgh, J. and B. Winter. 1980. Some causes of extinction. pp. 119-133. *In*. Soule' and B.A. Wilcox. (eds.), Conservation biology: an evolutionary-ecological perspective. Sinauer Associates, Sunderland, Mass.

Vankat, J.L. 1979. The natural vegetation of North America. John Wiley and Sons, New York, NY.

Veno, P.A. 1976. Successional relationships of five Florida plant communities. Ecology 57:498-508.

Vogl, R.J. 1973. Fire in the southeastern grasslands. Proc. Tall Timbers Fire Ecol. Conf. 12:175-198.

Wahlenberg, W.G. 1946. Longleaf pine. Charles Lathrop Pack Foundation, Washington, DC.

Walker, J. and R.K. Peet. 1983. Composition and species diversity of pine-wiregrass savannas of the Green Swamp, North Carolina. Vegetatio 55:163-179.

Walker, J. 1985. Production and species diversity in pine-wiregrass savannas of the Green Swamp, North Carolina. Ph.D. Dissertation, Univ. of No. Car. Chapel Hill, No. Car.

Walter, H. 1979. Vegetation of the earth. 2nd ed. Springer Verlag, New York, NY.

Wells, B.W. 1928. Plant communities of the Coastal Plain of North Carolina and their successional relations. Ecology 9:230-242.

Wells, B.W. and I.V. Shunk. 1928. A southern upland grass-sedge bog. No. Car. Agr. Exp. Sta. Tech. Bull. 32. Raleigh, No. Car.

Wells, B.W. and I.V. Shunk. 1931. The vegetation and habitat factors of the coarser sands of the North Carolina Coastal Plain. Ecol. Monogr. 1:465-520.

Wharton, C.H. 1978. The natural environments of Georgia, Dept. Natural Resources, Atlanta, Ga.

Wilson, E.O. and E.O. Willis. 1975. Applied biogeography. pp. 522-534. *In* M.L. Cody and J.M Diamond. (eds.). Ecology and evolution of communities. Belknap Press, Cambridge, Mass.

The Pine Barrens Of New Jersey And Associated Communities: Preservation Status And Management Problems

by

Scott L. Collins, Charles T. Roman and Ralph E. Good

ABSTRACT-- The Pine Barrens of southern New Jersey contain a 445,000 ha mosaic of upland and wetland vegetation. Common upland species include several pines (*Pinus rigida, P. echinata, P. virginiana*) and oaks (*Quercus alba, Q. coccinea, Q. ilicifolia, Q. marilandica, Q. prinus, Q. stellata, Q. velutina*). The more diverse wetland types include pitch pine lowlands, cedar swamps (*Chamaecyparis thyoides*), hardwood swamps (*Acer rubrum, Nyssa sylvatica*), bogs and heathlands (*Gaylussacia* spp., *Kalmia* spp. *Vaccinium* spp.), and marshes. The Pinelands are unique because they remain relatively intact, although they occur within the highly developed eastern seaboard. Because of increasing encroachment on the Pinelands from nearby metropolitan areas, a unique management plan was designed to preserve Pinelands ecosystems while providing for regulated land use. In 1978, the area was designated by the Federal Government as the Pinelands National Reserve. Subsequently, New Jersey enacted the Pinelands Protection Act to implement Federal legislation. A Comprehensive Management Plan was created to generate a strategy for regulating development within designated land capability areas and ensuring preservation of certain components of the Pinelands ecosystem. This is facilitated in part by a land acquisition program. Also, a wetlands buffer delineation model was proposed to ensure strict preservation of wetlands and aquifers. Despite regulated land use, portions of the Pinelands may still be threatened by acid deposition and ecosystem fragmentation. Because soils and water in the Pinelands are highly acidic, the impact of acid deposition is uncertain. Fragmentation, on the other hand, may alter vegetation dynamics through disruption of the natural disturbance regime, in particular fire frequency. The ecosystem approach to management embodied in the Pinelands National Reserve, however, will provide a means of protecting contiguous segments large enough to maintain regional patch dynamics.

KEYWORDS: comprehensive management plan, New Jersey, Pine Barrens, Pinelands National Reserve, Wetlands buffer delineation model.

The state of New Jersey is a study in contrasts. In particular, the heavily industrialized northeastern corridor from New York City to Philadelphia can be contrasted with the scenic areas to the north and south. Although New Jersey is the most densely populated state in the United States, the majority of people live in the northern half of the state. To the south, comprising approximately 25 percent of the state's land area, occurs the 445,000 ha Pine Barrens or Pinelands. The population of the Pine Barrens is sparse by comparison to the northern regions of New Jersey. The area is viewed by many only as they escape from Philadelphia on their summertime sojourns to the Jersey shore. Within this vast area of pine dominated vegetation exists a complex mosaic of upland and wetland plant communities that are protected by a comprehensive land use management plan (Pinelands Commission 1980). This plan was developed in response to federal and state legislation mandating that the natural and cultural resources of the region be protected while providing for environmentally compatible growth and development. The

purpose of this paper is to 1) briefly describe the environment and vegetation of the Pinelands, 2) describe some aspects of the land use management plan, and 3) discuss the potential impact of factors such as acid deposition and ecosystem fragmentation on the Pinelands landscape. In general, the management plan for the Pine Barrens can serve as a prototype for preservation of other ecologically important areas in the eastern United States and elsewhere.

SOILS AND CLIMATE

The Pine Barrens are located on the outer Coastal Plain of southern New Jersey (Fig. 1). This region was formed by sand and gravel deposits of the Kirkwood Formation during the Miocene. Overlying this Formation is a thick (7.9-61.3 m) and widespread layer of Cohansey Sands. This, and other more recent sands laid down by

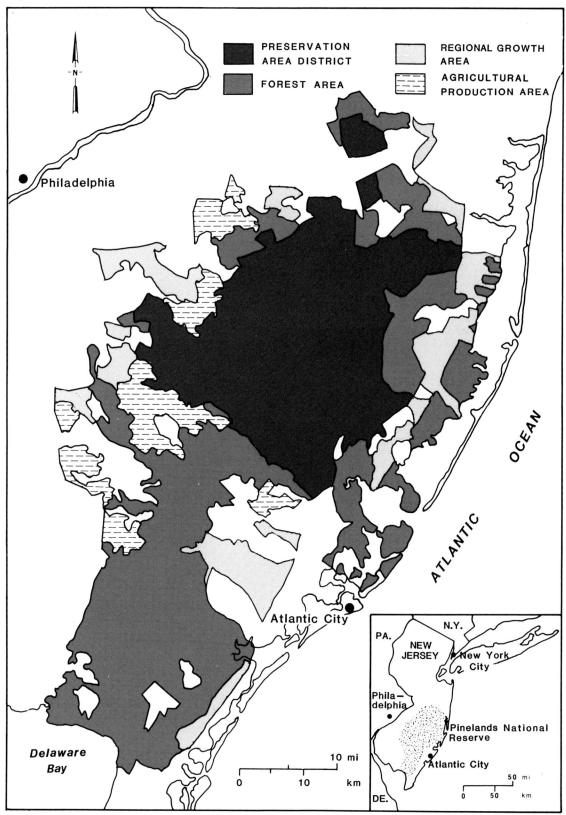

Figure 1. A map of New Jersey indicating the location of the Pine Barrens and several of the Land Capability Areas within the Pinelands National Reserve.

sea level fluctuations during the Pleistocene, comprise the majority of surface soils in the Pine Barrens (Rhodehamel 1979). Thirteen soil series occur in the Pinelands, ranging from the excessively well drained, coarse sands of the Lakewood, Woodmansee, and Evesboro series to the poorly drained sandy loams and loamy fine sands of the Pokomoke and Muck series (Tedrow 1979). The soils are highly acidic, ranging in pH from 3.6 to 5.0. Upland to wetland transitions are largely a function of depth to the seasonal high water table.

The area is characterized by a continental climate (Havens 1979). Temperatures range from an average of 23 degrees C during the three warmest months (June-August) to an average of 1 degree C during the three coldest months (December-February). Annual precipitation averages between 107-117 cm and is distributed evenly throughout the year. Nevertheless, the region experiences occasional droughts which are compounded by the coarse textured, well drained, sandy soils.

VEGETATION

The vegetation of the Pine Barrens was originally described in detail by Stone (1911) and Harshberger (1916). More recent descriptions include those by Robichaud and Buell (1973), McCormick (1979), and Olsson (1979). A brief synopsis of the plant communities will be provided here. The vegetation of the region is generally divided into upland and wetland assemblages based on hydrology,

soils, and plant species composition. Pitch pine (*Pinus rigida*) is the most common tree species in the Pine Barrens, occurring in both upland and wetland areas (Table 1). Uplands, which comprise approximately 70% of the Pinelands, are classified into three types: 1) pine-oak forests, 2) oak-pine forests, and 3) pygmy forest or pine plains. Pine-oak forests are those in which pines (mostly *P. rigida* with some *P. echinata*) account for greater than 50% of the stem density and basal area, and oaks (usually *Q. marilandica*, *Q. stellata*, and *Q. velutina*) are less abundant. Common understory shrubs include *Gaylussacia baccata*, *Vaccinium vacillans*, and *Q. ilicifolia* (Table 2). The herbaceous layer is sparce (Buell and Cantlon 1950), the most common species are *Carex pennsylvanica* and *Melampyrum lineare*. Pine-oak vegetation characterizes the Pine Barrens (McCormick 1979) although it is most widespread only in the northern half of the region. This vegetation occurs on well drained soils and is maintained by low intensity fires (Little 1979a, Forman and Boerner 1981).

Oak-pine forests differ considerably from the pine-oak

Table 1. Distribution of Common Tree Species among Vegetation Types in the New Jersey Pine Barrens.

Species	Pine-oak	Oak-pine	Pitch pine lowland	Cedar swamp	Hardwood swamp	Pine Plains
Acer rubrum			O	O	D	
Betula populifolia			O	O	O	
Chamaecyparis thyoides				D		
Liquidambar styraciflua			O	O	O	
Magnolia virginiana				O	O	
Nyssa sylvatica			O	O	D	
Pinus echinata	O	C				
P. rigida	D	O	D	O	O	D
Quercus alba		D				
Q. coccinea		C				
Q. falcata		C				
Q. marilandica	C					D
Q. prinus		D				
Q. stellata	C	O				
Q. velutina	D	D				

D = dominant, C = common, O = occasional

Table 2. Distribution of Some Common Shrubs among Vegetation Types in the New Jersey Pine Barrens.

Species	Pine-oak	Oak-pine	Pine plains	Pitch pine lowlands	Cedar swamp	Hardwood swamp	Shrub and bog
Chamaedaphne caliculata				D[a]			D
Clethra alnifolia					C	C	O
Gaylussacia baccata	C	D	C				
G. frondosa		O		O	C	O	
Kalmia angustifolia				D			D
K. latifolia	C	C	C				
Lyonia mariana				O	O	O	O
Rhododendron viscosum					C	O	O
Vaccinium vacillans	C	D	C				
V. corymbosum					C	C	D
V. macrocarpon					O		C
Comptonia peregrina	C	C	C				
Leocothoe racemosa				O		O	
Quercus illicifolia	D	O	D				

[a] D = dominant, C = common, O = occasional

type (Buell and Cantlon 1950). Oak-pine forests are taller, more diverse, and less dense than the pine-oak type. Common oaks include *Q. velutina* and *Q. alba* throughout the region, *Q. prinus* and *Q. coccinea* in the north and *Q. falcata* in the south. All oak forests include some pines, mostly *P. echinata* with a few individuals of *P. rigida* (Collins and Good 1985). *Gaylussacia baccata, G. frondosa*, and *V. vacillans* are common shrubs (Buell and Cantlon 1950). Herbaceous species are widely scattered, the most common are *C. pennsylvanica* and *M. lineare*. Oak-pine forests are scattered throughout the northern and eastern parts of the Pine Barrens and become more abundant in the southern half of the region. These forests develop under a reduced fire frequency (Little 1979a), but once established, fires may increase oak abundance via basal sprouts (Little and Moore 1949).

The most unique upland vegetation type is the pine plains, a dwarf forest (ca. 3.0-3.3 m tall) of *P. rigida* and shrub form oaks (*Q. ilicifolia, Q. marilandica*). Shrubs such as *Kalmia latifolia, V. vacillans*, and *G. baccata*, typical of other upland assemblages, are common in the plains. In addition *Leiophyllum buxifolium, Corema conradii*, and *Pyxidanthera barbulata* are locally abundant. Good *et al.* (1979) identify three areas containing dwarf forests: the east plains (2368 ha), the west plains (2467 ha), and the Spring Hill plains (108 ha), all of which occur in the northern half of the Pinelands. These pygmy forests have developed under conditions of frequent fires (Good *et al.* 1979). The pines in these forests have serotinous cones and the dwarf growth habit is genetically fixed (Ledig and Fryer 1972, Good and Good 1975).

About 30 percent of the Pine Barrens contains wetland plant communities such as: 1) pitch pine lowlands, 2) cedar swamps, 3) hardwood swamps, 4) bogs and heathlands, and 5) freshwater and coastal marshes. Pitch pine lowlands account for approximately one-third of the wetland vegetation in the Pinelands. These forests occur adjacent to other wetland types bordering streams and in local depressions. The canopy is almost exclusively *P. rigida* beneath which is dense shrub layer of *Gaylussacia frondosa* and/or *Kalmia angustifolia* may develop. Herbs such as *Pteridium aquilinum* and *Xerophyllum asphodeltoides* may be locally abundant and *Sphagnum* spp. occur in the wetter areas.

Dense, relatively even-aged stands of Atlantic white cedar (*Chamaecyparis thyoides*) form bands of forest vegetation along streams. At one time, cedar swamps were more extensive but logging, fires, and berry culture have eliminated many of the larger swamps. Most extant cedar swamps are less than 300 m wide (McCormick 1979). These forests contain an occasional individual of *P. rigida* and some hardwood species (*Acer rubrum, Nyssa sylvatica*), as well. Shrubs such as *Vaccinium corymbosum, Clethra alnifolia, Rhododendron viscosum*,

Figure 2. Oak-pine vegetation within Lebanon State Forest, New Jersey Pine Barrens. (Photograph by S. L. Collins)

and *Gaylussacia frondosa* are abundant especially along the margins of cedar swamps. *Sphagnum* spp. are common and several herbaceous taxa (*Sarracenia purpurea, Drosera* spp., *Utricularia* spp., *Schizaea pusilla* may be abundant beneath canopy openings (Ehrenfeld and Schneider 1983).

Hardwood swamps are also associated with streams and the borders of cedar swamps. The most common hardwood species are *Acer rubrum* and *Nyssa sylvatica*. Associated species include *Liquidambar syraciflua, Magnolia virginiana,* and *Betula populifolia* (Ehrenfeld and Gulick 1981). Individuals of *P. rigida* may occur, as well. Several species of shrubs (mostly *V. corymbosum* and *C. alnifolia*) are common and these can form a dense, continuous, understory canopy. Herbaceous plants are less common than in the cedar swamps, whereas, shrubs are more abundant (McCormick 1979).

Bogs and shrub-dominated heathlands often occur in isolated depressions (called spungs), immediately adjacent to streams, and in areas disturbed by fire or logging. *Chamaedaphne caliculata* and *Kalmia angustifolia* usually produce a continuous canopy. Other shrubs such as *V. corymbosum* and *V. macrocarpon* may be conspicuous in some abandoned bogs, and logged cedar swamps *Sphagnum* spp. produce a lush ground cover beneath the shrubs. Herbaceous communities develop in areas where peat has been removed down to the underlying sands. Several species of Orchidaceae, Cyperacea, and *Drosera* may be found in these habitats.

Coastal and inland marshes are extensive along the estuarine and river systems in the Pinelands. Coastal salt marshes contain several abundant taxa such as *Spartina alterniflora, S. patens,* and *Distichlis spicata*. Shrub species at the marsh-upland border may include *Iva frutescens* and *Baccharis halimifolia*, while drier, disturbed areas often are covered by the grass *Phragmites australis* (Good 1965). Marshes extend inland along rivers, grading from saline to freshwater environments. Freshwater tidal marshes include many herbaceous species occupying portions of a wet to dry continuum: *Nuphar advena, Zizania aquatica, Peltandra virginica,* and *Bidens* spp. (Simpson *et al.* 1983).

Vegetation dynamics in the Pine Barrens have been strongly influenced by disturbance, in particular fire frequency and intensity (Little 1979a,b). That fire has affected species composition, and community structure is amply demonstrated in the pine plains. In this vegetation type, the pines and oaks produce vigorous basal sprouts following fires and pines release seeds from serotinous cones. The percentage of individuals with serotinous cones approaches zero in most upland forests, whereas, it is nearly 100% in the plains (Good and Good 1975).

In the absence of fire, oaks tend to dominate upland forests and pines may comprise only 5 to 10% of tree species importance (Little 1979b, Collins and Good 1985). In addition, variables such as shrub density, litter depth, and ground cover increase during post-fire succession (Buell and Cantlon 1953, Collins and Good

1985). Forman and Boerner (1981) reported that the number of fires in the Pine Barrens has increased during the 1900's but the average area per fire has decreased. Much of this is a function of fire suppression activities during the early 1900's contrasted with the prescribed burning programs initiated in the late 1940's. Pines require a mineral seedbed for germination (Little and Moore 1949), whereas, some oak seedlings are favored by the accumulation of litter up to 5.0 cm (Wood 1938). Thus, oaks increase at the expense of pines on sites where fires are infrequent.

Although wetlands may occasionally serve as natural firebreaks, during dry periods fires may spread from uplands into adjacent pitch pine lowlands and cedar swamps. In cedar swamps, post-fire succession may return dominance of the site to cedar or hardwood forests. Forman and Boerner (1981) suggested that in the absence of fire, cedars are replaced by hardwoods. Overall, they suggest that reduced fire frequency may alter the Pine Barrens from its characteristic coarse-grained and patchy structure to a more fine-grained landscape.

Pine Barrens vegetation was originally more extensive along the eastern seaboard from southern New Jersey, northeastward through Long Island, Nantucket, Martha's Vinyard to Cape Cod (Kuchler 1964). Much of this vegetation has been fragmented, although some remaining forest is protected at the Brookhaven National Laboratory (Whittaker and Woodwell 1969) and in lands owned by the Nature Conservancy on Long Island. Additionally, pitch pine dominated barrens occur in upstate New York near Albany (Milne 1985) and in the Shawangunk Mountains (McIntosh 1959).

MANAGEMENT

Humans have had a tremendous impact on the Pine Barrens throughout its recent history (Wacker 1979). Nevertheless, the region has maintained its unique character partly because the low fertility, acid soils restrict traditional agricultural development. Because the Pine Barrens contains several endangered species (Table 3), exceptional water quality, and fragile ecosystems, it was imperative

Table 3. Threatened and Endangered Plant Species in Each Vegetation Type (from Pinelands Commission 1980).

Vegetation	Threatened	Endangered
Pine-oak[a]	3	4
Oak-pine	2	2
Pitch pine lowland	2	2
Cedar swamp	4	2
Hardwood swamp	15	6
Marshes[b]	11	6
Bog	18	11

[a] Includes pine plains.

[b] Includes inland and coastal marshes.

to protect this extensive natural resource. The area has been and continues to be threatened by encroachment from the industrial complex to the north, Philadelphia and its suburbs to the west, and the sprawl of Atlantic City to the southeast. There are occasional proposals to use the underlying Kirkwood-Cohansey aquifer system (estimated to contain 17 trillion gallons of potable water) as a water supply for nearby urban areas but this is unlikely to occur. Several retirement villages and housing developments have been sited in the Pinelands. These areas, especially, affect water quality and may threaten the integrity of wetland ecosystems (Ehrenfeld 1983). Developments also increase ecosystem fragmentation, the consequences of which have not been determined for the Pine Barrens (Good 1982).

A unique management plan was needed to preserve the Pine Barrens, while permitting necessary agricultural activities and restricted growth. In 1978, the Pinelands National Reserve was established by the Federal Government in Section 502 of the National Parks and Recreation Act. The purpose of this legislation was to "... direct, regulate and mitigate the effects of an increasing population on a regional ecosystem basis ..." (Good and Good 1984: 170). This act included a federally subsidized land acquisition program. The Governor of New Jersey established the Pinelands Commission as the state agency for review and implementation of land management policies. Subsequently, the State of New Jersey passed the Pinelands Protection Act in 1979 to implement the Federal legislation. This act required the development of a management plan for the Pinelands. The New Jersey Pinelands Comprehensive Management Plan (CMP) was completed and adopted by the Pinelands Commission in 1980 and received federal approval in 1981. In 1983, the Pinelands National Reserve was selected as a Biosphere Reserve in the UNESCO Man and the Biosphere Program.

The Comprehensive Management Plan designated specific land use capability areas based on environmental quality, cultural features, and existing land use (Fig. 1). The land capability areas are (in order of decreasing environmental quality and sensitivity to development): Preservation Area District, Forest Areas, Agricultural Production Areas, Rural Development Areas, Regional Growth Areas, Villages and Towns. Federal Installations are also included as a land capability type. Each capability area has a distinct set of rules specified in the CMP to govern growth and development. The CMP includes several management programs to insure that permitted development proceeds with minimal environmental impact. These programs pertain to wetlands, water quality and forestry to name a few. Also, land acquisition is designed to increase the amount of public holding and protect whole watersheds. Some of the land in the Preservation Area is state owned. The land acquisition program has focused on adding land to link together state owned lands in the Preservation Area as well as protect critical and unique habitats such as the pine

plains.

Of particular interest, is the strict maintenance of high water quality standards and wetlands protection in all of the land capability areas. Animal diversity and the number of threatened plant species are greatest in wetlands (Tables 3 and 4). Ehrenfeld (1983) has demonstrated that pollution associated with rural developments impacts wa-

Table 4. Number of Mammals, Breeding Birds and Selected Reptiles and Amphibians in Pine Barrens Vegetation Types (Compiled from Pinelands Commission 1980).

Vegetation	Mammals	Breeding Birds	Reptiles + Amphibians	Total
Pine-oak[a]	23	34	17	74
Oak-pine	24	40	17	83
Pitch pine lowlands	25	15	14	54
Cedar swamps	18	11	14	43
Hardwood swamps	27	41	14	82
Marshes[b]	13	61	12	86
Bogs	20	29	12	61

[a] Includes pine plains.

[b] Includes inland and coastal marshes.

ter quality and plant species composition in hardwood swamps. In cedar swamps receiving runoff from adjacent developments, typical Pine Barrens species were lost, while weeds and exotic plants increased. There was increased uptake by plants of lead and phosphorus in the most severely disturbed sites (Ehrenfeld and Schneider 1983).

The wetlands management program for the pinelands is particularly stringent. Development within wetlands is prohibited, and a maximum 91 m (300 ft) buffer is required between upland development and a wetland unless it can be demonstrated that the development will have no significant adverse impact on the wetland. Zampella and Roman (1983) assessed the effectiveness of this buffer provision and of the entire wetlands program and concluded that it provides a practical and successful approach to wetlands protection.

To aid in implementation of the wetland buffer provision, Roman and Good (1985) developed a model for determining the minimum site-specific buffer width needed to protect wetlands from impacts associated with upland development. The model includes Special Case Guidelines and a multifactor procedure. These Guidelines pertain to particular Pinelands land use areas (e.g. Preservation Area District), wetland types (e.g. Cedar Swamps), or developmental impacts (e.g. resource extraction, on-site waste water treatment) that deserve priority consideration, and thus, a buffer area of at least 91 m is recommended. For example, it is recommended that a minimum 91 m buffer be maintained between upland development and all wetlands of the environmentally sensitive Preservation Area District. If the proposed development does not meet one of the above guidelines, then a multifactor procedure is followed to determine buffer width. The buffer width may be reduced below 91 m based on an evaluation of relative wetland quality, an assessment of potential impacts associated with the proposed development, and incorporation of a land use factor based on the land capability area in which the development is to be located. Based on a systematic and consistent evaluation of these criteria, a numerical index is derived from which the minimum buffer width needed to protect the wetland is determined. Wetlands determined to have high relative quality and a high potential for impacts are assigned the maximum buffer of 91 m.

FUTURE IMPACTS

Despite a well-defined management plan, certain environmental impacts may have a deleterious effect on the Pinelands in the future. Good (1982) outlines several critical management concerns for the Pinelands including 1) fire management, 2) the effects of ecosystem fragmentation on Pinelands biota, and 3) effects of acid deposition on nutrient dynamics and hydrology. Acid deposition continues to threaten water quality and nutrient budgets in much of the eastern United States (Haines 1981). Johnson (1979) reported that pH of two Pine Barrens streams decreased from 1958-1978 as a result of acid deposition. Morgan (1984) analyzed pH data extending from 1958-1982 for the same two streams and found no significant decrease in pH during this time period. Instead, Morgan (1984) suggested that the trend of decreasing pH levels resulted from a pulse disturbance to the watershed. A large fire burned approximately 10% of the Pinelands in 1963. Following fire, leaching of base cations is increased (Boerner and Forman 1982) thus, stream pH values would be elevated. Leaching of cations is reduced during post-fire succession (Boerner and Forman 1982), therefore, pH levels decrease. Morgan (1984) concludes that current evidence does not support the notion that acid precipitation has lowered pH in the already acidic Pinelands ecosystem.

Much of the vegetation in the eastern United States has been reduced from large continuous forests to smaller more isolated units (Burgess and Sharpe 1981). The Pine Barrens is unusual in that much of the upland forest remains relatively intact despite the continuous presence of man in the region. Nevertheless, with the impending encroachment of development in portions of the Pinelands, ecosystem fragmentation becomes an increasing concern. Evidence is now being gathered on the effects of fragmentation on forest composition and dynamics. In general, not enough time has elapsed for changes in long-lived populations to become evident. One of the impacts of fragmentation, however, is isolation of fragments accompanied by a disruption of the natural disturbance regime (Pickett and Thompson 1978). Forest fragments in the Pine Barrens may burn less often than vegetation of non-fragmented areas. This can have a pro-

found affect on future vegetation dynamics (Forman and Boerner 1981). Tree seedling density of pines and some oaks was dramatically lower in a forest fragment compared to nearby continuous forest (Collins and Good 1985). Reduced seedling density was determined to be a function of increased litter depth, shrub density, and decreased amounts of light reaching the forest floor. These factors resulted from the long-term absence of fire in the forest fragment (e.g. Little 1979a). Fire suppression leads to accumulation of fuels which can result in catastrophic fires during seasonal droughts. Thus, the impacts of ecosystem fragmentation interact with the need for a fire management policy especially on privately-owned lands.

In summary, the New Jersey Pine Barrens are unique because they remain relatively intact despite surrounding urbanization, retain high water quality, and contain many threatened and endangered plant and animal species. By designating the region as the nation's first National Reserve, a novel approach to management was derived to promote conservation within a context of restricted development. This management program is continually being tested and refined. Such an approach requires cooperation at the federal, state, and local levels. These interactions have proved effective for the Pinelands and can serve as a model for regional management of other ecologically important areas in the United States and elsewhere.

LITERATURE CITED

Boerner, R.E.J. and R.T.T. Forman. 1981. Hydrologic and mineral budgets of New Jersey Pine Barrens upland forests following two fire intensities. Can. J. For. Res. 12:503-510.

Buell, M.F. and J.E. Cantlon. 1950. A study of two communities of the New Jersey Pine Barrens and a comparison of methods. Ecology 31:567-586.

Buell, M.F. and J.E. Cantlon. 1953. Effects of prescribed burning on ground cover in the New Jersey pine region. Ecology 34:520-528.

Burgess, R.L. and D.M. Sharpe. 1981. Forest island dynamics in man-dominated landscapes. Springer-Verlag, New York, N.Y.

Collins, S.L. and R.E. Good. 1985. A preliminary analysis of oak-pine vegetation in the New Jersey Pine Barrens. Tech. Rep., Div. Pinelands Res., Center for Coastal and Environmental Studies, Rutgers Univ., New Brunswick, New Jersey.

Ehrenfeld, J.G. 1983. The effects of changes in land-use on swamps of the New Jersey Pine Barrens. Biol. Conserv. 25:353-375.

Ehrenfeld, J.G. and M. Gulick. 1981. Structure and dynamics of hardwood swamps in the New Jersey Pine Barrens: contrasting patterns in trees and shrubs. Am. J. Bot. 68:471-481.

Ehrenfeld, J.G. and J.P. Schneider. 1983. The sensitivity of cedar swamps to the effects of non-point source pollution associated with suburbanization in the New Jersey Pine Barrens. Tech. Rep., Div. Water Res., Center for Coastal and Environmental Studies, Rutgers Univ., New Brunswick, NJ.

Forman, R.T.T. and R.E.J. Boerner. 1981. Fire frequency and the Pine Barrens of New Jersey. Bull. Torrey Bot. Club 108:34-50.

Good, R.E. 1965. Salt marsh vegetation, Cape May, New Jersey. Bull. New Jersey Acad. Sci. 10:1-11.

Good, R.E. 1982. Ecological solutions to environmental management concerns in the Pinelands National Reserve. Proceedings of a conference. Tech. Rep., Div. Pinelands Res., Center for Coastal and Environmental Studies, Rutgers Univ., New Brunswick, New Jersey.

Good, R.E. and N.F. Good. 1975. Growth characteristics of two populations of *Pinus rigida* Mill. from the Pine Barrens of New Jersey. Ecology 56:1215-1220.

Good, R.E. and N.F. Good. 1984. The Pinelands National Reserve: an ecosystem approach to management. BioScience 34:169-173.

Good, R.E., N.F. Good and J.W. Andreson. 1979 The pine barrens plains pp. 283-295. *In* R.T.T. Forman (ed.). Pine Barrens: Ecosystem and landscape. Academic Press, New York.

Haines, T.A. 1981. Acidic precipitation and its consequences for aquatic ecosystems: a review. Trans. Am. Fish. Soc. 110:669-707.

Harshberger, J.W. 1916. The vegetation of the New Jersey Pine-Barrens. Christopher Sower Co., Philadelphia, Penn.

Havens, A.V. 1979. Climate and microclimate of the New Jersey pine barrens. pp. 113-131, *In* R.T.T. Forman (ed.). Pine Barrens: ecosystem and landscape. Academic Press, New York, NY.

Johnson, A.H. 1979. Evidence of acidification of headwater streams in the New Jersey Pinelands. Science 206:834-836.

Kuchler, A.W. 1964. Potential natural vegetation of the conterminous United States. Am. Geogr. Soc. Special Publ. No. 36.

Ledig, F.T. and J.H. Fryer. 1972. A pocket of variability in *Pinus rigida*. Evolution 26:259-266.

Little, S. 1979a. Fire and plant succession in the New Jersey Pine Barrens. pp. 297-314. *In* R.T.T. Forman (ed.). Pine Barrens: ecosystem and landscape. Academic Press, New York.

Little, S. 1979b. The Pine Barrens of New Jersey. pp. 451-464, *In* R.L. Specht (ed.). Heathlands and related shrublands of the world. A. Descriptive studies. Elsevier Scientific Publ. Co., Amsterdam, The Netherlands.

Little, S. and E.B. Moore. 1949. The ecological role of prescribed burns in the pine-oak forests of southern New Jersey. Ecology 30:223-233.

Lutz, H.J. 1934. Ecological relations in the pitch pine plains of southern New Jersey. Yale Univ. School of Forestry Bull. No. 38, New Haven, Conn.

McCormick, J. 1979. The vegetation of the New Jersey Pine Barrens. pp. 229-243. *In* R.T.T. Forman (ed.). Pine Barrens: ecosystem and land-scape. Academic Press, New York, N.Y.

McIntosh, R.P. 1959. Presence and cover in pine-oak stands of the Shawangunk Mountains, New York. Ecology 40:482-485.

Milne, B.T. 1985. Upland vegetational gradients and post-fire succession in the Albany Pine Brush, New York. Bull. Torrey Bot. Club 112:21-34.

Morgan, M.D. 1984. Acidification of headwater streams in the New Jersey Pinelands: a re-evaluation. Limnol. Oceanogr. 29:1259-1266.

Olsson, H. 1979. Vegetation of the New Jersey Pine Barrens: a phytosociological classification. pp. 245-263. *In* R.T.T. Forman (ed.). Pine Barrens: ecosystem and landscape. Academic Press, New York.

Pickett, S.T.A. and J.N. Thompson. 1978. Patch dynamics and the design of nature reserves. Biol. Conserv. 13:27-37.

Pinelands Commission. 1980. New Jersey Pinelands comprehensive management plan. N.J. Pinelands Commission, New Lisbon, New Jersey.

Rhodehamel, E.C. 1979. Geology of the Pine Barrens of New Jersey. pp 39-60. *In* R.T.T. Forman (ed.). Pine Barrens: ecosystem and landscape. Academic Press, New York.

Robichaud, B. and M.F. Buell. 1973. Vegetation of New Jersey. Rutgers Univ. Press, New Brunswick, New Jersey.

Roman, C.T. and R.E. Good. 1985. Buffer delineation model for New Jersey Pinelands Wetlands. Tech. Rep., Div. Pinelands Res., Center for Coastal and Environmental Studies, Rutgers Univ., New Brunswick, New Jersey.

Simpson, R.L., R.E. Good, M.A. Leck and D.F. Whigham. 1983. The ecology of freshwater tidal wetlands. BioScience 33:255-259.

Stone, W. 1911. The plants of southern New Jersey with special reference to the flora of the Pine Barrens and the geographic distribution of the species. Annu. Rep., New Jersey State Museum, Trenton, New Jersey.

Tedrow, J.C.F. 1979. Development of Pine Barrens soils. pp. 61-80 *In* R.T.T. Forman, (ed.) Pine Barrens: ecosystem and landscape. Academic Press, New York.

Wacker, P.O. 1979. Human exploitation of the New Jersey Pine Barrens before 1900. pp. 3-23. *In* R.T.T. Forman, (ed.). Pine Barrens: ecosystem and landscape. Academic Press, New York.

Whittaker, R.H. and G.M. Woodwell. 1969. Structure, production and diversity of the oak-pine forest at Brookhaven, New York. J. Ecol. 57:155-174.

Wood, O.M. 1938. Seedling reproduction of oak in southern New Jersey. Ecology 19:276-293.

Zampella, R.A. and C.T. Roman. 1983. Wetlands protection in the New Jersey Pinelands. Wetlands 3:124-133.

Natural Forest Openings On Uplands Of The Eastern United States

by
H.R. DeSelm

ABSTRACT--Several kinds of natural openings occur in the forests of the eastern United States - some of these now occur on public lands where an agency is empowered to manage them. Many plants and animals, some more endangered than others, occur in these openings. Wet sites, that include marshes, flood zones, bogs and wet prairie, have experienced drainage and herbaceous weed and woody plant invasion. Prairie (barrens) and serpentine barrens and savanna also have experienced this invasion. Vegetation very shallow to bedrock, and vegetation such as cedar (cedar-pine) glades, shale barrens, granite, sandstone and limestone flatrocks and outcrops, are often grazed or quarried (on private land) and experience invasion by peripheral plants. Foot traffic is particularly damaging to this vegetation. High elevation sites, such as grassy balds with trails, erode badly because of the precipitation. Uncontrolled hog rooting is also a serious threat to these areas. Approaches to the containment of such problems vary from having public employees on the sites for educational, and foot and vehicle control purposes, to locate trails and roads, to patrol and clean-up litter, and to control invading vegetation with fire, cutting, or selective herbiciding.

KEYWORDS: barrens, prairies, glades, savannas, human impact, woody plant invasion, protection.

INTRODUCTION

This paper has three purposes. The first is to describe briefly the kinds of essentially herb-dominated natural plant communities which occur in the upland portion (inland from the lower Coastal Plain) of the eastern United States. I will indicate which types are currently being managed for public use, the problems which ensue with their management, and the kind of approaches being made toward their solution.

This area was mainly forested at the time of settlement by Europeans - forest and prairie occurred on the western borders and many kinds of natural openings occurred in the forest matrix. The area included in the discussion here extends from Illinois to New York and south to the Piedmont Physiographic Province on the east and southeast, to the upper Coastal Plain of Alabama and Mississippi and the Mississippi River alluvial plain of eastern Arkansas (Fenneman 1938). Several small scale, chiefly forest vegetation types have been mapped on the landscapes of these Provinces (Kuchler 1964).

The vegetation types, such as prairie (barrens) and glades (as cedar glades) included herein, are relatively stable ones on the landscape. Excluded are Amerind old fields, and fire and wind-ice-snow storm forest destruction noted by early diarists and surveyors (Steiner and DeSchweinitz 1799 *In* Williams 1928, Beatley 1959). Ex-

cluded are the small areas of tundra (Adams *et al.* 1920), block fields, of which some are open (Hack and Goodlet 1960, DePriest 1983), and debris avalanche scars (Clark 1973, Pomeroy 1980, Feldcamp 1984).

Modification of extant communities began in the sixteenth century along the east coast. Conversion of the landscape to crop fields, pastures, and farms proceeded inland. East Tennessee was settled, for the most part after the Revolutionary War, northern Alabama a little later, and the Coastal Plain of West Tennessee and the Jackson Purchase of Kentucky and the bottoms of nearby Arkansas after 1830 (Folmsbee *et al.* 1969). Plant communities on deep soil doubtless went into agricultural production immediately - if non-forest - or after clearing if forested where factors as slope steepness, soil rockiness, or the existence of soil pans did not inhibit this activity (cf. Cronon 1983 for New England). Some areas of moderately shallow soil were also plowed but then abandoned; some went through cycles of crop-use and abandonment as can be seen today. Areas of very shallow soil (ca. less than one dm.) have mostly been pastured since settlement unless a topographic or water hazard dictated otherwise. The forests that have remained have been logged repeatedly - thus the borders of natural openings have been disturbed. Often, the opening itself became the center of some activity such as a sawmill. The openings have also become the focal points of roads and paths. The above suggests that considerable modification, if not destruction, of certain communities, such as those noted by William Bartram (Harper 1958), had occurred by the beginning of the twentieth century (Braun 1950).

METHODS

The writer typifies the kinds of openings discussed below from the literature and personal experience. Information on management problems is summarized from my recent mail, and in some cases telephone contact, with natural area managers and other knowledgeable persons. Mailings went to 85 persons or organizations - there was a 68 percent return. I acknowledge with pleasure the assistance offered by these people.

RESULTS

General

The kinds of openings included in this report vary from those of extremely wet sites (marsh, bog, flood zone, wet prairie) to those of mesic to subxeric sites (prairie, barren, savanna) and to those on the xeric sites of shallow soil (cedar and cedar-pine glades, shale and serpentine barrens, limestone, sandstone and granite flatrocks and outcrops) and other types at considerable elevation, such as the grassy balds and southern Blue Ridge high, rocky domes and summits.

The flora of the community or mosaic of communities in each open site often includes plant taxa at various levels of recognition of rarity or endangerment. Recognition is at the national level (cf. Anonymous 1984b), proposed national level (Ayensu and DeFillips 1978), or state level (cf. Committee for Tennessee Rare Plants 1978); rare taxa occur in national parks (cf. White 1982) and national forests (cf. Kral 1983, Massey et al. 1983). Part of the flora of this open vegetation is rare; some are local endemics, some are particular floristic elements at the edge of their range (extraneous), and some are more or less widespread, but rare, in part or all of their range (intraneous).

Land ownership varies in these open sites from private and unknown, to the public, to private and posted, to government agency land including county parks, state parks or forests or natural areas, to national agency land such as national parks, national forests, national battlefield parks, national wild and scenic rivers, and land of other agencies. Agency use-control includes requiring permits for access, permits for collecting of biota (if allowed at all), limiting trail use to certain numbers of people, trail and road location, and roadblocks.

In the sections to follow, each type is located in general, described briefly, their ownerships and degree of endangerment are noted, and their management problems and current attacks on these problems are included.

Marshes

Marshes occur uncommonly on all parts of the study area, but are best developed along river bottoms and on upland flats (Shaw and Fredine 1956). In a central area, there may be open water marshes with submerged and/or floating aquatic plants. Circumferential bands of herbaceous, emergent vegetation on perennially wet soil occur. Herb communities are dominated by such taxa as cattail (*Typha*), sedges (Cyperaceae), and/or grasses (Pocaceae). They are invaded and replaced by such shrubs as buttonbush (*Cephalanthus*) or alder (*Alnus*) and then by the swamp forest in which willow (*Salix*) is usually conspicuous. Marshes occur in managed form on many state and federal Wildlife Management Areas; they also occur on the Oak Ridge National Laboratory, and Arnold Engineering and Development Center (Tullahoma, Tennessee). Many new marshes have been formed since we began manipulating our landscape: areas where drainage is blocked by roads and railroads, farm ponds, edges of new river reservoirs, swamps converted to pasture, and swamps with the water table raised by, for example, beaver dams. These, as those of presettlement lineage, may experience filling or drainage and conversion to another use, and invasion by weedy herbs (such as spiked lythrum, *Lythrum salicaria*, or the giant reed *Phragmites communis*) or shrubs and trees. On small areas, corrective measures are seldom used. On large areas managed by equipped personnel, ditching, dredging, manipulation of the water level, burning, and planting grain crops on nearby lands (cf. Good et al. 1978) is done. The flora of marshes contain chiefly intraneous taxa, but Coastal Plain disjuncts (as *Panicum hemitomon*) may occur in inland marshes.

Flood Zones

Energetic streams sweep their flood zones free of large trees leaving saplings, shrubs and/or herb dominated areas in this zone. Two such streams are the Hiwassee and Ocoee Rivers of the Blue Ridge of southeastern Tennessee and the Obed Wild and Scenic River of the Cumberland Plateau of Tennessee. On the Hiwassee - Ocoee Rivers, the boulder or bedrock covered valley bottom is vegetated by scattered colonies of herbs, including Ruths goldenaster (*Pityopsis ruthii*). On the extensive boulder and cobble bars of the Obed River, are shrub communities dominated by alder (*Alnus*) or buttonbush (*Cephalanthus*) and, for example, ninebark (*Physocarpus*). Interspersed are marshy stands dominated by grasses and sedges and drier stands of grass dominated by big bluestem (*Andropogan gerardii*) and little bluestem (*Schizachyrium scoparium*) and prairie forbs. In the study of the Obed River valley (Schmalzer and DeSelm 1982), virtually all of the rare taxa of the Wild and Scenic River area were in the flood zone communities rather than in valley slope or upland forests.

The Hiwassee and Ocoee Rivers are in the Cherokee National Forest. The goldenaster withstands the water level changes induced by the upstream dam and trampling by whitewater boaters. Populations are monitored by Forest Service personnel. The Obed Wild and Scenic River is currently being minimally developed to receive the public. Its Park Service personal are sensitive to the occurrence of rare plant taxa in the flood zone where little development is planned.

Bogs

Bogs once occurred extensively north of the glacial boundary in the eastern United States, extended south at elevations in the Appalachian Highlands, and occur extensively on the Coastal Plain from New Jersey to Texas. They are much less common elsewhere. The substrate is usually constantly wet; the soil is a histosol. These areas are vegetationally diverse. In small northern bogs (primary peat, Moore and Bellamy 1973), concentric zonation around the pool - which may represent the deepest water - is typical. The sedge (*Carex*) mat is replaced by a zone of bog meadow in which the base is of peat mosses (especially *Sphagnum* spp.) and cranberry (*Vaccinium macrocarpon*). The meadow is invaded by low and tall shrubs, and these by a hardwood swamp or boreal swamps forest. Southward, the meadow may be largely sedge and grass dominated. Rare plant species in this vegetation are usually endemics of such sites (*Sarracenia, Drosera*) and northern extraneous taxa (*Dalibarda repens, Listera cordata*) (Massy et al. 1983). Extending southward at high elevations, bog sites occur on the Appalachian Plateau of West Virginia in the Monogahela National Forest at Cranberry Glades (Edens 1973), and southward into Tennessee at Savage Gulf State Natural Area (Wofford et al. 1979). Similar vegetation occurs on private land and on the Jefferson National Forest in the Ridge and Valley of Virginia near Mountain Lake. This vegetation also occurs in the Blue Ridge, south from Pennsylvania to Georgia. These bogs are generally small (often less than one acre in size), occur on private land and in the National Forests and National Parks (Pittillo 1976, Pittillo and Govus 1978, Ogle 1982, Tucker 1972, Moore 1972). One small remnant of the Shady Valley bog in Johnson County Tennessee (Barclay 1957) has been purchased by the Nature Conservancy.

Many (perhaps most) bog sites have been eliminated by drainage and conversion to agriculture. Overgrowth of the

Figure 1. May Prairie, a State Natural Area, in Coffee County, Tennessee which illustrates the early invasion of woody species in the absence of fire or other treatments to restrict their growth. (Photograph by H. R. DeSelm)

meadow and shrub zones by forest is a general problem. Management includes, physical presence of responsible and educational personal, boardwalks (trails), patrolling, and litter removal where a funded agency is responsible.

Grassy Balds

Grassy balds occur chiefly on high Blue Ridge mountain peaks and ridges, which often have a southern or western aspect. They are areas of grassland dominated by mountain oatgrass (*Danthonia compressa*) and introduced Eurasian grasses. They are being actively invaded by shrubs (such as ericads) and trees from the adjacent spruce-fir, northern hardwood, or oak forests (Bruhn 1964, Lindsey and Bratton 1979). Well known balds are Big Meadows at Shenandoah National park, Whitetop Mountain Bald (Mount Rogers National Recreation Area), those at Roan Mountain (Cherokee and Pisgah National Forests), those in the Great Smoky Mountains National Park, and other balds in the Blue Ridge of the Tennessee and North Carolina National Forests.

The balds are the habitat of federally listed plants, federally proposed plants such as *Solidago spithamaea* (Anonymous 1984b), and state (Tennessee, North Carolina, Virginia) rare taxa. These include endemics such as *Geum geniculatum* and *G. radiatum* and a northern extraneous element, such as the sedge, *Carex aenea*.

The balds convert to shrub and tree vegetation at a rapid rate with the elimination of grazing (Lindsay and Bratton 1979). Other management problems are the considerable use by walkers (some of the above balds are on the Appalachian Trail). Relatively newly tested woody plant control procedures are fire, grazing, mowing, and hand-pruning (Baxter 1978, Lilly 1980, Barden 1978, Lindsay and Bratton 1979). Trampling and erosion, following intensive trail and off-trail use, cause gullying that is correctable by trail diversion and/or water-bar construction when funds are available. Another problem on balds is wild boar rooting - they literally plow the grass sod; roots and larger underground parts are eaten. Boar control measures now being used are ineffective. Hand seeding using local oatgrass seed has been attempted.

Wet Prairie

Wet prairie, at one time, occurred extensively throughout the tallgrass. These are sites dominated by such grasses as slough grass (*Spartina pectinata*), merging downslope into marsh and upslope into wet-mesic prairie dominated by switch grass (*Panicum virgatum*). The sites are known to have occurred along major drainageways and in upland, closed-drainage flats (Weaver 1954).

Most of the wet prairie has been placed in agriculture, or ditched and drained and/or grazed. With drainage modification and deceased fire frequency, tree invasion has been common. Stands today may be expected where large areas of grassland have been saved. In Prairie County, Arkansas on the Mississippi alluvial plain, privately owned prairies are burned annually by state heritage personnel.

Tallgrass Prairie (Barrens)

The vegetation of the tallgrass prairie is widely distrib-

uted in the central grasslands from Texas to Manitoba, and extends east as the "Prairie Peninsula" (Transeau 1935) into extensive areas of Illinois, parts of western Indiana, and isolated areas of central Ohio (Buffalo Beats, Wistendahl 1975), and western Pennsylvania (*Liatris* prairies, Jennings Nature Reserve, Erdman and Wiegman 1974), across the New York lowlands to the Pine Bush near Albany, and south in the Hudson River valley to Long Island at the Hempstead Plains (Cain *et al.* 1937). South of the glacial border, there were extensive areas of forest and prairie in the Kentucky Barrens, in the Black Belt of Alabama and Mississippi, and in the Jackson Prairie of Mississippi (Mohr 1901, Hilgard 1860). Many small outliers occur on dry sites, usually but not always, on limestone in the Interior Low Plateaus Appalachian Plateau, and Ridge and Valley Provinces (DeSelm *et al.* 1973, DeSelm 1981). This grassland vegetation, in the relatively high precipitation climates of the eastern United States, occurs chiefly on sites on which moisture storage is low; soils are often shallow, sandy or stoney, or a pan is present which inhibits water movement upward into the rooting zone in summer (Love *et al.* 1959). The vegetation is dominated by mid and tall grasses of the tallgrass prairie - occasionally taller grasses (*Erianthus* or *Tripsacum*) also occur. In the understory, are many species of shorter grasses sedges and rushes, and forbs. The prairie flora in the East includes many widely distributed intraneous taxa, some western taxa, and a few disjunct from the coastal plain.

In the main areas of prairie to be considered here, those in Illinois and Indiana, Kentucky, Alabama, and Mississippi have had a low percentage of these areas preserved because of the pressure of agriculture and because of the rapid invasion of forest following settlement. In the Ridge and Valley, barrens occur on private lands (DeSelm 1981, Bartgis 1985), on lands of the Oak Ridge National Laboratory, and in the Chickamauga - Chattanooga National Military Park. On the Cumberland Plateau they occur on private lands, on the Roosevelt Mountain State Forest, Tennessee, and at Buffalo Beats, Athens County, Ohio in the Wayne National Forest. On the Highland Rim and Pennyroyal barrens exist on private lands, on the Highland Rim Forest Experiment Station (Tullahoma, Tennessee), and at the May Prairie State Natural Area near Manchester, Tennessee, on Land Between the Lakes in Tennessee and Kentucky (Tennessee Valley Authority), and in the Little Mountain section of Alabama (private). Barrens occur on private land in the Central Basin of Tennessee and on uplands in West Tennessee (both rarely). They are known on the Mississippi River alluvial plain in Prairie County, Arkansas, on private land. Small outliers lie in the Knobs region of Estill County, Kentucky (private), and in the Blue Grass in Adams County, Ohio (Ohio Division of Natural Resources). They occur in southern Indiana (on private land, in Indiana State Nature Preserves, in Harrison State Forest, and in the Hoosier National Forest). In southern Illinois they occur on private land, on land of The Nature Conservancy, and on the

Shawnee National Forest. Of the larger areas of prairie in Ohio, Indiana, and Illinois, prairies occur on private land, in state Nature preserves (Illinois and Ohio), and State Parks (Indiana). The Nature Conservancy owns, or cooperates in management of, some of these preserves. The large area of prairie and forest in the Kentucky barrens is apparently unmarked by preserves - the same is apparently true of the Black Belt. The Jackson Prairie of Mississippi contains the Harrell Hill prairie, east of Jackson in the Bienville National Forest.

Barrens vegetation experiences woody plant and herbaceous weed invasion, changes in water regimes by ditching, and having been crossed when the soil is wet by motorcycles, cars, and trucks, and trash dumping and littering. The last two may be prevented by patrolling. Reversing the effects of long-standing ditches, especially those along roads, by blocking and or filling them, is a difficult matter to make road engineers understand. Plant invasion is generally approached by a program of fire use (Anderson and Schwegman 1971) or fire and, for example, hand cutting, or some combination of fire, cutting, and use of herbicides. Careful examination of the results of a one-season fire program may reveal differential responses of a variety of rare plants being protected. Thus, it seems likely that several burning programs should be attempted to determine the best response for the species and site. In Missouri, haying is also effective.

Glades (Cedar, cedar - pine glades)

This vegetation is centered in the Central Basin of Tennessee where these openings are called cedar glades. These are extensive and frequent openings in the forest of that area. The central part of this vegetation is a limestone outcrop sparingly covered by annual and perennial forbs and grasses. This "glade" is encircled by a thicket or forest of eastern redcedar, and this by an oak forest of xerophytic oaks, cedar, and other hardwoods (Quarterman 1950). Among the forbs are 20 taxa endemic, or nearly so, to these glades (Baskin *et al.* 1968). These glades extend south into Alabama and north into Kentucky, and sparingly into southern Indiana and Illinois (Aldrich *et al.* 1981, Bacone *et al.* 1982). They extend west into the Silurian limestone of the western Highland Rim, and eastward in the Ridge and Valley from Lee County Virginia (Carr 1944) to Georgia (VanHorn 1980) and Alabama. In the Ridge and Valley, the strip of evergreen forest around the glade may contain Virginia, shortleaf, or loblolly pines (*Pinus virginiana, P. echinata, P. taeda*). These glades are also mapped near Huntsville, Alabama (Kuchler 1964).

The open glade experiences both invasion by woody plants and death of the typical woody plants, such as eastern redcedar, during periodic droughts. As are the barrens, these areas are subject to automobile, motorcycle, and foot traffic, and littering.

Sites still may be found in the Central Basin of Tennessee at Cedars of Lebanon State Park, and State Forest and Cedar Glades State Natural Area, on Nature Conservancy land, and on private land. In Alabama, they occur on private land and at Monte Sano State Park. In northwest Georgia, they occur in the Chickamauga - Chattanooga National Military Park. In East Tennessee they occur on private and Oak Ridge National Laboratory land, and in southwestern Virginia, on private land. In Kentucky, they occur on private land and on the Blue Lick Battlefield State Park. In southern Indiana, they occur on private land, in southern Illinois on private and Shawnee National Forest land.

Shale Barrens

This vegetation occurs on Devonian shales in the Ridge and Valley Province from Pennsylvania to southern Virginia and eastern West Virginia. These barrens are sparsely forested vegetation on steep, south-facing slopes which are usually above actively cutting streams (Platt 1951). The canopy is occupied by eastern redcedar, Virginia, shortleaf, or pitch pines, and/or xerophytic hardwoods. The understory has a low percent cover of shrubs, such as southern red haw (*Viburnum rufidulum*) and herbs. Most of the herb cover is composed by taxa common to xeric Appalachian sites, but there are among them 18 endemic taxa (Keener 1970, 1983).

The vegetation occurs on private land and in the George Washington, Jefferson, and Monongahela National Forests. In the George Washington, 12 of these areas are identified as "special areas." Shale barrens also occur on the Green Ridge State Forest in western Maryland and around Raystown Lake (Corps of Engineers, Hesston, Pennsylvania). The slope angle on these sites inhibits use, but the low vegetation cover, the steep slopes, and the easily - moved substrate (shale fragments) make any use by people, or e.g. grazing animals, a cause of severe erosion. Protection includes none, site identification when within large managed areas, monitoring woody plant invasion, fencing to eliminate grazing, closing areas to the public, and public education.

Serpentine Barrens

This vegetation is uncommon in the eastern United States. The herbaceous communities are surrounded by thickets to low forest or savanna with eastern redcedar, pine, and/or xerophytic oaks. The vegetation occurs on a shallow soil derived from serpentine (a hydrous silicate of magnesium) in the Piedmont of southeastern Pennsylvania, eastern Maryland, and eastern Georgia, and Blue Ridge of southwestern North Carolina (Mansberg and Wentworth 1984, Radford and Martin 1975, Pennell 1910, Radford 1948, Proctor and Woodell 1980). This vegetation has 2-5 endemic taxa (Wherry *et al.* 1979, Pennell 1930). Shale barrens were, at one time, common in Southeast Pennsylvania, indeed the "barrens dot the Piedmont Plateau like islands in a sea of other rocks ... " (Wherry 1963).

Ownership varies from private to the Tyler Arboretum (Philadelphia), to a Baltimore County, Maryland Natural Area, a Chester County, Pennsylvania Park, and the Nantahala National Forest (Mansbery and Wentworth 1984, Radford and Martin 1975, Monteferrante 1973). These areas, like others of similar vegetation, have been converted to agriculture and urban uses but, of those remaining, quarrying is active in some, as is pasturing. Woody plant invasion and motorcycling are also problems, but solutions are not at hand.

Granite Flatrocks

Scattered through the Piedmont and to some extent the Blue Ridge, are outcrops of lesser or greater size of granite. These areas may be simply small, flat units of bedrock, but others are large, granite bodies and stand up as hills or low mountains often referred to as domes. Slow weathering to soil and steep slope angles makes soil accumulation slight. Open areas result, and these are encircled or invaded on islands of deeper soil by shrubs, pines, eastern redcedar, and hardwood trees. Outcrops are best developed on the Piedmont from Virginia to Alabama (McVaugh 1943). There are 17 endemics (McVaugh 1943), of which 10 are the best documented (Murdy 1968) in this well-described vegetation (Burbanck and Platt 1964). Murdy estimates that about 4,860 ha of these sites existed in the late 1960's scattered on hundreds of outcrops. Most of these are on private land. One, near Almond, Alabama is owned partly by Southern Union State College, Panola Mountain in Rockdale County, Georgia is a State Conservation Park, Stone Mountain, DeKalb County, Georgia is a state park, and Stone Mountain, Alleghany and Wilkins Counties, North Carolina is a state park (Radford and Martin 1975). Purchases by The Nature Conservancy continue (Anonymous 1984a).

Small granite outcrops on private land are grazed, and used as automobile runways and dumps. Those of all sizes may be quarried. Even those in public ownership experience littering and trampling.

Sandstone Flatrocks and Outcrops

Numerous small cliff and cliff-edge openings occur in the dissected topography of the Appalachian Plateau. Occasionally, also openings occur on flat uplands where areas of surface sandstone is hard enough that little soil develops and tree vegetation cannot occur. This open lichen - bryophyte - herb dominated vegetation is surrounded by and succeeded by trees such as pines and xerophytic hardwoods on deeper soils. It is described by Whetsone (1981) in Alabama, Perkins (1981) in Tennessee, Winterringer and Vestal (1956) in southern Illinois, and noted in southern Indiana (Jackson 1979, 1980) and in western Kentucky (Harker et al. 1980). Such openings in Illinois, Indiana, and western Kentucky are in the Interior Low Plateaus Province. In Ohio, West Virginia, and Kentucky, they occur on private land, in state parks, and in National Forests. They occur in Tennessee, Georgia, and Alabama state parks. They occur in the Cumberland Gap National Historical Park (White Rocks) and in the Obed Wild and Scenic River and Big South Fork National River and Recreation Area.

These areas, both public and private, experience littering, automobile and trail bike traffic, trampling, fire-building, and general hooliganism such as destruction of rock sculptures. Affecting cures for these problems involves public education and control of access to, and use of, public lands.

Limestone Outcrops (Calcareous Bedrock)

Areas included here are smaller and less floristically distinct sites than cedar glades. Some are simply cliff edges; but others are larger. The flora is that of the limestone, dolomite, or calcareous shale-derived soils of many sites in the eastern United States. Surrounding the lichen-bryophyte-herb covered opening may be open to closed stands of eastern redcedar, pines, and calciphilous hardwoods, such as yellow oak (Quercus muhlerbergii), blue ash (Fraxinus quadrangulata), North Carolina hickory (Carya carolinae-septentrionalis), hackberries (Celtis spp.), walnuts (Juglans spp.), and elms (Ulmus spp.). Other oaks occur and may be dominant.This stand bordering the opening merges into the upland forest. Several types of bedrocks support such vegetation in the Interior Low Plateaus and in limestone or dolomite underlain sites, such as dissections of the Appalachian Plateau, the Ridge and Valley, and the fensters of the Blue Ridge (Ozment 1967, White 1978, Jackson 1979, 1980, Martin et al. 1979, Quarterman and Powell 1978, DeSelm et al. 1969, DeSelm 1984). Similar sites on shale occur in southern Illinois (Anonymous 1984a).

These sites have the same problems as cedar glades-mainly dumping, littering, and traffic (foot and vehicle). Being small, they have a chance of being overlooked and, thus, a greater chance of survival of their floras; but small size also magnifies the effects of man's action. Most rock outcrops are unnamed and unmanaged. One unusual one on the Powell River in Tennessee is a debris-slide caused opening; white cedar (Thuja occidentalis), a northern extraneous tree here, has moved into the opening. It is owned by the Tennessee Chapter of The Nature Conservancy, who limit access to it.

Upland Savannas

Savannas were fairly widespread in the eastern United States at and before the time of settlement. For example, the chroniclers of the DeSoto expedition (Swanton 1939) saw them in the Southeast. These areas like the eastern grasslands, for the most part, grew up to forest upon settlement by European people.

Attempts at restoration using fire and native grass planting are in progress in Minnesota and Missouri, west of the main area of concern here (Papike 1984, White 1983, Anonymous 1983). Small areas on shallow soil near eastern redcedar glades or cedar-hardwood forest stands are to be found in the Central Basin of Tennessee, in southern Indiana, and in southern Illinois over sandstone (DeSelm and Schmalzer 1982, Jackson 1979, 1980, Quarterman and Powell 1978, Lindsey et al. 1969, Winterringer and Vestal 1956). A blue ash-oak savanna type in the Inner Blue Grass of Kentucky occurred in presettlement times - the forms with the grassy understory are apparently now gone (Bryant et al. 1980). Types dominated by post oak (Quercus stellata), or blackjack (Q. marilandica) or white oak (Q. alba) are noted in southern Indiana (Jackson 1980, Crankshaw 1964), in southern Illinois (Fralish 1976, Quarterman and Powell 1978), and in northern Alabama (Mohr 1901, Braun 1950) have been seen in the last one to three generations on private land.

Southern Blue Ridge High Rocky Domes and Summits

Scattered at middle to high elevations in the southern Blue Ridge on various bedrocks (usually granite under the domes), are sites which are not strictly grassy balds described above, nor heath balds (Whittaker 1956), nor *Rhododendron* gardens (Brown 1941). Rocky summits are small areas with exposed rock varying to areas of shallow soil over rock, to areas of deeper mineral or organic soil in cracks in the bedrock or in crevices between boulders of a rock field area. On and between the rocks are lichen and bryophyte communities (DePriest 1983). Rooted in the bryophytes or in the shallow soil are graminoids and forbs including Southern Appalachian endemics and northern extraneous taxa (including ones characteristic of the Mount Washington tundra, Bliss 1963) (Schafale and Weakley 1985).

Domes are areas of massive, usually exfoliating, granite bedrock with a central bare or lichen-bryophyte covered area encircled by a bryophyte-herb mat. This is invaded by woody taxa, such as red maple (*Acer rubrum*), fringe tree (*Chionanthus virginicus*), and several ericaceous shrubs (Oosting and Anderson 1937). The type location for Cain's reedgrass is on a cliff on Mt. LeConte in the Great Smoky Mountains (Hitchcock 1934). This grass is on the proposed list of nationally endangered plants (Ayensu and DeFilipps 1978).

Both of these types of areas occur in the southern Appalachian national parks and national forests. Being small, they get little intended damage, but much trampling and sometimes climbing damage. Trail construction around these areas, control of people on the trails, and public education are presently used to protect these areas when they are indeed recognized as being in need of protection.

SUMMARY AND CONCLUSIONS

Several kinds of natural openings occurred in the natural vegetation of the eastern United States at the time of settlement, inland from the lower Coastal Plain. Those considered below exclude old fields, fire and storm-damaged areas, as well as tundra, block fields, and debris avalanche scars. Of the types preserved today, some are managed in e.g. parks; their managers have been asked about management problems and their possible solutions. Wet site openings as marsh, flood zone, bog, and wet prairie experience water level manipulation and invasion by woody plants and marsh weeds. Prairie (barrens) and serpentine barrens and savanna also experience woody plant and herbaceous weed invasion. Rock dominated sites as cedar (cedar-pine) glades, shale barrens, granite flatrocks, sandstone and limestone flatrocks and outcrops are, at the onset, subject to grazing and quarrying (with the exception of shale barrens). They also are subject to woody plant and herbaceous weed invasion. Because of

the unyielding substrate, foot and vehicle traffic has a particularly large effect on these vegetation types. Middle to high elevation rocky domes and summits and grassy balds are subject to woody plant and weed invasion, and trampling. Here, trampling is a severe problem because of the high precipitation and resultant erosion. All of the areas experience littering which may cover the herbs being protected in the preserve.

Protection of these areas is often difficult. Sometimes private areas are protected by the absence of public knowledge or publicity. The private land may be posted. On public lands, the administering agency may be unaware of the existence of a unique area and so it never gets into a management plan and never becomes publicized in this way. Positive public use control is to have a visitor's center on the site with personnel whose main function is education. Or, these personnel may lead the public through the site on an educational walk. Self guided, leaflet-supported trails are an alternative. Patrolling the area by ranger-type personnel may inhibit destructive use of the area - these (and other) personnel also pick up litter. The placement of roads and trails and blocking of pre-existing roads are important where foot traffic occurs or off-road vehicles are used.

Natural forces at work consist mainly of invasion by herbaceous weeds and woody plants. These may be partially controlled by hand pruning or weeding and/or judicious use of point-spray or injection herbicides. On large areas, mowing or bush-hogging has been used. Fire is used where it can be controlled. Lowlands which require slow drainage are a special problem because of drainage features already installed before public acquisition - reversal of the installation (blocking ditches) may be necessary. Erosion on installed trails requires trail maintenance including water bars.

Much of the above implies the expenditure of public funds for maintenance of public lands. It is hoped that the availability of volunteers will continue and increase in the future. The same volunteer public may be trained to do some of the periodic (perhaps only annual) monitoring so necessary on these sites. The actions of nature (weather, drainage changes, plant or animal invasion) and those of man (trampling, littering, fire, woody plant cutting) may be considered treatments to the biotic communities of the sites. Monitoring of the constancy of the dominant species - whose cover controls the aspect - and of the special taxa such as rare ones - is a necessity as justification for maintaining the integrity of the areas. The results of monitoring become the baselines for evaluating results of other intended and unintended treatments.

Population shifts observed during long continued monitoring may form the basis for research into the nature of the species populations, their interactions with each other, or with man, or with community ecotone dynamics, or ecosystem function.

LITERATURE CITED

Adams, C.C., G.P. Burns, T.L. Hankinson, B. Moore and N. Tayor. 1920. Plants and animals of Mount Marcy, New York. Ecology 1:71-94, 204-233, 274-288.

Aldrich, J.R., J.A. Bacone, and M.D. Hutchison. 1981. Limestone glades of Harrison County, Indiana. Proc. Indiana Acad. Sci. 91:480-485.

Anderson, R.C. and J. Schwegman. 1971. The response of southern Illinois barren vegetation to prescribed burning. Trans. Illinois Acad. Sci. 64:287-291.

Anonymous. 1983. The savanna heritage of Ha Ha Tonka State Park. Park Leaflet. Missouri Department of Natural Resources.

Anonymous. 1984a. Projects-1984. The Nature Conservancy Annual Report 1984, pp. 9-28. Arlington, Virginia.

Anonymous. 1984b. Four plants in danger of extinction: Blue Ridge Goldenrod. Endangered Species Tech. Bull. 9:1, 5.

Ayensu, E.S. and R.A. DeFilipps. 1978. Endangered and threatened plants of the United States. Smithsonian Inst. and World Wildlife Fund, Inc. Washington, D.C.

Bacone, J.A., L.A. Casebere and M.D. Hutchison. 1982. Glades and barrens of Crawford and Perry Counties, Indiana. Indiana Acad. Sci. 92:367-373.

Barclay, F.H. 1957. The natural vegetation of Johnson County, Tennessee, past and present. Ph.D. Dissertation, University of Tennessee, Knoxville, Tennessee.

Barden, L.S. 1978. Regrowth of shrubs in grassy balds of the Southern Appalachians after prescribed burning. Castanea 43:238-246.

Bartgis, R.L. 1985. A limestone glade in West Virginia. Bartonia 51:34-36.

Baskin, J.M., E. Quarterman, and C. Caudle. 1968. Preliminary checklist of the herbaceous vascular plants of the cedar glades. J. Tenn. Acad. Sci. 43:65-71.

Baxter, E.E. 1978. Plant composition responses to single and repeated prescribed burns at Shenandoah National Park. M.S. Thesis. James Madison Univ., Harrisonburg, Virg.

Beatley, J.C. 1959. The primeval forests of a periglacial area in the Alleghany Plateau (Vinton and Jackson Counties, Ohio). Bull. Ohio Biol. Surv. 1:1-182.

Bliss, L.C. 1963. Alpine plant communities of the Presidential range, New Hampshire. Ecology 44:678-697.

Braun, E.L. 1950. Deciduous forests of eastern North America. Blakiston Publishing Co., Philadelphia, Penn.

Brown, D.M. 1941. Vegetation of Roan Mountain: a phytosociological and successional study. Ecol. Mong 11:61-97.

Bruhn, M.E. 1964. Vegetational succession in three grassy balds of the Great Smoky Mountains. M.S. Thesis. Univ. Tenn., Knoxville, Tenn.

Bryant, W.S., M.E. Wharton, W.H. Martin and J.B. Varner. 1980. The blue-ash oak savanna-woodland, a remnant of presettlement vegetation in the Inner Blue Grass of Kentucky. Castanea 45:149-164.

Burbanck, M.P. and R.B. Platt. 1964. Granite outcrop communities of the Piedmont Plateau in Georgia. Ecology 45:292-306.

Cain, S.A., M. Nelson and W. McLean. 1937. Androgonetum Hempsteadi: a Long Island grassland vegetation type. Amer. Mid. Nat. 18:334-350.

Carr, L.G. 1944. A new species of Houstonia from the cedar barrens of Lee County, Virginia. Rhodora 46:306-310.

Clark, G.M. 1973. Remote sensor utilization for environmental systems studies. Report to the Air Force Cambridge Research Laboratories. Processed. The Univ. of Tenn., Knoxville, Tenn. Contract No. F 19628-69-C-0016.

Committee for Tennessee Rare Plants. 1978. The rare vascular plants of Tennessee. J. Tenn. Acad. Sci. 53:128-133.

Crankshaw, W.B. 1964. The edaphology of tree species in presettlement Indiana south of the Late Wisconsin glacial border. Ph.D. Diss. Purdue Univ., West Lafayette, Indiana.

Cronon, W. 1983. Changes in the land. Hill and Wang. New York, New York.

DePriest, P.T. 1983. The macrolichen flora of Unaka Mountain, Unicoi County, Tennessee-Yancey County, North Carolina. M.S. Thesis, Univ. of Tenn., Knoxville, Tenn.

DeSelm, H.R. 1981. Characterization of some southeastern barrens, with special reference to Tennessee. pp. 86-88 In R.L. Stuckey and K.J. Reese, (eds.). The prairie peninsula-in the "shadow" of Transeau: Proc. Sixth North Amer. Prairie Conf., Ohio Biol. Surv. Biol. Note No. 15.

DeSelm, H.R. 1984. Potential National Natural Landmarks of the Appalachian Ranges Natural Region. Ecological Report. Prepared for the U.S. National Park Service. The University of Tennessee, Knoxville. Contract No. CX-0001-1-0079.

DeSelm, H.R. and P.A. Schmalzer. 1982. Final Report-Classification and description of the ecological themes of the Interior Low Plateaus. Prepared for the USDI National Park Service. Processed report, Univ. of Tenn., Knoxville, Tenn. N.P.S., PX-0001-1-0673.

DeSelm, H.R., P.B. Whitford and J.S. Olson. 1969. The barrens of the Oak Ridge area, Tennessee. Amer. Mid. Nat. 81:315-330.

DeSelm, H.R., E.E.C. Clebsch, G.M. Nichols, and E. Thor. 1973. Response of herbs, shrubs and tree sprouts in prescribed-burn hardwoods in Tennessee. Proc. Annual Tall Timbers Fire Ecology Conference. 11:331-344.

Edens, D.L. 1973. The ecology and succession of Cranberry Glades, West Virginia. Ph.D. Diss. North Carolina State University. Raleigh.

Erdman, K.S. and P.S. Wiegman. 1974. Preliminary list of natural areas in Pennsylvania. Western Pennsylvania Conservancy. Pittsburgh, Penn.

Feldcamp, S.M. 1984. Revegetation of upper elevation debris slide scars on Mount LeConte in the Great Smoky Mountains National park. M.S. Thesis. Univ. Tenn., Knoxville, Tenn.

Fenneman, N.E. 1938. Physiography of eastern United States. McGraw-Hill Book Co., New York, New York.

Folmsbee, S.J., R.E. Corlew and E.L. Mitchell. 1969. Tennessee A Short History. Univ. Tenn. Press. Knoxville, Tenn.

Fralish, J.S. 1976. Forest site-communities relationships in the Shawnee Hills region, Southern Illinois. pp. 65-87. In J.S. Fralish, G.T. Weaver, and R.C. Schlesinger (eds.). Proceedings Central Hardwoods Forest Conference I. Southern Illinois University, Carbondale, Ill.

Good, R.E., D.F. Whigham, R.L. Simpson and C.G. Jackson, Jr. (eds.). 1978. Freshwater wetlands. Academic Press. New York, New York.

Hack, J.R. and J.C. Goodlett. 1960. Geomorphology and forest ecology of a mountain region in the Central Appalachians. USGS Prof. Paper 347.

Harker, D.F. Jr., R.R. Hannan, M.L. Warren Jr., L.R. Phillippe, K.E. Camburn, R.S. Caldwell, S.M. Call, G.J. Fallo, and D. VanNorman. 1980. Western Kentucky Coal Field: Preliminary investigations of natural features and cultural resources. Volume 1. Part 1. Introduction and ecology and ecological features of the Western Kentucky Coal Field. Technical Report. Kentucky Nature Preserves Commission. Frankfort, Ky.

Harper, F. 1958. The travels of William Bartram. Yale Univ. Press. New Haven, Conn.

Hilgard, E.W. 1860. Report on the Geology and Agriculture of the State of Mississippi. E. Barksdale, Jackson, Miss.

Hitchcock, A.S. 1934. Two new grasses, one from Tennessee, one from Argentina. J. Washington Acad. Sci. 24:480-481.

Jackson, M.T. 1979. Landscape units of Indiana. Indiana Natural Heritage Program. Terre Haute, Ind.

Jackson, M.T. 1980. A classification of Indiana plant communities. Proc. Indiana Acad. Sci. 89:159-172.

Keener, C.S. 1970. The natural history of the Mid-Appalachian Shale Barren flora. pp. 215-248 In P.C. Holt and R.A. Paterson (eds.). The distributional history of the biota of the Southern Appalachians. Part II: Flora. Res. Div. Mong. No. 2. Virginia Polytechnic Institute and State Univ., Blacksburg, Va.

Keener, C.S. 1983. Distribution and biohistory of the endemic flora of the Mid-Appalachian shale barrens. Bot. Rev. 49:65-115.

Kral, R. 1983. A report of some rare, threatened or endangered forest-related vascular plants of the South. USDA For. Serv., R8-TP-2.

Kuchler, A.W. 1964. Potential natural vegetation of the conterminous United States. Amer. Geogr. Soc. Spec. Publ. No. 36.

Lilly, S.L. 1980. Plant community standing crop responses to single and repeated prescribed burns at Big Meadows, Shenandoah National Park. M.S. Thesis. James Madison Univ., Harrisonburg, Va.

Lindsay, M.M. and S.P. Bratton. 1979. Grassy balds of the Great Smoky Mountains: Their history and flora in relation to potential management. Envir. Manage. 3:417-430.

Lindsey, A.A., D.V. Schmelz, and S.A. Nichols. 1969. Natural areas in Indiana and their preservation. Indiana Natural Areas Survey. Dept. of Biological Science, Purdue Univ., Lafayette, Ind.

Love, T.R., L.D. Williams, W.H. Proffit, I.B. Epley, J. Elder and J.H. Winsor. 1959. Soil survey of Coffee County, Tennessee. USDA Survey Series 1956, No. 5.

Mansberg, L. and T.R. Wentworth. 1984. Vegetation and soils of a serpentine barren in Western North Carolina. Bull. Torrey Bot. Club 111:273-286.

Martin, W.H., W.S. Bryant, S.J. Lassetter and J.B. Varner. 1979. The Kentucky River Pallisades flora and vegetation. Inventory Report to the Kentucky Chapter of The Nature Conservancy.

Massey, J.R., D.K.S. Otle, T.A. Atkinson, and R.D. Whetstone. 1983. An atlas and illustrated guide to the threatened and endangered vascular plants of the mountains of North Carolina and Virginia. USDA For. Serv. Gen. Tech. Report SE-20.

McVaugh, R. 1943. The vegetation of the granite flat-rocks of the Southeastern United States. Ecol. Monog. 13:119-165.

Mohr, C. 1901. Plant life of Alabama. Contr. U.S. Nat. Herb. 6:1-921.

Monteferrante, F.J. 1973. A phytosociological study of Soldiers Delight, Baltimore County, Maryland. M.S. Thesis. Towson State College, Baltimore, Md.

Moore, P.D. and D.J. Bellamy. 1973. Peatlands. Springer Verlag, New York, New York.

Moore, T.A. 1972. The phytoecology of Boone Fork sphagnum bog. M.S. Thesis. Appalachian State Univ., Boone, N. Car.

Murdy, W.H. 1968. Plant speciation associated with granite outcrop communities of the southeastern Piedmont. Rhodora 70:394-407.

Ogle, D.W. 1982. Glades of the Blue Ridge of southwestern Virginia. pp. 143-147. In Symposium on Wetlands of the Unglaciated Appalachian Region. West Virginia Univ., Morgantown, W.Va.

Oosting, H.J. and L.E. Anderson. 1937. The vegetation of a barefaced cliff in western North Carolina. Ecology 18:280-292.

Ozment, J.E. 1967. The vegetation of limestone ledges of southern Illinois. Trans. Illinois State Acad. of Sci. 60:135-173.

Papike, R.V. 1984. Experimental burns, reintroductions in savanna restoration project Minnesota. Restoration and management Notes 2:73.

Pennell, F.W. 1910. Flora of the Conowingo Barrens of southeastern Pennsylvania. Proc. Acad. of Nat. Sci. of Philadelphia 62:541-584.

Pennell, F.W. 1930. On some critical species of the serpentine barrens. Bartonia 12:1-23.

Perkins, B. 1981. Vegetation of sandstone outcrops of the Cumberland Plateau. M.S. Thesis. Univ. Tenn., Knoxville, Tenn.

Pittillo, J.D. 1976. Potential natural landmarks of the southern Blue Ridge portion of the Appalachian Ranges natural region. Report to the National Park Service. Western Carolina Univ., Cullowhee, N. Car.

Pittillo, J.D. and T.E. Govus. 1978. A manual of important plant habitats of the Blue Ridge Parkway. Report to the National Park Service. Western Carolina Univ., Cullowhee, N. Car.

Platt, R.B. 1951. An ecological study of the Mid-Appalachian shale barrens and of the plants endemic to them. Ecol. Monog. 21:269-300.

Pomeroy, J.S. 1980. Storm-induced debris avalanching and related phenomena in the Johnstown area, Pennsylvania, with reference to other studies in the Appalachians. U.S. Geol. Surv. Prof. Paper 1191.

Proctor, J. and S.R.J. Woodell. 1980. The ecology of serpentine soils. Adv. Ecol. Res. 9:225-366.

Quarterman, E. 1950. Major plant communities of Tennessee cedar glades. Ecol. 31:234-254.

Quarterman, E. and R.L. Powell. 1978. Potential ecological/geological natural landmarks on the Interior Low Plateaus. Report to the National Park Service, Nashville, Tenn.

Radford, A.E. 1948. The vascular flora of the olivine deposits of North Carolina and Georgia. J. Elisha Mitchell Sci. Soc. 64:45-106.

Radford, A.E. and D.L. Martin. 1975. Potential ecological Natural Landmarks Piedmont region, eastern United States. Report to the National Park Service, Univ. N. Carolina, Chapel Hill, N. Car.

Schafale, M.P. and A.S. Weakley. 1985. Classification of the natural communities of North Carolina. Second Approximation. Processed report. North Carolina National Heritage Program, Raleigh, N.C.

Schmalzer, P.A. and H.R. DeSelm. 1982. Final report-vegetation, endangered and threatened plants, critical plant habitats and vascular flora of the Obed Wild and Scenic River. Report to the National Park Service, SER, Atlanta. Contract: CX5000-9-1149.

Shaw, S.P. and C.G. Fredine. 1956. Wetlands of the United States. Their extent and their value to waterfowl and other wildlife. U.S. Fish and Wildl. Serv. Circ. 39.

Swanton, J.R. 1939. The final report of the U.S. DeSoto Expedition Commission. House Document 71, 76th Congress, 1st Session. Government Printing Office, Washington, D.C.

Transeau, E.N. 1935. The prairie peninsula. Ecology 16:423-437.

Tucker, G.E. 1972. The vascular flora of Bluff Mountain, Ashe County, North Carolina. Castanea 37:2-26.

Van Horn, G.S. 1980. Additions to the cedar glade flora of northwest Georgia. Castanea 45:134-137.

Weaver, J.E. 1954. North American prairie. Johnson Publishing Co., Lincoln, Nebraska.

Wherry, E.T. 1963. Some Pennsylvania barrens and their flora. I. Serpentine. Bartonia 33:1-11.

Wherry, E.T., J.M. Fogg, Jr. and H.A. Wahl. 1979. Atlas of the flora of Pennsylvania. Morris Arboretum of the University of Pennsylvania, Philadelphia, Penn.

Whetstone, R.D. 1981. Vascular flora and vegetation of the Cumberland Plateau of Alabama including a computer-assisted spectral analysis and interpretive synthesis of the origin, migration and evolution of the flora. Ph.D. Dissertation. Univ. of N. Carolina, Chapel Hill, N. Car.

White, A.S. 1983. The effects of thirteen years of annual prescribed burning on a *Quercus ellipsoidalis* community in Minnesota. Ecology 64:1081-1085.

White, J. 1978. Illinois natural areas inventory technical report. Volume I. Survey methods and results. Illinois Natural Areas Inventory, Urbana, Ill.

White, P.S. 1982. The flora of Great Smoky Mountains National park: an annotated checklist of vascular plants and a review of previous floristic work. NPS-SER Research/Resources Management Report SER-55.

Whittaker, R.H. 1956. Vegetation of the Great Smoky Mountains. Ecol. Monogr. 26:1-80.

Williams, S.C. 1928. Early travels in the Tennessee country, 1580-1800. Watauga Press, Johnson City, Tenn.

Winterringer, G.S. and A.G. Vestal. 1956. Rock-ledge vegetation in southern Illinois. Ecol. Monogr. 26:105-130.

Wistendahl, W.A. 1975. Buffalo Beats, a relict prairie within a southeastern Ohio forest. Bull. Torrey Bot. Club 102:178-186.

Wofford, B.E., T.S. Patrick, L.R. Phillippe, and D.H. Webb. 1979. The vascular flora of Savage Gulf, Tennessee. Sida 8:135-151

Grasslands Of Missouri: Preservation Status And Management Problems

by
Thomas E. Toney

ABSTRACT--The central location of Missouri within the continent gives it a diversity of grassland and forest types. An estimated 41% of the state was covered by prairie in presettlement times. The original grasslands are broadly classified according to the major soil regions. Five agencies have been active since 1957 in the purchase and preservation of the native Missouri grasslands. Invasion by tall fescue presents the single greatest management problem. Housing development and the island effect of existing areas present additional concerns.

KEYWORDS: Missouri Prairies, grassland management, prairie preservation, Missouri Department of Conservation, fire, grazing, haying.

Missouri is a unique state where a vast array of rivers and streams, tall grass prairies, mountains, and forest meet to form an almost infinite variety of ecological types. The unique diversity of Missouri's forest, streams, and wildlife equally applies to the grasslands that covered over 40% of the state in presettlement times. A detailed study by Schroeder (1981) determined that a minimum of 26.7% of the state could be classified prairie according to early land surveyors. That large tracts of grassland were listed by the surveyors in such a way that proper classification could not be determined. Today, less than half of one percent (30,352 ha.) of the natural grasslands remain according to Christian (1972).

Botanists delayed too long behind the plow to properly classify the vast majority of northern Missouri prairies. The same fate occurred over much of the remainder of the state. Only within the southwest and west central regions of the state, were large tracts spared from the plow and urbanization. Fire control and overgrazing within the Ozarks resulted in the conversion of native grasslands to forest and tame pasture.

MISSOURI GRASSLANDS CHARACTERISTICS

The grasslands of Missouri are rich in species diversity, with over 400 plant species recorded (Toney 1980). The prairies are dominated by tall and medium height warm-season grasses including big and little bluestem, Indian grass, switchgrass, panicums, and dropseeds (Drew 1947, Toney 1980, Kelting 1982). The grasses make up from 70 to 90% of the total dry weight.

Grasslands of Missouri can be broadly classified into six types: Loess Hills, Loess Drift, Central Claypan, Missouri and Mississippi Alluvium, Cherokee, and Ozark Prairies. This classification follows that of the major soil regions of Missouri (Allgood 1979).

The Loess Hill Prairies are located in the extreme northwest portion of the state. They occur on moderate to steep slopes of south and west exposure. Forest occupies the north and east slopes. Loess deposits underlying the prairie exceeds 28 meters in some locations, with range of 3 to 28 m. Topographic changes up to 72 m occur on some slopes. The dominant grasses are little bluestem, plains muhly, Indian grass, side-oats, and hairy grama and buffalo grass on the ridges and steep slopes. On the gentle slopes and within the bottom flats, big blue stem, Indian grass and switchgrass take over dominance. The short grasses and plains broadleaf species are threatened by both forest invasion and from competition of the tall grass species.

The Loess Drift Prairies occupy that region of the state from the Loess Hills, eastward to the Central Claypan Prairies, and southward to the Missouri River. The topography consists of rolling hills to steep slopes along stream valleys. Grasses dominate the hills and gentle slopes, giving way to forest along the stream valleys and steep slopes. Little and big bluestem dominate with Indian grass, switchgrass, wildryes, and sideoats grama being characteristic. A few small remnants of this type still remain in private ownership. The majority of this region was plowed in the early twenties and later allowed to revert back to grassland. The incentive to produce bluegrass seed and the introduction of smoothbrome for pasture added to additional loss of the native grasses.

Figure 1. An important aspect of managing prairies in Missouri is educating the public about their natural and cultural history values. Here a group tours Diamond Grove Prairie, part of the Cherokee Prairies region. (Photograph by T. E. Toney)

377

The Central Claypan Prairies occupied the region within north central and eastern Missouri north of the Missouri River. The topography is nearly level to gentle sloping loess mantled, glacial till plain. The soils formed primarily from loess, and consists of deep claypan soils. Big bluestem and Indian grass dominated the landscape with pockets of switchgrass, sloughgrass, bluejoint and Canada wildrye. These were probably the most productive of the Missouri prairies. Tucker Prairie and a few small remnants on wildlife areas and state parks now represent the vast majority of this type. A few railroad right-of-ways and cemeteries still retain a small remnant.

The Missouri and Mississippi Alluvium Prairies occurred on nearly level flood plains of these two rivers and their tributaries. Soils are very fertile, but poorly drained, silts and clays that overflow yearly. The dominant grass was sloughgrass which often formed nearly pure stands. Associated species included rice cutgrass, barnyard grass, reedgrass, and a variety of sedges. Big bluestem, Indian grass, switchgrass, Canada and Virginia wildrye occupy the better drained soils. Only small remnants of this type have escaped the plow and inundation by reservoirs. The tracts along the Osage River in west central Missouri represent the highest quality preserved areas.

The Cherokee (unglaciated) Prairie occupies the greatest portion of southwest and west central Missouri. The nearly level to gentle sloping topography is underlain by shale, sandstone, and cherty limestone. These soils are listed as moderate to poor in natural fertility. The rocky, shallow soils in addition to the small farm economy helped to preserve large tracts in hay production. The extremes from rock outcrops to deep upland soils favored a more diverse flora and fauna than the other regions. The shallow uplands are dominated by little bluestem and other bunchgrasses, yielding to big bluestem and sod grasses on the deeper soils. It is within this region that the majority of preserves have been set aside.

The Ozark Prairies or Savannah occupied that portion of the state within the central and southwest Ozarks. The soils consists of shallow, cherty limestone on ridges and steep slopes. Gentle rolling slopes and nearly level plains occur intermittently along the streams. The dominant vegetation was forest with small openings called "glades." Reports by such early travelers as Schoolcraft (Park 1955) and by physical evidence today, indicate extensive grasslands at the head of tributaries and forest understory in numerous areas. Typical vegetation on and around many of the glades is little bluestem, big bluestem, Indian grass and various broadleaf plants common to the prairies. Evidence of the grasslands within the forest is often seen in manmade clearings or thinnings. Typical timber clearings are now converted to tame grasses suppressing the native species.

PRESERVE STATUS

Missouri's public prairies include 30 dry-mesic upland tracts within the Cherokee Region; 1 dry-mesic upland area within the Central Claypan Region; 2 Loess Hill Prairies; and 5 Alluvium Prairies (Table I). Not listed in this paper are the numerous small prairies found on Missouri Department of Conservation wildlife management areas and on state parks. Also not included are the glades of the Ozark Region.

Five agencies have been active, or contributed in part, in the purchase and preservation of 38 prairie tracts: University of Missouri, the Missouri Department of Conservation, the Missouri Prairie Foundation, The Nature Conservancy, and the Missouri Department of Natural Resources. In addition, tracts have been set aside for preservation by the Corps of Engineers, private industry and individuals.

Preservation of Missouri's grassland resource had its beginning in 1957 by the University of Missouri with the purchase of Tucker Prairie for a research prairie. Tucker continues to serve land managers with various studies.

In an effort to preserve the greater prairie chicken, two prairies were purchased by the Missouri Department of Conservation in 1959. The addition of a Natural History Section, and with a special tax fund, the Commission purchased 18 additional areas within the Cherokee Region. In 1984, a plan for restoration of the prairie chicken was approved by the Department which provides for an additional acquisition of 4,415 ha of grassland over the next several years. The Department has a cooperative lease agreement with the Nature Conservancy and Prairie Foundation for management of their respective areas. In addition, the Department manages 16 prairies for the Corps of Engineers on Truman Lake.

The Missouri Prairie Foundation was formed in the 1960's with the objective to help preserve the vanishing prairie. The Foundation has purchased 6 areas within the Cherokee Region. They have started working agreements with railroad companies in the Central Claypan Region for management of remnants along the lines. The Foundation in cooperative agreement with the Empire Mines of Joplin, Missouri has helped set aside a 32 ha prairie for future preservation.

The Nature Conservancy became active in preserving the dwindling Missouri prairies in the early 1970's. A number of the preserves have been purchased only by the cooperation between the Conservancy, Foundation and Conservation Department. The Conservancy, primarily with funds by Miss Katherine Ordway, purchased 13 areas between 1972 and 1984. The purchase of the Marmaton Bottoms Prairie, Alluvium type, preserved the highest quality site within the state.

The Department of Natural Resources, in cooperation with the Conservancy, purchased what is now the largest preserved prairie. This area, Prairie State Park, is located within the Cherokee Region. The parks also manage several remnants within other state parks, including the Cordgrass Bottoms and Locust Creek Prairies of the Alluvium type north of the Missouri River.

The effort to preserve the vanishing grasslands of Missouri has had its greatest success in the Cherokee Region.

Table I. Public Prairies of Missouri.

Prairie Name	Size (ha.)	Type	Owner*	Management
Brickyard Hill	5	Loess Hill	MDC	MDC
Bushwhacker	269	Cherokee	MDC	MDC
Catlin	60	Cherokee	MDC	MDC
Diamond Grove	208	Cherokee	MDC	MDC
Dorsett Hill	6	Cherokee	MDC	MDC
Drover	32	Cherokee	MPF	MDC
Flight Lake	22	Alluvium	MDC	MDC
Friendly	16	Cherokee	MPF	MDC
Gama Grass	32	Cherokee	TNC	MDC
Gay Feather	47	Cherokee	MPF/MDC	MDC
Golden	122	Cherokee	MPF	MPF
Hite	27	Cherokee	MDC	MDC
Hunkah	65	Cherokee	TNC	MDC
Indigo	16	Cherokee	MDC	MDC
La Petite Gemme	15	Cherokee	MPF	MDC
Little Osage	32	Cherokee	TNC	MDC
Locust Creek & Cordgrass Bottom	316	Alluvium	DNR	DNR
Marmaton Bottoms	45	Alluvium	TNC	TNC
McCormack Loess	4	Loess Hill	TNC/MDC	MDC
Mo-Ko	166	Cherokee	TNC	MDC
Monegaw	109	Cherokee	TNC/MDC	MDC
Mount Vernon	16	Cherokee	TNC	MDC
Niawathe	130	Cherokee	TNC/MDC	MDC
Osage	564	Cherokee	MDC	MDC
Paint Brush	62	Cherokee	MDC	MDC
Pawhuska	31	Cherokee	TNC	MDC
PennSylvania	65	Cherokee	MPF	MPF
Prairie State Park	595	Cherokee	DNR	DNR
Prairie Woods	8	Alluvium	MDC	MDC
Schell-Osage Upland	16	Cherokee	MDC	MDC
Schell-Osage Bottoms	53	Alluvium	MDC	MDC
Sky	81	Cherokee	MDC	MDC
Taberville	571	Cherokee	MDC	MDC
Tucker	59	Central Claypan	UM	UM
Tzi-Sho	65	Cherokee	TNC	MDC
Wah-Kon-Tah	283	Cherokee	TNC	MDC
Wah-Sha-She	65	Cherokee	TNC	MDC
Bentlage tract	65	Cherokee	MDC	MDC

*MDC = Missouri Department of Conservation, MPF = Missouri Prairie Foundation, TNC = The Nature Conservancy, DNR = Department of Natural Resources, UM = University of Missouri.

Efforts to preserve the Loess Hills and Loess Drift Prairies have met with little success. The Foundation will continue to work with railroad companies within the Central Claypan Region. The scarcity of the Alluvium prairies offers little hope of large acquisitions.

MANAGEMENT PROBLEMS

Even though the overall objective in purchase of the areas varies between the agencies, the management objective by the Conservation Department is to "maintain the highest diversity of indigenous plants/site and animals, giving special consideration to rare and endangered species when found" (Toney 1974). Management by the Conservation Department includes

haying, burning and grazing. The State Parks manage by control burning with the exception of a small herd of buffalo on Prairie State Park. The Conservation Department manages 32 of the 37 public areas.

A study was set up in 1984 to determine the effects of annual haying, two and three year hay-rest rotations, burning and grazing on the prairie flora and fauna. Management experience indicates that a summer disturbance is necessary to maintain the desired objective. The prairies managed by the Department contain 18 rare and endangered plant and animal species.

The single greatest problem on the preserves is the invasion of the introduced cool-season grass tall fescue for forage production. Unlike bluegrass, redtop, brome and other tame grasses, fescue is highly tolerant of fire. Fire has been effective in stopping fescue from spreading and may have reduced it to a limited degree. What often appears to be a reduction is later found to be of little effect after fire is removed for two to three years. Chemical treatment in future years may be the end solution.

The public prairies have become population centers for the prairie chicken and other grassland wildlife. The single island effect of the areas, increases the threat of natural or manmade disaster. A hail storm of October 16, 1983 destroyed 55% of the chicken population on one area. The Conservation Department's restoration plan should help offset such potentials with the purchase of additional areas in a continuous island pattern allowing for movement between populations.

Highway and housing projects near and around a number of the preserves are a potential problem with control burning in future years. At present, the safe use of fire with full consideration of smoke dispersion is the most effective tool to calm fears of homeowners.

The relationship of Missouri prairies to nesting and to wintering grounds of its migratory wildlife is in need of study. Is Missouri meeting the needs of nesting birds? Are we providing adequate habitat for wintering birds that nest further north? Loss of nesting habitat on any tract is not compensated for on adjacent lands. We must keep an open mind to techniques of management if we are to maintain the resource in future years.

LITERATURE CITED

Allgood, F.P. and I.D. Persinger. 1979. Missouri General Soil Map and Soil Association Descriptions. USDA, Soil Conserv. Serv., Columbia, Missouri.

Christisen, D.M. 1972. Prairie Preservation in Missouri, pp. 42-46. Third Midwest Prairie Conf. Proc. Kansas State Univ., Manhattan, Kansas.

Drew, W.B. 1947. Floristic Composition of Grazed and Ungrazed Prairie Vegetation in North Central Missouri. Ecology 28:26-41.

Kelting, R.W. 1982. Flora of Wah-Sha-She Prairie. Eighth Midwest Prairie Conf. Proc. Western Michigan Univ., Kalamazoo, Mich.

Park, H. 1955. Schoolcraft in the Ozarks. Press-Argus Printers, Van Buren, Ark.

Schroeder, W.A. 1981. Presettlement Prairie of Missouri. Nat. His. Ser. No. 2, Missouri Dept. Cons., Jeff. City., Missouri.

Toney, T.E. 1974. A Plan of Management for the Prairies Acquired by The Nature Conservancy. Missouri Dep. Conserv., Jeff. City., Missouri.

Toney, T.E. 1980. Vascular Plant Species of Taberville Prairie Handout. Missouri Dep. Conserv., Lockwood, Missouri.

Grasslands And Savannahs Of East Central Texas: Ecology, Preservation Status And Management Problems

by
Fred E. Smeins and David D. Diamond

ABSTRACT--The Eastern and Western Cross Timbers, the Post Oak Savannah and the Grand, Blackland, San Antonio, Fayette and Upper Coastal Prairies cover a 13 million ha northwest to southeast zone across central Texas. Post oak (*Quercus stellata*) is the characteristic tree species of the savannahs and woodlands, while little bluestem (*Schizachyrium scoparium*) is the dominant grass of late-successional communities in both savannahs and prairies. Increase in abundance of woody plants across this region as well as destruction or alteration of the natural vegetation have been major impacts since settlement. Less than 1% of the total area is contained within governmental or privately managed areas and less than 0.2% of the total area can be considered good or better quality. Landscape level management problems exist due to location and insularity of existing preserves. At the site level, manmade as well as naturally occurring ecological changes make management inevitable on most preserves. Controlled access, application of integrated management tools including fire, haying, controlled herbivory and selective treatment for weeds and pests may be necessary. Management planning is a continuous process and frequent alteration may be necessary to maintain the desired qualities of these natural areas.

KEYWORDS: tallgrass prairies, oak savannahs, fire, natural areas, integrated management, island biogeography, mowing/haying.

ECOLOGY

Location

Grasslands, savannahs and woodlands (physiognomic types defined according to the UNESCO physiognomic-ecologic classification by Mueller-Dombois and Ellenberg 1974) cover a large portion of the state of Texas. While these communities cross a wide variety of environments and have diverse faunistic and floristic affinities, only those with primarily eastern North American biogeographical affinities are considered here. Areas included are (Fig. 1):

Savannahs and Woodlands
  Western Cross Timbers
  Eastern Cross Timbers
  Post Oak Savannah/Woodland
Grasslands
  Grand Prairie
  Blackland Prairie
  San Antonio Prairie
  Fayette Prairie
Upper Coastal Prairie

These resource areas, which cover approximately 13 million ha, form alternating northeast to southwest zones that fall between 95 and 98 degrees west longitude and 29 and 35 degrees north latitude.

Environment

These northeast to southwest zones correspond generally with geological substrates deposited sequentially by receding sea levels. They vary in age from Pennsylvanian deposits underlying the western edge of the Western Cross Timbers to Quaternary and Recent deposits of the Coastal Prairie and Coastal Marshes (Sellards *et al.* 1966). Elevations vary from sea level to nearly 300 m. The Coastal Prairie region is a flat, subdued landscape, while inland the landscape takes on a gently rolling character. Several major rivers and their tributaries cross the region from northwest to southeast. The most northerly is the Trinity followed to the south by the Brazos and the Colorado (Fig. 1). These rivers with their wide valleys and terraces contribute diversity to the landscape as well as to the biotic components of the region.

The retreat of the sea left alternating arenaceous and calcareous materials which generally correspond to Alfisols and Vertisols, respectively (Godfrey *et al.* 1973). These soils in turn correspond generally with savannah/woodland and grassland. Alfisols often exhibit a landform called "mima" or "pimple" mound topography. These are sandy or loamy mounds which vary from 1 to over 10 m in diameter and from a few cm to over 1 m in height. Their origin is speculative but they do add a unique feature to some areas particularly where the landscape is flat (Butler 1979, Smeins *et al.* in press). Vertisols are characterized by shrink/swell clays that produce a microtopography referred to as "gilgai". On level areas these soils have "hogwallow" microtopography which are depressions up to 3 m in diameter that hold water for varying periods after a heavy rainfall. On slopes this topography is expressed as microvalleys and microridges that run parallel to the slope.

Mean annual precipitation varies from 70 cm in the northwest to 130 cm in the southeast. Mean annual temperatures range from 19 to 21 degrees C and frost free period from 225 to over 300 days. The more northerly portion experiences several days of freezing temperatures each year and occasional snowfalls are associated with "blue northers." Along the coast freezing temperatures are unusual, although not unheard of, and snowfall is rare.

Communities

Communities considered here are southwestern or southern extensions of the Eastern Deciduous Forest and the True Prairie Grassland (Braun 1950, Risser *et al.* 1981). Although western biotic elements do occur, the majority of species have eastern affinities (Butler 1979, Diamond and Smeins 1984). Woodlands and savannahs occur primarily on sandy or loam soils while the prairies are found mainly on calcareous, clayey soils, however, there is no exact correlation of community-type with soil

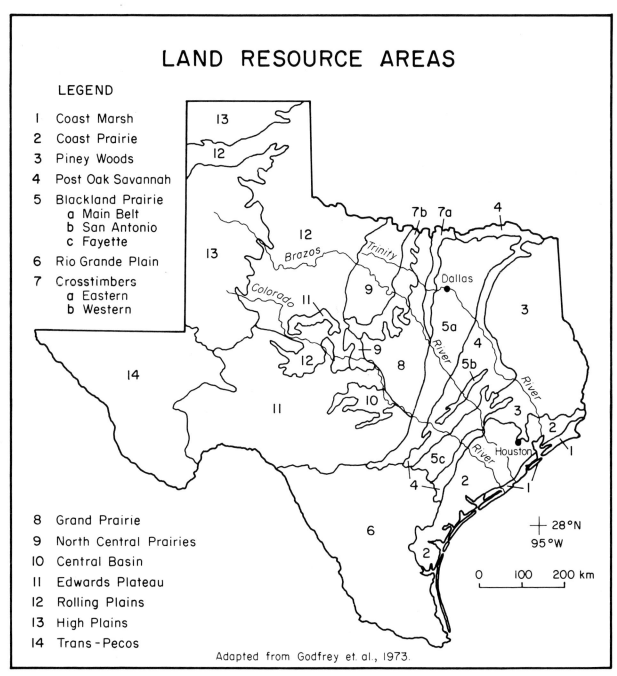

Figure 1. Land resource areas of Texas.

Figure 2. A remnant little bluestem *Schizachyrium scoparium*- Indiangrass *Sorghastrum nutans* prairie within the Blackland Prairie region. The prairie is mowed annually and the hay removed. Periodically (ca. 5 to 7 year interval) the prairie is burned in the spring. These treatments have maintained the grassland in excellent condition for over 75 years. (Photograph by Fred E. Smeins)

type (McCaleb 1954, Bell and Hulbert 1974). There is great interspersion of the two soil types in many locales.

Tharp (1926) provided the first general description of the vegetation of the entire area. Dyksterhuis (1948) gave the first comprehensive analysis of the Western Cross Timbers. The Eastern Cross Timbers have been described by Marcy (1982) and McClusky (1972), and Harrison (1974) conducted comparative studies of the Eastern and Western Cross Timbers. The Post Oak Savannah has been evaluated by McBryde (1933), McCaleb (1954) and Allen (1974). These areas are all characterized by post oak (*Quercus stellata*) (Taxonomic nomenclature in this paper follows Correll and Johnston (1970)). Blackjack oak *Q. marilandica*) is also widespread but not nearly so abundant. In the Post Oak Savannah region, particularly on deep sands, black hickory (*Carya texana*) may be locally abundant. Throughout the region liveoak (*Quercus virginiana*) may be found growing singly or in mottes often on the prairie soils and on river terraces.

Widespread tree species of lesser importance are hackberry (*Celtis laevigata*), cedar elm (*Ulmus crassifolia*), eastern red cedar (*Juniperus virginiana*), common persimmon (*Diospyros virginiana*) and mesquite (*Prosopis glandulosa* var. *glandulosa*), while winged elm (*Ulmus alata*), water oak (*Quercus nigra*) and green ash (*Fraxinus pennsylvanica*) occur sparingly in the eastern areas (Post Oak Savannah) and Texas oak (*Quercus texana*) in the west. Generally these tree species are short-statured and seldom exceed 12 m height. This height restriction is due to low fertility and poor water relations of the dense claypan subsoils that underlie most of the wooded areas.

Shrubs and vines found throughout are saw greenbriar (*Smilax bona-nox*), coralberry (*Symphoricarpos orbiculatus*), gum elastic (*Bumelia lanuginosa*) and prickly ash (*Zanthoxylum clava-herculis*). Within the Post Oak Savannah region a distinguishing characteristic of the vegetation is the great abundance of yaupon (*Ilex vomitoria*) which often forms dense understory thickets. The species is essentially absent from the Cross Timbers region. Often associated with yaupon but of much less importance are farkleberry (*Vaccinium arboreum*) and French mulberry (*Callicarpa americana*). Deciduous holly (*Ilex decidua*) occurs throughout the Post Oak Savannah and west through the Eastern and Western Cross Timbers but never is a major component of the vegetation. Fragrant sumac (*Rhus aromatica*) becomes a common shrub in the Western Cross Timbers.

The late seral herbaceous dominant of most savannah

areas is little bluestem (*Schizachyrium scoparium*). Indiangrass (*Sorghastrum avenaceum=nutans*) and big bluestem (*Andropogon Gerardi*) are secondary species throughout, while in the central and southern Post Oak Savannah brownseed paspalum (*Paspalum plicatulum*) is an important secondary grass. An abbreviated table of the vegetation of relict areas of the Western Cross Timbers is presented to illustrate composition and soil relationships (Table 1).

Riverine habitats add to the landscape and biotic diversity of the region. A cross-section of upland and bottomland habitats and dominance types of the Navasota River (tributary of the Brazos River) is presented to illustrate some relationships in the central region of the Post Oak Savannah (Table 2). The honey mesquite dominance-type occurs on prairie soils that have been invaded by this woody species. Other upland types are on Alfisols and the transition occurs at lower slope positions adjacent to the floodplain and on deep sands. Bottomland types are on a level floodplain and the ephemeral streams on periodically flooded stream channels, oxbows and backwater areas.

Grasslands of the region have been described by Dyksterhuis (1946), Launchbaugh (1955), Collins *et al.* (1975), Smeins and Diamond (1983), Diamond and Smeins (1984, 1985) and Smeins *et al.* (in press). General consensus indicates that the prevailing dominant grass of excellent condition grasslands across nearly all prairies is little bluestem (*Schizachyrium scoparium*) (Table 3). Secondary species throughout are Indiangrass (*Sorghastrum avenaceum*), big bluestem (*Andropogon Gerardi*) and tall dropseed (*Sporobolus asper*). On all Coastal Prairie soils and Alfisols of the Fayette Prairie brownseed paspalum (*Paspalum plicatulum*) becomes an important secondary species, while calcareous soils of the Fayette, Blackland and Grand Prairie have sideoats grama (*Bouteloua curtipendula*) as a secondary species.

Alfisols on the northern and northeastern margin of the Blackland Prairie that receive 90 cm or more annual

precipitation have Silveanus dropseed (*Sporobolus silveanus*) as the dominant grass and sedges as characteristic secondary species. Also the northern part of the Blackland Prairie over Vertisols with high precipitation is dominated by gamagrass (*Tripsacum dactyloides*) along with switchgrass (*Panicum virgatum*).

Rare Species

Several elements of the flora and fauna of this region are considered rare and/or endangered by the State or Federal government (Longley *et al.* 1979, Beaty *et al.* 1983, Federal Register 1980). A selected list of plant taxa would include:

Brazoria pulcherrima - Centerville brazosmint
Hymenoxys texana - Texas bitterweed
Machaeranthera aurea - Houston machaeranthera
Polygonella parksii - Parks jointweed
Spiranthes parksii - Navasota ladiestresses

Faunal taxa of note are:

Bufo houstonensis - Houston toad
Phrynosoma cornutum - Texas horned lizard
Haliaectus leucocephalus - Bald eagle
Tympanuchus cupido - Attwater's prairie chicken
Grus americanus - Whooping crane
Canis rufus - Red wolf (considered extinct, but hybrids with the coyote (*Canis latrans*) may exist)

Historical Changes

The natural ecosystems of this region have been greatly altered or destroyed since settlement. The exact character of the original communities is not well-documented, however, consensus from various studies indicates that woody vegetation has increased at the expense of herbaceous vegetation in both savannah/woodland and prairie areas (Smith 1899, Bray 1904, Foster 1917, Dyksterhuis 1946, 1948, Smeins 1982). That is not to conclude that dense areas of the woodland did not exist, but rather that the areal extent of thicketized, dense areas increased following settlement. As an example, early accounts of the Western Cross Timbers provide contrasting views of the vegetation. Kendall (1844) describes

Table 1. Samples from Two Tracts of Relict Vegetation for Each of the Three Major Edaphic Conditions of the Western Cross Timbers Showing Relative Coverage (%) by the Principal Species within Each.[1]

Principal Species	Podzolic Soils; Fine Sandy Loams: Gentle Relief		Immature Reddish Prairie Soils: Rough Relief		Mature Reddish Prairie Soils; Clays; Flat Relief	
	Cundiff[2]	Nocona	Alvord	Post oak	Bowie	Jacksboro
Little bluestem	62	68	47	70	70	72
Indiangrass	7	8	2	5	8	4
Big bluestem	3	—	P[3]	P	1	16
Sideoats grama	1	1	11	P	2	1
Tall dropseed	1	P	8	P	1	3
Hairy grama	—	3	5	12	1	P
Blue grama	—	—	—	6	—	—
Post oak	3	7	8	1	—	—
Blackjack oak	P	1	2	P	—	—

[1] Adapted from Dyksterhuis (1948).

[2] Name of town nearest to relict.

[3] "P" indicates that the species was present on the tract.

Table 2. Mean Importance Value (IV)[1] for Major Overstory and Middlestory[2] Species within Nine Dominance Types and Four Habitats of the Lower Navasota River Watershed. Data Collected using the Point-Centered Quarter Method with 30 Points per Stand.[3]

Species	Upland			Transition	Bottomland			Ephemeral Streams	
	Honey Mesquite	Post Oak	Postoak-Hickory	Winged Elm	Cedar Elm	Overcup Oak	Hackberry Cedar Elm	Swamp Privet	Water Elm
Overstory									
Honey mesquite	95	—	—	—	—	—	—	—	—
Blackjack oak	—	9	—	—	—	—	—	—	—
Eastern red cedar	—	4	—	—	—	—	—	—	—
Black hickory	—	7	35	—	—	—	—	—	—
Post oak	—	54	38	23	10	—	—	—	—
Winged elm	—	14	9	38	—	—	—	—	—
Water oak	—	2	2	9	—	—	—	—	—
Ash sp.	—	2	—	9	2	6	4	—	—
Bur oak	—	—	—	—	7	—	—	—	—
Willow oak	—	—	—	—	9	17	—	—	—
Overcup oak	—	—	—	—	6	35	—	—	3
Pecan	—	—	—	—	2	17	—	—	—
Cedar elm	—	—	—	—	47	14	53	—	3
Hackberry	—	—	—	—	7	2	52	—	—
Swamp privet	—	—	—	—	—	—	—	69	1
Water elm	—	—	—	—	—	—	—	18	63
Water hickory	—	—	—	—	—	—	—	—	10
Black tupelo	—	—	—	—	—	—	—	—	5
Nonliving	—	7	12	14	5	5	2	7	6
Others	5	1	5	7	7	4	—	7	9
Middlestory									
Yaupon	a[4]	62	77	83	—	—	—	a	a
Farkleberry	—	11	4	4	—	—	—	—	—
French mulberry	—	2	14	—	—	—	—	—	—
Hawthorne spp.	—	5	4	8	18	5	—	—	—
Deciduous holly	—	7	—	5	30	20	—	—	—
Cedar elm	—	—	—	—	37	8	58	—	—
Swamp privet	—	—	—	—	—	34	20	—	—
Overcup oak	—	—	—	—	—	12	—	—	—
Hackberry	—	—	—	—	—	—	17	—	—
Others	—	13	1	—	15	21	5	—	—

[1] IV = $\frac{\text{Relative Frequency + Relative Density + Relative Basal Area}}{3}$

[2] Overstory > 5 cm dbh and capable of obtaining a position on the canopy; middlestory trees > 5 cm dbh and shrubs > 0.6 m tall.

[3] Adapted from Allen 1974.

[4] Middlestory not present.

the area as follows: "The growth of timber is principally small gnarled, post oaks and black jacks, and in many places the traveller will find an almost inpenetrable undergrowth of brier and other thorny bushes." Marcy (1849) provides a somewhat different version: "At six different points where I have passed through it, I have found it characterized by the same peculiarities; the trees consisting principally of post-oak and blackjack, standing at such intervals that wagons can without difficulty pass between them in any direction." He later states: "Furthermore, dense thickets of saw greenbrier (*Smilax bonanox*) are common today on localized areas of deep sands."

Similar contrasting views concerning the relative openness of the savannah/woodlands can be found for the other resource areas under consideration. Generally, the past

150 years, however, has witnessed an increase in oaks, elms, junipers and various shrubs within the savannah/woodlands, and prairies have been invaded by these same species plus the ubiquitous mesquite.

Major changes have also occurred in the faunal components. Bear, bison, white-tailed deer, red wolves, passenger pigeons, prairie chickens and turkey were eliminated from the region (Yantis 1984). White-tailed deer were later re-introduced and today are widespread and locally overpopulation may be a problem. As the large native herbivores and predators were reduced they were replaced during the period 1750 to 1850 by large herds of mustangs and wild cattle that escaped from Spanish expeditions or missions. After the Civil War these animals were harvested for their hides, tallow or meat or

Table 3. Mean Relative Foliar Cover (%) of Selected Graminoids in Relict Stands for Five Major Upland Tallgrass Prairie Regions of Texas.[1]

Species	Central and Southern Blackland and Fayette Prairie Vertisols	Coastal Prairie Vertisols and Alfisols and Fayette and San Antonio Prairie Alfisols	Northern Blackland Prairie Alfisols with High Precipitation	Northern Blackland Prairie Vertisols with High Precipitation	Grand Prairie
Big bluestem	10	2	T[2]	—	2
Sideoats grama	5	T	—	T	8
Hairy grama	—	—	—	—	3
Mead's carex	—	—	10	—	1
Littletooth carex	4	2	—	5	—
Carolina jointtail	T	2	3	—	—
Schribners panic	1	2	6	—	—
Fimbry	2	3	12	—	—
Swithchgrass	1	4	5	13	1
Florida paspalum	4	5	4	T	—
Brownseed paspalum	—	14	—	—	—
Thin paspalum	—	2	1	—	—
Little bluestem	29	39	2	3	65
Indiangrass	18	13	T	13	5
Tall dropseed	5	4	T	10	2
Silveanus dropseed	—	—	37	—	—
Texas wintergrass	1	T	—	T	2
Easter gamagrass	2	—	—	38	—

[1] Adapted from Dyksterhuis (1946) and Diamond and Smeins (1985).

[2] Trace.

captured to become the nucleus of some domesticated herds. Other breeds of cattle as well as sheep and goats were introduced and increased in numbers and through time became more and more confined. By the late 1800's overgrazing had become a serious problem throughout the region (Smith 1899). Overgrazing not only reduced the herbaceous cover and changed species composition, it also reduced the fuel which carried fires across these communities. Naturally occurring fires were considered to have been a major retardant to the spread of woody species prior to settlement (Smeins 1982).

As settlement continued much of the land was cultivated. Many areas, however, due to exhaustion of the soil or soil erosion, have been returned to permanent grass. In most cases they have been planted to exotic tame pasture species such as bermudagrass (Cynodon dactylon) KR bluestem (Bothriochloa ischaemum var. songarica) and Johnsongrass (Sorghum halapense).

The productive soils of the Blackland Prairies caused an influx of people to the region for agricultural uses, while oil and gas development later contributed to increased population. Ultimately major centers of urbanization, epitomized by the metroplexes of Dallas-Fort Worth and Houston, covered much of the landscape.

Thus, long and continued overgrazing, elimination of fires, cultivation, urbanization and other associated human activities have collectively contributed to nearly total alteration of the natural communities of the region. Few relatively undisturbed remnants of these communities exist. A map of the current vegetation of Texas indicates that the oak savannah/woodlands are still predominantly woodlands, though variously altered from settlement times, while the prairies are largely cropland (McMahon et al. 1984).

PRESERVATION STATUS

Managed Natural Areas

A total of 11 Federal, 34 State and 15 major private managed areas occur within the region (Table 4). Most are within the Upper Coastal Prairie (37%) or Post Oak Savannah (30%). Less than 1% of the uplands of the Upper Coastal Prairie are within managed areas, while 11% of the wetlands are in managed areas. In the Post Oak Savannah, Western Cross Timbers and Blackland Prairie less than 1% of the land is in managed areas, while this figure is 7.0% and 5.0% for the Eastern Cross Timbers and Grand Prairie, respectively.

In most cases, only general community descriptions are available for these areas, and hence summaries are by resource area rather than community type. Also, statistics on amount of area occupied by fair or better quality examples of grassland or woodland are based on written descriptions or the best estimates of on-site managers and biologists and should not be taken as exact values. Fair or better quality communities are considered to occur over unbroken native sod with most component species of late successional stages (recoverable to near climax) present.

Federal Wildlife Refuges

Nine National Wildlife Refuges, administered by the U.S. Fish and Wildlife Service, are within the area. Eight of the nine refuges are within the Upper Coastal Prairie

(Table 5). Within these, an estimated 10,332 ha of fair or better quality grasslands occur. These include gulf cordgrass (*Spartina spartinae*) dominated flats as well as upland Coastal Prairie grasslands over unbroken native sod. The remaining refuge contains an estimated 300 ha of fair or better quality Grand Prairie bluestem grasslands and 400 ha of upland Eastern Cross Timbers oak woodland.

National Grasslands

Two National Grasslands occur within the region. They are administered by the U.S. Forest Service. A good deal of this land was acquired by the Federal government after the drought of the 1930's and had a previous history of cultivation and overgrazing. Thus, little of the land represents pristine conditions even though a good deal of it has been rehabilitated through reseeding and improved grazing management. Post Oak Savannah, Western Cross Timbers, Blackland Prairie and Grand Prairie are collectively represented by only 550 ha of fair or better quality communities within these Grasslands.

State Wildlife Management Areas

Four of the five State Wildlife Management Areas are within the Post Oak Savannah (Table 5). They contain an estimated 4500 ha of fair or better quality upland oak woodland. The remaining Wildlife Management Area occurs within the Upper Coastal Prairie and consists primarily of fresh, brackish and saline marsh.

State Parks

Four of the eight State Parks occur within the Post Oak Savannah (Table 5). These contain an estimated 752 ha of fair or better quality upland oak woodland plus 1263 ha of loblolly pine-post oak woodland (Lost Pines). Two state parks are within the Upper Coastal Prairie and contain approximately 456 ha of fair quality upland grassland and 278 ha of barrier island grassland on Galveston Island. An estimated 221 ha of fair or better quality upland oak woodland occurs within the Western Cross Timbers in two state parks.

State Historic Parks and Recreation Areas

The Kreische Brewery in Fayette County, which has a good quality 6 ha open oak savannah, was the only one of six historic parks to contain a significant natural area. Of fifteen State Recreation Areas, five contained fair or better quality upland oak woodland. In the Post Oak Savannah, Lake Somerville in Burleson and Lee Counties, contains 324 ha, Fairfield Lake in Freestone County about 243 ha and Lake Texana in Jackson County about 89 ha. In the Eastern Cross Timbers, Eisenhower in Grayson County contains 36 ha and Eagle Mountain Lake in Tarrant County about 721 ha of upland oak woodland.

There are additional Federal, State, County, Municipal and other government entities that control managed lands. These were not comprehensively surveyed in this study but general observations suggest they would add little to existing preserves, particularly areas that would be considered to be in good or better condition.

Private managed areas

The ecology of most private natural areas has not been well-documented. The Nature Conservancy's Peach Point preserve (scheduled for transfer to Texas Parks and Wildlife) in Brazoria County contains about 1377 ha of fair quality upland Coastal Prairie, while Slop Bowl, another Conservancy preserve in Brazoria County, contains about 40 ha of fair or better upland grassland. The Armand Bayou Nature Center in Chambers County contains about 243 ha of fair or better upland Coastal Prairie grassland. The Nature Conservancy's Dorthea Loenhart preserve in Falls County contains about 16 ha of upland *Schizachyrium-Andropogon-Sorghastrum* Blackland Prairie and the Thick-Spiked Tridens Prairie preserve in Lamar County contains about 39 ha of *Sporobolus silveanus-Carex meadii* tall grass prairie. The Conservancy's Marysee Prairie consists of about 3 ha of shrub-invaded grassland within the western edge of the Pineywoods. The Fort Worth Nature Center in Tarrant County contains about 61 ha of fair or better quality Grand Prairie and

Table 4. Area within Federal, State and Major Private Managed Natural Areas of East Central Texas.[1]

	Upper Coastal Prairie		Post Oak Savannah	Blackland Prairies	Eastern Cross Timbers	Western Cross Timbers	Grand Prairie
	Uplands	Wetlands					
Total Area (ha x 10^6)	2.50	0.36	2.10	5.10	0.34	0.83	1.70
Federal wildlife refuges (9)	15,841 (8)	36,785 (8)	—[2]	—	22,273 (1)	—	1,114 (1)
National grasslands (2)	—	2,347 (1)	323 (1)	7,114 (1)	—	1,187 (1)	6,130 (1)
State parks (8)	2,267 (2)	500 (2)	2,259 (4)	—	—	1,476 (2)	130 (1)
State wildlife management areas (5)	—	1,032 (1)	8,627 (3)	—	—	—	—
State recreation areas (15)	116 (1)	116 (1)	3,404 (6)	476 (2)	347 (2)	679 (2)	370 (2)
State historic parks (6)	203 (3)	106 (2)	102 (2)	—	—	—	—
Major private preserves (15)	3,256 (8)	1,864 (7)	137 (2)	153 (4)	1,377 (1)	—	—
Percent of total region in managed areas	<1%	11%	<1%	<1%	7%	<1%	5%

[1] The first number is area in hectares while the number in parentheses is the number of areas.

[2] Less than 10 ha.

440 ha of Eastern Cross Timbers oak woodland. Six of the remaining eight private natural areas are Audubon sanctuaries along the Upper Coast, including spoil islands, not known to contain good examples of grassland or savannah. The remaining two are within the Blackland Prairie, but consist primarily of tame pasture or old fields.

In addition to private managed areas there are numerous, usually small, private landholdings that harbor species and communities worthy of protection. In particular, within prairie areas many small haymeadows exist which contain relict plant communities. Some of these areas are under consideration for preservation by the Nature Conservancy, but the increasing rate of conversion to cultivation and other uses results in continued loss of some exceptional examples of natural communities.

As an example of the loss, in 1970 a survey was conducted across the main belt of the Blackland Prairie (Fig. 1). Approximately 100 ungrazed, excellent condition grasslands over uncultivated sod were located that collectively summed to 2,000 ha. Most sites were 20 ha or less in size but a few were as large as 300 ha. In 1980 the area was resurveyed. The number of sites had decreased from 100 to 35 and the area from 2000 to 800 ha.

Fair or better quality upland grasslands and oak woodland within refuges, parks and private natural areas comprise less than 1% of the total land area for all natural regions surveyed (Table 6). The total area of fair or better condition communities is lowest for the Blackland (0.004%) and Grand (0.02%) Prairies, and the current potential for restoration is lowest for these areas, where

Table 5. Location and Total Area (ha) of Grassland or Upland Oak Woodland for Federal Wildlife Refuges, National Grasslands, State Parks, and State Wildlife Management Areas of East Central Texas.

	County	Natural Region	Upland	Wetland[1]	Estimated fair or better quality Grassland	Upland Woodland
Federal Wildlife Refuges						
Anuhuac	Chambers	Upper Coastal Prairie	2591	7270	1000[2]	—[3]
Attwater's Prairie Chicken	Colorado	Upper Coastal Prairie	2951	243	1160	—
Big Boggy	Matagorda	Upper Coastal Prairie	289	1154	258	—
Brazoria	Brazoria	Upper Coastal Prairie	1488	2725	1084	—
Hagerman	Grayson	Eastern Cross Timbers & Grand Prairie	3342	1241	300	400
McFadden Ranch	Jefferson	Upper Coastal Prairie	3478	13,913	2500	—
Moody Ranch	Chambers	Upper Coastal Prairie	300	2700	—	—
San Bernard	Matagorda	Upper Coastal Prairie	4382	5518	4030	—
Texas Point	Jefferson	Upper Coastal Prairie	362	3262	300	—
National Grasslands						
Caddo	Fannin	Blackland Prairie	3231	—	100	—
		Post Oak Savannah	2347	1565	—	200
Lyndon B. Johnson	Wise, Montague	Grand Prairie	6130	—	50	—
		Western Cross Timbers	1187	813	—	200
State Wildlife Management Areas						
Engling	Anderson	Post Oak Savannah	3297	1133	—	2672
Murphee	Jefferson	Upper Coastal Prairie	—	3403	—	—
Neaslony	Gonzales	Post Oak Savannah	40	—	—	—
Pat Mayse	Lamar	Post Oak Savannah	2335	405	—	1545
Somerville	Burleson, Lee	Post Oak Savannah	729	688	—	283
State Parks						
Bastrop	Bastrop	Post Oak Savannah	1263	—	—	1263[4]
Brazos Bend	Fort Bend	Upper Coastal Prairie	1780	200	178	—
Buescher	Bastrop	Post Oak Savannah	402	10	—	351
Dinosaur Valley	Somerville	Western Cross Timbers & Grand Prairie	512	—	—	100
Galveston Island	Galveston	Upper Coastal Prairie	487	300	278	—
Lake Mineral Wells	Parker	Western Cross Timbers	1090	10	—	121
Palmetto	Gonzales	Post Oak Savannah	20	87	—	10
Purtis Creek	Vanzant, Henderson	Post Oak Savannah	462	15	—	391

[1] Includes palustrine forest and marsh.

[2] Includes *Spartina spartinae* grasslands for Federal Wildlife Refuges; upland prairie only for state areas.

[3] Less than 10 ha.

[4] Loblolly pine-post oak community.

Table 6. Fair or Better Quality Native Grassland and Upland Oak Woodland of Managed Natural Areas within Resource Areas of East Central Texas.

Resource Area	Estimated Area (ha) and Percent of Total Area in Managed Areas
Western Cross Timbers	421 (0.05%)
Grand Prairie	411 (0.02%)
Eastern Cross Timbers	1,147 (0.3%)
Blackland Prairie	205 (0.004%)
Post Oak Savannah	8,265 (0.4%)
Upper Coastal Prairie	12,208 (0.4%)

only 0.1% of the total land area is within managed areas (Table 4). This situation has been recognized on a national level where both oak savannahs and bluestem prairie are identified as critical areas for preservation (Klopatek *et al.* 1979).

MANAGEMENT

Natural areas exist to preserve biotic, physical or cultural features that have some aesthetic, educational, scientific or practical merit. Past and current changes (geological and ecological) have operated to produce the area's unique features and even though the area may be protected from outside, primarily manmade, forces ecological changes will continue to occur (Sousa 1984). Once established, however, an immediate problem faced by managers may be the elimination or alternation, often unintentional, of controlling factors that produced and maintained the features for which the preserve was originally established. While it is accepted that the best management of natural areas is the least necessary (Owen 1972), it is recognized by most scientists that a "hands-off" approach is inappropriate for maintenance of most preserves (White and Bratton 1980). A first objective of management then should be to identify and prioritize the features that make the preserve unique and the dynamic variables that control those features. A management plan can then be developed to simulate, as closely as current knowledge will permit, natural variables and processes to maintain the desired qualities of the preserve.

Landscape Considerations

Isolation of existing and potential preserves creates special problems for management. Insularity of these preserves and concomitant problems of longterm genetic isolation and alteration of species recruitment/extinction relationships have received considerable attention (Pickett and Thompson 1978, MacMahon 1979, Harris 1984, Risser - this volume). It is unknown how this island effect will influence the longterm integrity of a preserve.

Size of natural areas and their proximity to one another is of paramount importance and contributes to managerial decision-making. It is generally agreed that large preserves are more desirable because increased size tends to

increase the probability of greater floristic and faunistic diversity. While this is true several small but connected sites of minimum areas may provide greater habitat diversity, greater dispersal potential and, hence greater biotic diversity (Harris 1984). Unfortunately in east central Texas the latter approach is untenable since most remnant areas are isolated within highly altered landscapes. An interesting approach could be developed to provide connecting corridors between areas if highway right-of-ways were managed for native plant and animal communities (Ode 1972). These corridors could become preserves in their own right and provide a wider range of habitats, species and genetic diversity than could be contained within a single preserve. This approach holds some promise in Texas and would be a great contribution to maintenance of spatial and temporal biotic diversity.

The mosaic of associated natural and manmade communities in the immediate landscape and interspersion of communities in the landscape create some management problems and influence management approaches. Activities on adjacent lands that may have significant influences on the natural area are: 1) off-site drainage which may change the drainage regime of the natural area, 2) pesticide drift from adjacent areas, 3) soil drifting onto the area from adjacent unvegetated agricultural and urban development areas or during droughts, 4) trespass grazing by domestic livestock, 5) wildlife depredation during periods when food, water and escape cover are limited on adjacent lands, 6) off-road vehicle trespass, 7) air and water pollution, 8) sources of weeds and pests, and 9) littering and trash dumping. Of course, the greater the habitat diversity of adjacent areas, including rivers, ponds and marshes, the greater the potential for the natural area to contain a faunal component representative of the ecosystem or community being preserved. As an example, the Attwater's Prairie Chicken refuge may be sufficiently large to maintain viable populations of these birds, however, the character of adjacent rangeland and cropland greatly influences the longterm stability of this species (Cogar 1980).

Ownership pattern also influences management decisions. Since most natural areas of the region are surrounded by private land, it is necessary to integrate and schedule management practices that are compatible with adjacent landowner practices. For example, use of a herbicide to control invading weeds may have to be applied at times when susceptible crops on adjacent lands will not be harmed by possible drift. This restriction may, in fact, preclude herbicide use as a tool and other approaches may be necessary to deal with the problem.

An approach that integrates natural areas into a total landscape context (Godron and Forman 1983) would not only improve conditions for effective preservation and management of natural areas, but also increase our ability for more effective total landscape management for agriculture, urbanization and other purposes. We are unfortunately a long way from achieving this regional, landscape level approach to planning and management.

Site Considerations

Access, Monitoring, Research--On-site management, once a prioritized management plan has been developed, will first be required to determine the degree of allowable human access. It may be necessary to construct fences and controlled entry points, develop trails to direct traffic, initiate guided tours, disseminate educational information to explain reasons for restricted use or arrange for periodic patrol of the area.

Regardless of the degree of restricted access, there will be some impacts of human use and these impacts, in addition to the natural ecological processes that occur, will cause changes to occur within the natural area. Thus, very early a monitoring procedure must be developed to document temporal changes in biotic and physical features of the area. This will provide a baseline data set for development of an improved management plan. In this region of Texas, for example, woody plant invasion and increase in abundance can occur very rapidly and lack of an effective monitoring system may not detect initial subtle changes until a serious and often irreversible problem develops.

Since all biological and ecological responses of the communities under consideration are not known, natural areas usually serve not only as places to protect these communities but also as places to conduct research to better understand the various components of the system. This research along with an effective monitoring system will lead to eventual development of a more educated approach to perpetuation of the desired elements of the system. In the meantime, research activities must be integrated into the management plan.

Community Composition Control--Across nearly all of the region there is a tendency for woody vegetation to replace grassland or to become a greater portion of the cover and biomass of savannahs (Bragg and Hulbert 1976, Smeins 1982). Once converted to a woodland or shrubland a new steady state may be created that will persist indefinitely unless rather drastic treatments are applied to reverse the situation (Walker *et al.* 1981). Of course, a change in physiognomy of the plant community will be accompanied by changes in the kinds and densities of faunal components.

Several tools exist for manipulation of woody/herbaceous ratios in a plant community. Some are broadcast while others can be individual, species or area specific. These tools can be categorized as pyric, mechanical, chemical or biological (Scifres 1980). Within each of these categories there are many variations and types of equipment and procedures available for particular situations. None of the tools is a cureall and most must be applied on a prescribed, longterm basis to be effective. Also, combinations of these tools along with other treatments such as mowing and/or natural or domestic herbivory may more effectively promote desired results than any one treatment alone. Natural grasslands and savannahs evolved under the combined interactions of grazing, fire, weather fluctuations, insect outbreaks and a host of other impacts. Management likewise often requires the longterm application of integrated treatments to simulate as closely as possible natural processes.

Fire--There is little doubt that fires were a common phenomenon in this region at the time of settlement (Parker 1836, Kendall 1844) and evidence suggests fire was a factor in the original development of these areas for thousands, if not millions, of years (Komarek 1972, Smeins 1983). Fire is a complex, multifaceted factor that must be thoroughly understood in terms of its behavior, ecological impacts and methods of application if it is to be utilized to produce desired results (White 1980, Welch 1982). Atmospheric environmental conditions (temperature, humidity, wind) prior to, during and following the fire, fuel type and amount, vegetation physiognomy, soil moisture, season and frequency of burning are factors that influence the fire effect.

Size and location of the natural area influences the practicality of using fire as a management tool. With proper planning it can be used even in populated urban areas as exemplified by the Armand Bayou Nature Center in Houston, Texas where fire has been used to restore a native prairie on their property (Perkins *et al.* 1983). The Texas Parks and Wildlife Department, U.S. Fish and Wildlife Service, Nature Conservancy and other private groups are increasingly aware of the need and usefulness of fire as a tool for natural area management.

Ideally, if an area is of sufficient size, different parts should be burned at varying times and under different conditions to produce a mosaic of responses. Treating an entire area the same way over long periods may begin to shift the biotic components of the system. For example, Towne and Owensby (1984) have shown that dominant species composition of Kansas tallgrass prairies can be significantly altered over a 64 year period by simply changing the annual time of spring burning by a couple of weeks (Table 7). Likewise a single spring burn on a Texas prairie may alter density and reproductive relations of many plant species (Smeins 1972) (Table 8). Faunal composition and densities will also be influenced by fire, and burning may be scheduled to either enhance or perhaps control some species (Daubenmine 1968, Mueggler 1976, Ream 1981, James 1982).

The use of fire and the ecological responses of many ecosystems have been studied and at least short term changes have been evaluated (Wright and Bailey 1980, 1982). Its use on natural areas in Texas is a viable and sometimes necessary management option. Fire must be applied with caution and knowledge in order to produce desired results. Additionally, natural areas can serve as research sites to provide data on species and community fire responses that may not have been adequately documented elsewhere.

Herbivory--Defoliation by insects, small mammals and large herbivores is a natural process within grasslands and savannahs and herbivores may have been influential in the origin and evolution of these ecosystems (Mack and Thompson 1982). To eliminate herbivores from these

Table 7. Average Percent Composition of Four Grass Species from 1928 to 1982 under Different Burning Dates on Kansas Tallgrass Prairie. Means within Each Species Having the Same Letter Are Not Significantly Different (P < 0.05).

Species	Unburn	Late-Spring Burn	Mid-Spring Burn	Early-Spring Burn	Winter Burn
Big Bluestem	19d	46a	25c	23c	35b
Indiangrass	13b	19a	12b	7c	6d
Little Bluestem	30c	23d	41a	36b	35b
Bluegrass	14a	1b	1b	1b	1b

[1] Adapted from Towne and Ownsby (1984).

Table 8. Density (Stems/m^2) of Selected Species during August, 1972 following a Single Spring Burn on Texas Blackland Prairie.[1]

Species	Treatment				
	No Burn No Mow	Burn No Mow	No Burn Mow	Burn Mow	Mow Semiannually
Centaurea americana	3	3	3	0	26
Gaillardia pulchella	0	0	2	4	5
Shrankia uncinata	2	3	2	2	3
Schizachyrium scoparium (flowering culms)	15	37	26	21	25

[1] Adapted from Smeins 1972.

ecosystems is an unnatural, although on some preserves a necessary, approach to preservation. Because of size and location it may be difficult to manage native or domestic herbivores on many preserves. Research has shown, however, that proper understanding of grazing impacts and application of this knowledge to management of natural areas may be an effective way to maintain the integrity of the systems. The question is not whether grazing is natural to a given area but rather whether it can be applied at the right frequency and intensity and by the right combination of animals to produce a natural expression of herbivore impacts. Goats, for example, may be effectively used on a periodic basis to act as a biological agent for woody plant control (Merrill and Taylor 1981). This is a complex subject for which a growing research and management base continues to develop (Kothmann 1984). Grazing is, and should be considered, a viable option as a management tool and is being used on some areas (Heitlinger and Steuter 1984).

On the other hand, herbivores may require periodic control to reduce undesirable effects. For example, white-tailed deer often overpopulate local areas to the detriment of the vegetation and as a result it may be necessary to remove or harvest some of the animals. Insect outbreaks (e.g. grasshoppers) can be locally devastating and on a small natural area they may need to be controlled by insecticides for the good of the entire system. This approach requires judicious application. Certain carnivores may also require periodic control if they are selectively influencing a herbivore with limited numbers such as the endangered Attwater's Prairie Chicken.

Mowing and Hay Removal--Many grasslands and savannahs that have recently become natural areas in Texas have a history of use as hay meadows, and these areas often represent the best examples of uncultivated, natural communities that still exist (Launchbaugh 1955, Diamond and Smeins 1985). That is not to say that mowing, just as with burning and herbivory, does not have short and longterm effects on the character of the community and its influence is controlled by many of the same factors such as season and frequency and height of cutting (Conard 1953, Ehrenreich and Aikman 1963, Smeins 1972) (Table 8).

Annual mowing and hay removal effectively reduces or eliminates woody species in most native haymeadows over unbroken native sod. Haymeadows over native sod are observed throughout the region to be free of a significant woody plant component while immediately adjacent fields on the same soil type that are unutilized (i.e. ungrazed, unmowed, unburned) may be completely invaded.

A problem sometimes encountered with haying is prolonged presence of swaths and/or hay bales on the grassland which can smother the vegetation. On a small scale this may have positive effects on increased patchiness and species diversity, but at the other extreme it may produce open patches that allow exotic weed species to establish. Hay removal may also through time have significant impacts on soil fertility and nutrient cycling, although little data exist to deny or support this suggestion. Equipment disturbance must also be considered when conducting a haying operation.

Mechanical and Herbicide Treatments--In order to maintain an existing community or species compliment, particularly if fire, grazing and haying are not feasible, it may be necessary to selectively use mechanical or herbicide applications to manage the natural area. Even when the other tools can be used mechanical and herbicide treatments may be periodically integrated with burning, grazing and haying to produce a desired result (Scifres 1980).

Ownership

A final item of concern that relates to natural area management is ownership and objectives of land management under the jurisdiction of various land management agencies (Carls 1984). Texas Parks and Wildlife, while it has an admonition to manage for total ecosystem characteristics, tends to take a single species or economically valuable species approach to management of most of their areas. Of course, on much of their land human recreation development is of priority consideration. State natural areas are managed for total resource protection but these areas are limited in number and extent. State parks contain substantial acreage that could be restored to relatively natural communities but the likelihood of this happening is minimal based on limited resources available for management and emphasis on other priorities in the parks.

Federal lands are primarily managed to protect wildlife habitats but wildlife is often defined in a limited way to include primarily economically important species, although endangered species are given special consideration on some refuges (e.g. Attwater's Prairie Chicken). State and Federal lands in Texas could, with adequate resources and some redirection of emphasis, improve efforts to manage existing natural areas and restore others.

Several excellent potential natural areas exist on private land. While these areas may persist because of the landowners knowledge of their value there are many factors such as change in economic incentives or change in ownership that make preservation of these areas tentative. The land steward and conservation easement program of the Nature Conservancy and other private organizations attempts to deal with this issue but these are often only stop gap measures and the opportunity for management inputs may be very limited.

Management of natural areas in east central Texas is a complex problem. Application of existing knowledge can contribute greatly to proper stewardship of these lands, however, we are dealing with everchanging systems that require constant monitoring and evaluation. While management practices can be recommended for a given time and place it is almost certain that these practices will require alteration or change through time. Thus, management of these areas is an ongoing program of monitoring, application, education, research, modification and adjustment to new factors that continually enter the scene.

LITERATURE CITED

Allen, H.G. 1974. Woody vegetation of the Lower Navasota River Watershed. M.S. Thesis, Texas A&M Univ. College Station, Tex.

Beaty, H.E. (Chr.). 1983. Endangered, threatened, and watch lists of plants for Texas. Tex. Organization for Endangered Species, Austin, Tex.

Bell, E.L. and L.C. Hulbert. 1974. Effect of soil on occurrence of Cross Timbers and Prairie in southern Kansas. Trans. Kans. Acad. Sci. 77:203-209.

Bragg, T.B. and L.C. Hulbert. 1976. Woody plant invasion of unburned Kansas bluestem prairie. J. Range Manage. 29:19-24.

Braun, E.L. 1950. Deciduous Forest of Eastern North America. Blaikston Co., Philadelphia, Penn.

Bray, W.L. 1904. The timber of the Edwards Plateau of Texas: its relation to climate, water supply and soil. U.S. Dep. Agr., Bur. For. Bull. No. 49.

Butler, A.C. 1979. Mima mound grasslands of the Upper Coastal Prairie of Texas. M.S. Thesis, Texas A&M Univ., College Station, Tex.

Carls, E.G. 1984. Texas natural diversity: the role of parks and preserves. pp. 51-60 In E.G. Carls and J. Neal (eds.). Protection of Texas Natural Diversity: An Introduction for Natural Resource Planners and Managers. Tex. Agr. Exp. Sta. MP-1577.

Cogar, V.F. 1980. Food habits of Attwater's Prairie Chicken in Refugio County, Texas. Ph.D. Diss., Texas A&M Univ., College Station, Tex.

Collins, O.B., F.E. Smeins and D.H. Riskind. 1975. Plant communities of the Blackland of Texas. pp 75-88 In M.K. Wali (ed.). Prairie: A Multiple View. Univ. N. Dak. Press, Grand Forks, N.D.

Conard, E.C. 1953. Effect of time of cutting on yield and botanical composition of prairie hay in southeastern Nebraska. Ph.D. Diss., Texas A&M Univ., College Station, Tex.

Correll, D.S. and M.C. Johnston. 1970. Manual of the Vascular Plants of Texas. Tex. Res. Found., Renner, Tex.

Daubenmire, R. 1968. Ecology of fire in grasslands. Adv. Ecol. Res. 5:209-266.

Diamond, D.D. and F.E. Smeins. 1984. Remnant grassland vegetation and ecological affinities of the Upper Coastal Prairie of Texas. Southwest. Natur. 29:321-334.

Diamond, D.D. and F.E. Smeins. 1985. Composition, classification and species response patterns of remnant tallgrass prairies in Texas. Amer. Midl. Natur. 113:294-308.

Dyksterhuis, E.J. 1946. The vegetation of the Fort Worth Prairie. Ecol. Monogr. 16:2-29.

Dyksterhuis, E.J. 1948. The vegetation of the Western Cross Timbers. Ecol. Monogr. 18:325-376.

Ehrenreich, J.H. and J.M. Aikman. 1963. An ecological study of the effect of certain management practices on native prairies in Iowa. Ecol. Monogr. 33:113-130.

Federal Register. 1980. Endangered and threatened wildlife and plants: review of plant taxa for listing as endangered or threatened species. 45(242):82480-82569.

Foster, J.H. 1917. The spread of timbered areas in central Texas. J. For. 15:442-445.

Godfrey, C., G.S. McKee and H. Oakes. 1973 General soils map of Texas. Tex. Agr. Exp. Sta. Misc. Pub. MP-1304. 1:1,500,000 color map.

Godron, M. and R.T.T. Forman. 1983. Landscape modification and changing ecological characteristics. pp. 12-28 In H.A. Mooney and M. Godron (eds.). Disturbance and Ecosystems. Springer-Verlag, New York, New York.

Harrison, T.P. 1974. A floristic study of the woody vegetation of the North American Cross Timbers. Ph.D. Diss. N. Tex. St. Univ., Denton, Tex.

Harris, L.D. 1984. The Fragmented Forest: Island Biogeography Theory and the Preservation of Diversity. Univ. Chicago Press, Chicago, Ill.

Heitlinger, M. and A.A. Steuter. 1984. Grazing management in the Nature Conservancy. pp 77-78 In Research Natural Areas: Baseline Monitoring and Management. USDA For. Serv, Gen. Tech. Rep. INT-173.

James, S.V. 1982. Effects of fire and soil type on earthworm populations in a tallgrass prairie. Pedobiologica 24:37-40.

Kendall, G.W. 1844. Narrative of the Texan Sante Fe Expedition. Vol. I. Wiley and Putnam, London.

Klopatek, J.M., R.J. Olson, C.J. Emerson and J.L.. Jones. 1979. Land-use conflicts with natural vegetation in the United States. Environ. Cons. 6:191-200.

Komarek, E.V. 1972. Ancient fires. Tall Timbers Fire Ecol. Conf. Proc. 12:219-240.

Kothmann, M.M. 1984. Concepts and principles underlying grazing systems: a discussant paper. pp. 903-916 In Developing Strategies for Rangeland Management. Committee on Developing Strategies for Rangeland Management. Nat'l. Res. Council/Nat'l. Acad. Sci., Westview Press, Boulder Co.

Launchbaugh, J.L. 1955. Vegetational changes in the San Antonio Prairie associated with grazing, retirement from grazing, and abandonment from cultivation. Ecol. Monogr. 25:39-57.

Longley, G. (Chr.) 1979. TOES watch-list of endangered, threatened and peripheral vertebrates of Texas. Tex. Organization for Endangered Species, Austin, Tex.

Mack, R.N. and J.N. Thompson. 1982. Evolution in steppe with few large hooved animals. Amer. Natur. 119:757-773.

MacMahon, J.A. 1979. Thoughts on the optimum size of natural reserves based on ecological principles. pp. 128-134 In J.F. Franklin and S.L. Krugman, (Coords.) Selection, Management and Utilization of Biosphere Reservs. USDA For. Serv., GTR PNN-82.

Marcy, L.E. 1982. Habitat-types of the Eastern Cross Timbers of Texas. Ph.D. Diss., Texas A&M Univ., College Station, Tex.

Marcy, R.B. 1849. Report of Captain R.B. Marcy. House Exc. Doc. 45, 31st Congr., lst Session, Pub. Doc. 577, Wash., D.C.

McBryde, J.B. 1933. The vegetation and habitat factors of the Carrizo sands. Ecol. Mongr. 3:248-297.

McCaleb, J.E. 1954. An ecological and range vegetation analysis of the upland sites of the southern extension of the Oak-Hickory Forest Region in Texas. Ph.D. Diss., Texas A&M Univ., College Station, Tex.

McClusky, R.L. 1972. Some population parameters of Quercus stellata in the Texas cross timbers. Ph.D. Diss., N. Tex. St. Univ., Denton, Tex.

McMahan, C.A., R.G. Frye and K.L. Brown. 1984. Vegetation types of Texas including cropland. Wildl. Div., Tex. Pks. and Wildl. Dep., Austin, Tex. 1:1,000,000 color map.

Merrill, L.B. and C.A. Taylor. 1981. Diet selection, grazing habits and the place of goats in range management. pp. 233-252. In C. Gall (ed.). Goat Production. Academic Press, New York, New York.

Mueggler, W.F. 1976. Ecological role of fire in western woodland and range ecosystems. pp. 1-9 In Use of prescribed burning in western woodland and range ecosystems: a symposium. Utah St. Univ., Logan, Ut.

Mueller-Dombois, D. and H. Ellenberg. 1974. Aims and Methods of Vegetation Ecology. John Wiley and Sons, Inc., New York, New York.

Ode, A.H. 1972. A rationale for the use of prairie species in roadside vegetation management. Midwest Prairie Conf. Proc. 2:174-179.

Owen, J.S. 1972. Some thoughts on management in National Parks. Biol. Cons. 4:241-246.

Parker, A.A. 1836. Trip to the West and Texas, Comprising a Journey of 8,000 miles Through New York, Michigan, Illinois, Missouri, Louisiana and Texas in the Autumn and Winter of 1834-35. 2nd Edition, William White, Concord, NH.

Perkins, D. et al. 1983. Armand Bayou Nature Center. Fall Report to Membership. Houston, Tex.

Pickett, S.T.A. and J.N. Thompson. 1978. Patch dynamics and the design of nature reserves. Biol. Cons. 13:27-37.

Ream, C.H. 1981. The effect of fire and other disturbances on small mammals and their predators: an annotated bibliography. USDA For. Serv., Gen Tech. Rep. INT-106.

Risser, P.G., C.E. Girney, H.D. Blocker, S.W. May, M.J. Patton and J.A. Wiens. 1981. The True Prairie Ecosystem. Hutchinson Ross Pub. Co., Stroudsburg, Penn.

Scifres, C.J. 1980. Brush Management: Principles and Practices for Texas and the Southwest. Texas A&M Univ. Press, College Station, Tex.

Sellards, E.H., W.S. Adkins and F.B. Plummer. 1966. The Geology of Texas. Vol. I. Stratigraphy. Univ. Tex. Bull. 3232.

Smeins, F.E. 1972. Influence of fire and mowing on vegetation of the Blackland Prairie of Texas. Midwest Prairie Conf. Proc. 3:4-7.

Smeins, F.E. 1982. Natural role of fire in central Texas. pp. 3-15 In T.G. Welch (ed.). Prescribed Range Burning in Central Texas. Agr. Ext. Serv., College Station, Tex.

Smeins, F.E. 1983. Origin of the brush problem - a geological and ecological perspective of contemporary distributions. pp. 5-16. In K.W. McDaniel (ed.). Proceedings - Brush Management Symposium. Texas Tech. Univ. Press, Lubbock, Tex.

Smeins, F.E. and D.D. Diamond. 1983. Remnant grasslands of the Fayette Prairie, Texas. Amer. Midl. Natur. 110:1-13.

Smeins, F.E., D.D. Diamond and C.W. Hanselka. In press. Coastal prairie: Schizachyrium scoparium - Sorgahstrum nutans association. In R.T. Coupland (ed.). Natural Grasslands. Vol. VIII. Ecosystems of the World. Elsevier Sci. Pub., Amsterdam.

Smith, J.G. 1899. Grazing problems in the southwest and how to meet them. USDA, Agrost. Bull. 16:1-47.

Sousa, W.P. 1984. The role of disturbance in natural communities. Ann. Rev. Ecol. Syst. 15:353-391.

Tharp, B.C. 1926. Structure of Texas vegetation east of the 98th meridian. Univ. Tex. Bull. 2606.

Towne, G. and C. Owensby. 1984. Longterm effects of annual burning at different dates in ungrazed Kansas tallgrass prairie. J. Range Manage. 37:392-397.

Walker, B.H., D. Ludwig, C.S. Holling and R.M. Peterman. 1981. Stability of semiarid savannah grazing systems. J. Ecol. 69:473-498.

Welch, T.G. (ed.). 1982. Prescribed Range Burning in Central Texas. Tex. Agr. Ext. Serv., College Station, Tex.

White, L.D. (ed.). 1980. Prescribed Range Burning in the Edwards Plateau of Texas. Tex. Agr. Ext. Serv., College Station, Tex.

White, P.S. and S.P. Bratton. 1980. After preservation: philosophical and practical problems of change. Biol. Cons. 18:241-255.

Wright, H.A. and A.W. Bailey. 1980. Fire ecology and prescribed burning in the Great Plains - a research review. USDA For. Serv. Gen. Tech. Rep. INT-77.

Wright, H.A. and A.W. Bailey. 1982. Fire Ecology: United States and Southern Canada. John Wiley and Sons, Inc., Somerset, NJ.

Yantis, J.H. 1984. The Lexington-Marquez Wildlife Unit. Wildl. Div., Tex. Pks. Wildl. Dep., F.A. Series No.

Role Of Private Organizations In The Protection Of Grasslands And Savannahs

by
Rex R. Boner

ABSTRACT--The Nature Conservancy owns and manages over 40,500 ha of grasslands and savannahs in 12 Midwestern states and assists with the management of similar sites owned by other agencies, organizations, and individuals. Management needs of these sites currently being addressed by the Conservancy include funding; personnel training; information acquisition, management, and transfer; responding to research needs; applying appropriate monitoring techniques; managing to maintain rare species, and managing to control or eliminate pest species. Extensive internal planning and training is underway and cooperative partnerships are being established with many public agencies to efficiently address these stewardship challenges.

KEYWORDS: Nature Conservancy, Natural Heritage Programs, conservation partnerships, monitoring techniques, information transfer.

The Nature Conservancy is a private, non-profit conservation organization dedicated to the preservation of biological diversity. This is accomplished through the protection of ecologically significant habitat which supports endangered or threatened species or rare communities. Since its establishment in 1950, The Nature Conservancy has protected nearly 1 million ha of land, most of which has been transferred to other agencies for their management. The Conservancy continues to own and manage over 200,000 ha of preserved land in 49 states to perpetuate the significant elements of natural diversity that occur on these lands. This system of reserves represents the largest privately owned nature preserve system in the world.

Among this system of preserves is over 40,500 ha of grasslands and savannahs that protect examples of these vanishing community types and the common and rare species they support. Other papers in these proceedings discuss specific types of these communities and the management challenges associated with them. This paper will focus on a discussion of the role of a private organization's grassland and savannah management program and the management needs currently being addressed.

BACKGROUND

Traditionally, The Nature Conservancy's approach to the protection of biological diversity has been to identify where the best examples of the world's diversity occur, to protect these priority habitats primarily through outright acquisition, and to manage these habitats to maintain the species and communities occurring there.

The identification phase has been accomplished primarily through the network of state Natural Heritage Programs in existence throughout the world. These comprehensive, computer-assisted state by state ecological inventories are now in place in 35 states, the Navajo Nation, the Tennessee Valley Authority, and several Latin American countries. Regional programs are established in the Eastern U.S. and in the Rocky Mountain region and plans call for the establishment of similar regional heritage data bases in the Southeast and the Midwest. These programs are further described by Jenkins (1982).

Once identified as significant ecological habitat in need of protection, sites are protected through a variety of techniques ranging from simple landowner notification to outright purchase of fee title of the site. Hoose (1981) provides an excellent discussion of these land preservation techniques.

Following initial protection, the permanent preservation of a site requires proper ecological management. These stewardship activities attempt to manage the site to maintain the biological diversity for which the site was originally protected. This can range from periodic surveillance to intensive restoration and/or active interventionist management treatments such as the continual clearing of vegetated river sandbars to provide roosting or nesting habitat for shorebirds.

The key is to carefully plan this management, monitor

its success, and adjust it as necessary to meet the objectives for the site. This planning, management and monitoring of biological diversity is a major undertaking and has presented considerable challenges for The Nature Conservancy. These needs could be simplistically summarized as funding needs. That is, if the Conservancy had sufficient funding it could address these needs. More realistically, however, the major grassland/savannah management needs of The Nature Conservancy are the following: personnel and personnel training; information acquisition, management and transfer; responding to research needs; applying appropriate monitoring techniques; managing to maintain rare species; managing to control or eliminate pest species; and funding.

MANAGEMENT CHALLENGES

Personnel and Personnel Training

Grassland and savannah management planning, implementation, and monitoring require the availability of certain technical expertise. The Nature Conservancy attempts to utilize full-time staff, seasonal staff, volunteers, and contractors to efficiently plan for and carry out management on its preserves. Since grasslands and savannahs are dynamic, successional systems which require continual management, the personnel needs are great. In Minnesota alone, where the Conservancy owns and manages over 6,000 ha of grassland and savannahs, during 1984, 1 1/2 full-time staff, nine interns, five contractors, and many volunteers were used to carry out the management program which is not yet at the projected optimal level of performance. Many Conservancy programs elsewhere are still building their grassland/savannah management capability.

Having personnel available to plan and implement these programs is the first step. The second step is to properly train these personnel. The Conservancy utilizes a variety of techniques including on-the-job training, participation in other Conservancy management programs with similar preserve needs, intensive training sessions, and participation in other agency training sessions. Two brief examples related to prescribed burning training are: (1) a fire camp being planned for the fall of 1985 at the Niobrara Valley Preserve, a 22,000 ha preserve in north central Nebraska dominated by Sandhills Prairie, at which several Conservancy employees will receive intensive training in many aspects of prescribed burning to become certified as fire bosses; and (2) a compilation of fire train-

Figure 1. The Samuel H. Ordway Memorial Prairie located near Leola, South Dakota. The prairie is owned and managed by the Nature Conservancy. (Photograph by Rex R. Boner)

ing opportunities available within public agencies prepared by Heitlinger and Davis (1985).

Information Acquisition, Management and Transfer

As managers of nature preserves, the Conservancy has the need for information pertaining to the ecological requirements of the elements of natural diversity it is attempting to protect and the responsibility to record management actions taken and the apparent response of the elements to these actions. This quickly creates a major information management need. The Nature Conservancy is constantly assessing this need and is currently addressing it with a series of integrated data bases.

The Natural Heritage Programs have established data files on the distribution and taxonomy of species and communities. In addition to these important files, the Conservancy maintains a log of management needs, activities, and schedules on each preserve through a data file called the Site Stewardship Summary. From these summaries and the Natural Heritage Program files, a complete record of all occurrences of significant elements of natural diversity on Conservancy preserves is maintained in a data file called EOTNC. This file tracks the status of the species or community in question, what management techniques are being applied at that site, what monitoring is taking place, and who the contact is to obtain additional information. Finally, to investigate and record the ecological management needs of individual species and communities, the Conservancy is systematically producing literature reviews and recording research, management, and monitoring information as appropriate for these elements within a data file called the Element Stewardship Abstract.

Space limitations did not allow the publication of these forms or examples of these data bases as a part of this paper, but they are available by contacting the author. Internal transfer of this information takes place manually and through computer transfer. It is also exchanged at Conservancy meetings and conferences. Externally, this information is transferred through conferences and subsequent papers such as this, and through other publications such as the *Natural Areas Journal* and *Restoration and Management Notes*.

Responding to Research Needs

Often, managers find themselves responsible for maintaining a particular grassland or savannah community or species, but with little information as to the needs of those species or communities. An example has been the rare butterfly, the Dakota Skipper (*Hesperia dacotae*), which occurs on three Conservancy preserves in Minnesota and one in South Dakota. The Conservancy learned that it occurred there but knew nothing about the management required to maintain viable populations on these preserves. Through a cooperative project with the University of Minnesota, a Ph.D. student has been researching this species. Preliminary indications are that the preserves need to be periodically burned to prevent a heavy buildup of thatch and to stimulate flowering. The specific timing and frequency of burning necessary is still being investigated (Dana 1983).

This is only one example with one species; the research needs are immense and funding quickly becomes a major factor again. In an effort to efficiently address these research needs, the Conservancy works cooperatively with colleges and universities to identify mutual research interests. Likewise, the Conservancy coordinates with public agencies to avoid duplication and to combine efforts wherever and whenever possible.

Finally, the Conservancy has effectively initiated a small grants program in several states that provides funding on a competitive basis for researchers to investigate certain management-related needs. These programs have been quite successful as they often provide the seed money or travel expense necessary to attract researchers who otherwise simply could not afford to pursue the project.

Applying Appropriate Monitoring Techniques

Buttrick (1984) discussed the biological monitoring challenges facing The Nature Conservancy. The primary consideration is to clearly describe the objectives for any monitoring activities. Everyone is well aware of the costs of monitoring, so monitoring activities must be well focussed to address these objectives. In addition to cost, other considerations are methods, design, permanence, the ability of the initiating institution to continue the monitoring, data storage, and analysis over time.

Managing to Maintain Rare Species

A major component of the Conservancy's grassland/savannah management program is aimed at rare species protection. The Dakota Skipper mentioned earlier, the prairie white fringed orchid (*Platanthera leucophaea*), the whooping crane (*Grus americana*), are all examples of rare grassland species that are dependent on appropriate management of grassland preserves.

While Site Stewardship Summaries form the basis for preserve management plans for the Conservancy, rare species sites often require much more detailed plans. These plans attempt to prescribe the management treatments considered most appropriate for the rare species and to specify what type of monitoring should occur. Additional research on these species is often conducted if deemed necessary for proper management. Again, this information is recorded and tracked through the integrated data bases of the Conservancy.

Managing to Control or Eliminate Pest Species

As Paul Risser has pointed out elsewhere in this book, pest species are a major problem on grassland/savannah preserves. The Conservancy is developing Element Stewardship Abstracts for pest species in addition to rare species. To date, 15 (13 plants, 2 animals) have been completed and some of these have been published such as Evans (1982, 1983a, 1983b, 1984a, 1984b) and Heidel (1982).

The Conservancy attempts to manage pest species through natural processes if possible. Mechanical and physical control are often used to complement natural control such as fire or grazing. Occasionally, in very extreme cases chemical control is used, but only as a last resort and only after extensive review. Much further work needs to be done on assessing control options for pest species.

Funding

As mentioned earlier in this paper, a need common to all those above is funding. The Conservancy has been fortunate enough to endow certain preserves, but many preserves, especially grassland/savannah preserves in the Midwest, do not have sufficient funds to adequately meet all the management needs. The Conservancy is accumulating additional management funds by raising at least 20% over the fair market value of each new preserve purchased to be placed in a statewide management fund. This has been very effective and is being built into all fundraising campaigns.

The Conservancy is also experimenting with the restructuring of certain positions to minimize cost and to maximize stewardship capability. One such structure in operation is the transition of a full-time grassland preserve manager position into a 3 year term position with two-thirds of the time devoted to preserve management and one-third of the time applied to research. This has worked well to date as the two managers who have occupied the position have been able to handle the management needs with two-thirds of their time and use the remaining one-third of their time for research, investigating the role of fire and of bison grazing on the preserve.

Finally, the Conservancy has had excellent success utilizing seasonal or intern employees. These are usually graduate students eager to work and to gain experience and whose employment interests usually correspond with the work need during the summer season. This eliminates the year-long overhead of full-time employees when the actual work need is seasonal.

CONSERVATION PARTNERSHIPS

In recognition of the magnitude of the job of managing grassland/savannah preserves and the limited resources available to do the job, the Conservancy has attempted to develop conservation partnerships with public agencies. These vary tremendously in size and scope, but are designed to efficiently apply limited resources to management of these important systems. In Missouri, the Conservancy has lease agreements whereby both the Department of Conservation and the Department of Natural Resources assist with the on-site management of Conservancy preserves. This has worked out well as these state agencies have the local expertise and can more easily carry out the management than the Conservancy. Examples similar to this exist across the country. In Kansas, the Konza Prairie owned by The Nature Conservancy is leased to Kansas State University for their management and use. It has since become the site of a National

Science Foundation Long-term Ecological Research Project.

Another slightly different partnership has been established in Indiana. The Conservancy has long had a good working relationship with the Indiana Department of Natural Resources to preserve significant ecological habitat throughout the state. This year the Conservancy entered into a formal relationship through passage of legislation resulting in the Indiana Natural Heritage Protection Campaign. This authorizes the Indiana Legislature to provide $5 million to be matched by $5 million raised privately. These funds will be used to purchase additional nature preserves with 20% of the appraised value of each preserve placed in a stewardship trust account to provide on-going management funds. Several other states are considering entering into similar relationships with the Conservancy.

SUMMARY

The Nature Conservancy plays a key role in the management of grassland and savannah preserves in the United States. While major management challenges face the Conservancy, creative solutions are being found for many of these and the system of private grassland/savannah preserves owned and managed by The Nature Conservancy makes a major contribution to the protection of these communities across the country.

LITERATURE CITED

Buttrick, S.C. 1984. Biological monitoring: The Nature Conservancy's perspective. US For. Serv. Gen. Tech. Rep. Int-173:59-63.

Dana, R. 1983. The Dakota skipper: A now rare prairie butterfly. Nat. Areas J. 3:31-34.

Evans, J.E. 1982. A literature review of management practices for absinth sage (Artemisia absinthium). Nat. Areas J. 2:3-9.

Evans, J.E. 1983a. A literature review of management practices for multiflora rose (Rosa multiflora). Nat. Areas J. 3:6-15.

Evans, J.E. 1983b. A literature review of management practices for smooth sumac (Rhus glabra), poison ivy (Rhus radicans) and other sumac species. Nat. Areas J. 3:16-26.

Evans, J.E. 1984a. Japanese honeysuckle (Lonicera japonica): a literature review of management practices. Nat. Areas J. 4:4-10.

Evans, J.E. 1984b. Canada thistle (Cirsium arvense): a literature review of management practices. Nat. Areas J. 4:11-21.

Heidel, B. 1982. Leafy spurge: a challenge in natural areas management. Nat. Areas J. 2:10-13.

Heitlinger, M. and D. Davis, 1985. Training opportunities in prescribed fire management. Nat. Areas J. 5:25-30.

Hoose, P.M. 1981. Building an ark: tools for the preservation of natural diversity through land protection. Island Press, Covelo, Calif.

Jenkins, R.J. 1982. Planning and developing natural heritage protection programs. Indo-U.S. Workshop on Biosphere Reserves and Conservation of Biological Diversity. Bangalore, Karnataka State, India.

Wilderness And Natural Areas In The East: Symposium Summary

by
Robert C. Lucas

ABSTRACT--There were six main themes at this Symposium on Wilderness and Natural Areas in the East: (1) definition of wilderness, (2) the role of recreation, (3) wilderness East and West, (4) knowledge gaps, (5) cooperation, and (6) the management challenge.

KEYWORDS: wilderness management, wilderness recreation, research needs.

This symposium touched on many topics, but six major themes were woven through most of the discussions. These themes appeared and reappeared in different forms, sometimes in contradictory ways. The six themes, each of which will be discussed further, were:
1. Definition of wilderness and wilderness management
2. The role of recreation in wilderness
3. Wilderness East and West in relation to a national system
4. Knowledge gaps
5. Cooperation
6. The wilderness management challenge.

With over 65 presentations, and concurrent sessions most of the time, no one could capture every idea, but some that seemed important stick in my mind. I present these memorable ideas in this summary.

DEFINITION OF WILDERNESS AND WILDERNESS MANAGEMENT

The definition of wilderness--its basic nature and purpose--is fundamental. It drives management and sets the research agenda. Most of the keynote speakers emphasized the definition of wilderness, and most of the presentations expressed the authors' definitions directly or indirectly, with considerable variation.

Kent Adair, dean of the School of Forestry, Stephen F. Austin State University, stressed that wilderness is a long-term resource that needs to be considered at least in a 100-year timespan. Recreational and scientific uses of natural ecosystems are important, but educational values are also very important. Wilderness can teach future generations about natural values. The decision to establish wilderness has been made; the challenge now is to manage wilderness for the benefit of society.

Southern Regional Forester Jack Alcock echoed Dean Adair's statement that the task now is not to debate whether there should be wilderness, or how much, but to decide how the wilderness that has been established should be managed. This was also the starting point for the Wilderness Management Conference at the University of Idaho in 1983 and for the National Wilderness Research Conference at Colorado State University in 1985. Jack said that wilderness is an important part of multiple use, not an exception. The Wilderness Act states an ideal definition: "A wilderness, in contrast with those areas where man and his own works dominate the landscape, is hereby recognized as an area where the earth and its community of life are untrammeled by man . . . " But the Wilderness Act also provides managers the flexibility they need to deal practically with varying situations. It is a finely crafted, balanced piece of legislation, in his view.

John Hendee, Assistant Director of the Southeastern Forest Experiment Station, stressed that the primary definition of wilderness and its major value is as a naturally functioning, dynamic ecosystem. Wilderness is significant internationally, not just to the United States. Wilderness has broad, persistent public support. It is consistent with traditional conservative values and is also supported by people with liberal viewpoints.

Paul Barker, from the Forest Service Washington Office recreation staff, used Iago's lines in Shakespeare's Othello, "What's in a name?" to remind us of the importance of retaining the good name of wilderness by preserving its meaning and integrity. We should cherish the integrity of the name "Wilderness" as much as we do our own names. He posed the question, "Thirty years in the future, will wilderness be different than other nearby lands?". The answer will stem from the cumulative effect of management decisions, many of them seemingly small and innocuous. "Leaving it alone" is not possible: Congress intended wilderness to be used, and with use comes change. Change must be managed to retain an "enduring resource of wilderness." The definition of wilderness comes from the Wilderness Act. We need to **study** it, not merely read it. We must guard against the tendency to think the Act says what we want it to say. The exceptions in the Act are troublesome, but without them there would be no Wilderness Act. It is necessary to interpret each section based on all other sections. Two Acts define each wilderness: the Wilderness Act, and the particular area's establishing legislation if it extends or modifies any Wilderness Act provision. Paul also pointed out that the Secretary of Agriculture's Wilderness Regulations require the **restoration** of wilderness character. This regulation is particularly important for wildernesses with past use histories that diminish wilderness qualities.

Larry Phillips discussed the deep roots of the wilderness concept in religion, philosophy, and history, and reinforced Paul Baker's point about restoration by describing wilderness as a **renewable** resource now, in contrast to earlier views that stressed wilderness as once lost, forever lost. Recent Congressional action classifying areas as wilderness that have past disturbances of natural ecosystems and a number of man's works presents managers with the challenge of restoring or renewing the wilderness resource.

Peter Kirby of the Wilderness Society made it clear that wilderness is in the mainstream of resource management on the National Forests; 17 percent of the acres in the National Forest System are now classified as wilderness and 82 percent of all National Forests have wilderness. The main reason for wilderness, he said, is to have representative samples of naturally functioning ecosystems.

A key idea implied by those definitions is the central role of natural processes, which are dynamic, rather than a focus on any one stage. Some of the presentations in the concurrent sessions, however, seemed to assume that time should stop and one stage, usually old growth, should be preserved. For natural areas, as contrasted to wilderness, this view may be appropriate.

THE ROLE OF RECREATION IN WILDERNESS

The underlying question is "Is a wilderness a recreation area?" This theme is an extension of the first theme of wilderness definition. The answer given or implied by almost every speaker was "No." Certainly most wildernesses are used for recreation, and it is a major, important use of many. It is one of the authorized uses in the Wilderness Act. But there are many other uses, and recreation must take place within the basic wilderness definition.

Kent Adair stressed education values. John Hendee said, "We assign too much weight to recreation in wilderness, and too little to offsite vicarious uses and val-

ues." Paul Barker spoke on an "enduring resource of wilderness," which is not the same as a recreational resource. David Schmidly, from Texas A&M, in the concurrent session on wildlife ecology and management, described wilderness as a research laboratory because it is an island of natural conditions in a sea of modified environments.

At times, however, some conference participants tended to slip into thinking of wilderness almost exclusively as a recreation area, and into assuming that wilderness had to be beautiful and spectacular and provide good hunting.

WILDERNESS EAST AND WEST IN RELATION TO A NATIONAL SYSTEM

The question here is simple: "Are wildernesses in the East so different from those in the West that there really are two systems?" The symposium consensus, although it was not a landslide, was that there is only one National Wilderness System.

The clearest, shortest answer came from Paul Barker who said that the idea that there are two systems is "hogwash." He elaborated by pointing out that the 1975 "Eastern" Wilderness Act is not the "Eastern Wilderness Act." In fact, the act has **no** name, and this omission by Congress may have been deliberate to avoid the creation of two Wilderness Systems. However, the individual acts establishing particular areas sometimes provide special direction.

I must admit, at least at first, that some of us westerners experienced a little cultural shock at descriptions of conditions in some East Texas wildernesses--producing oil wells, D-9 cats, and clearcut logging to control southern pine beetle. David Drummond of Forest Service Pest Management also emphasized differences as he told the tale of a westerner who visited a southern wilderness for the first time. But the key idea, as a number of people pointed out, is that the entire National Wilderness Preservation System is diverse, and the East-West dichotomy is not the best way to account for this diversity. Wildernesses vary widely in size. Eastern wildernesses are smaller, on the average, than western areas, but there are small western wildernesses. A number in Washington and Oregon National Forests, for example are under 5,000 acres (2,025 ha). Alaska even has a 32-acre (13-ha) wilderness. A few eastern wildernesses are among the largest in the system; the Everglades and Boundary Waters Canoe Area Wildernesses are both over 1 million acres (0.4 million ha). Nonconforming uses are common in eastern wildernesses, but the East is far short of a monopoly on such marks of man. The eastern portion of the Selway-Bitterroot Wilderness, the section in Montana, which I can see from our laboratory, has well over half of all of the water storage dams in the entire wilderness system. Almost every lake in this area, and there are dozens of them, has a dam; many of these lakes date back to the 19th century.

Heavy recreation use occurs on many wildernesses both east and west, and so does light use. In fact, some eastern wildernesses, lacking spectacular scenery and well-developed trail systems, and with snakes and insects that are not overly benign, may well be some of the most lightly used wildernesses in the system for many years.

Frank Boteler, from West Virginia University, summed it up by saying the wildernesses in the East differed from those in the West in terms of averages for many factors, but there is a great deal of overlap.

Several speakers pointed out aspects that do not differ between East and West. Wilderness visitors are quite similar regardless of where they visit. Jeff Marion reported little difference in attitudes about the severity of recreation impacts on rivers in the East and West.

We also heard about some general differences, particularly the more rapid recovery of disturbed vegetation in many eastern, especially southern, areas in contrast to much of the West.

The challenge, as John Hendee said, is to work to integrate diversity into one system. Paul Barker said **every** wilderness needs to be managed differently, but within the same constraints of the Wilderness Act. Each area has certain problems and is spared others. For example, the heavy impact caused by horse use in many western wildernesses is rare in the East.

A common thread in discussion of this East-West theme was the need to manage for the same long-term ideal, while recognizing differences among individual areas.

KNOWLEDGE GAPS

The theme of numerous serious knowledge gaps that threaten our ability to manage wilderness effectively surfaced time and again, especially in the concurrent sessions. Rex Boner of the Nature Conservancy expressed the frustration many felt when he said, "We are best at pointing out our own ignorance," rather than supplying scientific answers.

Jack Alcock referred to wilderness management as a blend of art and science. Art will always be a required part of wilderness management, but one sometimes got the impression listening at the symposium that, currently, guesswork is standing in for the science component in many instances. New eastern wildernesses seem especially short on scientific knowledge to support management.

There was common agreement that managers and the public need more research. They need rigorous, well-designed research, experimental wherever possible, and descriptive and analytical where experiments are not possible.

The need more research focused specifically on the most critical wilderness management information gaps, and a number of these topics came out of symposium discussions, which will be mentioned below. But there is also a need for research scientists, in concert with wilderness managers, to work hard to relate research not done in wilderness, and not done with wilderness issues in mind, to wilderness management problems. Tom Ellis, Director of the Southern Forest Experiment Station, in his opening remarks, pointed out that the Station had no wilderness research as such, but that knowledge from wildlife, insect, disease, and other research was applicable to wilderness issues. This is certainly true, and applies as well to research done by scientists at universities and in other organizations. But it seems that before this application can achieve its potential, scientists and managers will need to work together to clarify what wilderness is meant to be, what management objectives are, and what the appropriate range of uses and management activities includes. Some scientific papers suggested that this dialogue and background understanding was limited, and researchers were operating from assumptions about wilderness off the tops of their heads.

A number of research needs stood out at the symposium:

1. The natural role of fire. This seems to be a critical need, especially in some southern wildernesses, where a number of speakers--Ross Wein, Geraldine Watson, Dick Conner, and others--indicated that fire was probably a frequent force that dominated natural conditions. How do present conditions depart from what would exist under a natural fire regime? How can a transition from present conditions to those resulting from natural fire be achieved? How would natural fire and its effects interact with insects, diseases, wildlife habitat. (especially for critical species such as the endangered Red-cockaded Woodpecker), and recreational use and values?

It became apparent at the symposium that the recently revised Forest Service wilderness fire policy permitting planned, manager-ignited, prescribed fires in wilderness under certain conditions is particularly relevant to conditions in many southern wildernesses. Because of the small size of many of these wildernesses, lightning-ignited fires inside their boundaries are infrequent. Fires ignited outside the boundaries that centuries ago would have burned into the wilderness are now controlled. Yet all indications are that many of these ecosystems are highly fire dependent. The new fire policy will probably be pilot-tested in the South, and wilderness managers elsewhere will benefit from the pioneer efforts there.

2. Insect population outbreaks. The southern pine beetle was a focus of much discussion at the symposium. It presents some extremely difficult challenges to southern wilderness managers. This is an unusual situation in my experience. I have participated in dozens of wilderness management conferences and workshops over the last 25 years, but insect problems have usually gone unmentioned and have never before been more than a secondary issue.

The potential for rapid expansion of southern pine beetle (SPB) populations, the rapid mortality of host trees, the small size of many affected wildernesses, the existence of adjacent lands with different objectives and sometimes different owners, and the drastic impacts of current control measures on natural conditions all serve to complicate the beetle issue. Jack Alcock reminded us that if the beetles would stay inside a wilderness they would not constitute a problem and no control would be required. Ron Billings, of the Texas Forest Service, reemphasized the same point when he explained that most of what we call "pests" elsewhere are not "pests" in wilderness, but rather part of the natural ecosystem. In his view, however, with SPB was an exception. Ron also told us that most SPB spots never affect more than 25 trees. Hazard rating systems that predict which spots are likely to expand were discussed by James Smith and Wesley Nettleton from Forest Service Pest Management. These systems could help avoid logging where large outbreaks are unlikely.

There seems to be a need for more knowledge about beetle populations in wildernesses, and about ways of limiting large outbreaks through less drastic modifications of stand conditions. Can fire play a useful role?

The demonstrators that were present throughout the symposium dramatized the controversy surrounding SPB control and emphasized the value of research to seek alternative ways of handling the dilemma the beetles present, to escape from "between a rock and a hard place" where southern wilderness managers now are.

3. Air pollution. Acid rain, acid deposition, ozone, and other types of pollution deeply concerned many symposium participants, such as Bob Jacobsen, Superintendent of Shenandoah National Park, and Keith McLaughlin of the Forest Service Southern Region. Air pollution is a pervasive potential threat to fundamental natural processes in naturally functioning, dynamic ecosystems, which are the basic purpose for wilderness. Research to understand the nature and magnitude of pollution effects is needed to document problems and help guide pollution control programs.

4. Education as a wilderness visitor management tool. This nonregulatory approach is appealing to many managers and the public, and it is being used widely in eastern wilderness. We were reminded again that the most distinguishing characteristic of wilderness visitors, both East and West, is very high educational level. Such visitors would seem to be excellent targets for education and information activities. Two main research issues were presented. One

is the validity of the content of messages to visitors, particularly recommended minimum impact practices. Jeff Marion, University of Wisconsin, River Falls, discussed this issue. The second research issue is effective communication to change visitor behavior. Joe Roggenbuck, VPI, presented an example of an experiment focused on various modes of communication to disperse campers.

COOPERATION

The cooperation needed in wilderness management is the fifth major theme of the symposium. Three types of needed cooperation were recognized. One type is cooperation between public and private groups, as between the Nature Conservancy and state and federal resource agencies, and between the visiting public and managers. A second type is cooperation between managers and researchers. A third is cooperation among managers and volunteers, both individuals and organizations. All of these were clearly felt by symposium participants to be essential for effective wilderness protection and management.

THE WILDERNESS MANAGEMENT CHALLENGE

The last and perhaps the most important word in the symposium title and my last word as well, is challenge. The challenge is critically important. That "leaving it alone" is impossible was obvious at the symposium.

The challenge must be met; it is a legal obligation, and it is a professional responsibility. It also is an opportunity for resource management professionals, with the support of resource scientists and with the involvement and cooperation of the public, to provide the American people something of great value--a value that is widely shared and treasured by the public.

The wilderness management challenge is very difficult, perhaps especially so for managers of many eastern wildernesses. But are any of us willing to admit that we lack the skill and commitment to find ways to manage for an enduring resource of wilderness? I hope not.

Contributors

Kent T. Adair
School of Forestry
Stephen F. Austin State University
Nacogdoches, Texas

Paul F. Barker
USDA Forest Service
National Forest System
Washington, DC

Pamela J. Behrman
School of Forestry
Stephen F. Austin State University
Nacogdoches, Texas

Ronald F. Billings
Texas Forest Service
Pest Control Section
Lufkin, Texas

W. H. Blackburn
Range Science Department
Texas A&M University
College Station, Texas

Rex R. Boner
The Nature Conservancy
Atlanta, Georgia

Frank E. Boteler
Department of Forestry
West Virginia University
Morgantown, West Virginia

John H. Burde
Department of Forestry
Southern Illinois State University
Carbondale, Illinois

Karen E. Cathey
School of Forestry
Stephen F. Austin State University
Nacogdoches, Texas

Scott L. Collins
Department of Botany and Microbiolgy
University of Oklahoma
Normal, Oklahoma

Richard N. Conner
Southern Forest Experiment Station
USDA Forest Service
Nacogdoches, Texas

Edward F. Connor
Department of Environmental Sciences
University of Virginia
Charlottesville, Virginia

H. Ken Cordell
Southeastern Forest Experiment Station
USDA Forest Service
Athens, Georgia

Robert N. Coulson
Department of Entomologyy
Texas A&M University
College Station, Texas

Hewlette S. Crawford
Northeastern Forest Experiment Station
USDA Forest Service
Orono, Maine

D.A. Crossley, Jr.
Department of Entomology
University of Georgia
Athens, Georgia

Kevin A. Curran
Department of Forestry
Southern Illinois University
Carbondale, Illinois

George D. Davis
Land Use Consultant
Chevre Hill Farm
Wadhams, New York

H.R. DeSelm
Botany Department
University of Tennessee
Knoxville, Tennessee

David D. Diamond
Range and Science Department
Texas A&M University
College Station, Texas

James G. Dickson
Southern Forest Experiment Station
USDA Forest Service
Nacogdoches, Texas

David B. Drummond
State and Private Forestry
USDA Forest Service
Pineville, Louisiana

Raymond D. Dueser
Department of Environmental Sciences
University of Virginia
Charlottesville, Virginia

Carol K. Evans
School of Forestry
Stephen F. Austin State University
Nacogdoches, Texas

Kent T. Evans
Sabine National Forest
USDA Forest Service
Hemphill, Texas

Michael S. Fountain
School of Forestry
Stephen F. Austin State University
Nacogdoches, Texas

James D. Fraser
Department of Fisheries and Wildlife Sciences
Virginia Polytechnic Institute and State University
Blacksburg, Virginia

Cecil C. Frost
Department of Biology
University of North Carolina
Chapel Hill, North Carolina

Ralph E. Good
Division of Pinelands Research Center
Rutgers University
New Brunswick, New Jersey

William D. Goodrum
Temple-EasTex Forests
Diboll, Texas

Lowell K. Halls
Southern Forest Experiment Station
USDA Forest Service
Nacogdoches, Texas

William E. Hammitt
Department of Forestry, Wildlife, & Fisheries
University of Tennessee
Knoxville, Tennessee

Jeff Haskins
US Fish & Wildlife Service
Albuquerque, New Mexico

Bruce C. Hastings
Department of Forestry, Wildlife, & Fisheries
University of Tennessee
Knoxville, Tennessee

John C. Hendee
Southeastern Forest Experiment Station
USDA Forest Service
Asheville, North Carolina

Gerard K. Hertel
Northeastern Forest Experiment Station
USDA Forest Service
Broomall, Pennsylvania

Edward P. Hill
Mississippi Cooperative Fish & Wildlife Research
Mississippi University
Mississippi State, Mississippi

Jimmy C. Huntley
Southern Forest Experiment Station
USDA Forest Service
Nacogdoches, Texas

Bette J. Schardien Jackson
Department of Biologecal Sciences
Mississippi State University
Mississippi State, Mississippi

Jerome A. Jackson
Department of Biological Sciences
Mississippi State University
Mississippi State, Mississippi

Robert R. Jacobsen
Shenandoah National Park
National Park Service
Luray, Virginia

Harry A. Jacobson
Department of Wildlife & Fisheries
Mississippi State University
Missipi State, Mississippi

Forrest L. Johnson
Oklahoma Biological Survey
University of Oklahoma
Norman, Oklahoma

Peter C. Kirby
The Wilderness Society
Washington, D.C.

James C. Kroll
School of Forestry
Stephen F. Austin State University
Nacogdoches, Texas

Edwin E. Krumpe
Wildland Recreation Management
University of Idaho
Moscow, Idaho

David L. Kulhavy
School of Forestry
Stephen F. Austin State University
Nacogdoches, Texas

Michael H. Legg
School of Forestry
Stephen F. Austin State University
Nacogdoches, Texas

David W. Lime
North Central Forest Experiment Station
USDA Forest Service
St. Paul, Minnesota

Robert C. Lucas
Intermountain Forest and Range Experiment Station
USDA Forest Service
Missoula, Montana

Jeffrey L. Marion
Plant Science Department
University of Wisconsin
River Falls, Wisconsin

Garland N. Mason
Northeastern Forest Experiment Station
USDA Forest Service
Morgantown, West Virginia

J. A. Matos
Department of Biology
Washington University
St. Louis, Missouri

Jack D. McCullough
Department of Biology
Stephen F. Austin State University
Nacogdoches, Texas

Cary D. McDonald
Department of Recreation and Leisure
Washington State University
Pullman, Washington

Keith R. McLaughlin
USDA Forest Service
National Forest System
Atlanta, Georgia

William J. McLaughlin
Wildland Recreation Management
University of Idaho
Moscow, Idaho

Paul A. Mistretta
State and Private Forestry
USDA Forest Service
Pineville, Louisana

Jim Neal
U.S. Fish and Wildlife Service
Nacogdoches, Texas

Wesley Nettleton
State and Private Forestry
USDA Forest Service
Pineville, Louisana

Elray S. Nixon
Department of Biology
Stephen F. Austin State University
Nacogdoches, Texas

Howard R. Orr
USDA Forest Service
National Forest System
Atlanta, Georgia

Robert K. Peet
Department of Biology
University of North Carolina
Chapel Hill, North Carolina

Michael R. Pelton
Department of Forestry, Wildlife & Fisheries
University of Tennessee
Knoxville, Tennessee

Larry N. Phillips
USDA Forest Service
National Forest System
Atlanta, Georgia

Clarence W. Reed
Department of Biology
Stephen F. Austin State University
Nacogdoches, Texas

Paul G. Risser
Illinois Natural History Survey
Champaign, Illinois

Joseph W. Roggenbuck
Department of Forestry
Virginia Polytechnic Institute and State University
Blacksburg, Virginia

Charles T. Roman
Division of Pinelands Research
Rutgers University
New Brunswick, New Jersey

D.C. Rudolph
Department of Biology
Stephen F. Austin State University
Nacogdoches, Texas

Victor A. Rudis
Southern Forest Experiment Station
USDA Forest Service
Starkville, Mississippi

Edward Rykiel
Department of Range Science
Texas A&M University
College Station, Texas

Paul R. Saunders
Agricultural Research Center
Washington State University
Pullman, Washington

David J. Schmidly
Department of Wildlife & Fisheries
Texas A&M University
College Station, Texas

Herman H. Shugart
Department of Environmental Sciences
University of Virginia
Charlottesville, Virginia

Jennifer A. Sidnell
Department of Biology
Stephen F. Austin State University
Nacogdoches, Texas

Fred E. Smeins
Range Science Department
Texas A&M University
College Station, Texas

James D. Smith
Forest Pest Management
USDA Forest Service
Pineville, Louisana

Robert K. Strosnider
Daniel Boone National Forest
USDA Forest Service
Winchester, Kentucky

Robert C. Thatcher
Southeastern Forest Experiment Station
USDA Forest Service
Pineville, Louisana

Thomas E. Toney
Missouri Conservation Department
Lockwood, Missouri

Forrest E. Varner
Texas Forest Service
Conroe, Texas

Joan Walker
Department of Botany
Duke University
Durham, North Carolina

William A. Wall
School of Forestry
Stephen F. Austin State University
Nacogdoches, Texas

John R. Ward
Texas Department of Water Resources
Deer Park, Texas

Alan E. Watson
Department of Recreation and Leisure Services
Georgia Southern College
Statesboro, Georgia

Geraldine E. Watson
Big Thicket National Preserve
National Park Service
Beaumont, Texas

Thomas M. Webb
Sam Houston National Forest
USDA Forest Service
New Waverly, Texas

Ross W. Wein
Fire Science Center
University of New Brunswick
Fredricton, New Brunswick

J.C. Wood
Range Science Department
Texas A&M University
College Station, Texas

James C. Woods
Big Thicket National Preserve
National Park Service
Beaumont, Texas

Paul J. Wright
Pisgah National Forest
USDA Forest Service
Pisgah Forest, North Carolina

TAXONOMIC INDEX

SUBJECT INDEX

Photo Credits

Francis E. Abernathy, Stephen F. Austin State University xvi, 306, 315, 321, 335; *Rex Bavousett* 217, 271, 272, 324, 334; *Big Thicket National Preserve* 168, 182; *Ronald F. Billings,* Texas Forest Service 113B, 120, 121, 128, 131, 132(2), 309, 316; *Tom Carbone,* Maine Fish and Wildlife Department 68; *Richard N. Conner,* U.S. Forest Service xiv, 33B, 35, 73, 93, 97, 198, 223, 273; *Bruce C. Cunningham,* Nacogdoches, Texas 53, 61, 137, 175, 180, 303, 404; *James G. Dickson,* U.S. Forest Service 87; *Kent Evans,* U.S. Forest Service 145B, 157, 159; *Michael S. Fountain,* Stephen F. Austin State University 289, 293; *James D. Fraser,* VPI & SU 82; *Edward P. Hill,* Mississippi Coop. Fish and Wildlife Research 40; *Jimmy C. Huntley,* U.S. Forest Service 56; *Lawrence G. Kolk,* U.S. Forest Service 17; *James C. Kroll,* Stephen F. Austin State University 84, 270, 295, 296, 297, 298; *Edwin E. Krumpe,* University of Idaho 219; *David L. Kulhavy,* Stephen F. Austin State University xv, 29, 243, 310, 337; *Michael Legg,* Stephen F. Austin University 2A, *Jim Neal,* USDI Fish and Wildlife Servpcie 273B; *National Park Service* 199, 202, 259,; *Fred Smeins,* Texas A&M University 337B; *Tommy Smith,* University of Tennessee 50; *USDA Forest Service* cover photo, xv (top), 32,63, 131(top), 136, 147, 178, 188, 204, 213, 224, 237, 244, 261, 262, 263, 399, 405.